Less managing. More teaching. Greater learning.

Q: INSTRUCTORS...

Would you like your **students** to show up for class **more prepared**?
(Let's face it, class is much more fun if everyone is engaged and prepared...)

Want an **easy way to assign** homework online and track student **progress**?
(Less time grading means more time teaching...)

Want an **instant view** of student or class performance?
(No more wondering if students understand...)

Need to **collect data and generate reports** required for administration or accreditation? *(Say goodbye to manually tracking student learning outcomes...)*

Want to **record and post your lectures** for students to view online?

A: With **McGraw-Hill's** *Connect™ Plus Finance,*

INSTRUCTORS GET:

- Simple **assignment management**, allowing you to spend more time teaching.

- **Auto-graded** assignments, quizzes, and tests.

- **Detailed visual reporting** where student and section results can be viewed and analyzed.

- Sophisticated **online testing** capability.

- A **filtering and reporting** function that allows you to easily assign and report on materials that are correlated to accreditation standards, learning outcomes, and Bloom's taxonomy.

- An easy-to-use **lecture capture** tool.

- The option to **upload course documents** for student access.

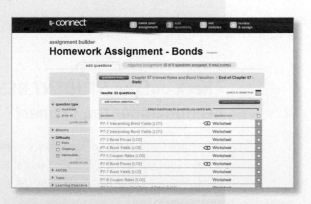

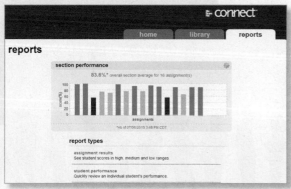

Want an online, **searchable version** of your textbook?

Wish your textbook could be **available online** while you're doing your assignments?

 ***Connect™ Plus Finance* eBook**

If you choose to use *Connect™ Plus Finance*, you have an affordable and searchable online version of your book integrated with your other online tools.

***Connect™ Plus Finance* eBook offers features like:**

- Topic search
- Direct links from assignments
- Adjustable text size
- Jump to page number
- Print by section

 Want to get more **value** from your textbook purchase?

Think learning finance should be a bit more **interesting**?

 Check out the STUDENT RESOURCES section under the *Connect™* Library tab.

Here you'll find a wealth of resources designed to help you achieve your goals in the course. Every student has different needs, so explore the STUDENT RESOURCES to find the materials best suited to you.

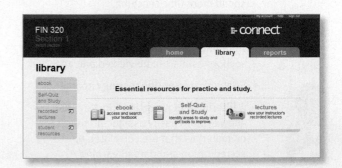

finance

Marcia Millon Cornett
Bentley University

Troy A. Adair, Jr.
Wilkes University

John Nofsinger
Washington State University

McGraw-Hill
Irwin

finance

VICE PRESIDENT AND EDITOR-IN-CHIEF: **BRENT GORDON**

PUBLISHER: **DOUGLAS REINER**

EXECUTIVE EDITOR: **MICHELE JANICEK**

EXECUTIVE DIRECTOR OF DEVELOPMENT: **ANN TORBERT**

DEVELOPMENT EDITOR II: **KAREN L. FISHER**

VICE PRESIDENT AND DIRECTOR OF MARKETING: **ROBIN J. ZWETTLER**

MARKETING DIRECTOR: **BRAD PARKINS**

SENIOR MARKETING MANAGER: **MELISSA S. CAUGHLIN**

VICE PRESIDENT OF EDITING, DESIGN, AND PRODUCTION: **SESHA BOLISETTY**

MANAGER OF PHOTO, DESIGN & PUBLISHING TOOLS: **MARY CONZACHI**

SENIOR BUYER: **CAROL A. BIELSKI**

SENIOR DESIGNER: **MARY KAZAK SANDER**

PHOTO RESEARCH COORDINATOR: **JOANNE MENNEMEIER**

SENIOR MEDIA PROJECT MANAGER: **SUSAN LOMBARDI**

MEDIA PROJECT MANAGER: **JOYCE J. CHAPPETTO**

COVER IMAGE: **© BUERO MONACO/CORBIS**

TYPEFACE: **10/12 MINION PRO REGULAR**

COMPOSITOR: **LASERWORDS PRIVATE LIMITED**

PRINTER: **QUAD/GRAPHICS**

M: FINANCE

Published by McGraw-Hill/Irwin, a business unit of The McGraw-Hill Companies, Inc., 1221 Avenue of the Americas, New York, NY, 10020.

Some ancillaries, including electronic and print components, may not be available to customers outside the United States.

This book is printed on acid-free paper.

Printed in the United States of America.

2 3 4 5 6 7 8 9 0 QDB/QDB 1 0 9 8 7 6 5 4 3 2 1

ISBN 978-0-07-338224-1
MHID 0-07-338224-8

Library of Congress Control Number: 2010939739

brief contents

chapter 1 Introduction to Financial Management   3

chapter 2 Reviewing Financial Statements   21

chapter 3 Analyzing Financial Statements   47

chapter 4 Time Value of Money 1: Analyzing Single Cash Flows   75

chapter 5 Time Value of Money 2: Analyzing Annuity Cash Flows   95

chapter 6 Valuing Bonds   123

chapter 7 Valuing Stocks   151

chapter 8 Understanding Financial Markets and Institutions   177

chapter 9 Characterizing Risk and Return   205

chapter 10 Estimating Risk and Return   229

chapter 11 Calculating the Cost of Capital   253

chapter 12 Estimating Cash Flows on Capital Budgeting Projects   273

chapter 13 Weighing Net Present Value and Other Capital Budgeting Criteria   297

chapter 14 Addressing Working Capital Policies and Managing Short-Term Assets and Liabilities   323

contents

CHAPTER ONE   INTRODUCTION TO FINANCIAL MANAGEMENT 3

FINANCE IN BUSINESS AND IN LIFE 4
  What Is Finance? 4
  Subareas of Finance 6
  Application and Theory for Financial Decisions 7

THE FINANCIAL FUNCTION 8
  The Financial Manager 8
  Finance in Other Business Functions 8
  Finance in Your Personal Life 9

BUSINESS ORGANIZATION 9
  Sole Proprietorships 9
  Partnerships 10
  Corporations 11
  Hybrid Organizations 11

FIRM GOALS 11

AGENCY THEORY 14
  Agency Problem 14
  Corporate Governance 15
  The Role of Ethics 16

FINANCIAL MARKETS, INTERMEDIARIES, AND THE FIRM 18

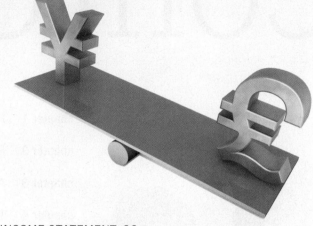

CHAPTER TWO   REVIEWING FINANCIAL STATEMENTS 21

BALANCE SHEET 22
  Assets 22
  Liabilities and Stockholders' Equity 23
  Managing the Balance Sheet 23

INCOME STATEMENT 26
  Corporate Income Taxes 27

STATEMENT OF CASH FLOWS 30
  Sources and Uses of Cash 30
  Free Cash Flow 33

STATEMENT OF RETAINED EARNINGS 35

CAUTIONS IN INTERPRETING FINANCIAL STATEMENTS 35

CHAPTER THREE   ANALYZING FINANCIAL STATEMENTS 47

LIQUIDITY RATIOS 48

ASSET MANAGEMENT RATIOS 48
  Inventory Management 49
  Accounts Receivable Management 50
  Accounts Payable Management 51
  Fixed Asset and Working Capital Management 51
  Total Asset Management 51

DEBT MANAGEMENT RATIOS 53
  Debt versus Equity Financing 53
  Coverage Ratios 54

PROFITABILITY RATIOS 55

MARKET VALUE RATIOS 57

DUPONT ANALYSIS 59

OTHER RATIOS 62
  Spreading the Financial Statements 62
  Internal and Sustainable Growth Rates 63

TIME SERIES AND CROSS-SECTIONAL ANALYSIS 65

CAUTIONS IN USING RATIOS TO EVALUATE FIRM PERFORMANCE 65

CHAPTER FOUR   TIME VALUE OF MONEY 1: ANALYZING SINGLE CASH FLOWS 75

ORGANIZING CASH FLOWS 76

FUTURE VALUE 76
Single Period Future Value 76
Compounding and Future Value 77

PRESENT VALUE 81
Discounting 81

USING PRESENT VALUE AND FUTURE VALUE 85
Moving Cash Flows 85

COMPUTING INTEREST RATES 88
Return Asymmetries 88

SOLVING FOR TIME 88

CHAPTER FIVE   TIME VALUE OF MONEY 2: ANALYZING ANNUITY CASH FLOWS 95

FUTURE VALUE OF MULTIPLE CASH FLOWS 96
Finding the Future Value of Several Cash Flows 96
Future Value of Level Cash Flows 96
Future Value of Multiple Annuities 98

PRESENT VALUE OF MULTIPLE CASH FLOWS 101
Finding the Present Value of Several Cash Flows 101
Present Value of Level Cash Flows 102
Present Value of Multiple Annuities 103
Perpetuity—A Special Annuity 105

ORDINARY ANNUITIES VERSUS ANNUITIES DUE 105

COMPOUNDING FREQUENCY 106
Effect of Compounding Frequency 106

ANNUITY LOANS 110
What Is the Interest Rate? 110
Finding Payments on an Amortized Loan 111

CHAPTER SIX   VALUING BONDS 123

BOND MARKET OVERVIEW 124
Bond Characteristics 124
Bond Issuers 126
Other Bonds and Bond-Based Securities 126
Reading Bond Quotes 128

BOND VALUATION 131
Present Value of Bond Cash Flows 131
Bond Prices and Interest Rate Risk 133
Bond Prices and the Term Structure of Interest Rates 134

BOND YIELDS 136
Current Yield 136
Yield to Maturity 136
Yield to Call 137
Municipal Bonds and Yield 138
Summarizing Yields 139

CREDIT RISK 140
Bond Ratings 140
Credit Risk and Yield 142

BOND MARKETS 143
Following the Bond Market 144

CHAPTER SEVEN   VALUING STOCKS 151

COMMON STOCK 152

STOCK MARKETS 152
Tracking the Stock Market 156
Trading Stocks 158

BASIC STOCK VALUATION 160
Cash Flows 160
Dividend Discount Models 162
Preferred Stock 163
Expected Return 165

ADDITIONAL VALUATION METHODS 166
Variable-Growth Techniques 166
The P/E Model 168
Estimating Future Stock Prices 171

CHAPTER EIGHT   UNDERSTANDING FINANCIAL MARKETS AND INSTITUTIONS 177

FINANCIAL MARKETS 178
Primary versus Secondary Markets 178
Money Markets versus Capital Markets 180
Other Markets 182

FINANCIAL INSTITUTIONS 183
Unique Economic Functions Performed by Financial Institutions 186

INTEREST RATES 187
Factors That Influence Interest Rates for Individual Securities 187
Theories Explaining the Shape of the Term Structure of Interest Rates 193
Forecasting Interest Rates 197

CHAPTER ELEVEN   CALCULATING THE COST OF CAPITAL 253

THE WACC FORMULA 254
  Calculating the Component Cost of Equity 254
  Calculating the Component Cost of Preferred Stock 255
  Calculating the Component Cost of Debt 256
  Choosing the Appropriate Tax Rate for the WACC 257
  Calculating the Weights 257

FIRM WACC VERSUS PROJECT WACC 257
  Project Cost Numbers That We Should Take from the Firm 259
  Project Cost Numbers That We Should Not Take from the Firm: The Pure-Play Approach 260

DIVISIONAL WACC 262
  Advantages and Disadvantages of a Divisional WACC 262
  Subjective versus Objective Approaches to Calculating Divisional WACCs 264

FLOTATION COSTS 265
  Adjusting the WACC 267

CHAPTER NINE   CHARACTERIZING RISK AND RETURN 205

HISTORICAL RETURNS 206
  Computing Returns 206
  Performance of Asset Classes 208

HISTORICAL RISKS 208
  Computing Volatility 208
  Risk of Asset Classes 210
  Risk versus Return 211

FORMING PORTFOLIOS 212
  Diversifying to Reduce Risk 212
  Modern Portfolio Theory 214

CHAPTER TEN   ESTIMATING RISK AND RETURN 229

EXPECTED RETURNS 230
  Expected Return and Risk 230
  Risk Premiums 232

MARKET RISK 233
  The Market Portfolio 234
  Beta, a Measure of Market Risk 235
  The Security Market Line 236
  Finding Beta 237
  Concerns about Beta 238

CAPITAL MARKET EFFICIENCY 240
  Efficient Market Hypothesis 240
  Behavioral Finance 242

IMPLICATIONS FOR FINANCIAL MANAGERS 244
  Using the Constant-Growth Model for Required Return 244

CHAPTER TWELVE   ESTIMATING CASH FLOWS ON CAPITAL BUDGETING PROJECTS 273

SAMPLE PROJECT DESCRIPTION 274

GUIDING PRINCIPLES FOR CASH FLOW ESTIMATION 274
  Opportunity Costs 275
  Sunk Costs 275
  Substitutionary and Complementary Effects 276
  Stock Dividends and Bond Interest 276

TOTAL PROJECT CASH FLOW 276
  Calculating Depreciation 277
  Calculating Operating Cash Flow 277
  Calculating Changes in Gross Fixed Assets 278
  Calculating Changes in Net Working Capital 279
  Bringing It All Together 280

ACCELERATED DEPRECIATION AND THE HALF-YEAR CONVENTION 281
  MACRS Depreciation Calculation 281
  Section 179 Deductions 281
  Impact of Accelerated Depreciation 282

"SPECIAL" CASES AREN'T REALLY THAT SPECIAL 283

CHOOSING BETWEEN ALTERNATIVE ASSETS WITH DIFFERING LIVES: EAC 285

FLOTATION COSTS REVISITED 288

APPENDIX: MACRS DEPRECIATION TABLES 292

CHAPTER THIRTEEN   WEIGHING NET PRESENT VALUE AND OTHER CAPITAL BUDGETING CRITERIA 297

THE SET OF CAPITAL BUDGETING TECHNIQUES 298

THE CHOICE OF DECISION STATISTIC FORMAT 298
  Decision Statistic Formats 299

PROCESSING CAPITAL BUDGETING DECISIONS 299

NET PRESENT VALUE 300
NPV Statistic 300
NPV Benchmark 300
NPV Strengths and Weaknesses 300

PAYBACK AND DISCOUNTED PAYBACK 302
Payback Statistic 302
Payback Benchmark 302
Discounted Payback Statistic 303
Discounted Payback Benchmark 303
Payback and Discounted Payback Strengths and Weaknesses 304

INTERNAL RATE OF RETURN AND MODIFIED INTERNAL RATE OF RETURN 306
Internal Rate of Return Statistic 306
Internal Rate of Return Benchmark 306
Problems with Internal Rate of Return 307
IRR and NPV Profiles with Non-Normal Cash Flows 308
Differing Reinvestment Rate Assumptions of NPV and IRR 308
Modified Internal Rate of Return Statistic 309
IRRs, MIRRs, and NPV Profiles with Mutually Exclusive Projects 309
MIRR Strengths and Weaknesses 313

PROFITABILITY INDEX 314
Profitability Index Statistic 314
Profitability Index Benchmark 315

CHAPTER FOURTEEN   ADDRESSING WORKING CAPITAL POLICIES AND MANAGING SHORT-TERM ASSETS AND LIABILITIES 323

REVISITING THE BALANCE-SHEET MODEL OF THE FIRM 324

TRACING CASH AND NET WORKING CAPITAL 324
The Operating Cycle 325
The Cash Cycle 326

SOME ASPECTS OF SHORT-TERM FINANCIAL POLICY 326
The Size of the Current Assets Investment 326
Alternative Financing Policies for Current Assets 328

THE SHORT-TERM FINANCIAL PLAN 329
Unsecured Loans 329
Secured Loans 330
Other Sources 330

CASH MANAGEMENT 331
Reasons for Holding Cash 331
Determining the Target Cash Balance: The Baumol Model 332
Determining the Target Cash Balance: The Miller-Orr Model 333
Other Factors Influencing the Target Cash Balance 333

FLOAT CONTROL: MANAGING THE COLLECTION AND DISBURSEMENT OF CASH 335
Accelerating Collections 335
Delaying Disbursements 336
Ethical and Legal Questions 337

INVESTING IDLE CASH 337
Why Firms Have Surplus Cash 337
What to Do with Surplus Cash 337

CREDIT MANAGEMENT 338
Credit Policy: Terms of the Sale 338
Credit Analysis 338
Collection Policy 338

VIEWPOINTS (revisited) 343

CREDITS   350

INDEX   351

finance

chapter **one**

introduction to
financial management

Do you know: What finance entails? How financial management functions within the business world? Why you might benefit from studying financial principles? This chapter is the ideal place to get answers to those questions.

Finance is largely the study of how to value all sorts of things, such as shares of stock, the payments left on a home mortgage, the purchase of an entire company, and the personal decision to retire early. In this text, we're going to focus primarily on one particular area of finance, **financial management,** which tends to concentrate on valuing things from the perspective of a company.

Financial management is critically important to the success of any business organization, and throughout the text, we will concentrate on describing the key financial concepts central to corporate finance. However, many of the tools and techniques we'll learn for handling the financial management of a firm are pretty widely applicable to broader types of financial problems, too, such as personal finance decisions.

continued on p. 4

LEARNING GOALS

LG1 Define the subareas of finance and their roles in corporate financial management.

LG2 Show why and how finance is at the heart of sound business decisions.

LG3 Apply finance in your personal life.

LG4 Compare and contrast the advantages and disadvantages of the three most common business organizational forms in the United States.

LG5 Differentiate between financial managers' appropriate and inappropriate goals.

LG6 Identify the firm's primary agency relationship and discuss why agency relationships can create conflicts.

LG7 Incorporate ethics into financial management.

LG8 Describe the complex and necessary relationships among firms, financial institutions, and financial markets.

continued from p. 3

In finance, we call the receiving and paying of money *cash flow,* and we'll start our discussion of finance off with a graphical depiction of the cash flows of finance, using this depiction to both help explain what finance is all about and to demonstrate the different aspects of finance. ■

The remainder of this chapter will be devoted to a discussion of several important environmental variables that will significantly impact the financial decisions of the firm, including the organizational form of the business, the agency relationship between the managers and owners of a firm, and ethical considerations in the application of finance.

FINANCE IN BUSINESS AND IN LIFE

Your perception of what finance is all about may have been negatively skewed by pop-culture entertainment. Most movies portray finance professionals as greedy and unethical people [see, for example, the movies *Trading Places* (1983), *Wall Street* (1987), *Barbarians at the Gate* (1993), *Rogue Trader* (1998), and *Boiler Room* (2000)]. While such characters make for good entertainment, those depictions do not reflect the truth about finance professionals and their contributions to society.

Successfully applying finance theories helps money flow from individuals who want to improve their financial future to businesses that want to expand the scale or scope of their operations. These exchanges lead to an expanding economy and more employment opportunities for people at all levels of society. So, two great things result from this simple exchange: the economy will be more productive now, and individuals' wealth will grow into the future.

In this section, we develop a comprehensive description of finance, its subareas, and the relevant decisions professionals in each subarea must make. As you will see, all of the subareas share a common set of ideas and application tools.

What Is Finance?

To envision what finance is all about, consider segmenting all of the participants in an economy along two dimensions. The first dimension is the availability of "extra" money (i.e., money above and beyond their current spending needs) for investment. The second dimension is the ability to develop economically viable business ideas.

Dividing everyone along these two dimensions will result in participants being divided into four types, as shown in Figure 1.1. Of course, people can move from one group to another over time.

Type 1 people really play no direct role in **financial markets** as either lenders of capital or users of capital, though they will probably play an indirect role by providing their labor to or consuming products from economic enterprises. Our discussion of finance is going to concentrate on only those participants who play a direct role, so we can set the type 1 participants aside.

Type 4 people will use tools to evaluate their own ideas to pick the ones that have the most potential and to create those enterprises that will implement those ideas most efficiently. However, the type 4 individuals have no need for the financial markets because they are self-funded, so the financial tools they use and the types of decisions they make will be fairly narrowly focused. Thus our discussion will not concentrate on type 4 individuals either.

Financial institutions and financial markets enhance the economy by empowering types 2 and 3 people to engage in a mutually advantageous exchange: the type 2 people temporarily lend their money to the type 3 people, who put that money into their good business ideas. In most developed economies, type 2 participants are usually individual **investors**—just as you will likely be for most of your life. Each of us individually may not have a lot of extra money, but by aggregating our available funds, we can provide sizable amounts. Type 3 participants may be individuals with innovative new ideas, but are more often corporations or

▼FIGURE 1.1 Participants in Our Hypothetical Economy

	NO EXTRA MONEY	EXTRA MONEY
No Economically Viable Business Ideas	Type 1: No money and no ideas	Type 2: Money, but no ideas
Economically Viable Business Ideas	Type 3: No money, but ideas	Type 4: Both money and ideas

personal APPLICATION

Dagmar is becoming interested in investing some of her money. However, she has heard about several corporations in which the investors lost all of their money. In the past several years, Dagmar has heard that Enron (2001), WorldCom (2002), and Delta Airlines (2005) have all filed for bankruptcy. These firms' stockholders lost their entire investments in these firms.

Many of the stockholders who lost money were employees of these companies who had invested some of their retirement money in the company stock. She wonders what guarantee she has as an investor against losing her money.

other types of companies with research and development (R&D) departments dedicated to developing innovative ideas.

Obviously, investors and companies can help one another. If investors lend their "extra" capital to companies, as shown in Figure 1.2, then companies can use this capital to fund expansion projects. Economically successful projects will eventually offer to repay the money (plus profit) to investors,

support ongoing operations) and *taxes*, which the government imposes on the company and individuals to help fund public services. Figure 1.4 on the next page shows an analysis of the resulting cash flows with the associated retained earnings and tax payments. Though simplistic, this figure provides a great overall intuitive explanation of finance in general and of the major subareas of finance.

For example, individuals must assess what investment opportunities are right for their needs and risk tolerance; financial institutions and markets must efficiently distribute the capital; and companies must evaluate their potential projects and wisely decide which projects to fund, what kind of capital to use, and how much capital to return to investors. All of these types of decisions deal with the basic cash flows of finance shown in Figure 1.4, but from different perspectives.

finance The ways people and organizations raise and allocate capital, use monetary resources, and account for the risks involved.

financial management The process for and the analysis of making financial decisions in the business context.

financial markets The places and processes that facilitate the trading of financial assets between investors.

investors Those who buy securities or other assets in hopes of earning a return and getting more money back in the future.

retained earnings The portion of company profits that are kept by the company rather than distributed to the stockholders as cash dividends.

ECONOMICALLY SUCCESSFUL PROJECTS WILL EVENTUALLY OFFER TO REPAY MONEY (PLUS PROFIT) TO INVESTORS.

as shown in Figure 1.3. The company has expanded its business, hired more employees, and created a promising future for itself. Meanwhile, the investor has increased his or her own wealth for the future.

Of course, not all of the cash will return to the investors. In reality, sources of friction arise in this system, which will reduce the amount of capital returned to investors. Two primary sources of friction will be **retained earnings** (which you can intuitively think of as funds that the firm retains to

▼**FIGURE 1.3** Return of Capital to Investors

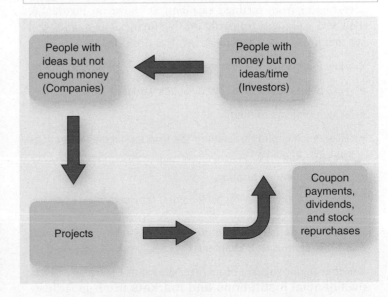

▼**FIGURE 1.2** Capital Flow from Investors to Companies

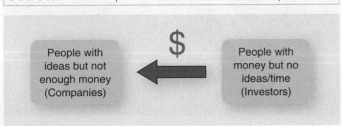

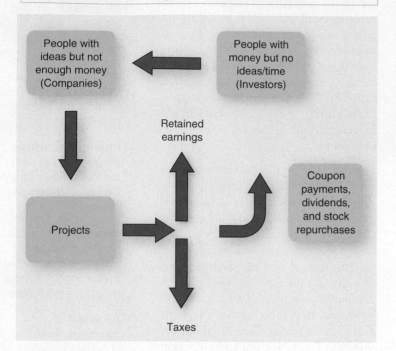

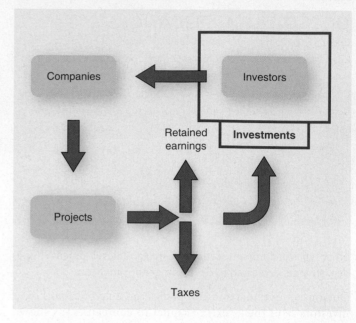

Subareas of Finance

Suppose we look at a set of cash flows from the investor's perspective as shown in Figure 1.5. The red arrows going into and out of the investor's perspective (represented by the blue-outlined box) represent the concerns of the study of **investments,** a subarea of finance which involves methods and techniques for making appropriate decisions about what kinds of securities to own (e.g., bonds versus stocks), which firms' securities to buy, and how to pay the investor back in the form that the investor wishes (e.g., the timing and certainty of the promised cash flows).

The next major subarea of finance, *financial management,* looks at firm decisions in acquiring and utilizing cash received from investors or from retained earnings, as shown in Figure 1.6. This text will focus primarily on this financial area, and we'll see that financial management involves decisions about:

• How to organize the firm in a manner that will attract capital.

• How capital should be raised (bonds versus stocks).

• Which projects to fund.

• How much capital to retain in the firm for ongoing operations and new projects.

• How to minimize taxation.

• How to go about paying back capital providers.

All of these decisions are quite involved, and we will discuss them throughout later chapters.

Another major subarea of finance, shown in Figure 1.7, covers the **financial institutions and markets** that help facilitate

the capital flows between investors and companies. This subarea involves the firm initially acquiring capital and then investors' ongoing securities trading. It also involves the function of financial institutions, like banks and pension administrators, and the dynamics of interest rates.

Risk tolerance varies among individuals.

FIGURE 1.6 Financial Management

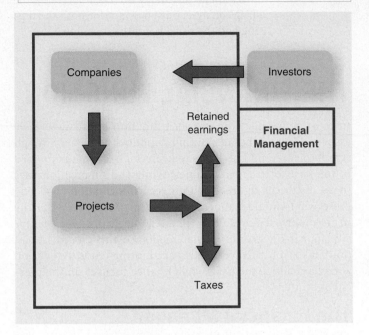

Finally, as the world has transformed into a global economy, finance has had to become much more innovative and sensitive to changes in other countries. As Figure 1.8 on the next page shows, investors, companies, business operations, and capital markets may all be located in different countries. Adapting to this environment requires the study of **international finance.** Until recently, international financial decisions were considered to be a straightforward application of the other three financial subareas. But experience has shown that the uncertainty about future exchange rates, political risk, and changing country business laws all add enough complexity to these decisions to warrant considering international finance as a subarea in its own right.

Application and Theory for Financial Decisions

Applying finance theory to real decisions requires that we realize that cash

financial institutions The organizations that facilitate the flow of capital between investors and companies.

international finance The use of finance theory in a global business environment.

risk A potential future negative impact to value and/or cash flows. It is often discussed in terms of the probability of loss and the expected magnitude of the loss.

financial asset A general term for securities like stocks, bonds, and other assets that represent ownership in a cash flow.

> "As the world has transformed into a global economy, finance has had to become much more innovative and sensitive to changes in other countries."

FIGURE 1.7 Financial Institutions and Markets

flows are neither instantaneous nor guaranteed. Future cash flows are uncertain in terms of both timing and size, and we refer to this uncertainty as **risk.** Investors experience risk about the return of their capital. Companies experience risk in funding and operating their business projects. Most financial decisions involve comparing the rewards of a decision to the risks that decision involves.

Comparing rewards with risks frequently involves assessing the value today of cash flows that we expect to receive in the future. For example, the price of a **financial asset,** like a stock or a bond, should depend on the cash flows you expect to receive from that asset in the future. A stock that's expected to deliver high cash flows in the future will be more valuable today than a stock with low expected future cash flows. Of course, investors would like to buy stocks whose market prices are currently lower then their actual values. They want to get stocks on sale! Similarly, a firm's goal is to fund projects that will give more value than their costs.

Despite the large number of stories about investors who've struck it rich in the stock market, it's actually more likely that a firm will find "bargain" projects than that investors will find

cash flows of either a business project or an investment are likely to be uncertain, the TVM analysis must account for both the timing and the risk level of the cash flows.

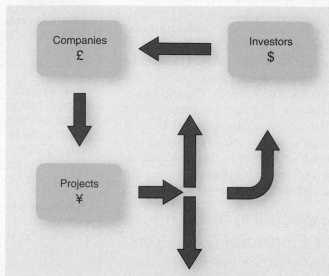

FIGURE 1.8 International Finance

time out!

1-1 What are the main subareas of finance and how do they interact?

THE FINANCIAL FUNCTION

In most companies, the financial function is usually closely associated with the accounting function. In a very rough sense, the accountant's job is to keep track of what happened *in the past* to the firm's money, while the finance job uses these historical figures with current information to determine what should happen *now and in the future* with the firm's money. The results of financial decisions will eventually appear in accounting statements, so this close association makes sense. Nevertheless, accounting tends to focus on and characterize the past, while finance focuses on the present and future.

The Financial Manager

The firm's highest-level financial manager is usually the chief financial officer, or CFO. Both the company treasurer and the controller report to the CFO. The treasurer is typically responsible for:

- Managing cash and credit.

- Issuing and repurchasing financial securities such as stocks and bonds.

- Deciding how and when to spend capital for new and existing projects.

- Hedging (reducing the firm's potential risk) against changes in foreign exchange and interest rates.

In larger corporations, the treasurer may also oversee other areas, such as purchasing insurance or managing the firm's pension fund investments. The controller oversees the accounting function, usually managing the tax, cost accounting, financial accounting, and data processing functions.

Finance in Other Business Functions

Though the CFO and treasurer positions tend to be the firm's most visible finance-related positions, finance affects the firm in many ways that are unrelated to such relatively high positions in a company's organizational chart. Finance permeates the entire business organization, providing guidance for both strategic and day-to-day decisions of the firm and collecting information for control and feedback about the firm's financial decisions.

underpriced stocks. Firms can find bargains because business projects involve **real assets** trading in **real markets,** where some level of monopoly power, special knowledge, and expertise can possibly make such projects worth more than they cost. Investors, however, are trading financial assets in *financial markets,* where the assets are more likely to be worth, on average, exactly what they cost.

The method for relating expected cash flows to a present value is called the **time value of money (TVM).** Since the expected

Operational managers use finance daily to determine how much overtime labor to use, or to perform cost/benefit analysis when they consider new production lines or methods. Marketing managers use finance to assess the cost effectiveness of doing follow-up marketing surveys. Human resource managers use finance in evaluating the company's cost for various employee benefit packages. No matter where you work in business, finance can help you do your job better.

Finance in Your Personal Life

Finance can also help you make good financial decisions in your personal life. Consider these common activities you will probably face in your life:

- Borrow money to buy a new car.
- Refinance your home mortgage at a lower rate.
- Make credit card or student loan payments.
- Save for retirement.

You will be able to perform all of these tasks better after learning about finance. Recent changes throughout our economy and the U.S. business environment make knowledge of finance even more valuable to you than before. For example, most companies have switched from providing **defined benefit** retirement plans to employees to offering **defined contribution** plans (such as **401k** plans) and self-funded plans like **individual retirement accounts (IRAs).** Tax changes in the early 1980s made this switch more or less inevitable. It appears that each of us will have to ensure adequate funds for our own retirement—much more so than previous generations.

1-2 How might the application of finance improve your professional and personal decisions?

BUSINESS ORGANIZATION

In the United States, people can structure businesses in any of several ways, with the primary driving factor being the

number of owners. Traditionally, single owners, partners, and corporations operate businesses. We can express the advantages and disadvantages of each organizational form through several dimensions. In describing these legal forms, we will use the following dimensions:

- Who controls the firm.
- Who owns the firm.
- What the owners' risks are.
- What access to capital exists.
- What the tax ramifications are.

Recently, small businesses have adopted hybrid structures that capture the benefits from multiple organizational forms, and we'll discuss those hybrid structures after we cover the more common, traditional types of business organizations.

Sole Proprietorships

Sole proprietorships represent, by far, the most common type of business in the United States.[1] A sole proprietorship is defined as any unincorporated business owned by a single individual.[2] Perhaps these businesses are so popular because they are relatively easy to start, and they're subject to a much lighter regulatory and paperwork burden than other business forms. The owner, or sole proprietor, of the business has complete control of the firm's activities. The owner also receives all of the firm's profits and is solely responsible for all losses.

The biggest disadvantage that sole proprietorships carry relative to other organizational forms is that they have **unlimited liability** for their companies' debts and actions. The owner's personal assets may be confiscated if the business is sued. The law recognizes no distinction between the owner's business assets and personal assets. The income of the business is also added to the owner's personal income and taxed by the government at the appropriate personal tax rate. Finally, sole proprietors have a difficult time obtaining capital to expand their business operations.

[1]According to the IRS' *SOI Tax Stats—Integrated Business Data* for 2002, 71.59% of all businesses in the U.S. were sole proprietorships.

[2]However, if you are the sole member of a domestic limited liability company (LLC, discussed below), you are not a sole proprietor if you elect to treat the LLC as a corporation.

defined benefit plan A retirement plan in which the employer sets aside money for the employees' retirement benefits.

defined contribution plan A retirement plan in which the employee contributes money and directs its investment. The amount of retirement benefits is directly related to the amount of money contributed and the success of its investment.

individual retirement account (IRA) A self-sponsored retirement program.

401k plan A defined contribution plan that is sponsored by corporate employers.

sole proprietorship A business entity that is not legally separate from its owner.

unlimited liability A situation in which a person's personal assets are at risk from a business liability.

equity An ownership interest in a business enterprise.

angel investors Individuals who provide small amounts of capital and expert business advice to small firms in exchange for an ownership stake in the firm.

venture capitalists Similar to angel investors except that they are organized as groups of investors and can provide larger amounts of capital.

general partnership A form of business organization where the partners own the business together and are personally liable for legal actions and debts of the firm.

Banks and other lenders are not typically interested in lending much money to sole proprietors because small firms have only one person liable for paying back the debt. A sole proprietor could raise capital by issuing **equity** to another investor. **Angel investors** and **venture capitalists** exchange capital for ownership in a business. But this requires re-forming the business as a partnership and the sole proprietor must give up some of the ownership (and thus control) of the firm. Table 1.1 summarizes sole proprietorships' characteristics.

Partnerships

A **general partnership,** or as it is more commonly known, a *partnership,* is an organizational form that features multiple individual owners. Each partner can own a different percentage of the firm. Firm control is typically determined by the size of partners' ownership stakes. Businesses' profits are split among the partners according to a prearranged agreement, usually by the percentage of firm ownership. Received profits are added to each partner's personal income and taxed at personal income tax rates.

Venture capital helped Starbucks become a success story.

▼ **TABLE 1.1** Characteristics of Business Organization

	Ownership	Control	Ownership Risk	Access to Capital	Taxes
Sole Proprietor	Single individual	Proprietor	Unlimited liability	Very limited	Paid by owner
Partnership	Multiple people	Shared by partners	Unlimited liability	Limited	Paid by partners
Corporation	Public investors who own the stock	Company managers	Stockholders can only lose their investment in the firm	Easy access	Corporation pays income tax and stockholders pay taxes on dividends
Hybrids: S-corp, LLP, LLC, LP	Partners or shareholders	Shared	Mostly limited	Limited by firm size restrictions	Paid by partners

EXAMPLE 1-1
LG1-3

For interactive versions of this example visit www.mhhe.com/canM

|||||||||||||||||||||||||||||||||||||||||||||||||||||||||||||||||||||||||||||||||||||||

Finance Applications

Chloe realizes how important finance will be for her future business career. However, some of the ways that she will see financial applications seem way off in the future. She is curious about how the theory applies to her personal litfe, both in the near term and in the long term.

SOLUTION:

Chloe will quickly find that her financial health now and in the future will depend upon many decisions she makes as she goes through life—starting now! For example, she will learn that the same tools that she applies to a business loan analysis can be applied to her own personal debt. After this course, Chloe will be able to evaluate credit card offers and select one that could save her hundreds of dollars per year. When she buys a new car and the dealership offers her a low interest rate loan or a higher rate loan with cash back, she will be able to pick the option that will truly cost her the least. Also, when Chloe gets her first professional job, she will know how to direct her retirement account so that she can earn millions of dollars for her future.

|||||||||||||||||||||||||||||||||||||||||||||||||||||||||||||||||||||||||||||||||||||||

The partners jointly share unlimited personal liability for the debts of the firm and all are obligated for contracts agreed to by any one of the partners. Banks are more willing to lend to partnerships than to sole proprietorships, because all partners are liable for repaying the debt. Partners would have to give up some ownership and control in the firm to raise more equity capital. In order to raise enough capital for substantial growth, a partnership often changes into a public corporation.

Corporations

Public corporations are legally *independent entities* entirely separate from their owners. This independence dramatically alters the firm's characteristics. Corporations hold many rights and obligations of individual persons, such as the ability to own property, sign binding contracts, and pay taxes. Federal and state governments tax corporate income once at the corporate level. Then shareholders pay taxes again at the personal level when corporate profits are paid out as dividends. This practice is generally known as **double taxation.**

Corporate owners are stockholders, also called *shareholders.* Public corporations typically have thousands of stockholders. The firm must hire managers to direct the firm, since thousands of individual shareholders could not direct day-to-day operations under any sort of consensus. As a result, managers control the company. Strong possibilities of conflicts of interests arise when one group of people owns the business, but another group controls it. We'll discuss conflicts of interest and their resolution later in the chapter.

As individual legal entities, corporations assume liability for their own debts, so the shareholders have only **limited liability.** That is, corporate shareholders cannot lose more money than they originally paid for their shares of stock. This limited liability is one reason that many people feel comfortable owning stock. Corporations are thus able to raise incredible amounts of money by selling stock (equity) and borrowing money. The largest businesses in the world are organized as corporations.

Hybrid Organizations

To promote the growth of small businesses, the U.S. government allows for several types of business organizations that simultaneously both offer limited personal liability for the owners *and* provide a pass-through of all firm earnings to the owners, so that the earnings are subject only to single taxation.

Hybrid organizations, such as *S corporations, limited liability partnerships (LLPs),* or *limited liability companies (LLCs),* offer single taxation and limited liability to all owners. Others, called *limited partnerships (LPs),* offer single taxation and limited liability to the *limited partners,* but also have *general partners,* who benefit from single taxation but also must bear personal liability for the firm's debts.

The U.S. government typically restricts hybrid organization status to relatively small firms. The government limits the maximum number of shareholders or partners involved,[3] the maximum amount of investment capital allowed, and the lines of business permitted. These restrictions are consistent with the government's stated reason for allowing the formation of these forms of business organization—to encourage the formation and growth of small businesses.

public corporation
A company owned by a large number of stockholders from the general public.

double taxation
A situation in which two taxes must be paid on the same income.

limited liability
Limitation of a person's financial liability to a fixed sum or investment.

time out!

1-3 Why must an entrepreneur give up some control of the business as it grows into a public corporation?

1-4 What advantages does the corporate form of organization hold over a partnership?

FIRM GOALS

Tens of thousands of public corporations operate in the United States. Many of them are the largest business organizations in the world. Because U.S. corporations are so large and because there are so many of them, corporations have a tremendous impact on society. Given the power that these huge firms wield, many people question what the corporate goals should be. Two different, well-developed viewpoints have arisen concerning

---

[3]For example, current federal regulations limit the number of shareholders in an S corporation to no more than 100.

finance at work //: corporate

Google Buys YouTube

In November 2006, Web search leader Google purchased the online video-sharing phenomenon YouTube for $1.65 billion. Google bought the firm by giving YouTube owners shares of Google stock in exchange for their ownership in YouTube. YouTube was a private corporation owned primarily by cofounders Chad Hurley and Steve Chen, who each received over $300 million of Google stock. Venture capital firm Sequoia Capital had backed YouTube and received $442 million of Google stock. Two dozen YouTube employees also had ownership stakes; some of them became millionaires from the deal.

YouTube was founded in February 2005. Imagine starting a business that was purchased for $1.65 billion less than two years later! Consider how many finance people and applications were needed to organize the buyout. Google's CFO George Reyes and team had to determine the value that YouTube could bring to Google. They also had to convince their own Google stockholders that Google did not overpay for the purchase. To do so, auditors had to evaluate YouTube's cash flows and the riskiness of those cash flows. The CFO, along with investment banker advisors, had to decide how to pay for YouTube. Google swapped its own stock for the firm but could have paid all cash or used a combination of cash and stock.

YouTube owners also had to assess the value of their stock to ensure that they received a fair price. Google's offer had to be compared to alternatives. For example, YouTube could have waited for a better offer from Google or sought an offer from another firm. Or YouTube owners could have decided to take the company public and sold shares to public investors.

This chapter illustrates the kinds of issues that finance addresses. The rest of the book describes the theories and tools needed to make these judgments. The practice of finance isn't just about numbers—the results of financial analysis are very dynamic and exciting!

Want to know more?

Key Words to Search for Updates: **Google, YouTube**

---

what the goal of the firm should be. The owners' perspective holds that the only appropriate goal is to **maximize shareholder wealth.** The competing viewpoint is from the **stakeholders'** perspective, which emphasizes social responsibility over profitability. This view maintains that managers must maximize the total satisfaction of all stakeholders in a business. These stakeholders include the owners and shareholders, but also include the business's customers, employees, and local communities.

While strong arguments speak in favor of both perspectives, financial practitioners and academics now tend to believe that the manager's primary responsibility should be to maximize

shareholder wealth and give only secondary consideration to other stakeholders' welfare. One of the first, and most well-known, proponents of this viewpoint was Adam Smith, an 18th-century economist who argued that, in capitalism, an individual pursuing his own interests tends also to promote the good of his community.[4]

Smith argued that the **invisible hand** of the market, acting through competition and the free price system, would ensure that only those activities most efficient and beneficial to society as a whole would survive in the long run. Thus, those same

[4]See Book IV of his *The Wealth of Nations.*

maximization of shareholder wealth A view that management should first and foremost consider the interests of shareholders in its business decisions.

stakeholder A person or organization that has a legitimate interest in a corporation.

invisible hand A metaphor used to illustrate how an individual pursuing his own interests also tends to promote the good of the community.

stock price The price of a share of stock trading on a stock market.

activities would also profit the individual most. When companies try to implement a goal other than profit maximization, their efforts tend to backfire. Consider the firm that tries to maximize employment. The high number of employees raises costs. Soon the firm will find that its costs are too high to allow it to compete against more efficient firms, especially in a global business environment. When the firm fails, all employees are let go and employment ends up being minimized, not maximized.

Regardless of whether you believe Smith's assertion or not, a more pragmatic reason supports the argument that maximizing owners' wealth is an admirable goal. As we discuss below, the owners of the firm hire managers to work on their behalf, so the manager is morally, ethically, and legally required to act in the owners' best interests. Any relationships between the manager and other firm stakeholders are necessarily secondary to the goal that shareholders give to their hired managers.

Maximizing owners' equity value means carefully considering:

- How best to bring additional funds into the firm.

- Which projects to invest in.

- How best to return the profits from those projects to the owners over time.

For corporations, maximizing the value of owners' equity can also be stated as *maximizing the current value per share, or* **stock price,** *of existing shares.* To the extent that the current stock price can be expected to include the present value of any future expected cash flows accruing to the owners, the goal of maximizing stock price provides us with a single, concrete, measurable gauge of value. You may be tempted to choose several other potential goals over maximizing the value of owners' equity. Common alternatives are:

Jodie Marks and four others like this.

Jodie Marks The live example about Disney and Michael Eisner helped me realize just how important this Finance stuff is.

7 hours ago · Like

write a comment...

- Maximizing net income or profit.
- Minimizing costs.
- Maximizing market share.

Though each may look appealing, each of these goals has some potentially serious shortcomings. For example, net income is measured on a year-by-year or quarter-by-quarter basis. When we say that we want to maximize profits, to which net income figure are we referring? We can maximize this year's net income in several legitimate ways, but many of these ways impose costs which will reduce future income. Or, current net income can be pushed into future years. Neither of these two extremes will likely encourage the firm's short-term and long-term stability. One more likely goal would be to maximize today's value of *all* future years of net income. Of course, this possible goal is very close to maximizing the current stock price, without the convenient market-oriented measure of the stock price. Another problem with considering maximizing all future profits as the goal is that net income (for reasons we'll go into later) does not really measure how much money the firm is actually earning.

Minimizing costs and *maximizing market share* also have fundamental problems as potential goals. Certainly minimizing costs would not make some stakeholders, like employees, very happy. In addition, without spending the money on R&D and new product development, many companies would not survive long in the ever-evolving economy without improving their products. A firm can always increase market share by lowering price. But if a firm loses money on every product sold, then selling more products will simply drive the firm into fiscal distress.

time out!

1-5 Describe why the primary objective of maximizing shareholder value may actually be the most beneficial for society in the long run.

AGENCY THEORY

Whenever one party (the *principal*) hires someone else (the *agent*) to work for him or her, their interaction is called an *agency relationship*. The agent is always supposed to act in the principal's best interests. For example, an apartment complex manager should ensure that tenants aren't doing willful damage to the property, that fire codes are enforced, and that the vacancy rate is kept as low as possible, because these are best for the apartment owner.

Agency Problem

In the context of a public corporation, we have already noted that stockholders hire managers to run the firm. Ideally, managers will operate the firm so that the shareholders realize maximum value for their equity. But managers may be tempted to operate the firm to serve their own best interests. Managers could spend company money to improve their own lifestyle instead of earning more profits for shareholders. Sometimes the manager's best interest does not necessarily align with shareholder goals. This creates a situation that we refer to as the **agency problem.**

For example, suppose it is time to buy a new corporate car for the firm's **chief executive officer (CEO).** Assuming

that the CEO has no extraordinary driving requirements, shareholders might wish for the CEO to buy a nice, conservative domestic sedan. But suppose that the CEO demands the newest, biggest luxury car available. It's tempting to say that the shareholders could just tell the CEO which car to buy. But remember, the CEO has most of the control in a public corporation. Organizational behavior specialists have identified three basic approaches to minimize this conflict of interest. First, ignore it. If the amount of money involved is small enough relative to the firm's cash flows, or if the suitability of the purchase in question is ambiguous enough, shareholders might be best served to simply overlook the problem. A good deal of research literature suggests that allowing the manager a certain amount of such **perks (perquisites)** might actually enhance owner value, in that such items may boost managers' productivity.[5]

The second approach to mitigating this conflict is to monitor managers' actions. Monitoring at too fine a level of detail is probably counterproductive and prohibitively expensive. However, major firm decisions are usually monitored at least roughly through the accounting auditing process. Also, shareholders can benefit indirectly from the fact that current debt holders with a relatively large stake in the firm will usually engage in

Perks can range from extra vacation to private transportation.

[5]See, for example, Raghuram Rajan and Julie Wulf, "Are Perks Really Managerial Excess?" *Journal of Financial Economics* 79(1), 2006, 1–33.

at least some additional monitoring of their own to insure their investments.[6]

The final approach for aligning managers' personal interests with those of owners is to make the managers owners—that is, to offer managers an equity stake in the firm so that management participates in any equity value increase. Many corporations take this approach, through explicitly granting shares to managers, by awarding them **options** on the firm's stock, or by allowing them to purchase shares at a subsidized price through an **employee stock option plan (ESOP).** When firm managers are also firm owners, their incentives are more likely to align with stockholders' best interests.

Corporate Governance

We refer to the process of monitoring managers and aligning their incentives with shareholder goals as **corporate governance.** Theoretically, managers work for shareholders. In reality, because shareholders are usually inactive,

[6]Potential acquirers will also often monitor firms for evidence that assets are being under- or misused by current management. To the extent that these acquirers may submit hostile takeover bids for the company (i.e., bids for enough of the company's shares to take control of the firm because existing management is not using firm assets in their highest use), current shareholders can benefit from this type of indirect monitoring, too.

the firm actually seems to belong to management. Generally speaking, the investing public does not know what goes on at the firm's operational level. Managers handle day-to-day operations, and they know that their work is mostly unknown to investors. This lack of supervision demonstrates the need for monitors. Figure 1.9 shows the people and organizations that help monitor corporate activities.

The monitors inside a public firm are the **board of directors,** who are appointed to represent shareholders' interests. The board hires the CEO, evaluates management, and can also design compensation contracts to tie management's salaries to firm performance.

The monitors outside the firm include auditors, analysts, investment banks, and credit rating agencies. **Auditors** examine the firm's accounting systems and comment on whether financial statements fairly

option The opportunity to buy stock at a fixed price over a specific period of time.

employee stock option plan (ESOP) An incentive program that grants options to employees (typically managers) as compensation.

corporate governance The set of laws, policies, incentives, and monitors designed to handle the issues arising from the separation of ownership and control.

board of directors The group of directors elected by stockholders to oversee management in a corporation.

auditor A person who performs an independent assessment of the fairness of a firm's financial statements.

▼**FIGURE 1.9** Corporate Governance Monitors

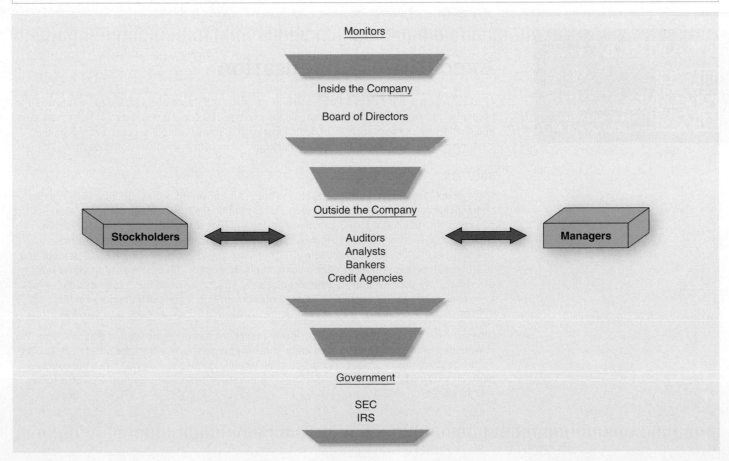

represent the firm's financial position. **Investment analysts** follow a firm, conduct their own evaluations of the company's business activities, and report to the investment community. **Investment banks,** which help firms access capital markets and advise managers about how to interact with those capital markets, also monitor firm performance. **Credit analysts** examine a firm's financial strength for its debt holders. The government also monitors business activities through the Securities and Exchange Commission (SEC) and the Internal Revenue Service (IRS).

The Role of Ethics

Ethics must play a strong role in any practice of finance. Finance professionals commonly manage other people's money. For example, corporate managers control the stockholder's firm, bank employees manage deposits, and

> Governments all over the world have passed laws and regulations meant to ensure compliance with ethical codes of behavior.

investment advisors manage people's investment portfolios. These **fiduciary** relationships create tempting opportunities for finance professionals to make decisions that either benefit the client or benefit the advisors themselves. Professional associations (such as for treasurers, bank executives, investment professionals, etc.) place a strong emphasis on ethical behavior and provide ethics training and standards. Nevertheless, as with any profession with millions of practitioners, a few are bound to act unethically.

The agency relationship between corporate managers and stockholders can create ethical dilemmas. Sometimes the corporate governance system has failed to prevent unethical managers from stealing from firms, which ultimately means stealing from shareholders. Governments all over the world have passed laws and regulations meant

EXAMPLE 1-2

LG1-6

For interactive versions of this example visit www.mhhe.com/canM

Executive Compensation

In 2005, firms in the Standard & Poor's 500 Index paid their CEOs, on average, $13.51 million, a 16.1 percent increase over the previous year. So the average CEO compensation was 411 times the average employee's compensation. In 2006, the increase in CEO pay was 8.9 percent. Every year, the controversy over CEO pay arises again. What arguments could be made on both sides?

SOLUTION:

Many people believe that CEOs are paid too much for the services they provide. They receive compensation that is far higher than workers' pay within their firms. Over the years, executive compensation has also increased at a faster and higher rate than has the value of the stockholders' wealth. For example, the return for stockholders of the S&P 500 Index firms was 15.6 percent in 2006 and 4.9 percent in 2005, compared to CEO pay increases of 8.9 percent and 16.1 percent, respectively. Each firm's board of directors sets CEO compensation. However, CEOs may have undue influence over director selection, tenure, and committee assignments— even over selecting the compensation advisors. This practice creates unhealthy conflicts of interest.

Others believe that a skilled CEO can positively affect company performance and that, therefore, the firm needs to offer high compensation and a bundle of perquisites to attract the best talent. To overcome agency problems, managers must be given incentives that pay very well when the company performs very well. If CEOs create a substantial amount of shareholder wealth, then who is to say that they are overpaid?

to ensure compliance with ethical codes of behavior.[7] And if professionals don't act appropriately, governments have set up strong punishments for financial malfeasance. In the end, financial managers must realize that they not only owe their shareholders the very best decisions to further shareholder interests, but they also have a broader obligation to society as a whole.

[7]The Sarbanes-Oxley Act of 2002 was passed in response to a number of recent major corporate accounting scandals including those affecting Enron, Tyco International, and WorldCom. The goal of the act was to make the accounting and auditing procedures more transparent and trustworthy.

finance at work //: corporate

The Amazing (Ongoing) Story of Apple Inc. and Steve Jobs

Steven Jobs and Stephen Wozniak started Apple Computer in 1976 as an equal partnership. Together, they built 50 computers in a garage using money borrowed from family, the proceeds from the sale of a VW bus, and credit from the parts distributor.

Jobs and Wozniak then designed the Apple II computer. But a higher production level to make more than 50 computers required more space and employees. They needed much more capital. They could not get a loan until angel investor Mike Markkula (an Intel executive) became a partner in the firm. He invested $92,000 and his personal guarantee induced a bank to loan Apple $250,000. As production ramped up in 1977, Apple Computer incorporated. Most shares were owned by Jobs, Wozniak, and Markkula, but the principals made some shares available to employees. They also hired an experienced manager (Mike Scott) to be the CEO and run the firm. Note that as the firm expanded, Jobs's ownership level and control got diluted. By 1980, Apple Computer had sold a total of 121,000 computers—against a potential demand of millions more. Apple needed even more capital.

At the end of 1980, Apple became a public corporation and sold $65 million worth of stock to public investors. Steve Jobs, cofounder of Apple, still owned more shares than anyone else (7.5 million), but he owned less than half of the firm. He gave up a great deal of ownership to new investors in exchange for the capital to expand the firm. Unhappy with Mike Scott's leadership, Steve Jobs also became CEO of Apple.

After a couple of years, Apple's board of directors felt that Jobs was not experienced enough to steer the firm through its rapid expansion. They hired John Sculley as CEO in 1983. In 1985, a power struggle ensued for control of the firm, and the board backed Sculley over Jobs. Jobs was forced out of Apple and no longer had a say in business operations, even though he was the largest shareholder and an original cofounder of the firm.

So, Steve Jobs bought Pixar in 1986 for $5 million and founded NeXT Computer. Over the next 10 years, Jobs's Pixar produced mega hit movies like *Toy Story, A Bug's Life,* and *Monsters, Inc.* This time, he kept 53 percent ownership of Pixar to ensure keeping full control. In the meantime, Apple Computer began to struggle, with losses of $800 million in 1996 and $1 billion in 1997. To get Steve Jobs back into the firm, Apple bought NeXT for $400 million and hired him as Apple's CEO. Over the next few years, Jobs introduced the iMAC, iPod, and iTunes, and Apple became very profitable again! Jobs was given the use of a $90 million Gulfstream jet as a perk. To realign his incentives, he became an Apple owner again via compensation that included options on 10 million shares of stock and 30 million shares of **restricted stock.** Then in 2006, Disney bought Pixar by swapping $7.4 billion worth of Disney stock for Pixar stock. When the deal closed, Steve Jobs became the largest owner of Disney stock (7 percent) and joined Disney's board of directors.

Wow! What a story of accessing capital, business organizational form, company control, and corporate governance.

Want to know more?

Key Words to Search for Updates: **Steve Jobs, Apple Computer, Pixar**

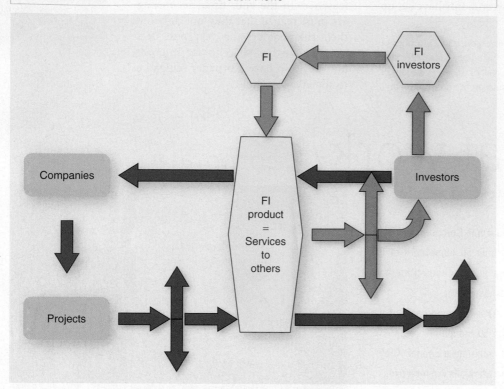

1-6 What unethical activities might managers engage in because of the agency problem?

1-7 Explain how the corporate governance system reduces the agency problem.

1-8 What is the role of financial institutions in a capitalist economy?

time out!

FINANCIAL MARKETS, INTERMEDIARIES, AND THE FIRM

Astute readers will note that we increased our emphasis on the role of financial markets and intermediaries throughout this chapter. This emphasis is intentional, as we feel that you must understand the role and impact of these institutions on the firm if you are to grasp the context in which professionals make financial management decisions.

There is one other important point we want to emphasize about these financial institutions (FI). Very astute readers may wonder how, if financial markets are competitive, investment banks and other financial institutions are able to make such impressive profits. Although FIs assist others with transactions involving financial assets in the financial markets, they do so as paid services. Successful execution of those services takes unique assets and expertise. As shown in Figure 1.10, it's the use of those unique assets and expertise that provides financial institutions with their high profit margins. ■

Get Online

mhhe.com/canM

for study materials including
quizzes, iPod downloads,
and video

Your Turn...

Questions

1. Describe the type of people who use the financial markets. *(LG1)*

2. What is the purpose of financial management? Describe the kinds of activities that financial management involves. *(LG1)*

3. What is the difference in perspective between finance and accounting? *(LG2)*

4. What personal decisions can you think of that will benefit from your learning finance? *(LG3)*

5. What are the three basic forms of business ownership? What are the advantages and disadvantages to each? *(LG4)*

6. Between the three basic forms of business ownership, describe the ability of each form to access capital. *(LG4)*

7. Explain how the founder of a business can eventually lose control of the firm. How can the founder ensure this will not happen? *(LG4)*

8. Explain the shareholder wealth maximization goal of the firm and how it can be measured. Make an argument for why it is a better goal than maximizing profit. *(LG5)*

9. Name and describe as many corporate stakeholders as you can. *(LG5)*

10. What conflicts of interest can arise between managers and stockholders? *(LG6)*

11. Figure 1.9 shows firm monitors. In your opinion, which group is in the best position to monitor the firm? Explain. Which group has the potential to be the weakest monitor? Explain. *(LG6)*

12. In recent years, governments all over the world have passed laws that increased the penalties for executives' crimes. Do you think this will deter unethical corporate managers? Explain. *(LG6)*

13. Every year, the media report on the vast amounts of money (sometimes hundreds of millions of dollars) that some CEOs earn from the companies they manage. Are these CEOs worth it? Give examples. *(LG6)*

14. Why is ethical behavior so important in the field of finance? *(LG7)*

15. Does the goal of shareholder wealth maximization conflict with behaving ethically? Explain. *(LG7)*

16. Describe how financial institutions and markets facilitate the expansion of a company's business. *(LG8)*

orporate managers must issue many reports to the public. Most stockholders, analysts, government entities, and other interested parties pay particular attention to annual reports. An annual report provides four basic **financial statements:** the balance sheet, the income statement, the statement of cash flows, and the statement of retained earnings.

These four statements provide an accounting-based picture of a firm's financial position. While accountants focus on reporting what happened in the past, financial managers use financial statements to draw inferences about the future. The statements often provide key information to firm managers, who make financial decisions, and to investors, who decide whether or not to invest in

reviewing
financial statements

the firm. In this chapter, we review these four vital financial statements, which you likely saw in accounting classes. We briefly examine each statement to identify its major features and uses. We highlight the differences between the accounting-based (or book) value of a firm as these statements report and the true market value of a firm. We also differentiate between accounting-based

continued on p. 22

LEARNING GOALS

LG1 Recall the major financial statements that firms must prepare and provide to the public.

LG2 Differentiate between book (or accounting) value and market value.

LG3 Explain how taxes influence corporate managers' and investors' decisions.

LG4 Differentiate between accounting income and cash flows.

LG5 Demonstrate how to use a firm's financial statements to calculate its cash flows.

LG6 Observe cautions that should be taken when examining financial statements.

continued from p. 21

income and actual cash flows, which we explore further in Chapter 3 as they are much more relevant to finance.

While firms must follow GAAP (generally accepted accounting principles), managers still have substantial discretion in preparing their firms' financial statements. For example, two firms with exactly the same operations may report financial statements that convey vastly different impressions about their firms' financial strengths, depending on managers' strategic plans for the future. We also discuss cautions that readers should take when they review and analyze financial statements in Chapter 3. ∎

viewpoints

business APPLICATION

The managers of DPH Tree Farm, Inc. believe the firm could double its sales if it had additional factory space and acreage. If DPH purchased the factory space and acreage in 2009, these new assets would cost $27 million to build and would require an additional $1 million in cash, $5 million in accounts receivable, $6 million in inventory, and $4 million in accounts payable. In addition to accounts payable, DPH Tree Farm would finance the new assets with the sale of a combination of long-term debt (40 percent of the total) and common stock (60 percent of the total). Assuming all else stays constant, what will these changes do to DPH Tree Farm's 2009 balance sheet assets, liabilities, and equity?

BALANCE SHEET

The **balance sheet** reports a firm's assets, liabilities, and equity at a particular point in time. A firm's assets must equal (balance) the liabilities and equity used to purchase the assets (hence the term *balance sheet*):

$$\text{Assets} = \text{Liabilities} + \text{Equity} \qquad (2\text{-}1)$$

Figure 2.1 illustrates a basic balance sheet and Table 2.1 on page 24 presents a simple balance sheet for DPH Tree Farm, Inc. as of December 31, 2007 and 2008. The left side of the balance sheet lists assets of the firm and the right side lists liabilities and

Assets

Figure 2.1 shows that assets fall into two major categories: current assets and fixed assets. **Current assets** will normally convert to cash within one year. They include cash and marketable securities, accounts receivable, and inventory. **Fixed assets** have a useful life exceeding one year. This class of assets includes physical (tangible) assets, such as net plant and equipment, and other, less tangible, long-term assets, such as patents and trademarks. We find the value of net plant and equipment by taking the difference between gross plant and equipment (or the fixed assets' original value) and the depreciation accumulated against the fixed assets since their purchase.

> "The balance sheet reports a firm's assets, liabilities, and equity at a particular point in time."

equity. Both assets and liabilities are listed in descending order of **liquidity,** that is, the time and effort it takes to convert the accounts to cash. The most liquid assets—called *current assets*—appear first on the asset side of the balance sheet. The least liquid, called *fixed assets,* appear last. Similarly, *current liabilities*—those obligations that the firm must pay within a year, appear first on the right side of the balance sheet. *Stockholders' equity*, which never matures, appears last on the balance sheet.

▼ FIGURE 2.1 The Basic Balance Sheet

Total Assets		Total Liabilities and Equity
Current assets	net working capital	Current liabilities
Cash and marketable securities		Accrued wages and taxes
Accounts receivable		Accounts payable
Inventory		Notes payable
Fixed assets		Long-term debt
Gross plant and equipment		
Less: Depreciation		Stockholders' equity
Net plant and equipment		Preferred stock
Other long-term		Common stock and paid-in surplus
		Retained earnings

Liabilities and Stockholders' Equity

Lenders provide funds, which become **liabilities** to the firm. Liabilities fall into two categories as well: current or long-term. **Current liabilities** constitute the firm's obligations due within one year, including accrued wages and taxes, accounts payable, and notes payable. **Long-term debt** includes long-term loans and bonds with maturities of more than one year.

The difference between total assets and total liabilities of a firm is the stockholders' (or owners') equity. The firm's preferred and common stock owners provide the funds known as **stockholders' equity. Preferred stock** appears on the balance sheet as the cash proceeds when the firm sells preferred stock in a public offering. Similarly, the proceeds from **common stock and paid-in surplus** appear as the other component of stockholders' equity. If the firm's managers decide to reinvest cumulative earnings rather than pay the dividends to stockholders, the balance sheet will record these funds as **retained earnings.**

Managing the Balance Sheet

Managers must monitor a number of issues underlying items reported on their firms' balance sheets. These include:

- The accounting method for fixed asset depreciation.
- The level of net working capital.
- The liquidity position of the firm.
- The method for financing the firm's assets—equity or debt.
- The difference between the book value reported on the balance sheet and the true market value of the firm.

Accounting Method for Fixed Asset Depreciation

Firm managers can choose the accounting method they use to record depreciation against their fixed assets. Two choices include the straight-line method and the modified accelerated cost recovery system (MACRS). Companies often calculate depreciation using MACRS when computing the firm's taxes and the straight-line method when reporting income to the firm's stockholders. The MACRS method accelerates depreciation, which results in higher depreciation expenses and lower taxable income and lower taxes in the early years of a project's life. The straight-line method results in lower depreciation expenses, but also results in higher taxes in the early years of a project's life. Firms seeking to lower their cash outflows from tax payments will favor the MACRS depreciation method.

Net Working Capital

We arrive at a **net working capital** figure by taking the difference between a firm's current assets and current liabilities. So, clearly, net working capital is positive when the firm has more current assets than current liabilities. Table 2.1 on page 24 shows the 2007 and 2008 year-end balance sheets for DPH Tree Farm, Inc. At year-end 2007, the firm had $190 million of current assets and $110 million of current liabilities. So the firm's net working capital was $80 million. A firm needs cash and other liquid assets to pay its bills as expenses come due. Liability holders monitor net working capital as a measure of a firm's ability to pay its obligations. Positive net working capital values are usually a sign of a healthy firm.

Liquidity

As we noted above, any firm needs cash and other liquid assets to pay its bills as debts come due. Liquidity actually refers to two dimensions: the ease with which the firm can convert an asset to cash, and the degree to which such a conversion takes place at a fair market value. You can convert any asset to cash quickly if you price the asset low enough. But clearly, you will wish to convert the asset without giving up a great portion of its value. So a highly liquid asset can be sold quickly at its fair market value. An illiquid asset, on the other hand, cannot be sold quickly unless you reduce the price far below fair value.

DPH TREE FARM, INC. Balance Sheet as of December 31, 2007 and 2008 (in millions of dollars)						
Assets	**2007**	**2008**	**Liabilities and Equity**	**2007**	**2008**
Current assets			Current liabilities		
Cash and marketable securities	$ 25	$ 24	Accrued wages and taxes	$ 15	$ 20
Accounts receivable	65	70	Accounts payable	50	55
Inventory	100	111	Notes payable	45	45
Total	190	205	Total	110	120
Fixed assets			Long-term debt	190	195
Gross plant and equipment	300	368	Total debt	300	315
Less: Depreciation	40	53	Stockholders' equity		
Net plant and equipment	260	315	Preferred stock (5 million shares)	5	5
Other long-term			Common stock and paid-in surplus (20 million shares)	40	40
assets	50	50	Retained earnings	155	210
Total	310	365	Total	200	255
Total assets	$500	$570	Total liabilities and equity	$500	$570

Current assets, by definition, remain relatively liquid, including cash and assets that will convert to cash within the next year. Inventory is the least liquid of the current assets. Fixed assets, and powerful machines—given a long enough lever, you can move almost anything. **Financial leverage** is likewise very powerful. Leverage in the financial sense refers to the extent to

> ## LEVERAGE IN THE FINANCIAL SENSE REFERS TO THE EXTENT TO WHICH A FIRM CHOOSES TO FINANCE ITS VENTURES OR ASSETS BY ISSUING DEBT SECURITIES.

then, remain relatively illiquid. In the normal course of business, the firm would have no plans to liquefy or convert these tangible assets such as buildings and equipment into cash.

Liquidity presents a double-edged sword on a balance sheet. The more liquid assets a firm holds, the less likely the firm will be to experience financial distress. However, liquid assets generate no profits for a firm. For example, cash is the most liquid of all assets, but it earns no return for the firm. In contrast, fixed assets are illiquid, but provide the means to generate revenue. Thus, managers must consider the trade-off between the advantages of liquidity on the balance sheet and the disadvantages of having money sit idle rather than generating profits.

Debt versus Equity Financing Ever since your high school physics class, you have known that levers are very useful

which a firm chooses to finance its ventures or assets by issuing debt securities. The more debt a firm issues as a percentage of its total assets, the greater its financial leverage. We discuss in later chapters why financial leverage can greatly magnify the firm's gains *and* losses for the firm's stockholders.

When a firm issues debt securities—usually bonds—to finance its activities and assets, debt holders usually demand first claim to a fixed amount of the firm's cash flows. Their claims are fixed because the firm must only pay the interest owed to bondholders and any principal repayments that come due within any given period. Stockholders—who buy equity securities or stocks—claim any cash flows left after debt holders are paid. When a firm does well, financial leverage increases shareholders' rewards, since the share of the firm's profits promised to debt holders is set and predictable.

The book value and market value of a classic car can be very different.

However, financial leverage also increases risk. Leverage can create the potential for the firm to experience financial distress and even bankruptcy. If the firm has a bad year and cannot make its scheduled debt payments, debt holders can force the firm into bankruptcy. But managers generally prefer to fund firm activities using debt, precisely because they can calculate the cost of doing business without giving away too much of the firm's value. So managers often walk a fine line as they decide upon the firm's **capital structure**—the amount of debt versus equity financing to hold on the balance sheet—because it can determine whether the firm stays in business or goes bankrupt.

Book Value versus Market Value Beginning finance students usually have already taken accounting, so they are familiar with the accounting point of view. For example, a firm's balance sheet shows its **book (or historical cost) value** based on generally accepted accounting principles (GAAP). Under GAAP, assets appear on the balance sheet at the price the firm paid for them, regardless of what those assets might be worth today if the firm were to sell them. Inflation and market forces make many assets worth more now than they were when the firm bought them. So in most cases, book values differ widely from the **market values** for the same assets—the amount that the assets would fetch if the firm actually sold them. For the firm's current assets—those that mature within a year—the book value and market value of any particular asset will remain very close. For example, the balance sheet lists cash and marketable securities at their market value. Similarly, firms acquire accounts receivable and inventory and then convert these short-term assets into cash fairly quickly, so the book value of these assets is generally close to their market value.

The "book value versus market value" issue really arises when we try to determine how much a firm's fixed assets are worth. In this case, book value is often very different from market value. For example, if a firm owns land for 100 years, this asset appears on the balance sheet at its historical cost (of 100 years ago). Most likely, the firm would reap a much higher price on the land upon its sale than the historical price would indicate.

financial leverage The extent to which debt securities are used by a firm.

capital structure The amount of debt versus equity financing to maintain on the balance sheet.

book (or historical cost) value Assets are listed on the balance sheet at the amount the firm paid for them.

market value Assets are listed at the amount the firm would get if it sold them.

EXAMPLE 2-1

For interactive versions of this example visit www.mhhe.com/canM

Calculating Book versus Market Value

EZ Toy, Inc. lists fixed assets of $25 million on its balance sheet. The firm's assets have recently been appraised at $32 million. EZ Toy, Inc.'s balance sheet also lists current assets at $10 million. Current assets were appraised at $11 million. Current liabilities' book and market values stand at $6 million and the firm's long-term debt is $15 million. Calculate the book and market values of the firm's stockholders' equity. Construct the book value and market value balance sheets for EZ Toy, Inc.

SOLUTION:

Recall the balance sheet identity in equation 2-1: Assets = Liabilities + Equity. Rearranging this equation: Equity = Assets − Liabilities. Thus, the balance sheets would appear as follows:

Value Assets	Book Value	Market Value	Liabilities and Equity	Book Value	Market Value
Current assets	$10m.	$11m.	Current liabilities	$ 6m.	$ 6m.
Fixed assets	25m.	32m.	Long-term debt	15m.	15m.
			Stockholders' equity	14m.	22m.
Total	$35m.	$43m.	Total	$35m.	$43m.

Again, accounting tools reflect the past: Balance sheet assets are listed at historical cost. Managers would thus see little relation between the total asset value listed on the balance sheet and the current market value of the firm's assets. Similarly, the stockowners' equity listed on the balance sheet generally differs from the true market value of the equity. In this case, the market value may be higher or lower than the value listed on the firm's accounting books. So financial managers and investors often find that balance sheet values are not always the most relevant numbers. The following example illustrates the difference between the book value and the market value of a firm's assets.

time out!

2-1 What is a balance sheet?

2-2 Which are the most liquid assets and liabilities on a balance sheet?

INCOME STATEMENT

You will recall that **income statements** show the total revenues that a firm earns and the total expenses the firm incurs to generate those revenues over a specific period of time—generally one year. Remember that while the balance sheet reports a firm's position at a point in time, the income statement reports performance over a period of time, for example, over the last year. Figure 2.2 illustrates a basic income statement and Table 2.2 on the next page shows a simple income statement for DPH Tree Farm, Inc. for the years ended December 31, 2007 and 2008. DPH's revenues (or net sales) appear at the top of the income statement. The income statement then shows various expenses (cost of goods sold, depreciation, interest, and taxes) subtracted from revenues to arrive at profit or income measures.

The top part of the income statement reports the firm's operating income. First, we subtract the cost of goods sold (the direct costs of producing the firm's product) from net sales to get **gross**

profit (so, DPH Tree Farm enjoyed gross profits of $140 million in 2007 and $165 million in 2008). Next, we deduct depreciation from gross profits to get operating profit or earnings before interest and taxes (**EBIT**) (so DPH Tree Farm's EBIT was $128 million in 2007 and $152 million in 2008). The EBIT figure represents the profit earned from the sale of the product without any financing cost or tax considerations.

The bottom part of the income statement summarizes the firm's financial and tax structure. First, we subtract interest expense (the cost to service the firm's debt) from EBIT to get earnings before taxes (**EBT**). So, as we follow our sample income statement, DPH Tree Farm had EBT of $110 million in 2007 and $136 million in 2008. Of course, firms differ in their financial structures and tax situations. These differences can cause two firms with identical operating income to report differing levels of net income. For example, one firm may finance its assets with only debt, while another finances with only common equity. The company with no debt would have no interest expense. Thus, even though EBIT for the two firms is identical, the firm with all-equity financing and no debt would report higher net income. We subtract taxes from EBT to get the last item on the income statement (the "bottom line"), or **net income.** DPH Tree Farm, Inc. reported net income of $70 million in 2007 and $90 million in 2008.

Below the net income, or bottom line, on the income statement, firms often report additional information summarizing income and firm value. For example, with its $90 million of net income

▼ **FIGURE 2.2** The Basic Income Statement

Net sales	
Less: Cost of goods sold	
Gross profits	Operating income
Less: Depreciation	
Earnings before interest and taxes (EBIT)	
Less: Interest	
Earnings before taxes (EBT)	Financing and tax considerations
Less: Taxes	
Net income before preferred dividends	
Preferred dividends	
Net income	

in 2008, DPH Tree Farm, Inc. paid its preferred stockholders cash dividends of $10 million and its common stockholders cash dividends of $25 million, and added the remaining $55 million to retained earnings. Table 2.1 shows that retained earnings on the balance sheet increased from $155 million in 2007 to $210 million in 2008. Other items reported below the bottom line include:

$$\text{Earnings per share (EPS)} = \frac{\text{Net income available to common stockholders}}{\text{Total shares of common stock outstanding}} \quad (2\text{-}2)$$

$$\text{Dividends per share (DPS)} = \frac{\text{Common stock dividends paid}}{\text{Number of shares of common stock outstanding}} \quad (2\text{-}3)$$

$$\text{Book Value per share (BVPS)} = \frac{\text{Common stockholders' equity}}{\text{Numbers of shares of common stock outstanding}} \quad (2\text{-}4)$$

$$\text{Market value per share (MVPS)} = \frac{\text{Market price of the firm's common stock}}{} \quad (2\text{-}5)$$

We discuss these items further in Chapter 3.

▼ **TABLE 2.2** Income Statement for DPH Tree Farm, Inc.

DPH TREE FARM, INC. Income Statement for Years Ending December 31, 2007 and 2008 (in millions of dollars)		
	2007	2008
Net sales (all credit)	$275	$315
Less: Cost of goods sold	135	150
Gross profits	140	165
Less: Depreciation	12	13
Earnings before interest and taxes (EBIT)	128	152
Less: Interest	18	16
Earnings before taxes (EBT)	110	136
Less: Taxes	40	46
Net income	$ 70	$ 90
Less: Preferred stock dividends	$ 10	$ 10
Net income available to common stock holders	$ 60	$ 80
Less: Common stock dividends	$ 25	$ 25
Addition to retained earnings	$ 35	$ 55
Per (common) share data:		
Earnings per share (EPS)	$ 3.00	$ 4.00
Dividends per share (DPS)	$ 1.25	$ 1.25
Book value per share (BVPS)	$ 9.75	$ 12.50
Market value (price) per share (MVPS)	$ 15.60	$ 17.25

Corporate Income Taxes

Firms pay out a large portion of their earnings in taxes. For example, in 2005, Microsoft had EBT of $16.6 billion. Of this amount, Microsoft paid $4.4 billion (over 26 percent of EBT) in taxes. Congress oversees the U.S. tax code, which determines corporate tax obligations. Corporate taxes can thus change with changes of administration or other changes in the business or public environment. As you might expect, the U.S. tax system is extremely complicated, so we do not attempt to cover it in detail here. However, firms recognize taxes as a major expense item and many financial decisions arise from tax considerations. In this section we provide a general overview of the U.S. corporate tax system.

The 2008 corporate tax schedule appears in Table 2.3 on the next page. Note from this table that the U.S. tax structure is progressive, meaning that the larger the income, the higher the taxes assessed. However, corporate tax rates do not increase in any kind of linear way based on this progressive nature: They rise from a low of 15 percent to a high of 39 percent, then drop to 34 percent, rise to 38 percent, and finally drop to 35 percent.

In addition to calculating their tax liability, firms also want to know their **average tax rate** and **marginal tax rate.** You can figure the average tax rate as the percentage of each dollar of taxable income that the firm pays in taxes.

$$\text{Average tax rate} = \frac{\text{Tax liability}}{\text{Taxable income}} \quad (2\text{-}6)$$

From your economics classes, you can probably guess that the firm's marginal tax rate is the amount of additional taxes a firm must pay out for every additional dollar of taxable income it earns.

income statement Financial statement that reports the total revenues and expenses over a specific period of time.

gross profit Net sales minus cost of goods sold.

EBIT Earnings before interest and taxes.

EBT Earnings before taxes.

net income The bottom line on the income statement.

average tax rate The average tax rate is the percentage of each dollar of taxable income that the firm pays in taxes.

marginal tax rate The amount of additional taxes a firm must pay out for every additional dollar of taxable income it earns.

▼ TABLE 2.3 Corporate Tax Rates as of 2008

Taxable Income	Pay This Amount on Base Income	Plus This Percentage on Anything over the Base
$0 − $50,000	$ 0	15%
$50,001 − $75,000	7,500	25
$75,001 − $100,000	13,750	34
$100,001 − $335,000	22,250	39
$335,001 − $10,000,000	113,900	34
$10,000,001 − $15,000,000	3,400,000	35
$15,000,001 − $18,333,333	5,150,000	38
Over $18,333,333	6,416,667	35

Interest and Dividends Received by Corporations

Any interest that corporations receive is taxable, though a notable exception arises: Interest on state and local government bonds is exempt from federal taxes. The U.S. tax code allows this exception to encourage corporations to be better community citizens by supporting local governments. Another exception of sorts arises when one corporation owns stock in another corporation. Seventy percent of any dividends received from other corporations is tax exempt. Only the remaining 30 percent is taxed at the receiving corporation's tax rate.[1]

Interest and Dividends Paid by Corporations

Corporate interest payments appear on the income statement as an expense item, so we deduct interest payments from operating income when the firm calculates taxable income. But any dividends paid by corporations to their shareholders are not tax deductible. This is one factor that encourages managers to finance projects with debt financing rather than to sell more stock. Suppose one firm uses mainly debt financing and another firm, with identical operations, uses mainly equity financing. The equity-financed firm will have very little interest expense to deduct for tax purposes. Thus, it will have higher taxable income and pay more taxes than the debt-financed firm. The debt-financed firm will pay fewer taxes and be able to pay more of its operating income to asset funders, that is, its bondholders and stockholders. So even stockholders prefer that firms finance assets primarily with debt rather than with stock. The debt-versus-equity financing issue is called *capital structure*, which we address more fully in Part Seven of the book.

[1]This tax code provision prevents or reduces any triple taxation that could occur: income could be taxed at three levels: (1) on the income from the dividend-paying firm, (2) as income for the dividend-receiving firm, and (3) finally, on the personal income of stockholders who receive dividends.

EXAMPLE 2-2

For interactive versions of this example visit www.mhhe.com/canM

Calculation of Corporate Taxes

Indian Point Kennels, Inc. earned $16.5 million taxable income (EBT) in 2008. Use the tax schedule in Table 2.3 to determine the firm's 2008 tax liability, its average tax rate, and its marginal tax rate.

SOLUTION:

From Table 2.3, the $16.5 million of taxable income puts Indian Point Kennels in the 38 percent marginal tax bracket. Thus

Tax liability = Tax on base amount + Tax rate (amount over base)

$$= \$5,150,000 + .38\,(\$16,500,000 - \$15,000,000) = \$5,720,000$$

Note that the base amount is the maximum dollar value listed in the previous tax bracket. In this example, we take the highest dollar value ($15,000,000) in the preceding tax bracket (35 percent). The additional percentage owed results from multiplying the income above and beyond the $15,000,000 (or $1,500,000) by the marginal tax rate (38%). The *average* tax rate for Indian Point Kennels, Inc. comes to:

$$\text{Average tax rate} = \frac{\text{Tax liability}}{\text{Taxable income}}$$

$$= \$5,720,000 / \$16,500,000 = 34.67\%$$

If Indian Point Kennels earned $1 more of taxable income, it would pay 38 cents (its tax rate of 38 percent) more in taxes. Thus, the firm's marginal tax rate is 38 percent.

Corporate Taxes with Interest and Dividend Income

In the example above, suppose that in addition to the $16.5 million of taxable income, Indian Point Kennels, Inc. received $250,000 of interest on state-issued bonds and $500,000 of dividends on common stock it owns in DPH Tree Farm, Inc. How do these items affect Indian Point Kennel's tax liability, average tax rate, and marginal tax rate?

SOLUTION:

In this case, interest on the state-issued bonds is not taxable and should not be included in taxable income. Further, the first 70 percent of the dividends received from DPH Tree Farm is not taxable. Thus, only 30 percent of the dividends received are taxed, so:

Taxable income = $16,500,000 + (.3)$500,000 = $16,650,000

Now Indian Point Kennel's tax liability will be:

Tax liability = $5,150,000 + .38 ($16,650,000 − $15,000,000) = $5,777,000

The $500,000 of dividend income increased Indian Point Kennel's tax liability by $57,000. Indian Point Kennels, Inc.'s resulting average tax rate is now:

Average tax rate = $5,77,000/$16,650,000 = 34.70%

Finally, if Indian Point Kennels earned $1 more of taxable income, it would still pay 38 cents (based upon its marginal tax rate of 38 percent) more in taxes.

Effect of Debt versus Equity Financing on Funders' Returns

Suppose that you are considering a stock investment in one of two firms (AllDebt, Inc. and AllEquity, Inc.), both of which operate in the same industry and have identical operating incomes of $5 million. AllDebt, Inc. finances its $12 million in assets with $11 million in debt (on which it pays 10 percent interest) and $1 million in equity. AllEquity, Inc. finances its $12 million in assets with no debt and $12 million in equity. Both firms pay 30 percent tax on their taxable income. Calculate the income that each firm has available to pay its debt and stockholders and the resulting return on assets for the two firms.

SOLUTION:

	AllDebt, Inc.	AllEquity, Inc.
Operating income	$5.00m.	$5.00m.
Less: Interest	1.10m.	0.00m.
Taxable income	3.90m.	5.00m.
Less: Taxes (30%)	1.17m.	1.50m.
Net income	$2.73m.	$3.50m.
Income available for asset funders (= operating income − taxes)	$3.83m.	$3.50m.
Return on asset-funders' investment	$3.83m/$12m = 31.92%	$3.50m/$12.0m = 29.17%

By financing most of its assets with debt and receiving the associated tax benefits from the interest paid on this debt, AllDebt, Inc. is able to pay more of its operating income to the funders of its assets, i.e., its debt holders and stockholders, than AllEquity, Inc.

time out!

2-3 What is an income statement?

2-4 When a corporation owns stock in another corporation, what percentage of dividends received on the stock is taxed?

STATEMENT OF CASH FLOWS

Clearly, income statements and balance sheets are the most common financial documents available to the public. But managers who make financial decisions may find themselves at something of a loss if they only have these two documents—reports on past performance—on which to base their decisions for today and into the future. Consider the following. Company accountants must prepare firm income statements following GAAP principles. GAAP procedures require that the firm recognize revenue at the time of sale, but sometimes the company receives the cash before or after the time of sale. Likewise, GAAP counsels the firm to show production and other expenses on the balance sheet as the sales of those goods take place. So production and other expenses associated with a particular product's sale only appear on the income statement (for example, cost of goods sold and depreciation) when that product sells. Of course, just as with the revenue recognition, actual cash outflows incurred with production may occur at a very different point in time—usually much earlier than GAAP principles allow the firm to formally recognize the expenses.

Further, income statements contain several noncash entries, the largest of which is depreciation. Depreciation attempts to capture the noncash expense incurred as fixed assets deteriorate from the time of purchase to the point when those assets must be replaced. Let's illustrate the effect of depreciation: Suppose a firm purchases a machine for $100,000. The machine has an expected life of five years

and at the end of those five years, the machine will have no expected salvage value. The firm lays out a $100,000 cash outflow at the time of purchase. But the entire $100,000 does not appear on the income statement in the year that the firm purchases the machine—in accounting terms, the machine is not *expensed* in the year of purchase. Rather, if the firm's accounting department uses the straight-line depreciation method, it deducts only $100,000/5, or $20,000, each year as an expense. This $20,000 equipment expense is not a cash outflow for the firm. The person in charge of buying the machine knows that the cash flow occurred at the time of purchase—and it totaled $100,000 rather than $20,000.

So, figures shown on an income statement may not represent the actual cash inflows and outflows for a firm during a particular period. Financial managers and investors, however, are far more interested in actual cash flows than they are in the somewhat artificial, backward-looking accounting profit listed on the income statement. This is a very important distinction between the accounting point of view and the finance point of view. Finance professionals know that the firm needs cash, not accounting profit, to pay the firm's obligations as they come due, to fund the firm's operations and growth, and to compensate the firm's ultimate owners: its shareholders. Thus, the **statement of cash flows** is a financial statement that shows the firm's cash flows over a given period of time. This statement reports the amounts of cash that the firm generated and distributed during a particular time period. The bottom line on the statement of cash flows—the difference between cash sources and uses—equals the change in cash on the firm's balance sheet from the previous year's cash account balance. That is, the statement of cash flows reconciles income statement items and noncash balance sheet items to show changes in the cash and marketable securities account on the balance sheet over the particular analysis period.

Sources and Uses of Cash

In general, some activities increase cash (cash sources) and some decrease cash (cash uses). Figure 2.3 classifies the firm's basic cash sources and uses. Cash sources include increasing liabilities (or equity) or decreasing noncash assets. For example,

▼ **FIGURE 2.3** Sources and Uses of Cash

Sources of Cash	Uses of Cash
Decrease a noncash current asset	Increase a noncash current asset
Decrease a fixed asset	Increase a fixed asset
Increase a current liability	Decrease a current liability
Increase long-term debt	Decrease long-term debt
Net income	Net losses
Depreciation	Pay dividends
Sell common or preferred stock	Repurchase common or preferred stock

if a firm sells new common stock, the firm has used primary markets to raise cash. Likewise, a drop in accounts receivable means that the firm has collected cash from its credit sales—also a cash source. The firm used cash to decrease a liability (paying off a bank loan) or to increase noncash assets (buying inventory). The statement of cash flows separates these cash flows into three categories or sections:

1. Cash flows from operating activities.
2. Cash flows from investing activities.
3. Cash flows from financing activities.

The basic setup of a statement of cash flows is shown in Figure 2.4 and a more detailed statement of cash flows for DPH Tree Farm, Inc. for the year ending December 31, 2008, appears as Table 2.4.

Cash flows from operations are those cash inflows and outflows that result directly from producing and selling the firm's products. These cash flows include:

- Net income.
- Depreciation.
- Working capital accounts other than cash and operations-related short-term debt.

Most finance professionals consider this top section of the statement of cash flows to be the most important. It shows quickly and compactly the firm's cash flows generated by and used for the production process. For example, DPH Tree Farm, Inc.

statement of cash flows Financial statement that shows the firm's cash flows over a period of time.

cash flows from operations Cash flows that are the direct result of the production and sale of the firm's products.

▼ **FIGURE 2.4** The Statement of Cash Flows

A. Cash flows from operating activities

Net income

Additions (sources of cash):

   Depreciation

   Decrease in noncash current asset

   Increase in accrued wages and taxes

   Increase in accounts payable

Subtractions (uses of cash):

   Increase in noncash current asset

   Decrease in accrued wages and taxes

   Decrease in accounts payable

B. Cash flows from investing activities

Additions:

   Decrease in fixed assets

   Decrease in other long-term assets

Subtractions:

   Increase in fixed assets

   Increase in other long-term assets

C. Cash flows from financing activities

Additions:

   Increase in notes payable

   Increase in long-term debt

   Increase in common and preferred stock

Subtractions:

   Decrease in notes payable

   Decrease in long-term debt

   Decrease in common and preferred stock

   Pay dividends

D. Net change in cash and marketable securities

▼ **TABLE 2.4** Statement of Cash Flows for DPH Tree Farm, Inc.

DPH TREE FARM, INC. Statement of Cash Flows for Year Ending December 31, 2008 (in millions of dollars)	
	2008
A. Cash flows from operating activities	
Net income	$90
Additions (sources of cash):	
Depreciation	13
Increase in accrued wages and taxes	5
Increase in accounts payable	5
Subtractions (uses of cash):	
Increase in accounts receivable	5
Increase in inventory	−11
Net cash flow from operating activities	$97
B. Cash flows from investing activities	
Subtractions:	
Increase in fixed assets	−$68
Increase in other long-term assets	0
Net cash flow from investing activities	−$68
C. Cash flows from financing activities	
Additions:	
Increase in notes payable	$0
Increase in long-term debt	5
Increase in common and preferred stock	0
Subtractions:	
Pay preferred stock dividends	−10
Pay common stock dividends	− 25
Net cash flow from financing activities	−$30
D. Net change in cash and marketable securities	−$1

generated $97 million in cash flows from its 2008 production. That is, producing and selling the firm's product resulted in a net cash inflow for the firm. Managers and investors look for positive cash flows from operations as a sign of a successful firm—positive cash flows from the firm's operations is precisely what gives the firm value. Unless the firm has a stable, healthy pattern in its cash flows from operations, it is not financially healthy no matter what its level of cash flow from investing activities or cash flows from financing activities.

Cash flows from investing activities are cash flows associated with buying or selling of fixed or other long-term assets. This section of the statement of cash flows shows cash inflows and outflows from long-term investing activities—most significantly the firm's investment in fixed assets. For example, DPH Tree Farm, Inc. used $68 million in cash to purchase fixed and other long-term assets in 2008. DPH funded this $68 million cash outflow with the $97 million cash surplus it produced from its operations.

Cash flows from financing activities are cash flows that result from debt and equity financing transactions. These include raising cash by:

- Issuing short-term debt.
- Issuing long-term debt.
- Issuing stock.
- Using cash to pay dividends.
- Using cash to pay off debt.
- Using cash to buy back stock.

In 2008, DPH Tree Farm, Inc.'s financing activities produced a net cash outflow of $30 million. As we saw with cash flows from financing activities, this $30 million cash outflow was funded (at least partially) with the $97 million cash surplus DPH Tree Farm produced from its operations. Managers, investors, and analysts normally expect the cash flows from financing activities to include small amounts of net borrowing along with dividend payments. If, however, a firm is going through a major period of expansion, net borrowing could reasonably be much higher.

The bottom line of the statement of cash flows shows the sum of cash flows from operations, investing activities, and financing activities. The bottom line will reconcile to the **net change in cash and marketable securities** account on the balance sheet over the period of analysis. For example, the bottom line of the statement of cash flows for DPH Tree Farm is −$1 million. This is also the change in the cash account on the balance sheet between 2007 and 2008 ($24 million − $25 million = − $1 million). In this case, the firm's operating, investing, and financing activities combined to produce a net drain on the firm's cash during 2008—cash outflows were greater than cash inflows, largely because of the $68 million investment in long-term and fixed assets. Of course, when the bottom line is positive, a firm's cash inflows exceed cash outflows for the period.

Even though a company may report a large amount of net income on its income statement during a year, the firm may actually receive a positive, negative, or zero amount of cash. For example, DPH Tree Farm, Inc. reported net income of $90 million on its income statement (in Table 2.2), yet reported a net change in cash and marketable securities of −$1 million on its

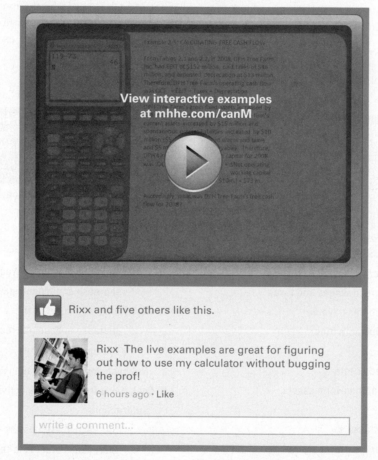

View interactive examples at mhhe.com/canM

Rixx and five others like this.

Rixx The live examples are great for figuring out how to use my calculator without bugging the prof!

6 hours ago · Like

write a comment...

statement of cash flows (in Table 2.4). Accounting rules under GAAP create this sense of discord: Net income is the result of accounting rules, or GAAP, that do not necessarily reflect the firm's cash flows. While the income statement shows a firm's accounting-based income, the statement of cash flows more often reflects reality today and is thus more important to managers and investors as they seek to answer such important questions as:

- Does the firm generate sufficient cash to pay its obligations, thus avoiding financial distress?

- Does the firm generate sufficient cash to purchase assets needed for sustained growth?

- Does the firm generate sufficient cash to pay down its outstanding debt obligations?

Free Cash Flow

The statement of cash flows measures net cash flow as net income plus noncash adjustments. However, to maintain cash flows over time, firms must continually replace working capital and depreciating fixed assets and develop new products. Thus, firm managers cannot use the available cash flows any way they please. Of particular interest to investors, **free cash flows** are the cash flows available to pay the firm's stockholders and debt holders after the firm has made the necessary working capital investments, fixed asset investments, and developed the necessary new products to sustain the firm's ongoing operations.

DPH Tree Farm reported net income of $90 million, yet reported a net change in cash and marketable securities of − $1 million on its statement of cash flows.

To calculate free cash flow (FCF), we use the mathematical equation that appears below:

$$FCF = [EBIT - Taxes + Depreciation] - [\Delta Gross\ fixed\ assets + \Delta Net\ operating\ working\ capital]$$

$$= Operating\ cash\ flow - Investment\ in\ operating\ capital \qquad (2\text{-}7)$$

Calculating Free Cash Flow

From Tables 2.1 and 2.2, DPH Tree Farm, Inc. had EBIT of $152 million, paid taxes of $46 million, and expensed deprecation at $13 million in 2008. Therefore, DPH Tree Farm's operating cash flow was

OCF = EBIT − Taxes + Depreciation

   = ($152m. − $46m. + $13m.) = $119m.

DPH Tree Farm's gross fixed assets increased by $68 million between 2007 and 2008. The firm's current assets increased by $15 million and spontaneous current liabilities increased by $10 million ($5 million in accrued wages and taxes and $5 million in accounts payable). Therefore, DPH's investment in operating capital for 2008 was

IOC = ΔGross fixed assets + ΔNet operating working capital

   = $68m. + ($15m. − $10m.) = $73m.

Accordingly, what was DPH Tree Farm's free cash flow for 2008?

SOLUTION:

FCF = Operating cash flow − Investment in operating capital

   = $119m. − $73m. = $46m.

In other words, in 2008, DPH Tree Farm, Inc. had cash flows of $46 million available to pay its stockholders and debt holders.

To calculate free cash flow, we start with operating cash flow. Firms generate operating cash flow (OCF) after they have paid necessary taxes. Depreciation, a noncash charge, is added back to operating cash flow to determine total OCF. We add other relevant noncash charges, such as amortization and depletion, back as well. Firms either buy physical assets or earmark funds for eventual equipment replacement to sustain firm operations; this is called *investment in operating capital (IOC)*. In accounting terms, IOC includes the firm's net investments (or changes) in fixed assets, current assets, and spontaneous current liabilities (such as accounts payable and accrued wages).

Like the bottom line shown on the statement of cash flows, the level of free cash flow can be positive, zero, or negative. A positive free cash flow value means that the firm may distribute funds to its investors (debt holders and stockholders.) When the firm's free cash flows come in as zero or negative, however, the firm's operations produce no cash flows available for investors. Of course, if free cash flow is negative because operating cash flow is negative, investors are likely to take up the issue with the firm's management. Negative free cash flows as a result of negative operating cash flows generally indicate that the firm is experiencing operating or managerial problems. A firm with positive operating cash flows but negative free cash flows, however, is not necessarily a poorly managed firm. Firms that invest heavily in operating capital to support growth often have positive operating cash flows but negative free cash flows, but in this case, the negative free cash flow will likely result in growing future profits.

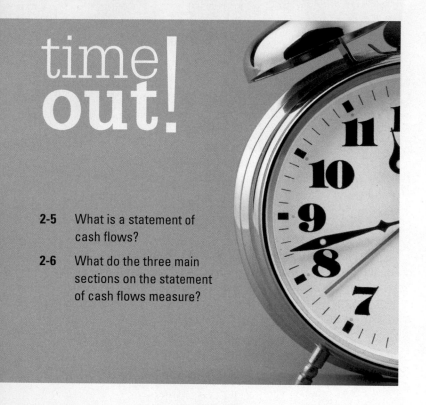

time out!

2-5   What is a statement of cash flows?

2-6   What do the three main sections on the statement of cash flows measure?

EXAMPLE 2-6

For interactive versions of this example visit www.mhhe.com/canM

Statement of Retained Earnings

Indian Point Kennels, Inc. earned net income in 2008 of $10.78 million. The firm paid out $1 million in cash dividends to its preferred stockholders and $2.5 million in cash dividends to its common stockholders. The firm ended 2007 with $135.75 million in retained earnings. Construct a statement of retained earnings to calculate the year-end 2008 balance of retained earnings.

SOLUTION:

The statement of retained earnings for 2008 is as follows:

INDIAN POINT KENNELS, INC. Statement of Retained Earnings as of December 31, 2008 (in millions of dollars)		
	2008	
Balance of retained earnings, December 31, 2007		$135.75
Plus: Net income for 2008		10.78
Less: Cash dividends paid		
Preferred stock	$1.0	
Common stock	2.5	
Total cash dividends paid		3.50
Balance of retained earnings, December 31, 2008		$143.03

▼ TABLE 2.5 Statement of Retained Earnings for DPH Tree Farm, Inc.

DPH TREE FARM, INC. Statement of Retained Earnings as of December 31, 2008 (in millions of dollars)		
		2008
Balance of retained earnings, December 31, 2007		$155
Plus: Net income for 2008		90
Less: Cash dividends paid		
Preferred stock	$10	
Common stock	25	
Total cash dividends paid		35
Balance of retained earnings, December 31, 2008		$210

STATEMENT OF RETAINED EARNINGS

The **statement of retained earnings** provides additional details about changes in retained earnings during a reporting period. This financial statement reconciles net income earned during a given period and any cash dividends paid within that period on one side with the change in retained earnings between the beginning and ending of the period on the other. Table 2.5 presents DPH Tree Farm, Inc.'s statement of retained earnings as of December 31, 2008. The statement shows that DPH Tree Farms brought in a net income of $90 million during 2008. The firm paid out $10 million in dividends to preferred stockholders and another $25 million to common stockholders. The firm then had $55 million to reinvest back into the firm, which shows as an increase in retained earnings. Thus, the retained earnings account on the balance sheet (Table 2.1) increased from $155 million at year-end 2007 to $210 million at year-end 2008.

Increased retained earnings occur not just because a firm has net income, but rather because the firm's common stockholders agree to let management reinvest net income back into the firm rather than pay it out as dividends. Reinvesting net income into retained earnings allows the firm to use investment to grow through additional funds spent in plant and equipment, inventory, and other assets needed to generate even more profit. So retained earnings represent a claim against all of the firm's assets and not against a particular asset.

CAUTIONS IN INTERPRETING FINANCIAL STATEMENTS

statement of retained earnings Financial statement that reconciles net income earned during a given period and any cash dividends paid with the change in retained earnings over the period.

As we mentioned earlier in the chapter, firms must prepare their financial statements according to GAAP. GAAP provides a common set of standards intended to produce objective and precise financial statements. But recall also that managers have significant discretion over their reported earnings. Managers and financial analysts have recognized for years that firms use considerable latitude in using accounting rules to manage their reported earnings in a wide variety of contexts. Indeed, within the GAAP framework, firms can "smooth" earnings. That is, firms often take steps to over- or understate earnings at various times. Managers may choose to smooth earnings to show investors that firm assets are growing steadily. Similarly, one firm may be using straight-line depreciation for its fixed assets, while another is using a modified accelerated cost recovery method (MACRS), which causes depreciation to accrue quickly. If the firm uses MACRS accounting methods, they write fixed asset values down quickly; assets will thus have lower book value than if the firm used straight-line depreciation methods.

2-7 What is a statement of retained earnings?

2-8 If, during a given period, a firm pays out more in dividends than it has net income, what happens to the firm's retained earnings?

finance at work //: markets

Coldwater Creek Inc. announced today that it received a Nasdaq Staff Determination on June 14, 2006, stating that Coldwater Creek (the "Company") failed to comply with Marketplace Rule 4310(c)(14) because its Quarterly Report on Form 10-Q for the quarter ended April 29, 2006 (the "Form 10-Q") filed on June 8, 2006, was incomplete. NASDAQ Staff Determination notices are generated automatically in these circumstances and indicate that, due to such noncompliance, Coldwater Creek's common stock will be subject to delisting.

As indicated in the Form 10-Q, the Company's independently registered public accounting firm had not completed its review of the financial information included in the Form 10-Q when it made the filing due to the Company's pending restatement of certain historical financial information. As a result, the Company was unable to provide the officer certifications required by [. . .] the Sarbanes-Oxley Act of 2002 with the Form 10-Q.

In the interim, the Company is working diligently to complete the amendment to its Form 10-K for the fiscal year ended January 28, 2006, to reflect the restated financial information so that the Company's independently registered public accounting firm can complete its review of the financial information in the Form 10-Q. Once this review is completed, the Company intends to file as soon as possible a fully compliant amended Form 10-Q/A, including the certifications required under [. . .] the Sarbanes-Oxley Act. It is currently expected that the Company's amended Form 10-K filing will be finalized prior to the Nasdaq hearing date, which will enable the Company to file

its amended Form 10-Q and return to compliance with Nasdaq's Marketplace Rules.

Want to know more?

Key Words to Search for Updates: **Sarbanes-Oxley Act of 2002, financial statements, 10Q filing, 10K filing.**

Source: *The Wall Street Journal*, June 20, 2006, p. A3.

This process of controlling a firm's earnings is called **earnings management.** At the extreme, earnings management has resulted in some widely reported accounting scandals involving Enron, Merck, WorldCom, and other major U.S. corporations that tried to artificially influence their earnings by manipulating accounting rules. Congress responded to the spate of corporate scandals that emerged after 2001 with the **Sarbanes-Oxley Act,** passed in June 2002. Sarbanes-Oxley requires public companies to ensure that their corporate boards' audit committees have considerable experience applying generally accepted accounting principles (GAAP) for financial statements. The act also requires that any firm's senior management must sign off on the financial statements of the firm, certifying the statements as accurate and representative of the firm's financial condition during the period covered. If a firm's board of directors or senior managers fail to comply with Sarbanes-Oxley (often referred to as SOX), the firm may be delisted from stock exchanges.

As illustrated in the Finance at Work reading, Coldwater Creek's accounting firm had not completed its review of the firm's financial statements when they were released to the public. As a result, the firm's common stock became subject to delisting. Congress's goal in passing SOX was to prevent deceptive accounting and management practices and to bring stability to jittery stock markets battered in 2002 by accounting and managerial scandals that cost employees their life savings and harmed many innocent shareholders as well. ■

time out!

2-9   What is earnings management?

Get Online

mhhe.com/canM

for study materials including quizzes, iPod downloads, and video

Your Turn...

Questions

1. List and describe the four major financial statements. *(LG1)*

2. On which of the four major financial statements (balance sheet, income statement, statement of cash flows, or statement of retained earnings) would you find the following items? *(LG1)*

   a. Earnings before taxes.

   b. Net plant and equipment.

   c. Increase in fixed assets.

   d. Gross profits.

   e. Balance of retained earnings, December 31, 20xx.

   f. Common stock and paid-in surplus.

   g. Net cash flow from investing activities.

   h. Accrued wages and taxes.

   i. Increase in inventory.

3. What is the difference between current liabilities and long-term debt? *(LG1)*

4. How does the choice of accounting method used to record fixed asset depreciation affect management of the balance sheet? *(LG1)*

5. What are the costs and benefits of holding liquid securities on a firm's balance sheet? *(LG1)*

6. Why can the book value and market value of a firm differ? *(LG2)*

7. From a firm manager's or investor's point of view, which is more important—the book value of a firm or the market value of the firm? *(LG2)*

8. What do we mean by a progressive tax structure? *(LG3)*

9. What is the difference between an average tax rate and a marginal tax rate? *(LG3)*

10. How does the payment of interest on debt affect the amount of taxes the firm must pay? *(LG3)*

11. The income statement is prepared using GAAP. How does this affect the reported revenue and expense measures listed on the balance sheet? *(LG4)*

12. Why do financial managers and investors find cash flow to be more important than accounting profit? *(LG4)*

13. Which of the following activities result in an increase (decrease) in a firm's cash? *(LG5)*

    a. Decrease fixed assets

    b. Decrease accounts payable

    c. Pay dividends

    d. Sell common stock

    e. Decrease accounts receivable.

    f. Increase notes payable

14. What is the difference between net cash flow from operating activities, net cash flow from investing activities, and net cash flow from financing activities? *(LG5)*

15. What are free cash flows for a firm? What does it mean when a firm's free cash flow is negative? *(LG5)*

16. What is earnings management? *(LG6)*

17. What does the Sarbanes-Oxley Act require of firm managers? *(LG6)*

Problems

BASIC PROBLEMS

2-1 **Balance Sheet** You are evaluating the balance sheet for Goodman's Bees Corporation. From the balance sheet you find the following balances: cash and marketable securities = $400,000, accounts receivable = $1,200,000, inventory = $2,100,000, accrued wages and taxes = $500,000, accounts payable = $800,000, and notes payable = $600,000. Calculate Goodman's Bees' net working capital. *(LG1)*

2-2 **Balance Sheet** Zoeckler Mowing & Landscaping's year-end 2009 balance sheet lists current assets of $256,000, fixed assets of $324,000, current liabilities of $245,000, and long-term debt of $185,000. Calculate Zoeckler's total stockholders' equity. *(LG1)*

2-3 **Income Statement** Reed's Birdie Shot, Inc.'s 2008 income statement lists the following income and expenses: EBIT = $538,000, interest expense = $63,000, and net income = $435,000. Calculate the 2008 taxes reported on the income statement. *(LG1)*

2-4 **Income Statement** Reed's Birdie Shot, Inc.'s 2009 income statement lists the following income and expenses: EBIT = $455,000, interest expense = $58,000, and taxes = $138,000.

Reed's has no preferred stock outstanding and 100,000 shares of common stock outstanding. Calculate the 2008 earnings per share. *(LG1)*

2-5   Corporate Taxes Oakdale Fashions Inc. had $245,000 in 2008 taxable income. Using the tax schedule in Table 2.3, calculate the company's 2008 income taxes. What is the average tax rate? What is the marginal tax rate? *(LG3)*

2-6   Corporate Taxes Hunt Taxidermy, Inc. is concerned about the taxes paid by the company in 2008. In addition to $26.5 million of taxable income, the firm received $1,750,000 of interest on state-issued bonds and $600,000 of dividends on common stock it owns in Hunt Taxidermy, Inc. Calculate Hunt Taxidermy's tax liability, average tax rate, and marginal tax rate. *(LG3)*

2-7   Statement of Cash Flows Ramakrishnan, Inc. reported 2008 net income of $15 million and depreciation of $2,650,000. The top part of Ramakrishnan, Inc.'s 2007 and 2008 balance sheets is listed below (in millions of dollars). Calculate the 2008 net cash flow from operating activities for Ramakrishnan, Inc. *(LG4)*

	2007	2008		2007	2008
Current assets:			Current liabilities:		
Cash and marketable securities	$ 15	$ 20	Accrued wages and taxes	$ 18	$ 19
Accounts receivable	75	84	Accounts payable	45	51
Inventory	110	121	Notes payable	40	45
Total	$200	$225	Total	$103	$115

2-8   Statement of Cash Flows In 2008, Usher Sports Shop had cash flows from investing activities of −$2,567,000 and cash flows from financing activities of −$3,459,000. The balance in the firm's cash account was $950,000 at the beginning of 2008 and $1,025,000 at the end of the year. Calculate Usher Sports Shop's cash flow from operations for 2008. *(LG4)*

2-9   Free Cash Flow You are considering an investment in Fields and Struthers, Inc. and want to evaluate the firm's free cash flow. From the income statement, you see that Fields and Struthers earned an EBIT of $62 million, paid taxes of $17 million, and its depreciation expense was $5 million. Fields and Struthers' gross fixed assets increased by $32 million from 2007 to 2008. The firm's current assets increased by $20 million and spontaneous current liabilities increased by $12 million. Calculate Fields and Struthers' operating cash flow, investment in operating capital, and free cash flow for 2008. *(LG5)*

2-10   Free Cash Flow Tater and Pepper Corp. reported free cash flows for 2008 of $23 million and investment in operating capital of $13 million. Tater and Pepper listed $8 million in depreciation expense and $17 million in taxes on its 2008 income statement. Calculate Tater and Pepper's 2008 EBIT. *(LG5)*

2-11   Statement of Retained Earnings Mr. Husker's Tuxedos Corp. began the year 2008 with $256 million in retained earnings. The firm earned net income of $33 million in 2008 and paid $5 million to its preferred stockholders and $10 million to its common stockholders. What is the year-end 2008 balance in retained earnings for Mr. Husker's Tuxedos? *(LG1)*

2-12   Statement of Retained Earnings Use the following information to find dividends paid to common stockholders during 2008. *(LG1)*

Balance of retained earnings, December 31, 2007		$785m.
Plus: Net income for 2008		25m.
Less: Cash dividends paid		
Preferred stock	$5m.	
Common stock	☐	
Total cash dividends paid		☐
Balance of retained earnings, December 31, 2008		$798m.

2-13 **Balance Sheet** Brenda's Bar and Grill has total assets of $15 million of which $5 million are current assets. Cash makes up 10 percent of the current assets and accounts receivable makes up another 40 percent of current assets. Brenda's gross plant and equipment has a book value of $11.5 million and other long-term assets have a book value of $500,000. Using this information, what is the balance of inventory and the balance of depreciation on Brenda's Bar and Grill's balance sheet? *(LG1)*

2-14 **Balance Sheet** Ed's Tobacco Shop has total assets of $54 million. Fifty percent of these assets are financed with debt of which $17 million is current liabilities. The firm has no preferred stock but the balance in common stock and paid-in surplus is $12 million. Using this information what is the balance for long-term debt and retained earnings on Ed's Tobacco Shop's balance sheet? *(LG1)*

2-15 **Market Value versus Book Value** Muffin's Masonry, Inc.'s balance sheet lists net fixed assets as $14 million. The fixed assets could currently be sold for $19 million. Muffin's current balance sheet shows current liabilities of $5.5 million and net working capital of $4.5 million. If all the current accounts were liquidated today, the company would receive $7.25 million cash after paying $5.5 million in liabilities. What is the book value of Muffin's Masonry's assets today? What is the market value of these assets? *(LG2)*

2-16 **Debt versus Equity Financing** You are considering a stock investment in one of two firms (AllDebt, Inc. and AllEquity, Inc.), both of which operate in the same industry and have identical operating income of $12.5 million. AllDebt, Inc. finances its $25 million in assets with $24 million in debt (on which it pays 10 percent interest annually) and $1 million in equity. AllEquity, Inc. finances its $25 million in assets with no debt and $25 million in equity. Both firms pay a tax rate of 30 percent on their taxable income. Calculate the income available to pay the asset funders (the debt holders and stockholders) and resulting return on assets for the two firms. *(LG1)*

2-17 **Income Statement** You have been given the following information for Corky's Bedding Corp.:

a. Net sales = $11,250,000.

b. Cost of goods sold = $7,750,000.

c. Addition to retained earnings = $1,000,000.

d. Dividends paid to preferred and common stockholders = $495,000.

e. Interest expense = $850,000.

The firm's tax rate is 35 percent. Calculate the depreciation expense for Corky's Bedding Corp. *(LG1)*

2-18 **Income Statement** You have been given the following information for Moore's HoneyBee Corp.:

a. Net sales = $54,500,000.

b. Gross profit = $27,500,000.

c. Addition to retained earnings = $8,000,000.

d. Dividends paid to preferred and common stockholders = $5,000,000.

e. Depreciation expense = $5,000,000.

The firm's tax rate is 35 percent. Calculate the cost of goods sold and the interest expense for Moore's HoneyBee Corp. *(LG1)*

2-19 **Corporate Taxes** The Dakota Corporation had a 2008 taxable income of $33,365,000 from operations after all operating costs but before (1) interest charges of $8,500,000; (2) dividends received of $750,000; (3) dividends paid of $5,250,000; and (4) income taxes.

a. Use the tax schedule in Table 2.3 to calculate Dakota's income tax liability. (LG3)

b. What are Dakota's average and marginal tax rates on taxable income? *(LG3)*

2-20 **Corporate Taxes** Suppose that in addition to $10.5 million of taxable income, Texas Taco, Inc. received $650,000 of interest on state-issued bonds and $450,000 of dividends on common stock it owns in Texas Taco, Inc.

a. Use the tax schedule in Table 2.3 to calculate Texas Taco's income tax liability. *(LG3)*

b. What are Texas Taco's average and marginal tax rates on taxable income? *(LG3)*

2-21 **Statement of Cash Flows** Use the balance sheet and income statement below to construct a statement of cash flows for Clancy's Dog Biscuit Corporation. *(LG5)*

CLANCY'S DOG BISCUIT CORPORATION Balance Sheet as of December 31, 2007 and 2008 (in millions of dollars)					
Assets	**2007**	**2008**	**Liabilities and Equity**	**2007**	**2008**
Current assets:			Current liabilities:		
Cash and marketable securities	$ 5	$ 5	Accrued wages and taxes	$ 6	$ 10
Accounts receivable	19	20	Accounts payable	15	16
Inventory	29	36	Notes payable	13	14
Total	53	61	Total	34	40
Fixed assets:			Long-term debt:	53	57
Gross plant and equipment	88	106	Stockholders' equity:		
Less: Depreciation	11	15	Preferred stock (2 million shares)	2	2
			Common stock and paid-in surplus (5 million shares)	11	11
Net plant and equipment	77	91			
Other long-term assets	15	15	Retained earnings	45	57
Total	92	106	Total	58	70
Total assets	$145	$167	Total liabilities and equity	$145	$167

CLANCY'S DOG BISCUIT CORPORATION Income Statement for Years Ending December 31, 2007 and 2008 (in millions of dollars)		
	2007	**2008**
Net sales	$80	$76
Less: Cost of goods sold	39	44
Gross profits	41	32
Less: Depreciation	4	4
Earnings before interest and taxes (EBIT)	37	28
Less: Interest	5	5
Earnings before taxes (EBT)	32	23
Less: Taxes	10	7
Net income	$22	$16
Less: Preferred stock dividends	$ 1	$ 1
Net income available to common stockholders	$21	$15
Less: Common stock dividends	$ 3	$ 3
Addition to retained earnings	$18	$12
Per (common) share data:		
Earnings per share (EPS)	$ 4.20	$ 3.00
Dividends per share (DPS)	$ 0.60	$ 0.60
Book value per share (BVPS)	$11.20	$13.60
Market value (price) per share (MVPS)	$14.60	$14.25

2-22 **Statement of Cash Flows** Use the balance sheet and income statement below to construct a statement of cash flows for Valium's Medical Supply Corporation. *(LG5)*

VALIUM'S MEDICAL SUPPLY CORPORATION Balance Sheet as of December 31, 2007 and 2008 (in thousands of dollars)					
Assets	**2007**	**2008**	**Liabilities and Equity**	**2007**	**2008**
Current liabilities:			Current assets:		
Cash and marketable securities	$ 123	$ 124	Accrued wages and taxes	$ 76	$ 98
Accounts receivable	321	339	Accounts payable	246	271
Inventory	494	548	Notes payable	222	222
Total	938	1,011	Total	544	591
Fixed assets:			Long-term debt:	937	963
Gross plant and equipment	1,507	1,843	Stockholders' equity:		
Less: Depreciation	197	261	Preferred stock (10 million shares)	10	10
Net plant and equipment	1,310	1,582	Common stock and paid-in surplus (100 million shares)	200	200
Other long-term assets	220	220	Retained earnings	777	1,049
Total	1,530	1,802	Total	987	1,259
Total assets	$2,468	$2,813	Total liabilities and equity	$2,468	$2,813

VALIUM'S MEDICAL SUPPLY CORPORATION Income Statement for Years Ending December 31, 2007 and 2008 (in thousands of dollars)		
	2007	**2008**
Net sales	$1,357	$1,509
Less: Cost of goods sold	666	740
Gross profits	691	769
Less: Depreciation	59	64
Earnings before interest and taxes (EBIT)	632	705
Less: Interest	68	79
Earnings before taxes (EBT)	564	626
Less: Taxes	190	219
Net income	$374	$407
Less: Preferred stock dividends	$10	$10
Net income available to common stockholders	364	397
Less: Common stock dividends	125	125
Addition to retained earnings	$239	$272
Per (common) share data:		
Earnings per share (EPS)	$3.64	$3.97
Dividends per share (DPS)	$1.25	$1.25
Book value per share (BVPS)	$9.77	$12.49
Market value (price) per share (MVPS)	$10.60	$14.25

2-23 **Statement of Cash Flows** Lane's Outdoor Furniture, Inc. has net cash flows from operating activities for the last year of $340 million. The income statement shows that net income is $315 million and depreciation expense is $46 million. During the year, the change in inventory on the balance sheet was $38 million, change in accrued wages and taxes was $15 million, and change in accounts payable was $20 million. At the beginning of the year, the balance of accounts receivable was $50 million. Calculate the end-of-year balance for accounts receivable. *(LG5)*

2-24   **Statement of Cash Flows** Dogs 4 U Corporation has net cash flow from financing activities for the last year of $20 million. The company paid $105 million in dividends last year. During the year, the change in notes payable on the balance was $23 million and change in common and preferred stock was $0. The end-of-year balance for long-term debt was $185 million Calculate the beginning-of-year balance for long-term debt. *(LG5)*

2-25   **Free Cash Flow** The 2008 income statement for Duffy's Pest Control shows that depreciation expense is $197 million, EBIT is $418 million, EBT is $240 million, and the tax rate is 30 percent. At the beginning of the year, the balance of gross fixed assets was $1,562 million and net operating working capital was $417 million. At the end of the year, gross fixed assets was $1,803 million. Duffy's free cash flow for the year was $424 million. Calculate the end-of-year balance for net operating working capital. *(LG5)*

2-26   **Free Cash Flow** The 2008 income statement for Egyptian Noise Blasters shows that depreciation expense is $50 million, EBIT is $215 million, and taxes are $70 million. At the end of the year, the balance of gross fixed assets was $385 million. The change in net operating working capital during the year was $43 million. Egyptian's free cash flow for the year was $112 million. Calculate the beginning-of-year balance for gross fixed assets. *(LG5)*

2-27   **Statement of Retained Earnings** Thelma and Louie, Inc. started the year with a balance of retained earnings of $543 million and ended the year with retained earnings of $589 million. The company paid dividends of $35 million to the preferred stockholders and $88 million to common stockholders. Calculate Thelma and Louie's net income for the year. *(LG1)*

2-28   **Statement of Retained Earnings** Jamaica Tours, Inc. started the year with a balance of retained earnings of $1,047 million. The company reported net income for the year of $168 million and paid dividends of $10 million to the preferred stockholders and $35 million to common stockholders. Calculate Jamaica Tours' end-of-year balance in retained earnings. *(LG1)*

ADVANCED PROBLEMS

2-29   **Income Statement** Listed below is the 2008 income statement for Tom and Sue Travels, Inc.

TOM AND SUE TRAVELS, INC. Income Statement for Year Ending December 31, 2008 (in millions of dollars)	
	2008
Net sales	$16.500
Less: Cost of goods sold	10.300
Gross profits	6.200
Less: Depreciation	2.900
Earnings before interest and taxes (EBIT)	3.300
Less: Interest	0.950
Earnings before taxes (EBT)	2.350
Less: Taxes	0.705
Net income	$ 1.645

The CEO of Tom and Sue's wants the company to earn a net income of $2.250 million in 2009. Cost of goods sold is expected to be 60 percent of net sales, depreciation expense is not expected to change, interest expense is expected to increase to $1.050 million, and the firm's tax rate will be 30 percent. Calculate the net sales needed to produce net income of $2.250 million. *(LG1)*

2-30 **Income Statement** You have been given the following information for Kellygirl's Athletic Wear Corp. for the year 2008:

a. Net sales = $22,500,000.

b. Cost of goods sold = $16,100,000.

c. Addition to retained earnings = $1,150,000.

d. Dividends paid to preferred and common stockholders = $1,125,000.

e. Interest expense = $1,050,000.

f. The firm's tax rate is 30 percent.

g. In 2009, net sales are expected to increase by $2.5 million.

h. Cost of goods sold is expected to be 70 percent of net sales.

i. Expensed depreciation is expected to be the same as in 2008.

j. Interest expense is expected to be $1,200,000.

k. The tax rate is expected to be 30 percent of EBT.

l. Dividends paid to preferred and common stockholders will not change.

Calculate the addition to retained earnings expected in 2009. *(LG1)*

2-31 **Free Cash Flow** Michelle's Flowers 4U, Inc. had free cash flow during 2008 of $43 million, EBIT of $110 million, tax expense of $25 million, and depreciation of $14 million. Using this information, fill in the blank on Michelle's balance sheet below. *(LG5)*

MICHELLE'S FLOWERS 4U, INC. Balance Sheet as of December 31, 2007 and 2008 (in millions of dollars)					
Assets	**2007**	**2008**	**Liabilities and Equity**	**2007**	**2008**
Current assets:			Current liabilities:		
Cash and marketable securities	$ 25	$ 28	Accrued wages and taxes	$ 15	$ 17
Accounts receivable	65	75	Accounts payable	50	
Inventory	100	118	Notes payable	45	45
Total	190	221	Total	110	118
Fixed assets:			Long-term debt:	190	195
Gross plant and equipment	300	333	Stockholders' equity:		
Less: Depreciation	40	54	Preferred stock (5 million shares)	5	5
Net plant and equipment	260	279	Common stock and paid-in surplus (20 million shares)	40	40
Other long-term assets	50	50	Retained earnings	155	192
Total	310	329	Total	200	237
Total assets	$500	$550	Total liabilities and equity	$500	$550

2-32 **Free Cash Flow** Wondy's Overhead Construction had free cash flows during 2008 of $12 million. The change in gross fixed assets on Wondy's balance sheet during 2008 was $10 million and the change in net operating working capital was $14 million. Using this information, fill in the blanks on Wondy's income statement below. *(LG5)*

WONDY'S OVERHEAD CONSTRUCTION, CORP. Income Statement for Year Ending December 31, 2008 (in millions of dollars)	
	2008
Net sales	$ ___
Less: Cost of goods sold	75.6
Gross profits	31.5
Less: Depreciation	6.0
Earnings before interest and taxes (EBIT)	___
Less: Interest	___
Earnings before taxes (EBT)	___
Less: Taxes (25%)	___
Net income	$ 15.5

chapter three

analyzing financial statements

We reviewed the major financial statements in Chapter 2. These financial statements provide information on a firm's financial position at a point in time or its operations over some past period of time. But these financial statements' real value lies in the fact that managers, investors, and analysts can use the information the statements contain to analyze the current financial performance or condition of the firm. More importantly, managers can use this information to plan changes that will improve the firm's future performance and, ultimately, its market value. Most commonly, managers, investors, and analysts use ratios to evaluate financial statements. **Ratio analysis** involves calculating and analyzing financial ratios to assess a firm's performance and to identify actions that could improve firm performance. The most commonly used ratios fall into five groups: (1) liquidity ratios, (2) asset management ratios, (3) debt management ratios, (4) profitability ratios, and (5) market value ratios. ■

LEARNING GOALS

- LG1 Calculate and interpret major liquidity ratios.
- LG2 Calculate and interpret major asset management ratios.
- LG3 Calculate and interpret major debt ratios.
- LG4 Calculate and interpret major profitability ratios.
- LG5 Calculate and interpret major market value ratios.
- LG6 Appreciate how various ratios relate to one another.
- LG7 Discuss the differences between time series and cross-sectional ratio analyses and decide which is most appropriate given an analytical situation.
- LG8 Explain cautions that should be taken when examining financial ratios and financial information in general.

ratio analysis
The process of calculating and analyzing financial ratios to assess the firm's performance and to identify actions needed to improve firm performance.

liquidity ratios Measure the relation between a firm's liquid (or current) assets and its current liabilities.

asset management ratios Measure how efficiently a firm uses its assets (inventory, accounts receivable, and fixed assets), as well as its accounts payable.

In this chapter, we review these ratios, describe what each ratio means, and identify the general trend (higher or lower) that managers and investment analysts look for in each ratio. Note as we review the ratios that the number calculated for a ratio is not always good or bad and that extreme values (either high or low) can be a bad sign for a firm. We will discuss how a ratio that seems too good can actually be bad for a company. We will also see how ratios interrelate—how a change in one ratio may affect the value of several ratios. It is often hard to make sense of a set of performance ratios. Thus, when managers or investors review a firm's financial position through ratio analysis, they often start by evaluating trends in the firm's financial ratios over time and by comparing their firm's ratios with that of other firms in the same industry. Finally, we discuss cautions that you should take when using ratio analysis to evaluate firm performance. As we go through the chapter, we show sample ratio analysis using the financial statements for DPH Tree Farm, Inc. listed in Tables 2.1 and 2.2 from the previous chapter.

LIQUIDITY RATIOS

As we stated in Chapter 2, firms need cash and other liquid assets (or current assets) to pay their bills (or current liabilities) as they come due. **Liquidity ratios** measure the relationship between a firm's liquid (or current) assets and its current liabilities. The three most commonly used liquidity ratios are the current ratio, the quick (or acid-test) ratio, and the cash ratio.

$$\text{Current ratio} = \frac{\text{Current assets}}{\text{Current liabilities}} \quad (3\text{-}1)$$

$$\text{Quick ratio} \atop (\text{acid-test ratio}) = \frac{\text{Current assets} - \text{Inventory}}{\text{current liabilities}} \quad (3\text{-}2)$$

$$\text{Cash ratio} = \frac{\text{Cash and marketable securities}}{\text{Current liabilities}} \quad (3\text{-}3)$$

The broadest liquidity measure, the current ratio, measures the dollars of current assets available to pay each dollar of current liabilities. Inventories are generally the least liquid of a firm's current assets. Further, inventory is the current asset for which book values are the least reliable measures of market value. In practical terms, what this means is that if the firm must sell inventory to pay upcoming bills, the firm is most likely to have to discount inventory items in order to liquidate them, and

therefore, they are the current assets on which losses are most likely to occur. Therefore, the quick (or acid-test) ratio measures a firm's ability to pay off short-term obligations without relying on inventory sales. The quick ratio measures the dollars of more liquid assets (cash and marketable securities and accounts receivable) available to pay each dollar of current liabilities.

Likewise, if the firm sells accounts receivable to pay upcoming bills, the firm must often discount the AR items to sell them—the assets once again bring less than their book value. Therefore, the cash ratio measures a firm's ability to pay short-term obligations with its available cash and marketable securities. The cash ratio measures the dollars of cash and marketable securities available to pay each dollar of current liabilities.

Of course, liquidity on the balance sheet is important. The more liquid assets a firm holds, the less likely it is that the firm will experience financial distress. Thus, the higher the liquidity ratios, the less liquidity risk a firm has. But as with everything else in business, high liquidity represents a painful trade-off for the firm. Liquid assets do not generate any profits for the firm. In contrast, fixed assets are illiquid, but generate revenue for the firm. Thus, extremely high levels of liquidity guard against liquidity crises but at the cost of lower returns on assets. High liquidity levels may actually show bad or indecisive firm management. Thus, in deciding the appropriate level of current assets to hold on the balance sheet, managers must consider the trade-off between the advantages of being liquid versus the disadvantages of reduced profits. Note that a company with very predictable cash flows can maintain low levels of liquidity without incurring much liquidity risk.

ASSET MANAGEMENT RATIOS

Asset management ratios measure how efficiently a firm uses its assets (inventory, accounts receivable, and fixed assets), as well as how efficiently the firm manages its accounts payable. The specific ratios allow managers and investors to evaluate

whether a firm is holding a reasonable amount of each type of asset and whether management uses each type of asset to effectively generate sales. The most commonly used asset management ratios are listed below, grouped by type of asset.

Inventory Management

The inventory turnover ratio measures the number of dollars of sales produced per dollar of inventory. Cost of goods sold is used in the numerator when managers want to emphasize that inventory is listed on the balance sheet at cost, that is, the

The inventory turnover ratio measures the number of dollars of sales produced per dollar of inventory.

EXAMPLE 3-1

For interactive versions of this example visit www.mhhe.com/canM

Calculating Liquidity Ratios

Use the balance sheet (Table 2.1) and income statement (Table 2.2) for DPH Tree Farm, Inc. to calculate the firm's 2008 values for the liquidity ratios.

SOLUTION:

The liquidity ratios for DPH Tree Farm, Inc. are calculated as follows.

$$\text{Current ratio} = \frac{\$205m.}{\$120m.} = 1.71 \text{ times}$$

Industry average = 1.50 times

$$\text{Quick ratio (acid-test ratio)} = \frac{\$205m. - \$11m.}{\$120m.} = 0.78 \text{ times}$$

Industry average = 0.50 times

$$\text{Cash ratio} = \frac{\$24m.}{\$120m.} = 0.20 \text{ times}$$

Industry average = 0.15 times

All three liquidity ratios show that DPH Tree Farm, Inc. has more liquidity on its balance sheet than the industry average (we discuss the process used to develop an industry average below). Thus, DPH Tree Farm has more cash and other liquid assets (or current assets) available to pay its bills (or current liabilities) as they come due than does the average firm in the tree farm industry.

cost of production per dollar of inventory purchased (equation 3-4). The days' sales in inventory ratio measures the number of days that inventory is held before the final product is sold (equation 3-5).

$$\text{Inventory turnover ratio} = \frac{\text{Sales or Cost of goods sold}}{\text{Inventory}} \quad (3\text{-}4)$$

$$\text{Days' sales in inventory} = \frac{\text{Inventory} \times 365 \text{ days}}{\text{Sales or Cost of goods sold}} \quad (3\text{-}5)$$

In general, a firm wants to produce a high level of sales per dollar of inventory, that is, it wants to turn inventory over (from raw materials to finished goods to sold goods) as quickly as possible. A high level of sales per dollar of inventory implies reduced warehousing, monitoring, insurance, and any other costs of servicing the inventory. So, a high inventory turnover ratio or a low days' sales in inventory is generally a sign of good management.

However, if the inventory turnover ratio is extremely high and the days' sales in inventory is extremely low, the firm may not be holding sufficient inventory to prevent running out (or stocking out) of the raw materials needed to keep the production process going. Thus, production and sales stop, which

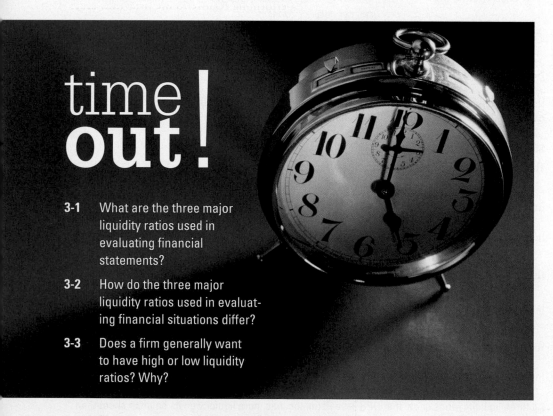

time out!

3-1 What are the three major liquidity ratios used in evaluating financial statements?

3-2 How do the three major liquidity ratios used in evaluating financial situations differ?

3-3 Does a firm generally want to have high or low liquidity ratios? Why?

wastes the firm's fixed resources. So, extremely high levels for the inventory turnover ratio and low levels for the days' sales in inventory ratio may actually be a sign of bad firm or production management.

As they decide the optimal inventory level to hold on the balance sheet, managers must consider the trade-off between the advantages of holding sufficient levels of inventory to keep the production process going versus the costs of holding large amounts of inventory. Note that companies with very good supply chain relations can maintain lower levels of inventory without incurring as much risk of stockouts.

Accounts Receivable Management

The average collection period (ACP) measures the number of days accounts receivable are held before the firm collects cash from the sale (equation 3-6). The accounts receivable turnover ratio measures the number of dollars of sales produced per dollar of accounts receivable (equation 3-7).

$$\frac{\text{Average collection}}{\text{period (ACP)}} = \frac{\text{Accounts receivable} \times 365 \text{days}}{\text{Credit sales}} \quad (3\text{-}6)$$

$$\text{Accounts receivable turnover} = \frac{\text{Credit sales}}{\text{Accounts receivable}} \quad (3\text{-}7)$$

In general, a firm wants to produce a high level of sales per dollar of accounts receivable, that is, it wants to collect its accounts receivable as quickly as possible to reduce any cost of financing accounts receivable. These costs include interest expense on liabilities used to finance accounts receivable and defaults associated with accounts receivable. In general, a high accounts receivable turnover ratio or a low ACP is a sign of good management, which is well aware of financing costs and customer remittance habits.

However, if the accounts receivable turnover ratio is extremely high and the ACP is extremely low, the firm's accounts receivable policy may be so strict that customers prefer to do business with competing firms. Firms offer accounts receivable terms as an incentive to get customers to buy products from their firm rather than a competing firm. By offering customers the accounts receivable privilege, management allows them to buy (more) now and pay later. Without this incentive, customers may choose to buy the goods from the firm's competitors who offer better credit terms. So extremely high accounts receivable turnover ratio levels and low ACP levels may be a sign of bad firm management. As they decide what level of accounts receivable to hold on the firm's balance sheet, managers must consider the trade-off between the advantages of increased sales by offering customers better terms versus the disadvantages of financing large amounts of accounts receivable.

Accounts Payable Management

The average payment period (APP) measures the number of days that the firm holds accounts payable before it has to extend cash to buy raw materials (equation 3-8). The accounts payable turnover ratio measures the dollar cost of goods sold per dollar of accounts payable (equation 3-9).

$$\text{Average payment period (APP)} = \frac{\text{Accounts payable} \times 365 \text{ days}}{\text{Cost of goods sold}} \quad (3\text{-}8)$$

$$\text{Accounts payable turnover} = \frac{\text{Costs of goods sold}}{\text{Accounts payable}} \quad (3\text{-}9)$$

In general, a firm wants to pay for its purchases as slowly as possible. The slower the firm pays for its supply purchases, the longer it can avoid obtaining other costly sources of financing such as notes payable or long-term debt. Thus, a high APP or a low accounts payable turnover ratio is generally a sign of good management.

However, if the APP is extremely high and the accounts payable turnover ratio is extremely low, the firm may be abusing the credit terms that its raw materials suppliers offer. At some point, the firm's suppliers may revoke its ability to buy raw materials on account and the firm will lose this source of free financing. If this situation is developing, extremely high levels for the APP and low levels for the accounts receivable turnover ratio may point to bad firm management.

As they decide the accounts payable level to hold on the balance sheet, managers must consider the trade-off between maximizing the use of free financing that raw material suppliers offer versus the risk of losing the opportunity to buy on account.

Fixed Asset and Working Capital Management

The fixed asset turnover ratio measures the number of dollars of sales produced per dollar of fixed assets (equation 3-10). Similarly, the sales to working capital ratio measures the number of dollars of sales produced per dollar of net working capital (current assets minus current liabilities) (equation 3-11).

$$\text{Fixed asset turnover ratio} = \frac{\text{Sales}}{\text{Fixed assets}} \quad (3\text{-}10)$$

$$\text{Sales to working capital} = \frac{\text{Sales}}{\text{Working capital}} \quad (3\text{-}11)$$

> A high accounts receivable turnover ratio or a low ACP is a sign of good management, which is well aware of financing costs and customer remittance habits.

In general, the higher the level of sales per dollar of fixed assets and working capital, the more efficiently the firm is being run. Thus, high fixed asset turnover and sales to working capital ratios are generally signs of good management. However, if either the fixed asset turnover or sales to working capital ratio is extremely high, the firm may be close to its maximum production capacity. If capacity is hit, the firm cannot increase production or sales. Accordingly, extremely high fixed asset turnover and sales to working capital ratio levels may actually indicate bad firm management if managers have allowed the company to approach maximum capacity without making any accommodations for growth.

Note a word of caution here. The age of a firm's fixed assets will affect the fixed asset turnover ratio level. A firm with older fixed assets, listed on its balance sheet at historical cost, will tend to have a higher fixed asset turnover ratio than will a firm that has just replaced its fixed assets and lists them on its balance sheet at a (most likely) higher value. Accordingly, the firm with newer fixed assets would have a lower fixed asset turnover ratio. But this is because it has updated its fixed assets, while the other firm has not. It is *not* correct to conclude that the firm with new assets is underperforming relative to the firm with older fixed assets listed on its balance sheet.

Total Asset Management

The final two asset management ratios put it all together. The total asset turnover ratio measures the number of dollars of sales produced per dollar of total assets (equation 3-12). Similarly, the capital intensity ratio measures the dollars of total assets needed to produce a dollar of sales (equation 3-13).

$$\text{Total assets turnover ratio} = \frac{\text{Sales}}{\text{Total assets}} \quad (3\text{-}12)$$

$$\text{Capital intensity ratio} = \frac{\text{Total assets}}{\text{Sales}} \quad (3\text{-}13)$$

In general, a well managed firm produces many dollars of sales per dollar of total assets, or uses few dollars of assets per dollar of sales. Thus, in general, the higher the total asset turnover and lower the capital intensity ratio, the more efficient the overall asset management of the firm will be. However, if the total asset turnover is extremely high and the capital intensity ratio is extremely low, the firm may actually have an asset management problem. As described above, inventory stockouts, capacity problems, or tight account receivables policies can all lead to a high total asset turnover and may actually be signs of poor firm management.

EXAMPLE 3-2

For interactive versions
of this example visit
www.mhhe.com/canM

Calculating Asset Management Ratios

Use the balance sheet (Table 2.1) and income statement (Table 2.2) for DPH Tree Farm, Inc. to calculate the firm's 2008 values for the asset management ratios.

SOLUTION:

We calculate the asset management ratios for DPH Tree Farm, Inc. as follows:

$$\text{Inventory turnover ratio} = \frac{\$315m.}{\$111m.} = 2.84 \text{ times}$$

Industry average = 2.15 times

$$\text{Days' sales in inventory} = \frac{\$111m. \times 365 \text{ days}}{\$315m.} = 129 \text{ days}$$

Industry average = 170 days

$$\text{Average collection period (ACP)} = \frac{\$70m. \times 365 \text{ days}}{\$315m.} = 81 \text{ days}$$

Industry average = 95 days

$$\text{Accounts receivable turnover} = \frac{\$315m.}{\$70m.} = 4.50 \text{ times}$$

Industry average = 3.84 times

$$\text{Average payment period (APP)} = \frac{\$55m. \times 365 \text{ days}}{\$150m.} = 134 \text{ days}$$

Industry average = 102 days

$$\text{Accounts payable turnover} = \frac{\$150m.}{\$55m.} = 2.73 \text{ times}$$

Industry average = 3.55 times

$$\text{Fixed asset turnover ratio} = \frac{\$315m.}{\$315m.} = 1.00 \text{ times}$$

Industry average = 0.85 times

$$\text{Sales to working capital} = \frac{\$315m.}{\$205m. - \$120m.} = 3.71 \text{ times}$$

Industry average = 3.20 times

$$\text{Total assets turnover ratio} = \frac{\$315m.}{\$570m.} = 0.55 \text{ times}$$

Industry average = 0.40 times

$$\text{Capital intensity ratio} = \frac{\$570m.}{\$315m.} = 1.81 \text{ times}$$

Industry average = 2.50 times

In all cases, asset management ratios show that DPH Tree Farm, Inc. is outperforming the industry average. The firm is turning over its inventory faster than the average firm in the tree farm industry, thus producing more dollars of sales per dollar of inventory. It is also collecting its accounts receivable faster and paying its accounts payable slower than the average firm. Further, DPH Tree Farm is producing more sales per dollar of fixed assets, working capital, and total assets than the average firm in the industry.

DEBT MANAGEMENT RATIOS

As we discussed in Chapter 2, financial leverage refers to the extent to which the firm uses debt securities in its capital structure. The more debt a firm uses as a percentage of its total assets, the greater is its financial leverage. **Debt management ratios** measure the extent to which the firm uses debt (or financial leverage) versus equity to finance its assets. The specific ratios allow managers and investors to evaluate whether a firm is financing its assets with a reasonable amount of debt versus equity financing, as well as whether the firm is generating sufficient earnings or cash to make the promised payments on its debt. The most commonly used debt management ratios are listed below.

Debt versus Equity Financing

The debt ratio measures the percentage of total assets financed with debt (equation 3-14). The debt-to-equity ratio measures the dollars of debt financing used for every dollar of equity financing (equation 3-15). The equity multiplier ratio measures the dollars of assets on the balance sheet for every dollar of equity (or just common stockholders' equity) financing (equation 3-16).

$$\text{Debt ratio} = \frac{\text{Total debt}}{\text{Total assets}} \qquad (3\text{-}14)$$

$$\text{Debt-to-equity ratio} = \frac{\text{Total debt}}{\text{Total equity}} \qquad (3\text{-}15)$$

$$\text{Equity multiplicr ratio} = \frac{\text{Total assets}}{\text{Total equity}} \text{ or}$$

$$\frac{\text{Total assets}}{\text{Common stockholders' equity}} \qquad (3\text{-}16)$$

As you might suspect, all three measures are related.[1] Specifically

$$\text{Debt-to-equity ratio} = \frac{1}{(1/\text{Debt ratio}) - 1}$$

$$= \text{Equity multiplier ratio} - 1$$

$$\text{Equity multiplier ratio} = \frac{1}{1 - \text{Debt ratio}}$$

$$= \text{Debt-to-equity ratio} + 1$$

[1]To see this remember the balance sheet identity is Assets (A) = Debt (D) + Equity (E). Dividing each side of this equation by equity, we get A/E = D/E + E/E, or A/E = D/E + 1. Also, rearranging this equation, D/E = A/E − 1.

So, the lower the debt, debt-to-equity, or equity multiplier ratios, the less debt and more equity the firm uses to finance its assets (i.e., the bigger the firm's equity cushion).

When a firm issues debt to finance its assets, it gives the debt holders first claim to a fixed amount of its cash flows. Stockholders are entitled to any residual cash flows—those left after debt holders are paid. When a firm does well, financial leverage increases the reward to shareholders since the amount of cash flows promised to debt holders is constant and capped. So when firms do

debt management ratios Measure the extent to which the firm uses debt (or financial leverage) versus equity to finance its assets.

capital structure The amount of debt versus equity to hold on the balance sheet.

time out!

3-4 What are the major asset management ratios?

3-5 Does a firm generally want to have high or low values for each of these ratios?

3-6 Explain why many of these ratios are mirror images of one another.

well, financial leverage creates more cash flows to share with stockholders—it magnifies the return to the stockholders of the firm. This magnification is one reason that stockholders encourage the use of debt financing.

However, financial leverage also increases the firm's potential for financial distress and even failure. If the firm has a bad year and cannot make promised debt payments, debt holders can force the firm into bankruptcy. Thus, a firm's current and potential debt holders (and even stockholders) look at equity financing as a safety cushion that can absorb fluctuations in the firm's earnings and asset values and guarantee debt service payments. Clearly, the larger the fluctuations or variability of a firm's cash flows, the greater the need for an equity cushion. Managers' choice of **capital structure**—the amount of debt versus equity to issue—affects the firm's viability as a long-term entity. In deciding the level of debt versus equity financing to hold on the balance sheet, managers must consider the trade-off between maximizing cash flows to the firm's stockholders versus the risk of being unable to make promised debt payments.

Coverage Ratios

The times interest earned ratio measures the number of dollars of operating earnings available to meet each dollar of

interest obligations on the firm's debt (equation 3-17). The fixed-charge coverage ratio measures the number of dollars of operating *earnings* available to meet the firm's interest dollars and other fixed charges (equation 3-18). The cash coverage ratio measures the number of dollars of operating *cash* available to meet each dollar of interest and other fixed charges that the firm owes (equation 3-19).

$$\text{Times interest earned} = \frac{\text{EBIT}}{\text{Interest}} \qquad (3\text{-}17)$$

EXAMPLE 3-3

Calculating Debt Management Ratios

Use the balance sheet (Table 2.1) and income statement (Table 2.2) for DPH Tree Farm, Inc. to calculate the firm's 2008 values for the debt management ratios.

SOLUTION:

The debt management ratios for DPH Tree Farm, Inc. are calculated as follows:

$$\text{Debt ratio} = \frac{\$120\text{m.} + \$195\text{m.}}{\$570\text{m.}} = 55.26\%$$

Industry average = 68.50%

$$\text{Debt-to-equity ratio} = \frac{\$120\text{m.} + \$195\text{m.}}{\$255\text{m.}} = 1.24 \text{ times}$$

Industry average = 2.17 times

$$\text{Equity multiplier ratio} = \frac{\$570\text{m.}}{\$255\text{m.}} = 2.24 \text{ times or } \frac{\$570\text{m.}}{\$250\text{m.}} = 2.28 \text{ times}$$

Industry average   = 4.10 times   or   4.14 times

$$\text{Times interest earned} = \frac{\$152\text{m.}}{\$16\text{m.}} = 9.50 \text{ times}$$

Industry average = 5.15 times

$$\text{Fixed-charge coverage ratio} = \frac{\$152\text{m.}}{\$16\text{m.}} = 9.50 \text{ times}$$

Industry average = 5.70 times

$$\text{Cash coverage ratio} = \frac{\$152\text{m.} + 13\text{m.}}{\$16\text{m.}} = 10.31 \text{ times}$$

Industry average = 7.78 times

In all cases, debt management ratios show that DPH Tree Farm, Inc. holds less debt on its balance sheet than the average firm in the tree farm industry. Further, the firm has more dollars of operating earnings and cash available to meet each dollar of interest obligations (there are no other fixed charges listed on DPH Tree Farm's income statement) on the firm's debt. This lack of financial leverage decreases the firm's potential for financial distress and even failure, but may also decrease equity shareholders' chance for magnified earnings. If the firm has a bad year, it has promised relatively few payments to debt holders. Thus, the risk of bankruptcy is small. However, when DPH Tree Farm, Inc. does well, the low level of financial leverage dilutes the return to the stockholders of the firm. This dilution of profit is likely to upset common stockholders of the firm.

$$\text{Fixed-charge coverage ratio} = \frac{\text{Earnings available to meet fixed charges}}{\text{Fixed charges}} \quad (3\text{-}18)$$

$$\text{Cash coverage ratio} = \frac{\text{EBIT + Depreciation}}{\text{Fixed charges}} \quad (3\text{-}19)$$

With the help of the times interest earned, fixed-charge coverage, and cash coverage ratios, managers, investors, and analysts can determine whether a firm has taken on a debt burden that is too large. These ratios measure the dollars available to meet debt and other fixed-charge obligations. A value of 1 for these ratios means that $1 of earnings or cash is available to meet each dollar of interest or fixed-charge obligations. A value of less (greater) than 1 means that the firm has less (more) than $1 of earnings or cash available to pay each dollar of interest or fixed-charge obligations.[2] Further, the higher the times interest

earned, fixed-charge coverage, and cash coverage ratios, the more equity and less debt the applicant uses to finance its assets. Thus, low levels of debt will lead to a dilution of the return to stockholders due to a greater increased usage of equity as well as to not taking advantage of the tax deductibility of interest expense.

PROFITABILITY RATIOS

The liquidity, asset management, and debt management ratios examined so far allow for an isolated or narrow look at a firm's performance. **Profitability ratios** show the combined effects of liquidity, asset management, and debt management on the overall operating results of the firm. Profitability ratios are among the most watched and best known of the financial ratios. Indeed, firm values (or stock prices) react quickly to unexpected changes in these ratios. The most commonly used profitability ratios are listed below.

The profit margin is the percentage of sales left after all firm expenses are paid (equation 3-20). The basic earnings power ratio measures the operating return on the firm's assets, irrespective of financial leverage and taxes (equation 3-21). This ratio measures the operating profit (EBIT) earned per dollar of assets on the firm's balance sheet. Return on assets (ROA) measures the overall return on the firm's assets, inclusive of financial leverage and taxes (equation 3-22). This ratio is the net income earned per dollar of assets on the firm's balance sheet. Return on equity (ROE) measures the return on the common stockholders' investment in the assets of the firm (equation 3-23). ROE is the net income earned per dollar of common stockholders' equity. The value of a firm's ROE is affected not only by net income, but also by the amount of financial leverage or debt that firm uses. As stated above, financial leverage

time out!

3-7 What are the major debt management ratios?

3-8 Does a firm generally want to have high or low values for each of these ratios?

3-9 What is the trade-off between using too much financial leverage and not using enough leverage? Who is likely to complain the most in each case?

[a] The fixed-charge and cash coverage ratios can be tailored to a particular firm's situation, depending on what really constitutes fixed charges that must be paid. One version of it follows: (EBIT + Lease payments)/[Interest + Lease payments + Sinking fund/$(1 - t)$], where t is the firm's marginal tax rate. Here, it is assumed that sinking fund payments must be made. They are adjusted by the division of $(1 - t)$ into a before-tax cash outflow so they can be added to other before-tax cash outflows.

A company's profit margin is inversely related to its sales.

magnifies the return to the stockholders of the firm. However, financial leverage also increases the firm's potential for financial distress and even failure. Generally, a high ROE is considered to be a positive sign of firm performance. However, if performance comes from a high degree of financial leverage, a high ROE can indicate a firm with an unacceptably high level of bankruptcy risk as well. Finally, the dividend payout ratio is the percentage of net income available to common stockholders that the firm actually pays as cash to these investors (equation 3-24).

$$\text{Profit margin} = \frac{\text{Net income available to common stockholders}}{\text{Sales}} \quad (3\text{-}20)$$

$$\text{Basic earnings power ratio (BEP)} = \frac{\text{EBIT}}{\text{Total assets}} \quad (3\text{-}21)$$

$$\text{Return on assets (ROA)} = \frac{\text{Net income available to common stockholders}}{\text{Total assets}} \quad (3\text{-}22)$$

EXAMPLE 3-4

For interactive versions of this example visit www.mhhe.com/canM

Calculating Profitability Ratios

Use the balance sheet (Table 2.1) and income statement (Table 2.2) for DPH Tree Farm, Inc. to calculate the firm's 2008 values for the profitability ratios.

SOLUTION:

The profitability ratios for DPH Tree Farm, Inc. are calculated as follows:

$$\text{Profit margin} = \frac{\$80\text{m.}}{\$315\text{m.}} = 25.40\%$$

Industry average = 23.25%

$$\text{Basic earnings power ratio (BEP)} = \frac{\$152\text{m.}}{\$570\text{m.}} = 26.67\%$$

Industry average = 22.85%

$$\text{Return on assets (ROA)} = \frac{\$80\text{m.}}{\$570\text{m.}} = 14.04\%$$

Industry average = 9.30%

$$\text{Return on equity (ROE)} = \frac{\$80\text{m.}}{\$40\text{m.} + \$210\text{m.}} = 32.00\%$$

Industry average = 38.50%

$$\text{Dividend payout ratio} = \frac{\$25\text{m.}}{\$80\text{m.}} = 31.25\%$$

Industry average = 30.90%

These ratios show that DPH Tree Farm, Inc. is more profitable than the average firm in the tree farm industry. The profit margin, BEP, and ROA are all higher than industry figures. Despite this, the ROE for DPH Tree Farm is much lower than the industry average. DPH's low debt level and high equity level relative to the industry is the main reason for DPH's strong figures relative to the industry. As we mentioned above, DPH's managerial decisions about capital structure dilute its returns, which will likely upset its common stockholders. To counteract common stockholders' discontent, DPH Tree Farm pays out a slightly larger percentage of its income to its common stockholders as cash dividends. Of course, this slightly high dividend payout ratio means that DPH Tree Farm retains less of its profits to reinvest into the business. A profitable firm that retains its earnings increases its equity capital level as well as its own value.

$$\text{Return on equity (ROE)} = \frac{\text{Net income available to common stockholders}}{\text{Common stockholders' equity}} \quad \text{(3-23)}$$

$$\text{Dividend payout ratio} = \frac{\text{Common stock dividends}}{\text{Net income available to common stockholders}} \quad \text{(3-24)}$$

For all but the dividend payout ratio, the higher the value of the ratio, the higher the profitability of the firm. But just as has been the case previously in this chapter, high profitability ratio levels may result from poor management in other areas of the firm as much as superior financial management. A high profit margin means that the firm has low expenses relative to sales. The BEP reflects how much the firm's assets earn from operations, irrespective of financial leverage and taxes. It follows logically that managers, investors, and analysts find BEP a useful ratio when they compare firms that differ in financial leverage and taxes. In contrast, ROA measures the firm's overall performance. It shows how the firm's assets generate a return inclusive of financial leverage and tax decisions made by management.

ROE measures the return on common stockholders' investment. Since managers seek to maximize common stock price, managers, investors, and analysts monitor ROE above all other ratios. The dividend payout ratio measures how much of the profit the firm retains versus how much it pays out to common stockholders as dividends. The lower the dividend payout ratio, the more profits the firm retains for future growth or other projects. A profitable firm that retains its earnings increases its level of equity capital as well as its own value.

MARKET VALUE RATIOS

As we note above, ROE is a most important financial statement ratio for managers and investors to monitor. Generally, a high ROE is considered to be a positive sign of firm performance. However, if a high ROE results from a highly leveraged position, it can signal a firm with a high level of bankruptcy risk. While ROE does not directly incorporate this risk, for publicly traded firms, market prices of the firm's stock do. (We look at

stock valuation in Chapter 7.)
Since the firm's stockholders earn their returns primarily from the firm's stock market value, ratios that incorporate stock market values are equally, and arguably more, important than other financial statement ratios.

The final group of ratios is market value ratios. **Market value ratios** relate a firm's stock price to its earnings and its book value. For publicly traded firms, market value ratios measure what investors think of the company's future performance and risk. The most commonly used market value ratios are

$$\text{Market-to-book ratio} = \frac{\text{Market price per share}}{\text{Book value per share}} \quad \text{(3-25)}$$

$$\text{Price-earnings (PE) ratio} = \frac{\text{Market price per share}}{\text{Earnings per share}} \quad \text{(3-26)}$$

market value ratios Ratios that relate a firm's stock price to its earnings and book value.

time out!

3-10 What are the major profitability ratios?

3-11 Does a firm generally want to have high or low values for each of these ratios?

3-12 What are the trade-offs to having especially high or low values for these ratios?

The market-to-book ratio measures the amount that investors will pay for the firm's stock per dollar of equity used to finance the firm's assets (equation 3-25). Book value per share is an accounting-based number reflecting the firm's assets' historical costs, and hence historical value (equation 3-26). The

EXAMPLE 3-5

For interactive versions
of this example visit
www.mhhe.com/canM

Calculating Market Value Ratios

Use the balance sheet (Table 2.1) and income statement (Table 2.2) for DPH Tree Farm, Inc. to calculate the firm's 2008 values for the market value ratios.

SOLUTION:

The market value ratios for DPH Tree Farm, Inc. are calculated as follows:

$$\text{Market-to-book ratio} = \frac{\$17.25}{\$12.50} = 1.38 \text{ times}$$

Industry average = 2.15 times

$$\text{Price-earnings (PE) ratio} = \frac{\$17.25}{\$4.00} = 4.31 \text{ times}$$

Industry average = 6.25 times

These ratios show that DPH Tree Farm's investors will not pay as much for a share of DPH's stock per dollar of book value and earnings as the average for the industry. DPH's low leverage level and high reliance on equity relative to the industry likely are the main reason for investors' disinterest. As mentioned above, DPH's seemingly intentional return dilution will likely upset the firm's common stockholders. Accordingly, stockholders lower the amount they are willing to invest per dollar of book value and EPS.

---

market-to-book ratio compares the market (current) value of the firm's equity to its historical cost. In general, the higher the market-to-book ratio, the better the firm. If liquidity, asset management, debt management, and accounting profitability are good for a firm, then the market-to-book ratio will be high. A market-to-book ratio greater than 1 (or 100 percent) means that stockholders will pay a premium over book value for their equity investment in the firm.

Probably the best known and most often quoted figure, the price-earnings (or PE) ratio measures how much investors are willing to pay for each dollar the firm earns per share of its stock. PE ratios are often quoted in multiples—the number of dollars per share—that fund managers, investors, and analysts compare within industry classes. Managers and investors often use PE ratios to evaluate the relative financial performance of the firm's stock. Generally, the higher the PE ratio, the better the firm's performance. Analysts and investors, as well as managers, expect companies with high PE ratios to experience future growth, to have rapid future dividend increases, or both, because retained earnings will support the company's goals. However, for value-seeking investors, high PE firms indicate expensive companies. Further, higher PE ratios carry greater risk because investors are willing to pay higher prices today for a stock in anticipation of higher earnings in the future. These earnings may or may not

time out!

3-13 What are the major market value ratios?

3-14 Does a firm generally want to have high or low values for each of these ratios?

3-15 Discuss the price-earnings ratio and address why it assumes particular importance among all of the other ratios we have presented.

materialize. Low PE firms are generally companies with little expected growth or low earnings. However, note that earnings depend on many factors (such as financial leverage or taxes) that have nothing to do directly with firm operations.

DUPONT ANALYSIS

Table 3.1 lists the ratios we discuss, their values for DPH Tree Farm, Inc. as of 2008, and the corresponding values for the tree farm industry. The value of each ratio for DPH Tree Farm is highlighted in green if it is generally stronger than the industry and is highlighted in red if it is generally a negative sign for the firm. As we noted in this chapter's introduction, many of the ratios we have discussed thus far are interrelated. So a change in one ratio may well affect the value of several ratios. Often these interrelations can help evaluate firm performance. Managers and investors often perform a detailed analysis of ROA (return on assets) and ROE (return on equity) using the **DuPont analysis system.** Popularized by the DuPont Corporation, the DuPont analysis system uses the balance sheet and income statement to break the ROA and ROE ratios into component pieces.

The basic DuPont equation looks at ROA as the product of the profit margin and the total asset turnover ratios:

$$\text{ROA} = \text{Profit margin} \times \text{Total asset turnover}$$

$$\frac{\text{Net income available to common stockholders}}{\text{Total assets}} = \frac{\text{Net income available to common stockholders}}{\text{Sales}} \times \frac{\text{Sales}}{\text{Total assets}} \quad (3\text{-}27)$$

The basic DuPont equation looks at the firm's overall profitability as a function of the profit the firm earns per dollar of sales (operating efficiency) and the dollar of sales produced per dollar of assets on the balance sheet (efficiency in asset use). With this tool, managers can see the reason for any changes in ROA in more detail. For example, if ROA increases, the DuPont equation may show that the net profit margin was constant, but the total asset turnover (efficiency in using assets) increased, or that total asset turnover remained constant, but profit margins (operating efficiency) increased. Managers can more specifically identify the reasons for an ROA change by using the ratios described above to further break down operating efficiency and efficiency in asset use.

DuPont system of analysis An analytical method that uses the balance sheet and income statement to break the ROA and ROE ratios into component pieces.

Next, the DuPont system looks at ROE as the product of ROA and the equity multiplier.

$$\text{ROE} = \text{ROA} \times \text{Equity multiplier}$$

$$\frac{\text{Net income available to common stockholders}}{\text{Common stockholders' equity}} = \text{ROA} \times \frac{\text{Total assets}}{\text{Common stockholders' equity}} \quad (3\text{-}28)$$

Notice that this version of the equity multiplier uses the return to common stockholders (the firm's owners) only. So the DuPont equity multiplier uses common stockholders' equity only, rather than total equity (which includes preferred stock).

Taking this breakdown one step further, the DuPont system breaks ROE into the product of the profit margin, the total asset turnover, and the equity multiplier.

$$\text{ROE} = \text{Profit margin} \times \text{Total asset turnover} \times \text{Equity multiplier}$$

$$\frac{\text{Net income available to common stockholders}}{\text{Common stockholders' equity}} = \frac{\text{Net income available to common stockholders}}{\text{Sales}} \times \frac{\text{Sales}}{\text{Total assets}} \times \frac{\text{Total assets}}{\text{Common stockholders' equity}} \quad (3\text{-}29)$$

This presentation of ROE allows managers, analysts, and investors to look at the return on equity as a function of the net profit margin (profit per dollar of sales from the income statement), total asset turnover (efficiency in the use of assets from the balance sheet), and the equity multiplier (financial leverage from the balance sheet). Again, we can break these components down to more specifically identify possible causes for a ROE change. Figure 3.1 illustrates the DuPont system analysis breakdown of ROA and ROE.

Ratio	Value for Dph Tree Farm, Inc.	Value for the Tree Farm Industry
Liquidity ratios:		
Current ratio $= \dfrac{\text{Current assets}}{\text{Current liabilities}}$	1.71 times	1.50 times
Quick ratio (acid-test ratio) $= \dfrac{\text{Current assets} - \text{Inventory}}{\text{Current liabilities}}$	0.78 times	0.50 times
Cash ratio $= \dfrac{\text{Cash and marketable securities}}{\text{Current liabilities}}$	0.20 times	0.15 times
Asset management ratios:		
Inventory turnover ratio $= \dfrac{\text{Sales or Cost of goods sold}}{\text{Inventory}}$	2.84 times	2.15 times
Days' sales in inventory $= \dfrac{\text{Inventory} \times 365 \text{ days}}{\text{Sales}}$	129 days	170 days
Average collection period $= \dfrac{\text{Accounts receivable} \times 365 \text{ days}}{\text{Credit sales}}$	81 days	95 days
Accounts receivable turnover $= \dfrac{\text{Credit sales}}{\text{Accounts receivable}}$	4.50 times	3.84 times
Average payment period (APP) $= \dfrac{\text{Accounts payable} \times 365 \text{ days}}{\text{Cost of goods sold}}$	134 days	102 days
Accounts payable turnover $= \dfrac{\text{Cost of goods sold}}{\text{Accounts payable}}$	2.73 times	3.55 times
Fixed asset turnover ratio $= \dfrac{\text{Sales}}{\text{Fixed assets}}$	1.00 times	0.85 times
Sales to working capital $= \dfrac{\text{Sales}}{\text{Working capital}}$	3.71 times	3.20 times
Total asset turnover ratio $= \dfrac{\text{Sales}}{\text{Total assets}}$	0.55 times	0.40 times
Capital intensity $= \dfrac{\text{Total assets}}{\text{Sales}}$	1.81 times	2.50 times
Debt management ratios:		
Debt ratio $= \dfrac{\text{Total debt}}{\text{Total assets}}$	55.26%	68.50%
Debt-to-equity ratio $= \dfrac{\text{Total debt}}{\text{Total equity}}$	1.24 times	2.17 times
Equity multiplier ratio $= \dfrac{\text{Total assets}}{\text{Total equity}}$	2.24 times	4.10 times
or $\dfrac{\text{Total assets}}{\text{Common stockholders' equity}}$	2.28 times	4.14 times

Times interest earned $= \dfrac{\text{EBIT}}{\text{Interest}}$	9.50 times	5.15 times
Fixed-charge coverage ratio $= \dfrac{\text{Earnings available to meet fixed charges}}{\text{Fixed charges}}$	9.50 times	5.70 times
Cash coverage ratio $= \dfrac{\text{EBIT} + \text{Depreciation}}{\text{Fixed charges}}$	10.31 times	7.78 times

Profitability ratios:

Profit margin $= \dfrac{\text{Net income available to common stockholders}}{\text{Sales}}$	25.40%	23.25%
Basic earnings power ratio $= \dfrac{\text{EBIT}}{\text{Total assets}}$	26.67%	22.85%
Return on assets $= \dfrac{\text{Net income available to common stockholders}}{\text{Total assets}}$	14.04%	9.30%
Return on equity $= \dfrac{\text{Net income available to common stockholders}}{\text{Common stockholders' equity}}$	32.00%	38.50%
Dividend payout ratio $= \dfrac{\text{Common stock dividends}}{\text{Net income available to common stockholders}}$	31.25%	30.90%

Market value ratios:

Market-to-book ratio $= \dfrac{\text{Market price per share}}{\text{Book value per share}}$	1.38 times	2.15 times
Price-earnings ratio $= \dfrac{\text{Market price per share}}{\text{Earnings per share}}$	4.31 times	6.25 times

▼**FIGURE 3.1** DuPont System Analysis Breakdown of ROA and ROE

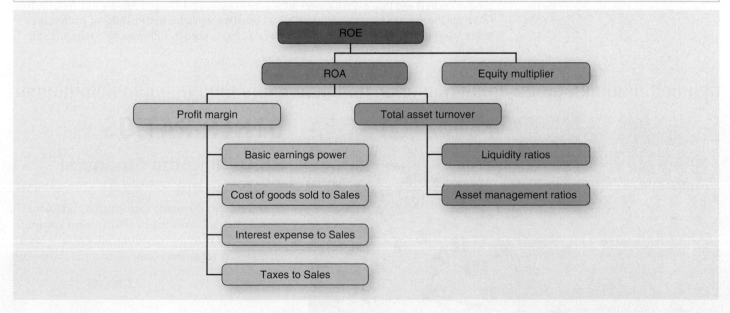

EXAMPLE 3-6

For interactive versions
of this example visit
www.mhhe.com/canM

Application of DuPont Analysis

Use the balance sheet (Table 2.1) and income statement (Table 2.2) for DPH Tree Farm, Inc. to calculate the firm's 2008 values for the ROA and ROE DuPont equations.

SOLUTION:

The ROA and ROE DuPont equations for DPH Tree Farm, Inc. are calculated as follows:

ROA	=	Profit margin	×	Total asset turnover	
14.04%	=	25.39683%	×	0.55263 times	
Industry average: 9.30%	=	23.25%	×	0.40 times	

$$\frac{\text{Net income available to common stockholders}}{\text{Stockholders' equity}} = \frac{\text{Net income available to common stockholders}}{\text{Sales}} \times \frac{\text{Sales}}{\text{Total assets}}$$

$$\frac{\$80m.}{\$570m.} = \frac{\$80m.}{\$315m.} \times \frac{\$315m.}{\$570m.}$$

ROE	=	Profit margin	×	Total asset turnover	×	Equity multiplier
32.00%	=	25.39683%	×	0.55263 times	×	2.28 times
Industry average: 38.50%	=	23.25%	×	0.40 times	×	4.13978 times

$$\frac{\text{Net income available to common stockholders}}{\text{Common stockholders' equity}} = \frac{\text{Net income available to common stockholders}}{\text{Sales}} \times \frac{\text{Sales}}{\text{Total assets}} \times \frac{\text{Total assets}}{\text{Common stockholders' equity}}$$

$$\frac{\$80m.}{\$40m. + \$210m.} = \frac{\$80m.}{\$315m.} \times \frac{\$315m.}{\$570m.} \times \frac{\$570m.}{\$40m. + \$210m.}$$

As we saw with profitability ratios, DPH Tree Farm, Inc. is more profitable than the average firm in the tree farm industry when it comes to overall efficiency expressed as return on assets, or ROA. The DuPont equation highlights that this superior performance comes from both profit margin (operating efficiency) and total asset turnover (efficiency in asset use). Despite this, the ROE for DPH Tree Farm lags the average industry ROE. The DuPont equation highlights that this inferior performance is due solely to the low level of debt and high level of equity used by DPH Tree Farm relative to the industry.

time out!

3-16 What are the DuPont ROA and ROE equations?

3-17 How do each of these equations help to explain firm performance and pinpoint areas for improvement?

OTHER RATIOS

Spreading the Financial Statements

In addition to the many ratios listed above, managers, analysts, and investors can also compute additional ratios by dividing all balance sheet amounts by total assets and all income statement amounts by net sales. These calculations, sometimes called *spreading the financial statements,* yield what we call **common-size financial statements** that correct for sizes. Using common-size financial statements, interested parties can identify

common-size financial statements Dividing all balance sheet amounts by total assets and all income statement amounts by net sales.

internal growth rate The growth rate a firm can sustain if it finances growth using only internal financing, that is, retained earnings growth.

sustainable growth rate The growth rate a firm can sustain if it finances growth using both debt and internal financing such that the debt ratio remains constant.

> ## The firm's ROA and ROE can be used to evaluate the firm's ability to grow and its market value to be maximized.

changes in corporate performance. Year-to-year growth rates in common-size balance sheets and income statement balances also provide useful ratios for identifying trends. They also allow for an easy comparison of balance sheets and income statements across firms in the industry. Common-size financial statements may provide quantitative clues about the direction that the firm (and perhaps the industry) is moving. They may thus provide roadmaps for managers' next moves.

Internal and Sustainable Growth Rates

Remember again that any firm manager's job is to maximize the firm's market value. The firm's ROA and ROE can be used to evaluate the firm's ability to grow and its market value to be maximized. Specifically, managers, analysts, and investors use these ratios to calculate two growth measures: the internal growth rate and the sustainable growth rate.

The **internal growth rate** is the growth rate a firm can sustain if it uses only internal financing—that is, retained earnings—to finance future growth. Mathematically, the internal growth rate is:

$$\text{Internal growth rate} = \frac{\text{ROA} \times \text{RR}}{1 - (\text{ROA} \times \text{RR})} \quad (3\text{-}30)$$

where RR is the firm's earnings retention ratio. The retention ratio represents the portion of net income that the firm reinvests as retained earnings:

$$\text{Retention ratio}\,(\text{RR}) = \frac{\text{Addition to retained earnings}}{\substack{\text{Net income available to} \\ \text{common stockholders}}} \quad (3\text{-}31)$$

Since a firm either pays its net income as dividends to its stockholders or reinvests those funds as retained earnings, the dividend payout and the retention ratios must always add to one:

$$\text{Retention ratio} = 1 - \text{Dividend payout ratio} \quad (3\text{-}32)$$

A problem arises when a firm relies only on internal financing to support asset growth: Through time, its debt ratio will fall because as asset values grow, total debt stays constant—only retained earnings finance asset growth. If total debt remains constant, as assets grow the debt ratio decreases. As we noted above, shareholders often become disgruntled if, as the firm grows, a decreasing debt ratio (increasing equity financing) dilutes their return. So as firms grow, managers must often try to maintain a debt ratio that they view as optimal. In this case, managers finance asset growth with new debt *and* retained earnings. The maximum growth rate that can be achieved this way is the **sustainable growth rate.** Mathematically, the sustainable growth rate is:

$$\text{Sustainable growth rate} = \frac{\text{ROE} \times \text{RR}}{1 - (\text{ROE} \times \text{RR})} \quad (3\text{-}33)$$

Maximizing the sustainable growth rate helps firm managers maximize firm value. Applying the DuPont ROE equation

EXAMPLE 3-7

For interactive versions
of this example visit
www.mhhe.com/canM

Calculating Internal and Sustainable Growth Rates

Use the balance sheet (Table 2.1) and income statement (Table 2.2) for DPH Tree Farm, Inc. to calculate the firm's 2008 internal and sustainable growth rates.

SOLUTION:

The internal and sustainable growth rates for DPH Tree Farm, Inc. are calculated as follows.

$$\text{Retention rate (RR)} = \frac{\$55m.}{\$80m.} = .6875 \text{ or } 68.75\%$$

$$\text{Industry RR} = 1 - \text{Industry dividend payout ratio}$$

$$= 1 - .3090$$

$$\text{Internal growth rate} = \frac{.1404 \times .6875}{1 - (.1404 \times .6875)} = .1068 \text{ or } 10.68\%$$

$$\text{Industry average internal growth rate} = \frac{.0930 \times (1 - .3090)}{1 - (.0930 \times (1 - .3090))} = .0687 \text{ or } 6.87\%$$

$$\text{Sustainable growth rate} = \frac{.3200 \times .6875}{1 - (.3200 \times .6875)} = .2821 \text{ or } 28.21\%$$

$$\text{Industry average sustainable growth rate} = \frac{.3800 \times (1 - .3090)}{1 - (.3800 \times (1 - .3090))} = .3561 \text{ or } 35.61\%$$

These ratios show that DPH Tree Farm, Inc. can grow faster than the industry if the firm uses only retained earnings to finance the growth. However, if DPH grows while keeping the debt *ratio* constant (e.g., both debt and retained earnings are used to finance the growth), industry firms can grow much faster than DPH Tree Farm. Once again, DPH's low debt level and high equity level relative to the industry creates this disparity. Therefore, DPH Tree Farm limits its growth as a result of its managerial decisions.

here, notice that a firm's sustainable growth depends on four factors:

1. The profit margin (operating efficiency).

2. The total asset turnover (efficiency in asset use).

3. Financial leverage (the use of debt versus equity to finance assets).

4. Profit retention (reinvestment of net income into the firm rather than paying it out as dividends).

Increasing any of these factors increases the firm's sustainable growth rate and hence helps to maximize firm value. Managers, analysts, and investors will want to focus on these areas as they evaluate firm performance and market value.

the Math Coach on...

" When putting values into the equation, enter them in decimal format, not percentage format

CORRECT $1 - (.1404 \times .6875)$

NOT CORRECT $1 - (14.04 \times 68.75)$ "

TIME SERIES AND CROSS-SECTIONAL ANALYSIS

We have explored many ratios that allow managers and investors to examine firm performance. But to really analyze performance in a meaningful way, we must interpret our ratio results against some kind of standard or benchmark. To interpret financial ratios, managers, analysts, and investors use two major types of benchmarks: (1) performance of the firm over time (**time series analysis**) and (2) performance of the firm against one or more companies in the same industry (**cross-sectional analysis**).

Analyzing ratio trends over time, along with absolute ratio levels, gives managers, analysts, and investors information about whether a firm's financial condition is improving or deteriorating. For example, ratio analysis may reveal that the days' sales in inventory is increasing. This suggests that inventories, relative to the sales they support, are not being used as well as they were in the past. If this increase is the result of a deliberate policy to increase inventories to offer customers a wider choice and if it results in higher future sales volumes or increased margins that more than compensate for increased capital tied up in inventory, the increased relative size of the inventories is good for the firm. Managers and investors should be concerned, on the other hand, if increased inventories result from declining sales but steady purchases of supplies and production.

Looking at one firm's financial ratios, even through time, gives managers, analysts, and investors only a limited picture of firm performance. Ratio analysis almost always includes a comparison of one firm's ratios relative to the ratios of other firms in the industry, or cross-sectional analysis. Key to cross-sectional analysis is identifying similar firms that compete in the same markets, have similar asset sizes, and operate in a similar manner to the firm being analyzed. Since no two firms are identical, obtaining such a comparison group is no easy task. Thus, the choice of companies to use in cross-sectional analysis is at best subjective. Note that as we calculated the financial ratios for DPH Tree Farm, Inc. throughout the chapter, we compared them to the industry average. Comparative ratios that can be used in cross-sectional analysis are available from many sources. For example, Value Line Investment Surveys, Robert Morris Associates, Hoover's Online (at www.hoovers.com), and the MSN Money Web site (at **moneycentral.msn.com**) are examples of four major sources of financial ratios for numerous industries that operate within the U.S. and worldwide.

time series analysis Analyzing firm performance by monitoring ratio trends.

cross-sectional analysis Analyzing the performance of a firm against one or more companies in the same industry.

time out!

3-18 What does "spreading the financial statements" mean?

3-19 What are retention rates and internal and sustainable growth rates?

3-20 What factors enter into sustainable growth rates?

3-21 What is time series analysis of a firm's operations?

3-22 What is cross-sectional analysis of a firm's operations?

3-23 How do time series and cross-sectional analyses differ, and what information would you expect to gain from each?

CAUTIONS IN USING RATIOS TO EVALUATE FIRM PERFORMANCE

Financial statement analysis allows managers, analysts, and investors to better understand a firm's performance. However, data from financial statements should not be received without certain cautions. These include:

1. Financial statement data are historical. Historical data may not reflect future performance. While we can make projections using historical data, we must also remember that projections may be inaccurate if historical performance does not persist.

2. As we discussed in Chapter 2, firms use different accounting procedures. For example, inventory methods can vary. One firm may use FIFO (first-in, first-out), transferring inventory at the first purchase price, while another uses LIFO (last-in, first-out), transferring inventory at the last purchase price. Likewise, the depreciation method used to value a firm's fixed assets over time may vary across firms. One firm may use straight-line depreciation, while another may use an accelerated depreciation method (e.g., MACRS). Particularly, when reviewing cross-sectional ratios, differences in accounting rules can affect balance sheet values and financial ratios. It is important to know which accounting rules the firms under consideration are using before making any conclusions about their performance from ratio analysis.

3. Similarly, a firm's cross-sectional competitors may often be located around the world. Financial statements for firms based outside the United States do not necessarily conform to GAAP. Even beyond inventory pricing and depreciation methods, different accounting standards and procedures make it hard to compare financial statements and ratios of firms based in different countries.

4. Sales and expenses vary throughout the year. Managers, analysts, and investors need to note the timing of these fund flows when performing cross-sectional analysis, otherwise they may draw conclusions from comparisons that are actually the result of seasonal cash flow differences. Similarly, firms end their fiscal years at different dates. For cross-sectional analysis, this complicates any comparison of balance sheets during the year. Likewise, one-time events, such as a merger, may affect a firm's financial performance. Cross-sectional analysis involving these events can result in misleading conclusions.

5. Large firms often have multiple divisions or business units engaged in different lines of business. In this case, it is difficult to truly compare a set of firms with which managers and investors can perform cross-sectional analysis.

6. Firms often window dress their financial statements to make annual results look better. For example, to improve liquidity ratios calculated with year-end balance sheets, firms often delay payments for raw materials, equipment, loans, and so on to build up their liquid accounts and thus their liquidity ratios. If possible, it is often more accurate to use other than year-end financial statements to conduct ratio analysis.

Financial statement ratio analysis is a major part of evaluating a firm's performance. If managers, analysts, or investors ignore the issues noted here, they may well draw faulty conclusions from their analysis. However, used intelligently and with good judgment, ratio analysis can provide useful information on a firm's current position and hint at future performance.

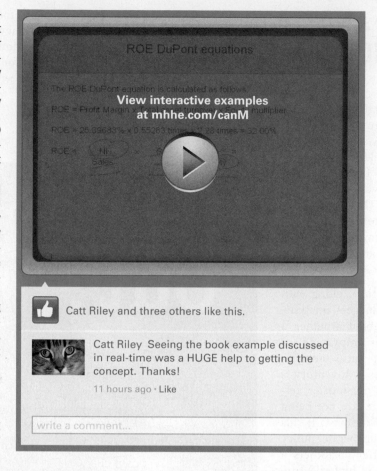

Catt Riley and three others like this.

Catt Riley Seeing the book example discussed in real-time was a HUGE help to getting the concept. Thanks!

11 hours ago · Like

write a comment...

3-24 What cautions should managers and investors take when evaluating a firm using ratio analysis?

Your Turn...

Questions

1. Classify each of the following ratios according to a ratio category (liquidity ratio, asset management ratio, debt management ratio, profitability ratio, or market value ratio). *(LG1–LG5)*
   a. Current ratio
   b. Inventory turnover ratio
   c. Return on assets
   d. Accounts payable period
   e. Times interest earned
   f. Capital intensity ratio
   g. Equity multiplier
   h. Basic earnings power ratio

2. For each of the actions listed below, determine what would happen to the current ratio. Assume nothing else on the balance sheet changes and that net working capital is positive. *(LG1)*
   a. Accounts receivable are paid in cash
   b. Notes payable are paid off with cash
   c. Inventory is sold on account
   d. Inventory is purchased on account
   e. Accrued wages and taxes increase
   f. Long-term debt is paid with cash
   g. Cash from a short-term bank loan is received

3. Explain the meaning and significance of the following ratios. *(LG1–LG5)*
   a. Quick ratio
   b. Average collection period
   c. Return on equity
   d. Days' sales in inventory
   e. Debt ratio
   f. Profit margin
   g. Accounts payable turnover
   h. Market-to-book ratio

4. A firm has an average collection period of 10 days. The industry average ACP is 25 days. Is this a good or poor sign about the management of the firm's accounts receivable? *(LG2)* Explain your response.

5. A firm has a debt ratio of 20 percent. The industry average debt ratio is 65 percent. Is this a good or poor sign about the management of the firm's financial leverage? *(LG3)* Explain your response.

6. A firm has an ROE of 20 percent. The industry average ROE is 12 percent. Is this a good or poor sign about the management of the firm? *(LG4)* Explain your response.

7. Why is the DuPont system of analysis an important tool when evaluating firm performance? *(LG6)*

8. A firm has an ROE of 10 percent. The industry average ROE is 15 percent. How can the DuPont system of analysis help the firm's managers identify the reasons for this difference? *(LG6)*

9. What is the difference between the internal growth rate and the sustainable growth rate? *(LG6)*

10. What is the difference between time series analysis and cross-sectional analysis? *(LG7)*

11. What information does time series and cross-sectional analyses provide for firm managers, analysts, and investors? *(LG7)*

12. Why is it important to know a firm's accounting rules before making any conclusions about its performance from ratios analysis? *(LG8)*

13. What does it mean when a firm window dresses its financial statements? *(LG8)*

Problems

BASIC PROBLEMS

3-1 **Liquidity Ratios** You are evaluating the balance sheet for Goodman's Bees Corporation. From the balance sheet you find the following balances: cash and marketable securities = $400,000; accounts receivable = $1,200,000; inventory = $2,100,000; accrued wages and taxes = $500,000; accounts payable = $800,000; and notes payable = $600,000. Calculate Goodman Bees' current ratio, quick ratio, and cash ratio. *(LG1)*

3-2 **Liquidity Ratios** The top parts of Ramakrishnan Inc.'s 2008 and 2009 balance sheets are listed below (in millions of dollars).

Calculate Ramakrishnan Inc.'s current ratio, quick ratio, and cash ratio for 2008 and 2009. *(LG1)*

	2008	2009		2008	2009
Current assets:			Current liabilities:		
Cash and marketable securities	$ 15	$ 20	Accrued wages and taxes	$ 18	$ 19
Accounts receivable	75	84	Accounts payable	45	51
Inventory	110	121	Notes payable	40	45
Total	$200	$225	Total	$103	$115

3-3 **Asset Management Ratios** Tater and Pepper Corp. reported sales for 2008 of $23 million. Tater and Pepper listed $5.6 million of inventory on its balance sheet. Using a 365-day year, how many days did Tater and Pepper's inventory stay on the premises? How many times per year did Tater and Pepper's inventory turn over? *(LG2)*

3-4 **Asset Management Ratios** Mr. Husker's Tuxedos, Corp. ended the year 2008 with an average collection period of 32 days. The firm's credit sales for 2008 were $33 million. What is the year-end 2008 balance in accounts receivable for Mr. Husker's Tuxedos? *(LG2)*

3-5 **Debt Management Ratios** Tiggie's Dog Toys, Inc. reported a debt-to-equity ratio of 1.75 times at the end of 2008. If the firm's total debt at year-end was $25 million, how much equity does Tiggie's have on its balance sheet? *(LG3)*

3-6 **Debt Management Ratios** You are considering a stock investment in one of two firms (LotsofDebt, Inc. and LotsofEquity, Inc.), both of which operate in the same industry. LotsofDebt, Inc. finances its $25 million in assets with $24 million in debt and $1 million in equity. LotsofEquity, Inc. finances its $25 million in assets with $1 million in debt and $24 million in equity. Calculate the debt ratio, equity multiplier, and debt-to-equity ratio for the two firms. *(LG3)*

3-7 Profitability Ratios Maggie's Skunk Removal Corp.'s 2008 income statement listed net sales of $12.5 million, EBIT of $5.6 million, net income available to common stockholders of $3.2 million, and common stock dividends of $1.2 million. The 2008 year-end balance sheet listed total assets of $52.5 million and common stockholders' equity of $21 million with 2 million shares outstanding. Calculate the profit margin, basic earnings power ratio, ROA, ROE, and dividend payout ratio. *(LG4)*

3-8 Profitability Ratios In 2008, Jake's Jamming Music, Inc. announced an ROA of 8.56 percent, ROE of 14.5 percent, and profit margin of 20.5 percent. The firm had total assets of $16.5 million at year-end 2008. Calculate the 2008 values of net income available to common stockholders, common stockholders' equity, and net sales for Jake's Jamming Music, Inc. *(LG4)*

3-9 Market Value Ratios You are considering an investment in Roxie's Bed & Breakfast Corp. During the last year the firm's income statement listed an addition to retained earnings of $4.8 million and common stock dividends = $2.2 million. Roxie's year-end balance sheet shows common stockholders' equity of $35 million with 10 million shares of common stock outstanding. The common stock's market price per share was $9.00. What are Roxie's Bed & Breakfast's book value per share and earnings per share? Calculate the market-to-book ratio and PE ratio. *(LG5)*

3-10 Market Value Ratios Gambit Golf's market-to-book ratio is currently 2.5 times and PE ratio is 6.75 times. If Gambit Golf's common stock is currently selling at $12.50 per share, what are the book value per share and earnings per share? *(LG5)*

3-11 DuPont Analysis If Silas 4-Wheeler, Inc. has an ROE of 18 percent, equity multiplier of 2, and a profit margin of 18.75 percent, what are the total asset turnover ratio and the capital intensity ratio? *(LG6)*

3-12 DuPont Analysis Last year Hassan's Madhatter, Inc. had an ROA of 7.5 percent, a profit margin of 12 percent, and sales of $10 million. Calculate Hassan's Madhatter's total assets. *(LG6)*

3-13 Internal Growth Rate Last year Lakesha's Lounge Furniture Corporation had an ROA of 7.5 percent and a dividend payout ratio of 25 percent. What is the internal growth rate? *(LG6)*

3-14 Sustainable Growth Rate Last year Lakesha's Lounge Furniture Corporation had an ROE of 12.5 percent and a dividend payout ratio of 20 percent What is the sustainable growth rate? *(LG6)*

INTERMEDIATE PROBLEMS

3-15 Liquidity Ratios Brenda's Bar and Grill has current liabilities of $15 million. Cash makes up 10 percent of the current assets and accounts receivable makes up another 40 percent of current assets. Brenda's current ratio is 2.1 times. Calculate the value of inventory listed on the firm's balance sheet. *(LG1)*

3-16 Liquidity and Asset Management Ratios Mandesa, Inc. has current liabilities of $5 million, current ratio of 2 times, inventory turnover ratio of 12 times, average collection period of 30 days, and sales of $40 million. Calculate the value of cash and marketable securities. *(LG1, LG2)*

3-17 Asset Management and Profitability Ratios You have the following information on Els' Putters, Inc.: sales to working capital is 4.6 times, profit margin is 20 percent, net income available to common stockholders is $5 million, and current liabilities are $6 million. What is the firm's balance of current assets? *(LG2, LG4)*

3-18 Asset Management and Debt Management Ratios Use the following information to complete the balance sheet below. Sales are $5.2 million, capital intensity ratio is 2.10 times, debt ratio is 55 percent, and fixed asset turnover ratio is 1.2 times. *(LG2, LG3)*

Assets		Liabilities and Equity	
Current assets	$_____	Total liabilities	$_____
Fixed assets	_____	Total equity	_____
Total assets	$_____	Total liabilities and equity	$_____

3-19 Debt Management Ratios Tiggie's Dog Toys, Inc. reported a debt-to-equity ratio of 1.75 times at the end of 2008. If the firm's total assets at year-end were $25 million, how much of their assets are financed with debt and how much with equity? *(LG3)*

3-20 Debt Management Ratios Calculate the times interest earned ratio for LaTonya's Flop Shops, Inc. using the following information. Sales = $1 million, cost of goods sold = $600,000, depreciation expense = $100,000, addition to retained earnings = $97,500, dividends per share = $1, tax rate = 30 percent, and number of shares of common stock outstanding = 60,000. LaTonya's Flop Shops has no preferred stock outstanding. *(LG3)*

3-21 Profitability and Asset Management Ratios You are thinking of investing in Nikki T's, Inc. You have only the following information on the firm at year-end 2008: net income is $250,000, total debt is $2.5 million, and debt ratio is 55 percent. What is Nikki T's ROE for 2008? *(LG2, LG4)*

3-22 Profitability Ratios Rick's Travel Service has asked you to help piece together financial information on the firm for the most current year. Managers give you the following information: sales are $4.8 million, total debt is $1.5 million, debt ratio is 40 percent, and ROE is 18 percent. Using this information, calculate Rick's ROA. *(LG4)*

3-23 Market Value Ratios Leonatti Labs' year-end price on its common stock is $35. The firm has total assets of $50 million, debt ratio of 65 percent, no preferred stock, and 3 million shares of common stock outstanding. Calculate the market-to-book ratio for Leonatti Labs. *(LG5)*

3-24 Market Value Ratios Leonatti Labs' year-end price on its common stock is $15. The firm has a profit margin of 8 percent, total assets of $25 million, a total asset turnover ratio of 0.75, no preferred stock, and 3 million shares of common stock outstanding. Calculate the PE ratio for Leonatti Labs. *(LG5)*

3-25 DuPont Analysis Last year, Stumble-on-Inn, Inc. reported an ROE of 18 percent. The firm's debt ratio was 55 percent, sales were $15 million, and the capital intensity ratio was 1.25 times. Calculate the net income for Stumble-on-Inn last year. *(LG6)*

3-26 DuPont Analysis You are considering investing in Nuran Security Services. You have been able to locate the following information on the firm: total assets are $16 million, accounts receivable are $2.2 million, ACP is 25 days, net income is $2.5 million, and debt-to-equity ratio is 1.2 times. Calculate the ROE for the firm. *(LG6)*

3-27 Internal Growth Rate Dogs R Us reported a profit margin of 10.5 percent, total asset turnover ratio of 0.75 times, debt-to-equity ratio of 0.80 times, net income of $500,000, and dividends paid to common stockholders of $200,000. The firm has no preferred stock outstanding. What is Dogs R Us's internal growth rate? *(LG6)*

3-28 Sustainable Growth Rate You have located the following information on Webb's Heating & Air Conditioning: debt ratio is 54 percent, capital intensity ratio is 1.10 times, profit margin is 12.5 percent, and dividend payout ratio is 40 percent. Calculate the sustainable growth rate for Webb. *(LG6)*

Use the following financial statements for Lake of Egypt Marina to answer Problems 3-29 through 3-32.

LAKE OF EGYPT MARINA, INC. Balance Sheet as of December 31, 2007 and 2008 (in millions of dollars)					
Assets	**2007**	**2008**	**Liabilities and Equity**	**2007**	**2008**
Current assets:			Current liabilities:		
Cash and marketable securities	$ 65	$ 75	Accrued wages and taxes	$ 43	$ 40
Accounts receivable	110	115	Accounts payable	80	90
Inventory	190	200	Notes payable	70	80
Total	365	390	Total	193	210
Fixed assets:			Long-term debt:	280	300
Gross plant and equipment	471	580	Stockholders' equity:		
Less: Depreciation	100	110	Preferred stock (5 million shares)	5	5
Net plant and equipment	371	470	Common stock and paid in surplus (65 million shares)	65	65
Other long term assets	49	50	Retained earnings	242	330
Total	420	520	Total	312	400
Total assets	$785	$910	Total liabilities and equity	$785	$910

LAKE OF EGYPT MARINA, INC. Income Statement for Years Ending December 31, 2007 and 2008 (in millions of dollars)		
	2007	**2008**
Net sales (all credit)	$ 432	$ 515
Less: Cost of goods sold	200	260
Gross profits	232	255
Less: Depreciation	20	22
Earnings before interest and taxes (EBIT)	212	233
Less: Interest	30	33
Earnings before taxes (EBT)	182	200
Less: Taxes	55	57
Net income	$ 127	$ 143
Less: Preferred stock dividends	$ 5	$ 5
Net income available to common stockholders	$ 122	$ 138
Less: Common stock dividends	65	65
Addition to retained earnings	$ 57	$ 73
Per (common) share data:		
Earnings per share (EPS)	$ 1.877	$ 2.123
Dividends per share (DPS)	$ 1.000	$ 1.000
Book value per share (BVPS)	$ 4.723	$ 6.077
Market value (price) per share (MVPS)	$12.550	$14.750

3-29 Spreading the Financial Statements Spread the balance sheets and income statements of Lake of Egypt Marina, Inc. for 2007 and 2008. *(LG1–LG7)*

3-30 Calculating Ratios Calculate the following ratios for Lake of Egypt Marina, Inc. as of year-end 2008. *(LG1–LG7)*

Lake of Egypt Marina, Inc.	Industry
a. Current ratio	2.00 times
b. Quick ratio	1.20 times
c. Cash ratio	0.25 times
d. Inventory turnover ratio	3.60 times
e. Days' sales in inventory	101.39 days
f. Average collection period	32.50 days
g. Average payment period	45 days
h. Fixed asset turnover ratio	1.25 times
i. Sales to working capital	4.25 times
j. Total asset turnover ratio	0.85 times
k. Capital intensity ratio	1.18 times
l. Debt ratio	62.50%
m. Debt-to-equity ratio	1.67 times
n. Equity multiplier	2.67 times
o. Times interest earned	8.50 times
p. Cash coverage ratio	8.75 times
q. Profit margin	28.75%
r. Basic earnings power ratio	32.50%
s. ROA	19.75%
t. ROE	36.88%
u. Dividend payout ratio	35%
v. Market-to-book ratio	2.55 times
w. PE ratio	15.60 times

3-31 DuPont Analysis Construct the DuPont ROA and ROE breakdowns for Lake of Egypt Marina, Inc. *(LG1–LG7)*

3-32 Internal and Sustainable Growth Rates Calculate the internal and sustainable growth rate for Lake of Egypt Marina, Inc. *(LG1–LG7)*

3-33 Cross-Sectional Analysis Using the ratios from Problem 3-30 for Lake of Egypt Marina, Inc. and the industry, what can you conclude about Lake of Egypt Marina's financial performance for 2008? *(LG1–LG7)*

ADVANCED PROBLEMS

3-34 Ratio Analysis Use the following information to complete the balance sheet below. *(LG1–LG5)*

Current ratio = 2.5 times

Profit margin = 10%

Sales = $2,100m.

ROE = 20%

Long-term debt to Long-term debt and equity = 55%

Current assets	_____	Current liabilities	$370m.
Fixed assets	_____	Long-term debt	_____
		Stockholders' equity	_____
Total assets	$ _____	Total liabilities and equity	$ _____

3-35 Ratio Analysis Use the following information to complete the balance sheet below. *(LG1–LG5)*

Current ratio = 2.2 times

Credit sales = $1,200m.

Average collection period = 60 days

Inventory turnover = 1.50 times

Total asset turnover = 0.75 times

Debt ratio = 60%

Cash	_____		
Accounts receivable	_____	Current liabilities	$500m.
Inventory	_____	Long-term debt	_____
Current assets	_____	Total debt	_____
Fixed assets	_____	Stockholders' equity	_____
Total assets	$ _____	Total liabilities and equity	$ _____

time value of money 1:
analyzing single cash flows

Both this chapter and the next illustrate time value of money (TVM) calculations, which we will use throughout the rest of this book. We hope that you will see what powerful tools they are for making financial decisions. Whether you're managing the financial or other functional area of a business, or making decisions in your personal life, being able to make TVM calculations will help you make financially sound decisions.

This background will also allow you to understand why CEOs, CFOs, and other professionals make the decisions that they do. Together, this chapter and the next will present all aspects of TVM. Since some students find this topic intimidating, we split the topic into two chapters as a way of providing more examples and practice opportunities. As you see the examples and work the practice problems, we believe that you will find that TVM is not difficult.

Factors to consider when making time value of money decisions include:

- Size of the cash flows.
- Time between the cash flows.
- Rate of return we can earn. ■

The basic idea behind the time value of money is that $1 today is worth more than $1 promised next year. But how much more? Is $1 today worth $1.05 next year? $1.08? $1.12? The answer varies depending on current interest rates. This chapter describes the time value of money concept and provides the tools needed to analyze single cash flows at different points in time.

LEARNING GOALS

LG1 Create a cash flow time line.

LG2 Compute the future value of money.

LG3 Show how the power of compound interest increases wealth.

LG4 Calculate the present value of a payment made in the future.

LG5 Move cash flows from one year to another.

LG6 Apply the Rule of 72.

LG7 Compute the rate of return realized on selling an investment.

LG8 Calculate the number of years needed to grow an investment to a specific amount of money.

ORGANIZING CASH FLOWS

Managing cash flow timing is one of the most important tasks in successfully operating a business. A helpful tool for organizing our analysis is the **time line,** which shows the magnitude of cash flows at different points in time, such as monthly, quarterly, semiannually, or yearly. Cash we receive is called an **inflow,** and we denote it with a positive number. Cash that leaves us, like a payment or contribution to a deposit, is an **outflow** designated with a negative number.

The time line below illustrates a $100 deposit you made at a bank that pays 5 percent interest. In one year, the $100 has become $105. *Given that interest rate,* having $100 now (in year 0) has the same value as having $105 one year from now.

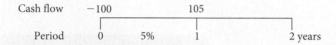

Cash flow	−100		105	
Period	0	5%	1	2 years

Here's one way to look at this example: suppose you allowed the bank to rent your $100 for a year at a cost of 5 percent, or $5. This cost is known as the **interest rate.** Interest rates

will affect you throughout your life, both in business and in your personal life. Companies borrow money to build factories and expand into new locations and markets. They expect the future revenues generated by these activities to more than cover the interest payments and repay the loan. People borrow money on credit cards and obtain loans for cars and home mortgages. They expect their purchases to give them the satisfaction in the future that compensates them for the interest payments charged on the loan. Understanding the dynamics between interest rates and cash inflows and outflows over time is key to financial success. The best place to start learning these concepts lies in understanding how money grows over time.

FUTURE VALUE

The $105 payment that your bank credits to your account in one year is known as the **future value (FV)** of $100 in one year at a 5 percent annual interest rate. If interest rates were higher than 5 percent, then the future value of your $100 would also be higher. If you left your money in the bank for more than one year, then its future value would continue to grow over time. Let's see why.

Single Period Future Value

Computing the future value of a sum of money one year from today is straightforward: add the interest earned cost to today's cash flow. In this case:

$$\text{Value in one year} = \text{Today's Cash flow} + \text{Interest earned}$$

$$\$105 \quad = \quad \$100 \quad + \quad \$5$$

We computed the $5 interest figure by multiplying the interest rate by today's cash flow ($100 × 5%). Note that in equations, interest rates appear in decimal format. So we use 0.05 for 5 percent:

$$\$100 + (\$100 \times 0.05) = \$105$$

Note that this is the same as:

$$\$100 \times (1 + 0.05) = \$105$$

We need the 1 in the parentheses to recapture the original deposit and the 0.05 is for the interest earned. We can generalize this computation to any amount of today's cash flow. In the general form of the future value equation, we call cash today **present value, or PV.** We compute the future value one year from now, called FV_1, using the interest rate, i:

$$FV_1 = PV \times (1 + i) \qquad (4\text{-}1)$$

Notice that this is the same equation we used to figure the future value of your $100. We've simply made it generic so we can use it over and over again. The 1 subscript means that we are calculating for only one period—in this case, one year. If interest rates were 6 percent instead of 5 percent per year, for

▼ **TABLE 4.1** Higher Interest Rates Lead to Higher Future Value

Today's Cash Flow	Interest Rate	Interest Earned (Dollars)	Next Year's Future Value
$ 100.00	5%	$ 5.00	$ 105.00
100.00	6	6.00	106.00
100.00	10	10.00	110.00
500.00	7.50	37.50	537.50
750.00	7.50	56.25	806.25
15,000.00	8	1,200.00	16,200.00
15,000.00	9	1,350.00	16,350.00

instance, we could use equation 4-1 to find that the future value of $100 in one year is $106 [=$100 × (1 + 0.06)].

Of course, the higher the interest rate, the larger the future value will be. Table 4.1 shows the interest cost and future value for a sample of different cash flows and interest rates. Notice from the first two lines of the table that, while the difference in interest earned between 5 percent and 6 percent ($1) doesn't seem like much on a $100 deposit, the difference on a $15,000 deposit (the last two lines) is substantial ($150).

Compounding and Future Value

After depositing $100 for one year, you must decide whether to take the $105 or leave the money at the bank for another year to earn another 5 percent (or whatever interest rate the bank currently pays). In the second year at the bank, the deposit earns 5 percent on the $105 value, which is $5.25 (= $105 × 0.05). Importantly, you get more than the $5 earned the first year, which would be a simple total of $110. The extra 25 cents earned in the second year is interest *on interest that was earned in the first year.* We call this process of earning interest on both the original deposit and on the earlier interest payments **compounding.**

So, let's illustrate a $100 deposit made for two years at 5 percent in the following time line:

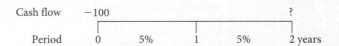

Cash flow	−100				?
Period	0	5%	1	5%	2 years

The question mark denotes the amount we want to solve for. As with all TVM problems, we simply have to identify what element we're solving for; in this case, we're looking for the FV. To compute the two-year compounded future value, simply use the one-year equation (4-1) twice.

$$\$100 \times (1 + 0.05) \times (1 + 0.05) = \$110.25$$

So the future value of $100 deposited today at 5 percent interest is $110.25 in period 2. You can see that this represents $10 of interest payments generated from the original $100 ($5 each year) and $0.25 of interest earned in the second year on previously earned interest payments. The $5 of interest earned every year on the original deposit is called **simple interest.**

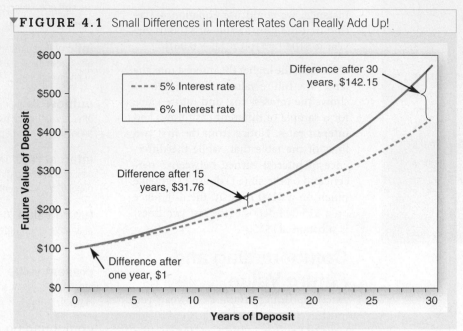

▼FIGURE 4.1   Small Differences in Interest Rates Can Really Add Up!

Any amount of interest earned above the $5 in any given year comes from compounding. Over time, the new interest payments earned from compounding can become substantial. The multiyear form of equation 4-1 is the future value in year N, shown as:

$$\text{Future value in N years} = FV_N = PV \times (1 + i)^N \qquad (4\text{-}2)$$

We can solve the two-year deposit problem more directly using equation 4-2 as $110.25 = $100 \times (1.05)^2$. Here, solving for FV

in the equation requires solving for only one unknown. In fact, all TVM equations that you will encounter only require figuring out what is unknown in the situation and solving for that one unknown factor.

We can easily adapt equation 4-2 to many different future value problems. What is the future value in 30 years of that $100 earning 5 percent per year? Using equation 4-2, we see that the future value is $100 × (1.05)^{30} = $432.19. The money has increased substantially! You have made a profit of $332.19 over and above your original $100. Of this profit, only $150 (=$5 × 30 years) came from simple interest earned on the original deposit. The rest, $182.19, is from the compounding effect of earning interest on previously earned interest.

Remember that the difference between earning 5 percent and 6 percent in interest on the $100 was only $1 the first year. So what is the future value difference after 15 years? Is it $15? No, as Figure 4.1 shows, the difference in future value substantially increases over time. The difference is $31.76 in year 15 and $142.15 in year 30.

The Power of Compounding
Compound interest is indeed a powerful tool for building wealth. Albert Einstein, the German-American physicist who developed the special and general theories of relativity and won the Nobel Prize for Physics in 1921, is supposed to have said, "The most powerful force in the universe is compound interest."[1] Figure 4.2 illustrates this point. It shows the original $100 deposited, the cumulative interest earned on that deposit, and the cumulative interest-on-interest earned. By the 27th year, the money from the interest-on-interest exceeds the interest earned on the original

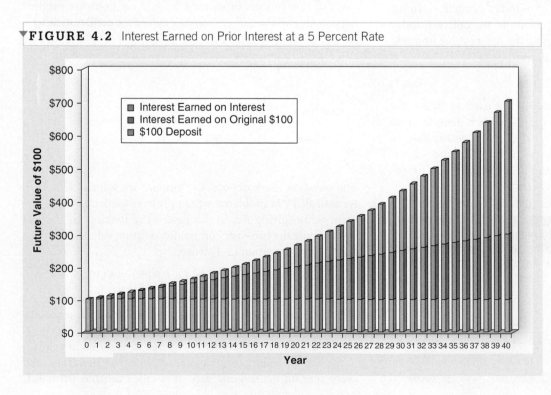

▼FIGURE 4.2   Interest Earned on Prior Interest at a 5 Percent Rate

[1]No one seems to know exactly what he said, when he said it, or to whom. Similar statements commonly attributed to Einstein are: (1) compound interest is the greatest wonder of the universe, (2) compound interest is the ninth wonder of the world, and (3) it is the greatest mathematical discovery of all time. If he did not say any of these things, he (or someone else) should have!

▼ **TABLE 4.2** Compounding Builds Wealth over Time

Future Value of $100 Deposited at 5%, 10%, and 15% Interest Rates				
	Future Value			
Interest Rate Earned	**5 Years**	**10 Years**	**20 Years**	**30 Years**
5%	$127.63	$162.89	$ 265.33	$ 432.19
10	161.05	259.37	672.75	1,744.94
15	201.14	404.56	1,636.65	6,621.18

deposit. By the 40th year, interest-on-interest contributes more than double the interest on the deposit. The longer money can earn interest, the greater the compounding effect.

Earning higher interest rates on the investment for additional time periods magnifies compounding power. Consider the future value of $100 deposited at different interest rates and over different time periods as shown in Table 4.2. The future value of $100 earning 5 percent per year for five years is $127.63, for a profit of $27.63. Would you double your profit by simply investing that same $100 at double the interest rate, 10 percent? No, because compounding changes the nature of the investment so that your money grows exponentially, not in a simple linear relationship. The future value of $100 in five years at 10 percent is $161.05. The $61.05 profit is *more* than double the profit of $27.63 earned at 5 percent. Tripling the interest rate to 15 percent shows a profit of $101.14 that is nearly *quadruple* the profit earned at 5 percent.

The same effect occurs when we increase the time. When the deposit earns 10 percent per year for five years, it makes a profit of $61.05. When we double the amount of time to 10 years, the return more than doubles to $159.37. After 30 years, the $100 deposit at 5 percent becomes a future value of $432.19. If the deposit earns 10 percent instead of 5 percent, the future value more than quadruples to $1,744.94. Interest rates and time are **both** important factors in compounding! These relationships are illustrated in Figure 4.3

Compounding at Different Interest Rates over Time
Interest rates have varied over time. In the past half-century, banks

have offered depositors rates lower than 1 percent and as high as double digit rates. They've also charged interest from about 4.5 percent to 21.6 percent to consumers for various kinds of loans. Let's look at how to compute future value when rates change, so that money earns interest at multiple interest rates over time. In our first example in this chapter, your deposit of $100 earned 5 percent interest. Now consider the future value when the bank announces it will pay 6 percent interest in the second year. How much will you earn now? We can illustrate the question with this time line:

Cash flow   −100   ?

Period   0   5%   1   6%   2 years

We already know that the $100 deposit will grow to $105 at the end of the first year. This $105 will then earn 6 percent in the second year and have a value of $111.30 [=$105 × (1.06)]. If we put the two steps together into one equation, the solution appears as $111.30 = $100 × (1.05) × (1.06). From this you should not be surprised that a general equation for future value of multiple interest rates is

$$\text{Future value in N periods} = FV_N = PV \times (1 + i_{\text{period 1}}) \times (1 + i_{\text{period 2}})$$

$$\times (1 + i_{\text{period 3}}) \times \cdots \times (1 + i_{\text{period N}}) \quad (4\text{-}3)$$

Note that the future value equation 4-2 is a special case of the more general equation 4-3. If the interest rate every period is the same, we can write equation 4-3 as equation 4-2.

▼**FIGURE 4.3** The Impact of Time and the Magnitude of the Interest Rate

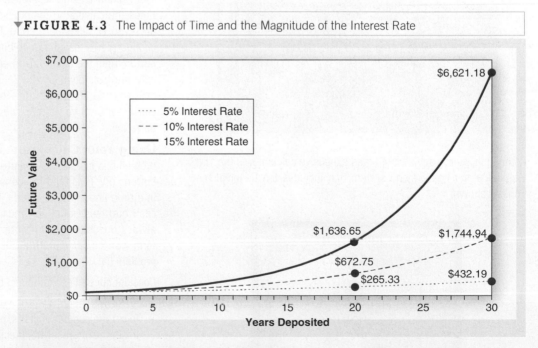

Future value of $100 deposited at 5%, 10%, and 15% interest rates

Using a Financial Calculator

Financial, or business, calculators are programmed to perform the time value of money equations we develop in this chapter and the next. The two most common types of inexpensive financial calculators that can perform such functions are the Hewlett/Packard 10B II Business Calculator and the Texas Instruments BA II (Plus or Professional). Among many useful financial shortcuts these calculators have five specific financial buttons. The relevant financial buttons for time value of money (TVM) calculations are listed below. The HP10BII calculator buttons look like this.

1. N (for the number of periods),
2. I/YR (for the interest rate),
3. PV (for present value),
4. PMT (for a constant payment every period), and
5. FV (for future value).

Notice that the TI BA II Plus financial calculator buttons appear to be very similar:

A common, more sophisticated, and expensive calculator is the TI-83. This calculator has a menu system that includes the financial functions as shown:

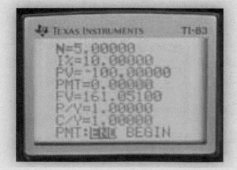

To get to the TVM menu, select APPLICATIONS and then choose FINANCE, and finally 1 TVM SOLVER on the previous screens.

Setting Up Your Calculator: Both of these calculators come from the factory with specific settings. You will find it useful to change two of them. The first is to set the number of digits shown after the decimal point on the calculator display. The factory setting is for two digits. However, consider a problem in which we use a 5.6 percent interest rate. The decimal version of this percentage is 0.056, which a two-digit display would round to 0.06. It's less worrisome to set the calculator to display the number of digits necessary to show the right number; this is called a *floating point display.* To set a floating point display for the HP calculator, press the color button, then the DISP button, and finally the decimal (.) button. To set the display for a floating point decimal on the TI calculator, push the 2ND button, followed by the FORMAT button, followed by the 9 button, and finally the ENTER button.

The second change you'll want to make is to set the number of times the calculator compounds each period. The settings may be preset to 12 times per period. Reset this to one time per period. To change the HP calculator to compound once per period, push the 1 button, then the color button, and finally the P/YR button. On the TI calculator, simply push the 2ND button, the P/Y button, the number one, and the ENTER button. These new settings will remain in the calculator until you either change them or remove the calculator's batteries.

Using Your Calculator: The calculators compute time-value problems in similar ways. Enter the cash flows into the time-value buttons (PV, PMT, and FV) consistent with the way they are shown in a time line. In other words, cash inflows should be positive and cash outflows negative. Thus, PV and FV cash flows are nearly always opposite in sign. Enter interest rates (I) in the percentage form, not the decimal form. Also enter the number of periods in the problem (N).

Consider our earlier example of the $100 deposit for two years earning a 5 percent interest rate.

1. To set the number of years, press 2 and then the N button.
2. To set the interest rate, press 5 and then the I button. (*Note* that interest rates are in percent format for using a financial calculator and in decimal format for using the equations.)

3. To enter the current cash flow: press 100, then make it negative by pressing the $+/-$ button, then press the PV button.
4. We won't use the PMT button, so enter 0 and then the PMT button.
5. To solve for future value, press the compute button (CPT) [for the TI] and then the FV button [press the FV button only for the HP].
6. Solution: the display should show FV = 110.25

Note that the answer is positive, consistent with an inflow and the time line diagram. These values remain in the TVM registers even after the calculator is turned off. So when you start a new problem, you should clear out old values first. For the HP calculator, clear the registers by pressing the shift/orange key before pressing C. You can clear the BAII Plus calculator with the 2nd and CLR Work.

You'll notice that throughout this book we use the equations in the main text to solve time value of money problems. We provide the calculator solutions in the margins.

EXAMPLE 4-1

For interactive versions of this example visit www.mhhe.com/canM

Graduation Celebration Loan

Dominic is a fourth-year business student who wants to go on a graduation celebration/ vacation in Mexico but he has no money to pay for the trip. After the vacation, Dominic will start his career. His job will require moving to a new town and buying professional clothes. He asked his parents to lend him $1,500, which he figures he will be able to pay back in three years. His parents agree to lend him the money, but they will charge 7 percent interest per year. What amount will Dominic need to pay back? How much interest will he pay?

SOLUTION:

Dominic will have to pay

$$FV_3 = \$1,500 \times (1.07)^3 = \$1,500 \times 1.225 = \$1,837.56$$

Of the $1,837.56 he owes his parents, $337.56 (=$1,837.56 − $1,500) is interest. We can illustrate this time-value problem in the following time line.

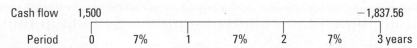

Cash flow	1,500						−1,837.56
Period	0	7%	1	7%	2	7%	3 years

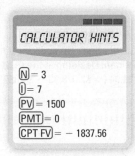

CALCULATOR HINTS

$N = 3$
$I = 7$
$PV = 1500$
$PMT = 0$
$CPT\ FV = -1837.56$

time out!

4-4 How does compounding help build wealth (or increase debt) over time?

4-5 In Example 4-1 above, how much of the $337.56 (=$1,837.56 − $1,500) paid in interest is actually interest-on-interest? (*Hint:* first compute the interest paid on the original $1,500 in each of the three years.)

PRESENT VALUE

We asked earlier what happens when you deposit $100 of cash in the bank to earn 5 percent interest for one year—the bank pays you a $105 future value. However, we could have asked the question in reverse. That is, if the bank will pay $105 in one year and interest rates are 5 percent, how much would you be willing to deposit now, to receive that payment in a year? Here, we start with a future value and must find the present value—a different kind of calculation called **discounting.**

Discounting

While the process of a present value growing over time into the future is called *compounding*, the process of figuring out how much an amount that you expect to receive in the future is worth today is discounting. Just as compounding significantly increases the present value into the future, discounting significantly decreases the value of a future amount to the present. Since discounting is the reverse of compounding, we can

discounting The process of finding present value by reducing future values using the discount, or interest, rate.

Celebration Loan with Payback Incentive

Reexamine the loan Dominic was seeking from his parents in the previous example. His parents want to give him an incentive to pay off the loan as quickly as possible. They structure the loan so they charge 7 percent interest the first year and increase the rate 1 percent each year until the loan is paid. How much will Dominic owe if he waits three years to pay off the loan? Say that in the third year he considers whether to pay off the loan or wait one more year. How much more will he pay if he waits one more year?

SOLUTION:

For a payment in the third year, Dominic will pay interest of 7 percent the first year, 8 percent the second year, and 9 percent the third year. He will have to pay

$$FV_3 = \$1{,}500 \times (1.07) \times (1.08) \times (1.09) = \$1{,}500 \times 1.2596 = \$1.889.41$$

The cash flow time line is

Cash flow	1,500						−1,889.41
Period	0	7%	1	8%	2	9%	3 years

Even worse, if he waits until the fourth year, he will pay one year of interest at 10 percent. The total payment will be

$$FV_4 = \$1{,}889.41 \times (1.10) = \$2{,}078.35$$

Because of both the escalating interest rate and the compounding effect, Dominic must make timely and increasing payments the longer he delays in paying off the loan. Deciding in the third year to put off the payment an extra year would cost him an additional \$188.94 (= \$2,078.35 − \$1,889.41).

---

rearrange equation 4-1 to solve for the present value of a cash flow received one year in the future.

$$\text{Present value of next period's cash flow} = PV = FV_1 \times \frac{1}{(1+i)} = \frac{FV_1}{(1+i)} \quad (4\text{-}4)$$

How much would you be willing to deposit now to receive a certain payment in a year?

Suppose the bank is going to pay \$105 in one year and interest rates are 5 percent. Then the present value of the payment is \$105/(1.05) = \$100. Present values are always smaller than future values (as long as interest rates are greater than zero!), and the difference between what an investment is worth today and what it's worth when you're supposed to redeem it gets larger as the interest rate increases. Likewise, if the amount of time until the expected payment date increases, the deposit will also increase in value.

Discounting over Multiple Periods Discounting over multiple periods is the reverse process of compounding over multiple periods. If we know that, we can find the general equation for present value by rearranging the terms in equation 4-2 to form:

$$\text{Present value of cash flow made in N years} = PV = FV_N \times \frac{1}{(1+i)^N}$$

$$= \frac{FV_N}{(1+i)^N} \quad (4\text{-}5)$$

The interest rate, i, which we use to calculate present value, is often referred to as the **discount rate.** How much is a $100 payment to be made in the future worth today? Of course, it depends on how far into the future you expect to receive the payment and the discount rate used. If you receive $100 cash flow in five years, then its present value is $78.35, discounted at 5 percent:

$$PV = \$100/(1.05)^5 = \$100/1.2763 = \$78.35$$

The time line looks like this:

Cash flow	−78.35					100
Period	0 5%	1 5%	2 5%	3 5%	4 5%	5 years

If the discount rate rises to 10 percent, the present value of our $100 to be paid to us in five years is only $62.09 today. At a 15 percent interest rate, the present value declines to less than half the future cash flow: $49.72. Higher interest rates discount future cash flows more quickly and dramatically. You can see this principle illustrated in Figure 4.4 on the next page.

Moving right from point A in the figure, notice that if interest rates are 0 percent, the present value will equal the future value. Also note from the curved lines that when the discount rate is greater than zero, the discounting to present value is not linear through time. The higher the discount rate, the more quickly the cash flow value falls. If the discount rate is 10 percent, a $100 cash flow that you would receive in 25 years is worth less than $10 today, as shown at point B in the figure. With a 15 percent discount rate, the $100 payment to be received in 33 years, at point C, is worth less than $1 today.

Discounting with Multiple Rates
We can also discount a future cash flow at different interest rates per period. We find the general form of the equation for present value with multiple discount rates by rearranging equation 4-3:

Present value with different discount rates

$$= PV = \frac{FV_N}{(1 + i_{\text{period 1}}) \times (1 + i_{\text{period 2}}) \times (1 + i_{\text{period 3}}) \times \cdots \times (1 + i_{\text{periodN}})} \quad (4\text{-}6)$$

Suppose that we expect interest rates to increase over the next few years, from 6 percent this year, to 8 percent next year, to 8.5 percent in the third year. In this environment, how would we work out the present value of a future $2,500 cash flow in year 3? The time line for this problem is

Cash flow	?			2,500
Period	0 7%	1 8%	2 8.5%	3 years

Using equation 4-6 shows that the present value is $1,993.90:

$$PV = \frac{\$2,500}{(1.07) \times (1.08) \times (1.085)} = \frac{\$2,500}{1.2538} = \$1,993.90$$

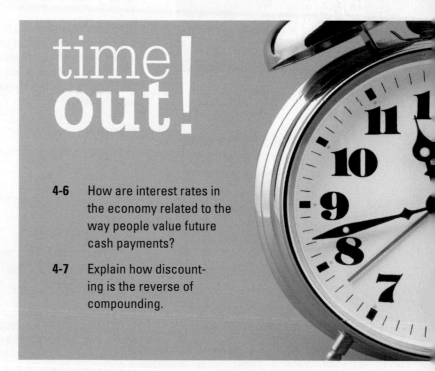

time out!

4-6 How are interest rates in the economy related to the way people value future cash payments?

4-7 Explain how discounting is the reverse of compounding.

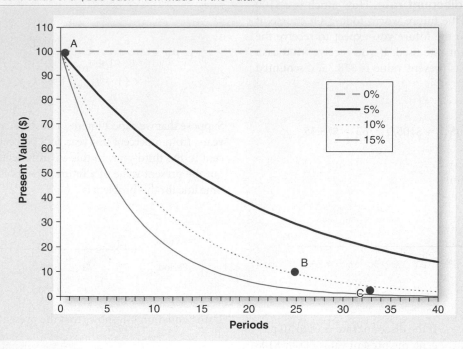

EXAMPLE 4-3

For interactive versions of this example visit www.mhhe.com/canM

Buy Now and Don't Pay for Two Years

Suppose that a marketing manager for a retail furniture company proposes a sale. Customers can buy now but don't have to pay for their furniture purchases for two years. From a time value of money perspective, selling furniture at full price with payment in two years is equivalent to selling furniture at a sale, or discounted, price with immediate payment. If interest rates are 7.5 percent per year, what is the equivalent sale price of a $1,000 sleeper-sofa when the customer takes the full two years to pay for it?

SOLUTION:

The time line for this problem is:

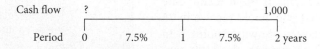

Using equation 4-5, the present value computation is

$$PV = \frac{FV_N}{(1 + i)^N} = \frac{\$1,000}{1.075^2} = \frac{\$1,000}{1.1556} = \$865.33$$

In this case, the marketing proposal for delaying payment for two years is equivalent to selling the $1,000 sleeper-sofa for a sale price of $865.33, or a 13.5 percent discount. When stores promote such sales, they often believe that customers will not be able to pay the full amount at the end of the two years and then must pay high interest rate charges and late fees. Customers who do pay on time are getting a good deal.

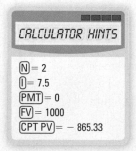

CALCULATOR HINTS

Ⓝ = 2
Ⓘ = 7.5
PMT = 0
FV = 1000
CPT PV = − 865.33

USING PRESENT VALUE AND FUTURE VALUE

Moving Cash Flows

As managers analyze investment projects, debt management, and cash flow, they frequently find it useful to move cash flows to different points in time. While you may be planning to keep money deposited in the bank for three years when you will buy a car, life often has a way of altering plans. What type of car might you purchase if the money earns interest for only two years, or for four years? How is a corporate financial forecast affected if the firm needs to remodel a factory two years sooner than planned? Moving cash flows around in time is important to businesses and individuals alike for sound financial planning and decision making.

Moving cash flows from one point in time to another requires us to use both present value and future value equations. Specifically, use the present value equation for moving cash flows *earlier* in time, and the future value cash flows for moving cash flows *later* in time. For example, what's the value in year 2 of a $200 cash flow to be received in three years, when interest rates are 6 percent? This problem requires moving the $200 payment in the third year to a value in the second year, as shown in the time line:

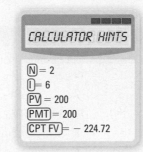

CALCULATOR HINTS

N = 2
I = 6
PV = 200
PMT = 200
CPT FV = − 224.72

Rule of 72 An approximation for the number of years it will take an investment to double in value.

What about moving the $200 cash flow to year 5? Since this requires moving the cash flow later in time by two years, we use the future value equation. In this case, the equivalent of $200 in the third year is a fifth-year payment of

$$FV_5 = PV_3 \times (1 + i)^2 = \$200 \times (1.06)^2$$

$$= \$200 \times 1.1236 = \$224.72$$

EXAMPLE : Delay Graduate School ?

As you finish your junior year, you have always planned ... school. Your grandma has prepared for ... a $40,000 gift to be used for further education and timed to happen when you graduate.

But you are a little tired ... and would like to travel Europe for a couple of years before going to graduate school. If interest rates are 6%, what would the value of the $40,000 to be received next year be after a two year delay?

View interactive examples at mhhe.com/canM

👍 FIFAfan92 and six others like this.

FIFAfan92 The example about delaying grad school really got me thinking about my own future.

5 hours ago · Like

write a comment...

Table 4.3 illustrates how we might move several cash flows. At an 8 percent interest rate, a $1,000 cash flow due in year 5 compounded to year 10 equals $1,469.33. We could also discount that same $1,000 cash flow to a value of $793.83 in year 2. At an 8 percent interest rate, the three cash flows ($793.83 in year 2, $1,000 in year 5, and $1,469.33 in year 10) become equivalent. Table 4.3 illustrates the movement of other cash flows given different interest rates and time periods.

Moving cash flows from one year to another creates an easy way to compare or combine two cash flows. Would you rather receive $150 in year 2 or $160 in year 2? Since both cash flows occur in the same year, the comparison is straightforward. But we can't directly add or compare cash flows in different years until we consider their time value. We can compare cash flows in different years by moving one cash flow to the same time as the other using the present value or future value equations. Once you have the value of each cash flow in the same year, you can directly compare or combine them.

Cash flow		?	200	
Period	0	1	2 6%	3 years

Since the cash flow is to be moved one year *earlier* in time, we use the present value equation

$$PV_2 = FV_3 / (1 + i)^1 = \$200 / (1.06)^1 = \$188.68.$$

When interest rates are 6 percent, a $188.68 payment in year 2 equates to a $200 payment in year 3.

CALCULATOR HINTS

N = 1
I = 6
PMT = 0
FV = 200
CPT PV = − 188.68

When Interest Rates Are	A Cash Flow of	In Year	Can Be Moved to Year	With Equation	Equivalent Cash Flow
8%	$1,000	5	10	$FV_{10} = PV_5 \times (1 + i)^5 = \$1,000 \times (1.08)^5 =$	$1,469.33
8	1,000	5	2	$PV_2 = FV_5 / (1 + i)^3 = \$1,000 / (1.08)^3 =$	793.83
10	500	9	10	$FV_{10} = PV_9 \times (1 + i)^1 = \$500 \times (1.10)^1 =$	550.00
10	500	9	8	$PV_8 = FV_9 / (1 + i)^1 = \$500 / (1.10)^1 =$	454.55
10	500	9	0	$PV_0 = FV_9 / (1 + i)^9 = \$500 / (1.10)^9 =$	212.05
12	100	4	20	$FV_{20} = PV_4 \times (1 + i)^{16} = \$100 \times (1.12)^{16} =$	613.04
12	100	4	30	$FV_{30} = PV_4 \times (1 + i)^{26} = \$100 \times (1.12)^{26} =$	1,904.01

EXAMPLE 4-4

For interactive versions of this example visit www.mhhe.com/canM

Pay Damages or Appeal?

Timber Inc. lost a lawsuit in a business dispute. The judge ordered the company to pay the plaintiff $175,000 in one year. Timber's attorney advises Timber to appeal the ruling. If so, Timber will likely lose again and will still have to pay the $175,000. But by appealing, Timber moves the $175,000 payment to year 2, along with the attorney's fee of $20,000 for the extra work. The interest rate is 7 percent. What decision should Timber make?

SOLUTION:

Timber executives must decide whether to pay $175,000 in one year or $195,000 in two years. To compare the two choices more directly, move the payment in year 2 to year 1 and then compare it to $175,000. Timber should choose to make the smaller payment. The computation is:

$$PV_1 = FV_2 / (1 + i)^1 = \$195,000 / (1.07)^1 = \$182,242.99$$

The value in year 1 of a year 2 payment of $195,000 is $182,242.99, which is clearly more than the $175,000 year 1 payment. So Timber should *not* appeal and should pay the plaintiff $175,000 in one year (and may want to look for another attorney).

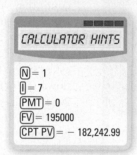

CALCULATOR HINTS

$N = 1$
$I = 7$
$PMT = 0$
$FV = 195000$
$CPT\ PV = -182,242.99$

Rule of 72 Albert Einstein is also credited with popularizing compound interest by introducing a simple mathematical approximation for the number of years required to double an investment. It's called the **Rule of 72.**

the Math Coach on...

When using a financial calculator to compute an interest rate between two cash flows, you must enter one cash flow as a negative number. This is because you must inform the calculator which payments are cash inflows and which are cash outflows. If you input all the cash flows as the same sign, the calculator will show an error when asked to compute the interest rate.

$$\text{Approximate number of years to double an investment} = \frac{72}{\text{Interest rate}} \quad (4\text{-}7)$$

The Rule of 72 illustrates the power of compound interest. How many years will it take to double money deposited at 6 percent per year? Using the Rule of 72, we find the answer is 12 years (72/6). A higher interest rate causes faster increases in future value. A 9 percent interest rate allows money to

finance at work //:investments

Fad "Investments"

Periodically, seemingly ordinary items become popular "investments." The past several decades have seen the rise and subsequent decline in popularity of collectible baseball cards, Beatles memorabilia, Pokèmon items, POGs, and other items. Without any real rationale, people collected them and treated them like investments.

Remember the Beanie Baby craze of the late 1990s? Beanie Babies are small beanbag animals with cute names like "Hissy the Snake." Ty, Inc. makes these toys in limited numbers and sells them for about $5 each. As they became popular, people tried to collect them all, insisting that one day their "collections" would become priceless. The demand for Beanie Babies skyrocketed, and so did their price. Many "retired" Beanies sold for $10 one year and $50 the next. Rare Beanies such as Peanut (the Royal Blue Elephant) sold for over $4,000 in online auctions. If you had bought Peanut for $5 and saw its price rise to $5,000 in three years, your annual return would have been 900 percent per year!

Then, seemingly overnight, the demand for Beanie Babies dried up. People who had bought dozens of the darlings at inflated prices all tried to sell at once. As collectors became sellers, the toys' prices plummeted. If you had bought Peanut for $5,000 at its peak, you would have experienced its price collapse six years later to $5.99, representing a –67.4 annual return. During the same period, Derby the Horse lost 70.8 percent per year, Pinchers the Lobster lost 72.2 percent per year, and Chilly the Polar Bear lost 66.8 percent per year.

Beware the fad "investment."

Hissy the Snake

Want to know more?

Key Words to Search for Updates: **collectible, Beanie Baby, bubble, memorabilia**

---

double in just eight years. Remember that this rule provides only a mathematical approximation. It's more accurate with lower interest rates. After all, with a 72 percent interest rate, the rule predicts that it will take one year to double the money. However, we know that it actually takes a 100 percent rate to double money in one year.

We can also use the Rule of 72 to approximate the interest rate needed to double an investment in a specific amount of time. What rate do we need to double an investment in 5 years? Rearranging equation 4-7 shows that the rate needed is 14.4 percent (72/5) per year.

time out!

4-8 In the problem above, could Timber Inc. have performed its analysis by moving the $175,000 to year 2 and comparing? Would the firm then have made the same decision?

4-9 At what interest rate (and number of years) does the Rule of 72 become too inaccurate to use?

COMPUTING INTEREST RATES

Time value of money calculations come in handy when we know two cash flows and need to find the interest rate. The investment industry often uses this analysis. Solving for the interest rate, or rate of return,[2] can answer questions like, "If you bought a gold coin for $350 three years ago and sell it now for $475, what rate of return have you earned?" The time line for this problem looks like this:

In general, computing interest rates is easiest with a financial calculator. To compute the answer using the time-value equations, consider how the cash flows fit into the future value equation 4-2:

$$FV_N = PV \times (1 + i)^N$$

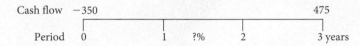

Cash flow	−350			475
Period	0	1 ?%	2	3 years

[2]The terms *interest rate* and *rate of return* are referring to the same thing. However, it is a common convention to refer to interest rate when you are the one paying the cash flows and refer to rate of return when you are the one receiving the cash flows.

4-10 Say you double your money in three years. Explain why the rate of return is NOT 33.3 percent per year.

4-11 Show that you must earn a 25 percent return to offset a 20 percent loss.

time out!

$$475 = 350 \times (1 + i)^3$$

Rearranging gives: $475/350 = (1 + i)^3$

or: $1.357 = (1 + i)^3$

To solve for the interest rate, *i*, take the third root of both sides of the equation. To do this, take 1.357 to the 1/3 power using the y^x button on your calculator.[3] Doing this leads to:

$$1.107 = (1 + i), \text{ or } i = 0.107 = 10.7\%$$

If you buy a gold coin for $350 and sell it three years later for $475, you earn a 10.7 percent return per year.

Time is an important factor in computing the return that you're earning per year. Turning a $100 investment into $200 is a 100 percent return. If your investments earn this much in two years, then they earned a 41.42 percent rate of return per year [computed as: $100 \times (1.4142)^2 = 200$]. Table 4.4 shows the annual interest rate earned for doubling an investment over various time periods. Notice how compounding complicates the solution: It's not as simple as just dividing by the number of years. Getting a 100 percent return in two years means earning 41.42 percent per year, not 50 percent per year. Table 4.4 also shows the Rule of 72 interest rate estimate.

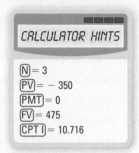

CALCULATOR HINTS

N = 3
PV = − 350
PMT = 0
FV = 475
CPT I = 10.716

Return Asymmetries

Suppose you bought a gold coin for $700 last year and now the market would only pay you $350. Clearly, the investment earned a negative rate of return. Use a financial calculator or a time-value equation to verify that this is a return of −50 percent. You lost half your money! So, in order to break even and get back to $700, you need to earn a positive 50 percent, right? Wrong. Note that to get from $350 to $700, your money needs to double! You need a 100 percent return to make up for a 50 percent decline. Similarly, you need a gain of 33.33 percent to make up for a 25 percent decline. If your investment declines by 10 percent, you'll need an 11.1 percent gain to offset the loss. In general, only a higher positive return can offset any given negative return.

SOLVING FOR TIME

Sometimes you may need to determine the time period needed to accumulate a specific amount of money. If you know the starting cash flow, the interest rate, and the future cash flow (the sum you will need), you can solve the time value equations for the number of years that you will need to accumulate that

[3]The general equation for computing the interest rate is $i = (FV_N/PV)^{\frac{1}{N}} - 1$.

EXAMPLE 4-5

For interactive versions of this example visit www.mhhe.com/canM

Growth in Staffing Needs

Say that you are the sales manager of a company that produces software for human resource departments. You are planning your staffing needs, which depend on the volume of sales over time. Your company currently sells $350 million of merchandise per year and has grown 7 percent per year in the past. If this growth rate continues, how long will it be before the firm reaches $500 million in sales? How long before it reaches $600 million?

SOLUTION:

You could set up the following time line to illustrate the problem:

Cash flow	350				500
			...		
Period	0	1	7%	2	? years

As shown in the margin, $350 million of sales growing at 7 percent per year will reach $500 million in five years and three months. To reach $600 million will take just two weeks short of eight years.

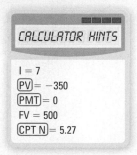

CALCULATOR HINTS

I = 7
PV = −350
PMT = 0
FV = 500
CPT N = 5.27

---

money. Just as with solving for different interest rates, solving for the number of periods is complicated and requires using natural logarithms.[4] Many people prefer to use a financial calculator to solve for the number of periods.

When interest rates are 9 percent, how long will it take for a $5,000 investment to double? Finding the solution with a financial calculator entails entering

[4]The equation for solving for the number of periods is $N = \dfrac{\ln(FV_N/PV)}{\ln(1 + i)}$.

- I = 9
- PV = −5,000
- PMT = 0
- FV = 10,000

The answer is 8.04 years, or eight years and two weeks. The Rule of 72 closely approximates the answer, which predicts eight years (72 ÷ 9). ■

▼ **TABLE 4.4** Interest Rate per Year to Double an Investment

Number of Years to Double Investment	Precise Annual Interest Rate	Rule of 72 Interest Rate Estimate
1	100.00%	72.00%
2	41.42	36.00
3	25.99	24.00
4	18.92	18.00
5	14.87	14.40
6	12.25	12.00
7	10.41	10.29
8	9.05	9.00
9	8.01	8.00
10	7.18	7.20
15	4.73	4.80
20	3.53	3.60
25	2.81	2.88
30	2.34	2.40

time out!

4-12 In the example above, how long will it take your company to double its sales?

4-13 In what other areas of business can these time-value concepts be used?

Your Turn...

Questions

1. List and describe the purpose of each part of a time line with an initial cash inflow and a future cash outflow. Which cash flows should be negative and which positive? Why? *(LG1)*

2. How are the present value and future value related? *(LG2)*

3. Would you prefer to have an investment earning 5 percent for 40 years or an investment earning 10 percent for 20 years? Explain. *(LG3)*

4. How are present values affected by changes in interest rates? *(LG4)*

5. What do you think about the following statement? "I am going to receive $100 two years from now and $200 three years from now, so I am getting a $300 future value."

How could the two cash flows be compared or combined? *(LG5)*

6. Show how the Rule of 72 can be used to approximate the number of years to quadruple an investment. *(LG6)*

7. Without making any computations, indicate which of each pair has a higher interest rate: *(LG7)*
   a. $100 doubles to $200 in five years *or* seven years.
   b. $500 increases in four years to $750 *or* to $800.
   c. $300 increases to $450 in two years *or* increases to $500 in three years.

8. A $1,000 investment has doubled to $2,000 in eight years because of a 9 percent rate of return. How much longer will it take for the investment to reach $4,000 if it continues to earn a 9 percent rate? *(LG8)*

Problems

BASIC PROBLEMS

4-1 **Time Line** Show the time line for a $300 cash inflow today, a $363 cash outflow in year 2, and a 10 percent interest rate. *(LG1)*

4-2 **Time Line** Show the time line for a $400 cash outflow today, a $518 cash inflow in year 3, and a 9 percent interest rate. *(LG1)*

4-3   **One Year Future Value** What is the future value of $500 deposited for one year earning a 9 percent interest rate annually? *(LG2)*

4-4   **One Year Future Value** What is the future value of $400 deposited for one year earning an interest rate of 11 percent per year? *(LG2)*

4-5   **Multiyear Future Value** How much would be in your savings account in eight years after depositing $150 today if the bank pays 7 percent per year? *(LG3)*

4-6   **Multiyear Future Value** Compute the value in 25 years of a $1,000 deposit earning 10 percent per year. *(LG3)*

4-7   **Compounding with Different Interest Rates** A deposit of $350 earns the following interest rates:

a. 8 percent in the first year.

b. 7 percent in the second year.

c. 5 percent in the third year.

   What would be the third year future value? *(LG3)*

4-8   **Compounding with Different Interest Rates** A deposit of $750 earns interest rates of 10 percent in the first year and 12 percent in the second year. What would be the second year future value? *(LG3)*

4-9   **Discounting One Year** What is the present value of a $250 payment in one year when the discount rate is 10 percent? *(LG4)*

4-10   **Discounting One Year** What is the present value of a $400 payment in one year when the discount rate is 7 percent? *(LG4)*

4-11   **Present Value** What is the present value of a $1,500 payment made in five years when the discount rate is 8 percent? *(LG4)*

4-12   **Present Value** Compute the present value of an $850 payment made in 10 years when the discount rate is 12 percent. *(LG4)*

4-13   **Present Value with Different Discount Rates** Compute the present value of $1,000 paid in three years using the following discount rates: 6 percent in the first year, 7 percent in the second year, and 6 percent in the third year. *(LG4)*

4-14   **Present Value with Different Discount Rates** Compute the present value of $5,000 paid in two years using the following discount rates: 8 percent in the first year and 7 percent in the second year. *(LG4)*

4-15   **Rule of 72** Approximately how many years does it take to double a $100 investment when the interest rate is 7 percent per year? *(LG6)*

4-16   **Rule of 72** Approximately how many years does it take to double a $500 investment when the interest rate is 10 percent per year? *(LG6)*

4-17   **Rule of 72** Approximately what interest rate is needed to double an investment over five years? *(LG6)*

4-18   **Rule of 72** Approximately what interest rate is earned when an investment doubles over 12 years? *(LG6)*

4-19   **Rates over One Year** Determine the interest rate earned on a $1,500 deposit when $1,700 is paid back in one year. *(LG7)*

4-20   **Rates over One Year** Determine the interest rate earned on a $2,300 deposit when $2,700 is paid back in one year. *(LG7)*

INTERMEDIATE PROBLEMS

4-21   **Interest-on-Interest** Consider a $1,000 deposit earning 8 percent interest per year for five years. What is the future value, and how much total interest is earned on the original deposit vs. how much is interest earned on interest? *(LG3)*

4-22 Interest-on-Interest Consider a $5,000 deposit earning 9 percent interest per year for 10 years. What is the future value, how much total interest is earned on the original deposit, and how much is interest earned on interest? *(LG3)*

4-23 Comparing Cash Flows What would be more valuable, receiving $500 today or receiving $625 in three years if interest rates are 9 percent? Why? *(LG5)*

4-24 Comparing Cash Flows Which cash flow would you rather pay, $400 today or $500 in two years if interest rates are 10 percent? Why? *(LG5)*

4-25 Moving Cash Flows What is the value in year 3 of a $700 cash flow made in year 7 if interest rates are 10 percent? *(LG5)*

4-26 Moving Cash Flows What is the value in year 4 of a $900 cash flow made in year 6 if interest rates are 8 percent? *(LG5)*

4-27 Moving Cash Flows What is the value in year 10 of a $1,000 cash flow made in year 5 if interest rates are 9 percent? *(LG5)*

4-28 Moving Cash Flows What is the value in year 15 of a $250 cash flow made in year 3 if interest rates are 12 percent? *(LG5)*

4-29 Solving for Rates What annual rate of return is earned on a $1,000 investment when it grows to $2,500 in six years? *(LG7)*

4-30 Solving for Rates What annual rate of return is earned on a $5,000 investment when it grows to $9,500 in five years? *(LG7)*

4-31 Solving for Time How many years (and months) will it take $2 million to grow to $5 million with an annual interest rate of 7 percent? *(LG8)*

4-32 Solving for Time How long will it take $2,000 to reach $6,000 when it grows at 10 percent per year? *(LG8)*

ADVANCED PROBLEMS

4-33 Future Value At age 30 you invest $1,000 that earns 9 percent each year. At age 40 you invest $1,000 that earns 12 percent per year. In which case would you have more money at age 60? *(LG2)*

4-34 Future Value At age 25 you invest $1,500 that earns 8 percent each year. At age 40 you invest $1,500 that earns 11 percent per year. In which case would you have more money at age 65? *(LG2)*

4-35 Solving for Rates You invested $2,000 in the stock market one year ago. Today, the investment is valued at $1,500. What return did you earn? What return would you need to get next year to break even overall? *(LG7)*

4-36 Solving for Rates You invested $3,000 in the stock market one year ago. Today, the investment is valued at $3,500. What return did you earn? What return would you suffer next year for your investment to be valued at the original $3,000? *(LG7)*

4-37 Solving for Rates What annual rate of return is earned on a $4,000 investment made in year 2 when it grows to $7,000 by the end of year 6? *(LG7)*

4-38 Solving for Rates What annual rate of return is implied on a $2,500 loan taken next year when $3,500 must be repaid in year 4? *(LG7)*

4-39 General TVM Ten years ago, Hailey invested $2,000 and locked in a 9 percent annual interest rate for 30 years (to end 20 years from now). Aidan can make a 20-year investment today and lock in a 10 percent interest rate. How much money should he invest now in order to have the same amount of money in 20 years as Hailey? *(LG2, LG4)*

4-40 Moving Cash Flows You are scheduled to *receive* a $500 cash flow in one year, a $1,000 cash flow in two years, and *pay* a $800 payment in three years. If interest rates are 10 percent per year, what is the combined present value of these cash flows? *(LG5)*

4-41 **Excel Problem** Oil prices have increased a great deal in the last decade. The table below shows the average oil price for each year since 1949. Many companies use oil products as a resource in their own business operations (like airline firms and manufacturers of plastic products). Managers of these firms will keep a close watch on how rising oil prices will impact their costs. The interest rate in the PV/FV equations can also be interpreted as a growth rate in sales, costs, profits, and so on (see Example 4-5).

a. Using the 1949 oil price and the 1968 oil price, compute the annual growth rate in oil prices during those 19 years.

b. Compute the annual growth rates between 1969 and 1988 and between 1989 and 2007.

c. Given the price of oil in 2007 and your computed growth rate between 1989 and 2007, compute the future price of oil in 2010, 2015, and 2020.

Average Oil Prices					
Year	Per Barrel	Year	Per Barrel	Year	Per Barrel
1949	$2.54	1969	$3.09	1989	$15.86
1950	2.51	1970	3.18	1990	20.03
1951	2.53	1971	3.39	1991	16.54
1952	2.53	1972	3.39	1992	15.99
1953	2.68	1973	3.89	1993	14.25
1954	2.78	1974	6.87	1994	13.19
1955	2.77	1975	7.67	1995	14.62
1956	2.79	1976	8.19	1996	18.46
1957	3.09	1977	8.57	1997	17.23
1958	3.01	1978	9.00	1998	10.87
1959	2.90	1979	12.64	1999	15.56
1960	2.88	1980	21.59	2000	26.72
1961	2.89	1981	31.77	2001	21.84
1962	2.90	1982	28.52	2002	22.51
1963	2.89	1983	26.19	2003	27.54
1964	2.88	1984	25.88	2004	38.93
1965	2.86	1985	24.09	2005	46.47
1966	2.88	1986	12.51	2006	58.30
1967	2.92	1987	15.40	2007	64.67
1968	2.94	1988	12.58		

time value of money 2:
analyzing annuity cash flows

We explained basic time value computations in the previous chapter. Those TVM equations covered moving a single cash flow from one point in time to another. While this circumstance does describe *some* problems that businesses and individuals face, most debt and investment applications of time value of money feature multiple cash flows. In fact, *most* situations require many equal payments over time. Since these situations require a bit more complicated analysis, this chapter continues the TVM topic for applications that require many equal payments over time. For example, car loans and home mortgage loans require the borrower to make the same monthly payment for many months or years. People save for the future through monthly contributions to their pension portfolios. People in retirement must convert their savings into monthly income. Companies also make regular payments. Johnson & Johnson (ticker: JNJ) will pay level semiannual interest payments through 2033 on money they borrowed. General Motors (ticker: GM) paid a 50¢ per share quarterly dividend to stockholders for six straight years until 2006, when it switched to a 25¢ dividend. These examples require payments (and compounding) over different time intervals (monthly for car loans and semiannually for company debt). How are we to value these payments into common or comparable terms? In this chapter, we illustrate how to value multiple cash flows over time, including many equal payments, and how to incorporate different compounding frequencies. ■

LEARNING GOALS

LG1 Compound multiple cash flows to the future.

LG2 Compute the future value of frequent, level cash flows.

LG3 Discount multiple cash flows to the present.

LG4 Compute the present value of an annuity.

LG5 Recognize the unique use of TVM methods to figure cash flows and present value of a perpetuity.

LG6 Recognize and adjust values for beginning-of-period annuity payments as opposed to end-of-period annuity payments.

LG7 Explain the impact of compound frequency and the difference between the annual percentage rate and the effective annual rate.

LG8 Compute the interest rate of annuity payments.

LG9 Compute payments and amortization schedules for car and mortgage loans.

L10 Calculate the number of payments on a loan

FUTURE VALUE OF MULTIPLE CASH FLOWS

Chapter 4 illustrated how to take single payments and compound them into the future. To save enough money for a down payment on a house or for retirement, people typically make many contributions over time to their savings accounts. We can add the future value of each contribution together to see what the total will be worth at some future point in time—such as age 65 for retirement or in two years for a down payment on a house.

Finding the Future Value of Several Cash Flows

Consider the following contributions to a savings account over time. You make a $100 deposit today, followed by a $125 deposit next year, and a $150 deposit at the end of the second year. If interest rates are 7 percent, what's the future value of your deposits at the end of the third year? The time line for this problem is illustrated as:

Cash flow	−100		−125		−150		?
Period	0		1	7%	2		3 years

Note that the first deposit will compound for three years. That is, the future value in year 3 of a cash flow in year 0 will compound 3 (= 3 − 0) times. The deposit at the end of the first year will compound twice (= 3 − 1). In general, a deposit in year m will compound $N − m$ times for a future value in year N. We can find the total amount at the end of three years by computing the future value of each deposit and then adding them together. Using the future value equation from Chapter 4, the future value of today's deposit is $100 \times (1 + 0.07)^3 = 122.50. Similarly, the future value of the next two deposits are $125 \times (1 + 0.07)^2 = 143.11 and $150 \times (1 + 0.07)^1 = 160.50, respectively.

Putting these three individual future value equations together would yield:

$$FV_3 = \$100 \times (1 + 0.07)^3 + \$125 \times (1 + 0.07)^2 + \$150 \times (1 + 0.07)^1 = \$426.11$$

The general equation for computing the future value of multiple and varying cash flows (or payments) is:

---

viewpoints

business APPLICATION

Walkabout Music, Inc. issued $20 million in debt 10 years ago to finance their factory construction. The debt allows Walkabout to make interest-only payments at a 7 percent coupon rate, paid semiannually for 30 years. Debt issued today would carry only 6 percent interest. The company CFO is considering whether or not to issue new debt (for 20 years) to pay off the old debt. To pay off the old debt early, Walkabout would have to pay a special "call premium" totaling $1.4 million to its debt holders. To issue new debt, the firm would have to pay investment bankers a fee of $1.2 million. Should the CFO replace the old debt with new debt?

$$FV_N = \frac{\text{Future value of}}{\text{first cash flow}} + \frac{\text{Future value of}}{\text{second cash flow}}$$

$$+ \cdots + \text{Future value of last cash flow} \qquad (5\text{-}1)$$

$$= PMT_m \times (1 + i)^{N-m} + PMT_n \times (1 + i)^{N-n} + \cdots$$

$$+ PMT_p \times (1 + i)^{N-p}$$

In this equation, the letters m, n, and p denote when the cash flows occur in time. Each deposit can be different from the others.

Future Value of Level Cash Flows

Now suppose that each cash flow is the same and occurs every year. Level sets of frequent cash flows are common in finance—we call them **annuities.** The first cash flow of an annuity occurs at the end of the first year (or other time period) and continues every year to the last year. We derive the equation for the future value of an annuity from the general equation for future value of multiple cash flows, equation 5-1. Since each cash flow is the same, and the cash flows are every period, the equation appears as:

$$FVA_N = \frac{\text{Future value of}}{\text{first payment}} + \frac{\text{Future value of}}{\text{second payment}}$$

$$+ \cdots + \text{Last payment}$$

$$= PMT \times (1 + i)^{N-1}$$

$$+ PMT \times (1 + i)^{N-2}$$

personal APPLICATION

Say that you obtained a mortgage for $150,000 three years ago when you purchased your home. You've been paying monthly payments on the 30-year mortgage with a fixed 8 percent interest rate and have $145,920.10 of principal left to pay. Recently, your mortgage broker called to mention that interest rates on new mortgages have declined to 7 percent. He suggested that you could save money every month if you refinanced your mortgage. You could find a 27-year mortgage at the new interest rate for a $1,000 fee. Should you refinance your mortgage?

$$+ PMT \times (1 + i)^{N-3}$$
$$+ \cdots + PMT(1 + i)^{0}$$

The term *FVA* is used to denote that this is the future value of an annuity. Factoring out the common level cash flow, PMT, we can summarize the equation as:

$$FVA_N = PMT \sum_{t=1}^{N} (1 + i)^{N-t}$$

And finally, we can reduce to the simpler equation:

$$FVA_N = PMT \times \frac{(1 + i)^N - 1}{i} \tag{5-2}$$

Suppose that $100 deposits are made at the end of each year for five years. If interest rates are 8 percent per year, the future value of this annuity stream is computed using equation 5-2 as:

$$FVA_N = \$100 \times \frac{(1 + 0.08)^5 - 1}{0.08} = \$100 \times 5.8666 = \$586.66$$

We can show these deposits and future value on a time line as:

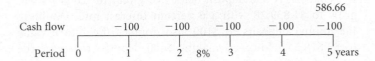

Cash flow		−100	−100	−100	−100	586.66 −100
Period	0	1	2 8%	3	4	5 years

EXAMPLE 5-1

Saving for a Car

Say that as a freshman in college, you will be working as a house painter in each of the next three summers. You intend to set aside some money from each summer's paycheck to buy a car for your senior year. If you can deposit $2,000 from the first summer, $2,500 in the second summer, and $3,000 in the last summer, how much money will you have to buy a car if interest rates are 5 percent?

SOLUTION:

The time line for the forecast is:

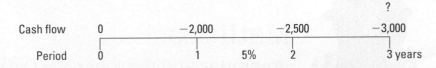

Cash flow	0	−2,000	−2,500	? −3,000
Period	0	1 5%	2	3 years

The first cash flow, which occurs at the end of the first year, will compound for two years. The second cash flow will be invested for only one year. The last contribution will not have any time to grow before the purchase of the car. Using equation 5-1, the solution is

$$FV_3 = 2,000 \times (1 + 0.05)^{3-1} + 2,500 \times (1 + 0.05)^{3-2} + 3,000 \times (1 + 0.05)^{3-3}$$

$$= 2,000 \times 1.1025 \times 2,500 \times 1.05 \times 3,000 \times 1 = \$7,830$$

You will have $7,830 in cash to purchase a car for your senior year.

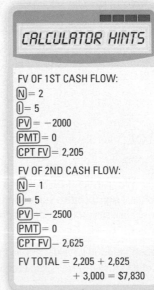

CALCULATOR HINTS

FV OF 1ST CASH FLOW:
N = 2
I = 5
PV = −2000
PMT = 0
CPT FV = 2,205

FV OF 2ND CASH FLOW:
N = 1
I = 5
PV = −2500
PMT = 0
CPT FV = 2,625

FV TOTAL = 2,205 + 2,625
+ 3,000 = $7,830

▼ **TABLE 5.1** Impact of Magnitude of Periodic Payments, Number of Years Invested, and Interest Rate on FV of Annuity

Annuity Cash Flow	Number of Years	Interest Rate	Future Value
$ 50	20	6%	$ 1,839.28
100	20	6	3,678.56
100	40	6	15,476.20
100	40	10	44,259.26

Five deposits of $100 each were made. So, the $586.66 future value represents $86.66 of interest paid. As with almost any TVM problem, the length of time of the annuity and the interest rate for compounding are very important factors in accumulating wealth within the annuity. Consider the examples in Table 5.1. A $50 deposit made every year for 20 years will grow to $1,839.28 with a 6 percent interest rate. Doubling the annual deposits to $100 also doubles the future value to $3,678.56. However, making $100 deposits for *twice* the amount of time, 40 years, more than *quadruples* the future value to $15,476.20! Longer time periods lead to more total compounding and much more wealth. Interest rates also have this effect. Increasing the interest rate from 6 percent to 10 percent on the 40-year annuity results in nearly tripling the future value to $44,259.26. Think about it: Depositing only $100 per year (about 25 lattes per year) can generate some serious money over time. See Figure 5.1. What would $2,000 annual deposits grow to?

Future Value of Multiple Annuities

At times, multiple annuities can occur in both business and personal life. For example, you may find that you can increase the amount of money you save each year because of a promotion or a new and better job. As an illustration, reconsider the annual $100 deposits made for five years at 8 percent per year. This time, the deposit is able to be increased to $150 for the fourth and fifth years. How can we use the annuity equation to compute the future value when we have two levels of cash flows? In this case, the cash flow can be categorized as two annuities. The first annuity is a $100 cash flow for five years. The second annuity is a $50 cash flow for two years. We demonstrate this as:

						?
					−50	−50
Cash flow	0	−100	−100	−100	−100	−100
Period	0	1	2 8%	3	4	5 years

To determine the future value of these two annuities, compute the future value of each one separately, and then simply add them together. The future value of the $100 annuity is the same as computed before, $586.66. The future value of the $50 annuity, using the TVM equation for the future value of a cash stream, is:

$$FVA_N = \$50 \times \frac{(1 + 0.08)^2 - 1}{0.08}$$

$$= \$50 \times 2.08 = \$104$$

So, the future value of both of the annuities is $690.66 (= $586.66 + $104). In this same way, we could easily compute the future value if the last two cash flows are $50 *lower* ($50 each), instead of $50 higher ($150 each). To solve this alternative version, we would simply *subtract* the $104 future value instead of adding it.

the
Math Coach on...
Annuities and the Financial Calculator

❝ In the previous chapter, the level payment button (PMT) in the financial calculator was always set to zero because no constant payments were made every period. We use the PMT button to input the annuity amount. For calculators, the present value is of the opposite sign (positive versus negative) from the future value. This is also the case with annuities. The level cash flow will be of the opposite sign as the future value, as the previous time line shows.

You would use the financial calculator to solve the above problem of depositing $100 for five years via the following inputs: $N = 5$, $I = 8$, $PV = 0$, $PMT = -100$. In this case, the input for present value is zero because no deposit is made today. The result of computing the future value is 586.66. ❞

FIGURE 5.1 Future Value of a $100 Annuity at 6 Percent

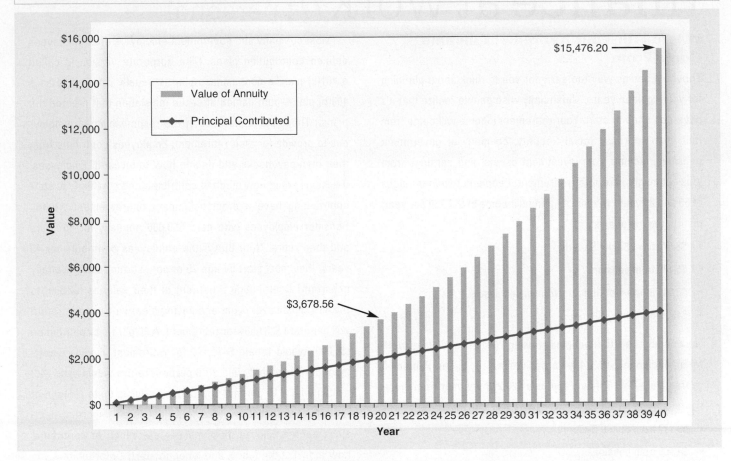

EXAMPLE 5-2

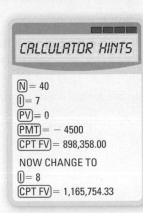

CALCULATOR HINTS

N = 40
I = 7
PV = 0
PMT = − 4500
$CPT FV$ = 898,358.00

NOW CHANGE TO

I = 8
$CPT FV$ = 1,165,754.33

Saving in the Company Pension Plan

You started your first job after graduating from college. Your company offers a retirement plan for which the company contributes 50 percent of what you contribute each year. So, if you contribute $3,000 per year from your salary, the company adds another $1,500. You get to decide how to invest the total annual contribution from several portfolio choices that the plan administrator provides. Suppose that you pick a mixture of stocks and bonds that is expected to earn 7 percent per year. If you plan to retire in 40 years, how big will you expect that retirement account to be? If you could earn 8 percent per year, how much money would be available?

SOLUTION:

Every year, you and your employer will set aside a total of $4,500 for your retirement. Using equation 5-2 shows that the future value of this annuity is:

$$FVA_{40} = \$4,500 \times \frac{(1 + 0.07)^{40} - 1}{0.07} = \$4,500 \times 199.635 = \$898,358.00$$

Note that you can build a substantial amount of wealth ($898,358) through your pension plan at work. If you can earn just 1 percent more each year, 8 percent total, you could be a millionaire!

$$FVA_{40} = \$4,500 \times \frac{(1 + 0.08)^{40} - 1}{0.08} = \$4,500 \times 259.057 = \$1,165,754.33$$

finance at work //: personal

Where Will Your Retirement Income Come From?

Though it seems way too early for you to think about planning for your "golden years," financially wise people realize that it's never too early to start. Your retirement income will come from four main sources: Social Security, company or government pensions, income from investment assets, and earnings from jobs you might take after retirement. People between the ages of 65 and 69 years receive an annual income of $17,708 per year, distributed as follows:

- $8,872 from Social Security.
- $5,140 from pensions.
- $3,244 interest or principal from saved assets.
- $452 from other sources.

No wonder, then, that people in this age group continue to work for an additional $10,374 in earned wages each year. People 10 years older (75 to 79) average only $20,278 per year from these sources:

- $9,772 from Social Security.
- $4,509 from pensions.
- $2,807 from saved assets.
- $2,874 from current jobs.
- $316 from other sources.

We can note several important things about the above. First, Social Security, while the largest contribution to retirees' income, doesn't provide very much money to live on. Second, the average retiree does not enjoy a very high living standard. Third, older people's savings have proved inadequate to provide a comfortable retirement lifestyle. Many of today's retirees aged 65 or above expected Social Security to meet a much greater portion of their income needs in retirement. These retirees also expected that their employers would provide adequate pensions for the retirees to live comfortably in retirement. So, what can you do to avoid the same situation when you retire?

Most company and government employers offer employees defined contribution plans. (The corporate version is called a 401(k) plan; a nonbusiness plan is usually referred to as a 403(b) plan—both named after the legislation that created the plans.) These plans place all of the responsibility on employees to provide for their retirement. Employees contribute from their own paychecks and decide how to invest it. Employees' decisions about how much to contribute and how early to start contributing have a dramatic impact on retirement wealth. Consider employees who earn $50,000 annually for 40 years and then retire. Note that if the employees contribute for 40 years, they must start by age 25 or so—starting early is vitally important! Contributing 5 percent of their salaries ($2,500) to the 401(k) plan every year and having it earn a 4 percent return will generate $237,564 for retirement. A 10 percent contribution ($5,000) would create $475,128 for retirement. Finally, investment decisions that yield an 8 percent return would yield $1.3 million with a 10 percent contribution. This is quite a range of retirement wealth generated from just three important decisions each employee must make—how much to contribute, how to invest the funds, and when to start! Unfortunately, too many people make poor decisions. The average 401(k) account value for people in their 60s is only $136,400—often because people start 401(k) contributions too late to allow the funds to compound much.

Saving and investing money through a defined contribution plan is a good way to build wealth for retirement. But you must Start Early, Save Much, and Don't Touch!

Want to know more?

Key Words to Search for Updates: **See the Employee Benefit Research Institute Web site (www.ebri.org) or Google retirement income.**

Sources: "Distribution of Older Population's Average Annual Income," *Fast Facts from EBRI, #18,* February 23, 2006, and "401(k) Account Balances, Asset Allocation by the Numbers," *Fast Facts from EBRI, #08,* October 3, 2005.

EXAMPLE 5-3

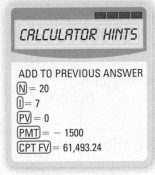

For interactive versions
of this example visit
www.mhhe.com/canM

Growing Retirement Contributions

In the previous example, you are investing a total of $4,500 per year for 40 years in your employer's retirement program. You believe that with raises and promotions, you will eventually be able to contribute more money each year. Consider that halfway through your career, you are able to increase your investment in the retirement program to $6,000 per year (your contribution plus the company match). What would be the future value of your retirement wealth from this program if investments are compounded at 7 percent?

SOLUTION:

You can compute the future value using two annuities. The first annuity is one with payments of $4,500 that lasts 40 years. The second is a $1,500 (= $6,000 − $4,500) annuity that lasts only 20 years. We already computed the future value of the first annuity in the previous example: $898,358. The future value of the second annuity is:

$$FVA_{20} = \$1,500 \times \frac{(1 + 0.07)^{20} - 1}{0.07} = \$1,500 \times 40.9955 = \$61,493.24$$

So, your retirement wealth from this program would be $959,851 (= $898,358 + $61,493).

CALCULATOR HINTS

ADD TO PREVIOUS ANSWER
N = 20
I = 7
PV = 0
PMT = − 1500
CPT FV = 61,493.24

PRESENT VALUE OF MULTIPLE CASH FLOWS

The future value concept is very useful to understand how to build wealth for the future. The present value concept will help you most particularly for personal applications such as evaluating loans (like car and mortgage loans) and business applications (like determining the value of business opportunities).

Finding the Present Value of Several Cash Flows

Consider the cash flows that we showed in the very beginning of the chapter: you deposit $100 today, followed by a $125 deposit next year, and a $150 deposit at the end of the second year. In the previous situation, we sought the future value when interest rates are 7 percent. Instead of future value, we compute the present value of these three cash flows. The time line for this problem appears as:

Cash flow	−100	−125		−150
Period	0	1	7%	2 years

The first cash flow is already in year zero, so its value will not change. We will discount the second cash flow one year and the third cash flow two years. Using the present value equation from the previous chapter, the present

value of today's payment is simply $100 ÷ $(1 + 0.07)^0$ = $100. Similarly, the present values of the next two cash flows are $125 ÷ $(1 + 0.07)^1$ = $116.82 and $150 ÷ $(1 + 0.07)^2$ = $131.02, respectively. Therefore, the present value of these cash flows is $347.84 (= $100 + $116.82 + $131.02).

Putting these three individual present value equations together would yield:

$$PV = \$100 \div (1 + 0.07)^0 + \$125 \div (1 + 0.07)^1$$
$$+ \$150 \div (1 + 0.07)^2$$
$$= \$347.84$$

CALCULATOR HINTS

PV OF 1ST CASH FLOW IS $100
PV OF 2ND CASH FLOW:
N = 1
I = 7
PMT = 0
FV = − 125
CPT PV = 116.82

PV OF 3RD CASH FLOW:
N = 2
I − 7
PMT = 0
FV = −150
CPT PV = 131.01
ADD THE 3 PVS

The general equation for discounting multiple and varying cash flows is:

$$PV = \frac{\text{Present value of}}{\text{first cash flow}} + \frac{\text{Present value of}}{\text{second cash flow}}$$

$$+ \cdots + \text{Present value of last cash flow}$$

$$= \frac{PMT_m}{(1 + i)^{N-m}} + \frac{PMT_n}{(1 + i)^{N-n}} + \cdots$$

$$+ \frac{PMT_p}{(1 + i)^{N-p}} \qquad (5\text{-}3)$$

In this equation, the letters m, n, and p denote when the cash flows occur in time. Each deposit can differ from the others in terms of size and timing.

time out!

5-1 Describe how compounding affects the future value computation of an annuity.

5-2 Reconsider your original retirement plan example to invest $4,500 per year for 40 years. Now consider the result if you don't contribute anything for four years (years 19 to 22) while your child goes to college. How many annuity equations will you need to find the future value of your 401(k) in this situation?

And finally, reduced to a simpler equation:

$$PVA_N = PMT \times \left[\frac{1 - \frac{1}{(1 + i)^N}}{i} \right] \quad (5\text{-}4)$$

Suppose that someone makes $100 payments at the end of each year for five years. If interest rates are 8 percent per year, the present value of this annuity stream is computed using equation 5-4 as:

$$PVA_5 = 100 \times \left[\frac{1 - \frac{1}{(1 + 0.08)^5}}{0.08} \right]$$

$$= 100 \times 3.9927 = 399.27$$

The time line for these payments and present value appears as:

	399.27					
Cash flow		−100	−100	−100	−100	−100
Period	0	1	2	8% 3	4	5 years

Present Value of Level Cash Flows

You will find that this present value of an annuity concept will have many business and personal applications throughout your life. Most loans are set up so that the amount borrowed (the present value) is repaid through level payments made every period (the annuity). Lenders will examine borrowers' budgets and determine how much each borrower can afford as a payment. The maximum loan offered will be the present value of that annuity payment. We derived the equation for the present value of an annuity from the general equation for the present value of multiple cash flows, equation 5-3. Since each cash flow is the same, and the borrower pays the cash flows every period, we can write the equation as:

PVA_N = Present value of first payment

+ Present value of second payment

+ · · · + Present value of last payment

$= PMT/(1 + i)^1 + PMT/(1 + i)^2$

$+ PMT/(1 + i)^3 + · · · + PMT/(1 + i)^N$

We denote the present value of an annuity as PVA. If we group the common level cash flow as PMT, the equation becomes

$$PVA_N = PMT \times \sum_{t=1}^{N} \frac{1}{(1 + i)^t}$$

Notice that although five payments of $100 each were made, $500 total, the present value is only $399.27. As we've noted previously, the span of time over which the borrower pays the annuity and the interest rate for discounting strongly affect present value computations. When you borrow money from the bank, the bank views the amount they lend as the

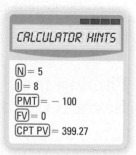

CALCULATOR HINTS

N = 5
I = 8
PMT = − 100
FV = 0
CPT PV = 399.27

present value of the annuity they receive over time from the borrower. Consider the examples in Table 5.2. A $50 deposit made every year for 20 years is discounted to $573.50 with a 6 percent discount rate. Doubling the annual cash flow to $100 also doubles the present value to $1,146.99. But extending the time period does not impact the present value as much as you might expect. Making $100 payments for twice the amount of time—40 years—does not double the present value. As you can see in Table 5.2, the present value increases less than 50 percent to only $1,504.63! If the discount rate increases from 6 percent to 10 percent on the 40-year annuity, the present value will shrink to $977.91.

The present value of a cash flow made far into the future is not very valuable today. That's why doubling the number of years in the table from 20 to 40 only increased the present value by approximately 30 percent. Figure 5.2 shows how the

EXAMPLE 5-4

For interactive versions of this example visit www.mhhe.com/canM

Value of Payments

Your firm needs to buy additional physical therapy equipment that costs $20,000. The equipment manufacturer will give you the equipment now if you will pay $6,000 per year for the next four years. If your firm can borrow money at a 9 percent interest rate, should you pay the manufacturer the $20,000 now or accept the four-year annuity offer of $6,000?

SOLUTION:

iWe can find the cost of the four-year, $6,000 annuity in present value terms using equation 5-4:

$$PVA_4 = \$6,000 \times \left[\frac{1 - \frac{1}{(1 + 0.09)^4}}{0.09} \right] = \$6,000 \times 3.2397 = \$19,438.32$$

The cost of paying for the equipment over time is $19,438.32. This is less, in present value terms, than paying $20,000 cash. The firm should take the annuity payment plan.

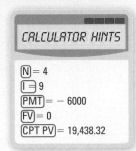

CALCULATOR HINTS

$N = 4$
$I = 9$
$PMT = -6000$
$FV = 0$
$CPT\ PV = 19,438.32$

▼ **TABLE 5.2** Impact of Magnitude of the Annuity, Number of Years Invested, and Interest Rate on PV

Annuity Cash Flow	Number of Years	Interest Rate	Present Value
$ 50	20	6%	$ 573.50
100	20	6	1,146.99
100	40	6	1,504.63
100	40	10	977.91

present value of $100 annuity payments declines for the cash flows made later in time, especially at higher discount rates. The $100 cash flow in year 20 is worth less than $15 today if we use a 10 percent discount rate; it's worth more than double, at nearly $38 today, if we use a discount rate of 5 percent. The figure also shows how quickly present value declines with a higher discount rate relative to a lower rate. As we showed above, the present values of the annuities in the figure are the sums of the present values shown. Since the present values for the 10 percent discount rate are smaller, the present value of an annuity is smaller as interest rates rise.

Present Value of Multiple Annuities

Just as we can combine annuities to solve various future value problems, we can also combine annuities to solve some present value problems with changing level cash flows. Consider Alex Rodriguez's (A-Rod's) baseball contract in 2000 with the Texas Rangers. This contract made A-Rod into the "$252 million man." The contract was structured so that the Rangers paid A-Rod a $10 million signing bonus, $21 million per year in

2001 through 2004, $25 million per year in 2005 and 2006, and $27 million per year in 2007 through 2010.[1] Note that adding the signing bonus to the annual salary equals the $252 million figure. However, Rodriguez will receive the salary in the future. Using an 8 percent discount rate, what is the present value of A-Rod's contract?

We begin by showing the salary cash flows with the time line:

Cash flow	?	21	21	21	21	25	25	27	27	27	27
				8%							
Period	0	1	2	3	4	5	6	7	8	9	10 years

First create a $27 million, 10-year annuity. Here are the associated cash flows:

			−6	−6	−6	−6	−2	−2				
Cash flow	?	27	27	27	27	27	27	27	27	27	27
				8%							
Period	0	1	2	3	4	5	6	7	8	9	10 years

Now create a $−2 million, six-year annuity:

			−4	−4	−4	−4					
			−2	−2	−2	−2	−2	−2			
Cash flow	?	27	27	27	27	27	27	27	27	27	27
				8%							
Period	0	1	2	3	4	5	6	7	8	9	10 years

Notice that creating the $−2 million annuity also resulted in the third annuity of $−4 million for four years. This time line shows three annuities. If you add the cash flows in any year, the

[1]The contract actually contains some complications like incentives to play well and salary deferral. We ignore those complicating factors here.

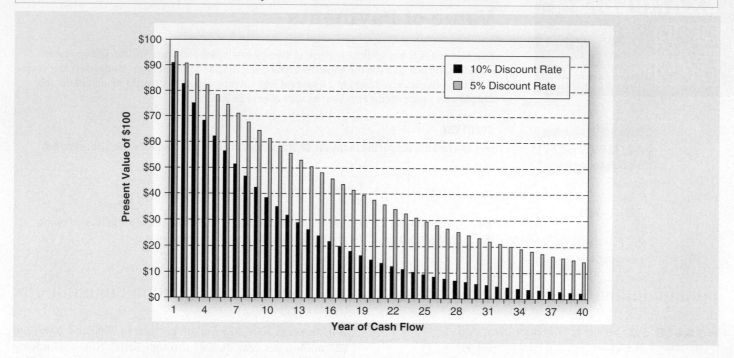

sum is A-Rod's salary for that year. Now we can find the present value of each annuity using equation 5-4 three times.

$$PVA_{10} = \$27 \times \left[\frac{1 - \frac{1}{(1 + 0.08)^{10}}}{0.08} \right] = \$27 \times 6.710$$

$$= \$181.17 \text{ million}$$

$$PVA_6 = \$-2 \times \left[\frac{1 - \frac{1}{(1 + 0.08)^6}}{0.08} \right] = \$-2 \times 4.623$$

$$= \$-9.25 \text{ million}$$

$$PVA_4 = \$-4 \times \left[\frac{1 - \frac{1}{(1 + 0.08)^4}}{0.08} \right] = \$-4 \times 3.312$$

$$= \$-13.25 \text{ million}$$

Adding the value of the three annuities reveals that the present value of A-Rod's salary was $158.67 million (= $181.17 −$9.25 −$13.25). Adding in the $10 million signing bonus produces a contract value of $168.67 million. So, the present value of A-Rod's contract turns out to be quite considerable, but you might not call him the $252 million man![2]

[2]Rodriguez opted out of the contract after the 2007 season and then re-signed with the New York Yankees with a new contract.

The reported values for many sports contracts may be misleading in present value terms.

consols Investment assets structured as perpetuities.

perpetuities An annuity with cash flows that continue forever.

annuity due An annuity in which cash flows are paid at the beginning of each time period.

Perpetuity—A Special Annuity

A perpetuity is a special type of annuity with a stream of level cash flows that are paid forever. These arrangements are called **perpetuities** because payments are perpetual. Assets that offer investors perpetual payments are preferred stocks and British 2½% Consolidated Stock, a debt referred to as **consols.**

The value of an investment like this is the present value of all future annuity payments. As the cash flow continues indefinitely, we can't use equation 5-4. Luckily, mathematicians have figured out that when the number of periods, N, in equation 5-4 goes to infinity, the equation reduces to a very simple one:

$$PV \text{ of a perpetuity} = \frac{PMT}{i} \quad (5\text{-}5)$$

For example, the present value of an annual $100 perpetuity discounted at 10 percent is $1,000 (= $100 ÷ 0.10). Compare this to the present value of a $100 annuity of 40 years as shown in Table 5.2. The 40-year annuity's value is $977.91. You'll see that extending the payments from 40 years to an infinite number of years adds only $22.09 (= $1,000 − $977.91) of value. This demonstrates once again how little value today is placed on cash flows paid many years into the future.

CALCULATOR HINTS

N = 10
I = 8
PMT = − 27
FV = 0
CPT PV = 181.17

NOW CHANGE TO
N = 6
PMT = 2
CPT PV = − 9.25

NOW CHANGE TO
N = 4
PMT = 4
CPT PV = − 13.25

ORDINARY ANNUITIES VERSUS ANNUITIES DUE

So far, we've assumed that every cash flow comes in at the end of every period. But in many instances, cash flows come in at the beginning of each period. An annuity in which the cash flows occur at the beginning of each period is called an **annuity due.**

Consider the five-year $100 annuity due. The cash flow in the beginning of year 1 looks like it's actually a cash flow today.

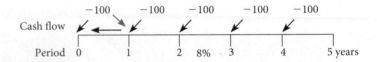

Note that these five annuity-due cash flows are essentially the same as a payment today and a four-year ordinary annuity.

Future Value of an Annuity Due So, how do we calculate the future value of the five-year annuity due shown in the time line? The first cash flow of an ordinary five-year annuity can compound for four years. The last cash flow does not compound at all. From the time line, you can see that the first cash flow of the annuity due essentially occurs in year zero, or today. So the first cash flow compounds for five years. The last cash flow of an annuity due compounds for one year. The main difference between an annuity due and an ordinary annuity is that all the cash flows of the annuity due compound one more year than the ordinary annuity. The future value of the annuity due will simply be the future value of the ordinary annuity multiplied by $(1 + i)$:

$$FVA_N \text{ due} = FVA_N \times (1 + i) \quad (5\text{-}6)$$

Earlier in the chapter, the future value of this ordinary annuity was shown to be $586.66. Therefore, the future value of the annuity due is $633.59 (= $586.66 × 1.08).

time out!

5-3 How important is the magnitude of the discount rate in present value computations? Do significantly higher interest rates lead to significantly higher present values?

5-4 Reconsider the physical therapy equipment example. If interest rates are only 7 percent, should you pay the up-front fee or the annuity?

Present Value of an Annuity Due. What is a five-year annuity due, shown above, worth today? Remember that we discount the first cash flow of an ordinary five-year annuity one year. We discount the last cash flow for the full five years. But since the first cash flow of the annuity due is already paid today, we don't discount it at all. We discount the last cash flow of an annuity due only four years. Indeed, we discount all the cash flows of the annuity due one year less than we would discount the ordinary annuity. Therefore, the present value of the annuity due is simply the present value of the ordinary annuity multiplied by $(1 + i)$:

$$PVA_N \text{ due} = PVA_N \times (1 + i) \qquad (5\text{-}7)$$

Earlier in the chapter, we discovered that the present value of this ordinary annuity was $399.27. So the present value of the annuity due is $431.21 (= $399.27 × 1.08).

Interestingly, we make the same adjustment, $(1 + i)$, to both the ordinary annuity present value and future value to compute the annuity due value.

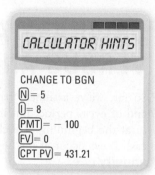

CALCULATOR HINTS

CHANGE TO BGN
N = 5
I = 8
PMT = − 100
FV = 0
CPT PV = 431.21

COMPOUNDING FREQUENCY

So far, all of our examples and illustrations have used annual payments and annual compounding or discounting periods. But many situations that use cash flow time-value-of-money analysis require more frequent or less frequent time periods than simple yearly entries. Bonds make semiannual interest payments; stocks pay quarterly dividends. Most consumer loans require monthly payments. Monthly payments require monthly compounding. In this section, we'll discuss the implications of compounding more than once a year.

Effect of Compounding Frequency

Consider a $100 deposit made today with a 12 percent annual interest rate. What's the future value of this deposit in one year? equation 4-2 from the previous chapter shows that the answer is $112. What would happen if the bank compounded the interest every six months instead of at the end of the year? Halfway through the year, the bank would compute that the deposit has grown 6 percent (half the annual 12 percent rate) to $106. At the end of the year, the bank would compute another 6 percent interest payment. However, this 6 percent is earned on $106, not the original $100 deposit. The end-of-year value is therefore $112.36 (= $106 × 1.06). By compounding twice per year instead of just once, the future value is $0.36 higher. Though this amount may seem negligible, you might be surprised to see how quickly the difference becomes significant.

Instead of compounding annually or semiannually, what might happen if compounding were quarterly? Since each year contains four quarters, the interest rate per quarter would be 3 percent (= 12 percent ÷ 4 quarters). The future value in one year, compounded quarterly, is $112.55 (= $100 × 1.03^4). Again, the compounding frequency increased and so did the future value. Table 5.3 shows the effect of various compounding frequencies. We'd like to draw your attention to two important points in the table. First, the higher the compound frequency, the higher the future value will be. Second, the relative increase in value

time out!

5-5 In what situations might you need to use annuity due analysis instead of an ordinary annuity analysis?

5-6 Reconsider your retirement plan earlier in this chapter. What would your retirement wealth grow to be if you started contributing today?

▼ TABLE 5.3 Future Value in One Year and Compounding Frequency of $100 at 12 percent

Frequency	Period Interest Rate	Future Value Equation	Future Value
Annual	12%	100×1.12^1	$112.00
Semiannual	6	100×1.06^2	112.36
Quarterly	3	100×1.03^4	112.55
Monthly	1	100×1.01^{12}	112.68
Daily	0.032877	$100 \times 1.00032877^{365}$	112.748
Hourly	0.00136986	$100 \times 1.0000136986^{8760}$	112.749

from increasing compounding frequency seems to diminish with increasing frequencies. For example, increasing frequency from annual to semiannual increased the future value by 36 cents. However, increasing frequency from daily to hourly compounding increases the future value by only 0.1 cents.[3]

When we work with annuity cash flows, the compound frequency used is the same as the timing of the cash flows. When annuity cash flows are paid monthly, then interest is also compounded monthly, as seen in the following two examples.

EARS and APRS

If you borrowed $100 at a 12 percent interest rate, you would expect to pay $112 in one year. If the loan compounded monthly, then Table 5.3 shows that you would owe $112.68 at the end of the year. So a 12 percent loan compounded monthly means that you really pay more than 12 percent. In fact, you would pay 12.68 percent. In this example, the 12 percent rate is called the **annual percentage rate (APR).** The higher rate, 12.68 percent, is called the **effective annual rate (EAR)**—a more accurate measurement of what you will actually pay.

> **annual percentage rate (APR)** The interest rate per period times the number of periods in a year.
>
> **effective annual rate (EAR)** An interest rate that reflects annualizing with compounding figured in.

[3]It is also possible to continuously compound. The future value of a continuously compounded deposit is $FV_N = PV \times e^{(i \times N)}$, where e has a value of 2.7183.

> When we work with annuity cash flows, the compound frequency used is the same as the timing of the cash flows.

EXAMPLE 5-5

For interactive versions of this example visit www.mhhe.com/canM

Car Loan Debt

Now you would like to buy a car. You have reviewed your budget and determined that you can afford to pay $500 per month as a car payment. How much can you borrow if interest rates are 9 percent and you pay the loan over four years? How much could you borrow if you agree to pay for six years instead?

SOLUTION:

The loan amount is the present value of the 48-month, $500 annuity. Note that the loan term will be 48 ($= 4 \times 12$) months and the interest rate is 0.75 ($= 9 \div 12$) percent. Using equation 5-4, you discover that you can borrow up to $20,092 to buy a car:

$$PVA_{48} = \$500 \times \left[\frac{1 - \dfrac{1}{(1 + 0.0075)^{48}}}{0.0075} \right] = \$500 \times 40.1848 = \$20,092.39$$

If you are willing to borrow money for six years instead of four, the small change to the equation results in your ability to borrow $27,738. Although this would allow you to buy a more expensive car, it would also require two more years of $500 payments (an additional $12,000 of payments!).

CALCULATOR HINTS

N = 48
I = 0.75
PMT = −500
FV = 0
CPT PV = 20,092.39

THEN CHANGE N TO 72
CPT PV = 27,738.42

EXAMPLE 5-6

Making Monthly Pension Contributions

Reexamine your original plan to contribute to your company retirement plan. Instead of a total contribution of $4,500 per year for 40 years, you are able to contribute monthly. Given your expected 7 percent per year investment return, how much money can you expect in your retirement account?

SOLUTION:

Now your total monthly contribution will be $375 (= $4,500 ÷ 12), which will continue for 480 months and earn a 0.58333 (= 7 ÷ 12) percent monthly return. The results of equation 5-2 show that the future value of this annuity is:

$$FVA_{40} = \$375 \times \frac{(1 + 7 \div 12 \div 100)^{480} - 1}{7 \div 12 \div 100} = \$375 \times 2{,}624.8135 = \$984{,}305.02$$

When you made contributions annually, the future value was $898,358. By changing to monthly contributions, your retirement nest egg increased by nearly $90,000 to $984,305!

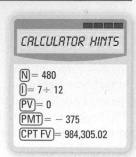

CALCULATOR HINTS

$\boxed{N}$ = 480
$\boxed{I}$ = 7 ÷ 12
$\boxed{PV}$ = 0
$\boxed{PMT}$ = − 375
$\boxed{CPT\ FV}$ = 984,305.02

For interactive versions of this example visit www.mhhe.com/canM

finance at work //: behavioral

Take Your Lottery Winnings Now or Later?

On February 18, 2006, a group of ConAgra Foods co-workers won a record Powerball jackpot of $365 million. The group had two choices for payment. They could take a much-discounted lump sum cash payment immediately, or take 30 annuity payments (one immediately and then one every year for 29 years, which is a 30-year annuity due). The annuity payment would be $12.17 million (= $365 million ÷ 30). The lump sum payment offered was $177.3 million. One way to decide between the two alternatives would be to use the time value of money concepts. They might have computed the present value of the annuity and compared it to the lump sum cash payment.

At the time, long-term interest rates were 5 percent. The present value of the annuity offered was $196.38 million. (Compute this yourself.) Notice that winning $365 million does not deliver $365 million of value! If the decision was made from this perspective, the group should take the annuity choice because it has more value than the cash alternative. However, this group selected the immediate cash option. Most winners do. Financial advisors tend to recommend that lottery winners take the lump sum because they believe that the money can earn a higher return than the 5 percent interest rate.

Good reasons arise for taking the annuity, however. To earn the higher return on the lump sum, the advisor (and the group of owners) would have to take risks. In addition, most of the lump sum would have to be invested. But most people who take a lump sum end up spending much of it in the first couple of years. Stories abound about lottery winners who declare bankruptcy a few years after receiving their money. Taking the money as an annuity helps instill financial discipline, since the winners can't waste money today that they won't receive for years.

Want to know more?

Key Words to Search for Updates: **See the Powerball Web site (www.powerball.com) or Google Powerball winners.**

Sources: "8 Win Record U.S. Lottery Jackpot, $365 million," *The New York Times,* February 23, 2006, page A24, and **www.powerball.com.**

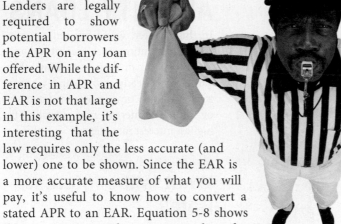

Lenders are legally required to show potential borrowers the APR on any loan offered. While the difference in APR and EAR is not that large in this example, it's interesting that the law requires only the less accurate (and lower) one to be shown. Since the EAR is a more accurate measure of what you will pay, it's useful to know how to convert a stated APR to an EAR. Equation 5-8 shows this conversion with a compounding frequency of *m* times per year:

$$EAR = \left(1 + \frac{APR}{m}\right)^m - 1 \qquad (5\text{-}8)$$

Table 5.4 shows various EAR conversions. If compounding occurs annually, you will see that the EAR and the APR will be the same. If compounding happens more than once a year, then the EAR will be higher than the APR. The table also demonstrates that the compound frequency effect grows substantially for higher interest rates or longer term loans. Compounded quarterly, the EAR is hardly different at all from a 5 percent

▼ **TABLE 5.4** The EAR Is Higher than the APR

APR	Compounding Periods	Equation	= EAR
5%	1	$(1 + 0.05/1)^1 - 1$	5.00%
5	4	$(1 + 0.05/4)^4 - 1$	5.09
5	12	$(1 + 0.05/12)^{12} - 1$	5.12
9	4	$(1 + 0.09/4)^4 - 1$	9.31
9	12	$(1 + 0.09/12)^{12} - 1$	9.38
12	4	$(1 + 0.12/4)^4 - 1$	12.55
12	12	$(1 + 0.12/12)^{12} - 1$	12.68

EXAMPLE 5-7

For interactive versions of this example visit www.mhhe.com/canM

Evaluating Credit Card Offers

As a college student, you probably receive many credit card offers in the mail. Consider these two offers. The first card charges a 16 percent APR. An examination of the footnotes reveals that this card compounds monthly. The second credit card charges 15.5 percent APR and compounds weekly. Which card has a lower effective annual rate?

SOLUTION:

Compute the EAR of each card to compare them in common (and realistic) terms. The first card has an EAR of:

$$EAR = \left(1 + \frac{0.16}{12}\right)^{12} - 1 = 0.17227 = 17.23\%$$

The EAR of the second card is:

$$EAR = \left(1 + \frac{0.155}{52}\right)^{52} - 1 = 0.16739 = 16.74\%$$

You should pick the second credit card because it has a lower effective annual rate. But note also that you will always be better off if you pay off your credit card balance whenever the bill comes due.

time out!

5-7 Why is EAR a more accurate measure of the rate actually paid than APR?

5-8 What would have a smaller present value, a future sum discounted annually or one discounted monthly?

APR: 5.09 percent versus 5 percent. The difference is larger when the APR is 12 percent. Compounded quarterly, the EAR is higher at 12.55 percent.

ANNUITY LOANS

In this chapter, we've focused on computing the future and present value of annuities. But in many situations, these values are already known and what we really need to compare are the payments or implied interest rate—usually, the highest interest rate offered.

What Is the Interest Rate?

Many business and personal applications already state the cost of an investment, as well as the annuity cash flows and time period. We need, then, to solve for the implied interest rate of this investment. Unfortunately, we have no general, easy equation to solve for the interest rate. Even financial calculators use an iterating process, which causes them to "think" a little longer before displaying the estimated interest rate result.

Consider the plight of a manager of a small doctor's office who has the opportunity to buy a piece of imaging equipment

---

EXAMPLE 5-8

For interactive versions of this example visit www.mhhe.com/canM

Computing Interest Rate Needed

After saving diligently your entire career, you and your spouse are finally ready to retire with a nest egg of $800,000. You need to invest this money in a mix of stocks and bonds that will allow you to earn $6,000 per month for 30 years. What interest rate do you need to earn?

SOLUTION:

Use a financial calculator and input N = 360, PV = −800000, PMT = 6000, and FV = 0. The interest rate result is 0.6860 percent. But remember, since the periods and payments are in months, the interest rate is too. It is customary to report this as an APR: 8.23 percent (= 0.6860 percent × 12). However, the EAR more accurately reflects the true interest rate, 8.55 percent (= $1.00686^{12} - 1$). In order for your money to last for 30 years while funding a $6,000 per month income, you must earn at least an 8.23 APR per year return.

for $100,000. The equipment will allow the office to generate $25,000 in profits for six years, at which time the equipment will be worn out and without value in the U.S.[4] What rate of return does this purchase offer the doctor's office? The time line for this problem appears as

Cash flow −100,000 25,000 25,000 25,000 25,000 25,000 25,000

Period   0   1   2   3   4   5   6 years

For the financial calculator solution, input N = 6, PV = −100000, PMT = 25000, and FV = 0. The interest rate result is then 12.98 percent. So, if this is a high enough return relative to other uses of the $100,000, the doctor's office should seriously consider purchasing the imaging machine.

Finding Payments on an Amortized Loan

Many consumers and small business owners already know how much money they want to borrow and the level of current interest rates. Usually, they really need to translate this information into the actual payments to determine if they can really afford the purchase. A loan structured for annuity payments that completely pay off the debt is called an **amortized loan.** To compute the annuity cash flow of an amortized loan, rearrange the present value of an annuity formula, equation 5-4, to solve for the payment:

$$PMT_N = PV \times \left[\frac{i}{1 - \dfrac{1}{(1 + i)^N}} \right] \qquad (5\text{-}9)$$

Most car loans require monthly payments for three to five years. Assume that you need a $10,000 loan to buy a car. The loan is for four years and interest rates are 9 percent per year

[4]Some charities are now gathering "obsolete" U.S. medical equipment and sending the materials to less developed countries—a situation in which everybody wins.

▼ **TABLE 5.5** Monthly Payments on a $225,000 Loan

APR Interest Rate (%)	Years to Repay Loan	Monthly Payment
10	30	$1,974.54
8	30	1,650.97
7	30	1,496.93
6	30	1,348.99
8	15	2,150.22
7	15	2,022.36
6	15	1,898.68

APR. To implement equation 5-9, use an interest rate of 0.75 percent (= 9 percent / 12) and 48 periods (= 4 × 12) as:

$$PMT_{48} = \$10,000 \times \left[\frac{0.0075}{1 - \dfrac{1}{(1 + 0.0075)^{48}}} \right]$$

$$= \$10,000 \times 0.024885 = \$248.85$$

So, when interest rates are 9 percent, it takes monthly payments of $248.85 to pay off a $10,000 loan in four years.

Interest rate levels and loan length strongly affect how large your payments will be. Table 5.5 shows the monthly payments needed to pay off a mortgage debt at various interest rates and lengths of time. (Try computing the payments yourself!) Note that as the interest rate declines, the monthly payment also declines. This is why people rush to refinance their mortgage after interest rates fall. A decline of 1 or 2 percent can save a homeowner hundreds of dollars every month. You will also see from the table that paying off

CALCULATOR HINTS

N = 48
I = 0.75
PV = 10000
FV = 0
CPT PMT = − 248.85

loan principal The balance yet to be paid on a loan.

amortization schedule A table detailing the periodic loan payment, interest payment, and debt balance over the life of the loan.

a mortgage in only 15 years requires larger payments, but generally saves thousands in interest.

Amortized Loan Schedules

When you pay a car loan or home mortgage, you will often find it useful to know how much of the debt, or **loan principal,** you still owe. For example, consider a case wherein you bought a car two years ago using a four-year loan. In order to sell the car now, the loan balance will have to be paid off. Being able to compute this principal balance may influence your chances of selling the car.

An interest-only loan allows the borrower to make payments that consist totally of interest payments, so none of the debt is reduced. A $10,000 interest-only loan with a 9 percent APR paid monthly will cost $75 per month (=$10,000 × 0.09 ÷ 12). Amortizing this loan over four years requires monthly payments of $248.85 (see earlier car loan problem). The difference in the first month's payment on the two loans is $173.85 (= $248.85 − $75) and represents the amount of the regular amortized loan's payment that goes to reducing the principal balance. So after the first month's payment, the amortized loan's balance has fallen to $9,826.15, while the interest-only loan still has a balance of $10,000.

In the second month, the interest incurred on the regular amortized loan is $73.70 (= $9,826.15 × 0.09 ÷ 12), so the $248.85 second month payment represents principal payment of $175.15. These numbers are shown in the **amortization schedule** of Table 5.6 on page 114. The table will show you that the early payments on a car loan go mostly to paying the interest rather than reducing the principal. That interest component declines over time, and then the principal balance declines.

The schedule shows that if you wish to sell the car after two years, you will have to pay the loan company a car loan (principal) debt of $5,447.13. Of course, if you had an interest-only loan,

Blaine-O and seven others like this.

Blaine-O Now I'll know what all that interest-rate jargon REALLY means when I go buy my next car!

8 hours ago · Like

write a comment...

you would still owe the full principal of $10,000 after two years. Amortization schedules are also useful for determining other things, like the total amount of interest that you will pay over the life of the loan. In this case, if you take a regular loan in which you pay both principal and interest, you pay $10,000 in principal and nearly $1,945 in interest during the four years of the loan. The interest component is an even larger component of longer-term loans, like 30-year mortgages. Depending on the interest rate charged, the first payment in a mortgage consists of 75 percent to 95 percent interest. The home mortgage principal balance falls very slowly in the first years of the loan.

We construct amortization schedules by showing the

Monthly Mortgage Payments

Say that you have your heart set on purchasing a beautiful, old Tudor-style house for $250,000. A mortgage broker says that you can qualify for a mortgage for 80 percent (or $200,000) of the price. If you get a 15-year mortgage, the interest rate will be 6.1 percent APR. A 30-year mortgage costs 6.4 percent. One of the factors that will help you decide which mortgage to take is the magnitude of the monthly payments. What will they be?[5]

SOLUTION:

To pay off the mortgage in only 15 years, the payments would have to be larger than for the 30-year mortgage. The higher payment will be eased somewhat because the interest rate is lower on the 15-year mortgage. The payment for the 15-year mortgage is

$$PMT_{180} = \$200,000 \times \left[\frac{0.0050833}{1 - \dfrac{1}{(1 + 0.0050833)^{180}}}\right] = \$200,000 \times 0.0849269 = \$1,698.54$$

The payment for the 30-year mortgage would be:

$$PMT_{360} = \$200,000 \times \left[\frac{0.0053333}{1 - \dfrac{1}{(1 + 0.0053333)^{360}}}\right] = \$200,000 \times 0.00622551 = \$1,251.01$$

So, the payments on the 15-year mortgage are nearly $450 more each month than the 30-year mortgage payments. You must decide whether the cost of paying the extra $450 each month is worth it to own the house with no debt 15 years sooner. The decision would depend on your financial budget and the strength of your desire to be debt free.

[5]Most homeowners are actually most interested in their total payment, which will include hazard insurance for the home and property taxes. Such payments are referred to as PITI—principal, interest, taxes, and insurance. For simplicity, we use only PI payments here—principal and interest only.

Time to Pay Off a Credit Card Balance

Through poor financial management, your friend has racked up $5,000 in debt on his credit card. The card charges a 19 percent APR and compounds monthly. His latest bill shows that he must pay a minimum of $150 this month. At this rate, how long will it take the friend to pay off his credit card debt?

SOLUTION:

Using the financial calculator, input I = 1.58333, PV = 5000, PMT = −150, FV = 0. The answer is 48 months, or 4 years. If the friend pays the minimum payment, then it will be a long time before he will be out of debt. The credit card company is very content to continue to earn the high return for many years—essentially, the interest on the loan and a very small portion of the principal. Your friend should pay more than the minimum charge to reduce his debt quicker.

Month	Beginning Balance	Total Payment	Interest Paid	Principal Paid	Ending Balance	Month	Beginning Balance	Total Payment	Interest Paid	Principal Paid	Ending Balance
1	$10,000.00	$248.85	$75.00	$173.85	$9,826.15	25	$5,447.13	$248.85	$40.85	$208.00	$5,239.14
2	9,826.15	248.85	73.70	175.15	9,651.00	26	5,239.14	248.85	39.29	209.56	5,029.58
3	9,651.00	248.85	72.38	176.47	9,474.53	27	5,029.58	248.85	37.72	211.13	4,818.45
4	9,474.53	248.85	71.06	177.79	9,296.74	28	4,818.45	248.85	36.14	212.71	4,605.74
5	9,296.74	248.85	69.73	179.12	9,117.61	29	4,605.74	248.85	34.54	214.31	4,391.43
6	9,117.61	248.85	68.38	180.47	8,937.15	30	4,391.43	248.85	32.94	215.91	4,175.52
7	8,937.15	248.85	67.03	181.82	8,755.32	31	4,175.52	248.85	31.32	217.53	3,957.99
8	8,755.32	248.85	65.66	183.19	8,572.14	32	3,957.99	248.85	29.68	219.17	3,738.82
9	8,572.14	248.85	64.29	184.56	8,387.58	33	3,738.82	248.85	28.04	220.81	3,518.01
10	8,387.58	248.85	62.91	185.94	8,201.64	34	3,518.01	248.85	26.39	222.46	3,295.55
11	8,201.64	248.85	61.51	187.34	8,014.30	35	3,295.55	248.85	24.72	224.13	3,071.41
12	8,014.30	248.85	60.11	188.74	7,825.56	36	3,071.41	248.85	23.04	225.81	2,845.60
13	7,825.56	248.85	58.69	190.16	7,635.40	37	2,845.60	248.85	21.34	227.51	2,618.09
14	7,635.40	248.85	57.27	191.58	7,443.81	38	2,618.09	248.85	19.64	229.21	2,388.88
15	7,443.81	248.85	55.83	193.02	7,250.79	39	2,388.88	248.85	17.92	230.93	2,157.94
16	7,250.79	248.85	54.38	194.47	7,056.32	40	2,157.94	248.85	16.18	232.67	1,925.28
17	7,056.32	248.85	52.92	195.93	6,860.40	41	1,925.28	248.85	14.44	234.41	1,690.87
18	6,860.40	248.85	51.45	197.40	6,663.00	42	1,690.87	248.85	12.68	236.17	1,454.70
19	6,663.00	248.85	49.97	198.88	6,464.12	43	1,454.70	248.85	10.91	237.94	1,216.76
20	6,464.12	248.85	48.48	200.37	6,263.75	44	1,216.76	248.85	9.13	239.72	977.04
21	6,263.75	248.85	46.98	201.87	6,061.88	45	977.04	248.85	7.33	241.52	735.51
22	6,061.88	248.85	45.46	203.39	5,858.49	46	735.51	248.85	5.52	243.33	492.18
23	5,858.49	248.85	43.94	204.91	5,653.58	47	492.18	248.85	3.69	245.16	247.02
24	5,653.58	248.85	42.40	206.45	5,447.13	48	247.02	248.87	1.85	247.02	0.00

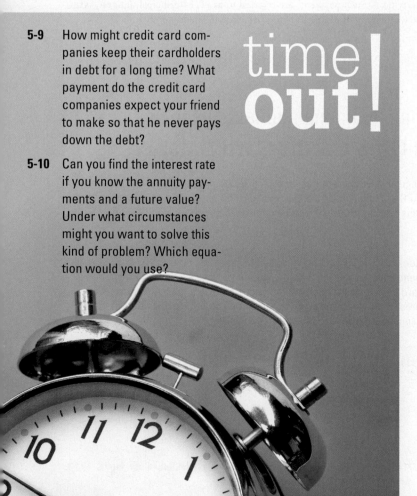

5-9 How might credit card companies keep their cardholders in debt for a long time? What payment do the credit card companies expect your friend to make so that he never pays down the debt?

5-10 Can you find the interest rate if you know the annuity payments and a future value? Under what circumstances might you want to solve this kind of problem? Which equation would you use?

loan's principal balance at the beginning of the month. This is the same as the balance at the end of the previous month (except for the very first payment). Then we compute the interest owed on that balance for the month. After paying that interest, what's left of the monthly payment reduces the loan balance for the next month. Because of these repetitive computations, spreadsheets make amortization schedules easy to construct.

Compute the Time Period You might well also find it useful to know how long it will take to pay off a loan with specific annuity payments. To find the number of periods, you can solve equation 5-9 for N—the number of payments—but the equation becomes quite complicated.[6] Many people just use a financial calculator or spreadsheet. We can check to see if the $248.85 monthly payment would indeed pay off the $10,000, 9 percent, car loan in four years. Finding the solution with a financial calculator entails entering I = 0.75, PV = 10000, PMT = −248.85, and FV = 0. The answer is 48 months. ■

[6]The equation for solving for the number of periods in an annuity is

$$N = \frac{\ln\left(\frac{PMT}{(PMT - PVA_N \times i)}\right)}{\ln(1 + i)}$$

Get Online

mhhe.com/canM

for study materials including
quizzes, iPod downloads,
and video

Your Turn...

Questions

1. How can you add a cash flow in year 2 and a cash flow in year 4 in year 7? *(LG1)*

2. People can become millionaires in their retirement years quite easily if they start saving early in employer 401(k) or 403(b) programs (or even if their employers don't offer such programs). Demonstrate the growth of a $250 monthly contribution for 40 years earning 9 percent APR. *(LG2)*

3. When you discount multiple cash flows, how does the future period that a cash flow is paid affect its present value and its contribution to the value of all the cash flows? *(LG3)*

4. How can you use the present value of an annuity concept to determine the price of a house you can afford? *(LG4)*

5. Since perpetuity payments continue forever, how can a present value be computed? Why isn't the present value infinite? *(LG5)*

6. Explain why you use the same adjustment factor, $(1 + i)$, when you adjust annuity due payments for both future value and present value. *(LG6)*

7. Use the idea of compound interest to explain why EAR is larger than APR. *(LG7)*

8. Would you rather pay $10,000 for a 5-year, $2,500 annuity or a 10-year, $1,250 annuity? Why? *(LG8)*

9. The interest on your home mortgage is tax deductible. Why are the early years of the mortgage more helpful in reducing taxes than in the later years? *(LG9)*

10. How can you use the concepts illustrated in computing the number of payments in an annuity to figure how to pay off a credit card balance? How does the magnitude of the payment impact the number of months? *(LG10)*

Problems

5-1   **Future Value** Compute the future value in year 8 of a $1,000 deposit in year 1 and another $1,500 deposit at the end of year 3 using a 10 percent interest rate. *(LG1)*

5-2   **Future Value** Compute the future value in year 7 of a $2,000 deposit in year 1 and another $2,500 deposit at the end of year 4 using an 8 percent interest rate. *(LG1)*

5-3   **Future Value of an Annuity** What is the future value of a $500 annuity payment over five years if interest rates are 9 percent? *(LG2)*

5-4   **Future Value of an Annuity** What is the future value of a $700 annuity payment over four years if interest rates are 10 percent? *(LG2)*

5-5   **Present Value** Compute the present value of a $1,000 deposit in year 1 and another $1,500 deposit at the end of year 3 if interest rates are 10 percent. *(LG3)*

5-6   **Present Value** Compute the present value of a $2,000 deposit in year 1 and another $2,500 deposit at the end of year 4 using an 8 percent interest rate. *(LG3)*

5-7   **Present Value of an Annuity** What's the present value of a $500 annuity payment over five years if interest rates are 9 percent? *(LG4)*

5-8   **Present Value of an Annuity** What's the present value of a $700 annuity payment over four years if interest rates are 10 percent? *(LG4)*

5-9   **Present Value of a Perpetuity** What's the present value, when interest rates are 7.5 percent, of a $50 payment made every year forever? *(LG5)*

5-10   **Present Value of a Perpetuity** What's the present value, when interest rates are 8.5 percent, of a $75 payment made every year forever? *(LG5)*

5-11   **Present Value of an Annuity Due** If the present value of an ordinary, seven-year annuity is $6,500 and interest rates are 8.5 percent, what's the present value of the same annuity due? *(LG6)*

5-12   **Present Value of an Annuity Due** If the present value of an ordinary, six-year annuity is $8,500 and interest rates are 9.5 percent, what's the present value of the same annuity due? *(LG6)*

5-13   **Future Value of an Annuity Due** If the future value of an ordinary, seven-year annuity is $6,500 and interest rates are 8.5 percent, what is the future value of the same annuity due? *(LG6)*

5-14   **Future Value of an Annuity Due** If the future value of an ordinary six-year annuity is $8,500 and interest rates are 9.5 percent, what's the future value of the same annuity due? *(LG6)*

5-15   **Effective Annual Rate** A loan is offered with monthly payments and an 11 percent APR. What's the loan's effective annual rate (EAR)? *(LG7)*

5-16   **Effective Annual Rate** A loan is offered with monthly payments and a 12 percent APR. What's the loan's effective annual rate (EAR)? *(LG7)*

5-17   **Future Value** Given a 6 percent interest rate, compute the year 6 future value of deposits made in years 1, 2, 3, and 4 of $1,000, $1,200, $1,200, and $1,500. *(LG1)*

5-18   **Future Value** Given a 7 percent interest rate, compute the year 6 future value of deposits made in years 1, 2, 3, and 4 of $1,000, $1,300, $1,300, and $1,400. *(LG1)*

5-19   **Future Value of Multiple Annuities** Assume that you contribute $200 per month to a retirement plan for 20 years. Then you are able to increase the contribution to $400 per month for another 20 years. Given a 7 percent interest rate, what is the value of your retirement plan after the 40 years? *(LG2)*

5-20 Future Value of Multiple Annuities Assume that you contribute $150 per month to a retirement plan for 15 years. Then you are able to increase the contribution to $350 per month for the next 25 years. Given an 8 percent interest rate, what is the value of your retirement plan after the 40 years? *(LG2)*

5-21 Present Value Given a 6 percent interest rate, compute the present value of payments made in years 1, 2, 3, and 4 of $1,000, $1,200, $1,200, and $1,500. *(LG3)*

5-22 Present Value Given a 7 percent interest rate, compute the present value of payments made in years 1, 2, 3, and 4 of $1,000, $1,300, $1,300, and $1,400. *(LG3)*

5-23 Present Value of Multiple Annuities A small business owner visits her bank to ask for a loan. The owner states that she can repay a loan at $1,000 per month for the next three years and then $2,000 per month for two years after that. If the bank is charging customers 7.5 percent APR, how much would it be willing to lend the business owner? *(LG2)*

5-24 Present Value of Multiple Annuities A small business owner visits his bank to ask for a loan. The owner states that he can repay a loan at $1,500 per month for the next three years and then $500 per month for two years after that. If the bank is charging customers 8.5 percent APR, how much would it be willing to lend the business owner? *(LG2)*

5-25 Present Value of a Perpetuity A perpetuity pays $100 per year and interest rates are 7.5 percent. How much would its value change if interest rates increased to 8.5 percent? Did the value increase or decrease? *(LG5)*

5-26 Present Value of a Perpetuity A perpetuity pays $50 per year and interest rates are 9 percent. How much would its value change if interest rates decreased to 8 percent? Did the value increase or decrease? *(LG5)*

5-27 Future and Present Value of an Annuity Due If you start making $50 monthly contributions today and continue them for five years, what's their future value if the compounding rate is 10 percent APR? What is the present value of this annuity? *(LG6)*

5-28 Future and Present Value of an Annuity Due If you start making $75 monthly contributions today and continue them for four years, what is their future value if the compounding rate is 12 percent APR? What is the present value of this annuity? *(LG6)*

5-29 Compound Frequency Payday loans are very short-term loans that charge very high interest rates. You can borrow $250 today and repay $300 in two weeks. What is the compounded *annual* rate implied by this 20 percent rate charged for only two weeks? *(LG7)*

5-30 Compound Frequency Payday loans are very short-term loans that charge very high interest rates. You can borrow $500 today and repay $575 in two weeks. What is the compounded *annual* rate implied by this 15 percent rate charged for only two weeks? *(LG7)*

5-31 Annuity Interest Rate What's the interest rate of a five-year, annual $5,000 annuity with present value of $20,000? *(LG8)*

5-32 Annuity Interest Rate What's the interest rate of a seven-year, annual $4,000 annuity with present value of $20,000? *(LG8)*

5-33 Annuity Interest Rate What annual interest rate would you need to earn if you wanted a $1,000 per month contribution to grow to $75,000 in five years?

5-34 Annuity Interest Rate What annual interest rate would you need to earn if you wanted a $500 per month contribution to grow to $45,000 in six years? *(LG8)*

5-35 Loan Payments You wish to buy a $25,000 car. The dealer offers you a four-year loan with a 10 percent APR. What are the monthly payments? How would the payment differ if you paid interest only? What would the consequences of such a decision be? *(LG9)*

5-36 Loan Payments You wish to buy a $10,000 dining room set. The furniture store offers you a three-year loan with an 11 percent APR. What are the monthly payments? How would the payment differ if you paid interest only? What would the consequences of such a decision be?

5-37 **Number of Annuity Payments** Joey realizes that he has charged too much on his credit card and has racked up $5,000 in debt. If he can pay $150 each month and the card charges 17 percent APR (compounded monthly), how long will it take him to pay off the debt? *(LG9)*

5-38 **Number of Annuity Payments** Phoebe realizes that she has charged too much on her credit card and has racked up $6,000 in debt. If she can pay $200 each month and the card charges 18 percent APR (compounded monthly), how long will it take her to pay off the debt? *(LG10)*

ADVANCED PROBLEMS

5-39 **Future Value** Given an 8 percent interest rate, compute the year 7 future value if deposits of $1,000 and $2,000 are made in years 1 and 3, respectively, and a withdrawal of $500 is made in year 4. *(LG1)*

5-40 **Future Value** Given a 9 percent interest rate, compute the year 6 future value if deposits of $1,500 and $2,500 are made in years 2 and 3, respectively, and a withdrawal of $700 is made in year 5. *(LG1)*

5-41 **Low Financing or Cash Back?** A car company is offering a choice of deals. You can receive $500 cash back on the purchase, or a 3 percent APR, four-year loan. The price of the car is $15,000 and you could obtain a four-year loan from your credit union, at 7 percent APR. Which deal is cheaper? *(LG4, LG9)*

5-42 **Low Financing or Cash Back?** A car company is offering a choice of deals. You can receive $1,000 cash back on the purchase, or a 2 percent APR, five-year loan. The price of the car is $20,000 and you could obtain a five-year loan from your credit union at 7 percent APR. Which deal is cheaper? *(LG4, LG9)*

5-43 **Amortization Schedule** Create the amortization schedule for a loan of $15,000, paid monthly over three years using a 9 percent APR. *(LG9)*

5-44 **Amortization Schedule** Create the amortization schedule for a loan of $5,000, paid monthly over two years using an 8 percent APR. *(LG9)*

5-45 **Investing for Retirement** Monica has decided that she wants to build enough retirement wealth that, if invested at 8 percent per year, it will provide her with $3,500 of monthly income for 30 years. To date, she has saved nothing, but she still has 25 years until she retires. How much money does she need to contribute per month to reach her goal? *(LG4, LG9)*

5-46 **Investing for Retirement** Ross has decided that he wants to build enough retirement wealth that, if invested at 7 percent per year it will provide him with $4,000 of monthly income for 30 years. To date, he has saved nothing, but he still has 20 years until he retires. How much money does he need to contribute per month to reach his goal? *(LG4, LG9)*

5-47 **Loan Balance** Rachel purchased a $15,000 car two years ago using an 8 percent, four-year loan. She has decided that she would sell the car now, if she could get a price that would pay off the balance of her loan. What is the minimum price Rachel would need to receive for her car? *(LG9)*

5-48 **Loan Balance** Hank purchased a $20,000 car two years ago using a 9 percent, five-year loan. He has decided that he would sell the car now, if he could get a price that would pay off the balance of his loan. What's the minimum price Hank would need to receive for his car? *(LG9)*

5-49 **Teaser Rate Mortgage** A mortgage broker is offering a $183,900 30-year mortgage with a teaser rate. In the first two years of the mortgage, the borrower makes monthly payments on only a 4 percent APR interest rate. After the second year, the mortgage interest rate charged increases to 7 percent APR. What are the monthly payments in the first two years? What are the monthly payments after the second year? *(LG9)*

5-50 Teaser Rate Mortgage A mortgage broker is offering a $279,000 30-year mortgage with a teaser rate. In the first two years of the mortgage, the borrower makes monthly payments on only a 4.5 percent APR interest rate. After the second year, the mortgage interest rate charged increases to 7.5 percent APR. What are the monthly payments in the first two years? What are the monthly payments after the second year? *(LG9)*

5-51 Excel Problem Consider a person who begins contributing to a retirement plan at age 25 and contributes for 40 years until retirement at age 65. For the first 10 years, she contributes $3,000 per year. She increases the contribution rate to $5,000 per year in years 11 through 20. This is followed by increases to $10,000 per year in years 21 through 31 and to $15,000 per year for the last 10 years. This money earns a 9 percent return. First compute the value of the retirement plan when she turns age 65. Then compute the annual payment she would receive over the next 40 years if the wealth was converted to an annuity payment at 8 percent. *(LG2, LG9)*

Combined Chapter 4 and Chapter 5 Problems

4&5-1 Future Value Consider that you are 35 years old and have just changed to a new job. You have $80,000 in the retirement plan from your former employer. You can roll that money into the retirement plan of the new employer. You will also contribute $5,000 each year into your new employer's plan. If the rolled-over money and the new contributions both earn a 7 percent return, how much should you expect to have when you retire in 30 years?

4&5-2 Future Value Consider that you are 45 years old and have just changed to a new job. You have $150,000 in the retirement plan from your former employer. You can roll that money into the retirement plan of the new employer. You will also contribute $8,000 each year into your new employer's plan. If the rolled-over money and the new contributions both earn an 8 percent return, how much should you expect to have when you retire in 20 years?

4&5-3 Future Value and Number of Annuity Payments Your client has been given a trust fund valued at $1 million. He cannot access the money until he turns 65 years old, which is in 25 years. At that time, he can withdraw $25,000 per month. If the trust fund is invested at a 5.5 percent rate, how many months will it last your client once he starts to withdraw the money?

4&5-4 Future Value and Number of Annuity Payments Your client has been given a trust fund valued at $1.5 million. She cannot access the money until she turns 65 years old, which is in 15 years. At that time, she can withdraw $20,000 per month. If the trust fund is invested at a 5 percent rate, how many months will it last your client once she starts to withdraw the money?

4&5-5 Present Value and Annuity Payments A local furniture store is advertising a deal in which you buy a $3,000 dining room set and do not need to pay for two years (no interest cost is incurred). How much money would you have to deposit now in a savings account earning 5 percent APR, compounded monthly, to pay the $3,000 bill in two years? Alternatively, how much would you have to deposit in the savings account each month to be able to pay the bill?

4&5-6 Present Value and Annuity Payments A local furniture store is advertising a deal in which you buy a $5,000 living room set with three years before you need to make any payments (no interest cost is incurred). How much money would you have to deposit now in a savings account earning 4 percent APR, compounded monthly, to pay the $5,000 bill in three years? Alternatively, how much would you have to deposit in the savings account each month to be able to pay the bill?

4&5-7 House Appreciation and Mortgage Payments Say that you purchase a house for $200,000 by getting a mortgage for $180,000 and paying a $20,000 down payment. If you get a 30-year mortgage with a 7 percent interest rate, what are the monthly payments?

What would the loan balance be in 10 years? If the house appreciates at 3 percent per year, what will be the value of the house in 10 years? How much of this value is your equity?

4&5-8   House Appreciation and Mortgage Payments Say that you purchase a house for $150,000 by getting a mortgage for $135,000 and paying a $15,000 down payment. If you get a 15-year mortgage with a 7 percent interest rate, what are the monthly payments? What would the loan balance be in five years? If the house appreciates at 4 percent per year, what will be the value of the house in five years? How much of this value is your equity?

4&5-9   Construction Loan You have secured a loan from your bank for two years to build your home. The terms of the loan are that you will borrow $100,000 now and an additional $100,000 in one year. Interest of 10 percent APR will be charged on the balance monthly. Since no payments will be made during the two-year loan, the balance will grow at the 10 percent compounded rate. At the end of the two years, the balance will be converted to a traditional 30-year mortgage at a 6 percent interest rate. What will you be paying as monthly mortgage payments (principal and interest only)?

4&5-10   Construction Loan You have secured a loan from your bank for two years to build your home. The terms of the loan are that you will barrow $100,000 now and an additional $50,000 in one year. Interest of 9 percent APR will be charged on the balance monthly. Since no payments will be made during the two-year loan, the balance will grow. At the end of the two years, the balance will be converted to a traditional 30-year mortgage at a 7 percent interest rate. What will you pay as monthly mortgage payments (principal and interest only)?

valuing
bonds

How important are bonds and the bond market to a capitalist economy? Those unfamiliar with the financial markets may have the impression that the stock market dominates capital markets in the United States and in other countries. Stock market performance appears constantly on 24-hour TV news channels and on the evening news. By contrast, we seldom hear any mention of the bond market. While bonds may not generate the same excitement that stocks do, they are an even more important capital source for companies, governments, and other organizations. The bond market is actually larger than the stock market. In late 2007, the U.S. bond market represented roughly $29.2 trillion in outstanding debt obligations. At the same time, the market value of all common stock issues was worth about half the value of the bond market, at roughly $14.2 trillion.

continued on p. 124

LEARNING GOALS

LG1 Describe bond characteristics.

LG2 Identify various bond issuers and their motivation for issuing debt.

LG3 Read and interpret bond quotes.

LG4 Compute bond prices using present value concepts.

LG5 Explain the relationship between bond prices and interest rates.

LG6 Compute bond yields.

LG7 Find bond ratings and assess credit risk's effects on bond yields.

LG8 Assess bond market performance.

continued from p. 123

Bonds also trade in great volume and frequency. In 2007, the total average daily trading in all types of U.S. bonds reached over $970 billion. Investors are often attracted to the stock market because it offers the potential for high investor returns—but great risks come with that high potential return. While some bonds offer more safe and stable returns than stocks, other bonds also offer high potential rewards and, consequently, higher risk. ■

In this chapter, we will explore bond characteristics and their price dynamics. You will see that bond pricing uses many time value of money principles that we've used in the preceding chapters.

viewpoints

business APPLICATION

You are the chief financial officer (CFO) for Beach Sand Resorts. The firm needs $150 million of new capital to renovate a hotel property. As you discuss the firm's plans with a credit rating agency, you learn that if 15-year bonds are used to raise this capital, the bonds will be rated BB and will have to offer a 7 percent return. How many bonds will you have to issue to raise the necessary capital? What semiannual interest payments will Beach Sand have to make?

BOND MARKET OVERVIEW

Bond Characteristics

Bonds are debt obligation securities that corporations, the federal government or its agencies, or states and local governments issue to fund various projects or operations. All of these organizations periodically need to raise capital for various reasons, which we formally discuss in Chapter 8. Bonds are also known as **fixed-income securities** because bondholders (investors) know both how much they will receive in interest payments and when their principal will be returned. From the bond issuer's point of view, the bond is a loan that requires regular interest payments and an eventual repayment of the borrowed **principal.** Investors—often pension funds, banks, and mutual funds—buy bonds to earn investment returns. Most bonds follow a relatively standard structure. A legal contract called the **indenture agreement** outlines the precise terms between the issuer and the bondholders. Any bond's main characteristics include:

- The date the principal will be repaid (the **maturity date**).

- The **par value** or face value of each bond, which is the principal loan amount that the borrower must repay.

- The interest rate.

- A description of any property to be pledged as collateral.

- Steps that the bondholder can take in the event that the issuer fails to pay the interest or principal.

Table 6.1 describes par value and other bond characteristics. Most bonds have a par value of $1,000. This is the amount of principal the issuer has promised to repay. Bonds have fixed lives. The bond's life ends when the issuer repays the par value to the buyer on the bond's maturity date. Although a bond will mature on a specific calendar date, the bond is usually referenced by its **time to maturity,** that is, 2 years, 5 years, 20 years, and so on. In fact, the market groups bonds together by their time to maturity and classifies them as short-term bonds, medium-term bonds, or long-term bonds, regardless of issuer. Long-term bonds carry 20 or 30 years to maturity. Of course, over time, the 30-year bond becomes a 20-year bond, 10-year bond, and eventually matures. But other time-periods-to-maturity bonds do exist. For example, Ford Motor issued bonds with 100 years to maturity on May 15, 1997. The bonds have a coupon (interest) rate of 7.70 percent and mature in 2097.

▼ **TABLE 6.1** Typical Bond Features

Characteristic	Description	Common Values
Par value	The amount of the loan to be repaid. This is often referred to as the *principal* of the bond.	$1,000
Time to maturity	The number of years left until the maturity date.	1 year to 30 years
Call	The opportunity for the issuer to repay the principal before the maturity date, usually because interest rates have fallen or issuer's circumstances have changed. When calling a bond, the issuer commonly pays the principal and one year of interest payments.	Many bonds are not callable. For those that are, a common feature is that the bond can be called any time after 10 years of issuance.
Coupon rate	The interest rate used to compute the bond's interest payment each year. Listed as a percentage of par value, the actual payments usually arrive twice per year.	2 to 10 percent
Bond price	The bond's market price reported as a percentage of par value.	80 to 120 percent of par value

personal APPLICATION

You would like to invest in bonds. Your broker suggests two different bonds. The first bond, issued by Liberty Media, will mature in 2013. Its price is quoted at 96.21 and it pays a 5.7 percent coupon. The second bond suggested, issued by Alcoa, Inc., also matures in 2013. This bond's price is 101.94 and pays a 5.375 percent coupon. To help you decide between the bonds bought in 2007, you want to know how much money it will cost to buy 10 bonds, what interest payments you will receive, and what return the bonds offer. Also, you want to understand the differences between what the two bonds imply about their risk.

When interest rates economywide fall several percentage points (which often takes several years), homeowners everywhere seek to refinance their home mortgages. They want to make lower interest payments (and sometimes want to pay down their mortgage principal) every month. Corporations that have outstanding bond debt will also want to refinance those bonds. Sometimes the indenture contract allows companies to do so; sometimes the indenture prohibits refinancing. Bonds that can be refinanced have a **call** feature, which means that the issuer can "call" the bonds back and repay the principal before the maturity date. To compensate the bondholders for getting the bond called, the issuer pays the principal and a **call premium.** The most common call premium is one year's worth of interest payments. In some indentures, the call premium declines over time.

The bond's **coupon rate** determines the dollar amount of interest paid to bondholders. The coupon rate appears on the bond and is listed as a percentage of the par value. So a 5 percent coupon rate means that the issuer will pay 5 percent of $1,000, or $50, in interest every year, usually divided into two equal semiannual payments. So a 5 percent coupon bond will pay $25 every six months. The name *coupon* is a holdover from the past, when bonds were actually issued with a coupon book. Every six months a bondholder would tear out a coupon and mail it to the issuer, who would then make the interest payment. These are sometimes referred to as *bearer bonds* (often a feature of spy or mystery movies) because whoever held the coupon book could receive the payments. Nowadays, issuers register bond owners and automatically wire interest payments to the owner's bank or brokerage account. Nevertheless, the term *coupon* persists today.

At original issue, bonds typically sell at par value, unless interest rates are very volatile. Bondholders recoup the par value on the bond's maturity date. However, at all times in between these two dates, bonds might trade among investors in the secondary bond market. The **bond's price** as it trades in the secondary market will not likely be the par value. Bonds trade for higher and lower prices than their par values. We'll thoroughly demonstrate the reasons for bond pricing in a later section of this chapter. Bond prices are quoted in terms of percent of par value rather than in dollar terms. Sources of trading information list a bond that traded at $1,150 as 115, and a bond that traded for $870 as 87.

EXAMPLE 6-1

For interactive versions of this example visit www.mhhe.com/canM

Bond Characteristics

Consider a bond issued 10 years ago with an at-issue time to maturity of 30 years. The bond's coupon rate is 8 percent and it currently trades in the bond market for 109. Assuming a par value of $1,000, what is the bond's current time to maturity, semiannual interest payment, and bond price in dollars?

SOLUTION:

Time to maturity = 30 years − 10 years = 20 years

Annual payment = 8 percent × $1,000 = $80, so semiannual payment is $40

Bond price = 109 percent × $1,000 = $1,090

FIGURE 6.1 Amount of Capital Raised Yearly from Bonds Issued by Local and Federal Government and Corporations

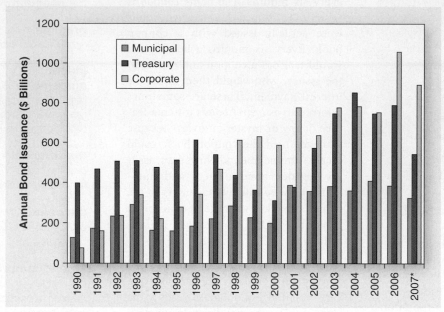

*Through September. *Data Source:* Securities Industry and Financial Markets Association.

Bond Issuers

For many years, bonds were considered stodgy, overly conservative investments. Not anymore! The fixed-income industry has seen tremendous innovation in the past couple of decades. The financial industry has created and issued many new types of bonds and fixed-income securities, some with odd-sounding acronyms, like TIGRs, CATS, COUGRs, and PINEs, all of which are securities based on U.S. Treasuries. Even with all the innovation, the traditional three main bond issuers remain:

to implement monetary policy. Technically, Treasury securities issued with 1 to 10 years until maturity are Treasury notes. Securities issued with 10 to 30 years until maturity are Treasury bonds. The figure shows that the number of new Treasuries being offered actually declined in the late 1990s as the federal budget deficit declined. However, this dramatically reversed in 2002 when the trend toward issuing more federal debt reversed.

Corporate Bonds Corporations raise capital to finance investments in inventory, plant and equipment, research and development, and general business expansion. As managers decide how to raise capital, corporations can issue debt, equity (stocks), or a mixture of both. The driving force behind a corporation's financing strategy is the desire to minimize its total capital costs. Through much of the 1990s, corporations tended to issue equity (stocks) to raise capital. Beginning in 1998 and into 2007, corporations switched to raising capital by issuing bonds to take advantage of low interest rates and issued $6.3 trillion in new bonds.

Municipal Bonds State and local governments borrow money to build, repair, or improve streets, highways, hospitals, schools, sewer systems, and so on. The interest and principal on these municipal bonds are repaid in two ways. Projects that benefit the entire community, such as courthouses, schools, and municipal office buildings, are typically funded by general obligation bonds and repaid using tax revenues. Projects that benefit only certain groups of people, such as toll roads and air-

> [Treasury securities issued with 1 to 10 years until maturity are Treasury notes. Securities issued with 10 to 30 years until maturity are Treasury bonds.]

U.S. treasury bonds, corporate bonds, and municipal bonds. Figure 6.1 shows the amount of money that these bond issuers have raised each year since 1990.

Treasury Bonds Treasury bonds carry the "full-faith-and-credit" backing of the U.S. government and investors have long considered them among the safest fixed-income investments in the world. The federal government sells Treasury securities through public auctions to finance the federal deficit. When the deficit is large, more bonds come to auction. In addition, the Federal Reserve System (the Fed) uses Treasury securities

ports, are typically funded by revenue bonds and repaid from user fees. Interest payments paid to municipal bondholders are not taxed at the federal level, or by the state for which the bond is issued.

Other Bonds and Bond-Based Securities

Treasury inflation-protected securities (TIPS) have proved one of the most successful recent innovations in the bond market. The U.S. Treasury began issuing this new type of Treasury bond, which is indexed to inflation, in 1997. TIPS have fixed coupon rates like traditional Treasuries. The new aspect is that the federal government adjusts the par value of the TIPS bond for inflation. Specifically, it increases at the rate of inflation (measured by the Consumer Price Index, CPI). As the bond's par value changes over time, interest payments also change. At maturity, investors receive an inflation-adjusted principal amount. If inflation has been high, investors will expect that the adjusted principal amount will be substantially higher than the original $1,000. Consider a new 10-year TIPS issued on January 15, 2005, that pays a 1 5/8 percent coupon. The reference CPI for these bonds is 190.94516. Three years later (on January 15, 2008) the reference CPI was 209.49645. So the par value of the TIPS in early 2008 was $1,097.16 (= $1,000 × 209.49645 ÷ 190.94516). Therefore, the 1 5/8 percent coupon

(paid semiannually) would be $8.91 (= 1 5/8% × $1, 097.16 ÷ 2). A TIPS' total return comes from both the interest payments and the inflation adjustment to the par value.

U.S. government agency securities are debt securities issued to provide low-cost financing for desirable private-sector activities such as home ownership, education, and farming. Fannie Mae, Freddie Mac, Student Loan Marketing Association (Sallie Mae), Federal Farm Credit System, Federal Home Loan Banks, and the Small Business Administration, among others, issue these **agency bonds** to support particular sectors of the economy. Agency securities do not carry the federal government's full-faith-and-credit guarantee, but the government

EXAMPLE 6-2

For interactive versions of this example visit www.mhhe.com/canM

TIPS Payments

A TIPS bond was issued on July 15, 2006, that pays a 2 ½ percent coupon. The reference CPI at issue was 201.95. The reference CPI for the following interest payments were:

January 2007	201.66
July 2007	207.26
January 2008	209.50

Given these numbers, what is the par value and interest payment of the TIPS at the three interest payments?

SOLUTION:

Compute the TIPS index ratio for each period as current CPI divided by the at-issue CPI: The par value for January 2007 is $1,000 × 201.66 ÷ 201.95 = $998.56, so the interest payment is 2 ½ percent × $998.56 ÷ 2 = $12.48. The answers for the next two dates are:

July 2007	par value = $1,026.29	interest payment = $12.83
January 2008	par value = $1,037.39	interest payment = $12.97

finance at work //:personal finance

Buy Treasuries Direct!

Treasury bonds are U.S. government-issued debt securities that investors trade on secondary markets. The government also issues nonmarketable debt, called "savings bonds," directly to investors. The common EE savings bonds, introduced in 1980, do not pay regular interest payments. Instead, interest accrues and adds to the bond's value. After a one-year holding period, they can be redeemed at almost any bank or credit union. You can now purchase savings bonds and other Treasury securities (bills, notes, bonds, and TIPS) electronically through the U.S. Treasury's Web site, TreasuryDirect. You can set up an account in minutes and buy savings bonds with cash from your bank account. You can also redeem your bonds and transfer the proceeds back to your bank account. Bonds can be purchased 24 hours a day, 7 days a week at no cost.

When bondholders redeem savings bonds, they receive the original value paid plus the accrued interest. Paper bonds sell at half of the face value; if investors hold them for the full 30 years, they receive the par value. Investors buy electronic bonds at face value and earn interest in addition to the par value. Unlike with other bonds, savers need not report income from these interest payments to the IRS until they actually redeem the bonds. So savings bonds count as tax-deferred investments.

About one in six Americans owns savings bonds. Savings bonds are used for a variety of purposes, such as personal savings instruments or gifts from grandparents to grandchildren. After the September 11, 2001, terrorist attacks, many Americans wanted to show support for the government. In December 2001, banks selling government EE savings bonds began printing "Patriot bond" on them. So EE savings bonds are now often called Patriot Bonds.

Want to know more?

Key Words to Search for Updates: **See the TreasuryDirect Web site (www.treasurydirect.gov).**

---

has never let one of its agencies fail. Because investors believe that the federal government will continue in this watchdog role, agency bonds are thought to be very safe and may provide a slightly higher return than Treasury securities do.

U.S. government agencies invented one popular type of debt security: **mortgage-backed securities** (MBS). Fannie Mae and Freddie Mac offer subsidies or mortgage guarantees for people who wouldn't otherwise qualify for mortgages, especially first-time homeowners. Fannie Mae started out as a government-owned enterprise in 1938 and became a publicly held corporation in 1968. Freddie Mac was chartered as a publicly held corporation at its inception in 1970. To increase the amount of money available (liquidity) for the home mortgage market, Fannie Mae and Freddie Mac purchase home mortgages from banks, credit unions, and other lenders. They combine the mortgages into diversified portfolios of such loans and then issue mortgage-backed securities (MBS), which represent a share in the mortgage debt, to investors. As homeowners pay off or refinance the underlying portfolio of mortgage loans, MBS investors receive interest and principal payments. After selling mortgages to Fannie Mae or Freddie Mac, mortgage lenders have "new" cash to provide more mortgage loans.

We could apply the same concept to any type of loans; indeed, the financial markets have already invented many such pooled-debt securities. Typical examples include credit card debt, auto loans, home equity loans, and equipment leases. Like mortgage-backed securities, investors receive interest and principal from **asset-backed securities** as borrowers pay off their consumer loans. The asset-backed securities market is one of the fastest-growing areas in the financial services sector.

Reading Bond Quotes

To those familiar with bond terminology, bond quotes provide all of the information needed to make informed investment decisions. The volume of Treasury securities traded each day is substantial. Treasury bonds and notes average more than a half billion dollars in trading daily. Investors exhibit much less enthusiasm for corporate or municipal bonds, perhaps because the markets for each particular bond or bonds with the same maturity, coupon rate, and credit ratings are much thinner and, therefore, less liquid. Most bond quote tables report only a small fraction of the outstanding bonds on any given day. Bond quotes can be found in *The Wall Street Journal* and online at places like Yahoo! Finance (**yahoo.finance.com**) and BondsOnline (**www.bonds-online.com**). Table 6.2 shows three bond quote examples.

▼ TABLE 6.2 Bond Quote Examples

Treasury Securities Maturity Rate	Mo/Yr	Bid	Asked	Chg	Ask Yld
6.500	Feb 10n	105:19	105:20	−9	4.57

Corporate Bond Company	Coupon	Last Maturity	Last Price	Yield	
Southwest Airlines Co.	5.570	Dec 15, 2016	97.876	6.036	

Municipal Bond Issue	Coupon	Maturity	Price	Chg	Bid Yld
NYC Muni Wtr Fin Auth	4.500	06-15-37	100.046	−.538	4.49

mortgage-backed securities Debt securities whose interest and par value payments originate from real estate mortgage payments.

asset-backed securities Debt securities whose payments originate from other loans, such as credit car debt, auto loans, and home equity loans.

premium bond A bond selling for greater than its par value.

discount bond A bond selling for lower than its par value.

A typical listing for Treasury bonds appears first. Here, this Treasury bond pays bondholders a coupon of 6.500 percent. On a $1,000 par value bond, this interest income would be $65 annually, paid as $32.50 every six months per bond. The bond will mature in February of 2010—since this is fairly soon, the bond is considered a short-term bond. The "n" in the quote indicates that this bond was originally issued as a note (1–10 years maturity). Both the bid and the ask quotes for the bond appear, expressed as percentages of the bond's par value of $1,000. The bid price is the price at which investors can sell the bond. Numbers after the colon represent 32nds of 1 percent. A bid of 105:19 means that a buyer paid $1,055.94 (= $1,000 × 105 19/32%). Investors can buy this bond at the ask price of 105:20, or $1,056.25. Since the price is higher than the par value of the bond, the bond is selling at a premium to par because its coupon rate is higher than current rates. Thus, investors call this kind of security a **premium bond.**

Notice that the ask price is higher than the bid price. The difference is known as the bid-ask spread. Investors buy at the higher price and sell at the lower price. The bid-ask spread is thus the cost of actively trading bonds. Investors buy and sell with a bond dealer. Since the bond dealer takes the opposite side of the transaction, the dealer buys at the low price and sells at the higher price. The bid-ask spread is part of the dealer's compensation for taking on risk. An investor who bought this bond and held it to maturity would experience a $56.25 capital loss (slightly more than −5.3 percent [= −$56.25/$1,056.25]). The bond lost −9/32 percent of its value during the day's trading—a change of $2.81 for a $1,000 par value bond. Last, the bond is offering investors who purchase it at the ask price and hold it to maturity a 4.57 percent annual return.

Corporate bond quotes provide similar information. The table shows the quote for a Southwest Airlines Co., bond, which offers bondholders a coupon of 5.570 percent, or $27.85 semiannually (= $1,000 × 5.57% ÷ 2). The bond would be considered a mid-term bond (usually 10–20 years to maturity), since it matures in the year 2016. Corporate bonds are also quoted in percentage of par value, but (thankfully) the 32nds convention is not used. The price quote of 97.876 indicates that the last trade occurred at a price of $978.76 per bond. Since the bond is selling for a price lower than its $1,000 par value, it's called a **discount bond.** An investor who bought this bond would reap a $21.24 capital gain if the bond were held to maturity. The Southwest bond represents an annual return of 6.036 percent for the investor who purchases the bond at $978.76. Notice that this corporate bond offers a higher return than does the Treasury bond's 4.57 percent return. This price relationship is no coincidence; it is consistent with financial theory. Southwest Airlines doesn't enjoy the luxury of virtually unlimited resources as the U.S. government does. The company therefore is more likely to have difficulty paying back its debt than the U.S. government would have in repaying its bond. Since the Southwest bond represents a riskier investment, it should offer investors a higher rate of return.

Companies set a bond's coupon rate when they originally issue the bond. A number of factors determine that coupon rate:

- The amount of uncertainty about whether the company will be able to make all the payments.

- The term of the loan.

- The level of interest rates in the overall economy at the time.

Bonds from different companies carry different coupon rates because some, or all, of these determining factors differ. Even a single company that has raised capital through bond issues many times may carry very different coupon rates on its various issues, because the bond issues would be offered in different years when the overall economic condition and interest rates differ.

Table 6.2 also shows a quote for a municipal bond issued by the New York City Municipal Water Finance Authority. This city government agency has raised capital by issuing municipal bonds to build reservoir facilities to provide water to New York City. The bond pays a 4.500 percent coupon, and since it matures in 2037, it's considered a long-term bond. According to Table 6.2, the bond is trading at a price close to par value—100.046 percent. Most municipal bonds, unlike other bonds, feature a $5,000 face value rather than the typical par value of $1,000. So, the 100.046 percent price quote represents a dollar amount of $5,002.30 (= 100.046% × $5,000). The low rate of return relative to Treasury bonds with similar maturities also has an explanation. Municipal bondholders do not have to pay federal income taxes on the interest payments that they receive from those securities. We explore this (sometimes) substantial advantage further in a later section of this chapter.

Investors are willing to pay a premium for bonds with rates higher than the market rate.

The Kohl's corporate bond shown in Example 6-3 pays a semi-annual interest payment of $36.88 (= 7.375% × $1,000 ÷ 2) and its price is $1,100.10 (= 110.01% × $1,000). This premium bond's 7.375 percent rate is likely well above market rates, which is why an investor would be willing to pay a premium for it.

The state of Florida issued the muni bond to fund bridge construction. With a $5,000 par value, the interest payments are $125 (= 5.0% × $5,000 ÷ 2) every six months. The bonds are priced at $5,339.00 (= 106.78% × $5,000).

EXAMPLE 6-3

For interactive versions of this example visit www.mhhe.com/canM

Bond Quotes

You note the following bond quotes and wish to determine each bond's price, term, and interest payments.

Treasury Securities Maturity Rate	Mo/Yr	Bid	Asked	Chg	Ask Yld
9.00	Nov 18	137:19	137:20	25	4.80

Corporate Bond Company	Coupon	Maturity	Last Price	Last Yield	
Kohl's	7.375	Oct 15, 2011	110.01	4.991	

Municipal Bond Issue	Coupon	Maturity	Price	Yld to Mat	
Florida St Aquis & Bridge Constr	5.00	July 1, 2025	106.78	4.458	

SOLUTION:

The Treasury bond matures in November of 2018 and pays 9 percent interest. Investors receive cash interest payments of $45 (= 9% × $1,000 ÷ 2) semiannually. Since the bond matures in less than 10 years but more than 1 year, we would consider it a mid-term bond. Since no "n" appears next to the maturity date, we can also tell that the security was issued as a bond that would mature in 30 years. Investors could sell this bond for $1,375.94 (= 137 19/32% × $1,000) and buy it for $1,376.25 (= 137 20/32% × $1,000). The price fell on this particular day by $1.56 (= −5/32% × $1,000). The dealer earned 31 cents on each trade of these premium bonds.

zero coupon bond A bond that does not make interest payments but generally sells at a deep discount and then pays the par value at the maturity date.

We compute the zero's price by finding the present value of the $1,000 cash flow received in 20 years. However, to be consistent with regular coupon-paying bonds, zero coupon bonds are priced using semiannual compounding. So the formula and calculator valuation would use 40 semiannual periods at a 3 percent interest rate rather than 20 periods at 6 percent. Using the present value equation of Chapter 4 results in

$$PV = \frac{FV_N}{(1 + i)^N} = \frac{\$1,000}{1.03^{40}} = \frac{\$1,000}{3.262} = \$306.56$$

So the zero coupon bond's price is indeed a steep discount to its par value. This makes sense because investors would only buy a security that pays $1,000 in many years for a price that is much lower to make enough profit to make up for the forgone semiannual interest payments. For comparison sake, instead of the 20-year zero, consider a 20-year bond with a 7 percent coupon. So this 20-year maturity bond pays $35 in interest payments every six months. We can think of these interest payments as an annuity stream. If the market discount rate is 6 percent annually, the time line appears as

BOND VALUATION

Present Value of Bond Cash Flows

Any bond's value computation directly applies time value of money concepts. Bondholders know the interest payments that they are scheduled to receive and the repayment of the par value at maturity. The current price of a bond is, therefore, the *present value of these future cash flows discounted at the prevailing market interest rate.* The prevailing market interest rate will depend on the bond's term to maturity, credit quality, and tax status.

The simplest type of bond for time value of money calculations is a **zero coupon bond.** As you might guess from its name, a zero coupon bond makes no interest payments. Instead, the bond pays only the par value payment at its maturity date. So a zero-coupon bond sells at a substantial discount from its par value. For example, a bond with a par value of $1,000, maturing in 20 years, and priced to yield 6 percent might be purchased for about $306.56. At the end of 20 years, the bond investor will receive $1,000. The difference between $1,000 and $306.56 (which is $693.44) represents the interest income received over the 20 years based upon the discount rate of 6 percent. The time line for this zero coupon bond valuation appears as

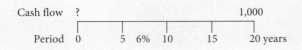

Cash flow	?				1,000
Period	0	5 6% 10	15	20 years	

```
Cash flow   ?   35  35  35  35  ...   35  35  35  35  1,000
Period      0   1   2   3   4   ...   37  38  39  40
                        3%                  semiannual periods
```

The time line shows the 40 semiannual payments (with the accompanying semiannual interest rate at 3%) of $35 and the par value payment at the bond's maturity. Think through this: When bonds pay semiannual payments, the discount rate must be a semiannual rate. Thus, the 6 percent annual rate becomes a 3 percent semiannual rate. So we then compute the price of this bond by adding the present value of the interest payment annuity cash flow to the present value of the future par value. A combination of the present value equations for the annuity cash flows and the value of the par redemption appear in the bond valuation equation 6-1:

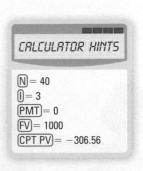

CALCULATOR HINTS

$N = 40$
$I = 3$
$PMT = 0$
$FV = 1000$
$CPT\ PV = -306.56$

$$\text{Present value} \atop \text{of bond} = \text{Present value of interest payments} \atop + \text{Present value of par value}$$

$$= PMT \times \left[\frac{1 - \dfrac{1}{(1 + i)^N}}{i} \right] + \frac{1,000}{(1 + i)^N} \quad (6\text{-}1)$$

EXAMPLE 6-4

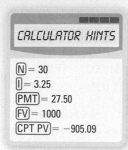

For interactive versions of this example visit www.mhhe.com/canM

Find the value of a bond

Consider a 15-year bond that has a 5.5 percent coupon, paid semiannually. If the current market interest rates is 6.5 percent, and the bond is priced at $940, should you buy this bond?

SOLUTION:

Compute the value of the bond using equation 6.1. Use semiannual compounding ($N = 2 \times 15 = 30$ and $I = 6.5 \div 2 = 3.25$, and $PMT = 5.5\% \times \$1,000 \div 2 = \$27.50$) as:

$$\text{Bond value} = \$27.50 \times \left[\frac{1 - \dfrac{1}{(1 + 0.0325)^{30}}}{0.0325} \right] + \frac{1,000}{(1 + 0.0325)^{30}} = \$522.00 + \$383.09 = \$905.09$$

So this bond's value is $905.09, which is less than the $940 price. The bond is overvalued in the market and you should not buy it.

CALCULATOR HINTS

N = 30
I = 3.25
PMT = 27.50
FV = 1000
$CPT\ PV$ = −905.09

---

where *PMT* is the interest payment, *N* is the number of periods until maturity, and *i* is the market interest rate per period on securities with the same bond characteristics. If this bond paid interest annually, then these variables would take yearly period values. Since this bond pays semiannually, *PMT*, *N*, and *i* are all denoted in semiannual periods. The price of this coupon bond should be

$$\text{Bond price} = \$35 \times \left[\frac{1 - \dfrac{1}{(1 + 0.03)^{40}}}{0.03} \right] + \frac{1,000}{(1 + 0.03)^{40}}$$

$$= \$809.017 + \$306.557 = \$1,115.57$$

Of the $1,115.57 bond price, most of the value comes from the semiannual $35 coupon payments ($809.017) and not the value from the future par value payment ($306.557).

Because equation 6-1 is quite complex, we usually compute bond prices using a financial calculator or computer program. An investor would compute the bond value using a financial calculator by entering $N = 40$, $I = 3$, PMT = 35, FV = 1,000, and computing the present value (PV). The calculator solution is $1,115.57.[1]

[1]In order to focus on the valuation concepts, we present these examples with the full six months until the bond's next interest payment. However, bonds can be sold anytime between interest payments. When this occurs, we simply add the interest accrued since the last payment to the price.

the
Math Coach on...
Bond Pricing and Periods

" Since most bonds have semiannual interest payments, we must use semiannual periods to discount the cash flows. Most errors in computing a bond price occur in the adjustment for semiannual periods. The errors happen whether you are using either the bond pricing equation or a financial calculator. To convert to semiannual periods, be sure to adjust the three variables: number of periods, interest rate, and payments.

The number of years needs to be multiplied by 2 for the number of semiannual periods. The interest rate should be divided by 2 for a six-month rate. Divide the annual coupon payment. Remember to adjust all three inputs for the semiannual periods.

A coupon paying bond's price should hover reasonably around the par value of the bond. For a $1,000 par value bond, we could expect a price in the range of $700 to $1,300. If you compute a price outside this range, check to see whether you made the semiannual period adjustments correctly. "

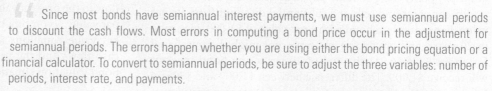

Bond Prices and Interest Rate Risk

At the time of purchase, the bond's interest payments and par value expected at maturity are fixed and known. Over time, economy-wide interest rates change, but the bond's coupon rate remains fixed. A rise in prevailing interest rates (also called *increasing the discount rate*) reduces all bonds' values. If interest rates fall, all bonds will enjoy rising values. Consider that when interest rates rise, newly issued bonds

Figure 6.2 demonstrates how the price of a 30-year Treasury bond may change over time. The 7.8 percent coupon exactly matches prevailing interest rate when the bond is issued in 1977. Consequently, the bond sells for its par value of $1,000. Shortly thereafter, interest rates quickly rose to very high levels (over 15 percent) in the economy. As interest rates rose, bond prices had to decline. Then

interest rate risk The chance of a capital loss due to interest rate fluctuations.

> "VERY SHORT-TERM BONDS EXPERIENCE LITTLE OR NO FLUCTUATION IN THEIR PRICES, AND THUS EXPOSE THE BONDHOLDER TO LITTLE INTEREST RATE RISK. LONG-TERM BONDHOLDERS EXPERIENCE SUBSTANTIAL INTEREST RATE RISK."

offer to pay higher interest rates than the rates offered on existing bonds. So to sell an existing bond with its lower coupon rate, its market price must fall so that the buyer can expect a profit similar to that offered by newly issued bonds. Similarly, when prevailing interest rates fall, market prices for outstanding bonds rise to bring the offered return on older bonds with higher coupon rates into line with new issues.

in 1984, interest rates started a prolonged descent to a low of 5 percent in 1993. Of course, bond prices rose during this nine-year period. Since the early 1990s, interest rates have generally declined, but have done so with many fluctuations. Note that while a bond is issued at $1,000 and returns $1,000 at maturity, its price can vary a great deal in between. Bond investors must be aware that bond prices fluctuate on a day-to-day basis as interest rates fluctuate. Bondholders can incur large capital gains or capital losses.

The fact that, as prevailing interest rates change, the prices of existing bonds will change has a specific name in the financial industry—interest rate risk. **Interest rate risk** means that during periods when interest rates change substantially (and quickly), bondholders experience distinct gains and losses in their bond inventories. But interest rate risk does not affect all bonds exactly the same. Very short-term bonds experience little or no fluctuation in their prices, and thus expose the bondholder to little interest rate risk. Long-term bondholders experience substantial interest rate risk. Table 6.3 illustrates the impact of interest rate risk on bonds with different coupons and times to maturity.[2]

[2]The prices are computed using semiannual periods, except for zero coupon bonds, which use annual periods.

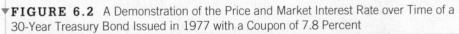

▼**FIGURE 6.2** A Demonstration of the Price and Market Interest Rate over Time of a 30-Year Treasury Bond Issued in 1977 with a Coupon of 7.8 Percent

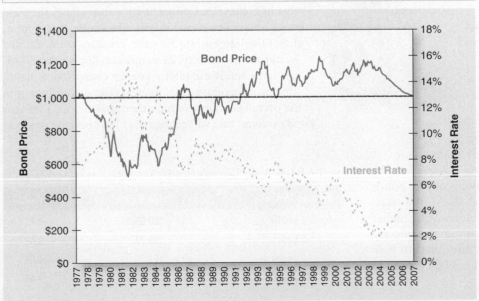

Time to Maturity	Coupon	Price at 6%	Price at 7%	Change
30 years	0%	$ 174.11	$ 131.37	−24.5%
30 years	5	861.62	750.55	−12.9
30 years	7	1,138.38	1,000.00	−12.2
30 years	10	1,553.51	1,374.17	−11.5
20 years	5	884.43	786.45	−11.1
10 years	5	925.61	857.88	−7.3
5 years	5	957.35	916.83	−4.2
2 years	5	981.41	963.27	−1.8

The first four rows show the prices and price changes for 30-year bonds with different coupon rates. Notice that the bonds with higher coupon rates also have higher prices. Bondholders as a rule find it more valuable to receive the large annuity payments. Also notice that a 1 percent increase in interest rates from 6 percent to 7 percent causes bond prices to fall. Bondholders with higher coupon bonds are not affected as much by interest rate increases because they can take the large coupon payments and reinvest those cash flows in new bonds that offer higher returns.

The price decline is greater for bonds with lower coupons because of **reinvestment rate risk.** When interest rates increase, these bondholders' lower future cash flows—both periodic payments and final payoff at maturity— are discounted at a higher rate, decreasing a bond's value. Because the cash flows from low coupon bonds are smaller, the holder of such bonds will have less money available from interest payments to buy the new, higher coupon bonds. Thus bondholders of lower coupon bonds have their capital tied up in assets that are not making them as much money. They face a bad dilemma: they can sell their lower coupon bonds and take a greater capital loss, using the (smaller) proceeds to buy new bonds with higher coupon rates. Or they can continue to receive the small income payments and hold their lower coupon bonds to maturity to avoid locking in the capital loss. Either way, they lose money relative to those bondholders with higher coupon rates. You can see this illustrated in the 30-year bonds shown in Table 6.3. Reinvestment rates tend to help partially offset changing discount rates for higher coupon paying bonds.

Another factor that influences the amount of reinvestment risk bondholders face is their bonds' time to maturity. The last four bonds in the table all have a 5 percent coupon but have different times to maturity. Note that when interest rates increase, the bond prices of longer-term bonds decline more than shorter-term bonds. This shows that bonds with longer maturities and lower coupons have the higher interest rate risk. Short-term bonds with high coupons have the lowest interest rate risk. High interest rate risk bonds experience considerable price declines when interest rates are rising. However, these bonds also experience dramatic capital gains when interest rates are falling. While a 1 percent change in market interest rates is not commonly seen on a daily or monthly basis, such a change is not unusual over the course of several months or a year.

Bond Prices and the Term Structure of Interest Rates

It may surprise you to discover that different interest rates apply to bonds with different terms to maturity. This concept is known as the **term structure of interest rates.** Consider the four Treasury bond quotes shown in Table 6.4. The price quote for each of the four bonds is associated with the yield shown. Note how the bonds with shorter time to maturity have smaller yields.

The maturity and yields of these bonds are depicted as dots in Figure 6.3. Connecting the dots shows the yield curve. This is an upward-sloping yield curve that demonstrates the interest rate for each Treasury bond, defined by its time to maturity. In an upward-sloping curve, longer-term bonds use higher interest rates. Notice that in this environment, even if interest rates do not change in the overall economy (which they always do!), a 20-year bond's interest rate will change over time because one year

▼ **TABLE 6.4** | Treasury Bond Information, December 19, 2007

Time to Maturity	Price Quote	Yield
2 years	100:00	3.11%
5 years	99:21	3.49
10 years	101:20	4.04
30 years	108:27	4.45

FIGURE 6.3   Interest Rates and Term to Maturity

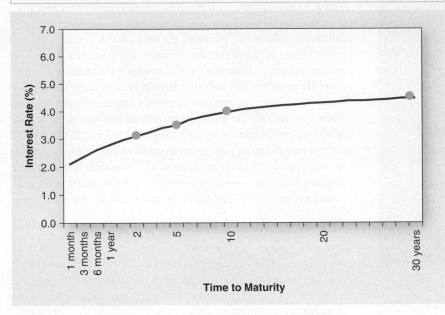

Interest Rate (%) — y-axis from 0.0 to 7.0
Time to Maturity — x-axis: 1 month, 3 months, 6 months, 1 year, 2, 5, 10, 20, 30 years

reinvestment rate risk The chance that future interest payments will have to be reinvested at a lower interest rate.

term structure of interest rates A comparison of market yields on securities, assuming all characteristics except maturity are the same.

While the upward-sloping example characterizes the relationship between interest rates and bond term to maturity during many periods in history, the yield curve can be flat, humped, and even downward sloping. The dynamics between time to maturity and interest rates is a very important topic. The relationship hints as to how interest rates might change in the future. Predicting future changes in interest rates can influence what bonds a company might issue or an investor may want to own. We'll explore these topics on a more macro level in Chapter 8. For this chapter, it's important to know that different maturities are associated with different interest rates. You can easily determine the current term structure of interest rates through financial Web sites. For example, you can choose the "Bonds" menu of Yahoo! Finance (**finance.yahoo.com**) or the "Bonds and Rates" menu of CNN Money.com (**money.cnn.com**).

later, it becomes a 19-year bond, and two years later it becomes an 18-year bond, and so on. As the bond's time to maturity gets shorter, it uses the appropriate interest rate for that maturity to determine its price.

EXAMPLE 6-5

For interactive versions of this example visit www.mhhe.com/canM

Capital Gains in the Bond Market

Say that you anticipate falling long-term interest rates from 6 percent to 5.5 percent during the next year. If this occurs, what will be the total return for a 20-year, 6.5 percent coupon bond through the interest rate decline?

SOLUTION:

To determine the total return, compute the capital gain or loss and the interest paid over the year. The capital gain or loss is determined from the change in price. The current bond price is:

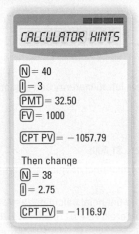

CALCULATOR HINTS

$N = 40$
$I = 3$
$PMT = 32.50$
$FV = 1000$

$CPT \ PV = -1057.79$

Then change
$N = 38$
$I = 2.75$

$CPT \ PV = -1116.97$

$$\text{Bond price} = \$32.50 \times \left[\frac{1 - \dfrac{1}{(1 + 0.03)^{40}}}{0.03} \right] + \frac{1,000}{(1 + 0.03)^{40}} = \$751.230 + \$306.557 = \$1,057.79$$

The price in one year would be:

$$\text{Bond price} = \$32.50 \times \left[\frac{1 - \dfrac{1}{(1 + 0.0275)^{38}}}{0.0275} \right] + \frac{1,000}{(1 + 0.0275)^{38}} = \$760.276 + \$356.690 = \$1,116.97$$

So, the capital gain is $59.18 (= \$1,116.97 − \$1057.79$). The interest payment during the year is $65 (= 6.5\% \times \$1,000$). If interest rates fall to 5.5 percent, then this bond should provide a total return of $124.18, which would be an 11.74 percent return (= \$124.18 \div \$1057.79$). Of course, this is only an anticipated interest rate change and it may not occur.

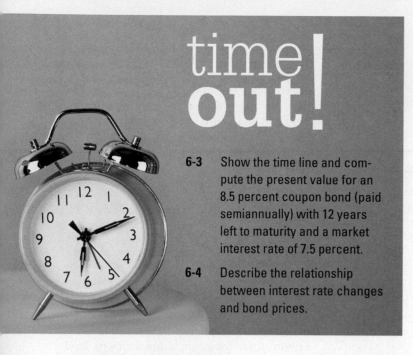

6-3 Show the time line and compute the present value for an 8.5 percent coupon bond (paid semiannually) with 12 years left to maturity and a market interest rate of 7.5 percent.

6-4 Describe the relationship between interest rate changes and bond prices.

BOND YIELDS

Current Yield

Although we speak about "the prevailing interest rate," bond relationships reflect many interest rates (also called *yields*). Some rates are difficult to calculate but accurately reflect the return the bond is offering. Others, like the **current yield,** are easy to compute but only approximate the bond's true return. A bond's current yield is defined as the bond's annual coupon rate divided by the bond's current market price. Current yield measures the rate of return a bondholder would earn annually from the coupon interest payments alone if the bond were purchased at a stated price. Current yield does not measure the total expected return because it does not account for any capital gains or losses that will occur from purchasing the bond at a discount or premium to par.

Yield to Maturity

Yield to maturity is a more meaningful equation for investors than the simple current yield calculation. The yield to maturity calculation tells bond investors the total rate of return that they might expect if the bond were bought at a particular price and held to maturity. While the yield to maturity calculation provides more information than the current yield calculation, it's also more difficult to compute, because we must compute the bond's cash flows' internal rate of return. This calculation seeks to equate the bond's current market price with the value of all anticipated future interest and par value payments. In other words, it is the discount rate that equates the present value of all future cash flows with the current price of the bond. To calculate yield to maturity, investors must solve for the interest rate, i, in equation 6-2, or solve for i in

$$\text{Bond price} = \text{PV of annuity } (pmt, i, N) + \text{PV } (FV, i, N) \quad \text{(6-2)}$$

Investors commonly compute the yield to maturity using financial calculators. For example, consider a 7 percent coupon bond (paid semiannually) with eight years to maturity and a current price of $1,150. The return that the bond offers investors, the yield to maturity, is computed as $N = 16$, $PV = -1150$, $PMT = 35$, and $FV = 1000$. Computing the interest rate (I) gives us 2.36 percent. We must remember, however, that 2.36 percent is only the return for six months because the bond pays semiannually. Yield to maturity always means an annual return. So, this bond's yield to maturity is 4.72 percent (2 × 2.36 percent).

Notice the link between a bond's yield to maturity and the prevailing market interest rates used to determine a bond's price as we discussed in the previous section. We use the market interest rate to compute the bond's value. We use the actual bond price to compute its yield to maturity. If the bond is correctly priced at its economic value, then the market interest rate will equal the yield to maturity. Thus, the relationship that we previously identified between bond prices and market interest

---

EXAMPLE 6-6

For interactive versions of this example visit www.mhhe.com/canM

Computing Current Yield and Yield to Maturity

You have identified a 3.5 percent Treasury bond with four years left to maturity and a quoted price of 96:09. Calculate the bond's current yield and yield to maturity.

SOLUTION:

(1) First, identify that the bond's price is $962.81 (= 96 09/32% × $1,000).

(2) The annual $35 in interest payments is paid in two $17.50 semiannual payments. Therefore, the current yield of the bond is 3.64 percent (= $35 ÷ $962.81).

(3) The yield to maturity is computed using equation 6-2 and the financial calculator as $N = 8$, $PV = -962.81$, $PMT = 17.50$, and $FV = 1,000$. Computing the interest rate (/) results in 2.26 percent and multiplying by 2 gives the yield to maturity of 4.53 percent.

(4) Note that the current yield is less than the yield to maturity because it does not account for the capital gain to be earned if held to maturity.

the Math Coach on...

Bond Yields and Financial Calculators

" People computing a bond's yield to maturity make three common mistakes. To avoid the first mistake, ensure that the bond price (PV) is a different sign than the interest and par value cash flows (PMT and FV). The second mistake: people forget to make the number of periods (N) and the per period interest payment (PMT) consistent. Both should be in semiannual terms if the coupon payment is paid semiannually. Lastly, many people forget to multiply the resulting calculator interest rate (I) output by 2 to convert the semiannual rate back to an annual rate. "

> **current yield** Return from interest payments; computed as the annual interest payment divided by the current bond price.
>
> **yield to maturity** The total return the bond offers if purchased at the current price and held to maturity.
>
> **yield to call** The total return that the bond offers if purchased at the current price and held until the bond is called.

rates applies to yields as well. Bond prices and bond yields are *inversely* related. As a bond's price falls, its yield to maturity increases and a rising bond price accompanies a falling yield. Look back at Figure 6.2 and you will see this relationship clearly.

Yield to Call

The yield to maturity computation assumes that the bondholder will hold the bond to its maturity. But remember that many bonds have call provisions that allow the issuers to repay the bondholder's par value prior to its scheduled maturity. Issuers often call bonds after large drops in market interest rates. In such cases, issuers commonly pay bondholders the bond's par value plus one year of interest payments. The reasons behind early bond redemptions are obvious. When interest rates fall, issuers can sell new bonds at lower interest rates. Companies want to refinance their debt—just as homeowners do—to reduce their interest payments.

Issuers gain important advantages with call provisions because they allow refinancing opportunities. Of course, the same provisions are disadvantages for bond investors. When bonds are called, investors receive the par value and call premium, but then investors must seek equally profitable bonds to buy with the proceeds. You will recall that investors can face reinvestment risk—the available bonds aren't as profitable because interest rates have declined. Bonds are called away at the worst time for investors. In addition, bond prices will rise as market interest rates fall, which could provide issuers opportunities to sell the bonds at a profit. But the price increases will be limited by the fact that the bond will likely be called early. The possibility that bonds can be called early dampens their upside price potential. We can even compute the price of a bond that's likely to be called from the equation

$$\text{Price of a callable bond} = \begin{array}{l}\text{Present value of interest}\\ \text{payments to call date}\\ + \text{ Present value of call price}\end{array}$$

$$= PMT \times \left[\frac{1 - \dfrac{1}{(1+i)^N}}{i}\right] + \frac{\text{Call price}}{(1+i)^N} \quad (6\text{-}3)$$

In this case, N is the number of periods until the bond can be called and *i* is the prevailing market rate. The prevailing market interest rate will probably differ from the rate for a noncallable bond. The previous section demonstrated via the yield curve that bonds with different maturities have different yields. A bond that matures in 20 years, but is likely to be called in 5 years, will carry a yield appropriate for a 5-year bond.

Now, reconsider the 20-year bond with a 7 percent coupon that we discussed previously. If the bond can be called in five years with a call price of $1,070, the appropriate discount rate happens to be 5.75 percent annually at that time (instead of the 6 percent in the original problem). This time line would be

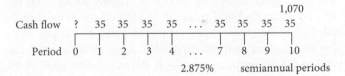

Cash flow	?	35	35	35	35	...	35	35	35	1,070 35
Period	0	1	2	3	4	...	7	8	9	10

2.875% semiannual periods

The changes in this time line are only 10 semiannual payments of $35 (rather than 40 such semiannual payments), a 2.875 percent semiannual discount rate, and the call price payment of $1,070. The price of this callable bond would be

$$\text{Bond price} = \$35 \times \left[\frac{1 - \dfrac{1}{(1+0.02875)^{10}}}{0.02875}\right] + \frac{1,070}{(1+0.02875)^{10}}$$

$$= \$300.47 + \$805.91 = \$1,106.38$$

In this example, the callable bond would be priced at $1,106.38, which is slightly lower than an identical bond that was not callable, priced at $1,115.57.

If a bond is likely to be called, then the yield to maturity calculation does not give investors a good estimate of their return. Bondholders can use instead a **yield to call** calculation, which differs from the yield to maturity only in that

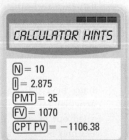

CALCULATOR HINTS

N = 10
I = 2.875
PMT = 35
FV = 1070
CPT PV = −1106.38

finance at work //: markets

its calculation assumes that the investor will receive the par value and call premium at the call date. For example, reconsider the 7 percent coupon bond (paid semiannually) with 8 years to maturity, which we examined previously. The current bond price is $1,130 (which is slightly lower than the yield to maturity bond price of $1,150). If the bond can be called in three years at a specific call price of the par value plus one annual coupon, then what is the yield to call? The yield to call is computed as $N = 6$, $PV = -1,130$, $PMT = 35$, and $FV = 1,070$. The resulting interest rate (I) is 2.26 percent. The yield to call for this bond is thus 4.52 percent (= 2×2.26 percent).

Municipal Bonds and Yield

Municipal bonds (munis) seem to offer low yields to maturity compared to the return that corporate bonds and Treasury securities offer. Munis offer lower rates because the interest income they generate for investors is tax-exempt—at least at the federal level.[3] Specifically, income from municipal bonds is not subject to taxation by the federal government or the state government where the bonds are issued. As a result, municipal bond investors willingly accept lower yields than

those they can obtain from taxable bonds. Generally speaking, investors compare the after-tax interest income earned on taxable bonds against the return earned on municipal bonds. For example, suppose an investor in the 35 percent *marginal* income tax bracket has $100,000 to invest in either corporate or municipal bonds. The $100,000 investment would earn a taxable $7,000 annually from 7 percent corporate bonds or $5,000 from tax exempt 5 percent municipal bonds. After taxes, the corporate bond leaves the investor with $4,550 [= $(1 - 0.35) \times \$7,000$]. Obviously, this is less than the tax-free income of $5,000 generated by the muni bond.

A common way to compare yields from muni bonds versus that from taxable bonds is to convert the yield to maturity of the muni to a **taxable equivalent yield,** as shown in equation 6-4.

$$\text{Equivalent taxable yield} = \frac{\text{Muni yield}}{1 - \text{Tax rate}} \qquad (6\text{-}4)$$

For high-income investors (in the 35 percent marginal tax bracket) a 5 percent muni bond has an equivalent taxable yield of 7.69 percent [= 5% ÷ $(1 - 0.35)$]. The 5 percent muni is more attractive for this investor than a 7 percent corporate bond. However, for an investor with lower income (in the 28 percent marginal tax bracket) the equivalent taxable yield is only 6.9 percent. The corporate bond provides more after-tax profit than the muni for this investor. It's easy to see why muni bonds are popular among high-income investors (those with substantial marginal tax rates).

---

[3]States have differing rules about whether they tax the income from a particular municipal bond—they will generally tax income from munis issued out of state. Further, capital gains arising from municipal bond sales may be taxed, and the income from municipal bonds must be added to overall income when determining the Alternative Minimum Tax consequences.

taxable equivalent yield Modification of a municipal bond's yield to maturity used to compare muni bond yields to taxable bond yields.

EXAMPLE 6-7

For interactive versions of this example visit www.mhhe.com/canM

Which Bond Has a Better After-Tax Yield?

Imagine a time when you have a high income, placing you in the 31 percent marginal tax bracket. You are interested in investing some money in a bond issue and have three alternatives. The first is a corporate bond with a 6.4 percent yield to maturity. The second bond is a Treasury that offers a 5.7 percent yield. The third choice is a municipal bond priced at a yield to maturity of 4.0 percent. Which bond gives you the highest after-tax yield?

SOLUTION:

The Treasury and corporate bonds are both taxable, so we can compare them directly with each other. The yield of 6.4 percent on the corporate is clearly higher than the 5.7 percent yield offered by the Treasury bond. To include a comparison with the nontaxable municipal bond, compute its equivalent taxable yield as in equation 6-4:

$$\text{Equivalent taxable yield} = \frac{4.0\%}{1 - 0.31} = 5.80\%$$

The municipal bond's equivalent taxable yield of 5.80 percent is higher than the Treasury but lower than the corporate bond.

▼ **TABLE 6.5** Price, Coupon, and Yield Relationships of a 10-Year Bond

	Price	Coupon Rate	Current Yield	Yield to Maturity	Yield to Call (In 5 Years)	Taxable Equivalent Yield (35% Tax Rate)
(1) Treasury	$1,000.00	5%	5 %	5 %		5 %
(2) Treasury	1,100.00	5	4.55	3.79		3.79
(3) Treasury	900.00	5	5.56	6.37		6.37
(4) Corporate	1,000.00	6	6	6	6 %	6
(5) Corporate	1,110.00	6	5.41	4.61	4.59	4.61
(6) Corporate	900.00	6	6.67	7.44	9.52	7.44
(7) Muni	1,000.00	4	4	4		6.15
(8) Muni	1,100.00	4	3.34	2.84		4.37
(9) Muni	900.00	4	4.44	5.30		8.16

Summarizing Yields

In this section, we have presented several different types of interest rates, or yields, associated with bonds. Many of these yields relate to one another. Consider the bonds and associated yields reported in Table 6.5. Treasury bonds (1) to (3) show how coupon rates, current yield, and yield to maturity relate. When a bond trades at its par value (usually $1,000), then the coupon rate, current yield, and yield to maturity are all the same. When that bond is priced at a premium (bond 2), then both the current yield and the yield to maturity will be lower than the coupon rate. They are both higher than the coupon rate when the bond trades at a discount. Notice that yield to maturity is higher than current yield for discount bonds, and

that yield to maturity is lower than current yield for premium bonds. In other words, the current yield always lies between the coupon rate and the yield to maturity. Both the current yield and the yield to maturity move in the opposite direction to the bond's price.

Bonds (4) to (6) are callable corporate bonds. Recall that all the yields (current yield, yield to maturity, and yield to call) are identical when the bond trades at par value. When interest rates fall and bond prices increase, as with bond (5), the issuing corporation has a strong incentive to call the bond after five years, as allowed in the indenture agreement. So investors should base their purchase decisions on the yield to call. When interest rates increase, bond prices decline (as bond 6 shows). In this case, investors could compute the yield to call (as shown), but the information isn't useful because the company will not likely call the bond while interest rates are high.

The last three bonds shown in the table are municipal bonds. Recall that these bonds typically offer lower yields because the income from munis is tax exempt. It is easier to compare municipal bonds with Treasuries and corporate bonds if you compute the municipal bond's taxable equivalent yield first. Here, we use a marginal tax rate of 35 percent in the calculation. The last column of the table shows that the taxable equivalent yield of the municipal bonds is really quite competitive with corporate bond yields. Any investor with income taxed at the 35 percent marginal tax bracket would prefer the municipal bond over the corporate bond if the muni's taxable equivalent yield is higher than the yield to maturity (or yield to call) of the corporate bond.

The table also shows that Treasury securities offer lower yields than corporate bonds with similar terms to maturity. The difference (or spread) between Treasury and corporate yields gives rise to a discussion of bond credit risk, which follows.

Bonds issued for municipal projects tend to offer lower yields because their income is tax exempt.

time out!

6-5 Calculate the yield to maturity for a zero coupon bond with a price of $525 and 10 years left to maturity.

6-6 Which is higher for a discount bond, the yield to maturity or the coupon rate? Why?

CREDIT RISK

Bond Ratings

Will a bond issuer make the promised interest and par value payments over the next 10, 20, or even 30 years? **Credit quality risk** is the chance that the bond issuer will not be able to make timely payments. To assess this risk, independent **bond rating** agencies, such as Moody's and Standard & Poor's, monitor corporate, U.S. agency, or municipal developments during the bond's lifetime and report their findings as a grade or rating. The U.S. government issues the highest credit quality debt; in fact, it's such high quality that it carries no rating. Rating agencies rate all other bonds and issuers who want to sell debt securities in the United States.

Bond credit rating agencies in the United States include Moody's Investors Service, Standard & Poor's Corporation, Fitch IBCA Inc., Dominion Bond Rating Service, and A.M. Best Co. Each of these credit analysis firms assigns similar ratings based on detailed analyses of issuers' financial condition, general economic and credit market conditions, and the economic value of any underlying collateral. The Standard & Poor's ratings are shown in Table 6.6. Their highest credit-quality rating is AAA. Bonds rated AAA, AA, A, or BBB are considered **investment grade** bonds. The issuers of these securities have the highest chance of making all interest and par value payments promised in the indenture agreement.

The investment community considers bonds rated BB and below to be below-investment grade bonds, and some investors, such as pension funds or other fiduciaries, cannot purchase these securities for their portfolios. These bonds are considered to be speculative because they carry a significant risk that the issuer will not make current or future payments. Speculative bonds are sometimes called **junk bonds** because of this risk. In order to attract buyers, issuers sell these bonds at a considerable discount from par and a high associated yield to maturity. Agencies often enhance ratings from "AA" to "CCC" with the addition of a plus (+) or minus (−) sign to show relative standing within the major rating categories. For example, PPG Industries, a manufacturer of coatings, glass, and chemicals, and member of the S&P 500 Index, saw its bonds downgraded from A to A− by Standard & Poor's on January 2, 2008.

Standard & Poor's signals that it's considering a rating change by placing an individual bond, or all of a given issuer's bonds, on CreditWatch (S&P). Rating agencies make their ratings information available to the public through their ratings information desks. In addition to published reports, ratings are made available in many public libraries and over the Internet.

Credit rating agencies conduct general economic analyses of companies' business and analyze firms' specific financial situations. A single

View interactive examples at mhhe.com/canM

👍 ROTCGrrl and three others like this.

ROTCGrrl The Excel examples show me what formulas to enter so I do the problem right the first time.

5 hours ago · Like

write a comment...

company may carry several outstanding bond issues. If these issues feature fundamental differences, then they may have different credit level risks. For example, **unsecured corporate bonds,** or

▼ **TABLE 6.6** Standard & Poor's Bond Credit Ratings

Credit Risk	Credit Rating	Description
Investment Grade		
Highest quality	AAA	The obligor's (issuer's) capacity to meet its financial commitment on the obligation is extremely strong.
High quality	AA	The obligor's capacity to meet its financial commitment on the obligation is very strong.
Upper medium grade	A	The obligor's capacity to meet its financial commitment on the obligation is still strong, though somewhat susceptible to the adverse effects of changes in circumstances and economic conditions.
Medium grade	BBB	The obligor exhibits adequate protection. However, adverse economic conditions or changing circumstances are more likely to lead to a weakened capacity to meet its financial commitment.
Below Investment Grade		
Somewhat speculative	BB	Faces major ongoing uncertainties or exposure to adverse business, financial, or economic conditions which could lead to the obligor's inadequate capacity to meet its financial commitment.
Speculative	B	Adverse business, financial, or economic conditions will likely impair the obligor's capacity or willingness to meet its financial commitment.
Highly speculative	CCC	Currently vulnerable to nonpayment, and is dependent upon favorable business, financial, and economic conditions for the obligor to meet its financial commitment.
Most speculative	CC	Currently highly vulnerable to nonpayment.
Imminent default	C	Used to cover a situation where a bankruptcy petition has been filed or similar action taken, but payments on this obligation are being continued.
Default	D	Obligations are in default or the filing of a bankruptcy petition has occurred and payments are jeopardized.

Source: Standard & Poor's Web page.

debentures
Unsecured bonds.

senior bonds Older bonds that carry a higher claim to the issuer's assets.

mortgage bonds Bonds secured with real estate as collateral.

equipment trust certificates Bonds secured with factory and equipment as collateral.

high-yield bonds Bonds with low credit quality that offer a high yield to maturity, also called junk bonds.

debentures, are backed only by the reputation and financial stability of the corporation. A **senior bond** has a priority claim over junior (more recently issued) securities in the event of default or bankruptcy. So, senior bonds carry less credit risk than junior bonds. Some bonds are secured with collateral. When you buy a car using a loan, the car is collateral for that loan. If you don't make the loan payments, the bank will repossess the car. Companies can also offer collateral when issuing bonds. When a firm uses collateral such as real estate or factory equipment, the bonds are called **mortgage bonds** or **equipment trust certificates,**

respectively. Bonds issued with no collateral generally carry higher credit risk.

Credit Risk and Yield

Investors will only purchase higher risk bonds if those securities offer higher returns. Therefore, issuers price bonds with high credit risk to offer high yields to maturity. So another common name for junk bonds is **high-yield bonds.** Differences in credit risk are a prime source of differences in yields between government and various corporate bonds. Figure 6.4 shows the historical average annual yields for long-term Treasury bonds and corporate bonds with credit ratings of AAA and BBB since 1980. Riskier low-quality bonds always offer a higher yield than the higher quality bonds. However, the yield spread between high- and low-quality bonds varies substantially over time. The yield difference between BBB bonds and Treasuries was as high as 3.7 percent and 3.3 percent in 1982 and 2003, respectively.

finance at work //: markets

Michael Milken, Controversial Financier

Michael Milken may be the most controversial financial figure of modern times. Some people consider him a financial genius. Others believe that he is a criminal who provided the capital to corporate raiders to break up companies and lay off masses of employees. Controversial indeed! Milken pioneered an active high-yield bond market in the late 1970s and 1980s that provided much needed capital to entrepreneurs and financial innovators, helping to drive the record-breaking stock market of the 1980s and early 90s.

Before the 1970s, the only junk bonds were those issued by once financially stable companies that had fallen on hard times, known as "fallen angels." When a bond was downgraded to junk status, its trading market dried up. Investors were simply unwilling to buy bonds with high credit risk. Using scholarly research, Milken showed investors that, historically, junk bonds rarely defaulted and offered a very high return to those willing to assume the risk of owning them. As investors became interested in buying these bonds, Milken and Drexel Burnham Lambert, the firm for which he worked, developed the market. When banks reduced the amount of risky capital they offered to the market in the 1970s, Milken used the strong demand for high-yield bonds to issue new junk bonds for growing companies and pioneers like Bill McGowan (telecommunications), Ted Turner (cable television), Craig McCaw (cellular telephones), and Steve Wynn (resorts). During the 1980s, Milken also used junk bonds to finance a new class of corporate raiders, such

as Kohlberg Kravis Roberts, who carried out numerous mergers, acquisitions, hostile takeovers, and leveraged buyouts.

Nicknamed "The Junk Bond King" in the 1980s, Milken earned $296 million in 1986 and $550 million in 1987 from trading more than $1 billion per day in bonds. He took much criticism for his obscene pay and for the lives ruined at companies targeted by corporate raiders, who tended to break companies up into smaller operating units and lay off many employees in the process. But in 1989, the government charged him with securities fraud. He originally faced a 98-count indictment, but pleaded guilty to only five of the more trivial offenses. He was sentenced to 10 years in prison and a $200 million fine. He paid an additional $750 million in civil settlements. He was released from prison after 22 months but is banned from the securities industry.

Milken has remained very active since being released from prison. He launched a venture called FastCures that is addressing cancer cures (he had prostate cancer). He also created an education empire formally known as Knowledge Universe (it has since changed its name to Monte LLC). The *Forbes* 2006 estimate of Milken's wealth was $2.1 billion. The junk bond market that he pioneered decades ago still thrives today.

Want to know more?

Key Words to Search for Updates: **See the Milken Institute (www.MilkenInstitute.org) or Google Michael Milken.**

Sources: Norman Barry, *Business Ethics,* Ichor Business Books, 1999, and "The Forbes 400," *Forbes,* October 19, 2006, Vol. 178, Issue 7.

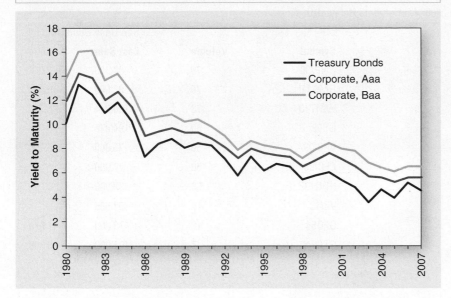

The spread has been as narrow as 1.3 percent and 1.4 percent in 1994 and 2006, respectively.

How do some corporations' debt obligations become junk bonds? Some companies that aren't economically sound or those that use a high degree of financial leverage issue junk bonds. In other cases, financially strong companies issue investment grade bonds and then, over time, begin to have

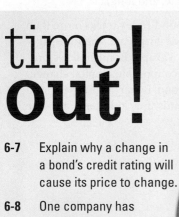

6-7 Explain why a change in a bond's credit rating will cause its price to change.

6-8 One company has issued two bond classes. One issue is a mortgage bond and the other is a debenture. Which issue will have a higher bond rating and which will offer a higher yield?

trouble. Eventually a company's bonds can be downgraded to junk status. For example, General Motors (GM) bonds were considered of the highest quality from the 1950s through the 1980s and much of the 1990s. On May 9, 2005, Standard & Poor's downgraded GM bonds to junk status. Junk bonds that were originally issued at investment grade status are still called *fallen angels.*

Bonds that experience credit-rating downgrades must offer a higher yield. As all the future cash flows are fixed, the bond price must fall to create a higher yield to maturity. Alternatively, bonds that are upgraded experience price increases and yield decreases. Bond upgrades often occur during strong economic periods because corporate issuers tend to perform better financially at these times. In a weak economy, high-yield bonds lose their luster because the default risk rises. More credit downgrades occur during economic recessions.

BOND MARKETS

The majority of trading volume in the bond market occurs in a decentralized, over-the-counter market. Most trades occur between bond dealers and large institutions (like mutual funds, pension funds, and insurance companies). Dealers bid for bonds that investors seek to sell and offer bonds from their own inventory when investors want to buy. This is especially true for the very active Treasury securities market. However, a small number of corporate bonds are listed on centralized exchanges.

The NYSE operates the largest centralized U.S. bond market. The majority of bond volume at the NYSE is in corporate debt, shown in Figure 6.5. Notice that even the most active bonds experience relatively low trading volume. A total of 73 of the Walmart Stores bonds traded on January 4, 2008. At a price of 100.744 percent of par value, the 73 bonds represent $73,543 of trading value. This is a paltry amount compared to the $930 million of Walmart stock traded the same day. Note that some of the bonds traded are short-term—the Goldman Sachs bond has just over one year left to maturity. Other bonds have many years to maturity, like 48 years for the Gulf Mobile & Ohio RR debenture. While the Goldman bond pays a 7.35 percent coupon, the mid-term bond from Hewlett-Packard that matures in 2017 is a zero coupon bond.

FIGURE 6.5 Daily Bond Trading Summary on the New York Stock Exchange

Powered by NYSE Euronext Data | as of 16:40 ET 4 Jan 2008 | Market data delayed 10 min.

Most Active Bonds by Volume   See Daily Bond Activity

Name	Symbol	Volume	Last Sale	Change
MISSOURI PACIFIC RR CO 4 3/4% 1/1/30	UNP/30	79	87.000	+2.000
GMAC LLC 6% DEEP DISC 4/1/11	GMA11	75	83.000	−0.510
Walmart Stores Inc 4.550% NTS 05/01/13	WMT13	73	100.744	+6.744
GOLDMAN SACHS GROUP 7.350% NTS 10/01/2009	GS09	60	104.875	+0.225
Countrywide Home Loans 5.625% SER K 07/15/09	CFC/09A	50	75.000	−6.000
Countrywide Home Loans 6.250% NTS 04/15/09	CFC/09	50	77.000	
HEWLETT-PACKARD CO ZR CPN LYON 10/14/2017	HPQ17Z	50	83.000	+3.000
Verizon Global Funding Co 4.375% NTS 06/01/13	VZ/13	12	97.586	
GULF MOBILE & OHIO RR 5% 12/1/56	GFO56	10	73.000	−4.625
Goldman Sachs Group 6.650% NTS 05/15/09	GS09A	7	101.000	−0.500

Source: NYSE Bond Web page.

Following the Bond Market

The entire bond market encompasses a wide variety of securities with varying credit quality from different issuers. Large differences also arise among bonds in terms of their characteristics such as term to maturity and size of the coupon. The biggest factor associated with changes in bond prices is changes in interest rates. So, one common way to describe the direction of bond prices is simply to report the changes in interest rates, since we know that interest rate changes will affect all bonds the same way. The interest rate referenced is the yield to maturity and daily yield change for the 10-year Treasury. Knowing how this interest rate changed today gives bond investors a good idea of the general price movement of all types of bonds.

Bond indexes track specific segments of the bond market. Various brokerage firms, such as Lehman Brothers or Merrill Lynch, maintain these indexes that capture bond price and yield changes in particular segments. You can find information about major bond indexes on the Internet and in publications like *The Wall Street Journal* (both in print and online). Figure 6.6 shows indexes that track bonds by type of issuer (federal government, corporation, local government, etc.) and time to maturity (short, intermediate, and long).

The Lehman Brothers Aggregate Bond Index tracks more than 5,000 government, investment-grade corporate, and mortgage-backed bonds. The Merrill Lynch Taxable Bond Indexes provide value-weighted total returns (coupon plus capital change) for a range of bond types. The Bond Buyer Municipal Bond Index tracks price and yield trends for long-term tax-free municipal bonds. ◼

6-9 Why can you use various interest rates to describe the performance of the entire bond market?

6-10 What bond segments are measured by which bond indexes?

time out!

Index	Close	% Chg	YTD total return	52-wk % Chg	YIELD (%), 52-WEEK RANGE Latest	Low	High
Broad Market							
U.S. Government/Credit	1486.21	−0.06	0.72	7.71	**4.370**	4.340	5.730
Aggregate Lehman	1290.52	−0.01	0.64	7.34	**4.760**	4.760	5.850
Hourly Treasury Indexes							
Composite (Price Return)	1355.59	0.02	0.74	4.46	**3.420**	−1.850	5.170
Composite (Total Return)	10213.61	0.03	0.78	9.52	**3.420**	0.210	5.170
Intermediate (Price Return)	1221.74	0.07	0.65	4.52	**3.180**	−1.160	5.120
Intermediate (Total Return)	8803.54	0.08	0.69	9.34	**3.180**	0.820	5.120
Long-Term (Price Return)	1803.61	−0.17	1.08	4.27	**4.310**	−4.420	5.390
Long-Term (Total Return)	15397.93	−0.16	1.13	10.22	**4.310**	−2.030	5.390
Mortgage-Backed							
Ginnie Mae (GNMA)	513.43	0.12	0.66	6.60	**5.218**	5.218	6.240
Fannie Mae (FNMA)	505.90	0.06	0.41	6.28	**5.067**	5.067	6.324
Freddie Mae (FHLMC)	312..01	0.08	0.43	6.21	**5.207**	5.207	6.354
U.S. Corporate Debt							
1-10 Year Maturities	1208.73	−0.03	0.67	5.28	**5.418**	3.373	6.007
10+ Year Maturities	1418.27	−0.31	0.92	3.21	**6.351**	5.950	6.694
Corporate Master	1701.60	−0.10	0.74	4.75	**5.668**	5.460	6.180
High Yield	845.80	−0.29	−0.30	1.61	**9.676**	7.353	9.676
Yankee Bonds	1274.70	−0.08	0.69	6.44	**5.176**	5.066	6.765
Tax-Exempt							
Muni Master	348.36	0.22	0.49	4.39	**3.720**	3.720	4.294
7-12 years	231.40	0.35	0.56	5.13	**3.631**	3.631	4.256
12-22 years	249.22	0.38	0.74	3.65	**4.205**	3.970	4.733
22-plus years	238.50	0.04	0.53	1.01	**4.847**	4.197	5.154
Bond Buyer 6% Muni	112.69	unch	0.61	−3.53	**4.820**	4.510	5.070

Source: The Wall Street Journal Online, Major Bond Indexes Web page.

Get Online

mhhe.com/canM

for study materials including
quizzes, iPod downloads,
and video

Your Turn...

Questions

1. What does a call provision allow issuers to do, and why would they do it? *(LG1)*

2. List the differences between the new TIPS and traditional Treasury bonds. *(LG2)*

3. Explain how mortgage-backed securities work. *(LG2)*

4. Provide the definitions of a discount bond and a premium bond. Give examples. *(LG3)*

5. Describe the differences in interest payments and bond price between a 5 percent coupon bond and a zero coupon bond. *(LG4)*

6. All else equal, which bond's price is more affected by a change in interest rates, a short-term bond or a longer-term bond? Why? *(LG5)*

7. All else equal, which bond's price is more affected by a change in interest rates, a bond with a large coupon or a small coupon? Why? *(LG5)*

8. Explain how a bond's interest rate can change over time even if interest rates in the economy do not change. *(LG5)*

9. Compare and contrast the advantages and disadvantages of the current yield computation versus yield to maturity calculations. *(LG6)*

10. What is the yield to call and why is it important to a bond investor? *(LG6)*

11. What is the purpose of computing the equivalent taxable yield of a municipal bond? *(LG6)*

12. Explain why high-income and wealthy people are more likely to buy a municipal bond than a corporate bond. *(LG6)*

13. Why does a Treasury bond offer a lower yield than a corporate bond with the same time to maturity? Could a corporate bond with a different time to maturity offer a lower yield? Explain. *(LG7)*

14. Describe the difference between a bond issued as a high-yield bond and one that has become a "fallen angel." *(LG7)*

15. What is the difference in the trading volume between Treasury bonds and corporate bonds? Give examples and/or evidence. *(LG8)*

16. Explain how the Lehman Brothers Intermediate Bond Index might increase one day while the Merrill Lynch High Yield Index decreases the same day. *(LG8)*

Problems

6-1 **Interest Payments** Determine the interest payment for the following three bonds: 3 ½ percent coupon corporate bond (paid semiannually), 4.25 percent coupon Treasury note, and a corporate zero coupon bond maturing in 10 years. (Assume a $1,000 par value.) *(LG1)*

6-2 **Interest Payments** Determine the interest payment for the following three bonds: 4 ½ percent coupon corporate bond (paid semiannually), 5.15 percent coupon Treasury note, and a corporate zero coupon bond maturing in 15 years. (Assume a $1,000 par value.) *(LG1)*

6-3 **Time to Maturity** A bond issued by Ford on May 15, 1997 is scheduled to mature on May 15, 2097. If today is November 16, 2008, what is this bond's time to maturity? *(LG1)*

6-4 **Time to Maturity** A bond issued by IBM on December 1, 1996, is scheduled to mature on December 1, 2096. If today is December 2, 2007, what is this bond's time to maturity? *(LG1)*

6-5 **Call Premium** A 7 percent corporate coupon bond is callable in five years for a call premium of one year of coupon payments. Assuming a par value of $1,000, what is the price paid to the bondholder if the issuer calls the bond? *(LG1)*

6-6 **Call Premium** A 6.5 percent corporate coupon bond is callable in 10 years for a call premium of 1 year of coupon payments. Assuming a par value of $1,000, what is the price paid to the bondholder if the issuer calls the bond? *(LG1)*

6-7 **TIPS Interest and Par Value** A 2 ¾ percent TIPS has an original reference CPI of 185.4. If the current CPI is 210.7, what is the current interest payment and par value of the TIPS? *(LG2)*

6-8 **TIPS Interest and Par Value** A 3 1/8 percent TIPS has an original reference CPI of 180.5. If the current CPI is 206.8, what is the current interest payment and par value of the TIPS? *(LG2)*

6-9 **Bond Quotes** Consider the following three bond quotes; a Treasury note quoted at 97:27, a corporate bond quoted at 103.25, and a municipal bond quoted at 101.90. If the Treasury and corporate bonds have a par value of $1,000 and the municipal bond has a par value of $5,000, what is the price of these three bonds in dollars? *(LG3)*

6-10 **Bond Quotes** Consider the following three bond quotes: a Treasury bond quoted at 106:14, a corporate bond quoted at 96.55, and a municipal bond quoted at 100.95. If the Treasury and corporate bonds have a par value of $1,000 and the municipal bond has a par value of $5,000, what is the price of these three bonds in dollars? *(LG3)*

6-11 **Zero Coupon Bond Price** Calculate the price of a zero coupon bond that matures in 20 years if the market interest rate is 6.5 percent. *(LG4)*

6-12 **Zero Coupon Bond Price** Calculate the price of a zero coupon bond that matures in 15 years if the market interest rate is 7.25 percent. *(LG4)*

6-13 **Current Yield** What's the current yield of a 5.5 percent coupon corporate bond quoted at a price of 102.08? *(LG6)*

6-14 **Current Yield** What's the current yield of a 7.2 percent coupon corporate bond quoted at a price of 96.78? *(LG6)*

6-15 **Taxable Equivalent Yield** What's the taxable equivalent yield on a municipal bond with a yield to maturity of 3.5 percent for an investor in the 28 percent marginal tax bracket? *(LG6)*

6-16 **Taxable Equivalent Yield** What's the taxable equivalent yield on a municipal bond with a yield to maturity of 2.9 percent for an investor in the 33 percent marginal tax bracket? *(LG6)*

6-17 **Credit Risk and Yield** Rank from highest credit risk to lowest risk the following bonds, with the same time to maturity, by their yield to maturity: Treasury bond with yield of 5.55 percent, IBM bond with yield of 7.49 percent, Trump Casino bond with yield of 8.76 percent, and Banc One bond with a yield of 5.99 percent. *(LG7)*

6-18   **Credit Risk and Yield**   Rank the following bonds in order from lowest credit risk to highest risk, all with the same time to maturity, by their yield to maturity: Treasury bond with yield of 4.65 percent, United Airline bond with yield of 9.07 percent, Bank of America bond with a yield of 6.25 percent, and Hewlett-Packard bond with yield of 6.78 percent. *(LG7)*

INTERMEDIATE PROBLEMS

6-19   **TIPS Capital Return**   Consider a 3.5 percent TIPS with an issue CPI reference of 185.6. At the beginning of this year, the CPI was 196.2 and was at 201.3 at the end of the year. What was the capital gain of the TIPS in dollars and in percentage terms? *(LG2)*

6-20   **TIPS Capital Return**   Consider a 2.25 percent TIPS with an issue CPI reference of 183.5. At the beginning of this year, the CPI was 197.1 and was at 203.8 at the end of the year. What was the capital gain of the TIPS in dollars and in percentage terms? *(LG2)*

6-21   **Compute Bond Price**   Compute the price of a 4.5 percent coupon bond with 15 years left to maturity and a market interest rate of 6.8 percent. (Assume interest payments are semiannual.) Is this a discount or premium bond? *(LG4)*

6-22   **Compute Bond Price**   Compute the price of a 5.6 percent coupon bond with 10 years left to maturity and a market interest rate of 7.0 percent. (Assume interest payments are semi-annual.) Is this a discount or premium bond? *(LG4)*

6-23   **Compute Bond Price**   Calculate the price of a 6.2 percent coupon bond with 18 years left to maturity and a market interest rate of 5.9 percent. (Assume interest payments are semi-annual.) Is this a discount or premium bond? *(LG4)*

6-24   **Compute Bond Price**   Calculate the price of a 5.7 percent coupon bond with 25 years left to maturity and a market interest rate of 4.8 percent. (Assume interest payments are semi-annual.) Is this a discount or premium bond? *(LG4)*

6-25   **Bond Prices and Interest Rate Changes**   A 5.75 percent coupon bond with 10 years left to maturity is priced to offer a 6.5 percent yield to maturity. You believe that in one year, the yield to maturity will be 6.0 percent. What is the change in price the bond will experience in dollars? *(LG5)*

6-26   **Bond Prices and Interest Rate Changes**   A 6.5 percent coupon bond with 14 years left to maturity is priced to offer a 7.2 percent yield to maturity. You believe that in one year, the yield to maturity will be 6.8 percent. What is the change in price the bond will experience in dollars? *(LG5)*

6-27   **Yield to Maturity**   A 6.85 percent coupon bond with 26 years left to maturity is offered for sale at $1,035.25. What yield to maturity is the bond offering? (Assume interest payments are paid semiannually.) *(LG6)*

6-28   **Yield to Maturity**   A 5.25 percent coupon bond with 14 years left to maturity is offered for sale at $955.75. What yield to maturity is the bond offering? (Assume interest payments are paid semiannually.) *(LG6)*

6-29   **Yield to Call**   A 6.75 percent coupon bond with 26 years left to maturity can be called in 6 years. The call premium is one year of coupon payments. It is offered for sale at $1,135.25. What is the yield to call of the bond? (Assume that interest payments are paid semiannually.) *(LG6)*

6-30   **Yield to Call**   A 5.25 percent coupon bond with 14 years left to maturity can be called in 4 years. The call premium is one year of coupon payments. It is offered for sale at $1,075.50. What is the yield to call of the bond? (Assume that interest payments are paid semiannually.) *(LG6)*

6-31   **Comparing Bond Yields**   A client in the 33 percent marginal tax bracket is comparing a municipal bond that offers a 4.5 percent yield to maturity and a similar-risk corporate bond that offers a 6.45 percent yield. Which bond will give the client more profit after taxes? *(LG6)*

6-32   **Comparing Bond Yields**   A client in the 28 percent marginal tax bracket is comparing a municipal bond that offers a 4.5 percent yield to maturity and a similar-risk corporate bond that offers a 6.45 percent yield. Which bond will give the client more profit after taxes? *(LG6)*

6-33 **TIPS Total Return** Reconsider the 3.5 percent TIPS discussed in problem 6-19. It was issued with CPI reference of 185.6. The bond is purchased at the beginning of the year (after the interest payment), when the CPI was 196.2. For the interest payment in the middle of the year, the CPI was 199.6. Now, at the end of the year, the CPI is 201.3 and the interest payment has been made. What is the total return of the TIPS in dollars and in percentage terms for the year? *(LG2)*

6-34 **TIPS Total Return** Reconsider the 2.25 percent TIPS discussed in problem 6-20. It was issued with CPI reference of 183.5. The bond was purchased at the beginning of the year (after the interest payment), when the CPI was 197.1. For the interest payment in the middle of the year, the CPI was 200.1. Now, at the end of the year, the CPI is 203.8 and the interest payment has been made. What is the total return of the TIPS in dollars and in percentage terms for the year? *(LG2)*

6-35 **Bond Prices and Interest Rate Changes** A 6.25 percent coupon bond with 22 years left to maturity is priced to offer a 5.5 percent yield to maturity. You believe that in one year, the yield to maturity will be 6.0 percent. If this occurs, what would be the total return of the bond in dollars and percent? *(LG5)*

6-36 **Bond Prices and Interest Rate Changes** A 7.5 percent coupon bond with 13 years left to maturity is priced to offer a 6.25 percent yield to maturity. You believe that in one year, the yield to maturity will be 7.0 percent. If this occurs, what would be the total return of the bond in dollars and percentage terms? *(LG5)*

6-37 **Yields of a Bond** A 3.75 percent coupon municipal bond has 14 years left to maturity and has a price quote of 98.45. The bond can be called in four years. The call premium is one year of coupon payments. Compute and discuss the bond's current yield, yield to maturity, taxable equivalent yield (for an investor in the 35 percent marginal tax bracket), and yield to call. (Assume interest payments are paid semiannually and a par value of $5,000.) *(LG6)*

6-38 **Yields of a Bond** A 4.25 percent coupon municipal bond has 18 years left to maturity and has a price quote of 97.65. The bond can be called in eight years. The call premium is one year of coupon payments. Compute and discuss the bond's current yield, yield to maturity, taxable equivalent yield (for an investor in the 35 percent marginal tax bracket), and yield to call. (Assume interest payments are paid semiannually and a par value of $5,000.) *(LG6)*

6-39 **Bond Ratings and Prices** A corporate bond with a 6.5 percent coupon has 15 years left to maturity. It has had a credit rating of BBB and a yield to maturity of 7.2 percent. The firm has recently gotten into some trouble and the rating agency is downgrading the bonds to BB. The new appropriate discount rate will be 8.5 percent. What will be the change in the bond's price in dollars and percentage terms? (Assume interest payments are paid semiannually.) *(LG7)*

6-40 **Bond Ratings and Prices** A corporate bond with a 6.75 percent coupon has 10 years left to maturity. It has had a credit rating of BB and a yield to maturity of 8.2 percent. The firm has recently become more financially stable and the rating agency is upgrading the bonds to BBB. The new appropriate discount rate will be 7.1 percent. What will be the change in the bond's price in dollars and percentage terms? (Assume interest payments are paid semiannually.) *(LG7)*

6-41 **Excel Problem** Say that in June 2008, a company issued bonds that are scheduled to mature in June 2011. The coupon rate is 5.75 percent and is paid semiannually. The bond issue was rated AAA.

    a. Build a spreadsheet that shows how much money the firm pays for each interest rate payment and when those payments will occur if the bond issue sells 50,000 bonds.

    b. If the bond issue rating would have been BBB, then the coupon rate would have been 6.30 percent. Show the interest payments with this rating. Explain why bond ratings are important to firms issuing capital debt.

    c. Consider that interest rates in the economy increased in the first half of 2008. If the firm would have issued the bonds in January of 2008, then the interest rates would have only been 5.40 percent. How much extra money per year is the firm paying because it issued the bonds in June instead of January?

chapter seven

valuing stocks

Businesses need capital to start up operations, expand product lines and services, and serve new markets. In the last chapter, we discussed debt, which is one source of financial capital upon which businesses can draw. Their other source of capital is called *equity,* or *business ownership.* Public corporations share business ownership and raise money by issuing stocks to investors. When the company sells this form of equity ownership to raise money, it gives up some ownership—and thus some control—over the business. Investors buy stock to receive the benefits of business ownership. Most citizens do not have the time or expertise to operate their own businesses. Buying stock allows them to participate in the profits of economic activities. Access to equity capital has allowed entrepreneurs like Steve Jobs of Apple (ticker: AAPL) and Larry Page of Google (ticker: GOOG) to take their companies public so that their businesses can become large corporations. Both the company founders and the new owners (stock investors) have amassed much wealth over the years under this arrangement.

continued on p. 152

LEARNING GOALS

LG1 Understand the rights and returns that come with common stock ownership.

LG2 Know how stock exchanges function.

LG3 Track the wider stock market with stock indices and differentiate among the kinds of information each index provides.

LG4 Know the terminology of stock trading.

LG5 Compute stock values using dividend discount and constant-growth models.

LG6 Calculate the stock value of a variable-growth-rate company.

LG7 Assess relative stock values using the P/E ratio model.

continued from p.151

One very important reason that investors are willing to buy company stock as an investment is that they know that they can sell the stock during any trading day. Investors buy and sell stocks among themselves in stock markets. Well-functioning stock markets are critical to any capitalist economy. In this chapter, we'll discuss stocks, stock market operations and stock valuation. ▪

COMMON STOCK

Equity securities (stocks) represent ownership shares in a corporation. **Common stock** offers buyers the potential for current income from dividends and capital appreciation from any stock price increases. Over time, some corporate profits are reinvested in the firm, which increases the value of each shareholder's stake in the business. At any point in time, the market value of a firm's common stock depends on many factors, including:

- The company's profitability.
- Growth prospects for the future.
- Current market interest rates.
- Conditions in the overall stock market.

Over periods of 30 to 40 years, stocks have offered investors the best opportunities to increase wealth. Because stocks are also susceptible to price declines and stock price fluctuations can be very volatile over short periods of time, stock investing requires a longer-term outlook.

viewpoints

business APPLICATION

As CEO of your firm, Dawa Tech, which makes computer components, you have been able to grow its dividends by 8 percent per year to a recent $2 per share. You expect this growth to continue. As a result, the stock price has risen to $65 and has a P/E ratio of 16.25.

Tomorrow, you are scheduled to meet with some stockholders and financial analysts. To prepare for the meeting, you should know what return the shareholders seem to expect and estimate where the Dawa stock price may be in three years. How will you go about preparing for this meeting?

what they are owed. As a company earns cash flows, it must pay suppliers, employees, expenses, taxes, and debt interest payments. Stockholders claim the leftover (or residual) cash flow. These profits can be used to reinvest in the firm to foster growth, to pay out as dividends to shareholders, or for a combination of the two.

Stocks of growing firms are valuable. Stocks in firms that pay dividends to shareholders are also valuable. Stocks issued by firms that have greater amounts of residual cash flow are even more valuable. The value is reflected in the stock price. Therefore, stock price values arise from the company's underlying business success. Many different investors and analysts may estimate a stock's fundamental value based upon some outlook or theory. But the actual stock price is determined in stock exchanges when investors seek to trade with one another. Let's discuss this trading process and then explore how stocks are valued.

> **VIRTUALLY ANY BUSINESS FIRM THAT IS ORGANIZED AS A CORPORATION MAY CHOOSE TO ISSUE PUBLICLY TRADED STOCK.**

Virtually any business firm that is organized as a corporation (see Chapter 1) may choose to issue publicly traded stock. Common stockholders vote to elect the board of directors; they also vote on various other proposals requested by other shareholders or the management team. As owners of the firm, common stockholders are considered to be **residual claimants.** This means that common stockholders have the right to claim any cash flows or value after all other claimants have received

STOCK MARKETS

In general, people will only invest significant amounts of their wealth in stocks if they know that they can convert their shares into cash at any time. Stock exchanges provide this liquidity, allowing buyers and sellers the means to transact stock trades with each other. This liquidity gives many people the confidence to invest in the first place and makes stocks (as well as

personal APPLICATION

You are impressed with the news and entertainment firm CBC Newscorp. The per-share dividends have increased from $1.25 per year three years ago to the recent $1.68 annual dividend. Then you discover that 15 analysts are following the firm and that their mean growth estimate for the future is 10.1 percent. Now you want to know if the current selling price of $54 seems like a good deal if the appropriate required return for the stock is 13.5 percent.

bonds) attractive investments relative to less-liquid assets like real estate or fine collectibles—which can be difficult to sell quickly at full value. The most well-known stock exchange in the world is the **New York Stock Exchange (NYSE).**

The New York Stock Exchange, located in New York City on the corner of Wall Street and Broad Street, is the largest U.S. stock exchange as measured by the value of companies listed and the dollar value of trading activity. The NYSE is the largest equities marketplace in the world and is home to nearly 2,700 companies (many with multiple securities listed). While other exchanges may boast more companies listed, the largest companies in the world tend to list in New York.

Consider this trade illustration. You decide to buy shares of McDonald's stock because of their new menu items and other initiatives. You place a buy order for 100 shares with your broker—either with a simple phone call or through an online brokerage service. The broker then sends the order to the NYSE electronically via the SuperDOT® System to the trading post assigned for McDonald's stock. At the trading post, the specialist makes sure the transaction is executed in a fair and orderly manner. Your buy order competes with other orders at the point of sale for the best price and an on-floor broker executes your purchase. You will receive a trade confirmation from your broker describing the trade and noting the exact amount you owe for the 100 shares of McDonald's plus any applicable commissions. The NYSE reports the transaction and it appears within seconds on displays across the country and around the world. Note that buy and sell orders are electronically routed from all over the world to the NYSE, which then routes trade results back.

Because most of the trade orders are already in electronic form, why not electronically match buy and

common stock An ownership stake in a public corporation.

residual claimants Ownership of cash flows and value after other claimants are paid.

New York Stock Exchange Large and prestigious stock exchange with a trading floor.

trading post Trading location on the floor of a stock exchange.

specialist Person charged with managing the trading process for several individual stocks on the trading floor.

brokers Floor traders who execute orders for others and themselves.

ticker symbol Unique code for a company consisting of one to five letters.

> The NYSE has joined many other exchanges in becoming increasingly electronic. Some floor specialist firms can see a time when no human intervention will be a part of floor trading at the NYSE.

Much of the stock buying and selling at the NYSE occurs at 17 stations called **trading posts** on the trading floor. Each post is staffed by a **specialist,** who oversees the orderly trading of the specific stocks assigned to that post. **Brokers,** located around the perimeter of the floor, act as agents for those buying and selling stocks. Brokers execute orders by matching buy and sell orders. Once the buy and sell orders match, the transaction is completed and the trade appears on trading screens viewed by people all over the world.

sell orders and bypass any human intervention in floor trading? Indeed, the NYSE has joined many other exchanges in becoming increasingly electronic. Some floor specialist firms can see a time when no human intervention will be a part of floor trading at the NYSE. Their claim that human intervention can detect and prevent problems with electronic trades has been widely questioned.

The NYSE will trade hundreds of thousands, even millions, of McDonald's stock shares in a given day. An intraday (during trading hours) stock quote for McDonald's stock, **ticker symbol**

The NYSE trades millions upon millions of stock shares in a given day

MCD, is shown in Figure 7.1. On January 8, 2008, over 5 million McDonald's shares traded by early afternoon. The stock traded at $58.12 per share, which was 4 cents higher than the closing price of the previous day. At this price, McDonald's stock is currently much closer to its 52-week high of $63.69 than to its 52-week low of $42.31.

To list its stock on the NYSE, a company must meet minimum requirements for its:

- Total number of stockholders.

- Level of trading volume.

- Corporate earnings.

- Firm size.

The Exchange also charges an initial list fee and an annual fee. Listing standards and fees are higher for the NYSE than for other stock exchanges, so many firms cannot (or choose not to) list their stocks there. They can find one alternative right down the street at the **American Stock Exchange (AMEX),** which uses a specialist trading system like the NYSE. As the nation's second largest floor-based stock auction exchange, the AMEX processes trades in both listed equities and equity derivative securities (options).

Another popular stock trading system is the **NASDAQ Stock Market,** an electronic stock market without a physical trading floor. Today, NASDAQ features many of the big-name high-tech companies investors have come to know, like Apple Computer (ticker: AAPL), Intel (ticker: INTC), Microsoft (ticker: MSFT), and Qualcomm (ticker: QCOM). Many newer high-tech companies like Google (ticker: GOOG), Netflix (ticker: NFLX), and Sirius Satellite Radio (ticker: SIRI), are also listed on NASDAQ. NASDAQ ranks second, behind the NYSE, among the world's equity markets in terms of total dollar volume. NASDAQ lists nearly 3,100 domestic and foreign companies.

Instead of having a trading floor, NASDAQ uses a vast electronic trading system that executes trades via computer rather than in person. Instead of one specialist overseeing the process for an individual stock on a trading floor, NASDAQ's system uses multiple **market makers,** called **dealers.** Market makers use their own stock inventory and capital to compete with other dealers to buy and sell the stocks they represent. When an investor places an order through a stockbroker for a NASDAQ-listed stock, the electronic system routes the order and the investor buys shares from the dealer offering the best (lowest) price. Typical NASDAQ stocks support 10 market makers actively competing with one another for investor trades.

Table 7.1 shows trading activity on the three main stock exchanges for one day in January 2008. The NYSE and NASDAQ each show over 3,000 securities trading, with a total volume of well over 1 billion shares each. Trading on the AMEX is much smaller at less than 50 million shares traded.

The business of providing platforms or forums for investors and speculators to trade stocks and other financial assets has been changing rapidly. Many exchanges that previously used physical floor trading systems with specialists and public outcry

American Stock Exchange Stock exchange with a trading floor.

NASDAQ Stock Market Large electronic stock exchange.

market makers Dealers and specialists who oversee an orderly trading process.

dealers NASDAQ market makers who use their own capital to trade with investors.

▼**FIGURE 7.1**
Read a Stock Quote, January 8, 2008, Yahoo! Finance

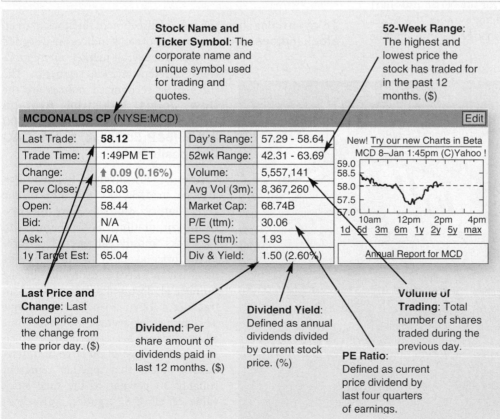

Stock Name and Ticker Symbol: The corporate name and unique symbol used for trading and quotes.

52-Week Range: The highest and lowest price the stock has traded for in the past 12 months. ($)

MCDONALDS CP (NYSE:MCD)   Edit

Last Trade:	**58.12**	Day's Range:	57.29 - 58.64
Trade Time:	1:49PM ET	52wk Range:	42.31 - 63.69
Change:	↑ 0.09 (0.16%)	Volume:	5,557,141
Prev Close:	58.03	Avg Vol (3m):	8,367,260
Open:	58.44	Market Cap:	68.74B
Bid:	N/A	P/E (ttm):	30.06
Ask:	N/A	EPS (ttm):	1.93
1y Target Est:	65.04	Div & Yield:	1.50 (2.60%)

New! Try our new Charts in Beta
MCD 8-Jan 1:45pm (C)Yahoo!
59.0 / 58.5 / 58.0 / 57.5 / 57.0
10am   12pm   2pm   4pm
1d 5d 3m 6m 1y 2y 5y max

Annual Report for MCD

Last Price and Change: Last traded price and the change from the prior day. ($)

Dividend: Per share amount of dividends paid in last 12 months. ($)

Dividend Yield: Defined as annual dividends divided by current stock price. (%)

PE Ratio: Defined as current price dividend by last four quarters of earnings.

Volume of Trading: Total number of shares traded during the previous day.

stock index Index of market prices of a particular group of stocks. The index is used to measure those stocks' performance.

Dow Jones Industrial Average A popular index of 30 large, industry-leading firms.

Standard & Poor's 500 Index A stock index of 500 large companies.

NASDAQ Composite Index A technology-firm weighted index of stocks listed on the NASDAQ Stock Exchange.

▼ **TABLE 7.1** Trading on the NYSE, NASDAQ, and AMEX, January 8, 2008

	NYSE	NASDAQ	AMEX
Number of securities traded	3,369	3,066	1,331
Advances	1,800	1,400	690
Declines	1,491	1,554	531
Unchanged	78	112	110
New high	53	60	33
New low	291	271	69
Total volume of shares	2,692,343,087	1,504,089,921	686,316,450

Source: Yahoo! Finance (http://finance.yahoo.com/advances).

to establish stock prices are shifting to electronic systems with no trading floors. Long-standing, traditional exchanges are also merging with other domestic and international exchanges to create fewer, but larger, forums that focus not just on U.S. securities but on many more internationally focused financial assets. The wider range of represented securities allows traders new opportunities to explore trading relationships among securities traded across the world. This worldwide trading will establish economically sound prices and additional financial stability around the world. Many exchanges have become public companies themselves. For example, in April 2007 the NYSE became a publicly traded company for the first time in its history when it merged with Euronext and became NYSE Euronext. So now, the common stock for the NYSE Euronext company is traded on the NYSE exchange under the ticker symbol: NYX. The NASDAQ stock exchange became a public company in 2002 and trades on its own exchange under the ticker symbol: NDAQ.

Tracking the Stock Market

With thousands of stocks trading every minute, many stock prices rise while others fall. Table 7.1 also shows that, throughout the trading day, 1,800 stocks increased in price on the NYSE while 1,491 stocks decreased in price. On the AMEX, too, more stocks increased in price than decreased but not on NASDAQ. In addition to the number of stocks advancing and declining, the table also shows the number of stocks that hit new 52-week price highs (53 listed on the NYSE) and new lows (291 on the NYSE) on that day. So, was this a good day or a bad day in the stock market?

To say anything about the *general* direction of the stock market, **stock indices** are useful. Dozens of stock indices are designed to track the overall market; many more track different market segments. The three most recognized indices are the **Dow Jones Industrial Average** (DJIA), the **Standard & Poor's 500 Index (S&P 500),** and the **NASDAQ Composite Index.**

Charles H. Dow invented the first stock average in 1884. At the turn of the 20th century, railroads were the first major corporations. So he began with 11 stocks, mostly railroads. Dow created a price average by simply adding up 11 stock prices and dividing by the number 11. Two years later, Dow began tracking a 12-stock industrial average. This industrial average would eventually evolve into the modern DJIA, which is a price average of 30 large, industry-leading stocks that together represent roughly 30 percent of the total stock value of all U.S. equities. DJIA level

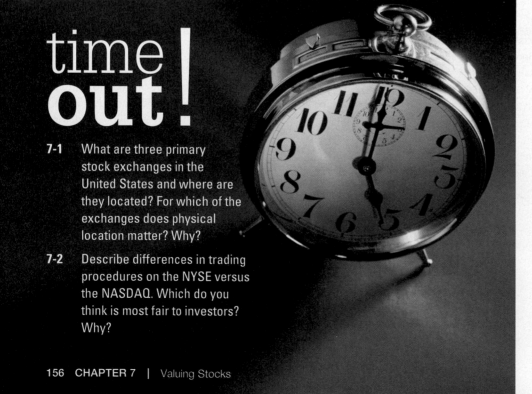

time out!

7-1 What are three primary stock exchanges in the United States and where are they located? For which of the exchanges does physical location matter? Why?

7-2 Describe differences in trading procedures on the NYSE versus the NASDAQ. Which do you think is most fair to investors? Why?

changes describe how the largest companies that participate in the stock market performed over a given period. The DJIA was at 12,866.59, a change of +39.10 (or 0.30 percent), on the day illustrated in Table 7.1.

The Standard & Poor's Corp. introduced its 500-stock index in 1957. Standard & Poor's chooses companies to include in the S&P 500 Index to represent the 10 sectors of the economy:

- Financial
- Information technology
- Health care
- Industrials
- Consumer discretionary
- Consumer staples
- Energy
- Telecom services
- Utilities
- Materials

market capitalization The size of the firm measured as the current stock price multiplied by the number of shares outstanding. (p. 224)

S&P uses **market capitalization** (a measure of company size using stock price times shares outstanding), not just stock prices, of the largest 500 U.S. firms to compute the index. These 500 firms represent roughly 80 percent of the overall stock market capitalization (number of shares times share price). Although the DJIA is a long-time favorite with the media and individual investors, the S&P 500 is much preferred in the

SINCE THE NASDAQ LISTS SO MANY LARGE, TECHNOLOGY-ORIENTED COMPANIES, MANY INVESTORS AND ANALYSTS CONSIDER THIS INDEX TO REFLECT THE TECH SECTOR PERFORMANCE MORE THAN THAT OF THE OVERALL STOCK MARKET.

Investors consider the NASDAQ to be a reflection of the tech sector's general performance.

investment industry because of its broader representation of the market as a whole. S&P 500 performance provides a standard against which most U.S. money managers and pension plan sponsors can compare their investment performance. During trading on January 8, 2008, the S&P 500 gained 8.124 (0.57 percent) to close at 1,424.30.

The NASDAQ Composite Index measures the market capitalization of all common stocks listed on the NASDAQ stock exchange. Since the NASDAQ lists so many large, technology-oriented companies, many investors and analysts consider this index to reflect the tech sector performance more than that of the overall stock market. The NASDAQ Composite gained 17.54 to 2,517.00 on January 8, 2008, a gain of 0.70 percent. Because all three popular indexes were up on this day, most reports would reflect a good day for the stock market.

Figure 7.2 shows the levels of all these stock indexes since 1980. The DJIA (black line) level appears on the left-hand axis. Both the S&P 500 (green line) and the NASDAQ Composite (orange line) run from the right-hand axis. The rapid price appreciation for NASDAQ stocks during the late 1990s—the tech boom years—is unprecedented for such a large and widely followed market index. The NASDAQ Composite soared from 817 in March 1995 to peak on March 10, 2000, at 5,048.62, for a 518 percent total return in only five years—a 43.9 percent annual rate of share-price appreciation for NASDAQ stocks.

FIGURE 7.2
Stock Market Index Levels Since 1980

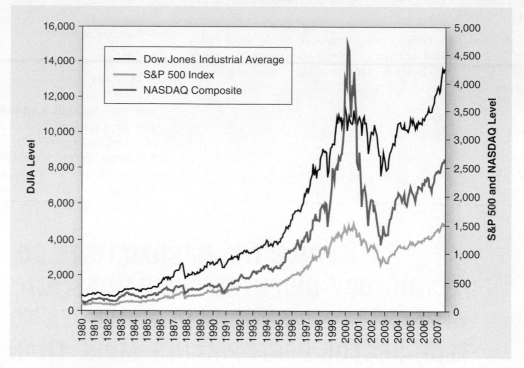

The NASDAQ index performed much better than did the DJIA (19.0 percent per year) or the S&P 500 (22.7 percent per year). The NASDAQ "price bubble" set the stage for one of the most dramatic stock price declines in history: The NASDAQ Composite Index plunged to 1,114.11 on October 9, 2002, losing 78 percent of its value. The other index values also fell during this period, albeit not as sharply. Note that the DJIA didn't climb back to its 2000 high until March 2006. The S&P 500 Index finally recovered in May 2007. The NASDAQ Composite still has a long way to go to recover from its fall from pre-2000 levels.

Trading Stocks

People who wish to buy and sell stocks need to open stock brokerage accounts. Traditional, full-service stockbrokers (e.g., Smith Barney, Merrill Lynch, Dean Witter) provide clients with research and advice in addition to executing trades. Their clients pay for this research and advice: Commission fees for these services may run well over $100 per trade. Discount brokerage firms (e.g., e-trade, Scottrade, TD Ameritrade) charge a much lower commission, $5 to $30 per trade, but do not provide the additional services. Investors at discount brokerages usually place trades through the brokerage's Internet sites.

Buy and sell orders go through the brokerage firm to a market maker (a dealer or a specialist) at a stock exchange. The quoted **bid** is the highest price at which the *market maker* offers to pay for the stock. Investors have little choice but to accept this selling price, because regardless of the broker used, the market maker offers the only place to sell the stock. The quoted **ask** price is the lowest price at which a market maker will sell a stock—so investors buy at the ask price. The difference between the bid and the ask price may be only 1 cent for high-volume stocks and can be as high as 20 cents for less-often traded companies. The spread between the bid and the ask price is a cost to the investor and a profit for the market maker. This profit compensates the market maker for providing a market and liquidity for that stock.

Investors can place a buy or sell **market order.** A market order to buy stock will be filled immediately at the current ask

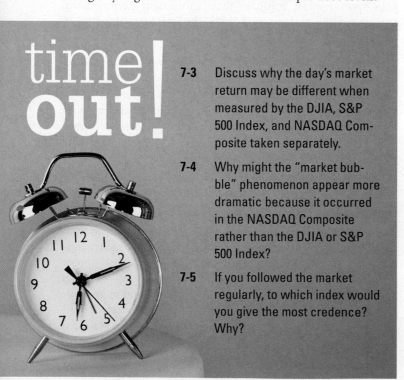

7-3 Discuss why the day's market return may be different when measured by the DJIA, S&P 500 Index, and NASDAQ Composite taken separately.

7-4 Why might the "market bubble" phenomenon appear more dramatic because it occurred in the NASDAQ Composite rather than the DJIA or S&P 500 Index?

7-5 If you followed the market regularly, to which index would you give the most credence? Why?

finance at work //: behavioral

Investor Psychology

To us today, it seems ludicrous that in the years 1634 to 1636, near the height of the "Tulip Mania" in Holland, the price for a single rare tulip bulb approached the equivalent of $35,000. Then, the bubble burst and tulip prices quickly plunged to less than the equivalent of $1. We may call those people who invested in a $35,000 tulip bulb irrational or even "crazy."

But this type of story seems to repeat itself throughout history. Investors paid extremely high prices for the new computer stocks in the 1960s, the "nifty fifty" companies in the 1970s, and Japanese stocks during the 1980s. And of course, the recent technology and Internet stock bubble of the late 1990s reflected equally irrational buying. The mania for stocks like Iomega drove its price from an equivalent of $1 per share in January of 1995 to over $75 in just 16 months. When the bubble burst, the price fell hard. Many years later, in 2007, the stock still trades for only about $3.50. But that's just one company. A portfolio full of Internet stocks experienced a similar price mania followed by a severe fall. Investors created a stock index (TheStreet.com Internet Index) designed to track Internet stocks in late 1998, but by that time, part-time investors and veterans alike were already well into the craze. The Internet index started at 250, quickly rose to 1,270 by March of 2000, and subsequently fell to a low of 63 in October of 2002. In retrospect, irrational bubble-like prices are not confined to tulips and the 17th century in Holland.

Seemingly irrational behavior may not occur only during highly emotional periods of a price bubble. Recently, a growing recognition has arisen that "normal" investors often behave in a way that might not be described as fully rational. Investors, being human, are subject to cognitive biases and emotions. Studies of investor

behavior have discovered that investors commonly succumb to psychological biases and:

- Trade too much.
- Sell winners too soon.
- Refuse to realize losses.
- Become overconfident—especially when trading online.
- Seek stocks that have already increased in price— perhaps up to their full potential price.
- Consider and react to what's happening with each stock in isolation, rather than remembering the purpose for forming an overall portfolio.

Investors who succeed in the long run are those who learn to avoid these psychological biases.

Want to know more?

Key Words to Search for Updates: **irrational exuberance, price bubble, mania**

---

price when routed to the stock exchange. A sell market order will be filled at the current bid price. The advantage of a market order is that it executes immediately at the best available price. The disadvantage of a market order is that the investor does not know in advance what that fill price will be. Investors can name their own prices by using **limit orders,** in which investors specify the price at which they are willing to execute the buy or sell order. With a buy limit order, a trade is executed if the ask quote is at or below the price target. For a sell limit order, a trade is executed if the bid quote moves through the specified price. If the current quote does not meet the price cited in the

limit order, the trade is not executed. The advantage of a limit order is that the investor makes the trade at the desired price; the disadvantage is that the trade might not be executed at all.

Consider a quote of McDonald's stock with a bid price of $58.10 and an ask price of $58.15. An investor placing a market buy order would purchase the stock at $58.10. A market sell order would execute as the price rises through $58.15. Note that an investor who simultaneously bought and sold 100 shares would pay $5,815 and receive $5,810—losing $5. An investor who places a buy limit order at $58.13 will only purchase the shares if the ask price falls to $58.13 or lower. If the ask does not fall, the order will not execute. Bid and ask prices tell investors at what prices the stock can currently be traded in general. But being able to buy at the ask price does not guarantee that the stock should be *valued* at that price. We'll discuss various ways to arrive at reasonable per-share stock values in the next section.

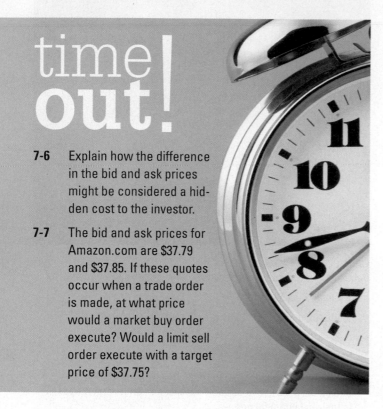

time out!

7-6 Explain how the difference in the bid and ask prices might be considered a hidden cost to the investor.

7-7 The bid and ask prices for Amazon.com are $37.79 and $37.85. If these quotes occur when a trade order is made, at what price would a market buy order execute? Would a limit sell order execute with a target price of $37.75?

BASIC STOCK VALUATION

Cash Flows

In the previous chapter, we showed how we value bonds by finding the present value of the future interest payments and the future par value. Stock valuation uses the same concept of finding the present value of future dividends and the future selling price. But of course uncertainty about both price appreciation and future dividend payment streams complicates stock valuation. Consider the simple case of valuing a stock to be held for one year shown in the time line.

Cash flow	?		$D_1 + P_1$
Period	0	i	1 year

The value of such a stock today, P_0, is the present value of the dividend to be received in the first year, D_1, plus the present value of the expected sales price in one year, P_1. The interest rate used to discount the cash flows is shown as i. Using the present value equation from Chapter 4 results in:

$$P_0 = \frac{D_1 + P_1}{1 + i} \qquad (7\text{-}1)$$

Whenever investors deal with future stock prices and future dividend payments, they must use expected values, not certain ones. Companies rarely decrease their dividends; most companies' dividends either remain constant or slowly grow. Examining a firm's dividend history over the past few years will give clues to that company's future dividend policy. For example, The Coca-Cola Company (ticker: KO) paid a $0.22 per share dividend for each quarter in 2003. The firm then raised the quarterly dividend to $0.25 for each quarterly dividend in 2004. The company paid quarterly dividends in 2005, 2006, and 2007 of $0.28, $0.31, and $0.34 respectively. This increase of 3¢ in the dividend every year seems fairly stable.

Stock prices, though, show much more volatility than dividend histories do. We face much uncertainty in trying to predict stock prices in the short term. Using a longer holding period to estimate stock value reduces *some,* but by no means all, of the uncertainty. A two-year holding period appears like this:

Cash flow	?		D_1		$D_2 + P_2$
Period	0	i	1		2 years

Coca-Cola increased its dividend by 3 cents per year over a five-year span.

The present value of the cash flows in years 1 and 2 is today's stock value:

$$P_0 = \frac{D_1}{1+i} + \frac{D_2 + P_2}{(1+i)^2} \qquad (7\text{-}2)$$

Notice that the divisor for the second term on the right-hand side of equation 7.2 is raised to the second power. This reflects the two years over which those cash flows must be discounted. You can do this analysis over any holding period. For a holding period of n years, the value of a stock is measured by the present value of dividends over the n years, and the eventual sale price, P_n.

$P_0 =$ sum of the present value of each payment received

$$P_0 = \frac{D_1}{1+i} + \frac{D_2}{(1+i)^2} + \cdots + \frac{D_n + P_n}{(1+i)^n} \qquad (7\text{-}3)$$

This formula incorporates both dividend income and capital appreciation or capital loss. It fully includes both major components of the investor's total return from investment.

As is often the case in finance, implementing equation 7.3 presents problems for some firms in practical terms. What will the future dividends of the firm be? What will the stock price be in 3, 5, or 10 years? While it seems that the dividend growth of Coca-Cola will be constant, consider the actual dividends and stock price of McDonald's Corp. since 2000 shown in Figure 7.3.

Unlike most firms, which pay quarterly dividends, McDonald's pays an annual dividend during the second week of November. On November 13, 2000, it paid a $0.215 per share dividend. McDonald's was able to increase that by 4¢ per share the following year (an 18.6 percent increase), but had to cut the dividend by 2¢ per share in 2002 (an 8.9 percent decline). However, since 2002, McDonald's has been able to increase its dividend every year—sometimes substantial increases. The dividend increases in 2003 and 2007 were 70.2 percent and 50.0 percent, respectively. The figure also shows that McDonald's stock price has been very volatile. The price fell from $37 in 2000 to nearly $12 in 2003 and then rapidly increased to over

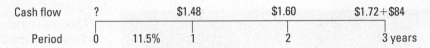

EXAMPLE 7-1

For interactive versions of this example visit www.mhhe.com/canM

Valuing Coca-Cola Stock

In January 2008, you are valuing Coca-Cola stock at the beginning of 2008 to compare its value to its market price. The current market price is $63.50. Given the history of Coca-Cola's dividends, you believe that the company will pay total dividends in 2008 of $1.48 ($= 4 \times \$0.37$). Your analysis indicates that the total dividends in 2009 and 2010 will be $1.60 and $1.72, respectively. In addition, you believe that the price of Coca-Cola stock at the end of 2010 will be $84 per share. If the appropriate discount rate is 11.5 percent, what is the value of Coca-Cola stock?

SOLUTION:

To organize your data, you first create the following timeline:

Cash flow	?		$1.48	$1.60	$1.72+$84
Period	0	11.5%	1	2	3 years

Using equation 7-3, you compute the stock value as:

$$P_0 = \frac{\$1.48}{1+0.115} + \frac{\$1.60}{(1+0.115)^2} + \frac{\$1.72 + \$84}{(1+0.115)^3} = \$1.33 + \$1.29 + \$61.84 = \$64.46$$

Since your analysis shows that Coca-Cola's stock should be valued at nearly $64.50 while it's selling for only $63.50, the stock appears to be slightly undervalued. You believe that this might be a good time to buy some Coca-Cola stock.

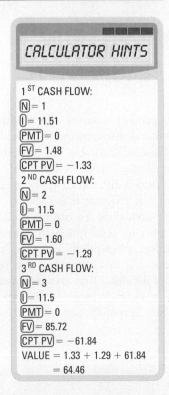

CALCULATOR HINTS

1ST CASH FLOW:
N = 1
I = 11.51
PMT = 0
FV = 1.48
CPT PV = −1.33

2ND CASH FLOW:
N = 2
I = 11.5
PMT = 0
FV = 1.60
CPT PV = −1.29

3RD CASH FLOW:
N = 3
I = 11.5
PMT = 0
FV = 85.72
CPT PV = −61.84
VALUE = 1.33 + 1.29 + 61.84
       = 64.46

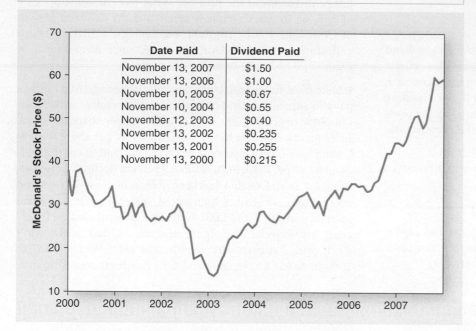

Date Paid	Dividend Paid
November 13, 2007	$1.50
November 13, 2006	$1.00
November 10, 2005	$0.67
November 10, 2004	$0.55
November 12, 2003	$0.40
November 13, 2002	$0.235
November 13, 2001	$0.255
November 13, 2000	$0.215

and stock prices. Indeed, short-term stock price changes seem almost random. Stock valuation can really only be viewed from a long-term perspective. Because predicting future dividends is uncertain at best, it's better to project valuation as a likely range of prices under reasonable assumptions rather than as a single price.

Dividend Discount Models

We can extend the discounted cash flow approach in equation 7-3 for an infinite stream of dividends, $n \to \infty$, and no final future selling price. If stockholders receive all future cash flows as future dividends, the stock's value to the investor is the present value of all these future dividends. In other words, embedded in any stock price is the value of all future dividends. We can demonstrate this value as:

$58 by the end of 2007. An investor in 2000 would have had a very difficult time accurately forecasting these future dividends

$$P_0 = \frac{D_1}{1+i} + \frac{D_2}{(1+i)^2} + \frac{D_3}{(1+i)^3} + \cdots \tag{7-4}$$

> **STOCK VALUATION CAN REALLY ONLY BE VIEWED FROM A LONG-TERM PERSPECTIVE.**

McDonald's pays an annual dividend instead of quarterly dividends.

This equation shows the general case of the **dividend discount model.** The dividend discount model provides a useful theoretical basis because it illustrates the importance of dividends as a fundamental stock price determinant. But, again, finance professionals find it difficult to apply the dividend discount model because it requires that they estimate an infinite number of future dividends. To use the model in practice, analysts make simplifying assumptions to make the model workable. One common assumption: The firm has a constant dividend growth rate, g. If this is the case, next year's dividend is simply this year's dividend that grew one year at the growth rate, that is, $D_1 = D_0 \times (1 + g)$. In fact, we can express each dividend as a function of D_0 and we can rewrite equation 7-4 as:

$$P_0 = \frac{D_0(1+g)}{1+i} = \frac{D_0(1+g)^2}{(1+i)^2} + \frac{D_0(1+g)^3}{(1+i)^3} + \cdots \tag{7-5}$$

So, with this version of the model, we need not forecast an infinite string of dividends; D_0 and g take care of that. However, we must still compute an infinite sum of numbers. Luckily, mathematicians know equations like these; they're known as power series. This power series can be simplified to the **constant-growth model,** and it assumes that the growth rate is smaller than the discount rate (i.e., for $g < i$):

$$\text{Constant-growth model} = P_0 = \frac{D_0(1+g)}{i-g} = \frac{D_1}{i-g} \quad \text{(7-6)}$$

If $g \geq i$, then the denominator would be zero or negative. Economically and mathematically, this is a nonsensical result. In the short run, a firm can grow very quickly. In the long run, no company can grow faster than the overall economic growth rate forever. You may hear the constant-growth model referred to as the *Gordon growth model,* after financial economist Myron J. Gordon.

Investors use several methods to estimate a firm's growth rate for this model. They can project the dividend trend into the future and determine the implied growth rate, compute the past growth rate, or even consider a financial analyst's growth rate predictions. Consider Coca-Cola's dividend behavior. If the 2007 dividend was $1.36 and the projected dividends will grow to $1.90 in 2011, the implied projected dividend growth rate is therefore 8.72 percent (N = 4, PV = −1.36, PMT = 0,

dividend discount model A valuation approach based on future dividend income.

constant-growth model A valuation method based on constantly growing dividends.

preferred stock A class of stock with fixed dividends.

FV = 1.72, CPT I = 8.14) annually. The growth rate in dividend changes from 2003 to 2007 was 11.50 percent (N = 4, PV = −0.88, PMT = 0, FV = 1.36, CPT I = 11.50) per year. You can find analyst forecasts many places online. The Yahoo! Finance Web page for Coca-Cola has an Analyst Estimates link, which shows the average analysts' forecast for the firm's growth in the next five years at 9.37 percent.

Preferred Stock

A special case of the constant-growth model occurs when the dividend does not grow but is the same every year. This zero-growth rate case describes a **preferred stock.** The phrase *preferred* comes from the fact that this type of stock takes preference over common stock in bankruptcy proceedings. Preferred stockholders have a higher priority for receiving proceeds from bankruptcy proceedings than do common stockholders. Preferred stock is largely owned by other companies, rather than by individual investors, because its dividends are mostly non-taxable income (70 percent of the income is exempt from taxes) to other corporations. Preferred stockholders do not have voting rights like common stockholders, though, which prevents one company from controlling another through preferred stock ownership.

EXAMPLE 7-2

For interactive versions of this example visit www.mhhe.com/canM

Constant Growth and Coca-Cola Stock

Assume that you are valuing Coca-Cola stock again. This time you are using the constant-growth model, assuming a discount rate of 11.5 percent.

SOLUTION:

You have a choice of three growth rates to use. The implied projected dividend growth rate is 8.72 percent. Past dividend growth has been 11.50 percent and analysts forecast a 9.37 percent growth. The 11.50 percent growth rate is the same as the 11.5 percent discount rate and is therefore not appropriate for the constant-growth-rate model. Compute the stock value using both the 8.72 percent and 9.37 percent growth rates.

Using a dividend growth rate of 8.72 percent and equation 7-6, the stock value is $53.24:

$$P_0 = \frac{\$1.36 \times (1 + 0.00872)}{0.115 - 0.0872} = \frac{\$1.48}{0.0278} = \$53.24$$

Using a dividend growth rate of 9.37 percent, the stock value is $69.83:

$$P_0 = \frac{\$1.36 \times (1 + 0.0937)}{0.115 - 0.0937} = \$69.83$$

Notice how a small change in the growth rate has a large impact on the stock value in this model. At a current price of $63.50 per share, Coca-Cola would be considered undervalued if future dividend growth is 9.37 percent and overvalued if dividends grow at 8.72 percent.

Using the Constant-Growth-Rate Model

" The distinction between the recent year's dividends, D_0, and next year's dividends, D_1, can be confusing in the constant-growth-rate model. The model's equation presents two different numerators. If you are given information about dividends last year or just paid, use the $D_0(1 + g)$ version of the equation. If you have information about expected dividends or next year's dividend, use the D_1 version of the equation. "

from the expectation that Coca-Cola's dividend will grow. In other words, investors value highly a growing firm.

Most companies issue only common stock, but nearly 1,000 preferred stock issues still exist. Table 7.2 compares the common stock and preferred stock for 10 firms. Many of the preferred stocks come from the finance, energy, and real estate sectors. Notice that the **dividend yield** for preferred stock is higher than for the common stock, because preferred stock investors should only expect a return from dividend payments. Common stockholders will also expect a return from capital appreciation over time. Common stocks also trade much more frequently than preferred stocks do.

The zero-growth-rate version of the constant-growth valuation model shows that, since dividends are fixed, a preferred

An interesting characteristic of preferred stock is that it pays a constant dividend. Because the dividend does not change, the preferred stock can be valued using the constant-growth-rate model with a zero growth rate expressed as $P = D/i$. What would Coca-Cola's stock be worth if its dividend stayed at $1.36 and never grew? Using the same 11.5 percent discount

[An interesting characteristic of preferred stock is that it pays a constant dividend.]

rate, the stock would be valued at $11.83 (= $1.36 ÷ 0.115). Given Coca-Cola's current stock price of $63.50, over 81 percent [= ($63.50 − $11.83) ÷ $63.50] of its stock value comes

stock's price changes because of changes in the discount rate, i. When interest rates throughout the economy change, the discount rate also changes. Preferred stock prices thus

▼ **TABLE 7.2** Common and Preferred Stock, July 11, 2007

Company	Ticker	Price	Annual Dividend (Yield%)	Volume	Ticker	Price	Annual Dividend (Yield%)	Volume
		Common Stock				Preferred Stock		
Alcoa Inc.	AA	$42.43	$0.68(1.5)	11,751,400	AA.PR	$71.75	$3.75(5.2)	1,300
Bear Stearns Cos.	BSC	138.03	1.28(0.9)	6,085,000	BSCPRG	48.40	2.74(5.7)	500
CIT Group Inc.	CIT	55.41	1.00(1.8)	1,110,100	CITPRA	24.85	1.59(6.4)	5,200
El Du Pont de Nemours & Co.	DD	51.18	1.48(2.9)	4,553,200	DDPRA	67.70	3.50(5.2)	300
Ford Motor Co.	F	8.90	0.20(2.5)	69,500,800	FPRS	39.24	3.25(8.3)	4,451,000
Host Hotels & Resorts Inc.	HST	24.53	0.80(3.3)	3,323,200	HSTPRE	26.80	2.22(8.3)	900
LaSalle Hotel Properties	LHO	47.53	2.04(4.3)	316,000	LHOD	24.10	1.88(7.7)	700
Northrop Grumman Corp.	NOC	76.79	1.48(1.9)	966,500	NOCPRB	140.96	7.00(4.9)	4,200
PG&E Corp.	PCG	44.80	1.44(3.2)	1,911,700	PCG.PRA	24.55	1.50(6.1)	300
Public Storage Inc.	PSA	76.55	2.00(2.6)	831,400	PSAPRL	24.27	1.68(6.9)	11,900

Source: New York Stock Exchange (**www.nyse.com**).

tend to act like bond prices. When interest rates rise, preferred stock prices fall. When interest rates decline, preferred stock prices rise. Preferred stock is usually categorized with bonds in the fixed-income security group because it acts so much like debt securities, even though a preferred stock represents equity ownership, like common stock.

Expected Return

Stock valuation models require a discount rate, i, in order to compute the present value of the future cash flows. The discount rate used should reflect the investment risk level. Higher risk investments should be evaluated using higher interest rates. For example, the previous chapter on bonds demonstrated that higher risk bonds, such as junk bonds, offer higher rates of return. Similarly, investors demand higher returns from higher risk stocks than they do from lower risk stocks. We discuss stock risk measurement and appropriate expected returns in the next section of this book.

However, one method for determining what return stock investors require from a stock is to use the constant-growth-rate model. If the current stock price fairly reflects its value, then the

dividend yield Last four quarters of dividend income expressed as a percentage of the current stock price.

growth stocks Companies expected to have above-average rates of growth in revenue, earnings, and/or dividends.

financial analyst Industry professional who makes predictions about a firm's future earnings and growth, and who may provide sell/hold opinions to investors.

discount rate, i, in equation 7-6 should be the expected return for the stock. Solving for this expected return results in equation 7-7:

$$\text{Expected return} = i = \frac{D_1}{P_0} + g$$
$$= \text{Dividend yield} + \text{Capital gain} \qquad (7\text{-}7)$$

Note that the expected return comes again from two sources: dividend yield and expected appreciation of the stock price, or capital gain. For example, consider that Coca-Cola's dividend next year (2008), D_1, is expected to be $1.48 per share. At a current price of $63.50, Coca-Cola offers a dividend yield of 2.33 percent (= $1.48 ÷ $63.50). Since analysts believe that the firm's stock price will grow at 9.37 percent in the future, investors expect a total return of 11.7 percent (= $2.33% + 9.37%). Dividend yield can represent a substantial portion of the profits for an investor. Many people get too enamored of high **growth stocks** that do not pay dividends and therefore miss out on an important source of stable returns.

finance at work //: investments

Financial Analysts' Predictions and Opinions

Financial analysts examine a firm's business and financial success and assess long-term prospects and management effectiveness. They combine this microeconomic analysis with a macroeconomic view of the conditions of the economy, financial markets, and industry outlooks. Their evaluation results in earnings predictions, stock price targets, and opinions about whether investors should buy the stock. Such recommendations can help investors decide whether to buy, hold, or sell the stock.

Analysts hired by brokerage firms and investment banks are called *sell-side analysts* because their firms make money by selling stocks and bonds. These analysts publicize their predictions and opinions publicly and in company "tip sheets" that are passed along to clients. Keep in mind that sell-side analysts often have incentives to be optimistic. Pension funds and mutual funds often hire analysts to give fund managers private opinions about securities. These analysts are referred to as *buy-side analysts* because they are hired by investment firms looking for advice on what stocks to buy for their portfolios. Because this is private, little buy-side research is made public.

Consider the 14 sell-side analyst predictions reported for Coca-Cola on the Yahoo! Finance Web site. The average five-year share price growth prediction from these analysts is 9.37 percent. This is lower than the growth prediction for the industry (9.51 percent) and sector (9.80 percent). While the current stock price for Coca-Cola this day was $63.50, the average target price that the analysts cited was $65.08, with the target prices ranging from $60 to $69. Last, analysts give opinions on whether investors should buy, sell, or hold Coca-Cola stock. Recommendations come in five levels: Strong Buy, Buy, Hold, Sell, and Strong Sell. Of the 17 analysts, five recommend a Strong Buy, eight recommend a Buy, and four recommend a Hold. Note that even though the analysts predict lower than average growth for the industry and sector, and that the analysts provide meager price targets, none of the analysts recommend a Sell or Strong Sell of the stock. This optimism in analysts' opinions is common. Knowledgeable investors know that a "hold" recommendation is as negative as most public or sell-side analysts get, and therefore a "hold" may actually represent a signal to sell.

Want to know more?

Key Words to Search for Updates: **analyst opinion, financial analyst bias**

variable growth rate A valuation technique used when a firm's current growth rate is expected to change some time in the future.

Corporate managers conduct an important application of the expected return concept to determine the return that their shareholders expect of them. We will discuss this application in detail later.

ADDITIONAL VALUATION METHODS

Variable-Growth Techniques

Some companies grow at such a high rate that we can't use the constant-growth-rate model to forecast their value. High-growth rates might be sustainable for several years, but they cannot continue forever. Consider what happens to a high-growth firm. Other companies will surely notice the market potential for high-growth rates and will enter those product markets to compete with the high-growth firm. The competition will soon drive down the growth rates for all companies in that product market. Companies that experience unusually high growth tend to see that growth become only average in the future unless they possess some kind of entry barrier such as a patent or government regulation due to economies of scale.

Remember that the constant-growth-rate model doesn't work for companies where $g > i$. And of course, we don't really expect the growth rate for these fast-growing firms to remain constant. To value these firms, we must use a **variable-growth-rate** technique. The variable-growth-rate method combines the present-value cash flow from equation 7-3 and the constant-growth-rate model from equation 7-6.

First, the investor chooses two different growth rates for two stages of the analysis. The first and higher growth rate, g_1, is the current growth rate, which we expect to last only a few years. A few years from now, we expect the firm to

time out!

7-8 Explain how valuable a firm's (and therefore its stock) growth is. Demonstrate this with growth and no-growth examples.

7-9 What proportion of the 11.7 percent of Coca-Cola's expected return discussed above comes from dividend yield?

" HIGH-GROWTH RATES MIGHT BE SUSTAINABLE FOR SEVERAL YEARS, BUT THEY CANNOT CONTINUE FOREVER. "

▼**FIGURE 7.4**
Variable Dividend Growth

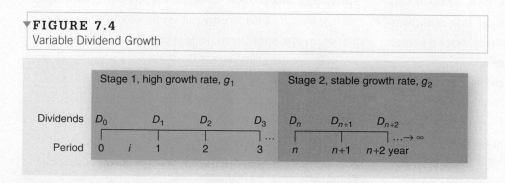

grow at a slower but more sustainable rate of growth, g_2. Figure 7.4 shows the cash flow time line when the first growth rate applies for the first n years, followed by the second growth rate, which applies forever.

When we analyze a variable-growth-rate stock like the one in the figure, we know the recent dividend, D_0, and the two expected growth rates. Therefore, we can calculate each of the dividends shown in general terms (i.e., D_1). For

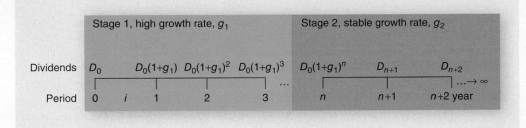

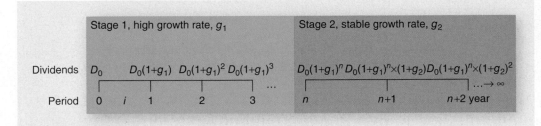

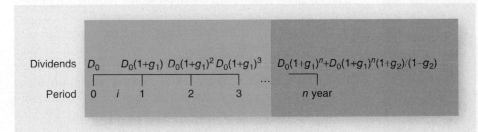

Once we've calculated all of the dividends, we can begin finding the value of the variable-growth stock by focusing on Stage 2 of the problem. Assume that the dividends in Stage 2 are growing at a modest rate, g_2, forever. As long as $g_2 < i$, Stage 2 can use the constant-growth-rate model, equation 7-6. Remember that the constant-growth-rate model, $P_0 = D_1/(i - g)$, replaces all future dividends with one value in the previous period. In previous applications, the growth began in year 1, so the value used for all future dividends came from the year 0 dividend. In this case, the change in the dividend rate occurs in year $n + 1$, so we will use the value from year n. So, using the constant-growth-rate model, we can replace all the cash flows in stage 2 with one value from year n, as:

$$P_n = \frac{D_{n+1}}{i - g_2} = \frac{D_0(1 + g_1)^n(1 + g_2)}{i - g_2}$$

The cash flows from Figure 7.6 now appear as shown in Figure 7.7.

By replacing all the Stage 2 cash flows that continued indefinitely with one terminal price in year n, we reduce the problem to a fixed number of cash flows. The value of this variable-growth-rate stock is finally computed as the present value of these cash flows, as solved with equation 7-3. Substituting the cash flows shown in Figure 7.7 into equation 7-3 gives us the general formula for finding the value of a variable-growth-rate stock:

General two-stage growth valuation model

$$P_0 = \frac{D_0(1 + g_1)}{1 + i} + \frac{D_0(1 + g_1)^2}{(1 + i)^2} + \frac{D_0(1 + g_1)^3}{(1 + i)^3} + \cdots \quad (7\text{-}8)$$

$$+ \frac{D_0(1 + g_1)^n + \dfrac{D_0(1 + g_1)^n(1 + g_2)}{i - g_2}}{(1 + i)^n}$$

The practical application of the variable-growth-rate valuation technique requires the investor to decide how long the current high-growth rate will last before declining to a more stable rate.

example, the dividend in the first year (D_1) is the year zero dividend that grows at g_1, specifically $D_1 = D_0 \times (1 + g_1)$. The dividend then grows at g_1 again for the second year dividend, $D_2 = D_0 \times (1 + g_1)^2$. The dividend continues to grow through the first stage to year n at $D_n = D_0 \times (1 + g_1)^n$. Figure 7.5 shows the first-stage dividends.

At this point, the company starts to move into stage 2 at the more modest growth rate, g_2, and the dividends reflect that slower growth rate. So D_{n+1} is the dividend D_n that grew at the rate g_2, or $D_{n+1} = D_0 \times (1 + g_1)n \times (1 + g_2)$. Similarly, the dividend in year $n + 2$ is $D_{n+2} = D_0 \times (1 + g_1)^n \times (1 + g_2)^2$. We can now substitute the known dividends as presented in Figure 7.5 into Figure 7.6.

Variable Growth and McDonald's Stock

The dividend has grown from $0.40 per share on November 12, 2003, to $1.50 on November 13, 2007. This represents an annual growth rate of 39.2 percent (N = 4, PV = −0.40, PMT = 0, FV = 1.50, CPT I = 39.16). You think this growth rate will continue for three years and then fall to the long-term growth rate of 9.4 percent predicted by analysts. You assume a 14 percent discount rate.

SOLUTION:

Figure 7.3 shows a $1.50 per share recent annual dividend. Modify equation 7-8 for a Stage 1 length of three years and then substitute $i = 0.14$, $g_1 = 0.392$, $g_2 = 0.094$, and $D_0 = \$1.50$. The valuation equation and solution becomes:

$$P_0 = \frac{\$1.50(1 + 0.392)}{1 + 0.14} + \frac{\$1.50(1 + 0.392)^2}{(1 + 0.14)^2} + \frac{\$1.50(1 + 0.392)^3 + \dfrac{\$1.50(1 + 0.392)^3(1 + 0.094)}{0.14 - 0.094}}{(1 + 0.14)^3}$$

$$= \$1.83 + \$2.24 + \frac{\$4.05 + \$96.22}{1.482}$$

$$= \$71.73$$

Given these parameters, McDonald's stock is worth nearly $72 per share. Figure 7.3 shows that the stock price at the end of 2007 was around $58. Comparing the stock's value to its market price, the stock is undervalued.

time out!

7-10 Explain how the variable-growth-rate technique could be used for a firm whose dividend is not expected to grow for three years and then will grow at 5 percent indefinitely.

7-11 Set up and solve the McDonald's valuation problem assuming that the first stage growth will last only two years.

The P/E Model

The valuation models that we've presented thus far help investors attempt to compute a stock's fundamental value based upon its cash flows to the investor. Another common approach is to assess a stock's **relative value.** This approach compares one company's stock valuation to other firms' stock values to evaluate whether your target company's stock is appropriately priced. The price of a stock taken in isolation doesn't give us a good measure of how expensive it is. Let's use an analogy: At the grocery store, we're less concerned with the total price of a bag of sugar than we are with the price per pound. Similarly, the price of the stock matters less than its price per one dollar of earnings.

Consider one company that earned $5 per share in profits for the year. Its stock sells for $100. Another company earned $2 per share and its stock price is $50 per share. At first glance, the first stock appears to be more expensive because its price is a high $100 compared to the lower $50 price of the second stock. However, the first company generated higher per-share profits than did the second company. Buying the first stock means that you purchase $5 in earnings. The $100 stock price implies a cost of $20 for every $1 in earnings (= $100 ÷ $5) generated. The $50 price of the second stock implies a cost of $25 for every $1 in earnings (= $50 ÷ $2). So in this regard, the second company becomes more expensive. The **price-earnings (P/E) ratio** represents the most common valuation yardstick in the investment industry; it allows investors to quickly compare the cost of earnings. The P/E ratio is simply the current price of the stock divided by the last four quarters of earnings per share:

relative value
A stock's pricy-ness measured relative to other stocks.

price-earnings (P/E) ratio Current stock price divided by the last four quarters of earnings per share.

trailing P/E ratio The P/E ratio computed using the *past* four quarters of earning per share.

$$P/E = \frac{\text{Current stock price}}{\text{Per-share earnings for last 12 months}} \qquad (7\text{-}9)$$

More accurately, this figure is the **trailing P/E ratio** and it's often denoted as P/E_0, where the 0 subscript denotes the past (or trailing) earnings.

Figure 7.8 shows two companies' trailing P/E ratios: Coca-Cola and McDonald's, as well as the Dow Jones Industrial Average's trailing P/E ratio over a 10-year period. The P/E ratio for the DJIA changes slowly and mostly stays in the 18-27 range. Historically, the DJIA's P/E ratio has fallen as low as single digits and climbed to over 30. Over the last decade, the P/E ratio for McDonald's has varied more than has the index's P/E ratio. The P/E ratio for Coca-Cola has experienced wild changes—as high as 63 and as low as 21. Figure 7.8 shows that investors valued Coca-Cola more than McDonald's in the late 1990s, but valued them nearly the same by the beginning of 2008.

Variations in P/E ratios between popular companies can be quite large. For example, in January of 2008, the P/E ratio for Google was 51, while the ratio for ConocoPhillips was only 13.1. Google stock is much more expensive than ConocoPhillips. But this does not mean the ConocoPhillips stock is a better deal than Google stock. Investors are willing to pay much more in relative terms for Google because they expect Google will grow much faster than ConocoPhillips. Indeed, analysts predict an annual growth rate of 34.4 percent per year for Google over the next five years, while they expect a growth rate of only 10.7 percent for ConocoPhillips. Remember that Example 7-2 shows how small changes in growth can result in large stock value changes. The large difference in expected growth between Google and ConocoPhillips causes a large difference in their relative value.

We can more directly see the impact that growth can have on the P/E ratio by modifying the constant-growth-rate model. Begin with the model, $P_0 = D_1 \div (i - g)$. Then divide both sides by the firm's earnings results in $P_0/E_0 = (D_1/E_0) \div (i - g)$. Note that the dividend payout ratio of the firm (D/E), the discount rate (i), and the growth rate (g), taken together, determine the P/E ratio. All else held equal, larger growth rates will lead to larger P/E ratios. Also, firms that have higher payout ratios will have higher P/E ratios. Of course, if a firm pays out a high portion of its earnings as dividends, then it may not have the cash to fund high growth. Thus, high dividend payout firms tend not to be the same as high-growth firms.

The value of a stock, and thus its price, relates directly to its future success. Note that valuation models use estimates of future dividends and growth rates. Because of this focus on the future, many people prefer to use a P/E ratio that

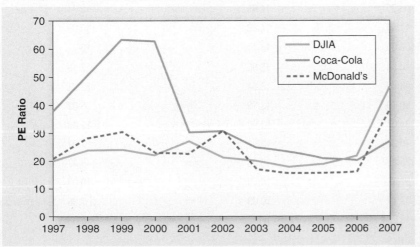

▼ FIGURE 7.8
Historical P/E Ratio of the DJIA, Coca-Cola, and McDonald's

forward P/E ratio The P/E ratio computed using the *estimated* next four quarters of earning per share.

value stocks Companies considered to be temporarily undervalued.

also looks forward rather than trailing. A **forward P/E ratio** uses analyst estimates of the earnings in the next 12 months instead of the past 12 months and can be denoted as P/E_1. The forward P/E ratio has the advantage over the trailing P/E ratio in that it incorporates investors' expectations of the firm's upcoming profits. A disadvantage is that expected earnings are harder to estimate and thus less accurate than past earnings. The media uses the trailing P/E ratio, while financial managers and investors use the forward P/E ratio more.

Knowledgeable investors who use the P/E ratio as a relative measure of value compare it to the firm's expected growth rate. Table 7.3 shows the forward P/E ratio and analysts' expected growth rates for the 27 of the 30 Dow Jones Industrial Average

Walmart qualifies as a value stock.

▼ **TABLE 7.3** P/E Ratios and Analyst Growth Estimates of DJIA Firms, July 11, 2007

Ticker	Company Name	Stock Price	Forward P/E Ratio	Next 5 Years Growth (%)
INTC	INTEL CP	$ 25.88	18.34	17.07%
KO	COCA-COLA CO THE	52.27	18.15	9.12
PG	PROCTER GAMBLE	62.74	17.69	11.69
MSFT	MICROSOFT CP	29.90	17.25	12.24
MCD	MCDONALD'S CP	51.58	17.14	8.92
HON	HONEYWELL INTL IN	60.33	16.69	11.83
MMM	3M COMPANY	89.46	16.27	11.12
DIS	WALT DISNEY-DISNE	34.15	16.26	13.24
MRK	MERCK CO INC	50.52	15.88	9.28
AXP	AMER EXPRESS INC	62.99	15.62	12.32
VZ	VERIZON COMMUN	41.23	15.45	7.28
MO	ALTRIA GROUP INC	71.95	15.44	7.25
UTX	UNITED TECH	73.66	15.37	11.48
GE	GEN ELECTRIC CO	38.28	15.34	10.56
DD	DUPONT E I DE NE	51.34	14.92	7.27
JNJ	JOHNSON AND JOHNS	63.20	14.65	8.31
HPQ	HEWLETT PACKARD C	47.14	14.63	13.95
IBM	INTL BUSINESS MAC	109.00	14.11	10.71
HD	HOME DEPOT INC	40.80	13.96	12.18
WMT	WALMART STORES	48.85	13.51	12.31
XOM	EXXONMOBIL CP	89.10	13.19	5.07
CAT	CATERPILLAR INC	84.07	12.98	12.83
T	AT&T INC.	40.24	12.97	7.37
PFE	PFIZER INC	25.89	10.88	5.47
C	CITIGROUP INC	52.82	10.18	10.03
GM	GEN MOTORS	37.42	10.09	7.90
JPM	JPMORGAN CHASE C	49.25	10.03	9.98

Source: Yahoo! Finance Screener.

EXAMPLE 7-4

The P/E Ratio Model for Caterpillar

Look at Table 7.3 and notice that the P/E ratio for Caterpillar seems low at 12.98 relative to the growth (12.8 percent) that analysts expect. Caterpillar earned $5.05 per share and paid a $1.10 dividend last year. You decide to explore this seeming anomaly and figure out what Caterpillar's stock price might reach in five years.

SOLUTION:

Compute the expected future price in five years under two different scenarios. The first assumption is that Caterpillar's P/E ratio will be the same in five years as it is today. But since this P/E ratio seems a bit low, the second scenario allows for a rise in the P/E ratio to 15. Under these two scenarios, the future price estimates are:

$$P_5 = \left(\frac{P}{E}\right)_n \times E_0 \times (1 + g)^n = 12.98 \times \$5.05 \times (1 + 0.128)^5 = \$119.70$$

$$P_5 = \left(\frac{P}{E}\right)_n \times E_0 \times (1 + g)^n = 15 \times \$5.05 \times (1 + 0.128)^5 = \$138.33$$

Note that if the P/E ratio increases from 12.98 to 15 in five years, the future price could be more than 15 percent higher than analysts expect without the change.

---

firms with positive earnings. The firms are sorted by their forward P/E ratios. Investors consider companies with high P/E ratios and high-growth rates to be appropriately priced. Companies with low P/E ratios and low growth also seem to be appropriately priced. Investors should be concerned about firms with high P/E ratios and only single digit growth rates. As such, Coca-Cola, McDonald's, Merck, and Verizon may be too expensive for their expected growth rates. Many investors like to buy growth stocks. They seek companies with high-growth rates. But growth stock investors are also concerned about paying too much for a stock. While examining growth stocks, they can use the P/E ratio to assess how expensive the stock is. On the other hand, investors consider companies with low P/E ratios and high expected growth to be undervalued, and they are often referred to as **value stocks.** Caterpillar, Walmart, and Home Depot would qualify as value stocks. Many investors like to buy value stocks because they feel they are getting a bargain price for a stable company.

Estimating Future Stock Prices

We can often find it useful to estimate a stock's future price. Consider equation 7-3's cash flow discount valuation model. The model requires estimates of future dividends and a future price. How can investors estimate this future price? They can use the P/E ratio model for this purpose. Upon reflection, you will see that multiplying the P/E ratio by earnings results in a stock price. So, in order to estimate a future price, simply multiply the expected P/E ratio by the expected earnings. This concept is captured in the following equation:

$$P_n = \left(\frac{P}{E}\right)_n \times E_n \qquad (7\text{-}10)$$
$$= \left(\frac{P}{E}\right)_n \times E_0 \times (1 + g)^n$$

As the formula shows, we can use assumptions about the earnings growth rate to estimate earnings in year n. Many investors believe the firm's P/E ratio in year n is best estimated using today's P/E ratio. However, if today's P/E ratio seems unusual compared with similar firms or even compared with a stock index, then adjustments might be wise. ■

time out!

7-12 Consider two firms with the same P/E ratio. Explain how one could be described as expensive compared to the other.

7-13 Compute the stock price for Caterpillar in five years if you expect the P/E ratio to decline to 11.

Get Online

mhhe.com/canM

for study materials including quizzes, iPod downloads, and video

Your Turn...

Questions

1. As owners, what rights and advantages do shareholders obtain? *(LG1)*

2. Describe how being a residual claimant can be very valuable. *(LG1)*

3. Obtain a current quote of McDonald's (MCD) from the Internet. Describe what has changed since the quote in Figure 7.1. *(LG2)*

4. Get the trading statistics for the three main U.S. stock exchanges. Compare the trading activity to that of Table 7.1. *(LG2)*

5. Why might the Standard & Poor's 500 Index be a better measure of stock market performance than the Dow Jones Industrial Average? Why is the DJIA more popular than the S&P 500? *(LG3)*

6. Explain how it is possible for the DJIA to increase one day while the NASDAQ Composite decreases during the same day. *(LG3)*

7. Which is higher, the ask quote or the bid quote? Why? *(LG4)*

8. Illustrate through examples how trading commission costs impact an investor's return. *(LG4)*

9. Describe the difference in the timing of trade execution and the certainty of trade price between market orders and limit orders. *(LG4)*

10. What are the differences between common stock and preferred stock? *(LG5)*

11. How important is growth to a stock's value? Illustrate with examples. *(LG5)*

12. Under what conditions would the constant-growth-rate model *not* be appropriate? *(LG5)*

13. The expected return derived from the constant-growth-rate model relies on dividend yield and capital gain. Where do these two parts of the return come from? *(LG5)*

14. Describe, in words, how to use the variable-growth-rate technique to value a stock. *(LG6)*

15. Can the variable-growth-rate model be used to value a firm that has a negative growth rate in Stage 1 and a stable and positive growth in Stage 2? Explain. *(LG6)*

16. Explain why using the P/E relative value approach may be useful for companies that do not pay dividends. *(LG7)*

17. How is a firm's changing P/E ratio reflected in the stock price? Give examples. *(LG7)*

18. Differentiate the characteristics of growth stocks and value stocks. *(LG7)*

19. What's the relationship between the P/E ratio and a firm's growth rate? *(LG7)*

20. Describe the process for using the P/E ratio to estimate a future stock price. *(LG7)*

Problems

BASIC PROBLEMS

7-1 **Stock Index Performance** On January 16, 2007, the Dow Jones Industrial Average set a new high. The index closed at 12,582.59, which was up 26.51 that day. What was the return (in percent) of the stock market that day? *(LG3)*

7-2 **Stock Index Performance** On January 16, 2007, the Standard & Poor's 500 Index reached the highest it had been since 2000. The index closed at 1,431.90, which was up 1.17 that day. What was the return (in percent) of the stock market that day? *(LG3)*

7-3 **Buying Stock with Commissions** At your discount brokerage firm, it costs $8.95 per stock trade. How much money do you need to buy 200 shares of Pfizer, Inc. (PFE), which trades at $27.22? *(LG4)*

7-4 **Buying Stock with Commissions** At your discount brokerage firm, it costs $9.50 per stock trade. How much money do you need to buy 300 shares of Time Warner, Inc. (TWX), which trades at $22.62? *(LG4)*

7-5 **Selling Stock with Commissions** At your full-service brokerage firm, it costs $120 per stock trade. How much money do you receive after selling 150 shares of Nokia Corporation (NOK), which trades at $20.13? *(LG4)*

7-6 **Selling Stock with Commissions** At your full-service brokerage firm, it costs $135 per stock trade. How much money do you receive after selling 250 shares of International Business Machines (IBM), which trades at $96.17? *(LG4)*

7-7 **Buying Stock with a Market Order** You would like to buy shares of Sirius Satellite Radio (SIRI). The current ask and bid quotes are $3.96 and $3.93, respectively. You place a market buy-order for 500 shares that executes at these quoted prices. How much money did it cost to buy these shares? *(LG4)*

7-8 **Buying Stock with a Market Order** You would like to buy shares of Coldwater Creek, Inc. (CWTR). The current ask and bid quotes are $20.70 and $20.66, respectively. You place a market buy-order for 200 shares that executes at these quoted prices. How much money did it cost to buy these shares? *(LG4)*

7-9 **Selling Stock with a Limit Order** You would like to sell 200 shares of WorldSpace, Inc. (WRSP). The current ask and bid quotes are $4.66 and $4.62, respectively. You place a limit sell-order at $4.65. If the trade executes, how much money do you receive from the buyer? *(LG4)*

7-10 **Selling Stock with a Limit Order** You would like to sell 100 shares of eCollege.com (ECLG). The current ask and bid quotes are $15.33 and $15.28, respectively. You place a limit sell-order at $15.31. If the trade executes, how much money do you receive from the buyer? *(LG4)*

7-11 **Value of a Preferred Stock** A preferred stock from Duquesne Light Company (DQU-PRA) pays $2.10 in annual dividends. If the required return on the preferred stock is 5.4 percent, what's the value of the stock? *(LG5)*

7-12 **Value of a Preferred Stock** A preferred stock from Hecla Mining Co. (HLPRB) pays $3.50 in annual dividends. If the required return on the preferred stock is 6.8 percent, what is the value of the stock? *(LG5)*

7-13 **P/E Ratio and Stock Price** Ultra Petroleum (UPL) has earnings per share of $1.56 and a P/E ratio of 32.48. What's the stock price? *(LG7)*

7-14 **P/E Ratio and Stock Price** JPMorgan Chase Co. (JPM) has earnings per share of $3.53 and a P/E ratio of 13.81. What is the price of the stock? *(LG7)*

7-15 **Value of Dividends and Future Price** A firm is expected to pay a dividend of $1.35 next year and $1.50 the following year. Financial analysts believe the stock will be at their price target of $75 in two years. Compute the value of this stock with a required return of 11.5 percent. *(LG5)*

7-16 **Value of Dividends and Future Price** A firm is expected to pay a dividend of $2.05 next year and $2.35 the following year. Financial analysts believe the stock will be at their price target of $110 in two years. Compute the value of this stock with a required return of 12 percent. *(LG5)*

7-17 **Dividend Growth** Annual dividends of AT&T Corp (T) grew from $0.96 in 2000 to $1.33 in 2006. What was the annual growth rate? *(LG5)*

7-18 **Dividend Growth** Annual dividends of General Electric (GE) grew from $0.66 in 2001 to $1.03 in 2006. What was the annual growth rate? *(LG5)*

7-19 **Value a Constant Growth Stock** Financial analysts forecast Safeco Corp. (SAF) growth for the future to be 10 percent. Safeco's recent dividend was $1.20. What is the value of Safeco stock when the required return is 12 percent? *(LG5)*

7-20 **Value a Constant Growth Stock** Financial analysts forecast Limited Brands (LTD) growth for the future to be 12.5 percent. LTD's recent dividend was $0.60. What is the value of Limited Brands stock when the required return is 14.5 percent? *(LG5)*

7-21 **Expected Return** Ecolap Inc. (ECL) recently paid a $0.46 dividend. The dividend is expected to grow at a 14.5 percent rate. At a current stock price of $44.12, what is the return shareholders are expecting? *(LG5)*

7-22 **Expected Return** Paychex Inc. (PAYX) recently paid an $0.84 dividend. The dividend is expected to grow at a 15 percent rate. At a current stock price of $40.11, what is the return shareholders are expecting? *(LG5)*

7-23 **Dividend Initiation and Stock Value** A firm does not pay a dividend. It is expected to pay its first dividend of $0.20 per share in three years. This dividend will grow at 11 percent indefinitely. Using a 12 percent discount rate, compute the value of this stock. *(LG6)*

7-24 **Dividend Initiation and Stock Value** A firm does not pay a dividend. It is expected to pay its first dividend of $0.25 per share in two years. This dividend will grow at 10 percent indefinitely. Using an 11.5 percent discount rate, compute the value of this stock. *(LG6)*

7-25 **P/E Ratio Model and Future Price** Kellogg Co. (K) recently earned a profit of $2.52 earnings per share and has a P/E ratio of 19.86. The dividend has been growing at a 5 percent rate over the past few years. If this growth rate continues, what would be the stock price in five years if the P/E ratio remained unchanged? What would the price be if the P/E ratio declined to 15 in five years? *(LG7)*

7-26 **P/E Ratio Model and Future Price** New York Times Co. (NYT) recently earned a profit of $1.21 earnings per share and has a P/E ratio of 19.59. The dividend has been growing at a 7.25 percent rate over the past six years. If this growth rate continues, what would be the stock price in five years if the P/E ratio remained unchanged? What would the price be if the P/E ratio increased to 22 in five years? *(LG7)*

7-27 **Value of Future Cash Flows** A firm recently paid a $0.45 annual dividend. The dividend is expected to increase by 10 percent in each of the next four years. In the fourth year, the stock price is expected to be $80. If the required return for this stock is 13.5 percent, what is its value? *(LG5)*

7-28 **Value of Future Cash Flows** A firm recently paid a $0.60 annual dividend. The dividend is expected to increase by 12 percent in each of the next four years. In the fourth year, the stock price is expected to be $110. If the required return for this stock is 14.5 percent, what is its value? *(LG5)*

7-29 Constant Growth Stock Valuation Walgreen Co. (WAG) paid a $0.137 dividend per share in 2000, which grew to $0.286 in 2006. This growth is expected to continue. What is the value of this stock at the beginning of 2007 when the required return is 13.7 percent? *(LG5)*

7-30 Constant Growth Stock Valuation Campbell Soup Co. (CPB) paid a $0.632 dividend per share in 2003, which grew to $0.76 in 2006. This growth is expected to continue. What is the value of this stock at the beginning of 2007 when the required return is 8.7 percent? *(LG5)*

7-31 Changes in Growth and Stock Valuation Consider a firm that had been priced using a 10 percent growth rate and a 12 percent required return. The firm recently paid a $1.20 dividend. The firm has just announced that because of a new joint venture, it will likely grow at a 10.5 percent rate. How much should the stock price change (in dollars and percentage)? *(LG5)*

7-32 Changes in Growth and Stock Valuation Consider a firm that had been priced using an 11.5 percent growth rate and a 13.5 percent required return. The firm recently paid a $1.50 dividend. The firm has just announced that because of a new joint venture, it will likely grow at a 12 percent rate. How much should the stock price change (in dollars and percentage)? *(LG5)*

7-33 Variable Growth A fast-growing firm recently paid a dividend of $0.35 per share. The dividend is expected to increase at a 20 percent rate for the next three years. Afterwards, a more stable 12 percent growth rate can be assumed. If a 13 percent discount rate is appropriate for this stock, what is its value? *(LG6)*

7-34 Variable Growth A fast-growing firm recently paid a dividend of $0.40 per share. The dividend is expected to increase at a 25 percent rate for the next four years. Afterwards, a more stable 11 percent growth rate can be assumed. If a 12.5 percent discount rate is appropriate for this stock, what is its value? *(LG6)*

7-35 P/E Model and Cash Flow Valuation Suppose that a firm's recent earnings per share and dividend per share are $2.50 and $1.30, respectively. Both are expected to grow at 8 percent. However, the firm's current P/E ratio of 22 seems high for this growth rate. The P/E ratio is expected to fall to 18 within five years. Compute a value for this stock by first estimating the dividends over the next five years and the stock price in five years. Then discount these cash flows using a 10 percent required rate. *(LG5, LG7)*

7-36 P/E Model and Cash Flow Valuation Suppose that a firm's recent earnings per share and dividend per share are $2.75 and $1.60, respectively. Both are expected to grow at 9 percent. However, the firm's current P/E ratio of 23 seems high for this growth rate. The P/E ratio is expected to fall to 19 within five years. Compute a value for this stock by first estimating the dividends over the next five years and the stock price in five years. Then discount these cash flows using an 11 percent required rate. *(LG5, LG7)*

7-37 Excel Problem Spreadsheets are especially useful for computing stock value under different assumptions. Consider a firm that is expected to pay the following dividends:

Year 1	2	3	4	5	6	
$1.20	$1.20	$1.50	$1.50	$1.75	$1.90	and grow at 5% thereafter

a. Using an 11 percent discount rate, what would be the value of this stock?

b. What is the value of the stock using a 10 percent discount rate? A 12 percent discount rate?

c. What would the value be using a 6 percent growth rate after Year 6 instead of the 5 percent rate using each of these three discount rates?

d. What do you conclude about stock valuation and its assumptions?

chapter eight

understanding financial
markets + institutions

ndividual investors and financial managers who wish to make sound decisions must understand how funds flow throughout the economy and how financial markets operate and relate to one another. Investors' funds flow through financial markets such as the New York Stock Exchange and mortgage markets. Financial institutions such as commercial banks (e.g., Bank of America), investment banks (e.g., Merrill Lynch), and mutual funds (e.g., Fidelity) act as intermediaries to channel funds from individual savers or investors to financial markets. In this chapter, we build on the information about stocks, bonds, and other securities covered in Chapters 6 and 7 to provide an overview of the U.S. financial system. That is, we look at various financial markets' nature and operations and the financial institutions (FIs) that participate in those markets.

We generally differentiate financial markets by their primary financial instruments' characteristics (such as bond

continued on p.178

LEARNING GOALS

LG1 Differentiate between primary and secondary markets and between money and capital markets.

LG2 List the types of securities traded in money and capital markets.

LG3 Identify different types of financial institutions and the services that each financial institution provides.

LG4 Analyze specific factors that influence interest rates.

LG5 Offer different theories that explain the shape of the term structure of interest rates.

LG6 Demonstrate how forward interest rates derive from the term structure of interest rates.

continued from p.177

maturities) or the market's location. FIs allow financial markets to function by providing the least costly and most efficient way to channel funds to and from these markets. FIs play a second crucial role by spreading risk among market participants. This risk-spreading function is vital to entrepreneurial efforts, for few firms or individuals could afford the risk of launching an expensive new product or process by themselves. Individual investors take on pieces of the risk by buying shares in risky enterprises. Investors then mitigate their own risks by diversifying their holdings into appropriate portfolios, which we cover in Chapters 9 and 10. ∎

viewpoints

business APPLICATION

DPH Corporation needs to issue new bonds either this year or in two years. DPH Corp. is a profitable firm, but if the U.S. economy were to experience a downturn, the company would see a big drop in sales over the next two years as its products are very sensitive to changes in the overall economy. DPH Corp. currently has $10 million in public debt outstanding, but its bonds are not actively traded. What questions must DPH Corp. consider as its managers decide whether to issue bonds today or in two years? How can DPH Corp. get these bonds to potential buyers and thus raise the needed capital?

FINANCIAL MARKETS

Financial markets exist to manage the flow of funds from investors to borrowers. We can distinguish markets along two major dimensions:

- Primary versus secondary markets.
- Money versus capital markets.

Primary versus Secondary Markets

Primary markets provide a forum in which demanders of funds (e.g., corporations or government entities such as IBM or the U.S. Treasury) raise funds by issuing new financial instruments, such as stocks and bonds. Corporations or government entities continually have new projects or expanded production needs, but do not have sufficient internally generated funds (such as retained earnings) to support their capital needs. Thus, corporations and governments issue securities in external primary markets to raise additional funds. Businesses sell new financial instrument issues to initial fund suppliers (e.g., households) in exchange for the funds (money) that the issuer requires.

fund demanders with a number of services, including advising the company or government agency about the securities issue (such as an appropriate offer price and number of securities to issue) and attracting initial public purchasers of the customer's securities offerings. Firms that need funds are seldom expert at raising capital themselves, so they avert risk and lower their costs by turning to expert investment banks to issue their primary market securities.

Figure 8.1 illustrates a time line for the primary market exchange of funds for a new issue of corporate bonds or equity. We will further discuss how companies, the U.S. Treasury, and government agencies that market primary government securities, such as Ginnie Mae and Freddie Mac, go about selling primary market securities in Chapter 16. Throughout this text, we focus on government securities from the *buyer's*, rather than the seller's, point of view. You can find in-depth discussions of government securities from the sellers' point of view in a public finance text.

Primary market financial instruments include stock issues from firms initially going public (e.g., allowing their equity shares to be publicly traded on stock markets for the first time). We usually refer to these first-time issues as **initial public offerings (IPOs).** For example, on April 29, 2004, Google announced

> [In the U.S., financial institutions called **investment banks** arrange most primary market transactions for businesses.]

In the U.S., financial institutions called **investment banks** arrange most primary market transactions for businesses. Some of the best-known examples of U.S. investment banks include Morgan Stanley, Goldman Sachs, and Lehman Brothers. These firms intermediate between issuing parties (fund demanders) and investors (fund suppliers). Investment banks provide

a $2.7 billion IPO of its common stock. Google used several investment banks, including Morgan Stanley, to underwrite the company's stock. Publicly traded firms may issue additional bonds or stocks as primary market securities. For example, in May 23, 2006, AngioDynamics Inc. announced that it would sell an additional 2,760,000 shares of common stock (at $24.07

per share) underwritten by investment banks such as RBC Capital Markets, KeyBank Capital Markets, and First Albany Capital. These funds augmented AngioDynamics, Inc.'s existing capital (equity) of $400 million.

FIGURE 8.1
Primary Market Transfer of Funds

Primary Markets
(Where new issues of financial instruments are offered for sale)

→→→→ Financial instrument flow
←←←← Funds flow

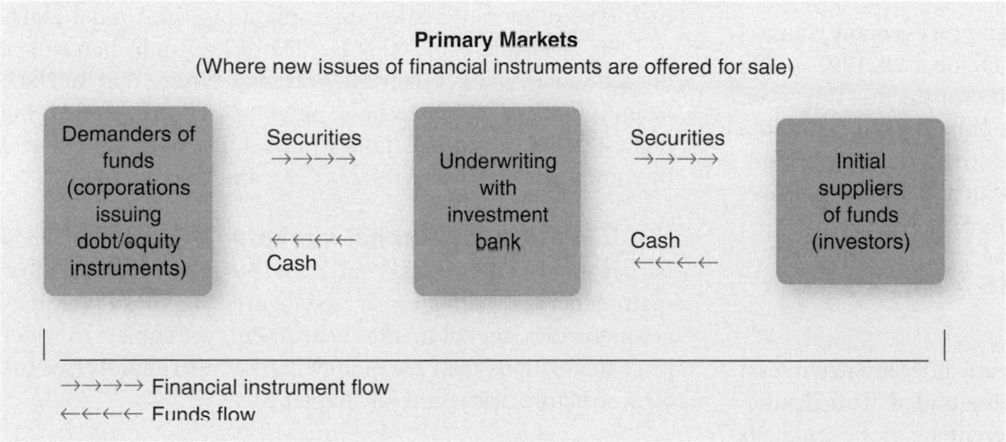

FIGURE 8.2
Secondary Market Transfer of Funds

Secondary Markets
(Where financial instruments, once issued, are traded)

→→→→→ Financial instruments flow
←←←← Funds flow

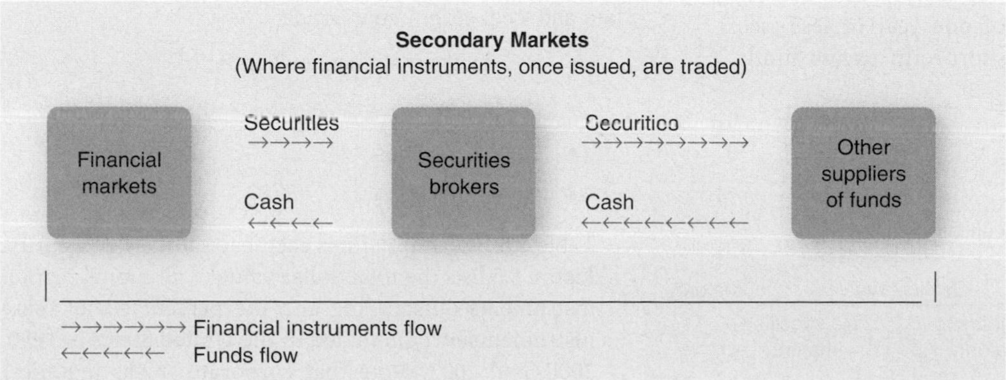

Secondary Markets Once firms issue financial instruments in primary markets, these same stocks and bonds are then traded—that is, bought and resold—in **secondary markets.** The New York Stock Exchange (NYSE), the American Stock Exchange (AMEX), and the National Association of Securities Dealers Automated Quotation (NASDAQ) system are three well-known examples of secondary markets for trading stocks, as you learned in Chapters 6 and 7. In addition to stocks and bonds, secondary markets also exist for financial instruments backed by mortgages and other assets, foreign exchange, and futures and options (i.e., derivative securities).

Buyers find sellers of secondary market securities in economic agents that need funds (fund demanders). Secondary markets provide a centralized marketplace where economic agents know that they can buy or sell most securities quickly and efficiently. Secondary markets, therefore, save economic agents the search costs of finding buyers or sellers on their own. Figure 8.2 illustrates a secondary market transfer of funds. Secondary market buyers often use securities brokers such as Charles Schwab or other brokerage firms to act as intermediaries as they exchange funds for securities (see Chapter 7). An important note: the firm that originally issued the stock or bond is not involved in secondary market transactions in any way—no money accrues to the company itself when its stock trades in a secondary market.

Secondary markets offer benefits to both investors (fund suppliers) and issuers (fund demanders). Investors gain liquidity and diversification benefits (see Chapter 10). And although corporate security issuers are not directly involved in secondary market transactions, issuers do

trading volume The number of shares of a security that are simultaneously bought and sold during a period.

money markets Markets that trade debt securities or instruments with maturities of less than one year.

over-the-counter market Markets that do not operate in a specific fixed location—rather, transactions occur via telephones, wire transfers, and computer trading.

capital markets Markets that trade debt (bonds) and equity (stock) instruments with maturities of more than one year.

gain information about their securities' current market value. Publicly traded firms can thus observe how investors perceive their corporate value and their corporate decisions by tracking their firms' securities' secondary market prices. Such price information allows issuers to evaluate how well they are using internal funds as well as the funds generated from previously issued stocks and bonds and provides indications about how well any subsequent bond or stock offerings might be received—and at what price.

Secondary market **trading volume** can be quite large. Trading volume is defined as the number of shares of a security that are simultaneously bought and sold during a given period. Each seller and each buyer actually contract with the exchange's clearinghouse, which then matches sell and buy orders for each transaction. The clearinghouse is a company whose stock trades on the exchange, and the clearinghouse runs on a for-profit basis.

The exchange and the clearinghouse can process many transactions in a single day. For example, on October 28, 1997, NYSE trading volume exceeded 1 billion shares for the first time ever. On August 16, 2007, NYSE trading volume topped 5.8 billion shares, the highest level to date. In contrast, during the mid-1980s, an NYSE trading day during which 250 million shares traded was considered a high-volume day.

Money Markets versus Capital Markets

We noted above that financial markets are differentiated in part by the maturity dates of the instruments traded. This distinction becomes important when we differentiate money markets from capital markets. Both of these markets deal in debt securities; the question becomes one of when the securities come due.

Money Markets
Money markets feature debt securities or instruments with maturities of one year or less (see Figure 8.3). Economic agents with short-term excess funds

can lend these excess funds (that is, they can buy money market instruments) to economic agents who need short-term funds (so, they sell money market instruments to raise funds). Because money market instruments trade for only short periods of time, fluctuations in secondary-market prices are usually quite small. With less volatility, money market securities are thus less risky than longer-term instruments. In the United States, many money market securities do not trade in a specific location; rather, transactions occur via telephones, wire transfers, and computer trading. Thus, most U.S. money markets are said to be **over-the-counter** (OTC) **markets.**

Money Market Instruments
Corporations and government entities issue a variety of money market securities to obtain short-term funds. These securities include:

- Treasury bills.
- Federal funds and repurchase agreements.
- Commercial paper.
- Negotiable certificates of deposit.
- Banker's acceptances.

Table 8.1 lists and defines each money market security. Figure 8.4 lists the total dollar value of all money market instruments outstanding and the percentages of the dollar value of each type of money market instruments in the United States in 1990, 2000, and 2007—that is, the breakdown by percentage of each money market instrument traded. Notice that, in 2007, federal funds and repurchase agreements commanded the highest dollar value of all money market instruments, followed by commercial paper, negotiable CDs, and Treasury bills.

Capital Markets
Capital markets are markets in which parties trade equity (stocks) and debt (bonds) instruments that mature in more than one year (see Figure 8.3). Given their longer maturities, capital market instruments are subject to wider price fluctuations than are money market instruments (see the term structure discussion in Chapter 6).

Capital Market Instruments
Capital market securities include:

- U.S. Treasury notes and bonds.
- State and local government bonds.
  - U.S. government agency bonds.
  - Mortgages and mortgage-backed securities.
  - Corporate bonds.
  - Corporate stocks.

Table 8.2 lists and defines each capital market security. Figure 8.5 lists the total dollar value of all capital market instruments outstanding and the percentages of these instruments by type traded in the United States in 1990, 2000, and 2007. Note that corporate stocks (equities)

▼FIGURE 8.3
Money versus Capital Market Maturities

	Capital Market Securities			
Money market securities	Notes and bonds	Stocks (equities)	Maturity
0	1 year to maturity	30 years to maturity	No specified maturity	

▼ **TABLE 8.1** Money Market Instruments

Treasury bills: short-term U.S. government obligations.

Federal funds: short-term funds transferred between financial institutions, usually for no more than one day.

Repurchase agreements (repos): agreements involving security sales by one party to another, with the promise to reverse the transaction at a specified date and price, usually at a discounted price.

Commercial paper (sometimes called Paper): short-term unsecured promissory notes that companies issue to raise short-term cash.

Negotiable certificates of deposit: bank-issued time deposits that specify an interest rate and maturity date and are negotiable—that is, traded on an exchange. Their face value is usually at least $100,000.

Banker acceptances (BAs): bank-guaranteed time drafts payable to a vendor of goods.

represent the largest capital market instrument, followed by mortgages and mortgage-backed securities and then corporate bonds. The relative size of capital markets depends on two factors: the number of securities issued and their market prices. The 1990s saw consistently rising bull markets; hence the sharp increase in equities' dollar value outstanding. Stock values fell in the early 2000s as the U.S. economy experienced a downturn—partly because of 9/11 and partly because interest rates began to rise—and stock prices fell. Stock prices in most sectors subsequently recovered and even surpassed their 1999 levels.

▼**FIGURE 8.4**
Money Market Instruments Outstanding

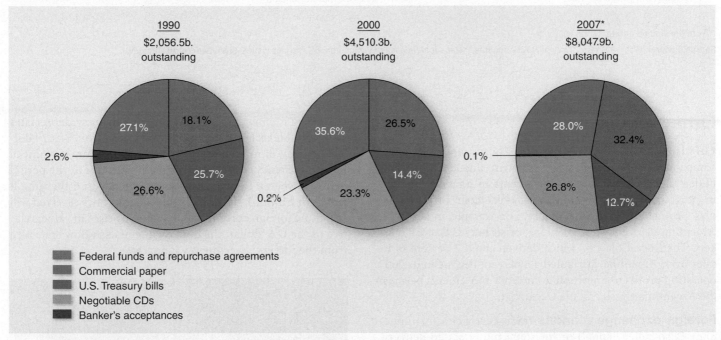

Federal funds and repurchase agreements
Commercial paper
U.S. Treasury bills
Negotiable CDs
Banker's acceptances

* As of the second quarter of the year.

Source: Federal Reserve Board, "Flow of Fund Accounts," *Statistical Releases,* Washington, DC, various issues, **www.federalreserve.gov**.

▼ **TABLE 8.2** Capital Market Instruments

Treasury notes and bonds: U.S. Treasury long-term obligations to finance the national debt and pay for other federal government expenditures.

State and local government bonds: debt securities issued by state and local (e.g., county, city, school) governments, usually to cover capital (long-term) improvements.

Mortgages: long-term loans to individuals or businesses to purchase homes, pieces of land, or other real property.

Mortgage-backed securities: long-term debt securities that offer expected principal and interest payments as collateral. These securities, made up of many mortgages, are gathered into a pool and are thus "backed" by promised principal and interest cash flows.

Corporate bonds: long-term bonds issued by corporations.

Corporate stocks: long-term equity securities issued by public corporations; stock shares represent fundamental corporate ownership claims.

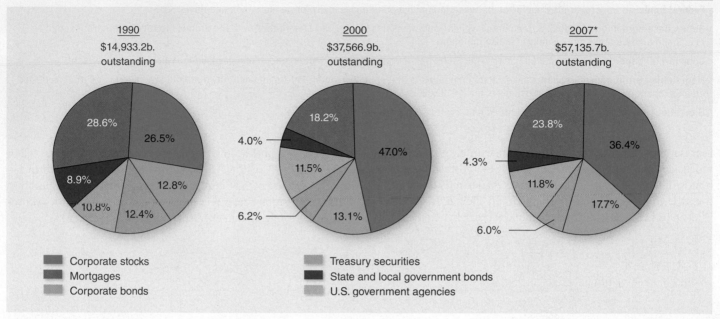

1990	2000	2007*
$14,933.2b.	$37,566.9b.	$57,135.7b.
outstanding	outstanding	outstanding

1990
- 28.6%
- 26.5%
- 8.9%
- 10.8%
- 12.4%
- 12.8%

2000
- 18.2%
- 4.0%
- 11.5%
- 6.2%
- 13.1%
- 47.0%

2007*
- 23.8%
- 4.3%
- 11.8%
- 6.0%
- 17.7%
- 36.4%

■ Corporate stocks
■ Mortgages
■ Corporate bonds

■ Treasury securities
■ State and local government bonds
■ U.S. government agencies

* As of the second quarter of the year.

Source: Federal Reserve Board, "Flow of Fund Accounts," *Statistical Releases,* Washington, DC, various issues, **www.federalreserve.gov**.

Other Markets

Foreign Exchange Markets Today, most U.S.-based companies operate globally. Competent financial managers understand how events and movements in financial markets in other countries can potentially affect their own companies' profitability and performance. For example, in late 2001, Argentina's currency and economic crisis hurt U.S. stock markets. The Coca-Cola Co., which derived about 2 percent of its sales from Argentina, attributed a 5 percent decline in its 2002 operating profits to unfavorable currency movements between the Argentinian peso and the U.S. dollar.

Foreign exchange markets trade currencies for immediate (also called "spot") or for some future stated delivery. When a U.S. corporation sells securities or goods overseas, the resulting cash flows denominated in a foreign currency expose the firm to **foreign exchange risk.** This is the risk arising from the unknown value at which foreign currency cash flows can be converted into U.S. dollars. Investors who deal in foreign-denominated securities face the same risk. For example, the actual number of U.S. dollars that a firm receives on a foreign investment depends on the exchange rate between the U.S. dollar and the foreign currency just as much as it does on the investment's performance. They will have to convert the foreign currency into U.S. dollars at the prevailing exchange rate. If the foreign currency depreciates (falls in value) relative to the U.S. dollar (say from $.1679 dollars per unit of foreign currency to $.1550 dollars per unit of foreign currency) over the investment period (i.e., the period between when a foreign investment is made and the time it comes to fruition), the dollar value of cash flows received will fall. If the foreign currency appreciates, or rises in value, relative to the U.S. dollar, the dollar value of cash flows received from the foreign investment will increase.

Foreign currency exchange rates are variable. They vary day to day with demand and supply of foreign currency and with demand and supply of dollars worldwide. Central governments sometimes intervene in foreign exchange markets directly—such as China's recent valuing of the yuan at artificially high rates relative to the dollar. Governments also affect foreign exchange rates indirectly by altering prevailing interest rates within their own countries. You will learn more about foreign exchange markets in Chapter 18.

Derivative Securities Markets A

derivative security is a financial security (such as a futures contract, option contract, or swap contract) linked to another, underlying security, such as a stock traded in capital markets or British pounds sterling traded in foreign exchange (forex) markets. Derivative securities generally involve an agreement between two parties to exchange a standard quantity of an asset or cash flow at a predetermined price and at a specified date in the future. As the value of the underlying security changes, the value of the derivative security changes.

While derivative security contracts, especially for physical commodities like corn or gold, have existed for centuries, derivative securities markets grew increasingly popular in the 1970s, 1980s, and 1990s as traders, firms, and academics figured out how to spread risk for more and more underlying commodities and securities by using derivative contracts. Derivative contracts generally feature a high degree of leverage; that is, the investor only has to put up a very small portion of the underlying commodity or security's value to affect or control the underlying commodity or security.

Derivative securities markets are the newest—and potentially the riskiest—financial security markets. Derivative securities traders can be either users of derivative contracts (for hedging and other purposes) or dealers (such as banks) that act as counterparties in customer trades for fees. An example of hedging involves commodities such as corn, wheat, or soybeans. For example, suppose you run a flour mill and will need to buy either soft wheat (Chicago) or hard red winter wheat (Kansas City) in the future. If you are concerned that the price of wheat will rise, you might lock in a price today to meet your needs six months from now by buying wheat futures on a commodities exchange. If you are correct and wheat prices rise over the

six months, you may purchase the wheat by closing out your futures positions, buying the wheat at the futures price rather than the higher market price. Likewise, if you know that you will be delivering a large shipment to, say, Europe, in three months, you might take an offsetting position in euro futures contracts to lock in the exchange rate between the dollar and the euro as it stands today—and (you hope) eliminate foreign exchange risk from the transaction.

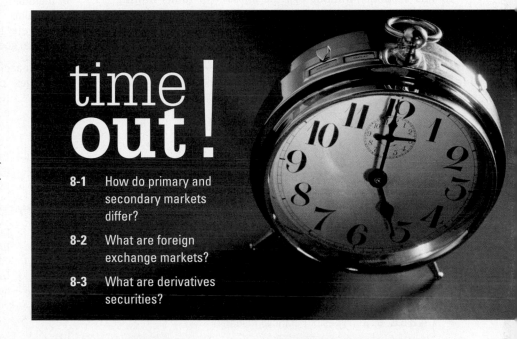

time out !

8-1 How do primary and secondary markets differ?

8-2 What are foreign exchange markets?

8-3 What are derivatives securities?

FINANCIAL INSTITUTIONS

Financial institutions (e.g., banks, thrifts, insurance companies, mutual funds) perform vital functions to securities markets of all sorts. Institutions channel funds from those with surplus funds (suppliers of funds) to those with shortages of funds (demanders of funds). In other words, FIs operate financial markets. Table 8.3 lists and summarizes the various types of FIs. The Finance at Work box highlights Walmart's ultimately unsuccessful attempts to operate as a financial institution.

To understand just how important FIs are to the efficient operation of financial markets, imagine a simple world in which FIs did not exist. In such a world, suppliers of funds (e.g., households), generating excess savings by consuming less than they earn, would have a basic choice. They could either hold cash as an asset or directly transfer that cash in the securities issued by users of funds (e.g., corporations, governments, or retail borrowers). In general, demanders (users) of funds issue financial claims (e.g., equity and debt securities) to finance the gap between their investment expenditures and their internally generated savings, such as retained earnings or tax funds. As shown in Figure 8.6, in a world without financial institutions, we would have **direct transfers** of funds from fund suppliers to fund users. In return, financial claims would flow directly from fund users to fund suppliers.

In this economy without FIs, the amount of funds flowing between fund suppliers and fund users through financial markets would likely be quite low for several reasons:

- Once they have lent money in exchange for financial claims, fund suppliers would need to monitor continually the use of their funds. Fund suppliers must ensure that fund users

neither steal the funds outright nor waste the funds on projects that have low or negative returns, since either theft or waste would lower fund suppliers' chances of being repaid and/or earning a positive return on their investments (such as through the receipt of dividends or interest). Monitoring against theft, misuse, or underuse of their funds would cost any given fund supplier a lot of time and effort, and of course each fund supplier, regardless of the dollar value of the investment, would have to carry out the same costly and time-consuming process. Further, many investors do not have the financial training to understand the necessary business information to assess whether a securities issuer is making the best use of their funds. In fact, so many investment opportunities are available to fund suppliers that even those trained in financial analysis rarely have the time to monitor how their funds are used in all of their investments. The resulting lack of monitoring increases the risk of directly investing in financial claims. Given these challenges, fund suppliers would likely prefer to delegate the task of monitoring fund borrowers to ensure good performance to others.

- Many financial claims feature a long-term commitment (e.g., mortgages, corporate stock, and bonds) for fund suppliers, thus creating another disincentive for fund suppliers to hold direct financial claims that fund users may issue. Specifically, given the choice between holding cash and holding long-term securities, fund suppliers may well choose to hold cash for its **liquidity,** especially if they plan to use their savings to finance consumption expenditures before their creditors expect to repay them. Fund suppliers may also fear that they will not find anyone to purchase their financial claim and free up their funds. When financial markets are not very developed, or deep, in terms of the number of active buyers and sellers in the market, such liquidity concerns arise.

▼FIGURE 8.6
Flow of Funds in a World without FIs

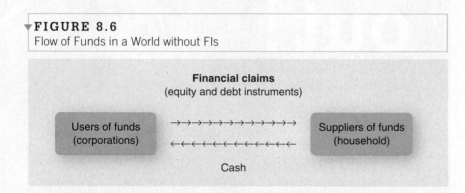

Financial claims
(equity and debt instruments)

Users of funds (corporations) →→→→→→→→→→→→ Suppliers of funds (household)
←←←←←←←←←←←←
Cash

▼ TABLE 8.3 Types of Financial Institutions

Commercial banks: depository institutions whose major assets are loans and whose major liabilities are deposits. Commercial bank loans cover a broader range, including consumer, commercial, and real estate loans, than do loans from other depository institutions. Because they are larger and more likely to have access to public securities markets, commercial bank liabilities generally include more nondeposit sources of funds, such as subordinate notes and debentures, than do those of other depository institutions.

Thrifts: depository institutions including savings associations, savings banks, and credit unions. Thrifts generally perform services similar to commercial banks, but they tend to concentrate their loans in one segment, such as real estate loans or consumer loans. Credit unions operate on a not-for-profit basis for particular groups of individuals, such as a labor union or a particular company's employees.

Insurance companies: protect individuals and corporations (policyholders) from financially adverse events. Life insurance companies provide protection in the event of untimely death or illness, and help in planning retirement. Property casualty insurance protects against personal injury and liability due to accidents, theft, fire, and so on.

Securities firms and investment banks: underwrite securities and engage in related activities such as securities brokerage, securities trading, and making markets in which securities trade.

Finance companies: make loans to both individuals and businesses. Unlike depository institutions, finance companies do not accept deposits, but instead rely on short- and long-term debt for funding, and many of their loans are collateralized with some kind of durable good, such as washer/dryers, furniture, carpets, and the like.

Mutual funds: pool many individuals' and companies' financial resources and invest those resources in diversified asset portfolios.

Pension funds: offer savings plans through which fund participants accumulate savings during their working years. Participants then withdraw their pension resources (which have presumably earned additional returns in the interim) during their retirement years. Funds originally invested in and accumulated in a pension fund are exempt from current taxation. Participants pay taxes on distributions taken after age 55, when their tax brackets are (presumably) lower.

finance at work //: markets

Retail Giant to Battle over Bank Plans

Walmart Stores Inc., ever looking for ways to expand its already huge empire, has asked the government for permission to move into an entirely different industry: running its own in-house bank. The world's largest retailer asked the Federal Deposit Insurance Corp. for permission to open a bank that can process millions of checks and credit card payments each month, operating out of its many stores. The company says it's not interested in running a consumer bank as well, but some of its opponents still fear that allowing Walmart into the banking industry in any way could hurt local banks in much the same way that Walmart decimated mom-and-pop stores during Walmart's rapid—some would even say ruthless—expansion.

This is Walmart's fourth bid at establishing its own bank—and its previous requests unleashed an unprecedented flood of comments to the FDIC. . . . "It's a landmark battle in both U.S. business and financial services history," said Jerry Comizio, a financial services lawyer for Thacher, Proffitt & Wood LLP in Washington D.C., and former senior attorney with the Securities and Exchange Commission and deputy general counsel of the U.S. Department of the Treasury's Office of Thrift Supervision.

Walmart says consumers and retail banks have nothing to fear. The retail giant pledges to stay out of branch banking and says it will not provide consumer lending, but for opponents, those assurances ring hollow. "There is reason to believe that these (Walmart's) plans could be expansive. Walmart has attempted on several occasions to enter the full-service banking business," said American Bankers Association's head of government relations Art Johnson, in testimony prepared for the FDIC hearing. "The ABA believes that banking is too important to the nation to try such a risky experiment."

Walmart says that it can save money if allowed to operate an in-house bank to handle the 140 million credit, debit card, and electronic check payments it handles each year. Concerns are twofold. One is the mixing of banking and commerce—parts of the economy that have traditionally been kept separate until the repeal of the

Glass-Steagall Act in 1999. The other worry stems from the fact that a Walmart bank could swallow local banks with its national presence and deep pockets, outcompeting even large institutions such as Bank of America, Chase, and Wachovia that have also grown at the expense of local ownership.

Want to know more?

Key Words to Search for Updates: **Walmart, banking; FDIC; ABA; Glass-Steagall repeal; electronic check payments**

Source: *The Wall Street Journal,* April 8, 2006, p. A3.

• Even though real-world financial markets provide some liquidity services by allowing fund suppliers to trade financial securities among themselves, fund suppliers face **price risk** when they buy securities—fund suppliers may not get their principal back, let alone any return on their investment. Trading securities on secondary markets involves various transaction costs. The price at which investors can sell a security on secondary markets such as the New York Stock Exchange (NYSE) or

NASDAQ may well differ from the price they initially paid for the security. The investment community as a whole may change the security's valuation between the time the fund supplier bought it and the time the fund supplier sold it. Further, dealers, acting as intermediaries between buyers and sellers, charge transaction costs for completing a trade. So even if an investor bought a security and then sold it the next day, the investor would likely lose money from transaction and other costs.

Unique Economic Functions Performed by Financial Institutions

Because of (1) monitoring costs, (2) liquidity costs, and (3) price risk, most average investors may well view direct investment in financial claims and markets as an unattractive proposition and, as fund suppliers, they will likely prefer to hold cash. As a result, financial market activity (and therefore savings and investment) would likely remain quite low. However, the financial system has developed an alternative, indirect way for investors (or fund suppliers) to channel funds to users of funds: financial intermediaries **indirectly transfer** funds to ultimate fund users. Because of monitoring, liquidity risk, and price risk costs, fund suppliers often prefer to hold financial intermediaries' financial claims rather than those directly issued by the ultimate fund users. Consider Figure 8.7, which more closely

represents the way that funds flow in the U.S. financial system than does Figure 8.6. Notice how financial institutions stand—or intermediate—between fund suppliers and fund users. That is, FIs channel funds from ultimate suppliers to ultimate fund users. Fund suppliers and users use these FIs to channel funds because of financial intermediaries' unique ability to reduce monitoring costs, liquidity costs, and price risk.

Monitoring Costs As we noted above, a fund supplier who directly invests in a fund user's financial claims faces a high cost of comprehensively monitoring the fund user's actions in a timely way. One solution to this problem is that a large number of small investors can group their funds together by holding claims issued by an FI. In turn, the FI will invest in direct financial claims that fund users issue. Financial institutions' aggregation of funds from fund suppliers resolves a number of problems:

- First, large FIs now have much greater incentive to collect information and monitor the ultimate fund user's actions, because the FI has far more at stake than any small individual fund supplier would have.

- Second, the FI performs the necessary monitoring function via its own internal experts, alleviating the "free-rider" problem that arises when small fund suppliers leave it to each other to collect information and monitor a fund user. In an economic sense, fund suppliers appoint the FI as a **delegated monitor** to act on their behalf. For example, full-service securities firms such as Merrill Lynch carry out investment research on new issues and make investment recommendations for their retail clients (investors), while commercial banks collect deposits from fund suppliers and lend these funds to ultimate users, such as corporations. An important part of these FIs' functions is their ability and incentive to monitor ultimate fund users.

Liquidity and Price Risk In addition to providing more and better information about fund users' activities, financial intermediaries provide additional liquidity to fund suppliers, acting as **asset transformers** as follows: FIs purchase the financial claims that fund users issue—primary securities such as mortgages, bonds, and stocks—and finance these purchases by selling financial claims to household investors and other fund suppliers as deposits, insurance policies, or other **secondary securities.** The secondary securities—packages or pools of primary claims—that FIs collect and then issue are often more liquid than are the primary securities themselves. For example, banks and thrift institutions (e.g., savings associations) offer draft deposit accounts with fixed principal values and (often) guaranteed interest rates. Fund suppliers can generally access the funds in those accounts on demand.

▼FIGURE 8.7
Flow of Funds in a World with FIs

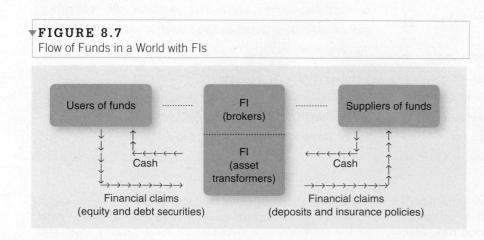

Money market mutual funds issue shares to household savers that allow the savers to maintain almost fixed principal amounts while earning somewhat higher interest rates than on bank deposits. Further, savers can also withdraw these funds on demand whenever the saver writes a check on the account. Even life insurance companies allow policyholders to borrow against their company-held policy balances at very short notice.

time out!

8-4   List the major types of financial institutions.

8-5   What three main issues would deter fund suppliers from directly purchasing securities?

INTEREST RATES

We often speak of "the interest rate" as if only one rate applies to all financial situations or transactions. In fact, we can list tens or hundreds of interest rates that are appropriate in various conditions or situations within the U.S. economy on any particular day. Let's explore a bit how the financial sector sets these rates and how the rates relate to one another. We actually observe **nominal interest rates** in financial markets—these are the rates most often quoted by financial news services. As we saw in Chapters 6 and 7, nominal interest rates (or, simply, interest rates) directly affect most tradable securities' value or price. Since any change in nominal interest rates has such profound effects on security prices, financial managers and individual investors spend a lot of time and effort trying to identify factors that may influence future interest rate levels.

Of course, interest rate changes influence investment performance and trigger buy or sell decisions for individual investors, businesses, and governmental units alike. Figure 8.8 illustrates the movement of several key U.S. interest rates over the past 35 years:

• The prime commercial loan rate.

• The three-month T-bill rate.

• The high-grade corporate bond rate.

• The home mortgage rate.

Figure 8.8 shows how interest rates vary over time. For example, the prime rate hit highs of over 20 percent in the early 1980s, yet fell as low as 4.75 percent in the early 1970s. The prime rate stayed below 10 percent throughout much of the 1990s, and fell back further to 4.00 percent in the early 2000s.

Factors That Influence Interest Rates for Individual Securities

Specific factors that affect nominal interest rates for any particular security include:

• Inflation.

• The real interest rate.

• Default risk.

• Liquidity risk.

• Special provisions regarding the use of funds raised by a particular security issuer.

• The security's term to maturity.

We will discuss each of these factors after summarizing them in Table 8.4.

Inflation The first factor that influences interest rates is the economywide *actual or expected inflation rate*. Specifically, the higher the level of actual or expected inflation, the higher will be the level of interest rates. The positive relationship between interest rates and inflation rates is fairly intuitive: When inflation raises the general price level, investors who buy financial assets must earn a higher interest rate (or inflation premium) to compensate for continuing to hold the investment. Holding on to their investments means that they incur higher costs of forgoing consumption of real goods and services today, only to have to buy these same goods and services at higher prices in the future. In other words, the higher the rate of inflation, the more expensive the same basket of goods and services will be in the future.

We define **inflation** of the general price index of goods and services (or the inflation premium, IP) as the (percentage) increase in the price of a standardized basket of goods and services over a given period of time. The U.S. Department of Commerce measures inflation using indexes such as the consumer price index (CPI) and the producer price index (PPI). For example, the annual inflation rate using the CPI index between years t and $t + 1$ would be equal to:

$$IP = \frac{CPI_{t+1} - CPI_t}{CPI_t} \times 100 \qquad (8\text{-}1)$$

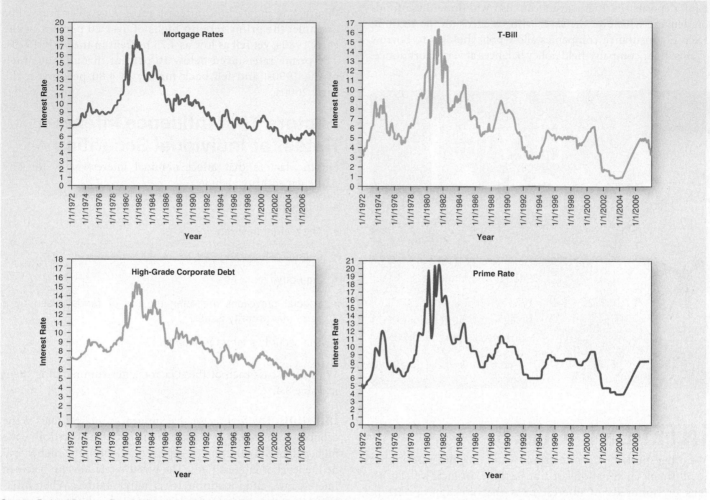

Source: Federal Reserve Board, Web site, various dates, **www.federalreserve.gov**.

▼ **TABLE 8.4** Factors Affecting Nominal Interest Rates

Inflation: A continual increase in the price level of a basket of goods and services throughout the economy as a whole.

Real interest rate: interest rate adjusted for inflation; generally lower than nominal interest rates at any particular time; interest rate adjusted so that a chosen date represents the base year. Thus, we can validly compare interest rates over various periods based upon a common denominator.

Default risk: risk that a security issuer will miss an interest or principal payment or continue to miss such payments.

Liquidity risk: risk that a security cannot be sold at a price relatively close to its value with low transaction costs on short notice.

Special provisions: provisions (e.g., taxability, convertibility, and callability) that impact a security holder beneficially or adversely and as such are reflected in the interest rates on securities that contain such provisions.

Time to maturity: length of time until a security is repaid, used in debt securities as the date upon which the security holders get their principal back.

▼FIGURE 8.9
Nominal Interest Rates versus Inflation

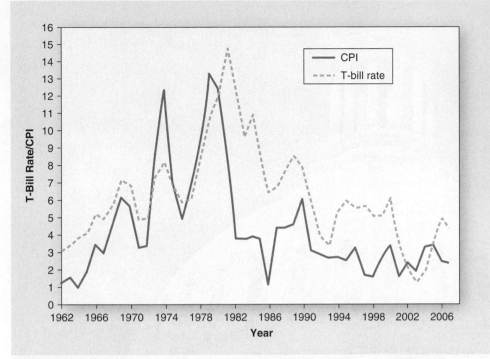

Source: Federal Reserve Board and U.S. Department of Labor Web sites, various dates, **www.federalreserve.gov** and **www.states.bls.gov/cpi/home.htm.**

early last century. The Fisher effect theorizes that nominal interest rates that we observe in financial markets must compensate investors for

- Any inflation-related reduction in purchasing power lost on funds lent or principal due.

- An additional premium above the expected rate of inflation for-going present consumption (which reflects the real interest rate issue discussed above).

$$i = \text{Expected } IP + RIR \quad (8\text{-}2)$$

Thus, the nominal interest rate will equal the real interest rate only when market participants expect inflation to be zero: Expected $IP = 0$. Similarly, the nominal interest rate will equal the expected inflation rate only when the real interest rate is zero. We can rearrange the nominal interest rate equation to show what determines the real interest rate:[1]

$$RIR = i - \text{Expected } IP \quad (8\text{-}3)$$

The one-year T-bill rate in 2004 was 1.89 percent, while the CPI for the year was 3.30 percent, which implies a real interest rate of −1.41 percent—that is, the real interest rate was actually negative. Thus, the real value of investments actually decreased in that year.

Real Interest Rates A **real interest rate** is the rate that a security would pay if no inflation were expected over its holding period (e.g., a year). As such, it measures only society's relative time preference for consuming today rather than tomorrow. The higher society's preference to consume today (i.e., the higher its time value of money or rate of time preference), the higher the real interest rate (RIR) will be.

Fisher effect Economists often refer to the relationship among real interest rates (RIR), expected inflation (expected IP), and nominal interest rates (i), described above, as the Fisher effect, named for Irving Fisher, who identified these economic relationships

[1]Often the Fisher effect formula is written as: $(1 + i) = (1 + IP) \times (1 + RIR)$, which, when solved for i, becomes: $i = \text{Expected } IP + RIR + (\text{Expected } IP \times RIR)$ where $RIR \times \text{Expected } IP$ is the inflation premium for the loss of purchasing power on the promised nominal interest rate payments due to inflation. For small values of RIR and Expected IP this term is negligible. The approximation formula used here assumes these values are small.

EXAMPLE 8-1

For interactive versions of this example visit www.mhhe.com/canM

Calculating Real Interest Rates

One-year Treasury bill rates in 2007 averaged 4.93 percent and inflation (measured by the consumer price index) for the year was 1.80 percent. If investors had expected the same inflation rate as that actually realized, calculate the real interest rate for 2007 according to the Fisher effect.

SOLUTION:

4.93% − 1.80% = 3.13%

The risk of the U.S. defaulting on debt payments is practically zero.

Figure 8.9 shows the nominal interest rate (one-year T-bill rate) versus the change in the CPI from 1962 through 2007. The expected inflation rate is difficult to estimate accurately, so the real interest rate can be difficult to measure accurately. Investors' expectations are not always realized either.

Default or Credit Risk **Default risk** is the risk that a security issuer may fail to make its promised interest and principal payments to its bondholders (or its dividend in the case of preferred stockholders). The higher the default risk, the higher the interest rate that security buyers will demand to compensate them for this default (or credit) risk relative to default-risk-free U.S. Treasury securities. Since the U.S. government has taxation powers and can print currency, the risk of its defaulting on debt payments is practically zero. But some borrowers, such as corporations or individuals, have less predictable cash flows (and no powers to tax anyone to raise funds immediately). So investors must charge issuers other

FIGURE 8.10
Default Risk Premiums on Corporate Bonds

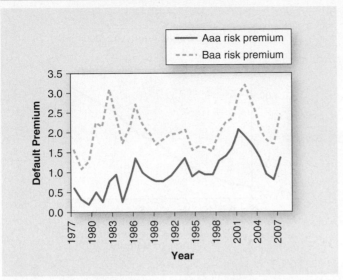

Source: Federal Reserve Board, Web site, various dates, **www.federalreserve.gov**.

$$DRP_{Aaa} = 5.53\% - 4.18\% = 1.35\%$$

$$DRP_{Baa} = 6.68\% - 4.18\% = 2.50\%$$

Figure 8.10 presents these risk premiums for the stated creditworthiness categories of bonds from 1977 through 2007. Notice from this figure and Figure 8.9 that default risk premiums tend to increase when the economy is contracting and decrease when the economy is expanding. For example, from 1981 to 1982, real interest rates (T-bills–CPI in Figure 8.9) increased from 5.90 percent to 8.47 percent. Over the same period, default risk premiums on Aaa-rated bonds increased from 0.25 percent to 0.78 percent. Baa-rated bonds showed a default risk premium increase from 2.12 percent to 3.10 percent.

Liquidity Risk A highly liquid asset can be sold at a predictable price with low transaction costs. That is, the holder can convert the asset at its fair market value at short notice. The interest rate on a security reflects its relative liquidity,

default risk The risk that a security issuer will default on that security by being late on or missing an interest or principal payment.

liquidity risk The risk that a security can be sold at a predictable price with low transaction costs on short notice.

term structure of interest rates A comparison of market yields on securities, assuming all characteristics except maturity are the same.

> # "Default risk premiums tend to increase when the economy is contracting and decrease when the economy is expanding."

---

than the U.S. government a premium for any perceived probability of default and the cost of potentially recovering the amount loaned built into their regular interest rate premium. The difference between a quoted interest rate on a security (security *j*) and a Treasury security with similar maturity, liquidity, tax, and other features is called a *default* or *credit risk premium* (DRP_j). That is:

$$DRP_j = i_{jt} - i_{Tt} \qquad (8\text{-}4)$$

where i_{jt} = Interest rate on a security issued by a non-Treasury issuer (issuer *j*) of maturity *m* at time *t*.

i_{Tt} = Interest rate on a security issued by the U.S. Treasury of maturity *m* at time *t*.

Various rating agencies, including Moody's and Standard & Poor's, evaluate and categorize the potential default risk on many corporate bonds, some state and municipal bonds, and some stocks. We covered these ratings in more detail in Chapter 7. For example, in 2007, the 10-year Treasury rate was 4.18 percent. Moody's Aaa-rated and Baa-rated corporate debt carried interest rates of 5.53 percent and 6.68 percent, respectively. Thus, the average default risk premiums on the Aaa-rated and Baa-rated corporate debt were:

with highly liquid assets carrying the lowest interest rates (all other characteristics remaining the same). Likewise, if a security is illiquid, investors add a **liquidity risk** premium (LRP) to the interest rate on the security. In the United States, most government securities sell in liquid markets, as do large corporations' stocks and bonds. Securities issued by smaller companies trade in relatively less liquid markets.

A different type of liquidity risk premium may also exist if investors dislike long-term securities because their prices (present values, as discussed in Chapters 4 and 6) react more to interest rate changes than short-term securities do. In this case, a higher liquidity risk premium may be added to a security with a longer maturity because of its greater exposure to price risk (loss of capital value) on the longer-term security as interest rates change.

Special Provisions or Covenants Sometimes a security's issuing party attaches special provisions or covenants to the security issued. Such provisions affect the interest rates on these securities relative to securities without such provisions attached to them. Some of these special provisions include the security's taxability, convertibility, and callability. For example, investors pay no federal taxes on interest payments received from municipal securities. So a municipal bondholder may demand a lower interest rate than that demanded on a comparable taxable bond—such as a Treasury bond (which is taxable at the federal level but not at the state or local levels) or a corporate bond (the interest on which is taxable at the state, local, and federal levels).

Another special covenant is convertibility: A convertible bond offers the holder the opportunity to exchange the bond for another type of the issuer's security—usually preferred or common stock—at a preset price (see Chapter 6). This conversion option can be valuable to purchasers, so convertible security buyers require lower interest rates than a comparable nonconvertible security holder would require (all else equal). In general, special provisions that benefit security holders (e.g., tax-free status and convertibility) bring with them lower interest rates, and special provisions that benefit security issuers (e.g., callability, by which an issuer has the option to retire, or call, the security prior to maturity at a preset price) require higher interest rates to encourage purchase.

Term to Maturity

Interest rates also change—sometimes daily—because of a bond's term to maturity. As we noted in Chapter 6, financial professionals refer to this daily or even hourly changeability in interest rates as the **term structure of interest rates,** or the yield curve. As we explained in Chapter 6, the shape of the yield curve derives directly from time value of money principles. The term structure of interest rates compares interest rates on debt securities based on their time to maturity, assuming that all characteristics (i.e., default risk, liquidity risk) are equal. Interest rates change as the maturity of a debt security changes; in general, the longer the term to maturity, the higher the required interest rate buyers will demand. This addition to the required interest rate is the maturity premium (MP). The MP, which is the difference between the required yield on long- versus short-term securities of the same characteristics except maturity, can be positive, negative, or zero.

The financial industry most often reports and analyzes the yield curve for U.S. Treasury securities. The yield curve for U.S. Treasury securities has taken many shapes over the years, but the three most common shapes appear in Figure 8.11. In graph (a), the yield curve on August 12, 2004, yields rise steadily with maturity when the yield curve slopes upward. This is the most common yield curve. On average, the MP is positive, as you might expect. Graph (b) shows an inverted, or downward-sloping, yield curve, reported on November 27, 2000, in which yields decline as maturity increases. Inverted yield curves do not generally last very long. In this case, the yield curve inverted as the U.S. Treasury began retiring long-term (30-year) bonds as the country began to pay off the national debt. Finally, graph (c) shows a flat yield curve, reported on February 28, 2006, when the yield to maturity is virtually unaffected by the term to maturity.

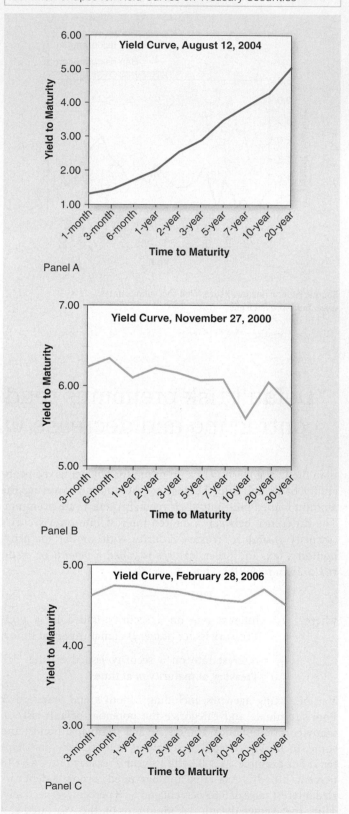

FIGURE 8.11
Common Shapes for Yield Curves on Treasury Securities

Source: U.S. Treasury, Office of Debt Management, Daily Treasury Yield Curves, various dates, **www.ustreas.gov.**

Note that yield curves may reflect factors other than investor's preferences for the maturity of a security. In reality, liquidity differences may arise among the securities traded at different points along the yield curve. For example, newly issued 20-year Treasury bonds offer a lower rate of return than previously issued Treasury bonds, all else being equal (so-called seasoned issues). Ten-year Treasury bonds may be more liquid if investors prefer new ("on the run") securities to previously issued ("off the run") securities. Specifically, since the U.S. Treasury has historically only issued new 10-year notes and 20-year bonds at the long end of the maturity spectrum, a seasoned 10-year Treasury bond would have to have been issued 10 years previously (i.e., it was originally a 20-year bond when it was issued 10 years previously). Increased demand for previously issued (and thus more liquid) 20-year Treasury bonds relative to the newly issued but less liquid 10-year Treasury bonds can be large enough to push the equilibrium interest rate on the 20-year Treasury bonds below that for the 10-year Treasury bonds and even below short-term rates. In the next section, we will review three major theories that financial analysts often use to explain the shape of the yield to maturity curve (or the shape of the term structure of interest rates).

Putting together the factors that affect interest rates in different markets, we can use the following general equation to note the influence of the factors that functionally impact the fair interest rate—the rate necessary to compensate investors for all security risks—(i_j^*) on an individual (jth) financial security.

$$i_j^* = f(IP, RIR, DRP_j, LRP_j, SCP_j, MP_j) \qquad (8\text{-}5)$$

where IP = Inflation premium.

       RIR = Real interest rate.

       DRP_j = Default risk premium on the jth security.

       LRP_j = Liquidity risk premium on the jth security.

       SCP_j = Special covenant premium on the jth security.

       MP_j = Maturity premium on the jth security.

The first two factors, IP and RIR, are common to all financial securities, while the other factors can uniquely influence the price of a single security.

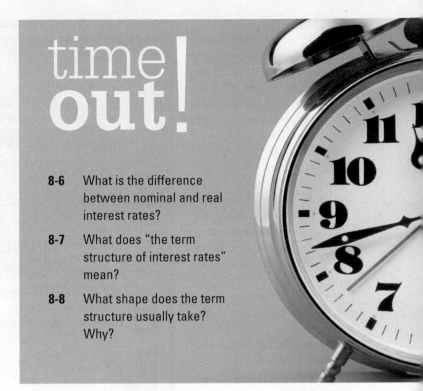

time out!

8-6 What is the difference between nominal and real interest rates?

8-7 What does "the term structure of interest rates" mean?

8-8 What shape does the term structure usually take? Why?

Theories Explaining the Shape of the Term Structure of Interest Rates

We just explained the necessity of a maturity premium, the relationship between a security's interest rate and its remaining term to maturity. We can illustrate these issues by showing that the term structure of interest rates can take a number of different shapes. As you might expect, economists and financial theorists with various viewpoints differ among themselves in theorizing why the yield curve takes different shapes. Explanations for the yield curve's shape fall predominantly into three categories:

• The unbiased expectations theory.

• The liquidity premium theory.

• The market segmentation theory.

Look again at Figure 8.11 (a), which presents the Treasury yield curve as of August 12, 2004. We see that the yield curve on this date reflected the normal upward-sloping relationship between yield and maturity. Now let's turn to explanations for this shape based on the three predominant theories noted above.

Unbiased Expectations Theory

According to the unbiased expectations theory of the term structure of interest

▼**FIGURE 8.12**
Unbiased Expectations Theory of the Term Structure of Interest Rates

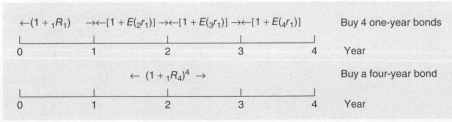

rates, at any given point in time, the yield curve reflects the *market's current expectations of future short-term rates.* As illustrated in Figure 8.12, the intuition behind the unbiased expectations theory is this: If investors have a four-year investment horizon, they could either buy current four-year bonds and earn the current (or spot) yield on a four-year bond ($_1R_4$, if held to maturity) each year, or they could invest in four successive one-year bonds (of which they know only the current one-year spot rate ($_1R_1$). But investors also expect what the unknown future one-year rates [$E(_2r_1)$, $E(_3r_1)$, and $E(_4r_1)$] will be. Note that each interest rate term has two subscripts, e.g., $_1R_4$. The first subscript indicates the period in which the security is bought, so that 1 represents the purchase of a security in period 1. The second subscript indicates the maturity on the security. Thus, 4 represents the purchase of a security with a four-year life. Similarly, $E(_3r_1)$ is the expected return on a security with a one-year life purchased in period 3.

According to the unbiased expectations theory, the return for holding a four-year bond to maturity should equal the expected return for investing in four successive one-year bonds (as long as the market is in equilibrium). If this equality

ILuvTrixie and nine others like this.

ILuvTrixie Now I don't have to hassle my roommate to show me how to use my BA II Plus!

11 hours ago · Like

write a comment...

does not hold, an arbitrage opportunity exists. That is, if investors could earn more on the one-year bond investments, they could short (or sell) the four-year bond, use the proceeds to buy the four successive one-year bonds, and earn a guaranteed profit over the four-year investment horizon. So, according to the unbiased expectations hypothesis, if the market expects future one-year rates to rise each successive year into the future, then the yield curve will slope upwards. Specifically, the current four-year T-bond rate or return will exceed the three-year bond rate, which will exceed the two-year bond rate, and so on. Similarly, if the market expects future one-year rates to remain constant each successive year into the future, then the four-year bond rate will equal the three-year bond rate. That is, the term structure of interest rates will remain constant (flat) over the relevant time period. Specifically, the unbiased expectation theory states that current long-term interest rates are geometric averages of current and expected *future* short-term interest rates. The mathematical equation representing this relationship is

$$(1 + {_1R_N})^N = (1 + {_1R_1})[1 + E(_2r_1)] \ldots [1 + E(_Nr_1)] \quad (8\text{-}6)$$

therefore:

$$_1R_N = \{[1 + {_1R_1}][1 + E(_2r_1)] \ldots [1 + E(_Nr_1)]\}^{1/N} - 1 \quad (8\text{-}7)$$

where $_1R_N$ = Actual N-period rate today (i.e., the first day of year 1).

N = Term to maturity.

$_1R_1$ = Actual one-year rate today.

$E(_ir_1)$ = Expected one-year rates for years 2, 3, 4, ... N in the future.

Notice, as above, that uppercase interest rate terms, $_1R_t$, are the actual current interest rates on securities purchased today with a maturity of t years. Lowercase interest rate terms, $_tr_1$, represent estimates of future one-year interest rates starting t years into the future.

the
Math Coach on...

Using the Constant Growth-Rate Model

" When putting interest rates into the equation, enter them in decimal format, not percentage format:

Correct: (1 + .0294)

Not correct: (1 + 2.94) "

Calculating Yield Curves

Suppose that the current one-year rate (one-year spot rate) and expected one-year T-bond rates over the following three years (i.e., years 2, 3, and 4, respectively) are as follows:

$$_1R_1 = 2.94\% \qquad E(_2r_1) = 4\% \qquad E(_3r_1) = 4.74\% \qquad E(_4r_1) = 5.10\%$$

Construct a yield curve using the unbiased expectations theory.

SOLUTION:

Using the unbiased expectations theory, current (or today's) rates for one-, two-, three-, and four-year maturity Treasury securities should be:

$$_1R_1 = 2.94\% \quad \text{(Expected return of security with one-year life purchased in period 1)}$$

$$_1R_2 = [(1 + .0294)(1 + .04)]^{1/2} - 1 = 3.469\%$$

$$_1R_3 = [(1 + .0294)(1 + .04)(1 + .0474)]^{1/3} - 1 = 3.891\%$$

$$_1R_4 = [(1 + .0294)(1 + .04)(1 + .0474)(1 + .051)]^{1/4} - 1 = 4.192\%$$

and the current yield to maturity curve will be upward sloping as shown:

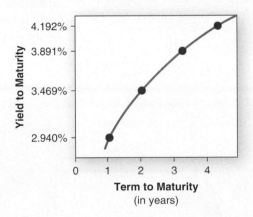

This upward-sloping yield curve reflects the market's expectation of persistently rising one-year (short-term) interest rates over the future horizon.[2]

[2] That is, $E(_4r_1) > E(_3r_1) > E(_2r_1) > {_1R_1}$.

Liquidity Premium Theory The second popular explanation—the liquidity premium theory of the term structure of interest rates—builds on the unbiased expectations theory. The liquidity premium idea is as follows: Investors will hold long-term maturities only if these securities with longer-term maturities are offered at a premium to compensate for future uncertainty in the security's value. Of course, uncertainty or risk increases with an asset's maturity. This theory is thus consistent with our discussions of market risk and liquidity risk, above. Specifically, in a world of uncertainty, short-term securities provide greater marketability (due to their more active secondary markets) and have less price risk than long-term securities do. As a result (due to smaller price fluctuations for a given change in interest rates) investors will prefer to hold shorter-term securities because this kind of paper can be converted into cash with little market risk. Said another way, investors face little risk of a capital loss, i.e., a fall in the price of the security below its original purchase price. So, investors must be offered a liquidity premium to buy longer-term securities that carry higher capital loss risk. This difference in market and liquidity risk can be directly related to the fact that longer-term securities are more sensitive to interest rate changes in the market than are shorter-term securities—Chapter 6 discussed bond interest rate sensitivity and the link to a bond's maturity. Because longer maturities on securities mean greater market and liquidity risk, the liquidity premium increases as maturity increases.

The liquidity premium theory states that long-term rates are equal to geometric averages of current and expected short-term rates (like the unbiased expectations theory), plus liquidity risk premiums that increase with the security's maturity (this is the extension of the liquidity premium added to the unbiased expectations theory). Figure 8.13 illustrates the differences in the shape of the yield curve under the unbiased expectations hypothesis versus the liquidity premium hypothesis. For example, according to the liquidity premium theory, an upward-sloping yield curve may reflect investors' expectations that future short-term rates will be flat, but because liquidity premiums increase with maturity, the yield curve will nevertheless slope upward. Indeed, an upward-sloping yield curve may reflect expectations that future interest rates will rise, be flat, or even fall as long as the liquidity premium increases with maturity fast enough to produce an upward-sloping yield curve. The liquidity premium theory can be mathematically represented as

$$_1R_N = \{[1 + {_1R_1}][1 + E({_2r_1}) + L_2] \ldots$$

$$[1 + E({_Nr_1}) + L_N]\}^{1/N} - 1 \qquad (8\text{-}8)$$

where L_t = Liquidity premium for a period t and $L_2 < L_3 < L_N$.

Comparing the yield curves in Examples 8.2 (using the unbiased expectations hypothesis) and 8.3 on the next page, notice that the liquidity premium in year 2 ($L_2 = 0.10\%$) produces a 0.05 percent premium on the yield to maturity on a two-year T-note, the liquidity premium for year 3 ($L_3 = 0.20\%$) produces a 0.10 percent premium on the yield to maturity on the three-year T-note, and the liquidity premium for year 4 ($L_4 = 0.30\%$) produces a 0.15 percent premium on the yield to maturity on the four-year T-note.

Market Segmentation Theory The market segmentation theory does not build on the unbiased expectations theory or the liquidity premium hypothesis, but rather argues that individual investors and FIs have specific maturity preferences, and convincing them to hold securities with maturities other than their most preferred requires a higher interest rate (maturity premium). The main thrust of the market segmentation theory is that investors do not consider securities with different maturities as perfect substitutes. Rather, individual investors and FIs have distinctly preferred investment horizons dictated by the dates when their liabilities will come due. For example, banks might prefer to hold relatively short-term U.S. Treasury bonds because their deposit liabilities also tend to be short term—recall that bank customers can access their funds on demand. Insurance companies, on the other hand, may prefer to hold long-term U.S. Treasury bonds because life insurance contracts usually expose insurance firms to long-term liabilities. Accordingly, distinct supply and demand conditions within a particular maturity segment—such as the short end and long end of the bond market—determine interest rates under the market segmentation theory.

The market segmentation theory assumes that investors and borrowers generally do not want to shift from one maturity sector to another without adequate compensation—that is, an interest rate premium. Figure 8.14 demonstrates how changes in supply for short- versus long-term bond market segments result in changing shapes of the yield to maturity curve. Specifically, as shown in Figure 8.14, the higher the yield on securities is (which means the lower the price), the higher the demand for those securities is.[3]

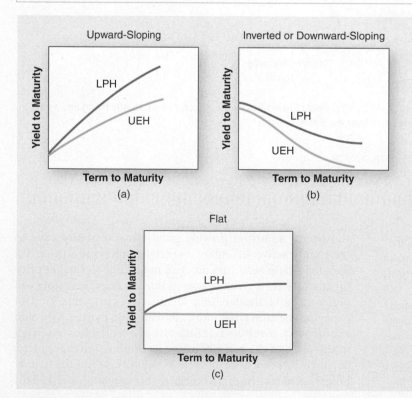

▼**FIGURE 8.13**
Yield Curve under the Unbiased Expectations Hypothesis (UEH) versus the Liquidity Premium Hypothesis (LPH)

[3]In general, the price and yield on a bond are inversely related. Thus, as the price of a bond falls (becomes cheaper), the demand for the bond will rise. This is the same as saying that as the yield on a bond rises, it becomes cheaper and the demand for it increases. See Chapter 6.

Calculating Yield Curves Using the Liquidity Premium Hypothesis

Suppose that the current one-year rate (one-year spot rate) and expected one-year T-bond rates over the following three years (i.e., years 2, 3, and 4, respectively) are as follows:

$$_1R_1 = 2.94\%, \quad E(_2r_1) = 4.00\%, \quad E(_3r_1) = 4.74\% \quad E(_4r_1) = 5.10\%$$

In addition, investors charge a liquidity premium on longer-term securities such that,

$$L_2 = 0.10\% \quad L_3 = 0.20\%, \quad L_4 = 0.30\%$$

Using the liquidity premium theory, construct the yield curve.

SOLUTION:

Using the liquidity premium theory, current rates for one-, two-, three-, and four- year maturity Treasury securities should be:

$$_1R_1 = 2.94\%$$

$$_1R_2 = [(1 + .0294)(1 + .04 + .001)]^{1/2} - 1 = 3.52\%$$

$$_1R_3 = [(1 + .0294)(1 + .04 + .001)(1 + .0474 + .002)]^{1/3} - 1 = 3.99\%$$

$$_1R_4 = [(1 + .0294)(1 + .04 + .001)(1 + .0474 + .002)(1 + .051 + .003)]^{1/4} - 1 = 4.34\%$$

and the current yield to maturity curve will be upward sloping as shown:

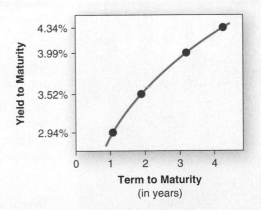

Thus, as the supply of securities decreases in the short-term market and increases in the long term market, the slope of the yield curve becomes steeper. If the supply of short-term securities had increased while the supply of long-term securities had decreased, the yield curve would have a flatter slope and might even have sloped downward. Indeed, the U.S. Treasury's large-scale repurchase of long-term Treasury bonds (i.e., reductions in supply) in early 2000 has been viewed as the major cause of the inverted yield curve that appeared in February 2000.

Forecasting Interest Rates

We noted in the time value of money (TVM) chapters (Chapters 4 and 5) that as interest rates change, so do the values of financial securities. Accordingly, both individual investors and public corporations want to be able to predict or forecast interest rates if they wish to trade profitably. For example, if interest rates rise, the value of investment portfolios of individuals and corporations will fall, resulting in a loss of wealth. So, interest rate forecasts are extremely important for the financial wealth of both public corporations and individuals.

Recall our discussion of the unbiased expectations hypothesis in the previous section of this chapter. That hypothesis indicated that the market's expectation of future short-term interest rates determines the shape of the yield curve. For example, an upward-sloping yield curve implies that the market expects future short-term interest rates to rise. So, we can use the unbiased expectations hypothesis to forecast (short-term) interest rates in the future (i.e., forward one-year interest rates). A **forward rate** is an expected, or implied, rate

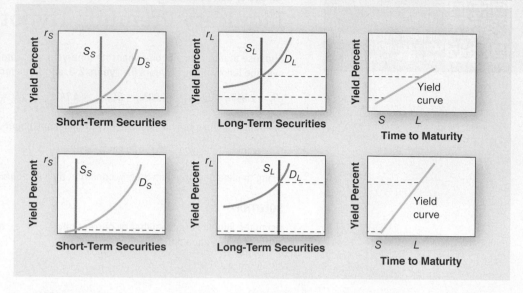

▼FIGURE 8.14
Market Segmentation and Determination of the Slope of Yield Curve

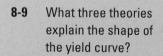

8-9 What three theories explain the shape of the yield curve?

8-10 Explain how arbitrage plays a role in the unbiased expectations explanation of the shape of the yield curve.

8-11 What is a forward rate?

8-12 How can we obtain an implied forward rate from current short- and long-term interest rates?

8-13 Why is it useful to calculate forward rates?

on a short-term security that will originate at some point in the future. Using the equations in the unbiased expectations theory, we can directly derive the market's expectation of forward rates from existing or actual rates on spot market securities.

To find an implied forward rate on a one-year security to be issued one year from today, we can rewrite the unbiased expectations hypothesis equation as follows:

$$_1R_2 = \{[1 + {}_1R_1][1 + ({}_2f_1)]\}^{1/2} - 1 \qquad (8\text{-}9)$$

where ${}_2f_1$ = expected one-year rate for year 2, or the implied forward one-year rate for next year.

Saying that ${}_2f_1$ is the expected one-year rate for year 2 is the same as saying that, once we isolate the ${}_2f_1$ term, the equation will give us the market's estimate of the expected one-year rate for year 2. Solving for ${}_2f_1$ we get:

$$_2f_1 = [(1 + {}_1R_2)^2/(1 + {}_1R_1)] - 1 \qquad (8\text{-}10)$$

In general, we can find the forward rate for any year, N, into the future using the following generalized equation derived from the unbiased expectations hypothesis:

$$_Nf_1 = [(1 + {}_1R_N)^N/(1 + {}_1R_{N-1})^{N-1}] - 1 \qquad (8\text{-}11)$$

Estimating Forward Rates

In the mid-2000s, the existing or current (spot) one-year, two-year, three-year, and four-year zero-coupon Treasury security rates were as follows:

$$_1R_1 = 5.00\%, \quad _1R_2 = 4.95\%, \quad _1R_3 = 4.93\%, \quad _1R_4 = 4.94\%$$

Using the unbiased expectations theory, calculate one-year forward rates on zero-coupon Treasury bonds for years 2, 3, and 4.

SOLUTION:

$$_2f_1 = [(1.0495)^2/(1.0500)] - 1 = 4.900\%$$

$$_3f_1 = [(1.0493)^3/(1.0495)^2] - 1 = 4.890\%$$

$$_4f_1 = [(1.0494)^4/(1.0493)^3] - 1 = 4.970\%$$

Your Turn...

Questions

1. Classify the following transactions as taking place in the primary or secondary markets *(LG1)*:

    a. IBM issues $200 million of new common stock.

    b. The New Company issues $50 million of common stock in an IPO.

    c. IBM sells $5 million of GM preferred stock out of its marketable securities portfolio.

    d. The Magellan Fund buys $100 million of previously issued IBM bonds.

    e. Prudential Insurance Co. sells $10 million of GM common stock.

2. Classify the following financial instruments as money market securities or capital market securities *(LG2)*:

    a. Federal Funds

    b. Common Stock

    c. Corporate Bonds

    d. Mortgages

    e. Negotiable Certificates of Deposit

    f. U.S. Treasury Bills

    g. U.S. Treasury Notes

    h. U.S. Treasury Bonds

    i. State and Government Bonds

3. What are the different types of financial institutions? Include a description of the main services offered by each. *(LG3)*

4. How would economic transactions between suppliers of funds (e.g., households) and users of funds (e.g., corporations) occur in a world without FIs? *(LG3)*

5. Why would a world limited to the direct transfer of funds from suppliers of funds to users of funds likely result in quite low levels of fund flows? *(LG3)*

6. How do FIs reduce monitoring costs associated with the flow of funds from fund suppliers to fund investors? *(LG3)*

7. How do FIs alleviate the problem of liquidity risk faced by investors wishing to invest in securities of corporations? *(LG3)*

8. What are six factors that determine the nominal interest rate on a security? *(LG4)*

9. What should happen to a security's equilibrium interest rate as the security's liquidity risk increases? *(LG4)*

10. Discuss and compare the three explanations for the shape of the yield curve. *(LG5)*

11. Are the unbiased expectations and liquidity hypothesis explanations for the shape of the yield curve completely independent theories? Explain why or why not. *(LG5)*

12. What is a forward interest rate? *(LG6)*

13. If we observe a one-year Treasury security rate higher than the two-year Treasury security rate, what can we infer about the one-year rate expected one year from now? *(LG6)*

Problems

BASIC PROBLEMS

8-1 Determinants of Interest Rates for Individual Securities A particular security's default risk premium is 2 percent. For all securities, the inflation risk premium is 1.75 percent and the real interest rate is 3.5 percent. The security's liquidity risk premium is 0.25 percent and maturity risk premium is 0.85 percent. The security has no special covenants. Calculate the security's equilibrium rate of return. *(LG4)*

8-2 Determinants of Interest Rates for Individual Securities You are considering an investment in 30-year bonds issued by Moore Corporation. The bonds have no special covenants. *The Wall Street Journal* reports that one-year T-bills are currently earning 3.25 percent. Your broker has determined the following information about economic activity and Moore Corporation bonds:

Real interest rate = 2.25%

Default risk premium = 1.15%

Liquidity risk premium = 0.50%

Maturity risk premium = 1.75%

a. What is the inflation premium? *(LG4)*

b. What is the fair interest rate on Moore Corporation 30-year bonds? *(LG4)*

8-3 **Determinants of Interest Rates for Individual Securities** Dakota Corporation 15-year bonds have an equilibrium rate of return is 8 percent. For all securities, the inflation risk premium is 1.75 percent and the real interest rate is 3.5 percent. The security's liquidity risk premium is 0.25 percent and maturity risk premium is 0.85 percent. The security has no special covenants. Calculate the bond's default risk premium. *(LG4)*

8-4 **Determinants of Interest Rates for Individual Securities** A two-year Treasury security currently earns 4.14 percent. Over the next two years, the real interest rate is expected to be 2.25 percent per year and the inflation premium is expected to be 1.75 percent per year. Calculate the maturity risk premium on the two-year Treasury security. *(LG4)*

8-5 **Unbiased Expectations Theory** Suppose that the current one-year rate (one-year spot rate) and expected one-year T-bill rates over the following three years (i.e., years 2, 3, and 4, respectively) are as follows:

$$_1R_1 = 6\%, \quad E(_2r_1) = 7\%, \quad E(_3r_1) = 7.5\%, \quad E(_4r_1) = 7.85\%$$

Using the unbiased expectations theory, calculate the current (long-term) rates for one-, two-, three-, and four-year-maturity Treasury securities. Plot the resulting yield curve. *(LG5)*

8-6 **Unbiased Expectations Theory** One-year Treasury bills currently earn 3.45 percent. You expect that one year from now, one-year Treasury bill rates will increase to 3.65 percent. If the unbiased expectations theory is correct, what should the current rate be on two-year Treasury securities? *(LG5)*

8-7 **Liquidity Premium Hypothesis** One-year Treasury bills currently earn 3.45 percent. You expect that one year from now, one-year Treasury bill rates will increase to 3.65 percent. The liquidity premium on two-year securities is 0.05 percent. If the liquidity theory is correct, what should the current rate be on two-year Treasury securities? *(LG5)*

8-8 **Liquidity Premium Hypothesis** Based on economists' forecasts and analyses, one-year Treasury bill rates and liquidity premiums for the next four years are expected to be as follows:

$$R_1 = 5.65\%$$

$E(_2r_1) = 6.75\%$	$L_2 = 0.05\%$
$E(_3r_1) = 6.85\%$	$L_2 = 0.10\%$
$E(_4r_1) = 7.15\%$	$L_2 = 0.12\%$

Using the liquidity premium hypothesis, plot the current yield curve. Make sure you label the axes on the graph and identify the four annual rates on the curve both on the axes and on the yield curve itself. *(LG5)*

INTERMEDIATE PROBLEMS

8-9 **Determinants of Interest Rates for Individual Securities** *The Wall Street Journal* reports that the rate on three-year Treasury securities is 6.00 percent, and the six-year Treasury rate is 6.20 percent. From discussions with your broker, you have determined that expected inflation premium is 2.25 percent next year, 2.50 percent in Year 2, and 2.60 percent in Year 3 and beyond. Further, you expect that real interest rates will be 3.4 percent annually for the foreseeable future.

a. Calculate the maturity risk premium on the three year Treasury security. *(LG4)*

b. Calculate the maturity risk premium on the six-year Treasury security. *(LG4)*

8-10 **Determinants of Interest Rates for Individual Securities** Nikki G's Corporation's 10-year bonds are currently yielding a return of 8.15 percent. The expected inflation premium is 2.5 percent annually and the real interest rate is expected to be 3.10 percent annually over the next 10 years. The liquidity risk premium on Nikki G's bonds is 0.25 percent. The maturity risk premium is 0.10 percent on two-year securities and increases by 0.05 percent for each additional year to maturity. Calculate the default risk premium on Nikki G's 10-year bonds. *(LG4)*

8-11 **Unbiased Expectations Theory** Suppose we observe the following rates:

$$_1R_1 = 8\%, \ _1R_2 = 10\%.$$

If the unbiased expectations theory of the term structure of interest rates holds, what is the one-year interest rate expected one year from now, $E(_2r_1)$? *(LG4)*

8-12 **Unbiased Expectations Theory** *The Wall Street Journal* reports that the rate on four-year Treasury securities is 5.60 percent and the rate on five-year Treasury securities is 6.15 percent. According to the unbiased expectations hypotheses, what does the market expect the one-year Treasury rate to be four years from today, $E(_5r_1)$? *(LG5)*

8-13 **Liquidity Premium Hypothesis** *The Wall Street Journal* reports that the rate on three-year Treasury securities is 5.25 percent and the rate on four-year Treasury securities is 5.50 percent. The one-year interest rate expected in three years is $E(_4r_1)$, is 6.10 percent. According to the liquidity premium hypotheses, what is the liquidity premium on the four-year Treasury security, L_4? *(LG5)*

8-14 **Liquidity Premium Hypothesis** Suppose we observe the following rates:

$$_1R_1 = 10\%, \ _1R_2 = 14\%, \text{ and } E(_2r_1) = 10\%.$$

If the liquidity premium theory of the term structure of interest rates holds, what is the liquidity premium for year 2, L_2? *(LG5)*

Maturity	Yield
One day	2.00%
One year	5.50
Two years	6.50
Three years	9.00

8-15 **Forecasting Interest Rates** You note the following yield curve in *The Wall Street Journal.* According to the unbiased expectations hypothesis, what is the one-year forward rate for the period beginning one year from today, $_2f_1$? *(LG6)*

8-16 **Forecasting Interest Rates** On May 23, 20XX, the existing or current (spot) one-year, two-year, three-year, and four-year zero-coupon Treasury security rates were as follows:

$$_1R_1 = 4.75\%, \quad _1R_2 = 4.95\%, \quad _1R_3 = 5.25\%, \quad _1R_4 = 5.65\%$$

Using the unbiased expectations theory, calculate the one-year forward rates on zero-coupon Treasury bonds for years 2, 3, and 4 as of May 23, 20XX. *(LG6)*

ADVANCED PROBLEMS

8-17 **Determinants of Interest Rates for Individual Securities** *The Wall Street Journal* reports that the current rate on 10-year Treasury bonds is 7.25 percent, on 20-year Treasury bonds is 7.85 percent, and on a 20-year corporate bond is 8.75 percent. Assume that the maturity risk premium is zero. If the default risk premium and liquidity risk premium on a 10-year corporate bond are the same as that on the 20-year corporate bond, calculate the current rate on a 10-year corporate bond. *(LG4)*

8-18 **Determinants of Interest Rates for Individual Securities** *The Wall Street Journal* reports that the current rate on five-year Treasury bonds is 6.85 percent and on 10-year Treasury bonds is 7.35 percent. Assume that the maturity risk premium is zero. Calculate the expected rate on a five-year Treasury bond purchased four years from today, $E(_5r_5)$. *(LG4)*

8-19 **Unbiased Expectations Theory** Suppose we observe the three-year Treasury security rate $(_1R_3)$ to be 8 percent, the expected one-year rate next year—$E(_2r_1)$—to be 4 percent, and the expected one-year rate the following year—$E(_3r_1)$—to be 6 percent. If the unbiased expectations theory of the term structure of interest rates holds, what is the one-year Treasury security rate, $_1R_1$? *(LG5)*

8-20 **Unbiased Expectations Theory** *The Wall Street Journal* reports that the rate on three-year Treasury securities is 5.60 percent and the rate on five-year Treasury securities is 6.15 percent. According to the unbiased expectations hypothesis, what does the market expect the two-year Treasury rate to be two years from today, $E(_3r_2)$? *(LG5)*

8-21 **Forecasting Interest Rates** Assume the current interest rate on a one-year Treasury bond ($_1R_1$) is 4.50 percent, the current rate on a two-year Treasury bond ($_1R_2$) is 5.25 percent, and the current rate on a three-year Treasury bond ($_1R_3$) is 6.50 percent. If the unbiased expectations theory of the term structure of interest rates is correct, what is the one-year interest rate expected on Treasury bills during year 3, $_3f_1$? *(LG6)*

8-22 **Forecasting Interest Rates** A recent edition of *The Wall Street Journal* reported interest rates of 2.25 percent, 2.60 percent, 2.98 percent, and 3.25 percent for three-year, four-year, five-year, and six-year Treasury security yields, respectively. According to the unbiased expectation theory of the term structure of interest rates, what are the expected one-year rates for years 4, 5, and 6? *(LG6)*

characterizing
risk + return

The risk-return relationship funda-
mentally affects finance theory.
You can invest your money very
safely by opening a savings account
at a bank or by buying Treasury bills. If
you can take advantage of these low-
risk opportunities, why would you invest
your money in risky stocks and bonds?
The answer: Very low risk investments
also provide a very low return. Investors take on higher risk investments in
expectation of earning higher returns.
Likewise, businesses also take on risky
capital investments only if they expect
to earn higher returns that at least cover
their costs, including investors' required
return. Both investor and business sen-
timents create a positive relationship
between risk and expected return. Of
course, taking risk means that you get

continued on p. 206

LEARNING GOALS

LG1 Compute an investment's dollar and
percentage return.

LG2 Find information about the
historical returns and volatility for
the stock, bond, and cash markets.

LG3 Measure and evaluate the total
risk of an investment using several
methods.

LG4 Recognize the risk / return
relationship and its implications.

LG5 Plan investments that take
advantage of diversification and
its impact on total risk.

LG6 Find efficient and optimal
portfolios.

LG7 Compute a portfolio's return.

continued from p. 205

no guarantee that you will recoup your investment. In the short run, higher risk investments often significantly underperform lower risk investments. Companies and investors should expect higher risk investments to earn higher returns only over the long term (many years). In addition, not all forms of risk are rewarded. In this chapter, we focus on using historical information to characterize past returns and risks. We show how you can diversify to eliminate some risk and expect the highest return possible for your desired risk level. In Chapter 10, we'll turn to estimating the risks and returns you should expect in the future. ■

viewpoints

business APPLICATION

Managers from the production and marketing departments have proposed some risky new business projects for your firm. These new ideas appear to be riskier than the firm's current business operations.

You are concerned that taking on these new projects will make the firm's stock too risky. However, you also know that diversifying the firm's product offerings could reduce the firm's overall risk. How can you determine whether these project ideas would make the firm's stock riskier or less risky?

HISTORICAL RETURNS

Let's begin our discussion of risk and return by characterizing the concept of return. First, we need a method for calculating returns. After computing a return, investors need to assess whether it was a good, average, or bad investment return. Examining returns from the past gives us a general idea of what we might expect to see in the future. We should think in terms of return for the long run because a return for any one year can be quite different from the average returns from the past couple of decades.

Computing Returns

How much have you earned on each of your investments? Two ways to determine this are to compute the actual dollar return and to compute the dollar return as a percentage of the money invested.

Dollar Return The **dollar return** earned includes any capital gain (or loss) that occurred as well as any income that you received over the period. Equation 9-1 illustrates the dollar return calculation:

$$\text{Dollar return} = (\text{Capital gain or loss}) + \text{Income} \quad (9\text{-}1)$$
$$= (\text{Ending value} - \text{Beginning value}) + \text{Income}$$

For example, say you held 200 shares of RadioShack Corp's (RSH) stock. The consumer electronic goods retailer had a market price of $16.78 per share at the end of 2006. RadioShack also paid 25¢ in dividends per share during 2006. At the end of 2007, RadioShack's stock price was $16.86. For the whole of 2007, you earned a capital gain of ($16.86 − $16.78) × 200 shares, or $16, and received a dividend payment of 200 shares × $0.25, or $50. So the total dollar return on your investment was $66 (= $16 + $50) for 2007.

In RadioShack's case, the stock price increased slightly, so you experienced a capital gain. On the other hand, the stock price of toy and game producer Mattel Inc. (MAT) started the year at $22.66 per share, paid a 75¢ dividend, and ended 2007 at $19.04. If you owned 200 shares of Mattel, you would have experienced a capital loss of $724. This loss would have been partially offset by the $150 of dividends received. However, the total dollar return would still have been −$574. Stock prices can fluctuate substantially and cause large positive or negative dollar returns.

Does your dollar return depend on whether you continue to hold the Mattel and RadioShack stock or sell it? No. In general, finance deals with *market* values. RadioShack stock was worth $16.86 at the end of 2007 regardless of whether you held the stock or sold it. If you sell it, then we refer to your gains as "realized" gains. If you continue to hold the stock, the gains are "unrealized" gains.

Percentage Return We usually find it more useful to characterize investment earnings as **percentage returns** so that we can easily compare one investment's return to other alternatives' returns. We calculate percentage return by dividing the dollar return by the investment's value at the beginning of the time period.

$$\text{Percentage return} = \frac{\text{Ending value} - \text{Beginning value} + \text{Income}}{\text{Beginning value}} \times 100\% \quad (9\text{-}2)$$

Because it's standardized, we can use percentage returns for almost any type of investment. We can use beginning and ending values for stock positions, bond prices, real estate values, and so on. Investment income may be stock dividends, bond interest payments, or other receipts. The percentage return for

personal APPLICATION

Suppose an investor owns a portfolio of 100 percent long-term Treasury bonds because the owner prefers low risk. The investor has avoided owning stocks because of their high volatility.

The investor's stockbroker claims that putting 10 percent of the portfolio in stocks would actually reduce total risk and increase the portfolio's expected return. The investor knows that stocks are riskier than bonds. How can adding the risky stocks to the bond portfolio reduce the risk level?

The 2007 return of −12.7 percent is quite poor for Mattel. Both firms belong to the S&P 500 Index, which earned 3.5 percent in 2007.

Are the 2007 returns for Mattel and RadioShack typical? We look to **average returns** to examine performance over time. The arithmetic average return provides an estimate for how the investment has performed over longer periods of time. The formula for the average return is:

$$\text{Average return} = \frac{\sum_{t=1}^{N} \text{Return}_t}{N} \qquad (9\text{-}3)$$

where the return for each subperiod is summed up and divided by the number of subperiods. You can state the returns in either percentage or decimal format. Table 9.1 shows the annual returns for Mattel and RadioShack during 1985 to 2007. First, notice that over time, the returns are quite varied for both firms. The stock return for Mattel has ranged from a low of −42.2 percent in 1999 to a high of 108.8 percent in 1991. RadioShack's stock return varied between −37.1 percent (2002) and 140.1 percent (1999). Also note that the returns appear unpredictable or random. Sometimes a large negative return is followed by another bad year, like Mattel's returns in 1986 and 1987. Other times, a poor year is followed by a very good year, like 1987 and 1988 for RadioShack. The table also reports average annual returns for Mattel and RadioShack of 16.1 percent and 12.5 percent, respectively. Over the years, these stocks have earned investors a good average rate of return.

holding the RadioShack stock during calendar year 2007 was 1.97 percent, computed as:

$$\text{RadioShack percentage return} = \frac{\begin{array}{c}\$16.86 \times 200 - \$16.78 \times 200 + \\ \$0.25 \times 200\end{array}}{\$16.78 \times 200}$$

$$= 0.0197, \text{ or } 1.97\%$$

The return for the Mattel position during the same period was −12.7 percent:

$$\text{Mattel percentage return} = \frac{\begin{array}{c}\$19.04 \times 200 - \$22.66 \times \\ 200 + \$0.75 \times 200\end{array}}{\$22.66 \times 200}$$

$$= -0.1266, \text{ or } -12.7\%$$

EXAMPLE 9-1

For interactive versions of this example visit www.mhhe.com/canM

Computing Returns

You are evaluating a stock's short-term performance. On January 29, 2007, pharmaceutical giant Bristol-Myers Squibb (BMY) saw its stock price surge on merger news regarding another firm, Schering-Plough. Bristol-Myers stock had closed the previous trading day at $26.21 and was up to $27.69 within hours of trading. BMY had ended 2006 at $26.32 and paid a 28¢ dividend in January. What is the dollar return and percentage return of 300 shares of BMY for the day and year to date?

SOLUTION:

For the day, realize that no income is paid. Therefore, the dollar return is $444 = 300 × ($27.69 − $26.21) + 0 and the percent return is 5.65% = $444 ÷ (300 × $26.21). The year to date (YTD) return does include dividend income. So the dollar YTD return is $495 = 300 × ($27.69 − $26.32) + (300 × $0.28). The Bristol-Myer YTD percentage return is

$$\text{BMY YTD return} = \frac{(\$27.69 \times 300) - (\$26.32 \times 300) + (\$0.28 \times 300)}{\$26.32 \times 300} = 0.063, \text{ or } 6.3\%$$

Note that most of the YTD return of 6.3% occurred during the 5.65% return from one day of trading.

	Mattel	RadioShack		Mattel	RadioShack
1985	20.0%	68.0%	1997	36.6%	77.5%
1986	−32.9	4.3	1998	−35.8	7.7
1987	−16.8	−21.2	1999	−42.2	140.1
1988	38.8	26.0	2000	13.9	−12.6
1989	107.5	3.2	2001	20.0	−29.3
1990	2.9	−23.7	2002	11.6	−37.1
1991	108.8	0.8	2003	2.8	65.1
1992	16.9	5.3	2004	3.6	8.0
1993	11.0	69.3	2005	−16.3	−35.3
1994	15.8	2.6	2006	47.3	−19.0
1995	55.8	−15.7	2007	−12.7	2.0
1996	14.8	7.9	**Average =**	**16.1**	**12.5**

Data Source: Yahoo! Finance.

Performance of Asset Classes

During any given year, the stock market may perform better than the bond market, or it may perform worse. Over longer time periods, how do stocks, bonds, or cash securities perform? Historically, stocks have performed better than either bonds or cash. Table 9.2 shows the average returns for these three asset classes over the period 1950 to 2007, as well as over various subperiods. Over the entire period, stocks (as measured by the S&P 500 Index) earned an average 13.2 percent return per year. This is double the 6.4 percent return earned by long-term Treasury bonds. Cash securities, measured by U.S. Treasury bills, earned an average 4.9 percent return.

The table also shows each asset class's average return for each decade since 1950. The best decade for the stock market was the 1950s, when stocks earned an average 20.9 percent per year. The 1990s ran a close second with a 19 percent per year return. The best decade for the bond market was the 1980s, when it earned an average 13.5 percent per year return due to capital gains as interest rates fell. Stocks have outperformed bonds in every decade since 1950. Notice that the average return in the stock and bond markets has not been negative during any decade since 1950. But average stock returns do not really paint a very accurate picture of annual returns. Individual annual returns from 2000 to 2007 show that returns can vary strongly and be quite negative in any particular year. Indeed, this annual variability defines risk. Note that even the bond market outperformed the stock market between 2000 and 2007.

HISTORICAL RISKS

When you purchase a U.S. Treasury bill, you know exactly what your dollar and percentage return are going to be. Many people find comfort in the certainty from this safe investment. On the other hand, when you purchase a stock, you do not know what your return is going to be—either in the short term or in the long run. This uncertainty is precisely what makes stock investing risky. It's useful to evaluate this uncertainty quantitatively so that we can compare risk among different stocks and asset classes.

Computing Volatility

Financial theory suggests that investors should look at an investment's historical returns to assess how much uncertainty to expect in the future. If you see high variability in historical returns, you should expect a high degree of future uncertainty. Table 9.2 shows that between 2000 and 2007, the stock market experienced a range of −22.2 percent return in 2002 to a 28.7 percent return in 2003. Bonds

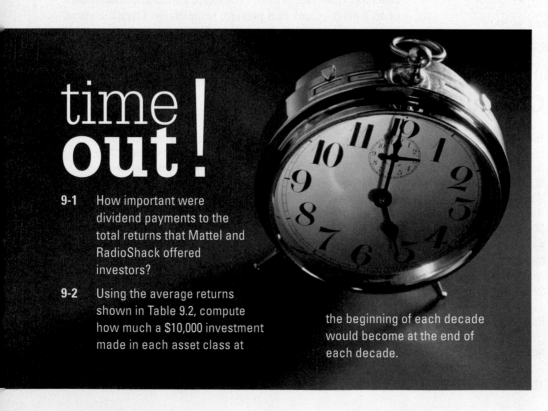

9-1 How important were dividend payments to the total returns that Mattel and RadioShack offered investors?

9-2 Using the average returns shown in Table 9.2, compute how much a $10,000 investment made in each asset class at the beginning of each decade would become at the end of each decade.

standard deviation as the square root of the variance, and this figure represents the security's or portfolio's **total risk.** We'll discuss other risk measurements in the next chapter.

Our process of computing standard deviation starts with the average return over the period. The average annual return for the stock market since 1950 is 13.2 percent. How much can the return in any given year deviate from this average? We compute the actual annual deviation by subtracting the return each year from this average return: $Return_{(1950)}$ − Average return; $Return_{(1951)}$ − Average return; $Return_{(1952)}$ − Average return, and so on. Note that many of these deviations will be negative (from a lower-than-average return that year) and others will be positive (from a higher-than-average return). If we computed the *average* of these return deviations, our result would be zero. Large positive deviations cancel out large negative deviations and hide the variability. To really see the size of the variations without the distractions that come with including a positive or negative sign, we square each deviation before adding them up. Dividing by the number of returns in the sample minus one provides the return *variance.*[1] The square root of the return variance is the standard deviation:

Mattel's stock returns have ranged from -42.2 percent to 108.8 percent.

experienced a smaller variability—1.9 percent return in 2006 to 20.1 percent return in 2000. Examining the range of historical returns provides just one way to express the return volatility that we can expect. In practical terms, the finance industry uses a statistical return volatility measure known as the **standard deviation** of percentage returns. We calculate

$$\text{Standard deviation} = \sqrt{\frac{\sum_{t=1}^{N} (\text{Return}_t - \text{Average return})^2}{N - 1}} \qquad (9\text{-}4)$$

A large standard deviation indicates greater return volatility— or high risk. Table 9.3 shows the standard deviations of Mattel stock returns over 23 years. The Deviation column shows the annual return minus Mattel's average return of 16.1 percent. The last column squares each deviation. Then we sum up these squared deviations and divide the result by the number of observations less one (22), to compute the return variance. If we want to use a measure that makes sense in the real world (how would you interpret a squared percentage, anyway?), we take the square root of the variance to get the standard deviation. Mattel's standard deviation of returns during this sample period comes to 38.4 percent. In comparison, the standard deviation of RadioShack stock returns for this same

▼ **TABLE 9.2** Annual and Average Returns for Stocks, Bonds, and T-Bills, 1950 to 2007

		Stocks (S&P 500)	Long-Term Treasury Bonds	T-Bills
1950 to 2007	Average	13.2%	6.4%	4.9%
1950 to 1959	Average	20.9	0.0	2.0
1960 to 1969	Average	8.7	1.6	4.0
1970 to 1979	Average	7.5	5.7	6.3
1980 to 1989	Average	18.2	13.5	8.9
1990 to 1999	Average	19.0	9.5	4.9
2000	Annual return	−9.1	20.1	5.9
2001	Annual return	−11.9	4.6	3.5
2002	Annual return	−22.1	17.2	1.6
2003	Annual return	28.7	2.1	1.0
2004	Annual return	10.9	7.7	1.4
2005	Annual return	4.9	6.5	3.1
2006	Annual return	15.8	1.9	4.7
2007	Annual return	3.5	9.8	3.4
2000 to 2007	Average	2.6	8.7	3.1

[1]We use the denominator of $N - 1$ to compute a sample's standard deviation, which is the most common for finance applications. We would divide the standard deviation of a population simply by N.

Because RadioShack's standard deviation is higher than Mattel's, its stock features more total risk.

period is 43.6 percent. Since RadioShack's standard deviation is higher, its stock features more total risk than Mattel's stock does.

Although analysts and investors use a stock return's standard deviation as an important and common measure of risk, it's laborious to compute by hand. Most people use a spreadsheet or statistical software to calculate stock return standard deviations.

Risk of Asset Classes

We report the standard deviations of return for stocks, bonds, and T-bills in Table 9.4 for 1950 to 2007 and for each decade since 1950. Over the entire sample, the stock market returns' standard deviation is 17.0 percent. As we would expect, stock market volatility is higher than bond market volatility (10.3 percent) or for T-bills (2.8 percent). These volatility estimates are consistent with our previously stated position that the stock market carries more risk than the bond and cash markets do. Every decade since 1950 has seen a lot of stock market volatility. The bond market experienced the most volatility in the 1980s and 1990s as interest rates varied.

You will recall from Chapter 6 that since any bond's par value and coupon rate are fixed, bond prices must fluctuate to adjust for changes in interest rates. Bond prices respond inversely to interest rate changes: As interest rates rise, bond prices fall, and if interest rates fall, bond prices rise. T-bills returns have experienced very low volatility over each decade. Indeed, T-bills are commonly considered to be one of the only risk-free assets. Higher-risk investments offer higher returns over time. But short-term fluctuations in the value of higher risk investments can be substantial. The stock market is risky—while it has offered a good annual return of 13.2 percent, that

▼ **TABLE 9.3** Computation of Mattel Stock Return Standard Deviation

	Mattel Return	Deviation	Squared Deviation
1985	20.0%	3.9%	0.1%
1986	−32.9	−49.0	24.1
1987	−16.8	−32.9	10.9
1988	38.8	22.7	5.1
1989	107.5	91.4	83.4
1990	2.9	−13.2	1.8
1991	108.8	92.7	85.8
1992	16.9	0.8	0.0
1993	11.0	−5.1	0.3
1994	15.8	−0.3	0.0
1995	55.8	39.7	15.7
1996	14.8	−1.3	0.0
1997	36.6	20.5	4.2
1998	−35.8	−51.9	27.0
1999	−42.2	−58.3	34.0
2000	13.9	−2.2	0.1
2001	20.0	3.9	0.1
2002	11.6	−4.5	0.2
2003	2.8	−13.3	1.8
2004	3.6	−12.5	1.6
2005	−16.3	−32.4	10.5
2006	47.3	31.2	9.7
2007	−12.7	−28.8	8.3
Average =	16.1		
		Sum =	324.9
		Variance =	14.8
		Std Dev =	38.4

Data Source: Yahoo! Finance.

return comes with volatility of 17.0 percent standard deviation. Many investors may intellectually understand that this high risk means that they may receive very poor returns in the short term. Investors really felt the full force of this risk when the stock market declined three years in a row (2000 to 2002). Some investors even decided that this was too much risk for them and they sold out of the stock market before the 2003 rally.

The stock market return standard deviations that appear in Table 9.4 are all considerably lower than the standard deviations of Mattel and of RadioShack stocks (38.4 percent and 43.6 percent, respectively). In this case, we measure stock market return and standard deviation using the S&P 500 Index. Mattel and RadioShack are both included in the S&P 500 Index. Why

▼ **TABLE 9.4** Annual Standard Deviation of Returns for Stocks, Bonds, and T-Bills, 1950 to 2007

	Stocks	Long-Term Treasury Bonds	T-Bills
1950 to 2007	17.0%	10.3%	2.8%
1950 to 1959	19.8	4.9	0.8
1960 to 1969	14.4	6.2	1.3
1970 to 1979	19.2	6.8	1.8
1980 to 1989	12.7	15.1	2.6
1990 to 1999	14.2	12.8	1.2
2000 to 2007	16.4	6.7	1.7

do these two large firms have measures of total risk—standard deviations—that are at least twice as large as the standard deviations on the stock market returns? Are Mattel and RadioShack just two of the most risky firms in the Index? Actually, no.

The differences in standard deviations between these individual companies and the entire market have much more to do with *diversification*. Owning 500 companies, such as all of those included in the S&P 500 Index, generates much less risk than owning just one company. This phenomenon appears in the standard deviation measure. We'll discuss the effects of diversification in detail later in this chapter.

Risk versus Return

Investors can buy very safe T-bills. Or they can take some risk to seek higher returns. How much extra return can you expect for taking more risk? This is known as the *trade-off between risk and return*. The **coefficient of variation** (CoV) is a common *relative* measure of this risk vs. reward relationship. The equation for the coefficient of variation is simply

EXAMPLE 9-2

For interactive versions of this example visit www.mhhe.com/canM

Risk and Return

Find the average return and risk (as measured by standard deviation) for Mattel since 2000. Table 9.3 shows the annual returns for years 2000 to 2007.

SOLUTION:

First, compute the average annual return for the period. Using equation 9-3:

$$\frac{13.9\% + 20.0\% + 11.6\% + 2.8\% - 3.6\% - 16.3\% + 47.3\% - 12.7\%}{8} = \frac{70.2\%}{8} = 8.8\%$$

Mattel has averaged an 8.8 percent return per year since 2000. To compute the risk, use the standard deviation equation 9-4. First, find the deviations of return for each year:

Year 2000	2001	2002	2003	2004	2005	2006	2007
13.9% − 8.8%	20.0% − 8.8%	11.6% − 8.8%	2.8% − 8.8%	3.6% − 8.8%	− 16.3% − 8.8%	47.3% − 8.8%	− 12.7% − 8.8%

Square those deviations:

YEAR 2000	2001	2002	2003	2004	2005	2006	2007
$(13.9\% − 8.8\%)^2$	$(20.0\% − 8.8\%)^2$	$(11.6\% − 8.8\%)^2$	$(2.8\% − 8.8\%)^2$	$(3.6\% − 8.8\%)^2$	$(−16.3\% − 8.8\%)^2$	$(47.3\% − 8.8\%)^2$	$(−12.7\% − 8.8\%)^2$

Then add them up, divide by $N − 1$, and take the square root:

$$\sqrt{\frac{\begin{array}{c}(13.9\% − 8.8\%)^2 + (20.0\% − 8.8\%)^2 + (11.6\% − 8.8\%)^2 + (2.8\% − 8.8\%)^2 + (3.6\% − 8.8\%)^2 \\ + (−16.3\% − 8.8\%)^2 + (47.3\% − 8.8\%)^2 + (−12.7\% − 8.8\%)^2\end{array}}{8 − 1}}$$

$$= \sqrt{\frac{26.01 + 125.44 + 7.84 + 36.00 + 27.04 + 630.01 + 1482.25 + 462.25}{7}} = \sqrt{399.549} = 19.99\%$$

Mattel stock has averaged an 8.8 percent return with a standard deviation of 19.99 percent since 2000.

the standard deviation divided by average return. It is interpreted as the amount of risk (measured by volatility) per unit of return:

$$\text{Coefficient of variation} = \frac{\text{Standard deviation}}{\text{Average return}} \quad (9\text{-}5)$$

As an investor, you would want to receive a very high return (the denominator in the equation) with a very low risk (the numerator). So, a smaller CoV indicates a better risk-reward relationship. Since the average return and standard deviation for Mattel stock are 16.1 percent and 38.4 percent, its CoV is 2.39 (= 38.4 ÷ 16.1). This is better than RadioShack's CoV of 3.49 (= 43.6 ÷ 12.5). For all asset classes since 1950, the stock market earned a higher return than bonds and was also riskier. But which one had a better risk-return relationship? The CoV for common stock is 1.29 (= 17.0 ÷ 13.2). For Treasury bonds, the coefficient of a variation is 1.61 (= 10.3 ÷ 6.4). Even though stocks are riskier than bonds, they involve a somewhat better risk-reward trade-off.

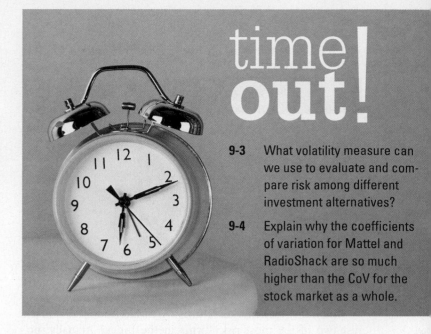

time out!

9-3 What volatility measure can we use to evaluate and compare risk among different investment alternatives?

9-4 Explain why the coefficients of variation for Mattel and RadioShack are so much higher than the CoV for the stock market as a whole.

FORMING PORTFOLIOS

As we noted previously, Mattel and RadioShack stocks' risk as measured by their standard deviations appear quite high compared to the standard deviation of the S&P 500 Index. This is by no means a coincidence. Combining stocks into **portfolios** can reduce many sources of stock risk. **Diversification** reduces risk. The S&P 500 Index, for example, tracks 500 companies, which allows for a great deal of diversification.

EXAMPLE 9-3

For interactive versions of this example visit www.mhhe.com/canM

Risk versus Return

You are interested in the risk-return relationship of stocks in each decade since 1950. Obtain the average returns and risks in Tables 9.2 and 9.4.

SOLUTION:

Using the coefficient of variation, the average returns, and standard deviation of return, compute the following risk-return relationships:

$$CoV_{1950s} = \frac{19.8\%}{20.9\%} = 0.95 \qquad CoV_{1960s} = \frac{14.4\%}{8.7\%} = 1.66$$

$$CoV_{1970s} = \frac{19.2\%}{7.5\%} = 2.56 \qquad CoV_{1980s} = \frac{12.7\%}{18.2\%} = 0.70$$

$$CoV_{1990s} = \frac{14.2\%}{19.0\%} = 0.75 \qquad CoV_{2000s} = \frac{16.4\%}{2.6\%} = 6.31$$

Note that over short time periods, the stock risk-return relationship varies significantly.

Diversification reduces risk.

Diversifying to Reduce Risk

Think about a stock's total risk as having two components. The first component includes risks that are both specific to that company and common to other companies in the same industry. We call this risk **firm-specific risk.** The stock's other risk component is general risk that all firms—and all individuals, for that matter—face based upon economic strength both domestically and globally. We call this type of risk **market risk.** These risks appear in the equation:

$$\text{Total risk} = \text{Firm-specific risk} + \text{Market risk} \qquad (9\text{-}6)$$

change to some degree. Macroeconomic events represent market risks because such events—unemployment claims, interest rate changes, national budget deficits or surpluses—affect all companies.

Suppose that you own only RadioShack stock and have earned the annual returns shown in Table 9.5. Then someone suggests that you add Mattel to your RadioShack stock to form a two-stock portfolio. Both Mattel and RadioShack stocks carry a lot of total risk. But look at the risk and return characteristics of a portfolio consisting of 50 percent RadioShack stock and 50 percent Mattel stock. You start with RadioShack stock, which provided an average return of 12.5 percent with a risk of 43.6 percent. The two-stock portfolio earns an average 14.3 percent return with a standard deviation of only 26.2 percent. You added a high-risk stock to a high-risk stock and you ended up with a portfolio with much lower risk! This is a hallmark of most portfolios, which pool market risk but often provide offsetting, reduced firm-specific risks overall.

Next, add IBM stock to your Mattel and RadioShack stock portfolio. Figure 9.1 shows that the total risk of this three-stock portfolio declines to 20.8 percent. Note that adding Newmont Mining, Disney, and General Electric also reduces

> ## MACROECONOMIC EVENTS REPRESENT MARKET RISKS BECAUSE SUCH EVENTS—UNEMPLOYMENT CLAIMS, INTEREST RATE CHANGES, NATIONAL BUDGET DEFICITS OR SURPLUSES—AFFECT ALL COMPANIES.

Standard deviations measure total risk. Individual stocks are subject to many firm-specific risks. We can reduce firm-specific risk by combining stocks into a portfolio. Since we can reduce firm-specific risk by diversifying, this risk is sometimes referred to as **diversifiable risk.** If RadioShack announces lower-than-expected profits, its stock price will decline. However, since this news is *specific* to RadioShack, the news should not affect Mattel stock's price. On the other hand, if the government announces a change in unemployment, both stocks' prices will

the total risk of the stock portfolio. As you add more stocks, the firm-specific risk portion of the total portfolio risk declines. The total risk falls rapidly as we add the first few stocks. Diversification's power to reduce firm-specific risk weakens for the later stocks added to the portfolio, because we have already eliminated much of the firm-specific risk. We could continue to add stocks until the portfolio comprises all S&P 500 Index firms, in which case the standard deviation of the portfolio would be 17.0 percent. At this point, virtually

	RadioShack	Mattel	Portfolio of RadioShack and Mattel
1985	68.0%	20.0%	44.0%
1986	4.3	−32.9	−14.3
1987	−212.0	−16.8	−19.0
1988	26.0	38.8	32.4
1989	−3.2	107.5	52.2
1990	−23.0	2.9	−10.4
1991	0.8	108.8	54.8
1992	5.3	16.9	11.1
1993	69.3	11.0	40.2
1994	2.6	15.8	9.2
1995	−15.7	55.8	20.1
1996	7.9	14.8	11.4
1997	77.5	36.6	57.1
1998	7.7	−35.8	−14.1
1999	140.1	−42.2	49.0
2000	−12.6	13.9	0.7
2001	−29.3	20.0	−4.7
2002	−37.1	11.6	−12.8
2003	65.1	2.8	34.0
2004	8.0	3.6	5.8
2005	−35.3	−16.3	−25.8
2006	−19.0	47.3	14.2
2007	2.0	−12.7	−5.3
Average =	12.5	16.1	14.3
Std Dev =	43.6	38.4	26.2

Data Source: Yahoo! Finance

all of the firm-specific risk has been purged and the portfolio carries only market risk, which is sometimes called **nondiversifiable risk.**

Modern Portfolio Theory

The concept that diversification reduces risk was formalized in the early 1950s by Harry Markowitz, who eventually won the Nobel Prize in Economics for his work. Markowitz's **modern portfolio theory** shows how risk reduction occurs when securities are combined. The theory also describes how to combine stocks to achieve the lowest total risk possible for a given expected return. Or, said differently, it describes how to achieve the highest expected return for the desired risk level. The combination of securities that achieves the highest expected return for a given risk level is called the investor's **optimal portfolio.**

In our Mattel and RadioShack portfolio example above, we allocated 50 percent of the portfolio to Mattel and 50 percent to RadioShack. Is this the best allocation for the portfolio? Consider the different allocations shown in Figure 9.2 for the two stocks. The graph shows the expected return (computed as average return) and risk (computed as standard deviation) of various portfolios. It would be terrific if you could find a portfolio located in the upper left-hand corner. That is, investors would like a high expected return with low risk. One large dot shows the risk-return point for owning only Mattel. The other large dot shows owning only RadioShack. The smaller diamonds show 10/90, 25/75,

▼**FIGURE 9.1** Adding Stocks to a Portfolio Reduces Risk

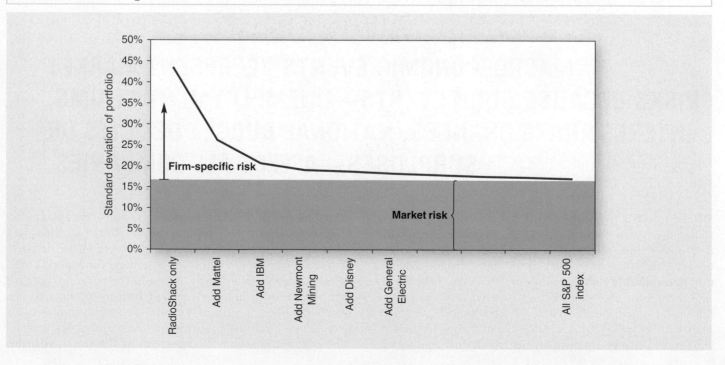

Adding IBM to the portfolio reduces total risk.

40/60, 50/50, 60/40, 75/25, and 90/10 allocations of Mattel/RadioShack stocks.

While all these portfolios are possible, not all are desirable. For example, the portfolio of 25 percent Mattel and 75

percent RadioShack is not desirable. Other portfolios provide *both* higher return and lower risk. The dominating portfolios appear higher and to the left in the figure. One such portfolio consists of 75 percent Mattel stock and 25 percent RadioShack stock. The 50/50 portfolio (circled in the figure) is also better than the 25/75 portfolio. However, the 50/50 portfolio isn't desirable because a portfolio with slightly higher return and slightly lower risk appears above and to the left of the 50/50 portfolio: the 60/40 portfolio. Portfolios with the highest return possible for each risk level are called **efficient portfolios.** Notice that if you drew a line connecting the dots, the figure would appear like the end of a bullet. The portfolios on the top of the bullet dominate the portfolios on the bottom; the top portfolio dots show the efficient portfolios for these two stocks.

Figure 9.3 shows efficient portfolios for combining the four stocks: RadioShack, Mattel, IBM, and Newmont Mining. These portfolios appear as diamonds in the figure with each diamond representing a different allocation of the four stocks. The single square represents the portfolio that consists of 25 percent in each of the four stocks. We used this portfolio to demonstrate how diversification reduces risk in Figure 9.1. Notice that other, efficient portfolios dominate this portfolio.

If we showed all efficient portfolios, they would appear as a line that connects the upper side of the bullet shape. If we added all available securities to the graph, then all of the efficient portfolios of those securities form the efficient frontier. Efficient frontier portfolios dominate all other possible stock portfolios. The shape of the efficient frontier implies that diminishing returns apply to risk taking in the investment world. To gain ever-higher expected rates of return, investors must be willing to take on ever-increasing amounts of risk. The optimal portfolio for you is one on the efficient frontier that reflects the amount of risk that you're willing to take. Clearly, optimal portfolio choice depends on individual risk

▼**FIGURE 9.2** Risk and Return Ramifications of Portfolio Allocations to Mattel and RadioShack

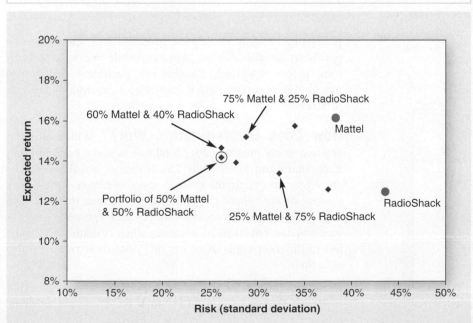

finance at work //: personal

Investor Diversification Problems

Experts have examined investor behavior using detailed data-sets of stock brokerage accounts, employee pension plans, and the Survey of Consumer Finances. Studies have identified many investor behaviors that are inconsistent with the principle of full diversification:

- Many households own relatively few individual stocks—they held a median number of two stocks until 2001, when it rose to three. Of course, many households own equity indirectly, through mutual funds or retirement accounts, and these indirect holdings tend to be much better diversified.

- Ten to fifteen percent of households with between $100,000 and $1 million in financial asset wealth own no stocks (neither directly nor indirectly through funds).

- Investors seem to prefer securities of local firms. Many geographic regions feature companies that are heavily concentrated in few industries. Thus, a local preference could reduce diversification opportunities.

- Many employees hold mostly their employers' stocks (more than 50 percent of employee holdings), particularly within their 401(k) retirement savings accounts. Holding a lot of a single stock creates a "portfolio" with high total risk.

Finance professionals and the investment industry have established diversification concepts for many decades and can help investors maximize their returns with appropriate risk levels. But

Ten to fifteen percent of households with between $100,000 and $1 million in financial asset wealth own no stocks.

many investors do not consult professionals; they fail to diversify and thus take unnecessary diversifiable risk.

Want to know more?

Key Words to Search for Updates: **diversification, pension plan choices, asset allocation**

Sources: John Y. Campbell, "Household Finance," *Journal of Finance* 61 (2006): 1553–1604; Valery Polkovichenko, "Household Portfolio Diversification: A Case for Rank-Dependent Preferences," *Review of Financial Studies* 18 (2005): 1467–1500; and Shlomo Benartzi, Richard Thaler, Stephen Utkus, and Cass Sunstein, "The Law and Economics of Company Stock in 401(k) Plans," *Journal of Law and Economics* 50 (2007):45–79.

FIGURE 9.3
Efficient Portfolios from Four Stocks

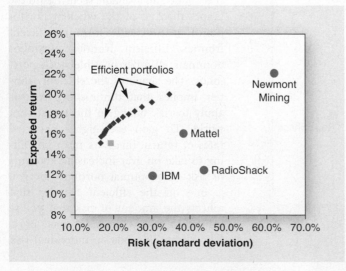

preferences. Highly risk-averse investors will select low-risk portfolios on the efficient frontier, while more adventuresome investors will select higher-risk portfolios. Any choice may be appropriate, given differences in individual risk preferences.

How Does Diversification Work? Will combining any two stocks greatly reduce total risk as much as combining RadioShack and Mattel did? The answer is no. If two stocks are subject to exactly the same kinds of events such that their returns always behave the same way over time, then we have no need to own both stocks—simply pick the one that performs better. Diversification comes when two stocks are subject to different kinds of events such that their returns differ over time.

Consider the illustration in Figure 9.4. You own Stock A in Panel A of the figure. The stock features risk, as demonstrated by its price volatility over time. You would like to reduce the risk by combining your position in Stock A with an equal position in Stock B. In this case, the alternative stock, Stock B, moves the same way over time as Stock A does. When Stock A goes up, so does Stock B. They also decline together. A portfolio of both stocks is illustrated. Notice how the portfolio has the same volatility of Stocks A and B separately. Combining these two stocks didn't reduce volatility, or total risk.

Now consider Stock C, shown in Panel B. Stock C has the same volatility as

> ## INVESTORS SEEKING DIVERSIFICATION LOOK FOR STOCKS WHERE THE RETURNS HAVE LOW OR NEGATIVE CORRELATIONS WITH EACH OTHER.

▼FIGURE 9.4
Efficient Portfolios from Four Stocks

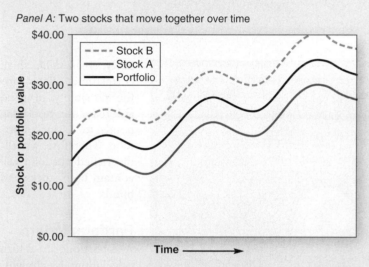

Panel A: Two stocks that move together over time

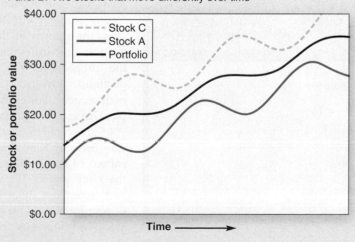

Panel B: Two stocks that move differently over time

Stock A, but its price moves in different directions than does the price of Stock A. When Stock A's price increases, Stock C's price increases sometimes and decreases sometimes. As shown, a portfolio of Stock A and Stock C features much lower volatility than either Stock A or Stock C alone. Combining Stocks A and C reduces risk because their price movements often counteract one another. In short, combining stocks with similar characteristics does not provide much diversification and thus risk reduction. Combining stocks with many differences does provide diversification and thus lowers risk.

The ways that stocks co-move over time determines how much diversification and thus risk reduction we can achieve by combining them. So what we need is some measure of co-movement to help investors form diversified portfolios. That measure, called **correlation,** is denoted with Greek symbol ρ (rho). Correlation is a statistical measure with some very useful characteristics that make it easy to interpret. Its value is bounded between −1 and +1. A correlation value of +1 means that returns from two different securities move perfectly in sync. They change lock-step up and down together. A value of −1 means that returns from two securities are perfectly inversely correlated—they move exactly opposite. A value of 0 means that the movements of the two returns over time are unrelated to one another. Investors seeking diversification look for stocks where the returns have low or negative correlations with each other.

What return correlations are common between stocks? Panel A of Table 9.6 shows the correlations between many companies. One high correlation shown is the 0.598 correlation between Citigroup and the Bank of New York. This shouldn't be surprising, because these are two similar firms in the same industry. Combining

Panel A: Company Annual Returns, 1985 to 2007							
	RadioShack	Mattel	IBM	Newmont Mining	Disney	General Electric	Citigroup
RadioShack	1						
Mattel	−0.188	1					
IBM	0.253	−0.197	1				
Newmont Mining	−0.053	−0.152	−0.241	1			
Disney	0.256	0.317	−0.128	0.206	1		
General Electric	0.625	0.203	0.339	−0.079	0.508	1	
Citigroup	0.493	0.368	0.056	−0.220	0.298	0.725	1
Bank of New York	0.265	0.466	0.043	−0.372	0.405	0.583	0.598

Panel B: Asset Class Annual Returns, 1950 to 2007			
	Stocks	Long-Term Treasury Bonds	T-Bills
Stocks	1		
Long-term Treasury bonds	0.106	1	
T-bills	−0.109	0.203	1

these two stocks wouldn't reduce risk very much in a portfolio. The largest negative correlation is the correlation of −0.372 between Newmont Mining and the Bank of New York. These firms practice in very different industries and provide large risk reduction possibilities. Note that the correlation between RadioShack and Mattel is − 0.188. This negative correlation gives us an answer to the question of why total risk (in the form of standard deviations) fell so much when we combined the two stocks relative to their individual standard deviations as shown in Figure 9.2. Most of the correlations in Table 9.6 are positive. Because most stocks are positively correlated, we typically add many stocks together to fully eliminate all the firm-specific risk in the portfolio, as we showed in Figure 9.1.

Panel B of Table 9.6 shows correlations between stocks, bonds, and T-bills. At 0.11, the correlation between stocks and bonds is

JustRon and six others like this.

JustRon Cool vids. The "Choose your own adventure" decision points are fun.
2 hours ago · Like

write a comment...

fairly small. The small correlation allows for the possibility of good risk reduction by adding bonds to a stock portfolio. Therefore, a well-diversified portfolio will contain both stocks and bonds.

Portfolio Return

A portfolio's return calculation is straightforward. A portfolio's return comes directly from the returns of the portfolio securities and the proportion of the portfolio invested in each security. For example, Disney stock earned −4.8 percent in 2007. The Bank of New York earned 19.4 percent over the same period. If you had invested a quarter of your money in Disney stock and three quarters

finance at work //: markets

International Opportunities for Diversification

The U.S. stock market represents nearly 47 percent of all stock value worldwide. Japanese and U.K. stock markets represent 11 percent and 8 percent of the worldwide stock market value, respectively. Many investment and diversification opportunities present themselves internationally! However, most people allocate very little or none of their portfolios to international securities. If worldwide opportunities can create greater diversification, then those who don't invest in international stocks miss out on an important opportunity to reduce risk in their portfolios.

MSCI, Inc., is the leading provider of global stock market indexes. Some MSCI Barra indexes follow individual countries. In addition, MSCI, Inc., compiles composite indexes for groups of companies in developed markets, emerging markets, frontier markets, and by geographic regions. Investment managers use the MSCI World Index, the MSCI EAFE (Europe, Australasia, Far East) Index, and the MSCI Emerging Markets Index as premier benchmarks to measure global stock market performance.

The table below shows the average annual returns and standard deviations for the U.S. stock market, Treasury bonds, and the MSCI EAFE and MSCI Emerging Markets indexes for the period 1988 to 2007. Note that both the EAFE and the Emerging Markets indexes feature higher risk than the S&P 500 Index. The Emerging Markets return has been high, but the EAFE return has been low compared to the U.S. stock and bond markets.

	S&P 500	Bonds	EAFE	Emerging Markets
Average	12.9%	9.6%	7.1%	17.8%
Std. Deviation	16.7	9.9	17.9	32.1

The correlations among these markets appear below:

Correlation	S&P 500	Bonds	EAFE
S&P 500	1		
Bonds	0.17	1	
EAFE	0.61	−0.14	1
Emerging Markets	0.33	−0.14	0.66

The correlation between the S&P 500 Index and the MSCI EAFE is 0.61 and between the Emerging Markets is 0.33. These correlations indicate that diversification might work. Even better diversification appears to be possible between the U.S. Treasury Bond Market and the EAFE and Emerging Markets indexes—look at the negative correlations!

Want to know more?

Key Words to Search for Updates: **international diversification, global asset allocation**

Source: www.msci.com

---

of it in Bank of New York stock, then your portfolio return would be:

Return contribution from Disney
+ Contribution from BNY

$= (0.25 \times -4.8\%) + (0.75 \times 19.4\%)$
$= 13.35\%$

To calculate the return on a three-stock portfolio, you will need the proportion of each stock in the portfolio and each stock's return. We typically call these proportions *weights*, signified by *w*. So, a portfolio with *n* securities will have a return of

$R_p = $ (Proportion of portfolio in first stock $\times$
That stock's return) + (Second stock portion (9-7)
$\times$ Second stock return) + $\cdots$

$= (w_1 \times R_1) + (w_2 \times R_2) + (w_3 \times R_3)$

$+ \cdots + (w_n \times R_n) = \sum_{i=1}^{n} w_i R_i$

the Math Coach on...

" When computing portfolio returns, use the decimal format for the portfolio weights and the percentage format for the security returns. The result of equation 9-7 will then be in percentage format. "

Computing Portfolio Returns

At the beginning of 2007, you owned $5,000 of Disney stock, $10,000 of Bank of New York stock, and $15,000 of IBM stock. In 2007, Disney, Bank of New York, and IBM returned −4.8 percent, 19.4 percent, and 12.8 percent, respectively. What is your portfolio's return?

SOLUTION:

First determine your portfolio weights. The three stocks make up a $30,000 portfolio. Disney makes up a 16.67 percent (= $5,000 ÷ $30,000) portion of the portfolio. Bank of New York stock makes up a 33.33 percent (=$10,000 ÷ $30,000) portion and IBM a 50.0 percent (=$15,000 ÷ $30,000) portion. The portfolio return can now be computed as:

$$R_P = (0.1667 \times -4.8\%) + (0.3333 \times 19.4\%) + (0.50 \times 12.8\%) = -0.80\% + 6.47\% + 6.40\% = 12.07\%$$

where the sum of the weights, w, must equal one. The portfolio's rate of return is a simple weighted sum of the returns of each stock in the portfolio. Investors choose portfolio weights by determining how much of each stock they want in their portfolios. Ideally, investors will choose weights for their portfolios located on the efficient frontier (shown in Figure 9.3). ■

time out!

9-5 Describe characteristics of companies that would be good to combine into a portfolio.

9-6 Explain why one portfolio made up of the same companies (but not in the same proportions) as another portfolio can be undesirable in comparison.

9-7 Combining which two companies in Table 9.6 would reduce risk the most? Combining which two would create the least diversification?

Your Turn...

Questions

1. Why is the percentage return a more useful measure than the dollar return? *(LG1)*

2. Characterize the historical return, risk, and risk-return relationship of the stock, bond, and cash markets. *(LG2)*

3. How do we define risk in this chapter and how do we measure it? *(LG3)*

4. What are the two components of total risk? Which component is part of the risk-return relationship? Why? *(LG3)*

5. What's the source of firm-specific risk? What's the source of market risk? *(LG3)*

6. Which company is likely to have lower total risk, General Electric or Coca-Cola? Why? *(LG3)*

7. Can a company change its total risk level over time? How? *(LG3)*

8. What does the coefficient of variation measure? Why is a lower value better for the investor? *(LG4)*

9. You receive an investment newsletter advertisement in the mail. The letter claims that you should invest in a stock that has doubled the return of the S&P 500 Index over the last three months. It also claims that this stock is a surefire safe bet for the future. Explain how these two claims are inconsistent with finance theory. *(LG4)*

10. What does diversification do to the risk and return characteristics of a portfolio? *(LG5)*

11. Describe the diversification potential of two assets with a −0.8 correlation. What's the potential if the correlation is +0.8? *(LG5)*

12. You are a risk-averse investor with a low-risk portfolio of bonds. How is it possible that adding some stocks (which are riskier than bonds) to the portfolio can lower the total risk of the portfolio? *(LG5)*

13. You own only two stocks in your portfolio but want to add more. When you add a third stock, the total risk of your portfolio declines. When you add a tenth stock to the portfolio, the total risk declines. Adding which stock, the third or the tenth, likely reduced the total risk more? Why? *(LG5)*

14. Many employees believe that their employer's stock is less likely to lose half of its value than a well diversified portfolio of stocks. Explain why this belief is erroneous. *(LG5)*

15. Explain what we mean when we say that one portfolio dominates another portfolio. *(LG6)*

16. Explain what the efficient frontier is and why it is important to investors. *(LG6)*

17. If an investor's desired risk level changes over time, should the investor change the composition of his or her portfolio? How? *(LG6)*

18. Say you own 200 shares of Mattel and 100 shares of RadioShack. Would your portfolio return be different if you instead owned 100 shares of Mattel and 200 shares of RadioShack? Why? *(LG7)*

Problems

9-1 **Investment Return** FedEx Corp. stock ended the previous year at $103.39 per share. It paid a $0.35 per share dividend last year. It ended last year at $106.69. If you owned 300 shares of FedEx, what was your dollar return and percent return? *(LG1)*

9-2 **Investment Return** Sprint Nextel Corp. stock ended the previous year at $23.36 per share. It paid a $2.37 per share dividend last year. It ended last year at $18.89. If you owned 500 shares of Sprint, what was your dollar return and percent return? *(LG1)*

9-3 **Total Risk** Rank the following three stocks by their level of total risk, highest to lowest. Rail Haul has an average return of 12 percent and standard deviation of 25 percent. The average return and standard deviation of Idol Staff are 15 percent and 35 percent; and of Poker-R-Us are 9 percent and 20 percent. *(LG3)*

9-4 **Total Risk** Rank the following three stocks by their total risk level, highest to lowest. Night Ryder has an average return of 13 percent and standard deviation of 29 percent. The average return and standard deviation of WholeMart are 11 percent and 25 percent; and of Fruit Fly are 16 percent and 40 percent. *(LG3)*

9-5 **Risk versus Return** Rank the following three stocks by their risk-return relationship, best to worst. Rail Haul has an average return of 12 percent and standard deviation of 25 percent. The average return and standard deviation of Idol Staff are 15 percent and 35 percent; and of Poker-R-Us are 9 percent and 20 percent. *(LG4)*

9-6 **Risk versus Return** Rank the following three stocks by their risk-return relationship, best to worst. Night Ryder has an average return of 13 percent and standard deviation of 29 percent. The average return and standard deviation of WholeMart are 11 percent and 25 percent; and of Fruit Fly are 16 percent and 40 percent. *(LG4)*

9-7 **Dominant Portfolios** Determine which one of these three portfolios dominates another. Name the dominated portfolio and the portfolio that dominates it. Portfolio Blue has an expected return of 12 percent and risk of 18 percent. The expected return and risk of portfolio Yellow are 13 percent and 17 percent, and for the Purple portfolio are 14 percent and 20 percent. *(LG6)*

9-8 **Dominant Portfolios** Determine which one of the three portfolios dominates another. Name the dominated portfolio and the portfolio that dominates it. Portfolio Green has an expected return of 15 percent and risk of 21 percent. The expected return and risk of portfolio Red are 13 percent and 17 percent, and for the Orange portfolio are 13 percent and 16 percent. *(LG6)*

9-9 **Portfolio Weights** An investor owns $4,000 of Adobe Systems stock, $5,000 of Dow Chemical, and $6,000 of Office Depot. What are the portfolio weights of each stock? *(LG7)*

9-10 **Portfolio Weights** An investor owns $3,000 of Adobe Systems stock, $6,000 of Dow Chemical, and $7,000 of Office Depot. What are the portfolio weights of each stock? *(LG7)*

9-11 Portfolio Return Year-to-date, Oracle has earned a -1.34 percent return. During the same time period, Valero Energy earned 7.96 percent and McDonald's earned 0.88 percent. If you have a portfolio made up of 30 percent Oracle, 20 percent Valero Energy, and 50 percent McDonald's, what is your portfolio return? *(LG7)*

9-12 Portfolio Return Year-to-date, Yum Brands has earned a 3.80 percent return. During the same time period, Raytheon earned 4.26 percent and Coca-Cola earned -0.46 percent. If you have a portfolio made up of 30 percent Yum Brands, 30 percent Raytheon, and 40 percent Coca-Cola, what is your portfolio return? *(LG7)*

INTERMEDIATE PROBLEMS

9-13 Average Return The past five monthly returns for Kohl's are 3.54 percent, 3.62 percent, -1.68 percent, -1.42 percent, and 8.75 percent. What is the average monthly return? *(LG1)*

9-14 Average Return The past five monthly returns for PG&E are 2.14 percent, -1.37 percent, 3.77 percent, 6.47 percent, and 3.58 percent. What is the average monthly return? *(LG1)*

9-15 Standard Deviation Compute the standard deviation of Kohl's monthly returns shown in problem 9-13. *(LG3)*

9-16 Standard Deviation Compute the standard deviation of PG&E's monthly returns shown in problem 9-14. *(LG3)*

9-17 Risk versus Return in Bonds Assess the risk-return relationship of the bond market (see Tables 9.2 and 9.4) during each decade since 1950. *(LG2, LG4)*

9-18 Risk versus Return in T-bills Assess the risk-return relationship in T-bills (see Tables 9.2 and 9.4) during each decade since 1950. *(LG2, LG4)*

9-19 Diversifying Consider the characteristics of the following three stocks:

	Expected Return	Standard Deviation
Thumb Devices	13%	23%
Air Comfort	10	19
Sport Garb	10	17

The correlation between Thumb Devices and Air Comfort is -0.12. The correlation between Thumb Devices and Sport Garb is -0.13. The correlation between Air Comfort and Sport Garb is 0.85. If you can pick only two stocks for your portfolio, which would you pick? Why? *(LG4, LG5)*

9-20 Diversifying Consider the characteristics of the following three stocks:

	Expected Return	Standard Deviation
Pic Image	11%	19%
Tax Help	10	19
Warm Wear	14	24

The correlation between Pic Image and Tax Help is 0.88. The correlation between Pic Image and Warm Wear is -0.21. The correlation between Tax Help and Warm Wear is -0.19. If you can pick only two stocks for your portfolio, which would you pick? Why? *(LG4, LG5)*

9-21 **Portfolio Weights** If you own 300 shares of Alaska Air at $42.88, 350 shares of Best Buy at $51.32, and 250 shares of Ford Motor at $8.51, what are the portfolio weights of each stock? *(LG7)*

9-22 **Portfolio Weights** If you own 400 shares of Xerox at $17.34, 500 shares of Qwest at $8.15, and 350 shares of Liz Claiborne at $44.73, what are the portfolio weights of each stock? *(LG7)*

9-23 **Portfolio Return** At the beginning of the month, you owned $5,500 of General Motors, $7,500 of Starbucks, and $9,000 of Nike. The monthly returns for General Motors, Starbucks, and Nike were 6.80 percent, −1.36 percent, and −0.22 percent. What is your portfolio return? *(LG7)*

9-24 **Portfolio Return** At the beginning of the month, you owned $6,000 of News Corp, $5,000 of First Data, and $8,500 of Whirlpool. The monthly returns for News Corp, First Data, and Whirlpool were 8.24 percent, −2.59 percent, and 10.13 percent. What's your portfolio return? *(LG7)*

ADVANCED PROBLEMS

9-25 **Asset Allocation** You have a portfolio with an asset allocation of 50 percent stocks, 40 percent long-term Treasury bonds, and 10 percent T-bills. Use these weights and the returns in Table 9.2 to compute the return of the portfolio in the year 2000 and each year since. Then compute the average annual return and standard deviation of the portfolio and compare them with the risk and return profile of each individual asset class. *(LG2, LG5)*

9-26 **Asset Allocation** You have a portfolio with an asset allocation of 60 percent stocks, 30 percent long-term Treasury bonds, and 10 percent T-bills. Use these weights and the returns in Table 9.2 to compute the return of the portfolio in the year 2000 and each year since. Then compute the average annual return and standard deviation of the portfolio and compare them with the risk and return profile of each individual asset class. *(LG2, LG5)*

9-27 **Portfolio Weights** You have $15,000 to invest. You want to purchase shares of Alaska Air at $42.88, Best Buy at $51.32, and Ford Motor at $8.51. How many shares of each company should you purchase so that your portfolio consists of 30 percent Alaska Air, 40 percent Best Buy, and 30 percent Ford Motor? Report only whole stock shares. *(LG7)*

9-28 **Portfolio Weights** You have $20,000 to invest. You want to purchase shares of Xerox at $17.34, Qwest at $8.15, and Liz Claiborne at $44.73. How many shares of each company should you purchase so that your portfolio consists of 25 percent Xerox, 40 percent Qwest, and 35 percent Liz Claiborne? Report only whole stock shares. *(LG7)*

9-29 **Portfolio Return** The table below shows your stock positions at the beginning of the year, the dividends that each stock paid during the year, and the stock prices at the end of the year. What is your portfolio dollar return and percentage return? *(LG7)*

Company	Shares	Beginning-of-Year Price	Dividend per Share	End-of-Year Price
Washington Mutual	300	$43.50	$2.06	$43.43
PepsiCo	200	59.08	1.16	62.55
JDS Uniphase	500	18.88		16.66
Duke Energy	250	27.45	1.26	33.21

9-30 Portfolio Return The table below shows your stock positions at the beginning of the year, the dividends that each stock paid during the year, and the stock prices at the end of the year. What is your portfolio dollar return and percentage return? *(LG7)*

Company	Shares	Beginning of Year Price	Dividend per Share	End of Year Price
Johnson Controls	300	$72.91	$1.17	$85.92
Medtronic	200	57.57	0.41	53.51
DIRECTV	500	24.94		24.39
Qualcomm	250	43.08	0.45	37.79

9-31 Risk, Return, and Their Relationship Consider the following annual returns of Estée Lauder and Lowe's Companies:

	Estee Lauder	Lowe's Companies
2006	23.4%	−6.0%
2005	−26.0	16.1
2004	17.6	4.2
2003	49.9	48.0
2002	−16.8	−19.0

Compute each stock's average return, standard deviation, and coefficient of variation. Which stock appears better? Why? *(LG3, LG4)*

9-32 Risk, Return, and Their Relationship Consider the following annual returns of Molson Coors and International Paper:

	Molson Coors	International Paper
2006	16.3%	4.5%
2005	−9.7	−17.5
2004	36.5	−0.2
2003	−6.9	26.6
2002	16.2	−11.1

Compute each stock's average return, standard deviation, and coefficient of variation. Which stock appears better? Why? *(LG3, LG4)*

9-33 **Excel Problem** Below are the monthly returns for May 2002 to June 2007 of three international stock indices: All Ordinaries of Australia, Nikkei 225 of Japan, and FTSE 100 of England.

Date	All Ordinaries (Australia)	Nikkei 225 (Japan)	FTSE 100 (England)	Date	All Ordinaries (Australia)	Nikkei 225 (Japan)	FTSE 100 (England)
Jun 2007	1.82%	0.55%	1.65%	Nov 2004	2.80%	5.41%	2.36%
May 2007	−0.49	1.47	−0.20	Oct 2004	4.13	1.19	1.71
Apr 2007	2.98	2.73	2.67	Sep 2004	3.04	−0.48	1.17
Mar 2007	3.00	0.65	2.24	Aug 2004	3.17	−2.33	2.50
Feb 2007	2.79	−1.80	2.21	Jul 2004	0.45	−2.15	1.05
Jan 2007	1.02	1.27	−0.51	Jun 2004	0.45	−4.50	−1.14
Dec 2006	2.01	0.91	−0.28	May 2004	2.12	5.54	0.75
Nov 2006	3.35	5.85	2.84	Apr 2004	1.44	−4.47	−1.31
Oct 2006	2.03	−0.76	−1.31	Mar 2004	−0.25	0.40	2.37
Sep 2006	4.69	1.69	2.83	Feb 2004	1.30	6.10	−2.37
Aug 2006	0.65	−0.08	0.93	Jan 2004	2.71	2.40	2.31
Jul 2006	2.48	4.42	−0.37	Dec 2003	−0.68	1.00	−1.93
Jun 2006	−1.53	−0.31	1.63	Nov 2003	3.45	5.70	3.09
May 2006	1.24	0.24	1.91	Oct 2003	−2.64	−4.35	1.28
Apr 2006	−4.51	−8.51	−4.97	Sep 2003	3.34	3.33	4.80
Mar 2006	2.35	−0.90	0.98	Aug 2003	−0.83	−1.20	−1.68
Feb 2006	4.28	5.27	2.99	Jul 2003	3.10	8.16	0.10
Jan 2006	−0.04	−2.67	0.54	Jun 2003	3.59	5.29	3.12
Dec 2005	3.64	3.34	2.52	May 2003	0.64	7.82	−0.42
Nov 2005	2.73	8.33	3.61	Apr 2003	0.30	7.57	3.11
Oct 2005	3.87	9.30	1.99	Mar 2003	4.29	−1.77	8.65
Sep 2005	−3.92	0.24	−2.93	Feb 2003	2.53	−4.67	−1.16
Aug 2005	4.06	9.35	3.41	Jan 2003	−5.35	0.28	2.47
Jul 2005	1.54	4.32	0.28	Dec 2002	−1.35	−2.79	−9.47
Jun 2005	2.76	2.72	3.31	Nov 2002	−1.64	−6.91	−5.49
May 2005	3.92	2.73	3.01	Oct 2002	1.01	6.66	3.21
Apr 2005	3.23	2.43	3.38	Sep 2002	2.28	−7.92	8.54
Mar 2005	−3.84	−5.66	−1.89	Aug 2002	−4.73	−2.45	−11.96
Feb 2005	−1.34	−0.61	−1.49	Jul 2002	1.36	−2.62	−0.45
Jan 2005	1.21	3.10	2.39	Jun 2002	−4.13	−7.00	−8.81
Dec 2004	1.32	−0.88	0.79	May 2002	−4.87	−9.71	−8.43

a. Compute and compare each index's monthly average return and standard deviation.

b. Compute the correlation between (1) All Ordinaries and Nikkei 225, (2) All Ordinaries and FTSE 100, and (3) Nikkei 225 and FTSE 100, and compare them.

c. Form a portfolio consisting of one-third of each of the indices and show the portfolio return each year, and the portfolio's return and standard deviation.

chapter ten

estimating
risk + return

In Chapters 9 and 10, we explore methods to find the return that individual or institutional investors require to make a particular investment attractive. In Chapter 9, we established a positive relationship between risk and return using historical data. Risk and return play an undeniable role as investors seek the best return for the least risk. But financial managers and investors must make investment decisions armed only with their *expectations* about future risk and return. We need an exact specification that shows directly the amount of reward required for investors to take the level of risk in a given firm's stock or portfolio of securities.

Investors need to know how much risk they have to take to confidently expect a 10 percent return. Managers also want to know what return shareholders require so that they can decide how to meet those expectations.

continued on p. 230

LEARNING GOALS

LG1 Compute forward-looking expected return and risk.

LG2 Understand risk premiums.

LG3 Know and apply the Capital Asset Pricing Model (CAPM).

LG4 Calculate and apply beta, a measure of market risk.

LG5 Differentiate among the different levels of market efficiency and their implications.

LG6 Calculate and explain investors' required return and risk.

LG7 Use the constant growth rate model to compute required return.

continued from p. 229

If we want to specify the exact risk-return relationship, we need to develop a better measure of *risk* for individuals and institutional investors. As we saw in Chapter 9, any firm's total risk is specific to that particular firm. But the market doesn't reward firm-specific risk, because investors can easily diversify away any single firm's specific risks by owning other offsetting firms' stocks to create a portfolio subject only to market or undiversifiable risk. So, we need to find just the market risk portion of total risk for investors. The theory to find the market risk portion of stock ownership extends modern portfolio theory. Our search to find market risk will lead us to the capital asset pricing model (CAPM), which utilizes a measure of market risk called beta. CAPM's risk-return specification provides us a powerful tool to make better investment decisions.

Corporate finance managers and investment professionals use the beta measure commonly. But like any theory, CAPM has its limitations. We'll discuss the CAPM's limitations and concerns about beta and propose an alternative required return measure. Whether beta or any other risk-return specification is useful relies in part on whether a stock's price represents a fair estimate of the true company value. Stock price validity and reliability—their general correctness—is vitally important both to investors and to corporate managers. ■

EXPECTED RETURNS

In the previous chapter, we characterized risk and return in historical terms. We defined a stock's return as the actual profit realized while holding the stock or the average return over a longer period. We described risk simply as the standard deviation of those returns—a term already familiar to you from your statistics classes. So, we did a good job describing the risk and return that the stock experienced *in the past*. But do those risk-and-return figures hold into the future? Firms can quite possibly change their stocks' risk level by substantially changing their business. If a firm takes on riskier new projects over time, or changes the nature of its business, the firm itself will become riskier. Similarly, firms can reduce their risk level—and hence, their stock's riskiness—by choosing low-risk new projects. Both investors and firms find expected return, a forward-looking return calculation that includes risk measures, very useful to estimate future stock performance.

viewpoints

business APPLICATION

Consider that you work in the finance department of a large corporation. Your team is analyzing several new projects the firm can pursue. To complete the analysis, the team needs to know what return stockholders require from the firm.

You are to estimate this required return. Shareholders' expected return will depend on your company's risk level. What information do you need to gather and how might you compute this return?

Expected Return and Risk

We can attribute a company's business success over a year partly to its management talent, strategies, and other firm-specific activities. Overall economic conditions will also

A company's success depends partly on management talent, strategies, and other activities.

personal APPLICATION

You have just started your first job in the corporate world and need to make some retirement plan decisions. The company's 401(k) retirement plan offers three investment choices: a stock portfolio, a bond portfolio, and a money market deposit. For your allocation, you decide to contribute $200 per month to the stock portfolio, $100 to the bond portfolio, and $50 to the money market deposit.

What risk level are you taking in your retirement portfolio and what return should you expect over the long run?

Economists seldom predict simple two-state views of the economy as in the above example. Rather, economists give much more detailed forecasts (like three states: red-hot economy, average expansion, and recession). So our general equation for a stock's expected return with S different conditions of the economy is:

$$\text{Expected return} = (p_1 \times \text{Return}_1) + (p_2 \times \text{Return}_2)$$
$$+ (p_3 \times \text{Return}_3) \qquad (10\text{-}1)$$
$$+ \cdots + p_s \times \text{Return}_s = \sum_{j=1}^{s} p_j \times \text{Return}_j$$

The result of this expected return calculation has some interesting properties. First, the expected return figure expresses what the average return would be over time if the probabilistic states of the economy occur as predicted. For example, the 70/30 **probability distribution** for good/recession economic states suggests that the economy will be good in 7 of the next 10 years, earning Nucor shareholders a 20 percent return in each of those years. Shareholders would lose 10 percent in each of the three recession years. So the *average return* over those 10 years would be 11 percent, the same as the expected return. The second interesting property: The expected return itself will not likely occur during any one year. Remember that Nucor will earn a return of either 20 percent or 10 percent. Yet its expected return is 11 percent, a value that it cannot earn because we have no economic condition for which the return is 11 percent. This illustration seems extreme because we used only two economic states. Any real economic forecast would instead include a probability distribution of many potential economic conditions.

We can also characterize risk via this expected return figure. The expected return procedure shows potential return possibilities, but we don't know which one will actually occur, so we face uncertainty. In the last chapter, we measured risk using the standard deviation of returns over time. We can use the same principle to measure risk for expected return. What range of different expected returns will Nucor exhibit from the expected return of 11 percent? In our two-state description of the economy, the deviation could be either 9 percent (= 20% − 11%) or −21 percent (= −10% − 11%). We compute the standard deviation of

affect a firm's level of success or failure. Consider a steel manufacturer—Nucor Corp. The steel business closely follows economic trends. In a good economy, demand for steel is strong as builders and manufacturers step up building and production. During economic recessions, demand for steel falls off quickly. So, if we want to assess Nucor's probabilities for success next year, we know that we must look partly at Nucor's managerial ability and partly at the economic outlook.

Unfortunately, we cannot accurately predict what the economy will be like next year. Predicting economic activity is like predicting the weather—forecasts give the **probability** of rain or sunshine. Economists cannot say for sure whether the economy will be good or bad next year. Instead, they may forecast a 70 percent chance that the economy will be good and a 30 percent chance of a recession. Similarly, analysts might say that given Nucor's managerial talent, if the economy is good, Nucor will perform well and the stock will increase 20 percent. If the economy goes into a recession, then Nucor's stock will fall 10 percent. So what return do you expect from Nucor? The return still depends on the state of the economy.

This leads us directly to a key concept: **expected return.** We compute expected return by multiplying each possible return by the probability, p, of that return occurring. We then sum them (recall that all probabilities must add to one). In Nucor's case, the expected return would be 11 percent [= (0.7 × 20%) + (0.3 × −10%)]. Of course, nothing is quite that simple.

the Math Coach on...

Expected Return and Standard Deviation

" When you compute expected return and standard deviation, you'll find it helpful to use the decimal format for the probability of the economic state and percentages to state the return in each state. "

expected returns the same way we did for historical returns. We square the deviations, then multiply by the probability of that deviation occurring, and then sum them all up. So Nucor's return variance is 189.0 [$=(0.7 \times 9^2) + (0.3 \times -21^2)$]. As a final step, we take the square root of our result to put the figure back into sensible terms. The standard deviation for Nucor is 13.75 percent ($= \sqrt{189}$). The general equation for the standard deviation of S different economic states is:

$$\text{Standard deviation} = \sqrt{\begin{array}{l} p_1 \times (\text{Return}_1 - \text{Expected return})^2 + p_2 \\ \times (\text{Return}_2 - \text{Expected return})^2 + \cdots \end{array}} \quad (10\text{-}2)$$

$$= \sqrt{\sum_{j=1}^{s} p_j \times (\text{Return}_j - \text{Expected return})^2}$$

Risk Premiums

Throughout the book, we have mentioned the positive relationship between expected return and risk. Consider this key question: You have a riskless investment available to you. The short-term government debt security, the T-bill, offers you a low return with no risk. Why would you invest in anything risky, when you could simply buy T-bills? The answer, of course, is that some investors want a higher return and are willing to take

EXAMPLE 10-1

For interactive versions of this example visit www.mhhe.com/can1e

Expected Return and Risk

Bailey has a probability distribution for four possible states of the economy, as shown below. She has also calculated the return that Motor Music stock would earn in each state. Given this information, what's Motor Music's expected return and risk?

Economic State	Probability	Return
Fast growth	0.15	25%
Slow growth	0.60	15%
Recession	0.20	−5%
Depression	0.05	−20%

SOLUTION:

Bailey can compute the expected return using equation 10-1:

Expected return $= (0.15 \times 25\%) + (0.60 \times 15\%) + (0.20 \times -5\%) + (0.05 \times -20\%) = 10.75\%$

Then Bailey can compute the expected return by computing the standard deviation using equation 10-2:

$$\text{Standard deviation} = \sqrt{\begin{array}{l} 0.15 \times (25\% - 10.75\%)^2 + 0.60 \times (15\% - 10.75\%)^2 + 0.20 \\ \times (-5\% - 10.75\%)^2 + 0.05 \times (-20\% - 10.75\%)^2 \end{array}}$$

$$= \sqrt{30.46 + 10.84 + 49.61 + 47.28} = 11.76\%$$

The expected return and standard deviation are 10.75 percent and 11.76 percent, respectively. We could also show these equations in a table, such as:

Economic State	Probability	Return	p × Return	Deviation	Squared Dev.	× p
Fast growth	0.15	25%	3.75%	14.25%	203.06	30.46
Slow growth	0.60	15	9.00	4.25	18.06	10.84
Recession	0.20	−5	−1.00	−15.75	248.06	49.61
Depression	0.05	−20	−1.00	−30.75	945.56	47.28
Sum =	1.0		10.75%	Square root =	138.19	11.76%

some risk to raise their returns. Investors who take on a little risk should expect a slightly higher return than the T-bill rate. People who take on higher risk levels should expect higher returns. Indeed, it's only logical that investors require this extra return to willingly take the added risk.

The expected return of an investment is often expressed in two parts, a risk-free return and a risky contribution. The return investors require for the risk level they take is called the **required return:**

$$\text{Required return} = \text{Risk-free rate} + \text{Risk premium} \quad (10\text{-}3)$$

The *risk-free rate* is typically considered the return on U.S. government bonds and bills and equals the real interest rate and the expected inflation premium that we discussed in Chapter 8. The **risk premium** is the reward investors require for taking risk. How large are the rewards for taking risk? As we discussed in the previous chapter, the market doesn't reward all risks. The firm-specific portion of total risk for any stock can be diversified away, and since the investor takes on such risk out of ignorance or by mistake, an efficient market will not reward anyone for taking on this "superfluous" risk. So as we examine historical risk premiums, we do so with a diversified portfolio that contains no firm-specific risk.

Table 10.1 shows the average annual return on the S&P 500 Index minus the T-bill rate for different time periods. The remainder after we subtract the T-bill rate is the risk premium; in this case, it's the **market risk premium**—the reward for taking general (unsystematic) stock market risk. Since 1950, the average market risk premium has been 8.2 percent per year. Over the long run, this is the reward for taking stock market risk. The actual, realized risk premium during particular decades has varied. The average risk premium has been as high as 18.8 percent for the 1950s and as low as 1.2 percent during

the 1970s. So far in the 2000s, the stock market return has been so poor that it has not beaten the risk-free rate. Investors require a risk premium for taking on market risk. But taking that risk also means that they will periodically experience poor returns.

10-1 Describe the similarities between computing average return and expected return. Also, describe the similarities between expected return risk and historical risk.

10-2 Why would people take risks by investing their hard-earned money?

MARKET RISK

How much risk should you take to achieve the return you want over time? In the previous chapter we demonstrated that individual stocks and different portfolios exhibit different levels of total risk. Recall that the rewards for carrying risk apply only to the market risk (or undiversifiable) portion of total risk. But how do investors know how much of the 38.8 percent standard

▼ **TABLE 10.1** The Realized Average Annual Risk Premium for Stocks

	1950 to 2007	1950 to 1959	1960 to 1969	1970 to 1979	1980 to 1989	1990 to 1999	2000 to 2007
Risk premium	8.2%	18.8%	4.7%	1.2%	9.3%	14.1%	−0.5%

S&P 500 Index and T-bill rate data.

asset pricing The process of directly specifying the relationship between required return and risk.

capital asset pricing model (CAPM) An asset pricing theory based on a beta, a measure of market risk.

capital market line The line on a graph of return and risk (standard deviation) from the risk-free rate through the market portfolio.

market portfolio In theory, the market portfolio is the combination of securities that places the portfolio on the efficient frontier and on a line tangent to the risk-free rate. In practice, the S&P 500 Index is used to proxy for the market portfolio.

financial leverage The use of debt to increase an investment position.

deviation of returns for Mattel Inc. is firm-specific risk and how much of that deviation is market risk? The answer to this important question will determine how much of a risk premium investors should require for Mattel. The attempt to specify an equation that relates a stock's required return to an appropriate risk premium is known as **asset pricing.**

The Market Portfolio

The best-known asset pricing equation is the **capital asset pricing model,** typically referred to as CAPM. Though many theorists formulated theories that, in the end, supported the CAPM's effectiveness, credit for the model goes to William Sharpe and John Lintner. Sharpe eventually won a Nobel Prize for his work in 1990. (Lintner passed away in 1983, and Nobel Prizes are not awarded posthumously.) Today, both investors and corporate finance professionals use CAPM widely. In developing the CAPM, Lintner and Sharpe sought to emphasize the individual investor's best strategy to maximize returns for a given amount of market risk.

CAPM starts with modern portfolio theory. Remember from the previous chapter that when you combine securities into a portfolio, you can find a set of portfolios that dominate all others. The best combinations possible use all the risky securities available (but not the risk-free asset) to create efficient frontier portfolios, as shown by the curved line in Figure 10.1, panel A. These portfolios represent combinations of various risky securities that give the highest expected return for each potential level of risk.

The idea of a risk premium in equation 10-3 implies a risk-free investment, like T-bills. Panel B shows where the risk-free asset would appear on the **capital market line** (CML). The risk-free asset must lie on the *y* axis precisely because it carries no risk. Now we draw a line from the risk-free security to a point tangent to the efficient frontier. The CML relationship appears as a line because investments show a direct risk-reward relationship. You may recall from your economics classes that only one tangency point will be possible between this kind of curve and a straight line. The spot where the tangency occurs is called the **market portfolio,** which has a special significance. The market portfolio represents ownership in all traded assets in the economy, so this portfolio provides maximum diversification. You can locate your optimal portfolio on this line by owning various combinations of the risk-free security and the market portfolio. If most of your money is invested in the market portfolio, then you will have a portfolio on the line that lies just

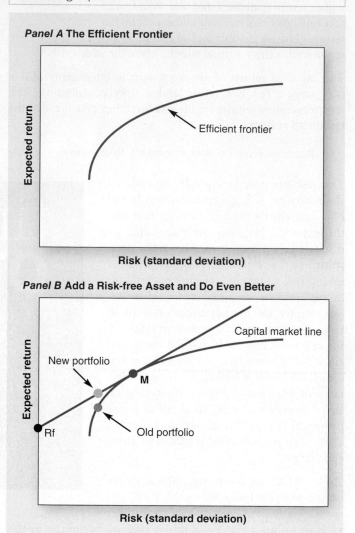

▼FIGURE 10.1
Maximizing Expected Return

Panel A The Efficient Frontier

Efficient frontier

Expected return

Risk (standard deviation)

Panel B Add a Risk-free Asset and Do Even Better

Capital market line

New portfolio

M

Expected return

Rf

Old portfolio

Risk (standard deviation)

to the left of the market portfolio dot in the graph. If you own just a little of the market portfolio and hold mostly risk-free securities, then your portfolio will lie on the line near the risk-free security dot. For your investments to lie on the line to the right of the market portfolio, you would have to invest all your money in the market portfolio, then borrow more money and invest these additional funds in the market portfolio. Borrowing money to invest is known as using **financial leverage.** Using financial leverage increases the overall risk of the portfolio.

Notice that if you had a portfolio on the efficient frontier (labeled "old portfolio"), you could do better. Instead of owning the old portfolio, you can put some of your money in the market portfolio and some in the risk-free security to obtain the "new portfolio." See how the new portfolio dominates that old one? It carries the same risk level, but offers a higher return. In fact, notice that the line drawn between the risk-free investment and the market portfolio dominates all of the efficient frontier portfolios (except the market portfolio itself). All portfolio allocations between the risk-free security and the market

▼ TABLE 10.2 Dow Jones Industrial Average Stock Betas

Company	Beta	Company	Beta
3M Company	0.75	Home Depot	1.08
Alcoa	1.69	Honeywell International	1.38
Altria	0.24	Intel	1.44
American International	1.38	International Business Mach.	1.59
American Express	1.12	Johnson & Johnson	0.14
AT&T	1.01	JPMorgan	0.99
Boeing	0.81	McDonald's	1.67
Citigroup	1.20	Merck	1.11
Caterpillar	1.43	Microsoft	1.36
Coca-Cola	0.62	Pfizer	1.16
Du Pont de Nemours	1.10	Procter & Gamble	0.61
ExxonMobil	1.26	United Technologies	0.64
General Electric	0.59	Verizon Communications	1.11
General Motors	1.94	Walmart	0.05
Hewlett-Packard	1.24	Walt Disney	0.56

Data Source: Yahoo! Finance, January 18, 2008.

beta A measure of the sensitivity of a stock or portfolio to market risk.

If Mattel's total risk level is measured by its standard deviation, σ_{Mattel}, then we can find the risk contribution attributable to the market in general by multiplying Mattel's total risk by its correlation with the market portfolio, $\sigma_{Mattel} \times \rho_{Mattel, Market}$. The beta computation is scaled so that the market portfolio itself has a beta of one and is done by dividing by standard deviation of the market portfolio; $\sigma_{Mattel} \times \rho_{Mattel, Market} \div \sigma_{Market}$.[1] Stocks with betas larger than one are considered riskier than the market portfolio, while betas of less then one indicate lower risk. Mattel has a beta of 1.5, meaning that Mattel stock is very sensitive to market risk. When the market portfolio moves, you can expect Mattel stock to move in the same direction. Technically, you should expect Mattel's realized risk premium to be 50 percent more than the realized market risk premium.

portfolio constitute the capital market line. All investors should want to locate their portfolios on the CML, rather than the efficient frontier. Portfolios on the CML offer the highest expected return for any level of desired risk, which the investor controls by deciding how much of the market portfolio and how much of the risk-free asset to hold. Risk-averse investors can put more of their money in T-bills and less into the market portfolio. Investors willing to take on higher risk for larger returns can put more of their money in the market portfolio.

Beta, a Measure of Market Risk

The CML demonstrates that the market portfolio is crucial. Indeed, its return less the risk-free rate represents the expected average market risk premium. The market portfolio features no firm-specific risk; all such risk is diversified away. So the market portfolio carries only market risk. So the market portfolio's risk factor allows us to compute a measure of firm-specific risk for any individual stock or portfolio. We can now examine the question posed at the beginning of this section: "How much of Mattel's total risk is attributable to market risk?" The standard deviation of returns includes all of Mattel stock's risk—it quantifies how much the stock price rises and falls. The market risk portion will rise and fall along with the market portfolio. If we subtract the market risk portion from the total risk measure, we're left with firm-specific risk. This part of risk rises and falls in ways unrelated to market changes.

Remember that portfolio theory describes a measure—correlation—that measures how two stocks move together through time. Instead of measuring how any two stocks or portfolios move together, we now want to know how a stock or portfolio moves relative to market portfolio movements. This measure is known as **beta (β).** Beta measures the comovement between a stock and the market portfolio.

Table 10.2 shows the beta for each of the 30 companies in the Dow Jones Industrial Average. Investors consider many of these companies high risk, like General Motors (β = 1.94) and Alcoa (1.69). These firms' stocks carry high market risk because the demand for their products is very sensitive to the overall economy's strength. People buy new cars and firms buy more construction materials when the economy is good. They buy less when they think that the economy is likely to go sour. Investors consider

[1] A mathematically equivalent equation for beta is $\beta = cov(R_s, R_M)/var(R_M)$, where cov() is the covariance between the stock and market portfolio returns, and var() is the variance of the market portfolio.

AT&T has nearly the same risk as the market portfolio.

other companies safe bets with low risk, like Walmart (0.05), Johnson & Johnson (0.14), and Altria (0.24). Many lower-beta firms sell consumer goods that we consider the necessities of life, which we will buy whether the economy is in recession or expansion. The demand for these products is price inelastic and not sensitive to economic conditions. Some companies have nearly the same risk as the market portfolio, like JPMorgan (0.99) and AT&T (1.01).

The Security Market Line

Beta indicates the market risk that each stock represents to investors. So the higher the beta, the higher the risk premium investors will demand to undertake that security's market risk. Since beta sums up precisely what investors want to know about risk, we often replace the standard deviation risk measure shown in Figure 10.1 with beta. Figure 10.2 shows required return versus beta risk. We call the line in this figure the **security market line** (SML), which illustrates how required return relates to risk at any particular time, all else held equal. The SML also shows the market portfolio's risk premium or any stock's risk premium. When a stock like Home Depot carries a beta greater than one, then its risk premium must be larger than the market risk premium. A stock like Boeing carries a lower beta than does the overall market; therefore, Boeing would offer a lower risk premium to investors.

We can use the SML to show the relationship between risk and return for any stock or portfolio. To precisely quantify this relationship, we need the equation for the SML. The equation of any line can be defined as $y = b + m\,x$, where b is the intercept and m is the slope. In this case, the y axis is required return and the x axis is beta. The intercept is R_f. You may remember that the slope is the "rise over run" between two points on the line. The rise between the risk-free security and

the market portfolio is $R_M - R_f$ and the run is $1 - 0$. Substituting into the line equation results in the CAPM:

$$\text{Required return} = R_f + \beta(R_M - R_f) \qquad (10\text{-}4)$$

So, we have determined a way to estimate any stock's required return once we have determined its beta. Consider this: We expect the market portfolio to earn 12 percent and T-bill yields are 5 percent. Then Home Depot's required return, with a $\beta = 1.08$, is $5\% + 1.08 \times (12\% - 5\%) = 12.56$ percent. Table 10.3 shows the 30 Dow Jones Industrial Average stocks'

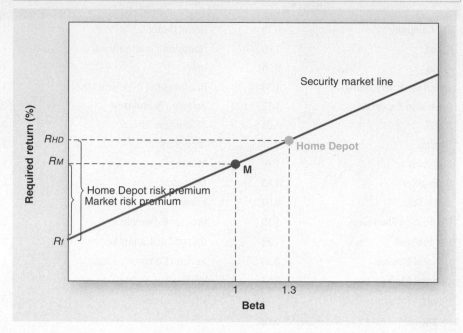

▼ FIGURE 10.2 The Security Market Line Uses Beta as the Risk Measure

▼ TABLE 10.3 Required Returns for DJIA Stocks

Company	Required Return	Company	Required Return
3M Company	10.2%	Home Depot	12.6%
Alcoa	16.8	Honeywell International	14.7
Altria	6.7	Intel	15.1
American International	14.7	International Business Mach.	16.1
American Express	12.8	Johnson & Johnson	6.0
AT&T	12.1	JPMorgan	11.9
Boeing	10.7	McDonald's	16.7
Citigroup	13.4	Merck	12.8
Caterpillar	15.0	Microsoft	14.5
Coca-Cola	9.3	Pfizer	13.1
Du Pont de Nemours	12.7	Procter & Gamble	9.3
ExxonMobil	13.8	United Technologies	9.5
General Electric	9.1	Verizon Communications	12.8
General Motors	18.6	Walmart	5.4
Hewlett-Packard	13.7	Walt Disney	8.9

Assumptions: market return = 12% and risk-free rate = 5%.

EXAMPLE 10-2

CAPM and Under- or Overvalued Stock

Say that you are a corporate CFO. You know that the risk-free rate is currently 4.5 percent and you expect the market to earn 11 percent this year. Through your own analysis of the firm, you think it will earn a 13.5 percent return this year. If the beta of the company is 1.2, should you consider the firm undervalued or overvalued?

SOLUTION:

You can compute shareholders' required return with CAPM as $4.5\% + 1.2 \times (11\% - 4.5\%) = 12.3\%$. Since you think the firm will actually earn more than this required return, the firm appears to be currently undervalued. That is, its price must rise more then predicted by CAPM to obtain the return you estimated.

---

required returns, using these same market and risk-free rate assumptions. Higher-risk companies have higher betas, and thus require higher returns.

Portfolio Beta As you might expect, a stock **portfolio's beta** is the weighted average of the portfolio stocks' betas. The portfolio beta equation resembles equation 9-7, which gives the return of a portfolio:

$$\beta_p = (w_1 \times \beta_1) + (w_2 \times \beta_2) + (w_3 \times \beta_3) + \cdots + (w_n \times \beta_n)$$

$$= \sum_{j=1}^{n} w_j \beta_j \qquad (10\text{-}5)$$

With this equation, you can easily determine whether adding a particular stock to the portfolio will increase or decrease the portfolio's total market risk. If you add a stock with a higher beta than the existing portfolio, then the new portfolio will carry higher market risk than the old one did. Although we can find the effects on total portfolio risk of adding particular stocks using beta, the same is not necessarily true if we use standard deviations as our risk measure. The new stock, however risky, might have low correlations with the other stocks in the portfolio—offsetting (negative) correlations would reduce total risk.

Finding Beta

The CAPM is an elegant explanation that relates the return you should require for taking on various levels of market risk. Although CAPM provides many practical applications, you need a company's beta to use those applications. Where or how can you obtain a beta? You have two ways to get beta. First, given the returns of the company and the market portfolio, you can compute the beta yourself. Second, you can find the beta that others have computed through financial information data providers.

Many financial outlets publish company betas. One publication that your library may have been subscribing to for decades is the *Value Line Investment Survey*. Value Line prints a terrific one-page summary of each company that includes beta. Value Line is now also online **(www.valueline.com)**, but you need to subscribe to access this information. Nevertheless, many Web sites provide company betas for free. Hoovers, MSN Money, Yahoo! Finance, and Zacks, to name just a few. For example, in January 2008, the beta these Web sites listed for AT&T were: Hoovers (1.2), MSN Money (1.14), Yahoo! Finance (1.01), and Zacks (1.23). Note that these reported betas have some differences. To know why differences might arise, consider how you would go about gathering information and computing beta yourself.

EXAMPLE 10-3

Portfolio Beta

You have a portfolio consisting of 20 percent Boeing stock ($\beta = 0.81$), 40 percent Hewlett-Packard stock ($\beta = 1.24$), and 40 percent McDonald's stock ($\beta = 1.67$). How much market risk does the portfolio have?

SOLUTION:

Compute a beta for the portfolio. Using equation 10-5, the portfolio beta is $0.2 \times 0.81 + 0.4 \times 1.24 + 0.4 \times 1.67 - 1.33$. Note that this portfolio carries 33 percent more market risk than the general market does.

To compute your own beta, first obtain historical returns for the company of interest and of the market portfolio. Then run a regression of the company return as the dependent variable and the market portfolio return as the independent variable. The resulting market portfolio return coefficient is beta. Many important questions may come to mind. First, what do you use as the market portfolio? People typically use a major stock index like the S&P 500 Index to proxy for the market portfolio. Second, what time frame should you use? You can use daily, weekly, monthly, or even annual returns. Using monthly returns is the most common. How long of a time series is needed? As you will recall, statistical estimates become more reliable and valid as more data are used. But you'll have to weigh those statistical advantages against the fact that companies change their business enterprises and thus their risk levels over time. Using data from too far back will distort your beta estimate, reflecting both risk today and risk from previous company activities. Generally speaking, using a time series data of three to five years is common. Whatever decisions you make

returns versus annual returns), and different time periods. A problem at the end of this chapter explores these differences.

In addition to these estimation problems, a company can change its risk level, and thus its beta, by changing the way it operates within its business, by expanding into new businesses, and/or by changing its debt load. So even if beta is an accurate measure of what the firm's risk level was in the past, does it apply to the future? Beta's applicability will depend on the firm's future plans.

Both financial managers and investors share these concerns about beta. In the end, beta's usefulness depends on its reliability. Unfortunately, beta's empirical record is not as good as we would like. We should expect that companies with high betas yield higher returns than companies with low betas. On average, though, this does not turn out to be the case. A company's beta does not appear to predict its future return very well. Since characterizing the risk-return relationship is so important, finance researchers have introduced other asset pricing models. One promising model adds more risk factors to the

> "Unfortunately, beta's empirical record is not as good as we would like. We should expect that companies with high betas yield higher returns than companies with low betas. On average, though, this does not turn out to be the case."

to address these questions, be consistent by making the same decisions for all the company betas you compute. You'll find an example of computing beta in the Excel problem in this chapter. (It's not a calculation that you would want to make by hand!)

Concerns about Beta

Consider the estimation choices just mentioned. Say you estimate a firm's beta using monthly data for five years and the Dow Jones Industrial Average return as the market portfolio. Suppose that the result is a beta of 1.3. Then you try again using weekly returns for three years and the return from the S&P 500 Index as the market portfolio's yield, resulting in a beta of 0.9. These estimates are quite different and would create a large variation in required return if you plugged them into the CAPM. So, which is the more accurate estimate? Unfortunately, we may not be able to determine which is most representative, or "true." In general, you may estimate a little different beta using different market portfolio proxies, different return intervals (like monthly

predictive relationship other than just market risk. Firm size and book-to-market ratio have had some success predicting returns, so new models often include factors derived from these characteristics along with beta as a measure of market risk.

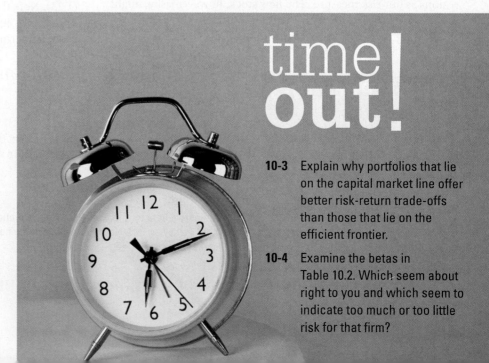

time out!

10-3 Explain why portfolios that lie on the capital market line offer better risk-return trade-offs than those that lie on the efficient frontier.

10-4 Examine the betas in Table 10.2. Which seem about right to you and which seem to indicate too much or too little risk for that firm?

finance at work //: markets

Asset Pricing and Hedge Funds

Hedge funds are professionally managed portfolios, much like mutual funds. But differences between the two fund types carry very important ramifications for investors. While mutual funds typically just buy stocks and bonds, hedge funds often take short positions—that is, they sell stock they don't even own by borrowing it because they anticipate price declines. Once the price falls, the short seller covers the short by buying back the securities and returning them to the original owner to close out the transaction. Hedge funds short stocks and take sophisticated positions in commodities, futures, options, and other complicated derivative securities. They also maintain secrecy about their holdings, trading, and strategies. In return for the ability to use these kinds of strategies and maintain privacy, they can't advertise for new clients, so they are limited to sophisticated investors (a net worth in excess of $1 million or an annual income of greater than $200,000). Over $1.2 trillion is currently invested in hedge funds worldwide and the hedge fund industry is growing fast as more and more money managers think that they understand complex positions and can "make a killing" with unorthodox positions and financial instruments.

Some hedge funds use sophisticated asset pricing models to assess risks and rewards of unusual investment strategies. But just as with beta, sometimes asset prices do not behave as indicated in the models. This can lead to spectacular "blow ups." The most famous hedge funds implosion was the Long Term Capital Management debacle in 1998. Partners in LTCM included the likes of David Mullins (former Harvard Business School professor and vice chairman of the Federal Reserve Board) and Nobel Laureates Myron Scholes (from Stanford University) and Robert Merton (from MIT)—very smart and sophisticated investors indeed. The LTCM's traders, economists, and mathematicians used computers to detect suspected mispricings in bond and financial derivative values.

In August 1998, LTCM took a huge position based on their assumption that the "spread" or difference in interest rates between U.S. Treasury bonds and Danish mortgage securities would narrow. They were very wrong. Like many hedge funds, they had taken on enormous financial leverage. Say that you have $100 to invest and you buy a very safe investment. Say further that this investment will very likely pay you a profit of $1. You also face a

Even a low-risk venture, when highly leveraged, can become high-risk.

slight risk that you may lose $1. This is a low-risk endeavor! Now say that you *borrow* an additional $9,900 to buy more of this safe investment. Now you are financially leveraged to a high degree. The investment will *likely* pay you a total of $100, in which case you will have doubled your $100 investment. But remember that slight chance that you will lose $100, which is all of your money. Either way, you must repay the borrowed $9,900 plus whatever interest you owe on that sum. The leverage you have taken on magnifies your return—and your risk. A low-risk investment with no leverage can become a high-risk investment when levered. LTCM made a low-risk investment, but it was so highly levered that the loss wiped out more than 90 percent of the hedge fund value—a loss of two billion dollars!

The LTCM loss pales in comparison to the Amaranth hedge fund implosion in the fall of 2006. Amaranth lost $6.6 billion by taking a highly leveraged position based on their belief that short-term natural gas prices would rise. Instead, short-term gas prices fell.

Incidents like these can create ripple effects throughout the economy. So the U.S. Securities and Exchange Commission (SEC) has decided to monitor the hedge fund industry more closely, though the Commission has stopped short of actually regulating the industry at this time.

Want to know more?

Key Words to Search for Updates: **hedge funds, U.S. SEC, LTCM, Amaranth**

CAPITAL MARKET EFFICIENCY

The risk and return relationship rests on an underlying assumption that stock prices are generally "correct"—they are not predictably too high or too low. Imagine having a system that identified undervalued stocks with low risks (i.e., relatively high returns with a low beta). Because those stocks are undervalued, they will earn you a high return, on average, as their stock prices rise to their correct value. Note that the CAPM's risk-return relationship would be incorrect. You would be consistently getting high returns with low risk. On the other hand, if you consistently picked overvalued stocks, you wouldn't be earning enough return to compensate you for the risks you are taking. Investors move their money to the best alternatives by selling overvalued stocks and buying undervalued stocks. This causes the prices of the overvalued stocks to drop and the prices of the undervalued stocks to rise until both stocks' returns stand more in line with their riskiness. Thus, the risk-return relationship relies on the idea that prices are generally accurate.

What conditions are necessary for an **efficient market?** Efficient, or perfectly competitive, markets feature:

- Many buyers and sellers.

- No prohibitively high barriers to entry.

- Free and readily available information available to all participants.

- Low trading or transaction costs.

Are these conditions met for the U.S. stock market? Certainly millions of stock investors trade every day, buying and selling securities. With discount brokers and online traders, the costs to trade are fairly minimal and don't represent any real barriers to enter the market. Information is increasingly accessible from many sources and trading philosophies, and commission costs and bid-ask spreads have steadily declined. With millions of the larger companies' shares (say the S&P 500) of stock trading every day, the U.S. stock exchanges appear to meet efficiency conditions. But other segments of the market, like those exchanges that trade in **penny stocks,** feature very thin trading. The prices of these very small companies' stock may not be fair and these equities may be manipulated in fraudulent scams. In the 1970s and 1980s, penny stock king Meyer Blinder and his firm Blinder-Robinson were known as "blind 'em and rob 'em" as they practiced penny stock price manipulation to rob many small investors of their entire investments in these small markets. These days, penny stock price manipulation is typically conducted through e-mail and Web posting scams.

Efficient Market Hypothesis

Our concept of market efficiency provides a good framework for understanding how stock prices change over time. This theory is described in the **efficient market hypothesis (EMH),** which states that *security prices fully reflect all available information.* At any point in time, the price for any stock or bond reflects the collective wisdom of market participants about the company's future prospects. Security prices change as new information becomes available. Since we cannot predict whether new information about a company will be good news or bad news, we cannot predict whether its stock price will go up or go down. This makes short-term stock-price movements unpredictable. But in the longer run, stock prices will adjust to their proper level as market participants gather and digest all available information.

The EMH brings us to the question of what type of information is embedded within current stock prices. Segmenting information into three categories leads to the three basic levels of market efficiency, described as:

1. Weak-form efficiency—current prices reflect all information derived from trading. This stock market information generally includes current and past stock prices and trading volume.

2. Semistrong-form efficiency—current prices reflect all **public information.** This includes all information that has already been revealed to the public, like financial statements, news, analyst opinions, and so on.

3. Strong-form efficiency—current prices reflect *all* information. In addition to public information, prices reflect the **privately held information** that has not yet been released to the but may be known to some people, like managers, accountants, auditors, and so on.

Each of the EMH's three forms rests on different assumptions regarding the extent of information that is incorporated into stock prices at any point in time. A fourth possibility—that markets may not be efficient and prices may not reflect all the information known about a company—also arises.

The *weak-form* efficiency level involves the lowest information hurdle, stating that stock prices reflect all past price and trading volume activity. If true, this level of efficiency would have important ramifications. A segment of the investment industry uses price and volume charts to make investment timing decisions. Technical analysis has a large following and its own vocabulary of patterns and trends (resistance, support, breakout, momentum, etc.). If the market is at least weak-form efficient, then prices already reflect this information and these activities would not result in useful predictions about future price changes, and thus would be a waste of time. Indeed, the people who make the most money from price charting services are the people who sell the services, not the investors who buy and use those services.

The *semistrong-form* efficiency level assumes that stock prices include all public information. Notice that past stock prices and volumes are publicly available information, so this level includes the weak form as a subset. Important investment implications arise if markets are efficient to public information. Many investors conduct security analysis in which they obtain financial data and other public information to assess whether a company's stock is undervalued or overvalued. But in a semistrong-form efficient market, stock prices already reflect this information and are thus "correct." Using only public information, you would not be able to determine whether a stock is misvalued because that information is already reflected in the price.

If prices reflect all public information, then those prices will react as traders hear new (or private) information. Consider a company that announces surprisingly good quarterly profits. Traders and investors will have factored the old profit expectations into the stock price. As they incorporate the new information, the stock price will quickly rise to a new and accurate price as shown in the solid black line in Figure 10.3. Note that the stock price was $35 before the announcement and $40 immediately following. If you tried to buy the stock after hearing the news, then you would have bought at $40 and not received any benefit of the good quarterly profit news. On the other hand, if the market is not semistrong-form efficient, then the price might react quickly, but not accurately. The dashed green line shows a reaction in a non-semistrong efficient market where the price continues to drift up well after the announcement. This gradual drift to the "correct" price indicates that the

market initially underreacted to the news. In this case, you could have bought the stock after the announcement and still earned a profit. The dotted blue line shows an overreaction to the firm's better-than-expected profits announcement. If markets consistently either underreact or consistently overreact to announcements that would change stock prices (earnings, stock split, dividend, etc.), then we would believe that the market is not semistrong efficient.

The *strong-form* market efficiency level presents the highest hurdle to test market reaction to information. The strong-form level includes information considered by the weak-form, the semistrong-form, as well as privately known information. People within firms, like CEOs and CFOs, know information that has not yet been released to the public. They may trade on this privately held, or insider, information and their trading may cause stock prices to change as it reflects that private information. In this way, stock prices could reflect even privately known information. Note that the firm managers, accountants, and auditors know several days in advance that a firm has earned unexpectedly high quarterly profits. If the stock price already incorporated this closely held private knowledge, then the big price reaction shown in Figure 10.3 would not occur.

▼**FIGURE 10.3**
Potential Price Reaction to a Good News Announcement

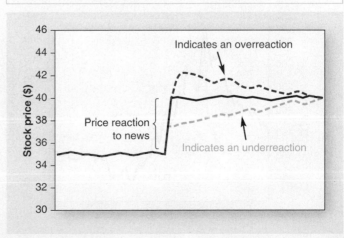

So, is the stock market efficient? If it is, at what level? This has been a hotly debated topic for decades and continues to be. It is not likely that the market is strong-form efficient. Since insider trading is punished, insider information must be valuable. However, much evidence suggests that the market could be weak-form or semistrong-form efficient. Of course, we also have evidence that the market is not efficient at any of the three levels.

Behavioral Finance

The argument for the market being efficient works as follows: Many individual and professional investors constantly look for mispriced stocks. If they find a stock that is undervalued, they will buy it and drive up its price until it's correctly priced. Likewise, investors would sell an overpriced stock, driving down its price until it's correctly valued. With so many investors looking for market "mistakes," it's unlikely that any mispriced stock opportunities will be left in the market.

The argument against the market being efficient is equally convincing. The market comprises many people transacting with

finance at work //: markets

Bubble Trouble

Many professionals criticize the EMH because the overall market sometimes seems too high or too low. A very dramatic example of the market level being artificially high is the market bubble. During a market bubble, the market quickly inflates on rampant speculation and subsequently crashes. Investors who buy near the peak of the bubble risk losing nearly all their investment.

One of the United States' earliest stock market bubbles was the bubble and crash of 1929. Note from the figure that the DJIA started in 1927 at around 160. By October 1929, the DJIA had reached nearly 400 and then crashed. By mid-1932, the DJIA had fallen to the 40s. The sustained fall coincided with an economic depression. Panel A of the figure also shows a price bubble in gold. The price of gold was $230 per ounce in January 1979. The late 1970s and early 1980s saw double-digit inflation throughout the economy, and many investors felt that gold represented a safe and inflation-proof investment. Just one year later, the price

had skyrocketed to $870. It then fell below $300 in less than two and a half years.

See the spectacular tech bubble during the 1990s? The NASDAQ 100, which started in 1985 at 250, soared to a peak of 4,816.35 on March 24, 2000. It then fell to less than 1,000 in two and a half years. The rise and fall of the NASDAQ 100 seems much more pronounced than the Japanese stock bubble of the 1980s. From a January 2, 1985, start at 11,543, the Nikkei 225 soared to a closing high of 38,916 on December 29, 1989. The bubble then burst and the Japanese stock market plummeted. The Nikkei has yet to fully recover, trading today at around the 16,500 level.

EMH critics do not believe that the entire stock market, or a substantial segment of it, can be correctly valued before, during, or after a bubble. It certainly appears to be overvalued during the time the bubble is inflating.

Want to know more?

Key Words to Search for Updates: **stock bubble, irrational exuberance**

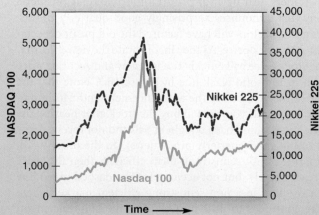

The technology sector fell victim to a stock market bubble in 2000.

> **Whenever a set of stock prices goes unnaturally high and subsequently crashes down, the market experiences what we call a stock market bubble.**

one another. When someone makes trading decisions influenced by emotion or psychological bias, those decisions may not seem rational. When many people fall under such influences, their trading decisions may actually drive stock prices away from the correct price as emotion carries the traders away from rationality. For example, many people believe that investors were "irrationally exuberant" about technology stocks in the late 1990s—and that their buying excitement drove prices to an artificially high level. In 2000, the excitement wore off and tech stock prices plummeted. Whenever a set of stock prices go unnaturally high and subsequently crash down, the market experiences what we call a **stock market bubble.**

In the past couple of decades, finance researchers have studied **behavioral finance** and found that people often behave in ways that are very likely "irrational." At times, investors appear to be too optimistic, as though they are looking through rose-colored glasses. At other times they appear to be too pessimistic. Common investment decisions aren't necessarily optimal ones, which flies in the face of the economist's expectation of rational economic actors. Perhaps, then, capital markets don't

represent perfectly competitive or efficient markets if buyers and sellers do not always make rational choices.

time out!

10-5 Can the market be semistrong-form efficient but not weak-form efficient? Explain.

10-6 If the market usually overreacts to bad news announcements, what would your return be like if you bought after you heard the bad news?

IMPLICATIONS FOR FINANCIAL MANAGERS

Financial managers must understand the crucial relationship between risk and return for several reasons. First, while the relationship between risk and return is demonstrated here using the capital markets, it equally applies to many business decisions. A firm's product mix, marketing campaign combination, and research and development programs all entail risk and potential rewards. Being able to understand and characterize these decisions within a risk and return framework can help managers make better decisions. In addition, managers must understand what return their stockholders require at various times of firm operations. After all, a firm must receive enough revenue from its variously risky activities to pay its business costs, debt costs, and reward the owners (the stockholders). Managers must thus include the return to shareholders when they analyze new business opportunities.

Firms and capital markets also interact directly. For example, a good understanding of market efficiency helps managers understand how their stock prices will react to different types of decisions (like dividend changes) and news announcements (like unexpectedly high or low profitability). In fact, many managers own company stock and are thus compensated through programs that rely on the stock price, like **restricted stock** and **executive stock options.** Companies also periodically issue (sell) additional shares of stock to raise more capital, and these sales depend upon market efficiency assumptions. The firm would not want to sell additional shares if the stock price is too low (i.e., undervalued). They *would* want to sell more shares at any time that they thought their shares are overvalued. Other times, firms repurchase (buy back) shares of stock. The firm might want to do this if its shares were undervalued, but not if its shares were overvalued. Of course, valuation is not an issue if security markets are efficient.

Using the Constant Growth Model for Required Return

For decades, financial managers have used the CAPM to compute shareholders' required return. Given recent concerns about beta's limitations, many see the CAPM as a less useful model for calculating appropriate returns. Some have turned instead to another model useful for computing required return—the constant growth rate model discussed in Chapter 7. We can arrange the terms of that model as:

$$i = \frac{D_1}{P_0} + g = \text{Dividend yield} + \text{Constant growth} \quad (10\text{-}6)$$

Of course, this model assumes that the stock is efficiently priced. This model holds an advantage in that it uses current firm data (dividend, D, and price, P_0) and a simple forward estimate (growth, g) to assess what investors currently expect the stock to return, i. For example, Table 10.2 shows Walmart's beta as 0.05. Using this beta, Table 10.3 shows that shareholders require only 5.4 percent return to hold Walmart stock, given its low risk profile. You may find it hard to believe that Walmart's owners (the shareholders) expect such a low return from one of the world's most profitable firms. So perhaps this is a case in which the CAPM result isn't very useful. Applying the constant-growth model looks something like this: Walmart is expected to pay a $1 dividend this year and say the stock price currently stands at $48 per share. Financial analysts believe Walmart will grow at 12 percent per year for the next five years. The constant growth rate model suggests that Walmart shareholders expect a 14.1 percent [= ($1 ÷ $48) + 0.12] return. So, which required return seems more likely, the 5.4 percent computed from CAPM or the 14.1 percent suggested by the constant growth rate model? Since Walmart shareholders have enjoyed an average annual return of 15.8 percent per year for the past 10 years, the constant growth rate estimate looks better and more accurate.

Financial managers need an estimate of their shareholders' required return in order to make appropriate decisions about their companies' future growth. Good financial managers will compute shareholders' required return using as many methods as they can to determine the most realistic value possible. ■

time out!

10-7 Why is the shareholders' required return important to corporate managers?

Required Return

Note from Table 10.3 that the required returns for 3M, Home Depot, and Intel are 10.2 percent, 12.6 percent, and 15.1 percent, respectively. These expectations may seem quite far apart, considering that all three firms are in the DJIA and are leaders in their market sectors. Use the following information to compute the constant growth rate model estimate of the required return:

	Expected Dividend	Current Price	Analyst Growth Estimate
3M Company	$2.00	$75.40	10.9%
Home Depot	0.90	26.30	12.3
Intel	0.50	19.00	17.0

SOLUTION:
You can now use equation 10-6 to find each company's required return as:

$$\text{3M required return} = (\$2.00 \div \$75.40) + 0.109 = 13.6\%$$

$$\text{Home Depot required return} = (\$0.90 \div \$26.30) + 0.123 = 15.7\%$$

$$\text{Intel required return} = (\$0.50 \div \$19.00) + 0.170 = 19.6\%$$

Note that the constant growth rate model estimates are 2 to 5 percent higher than the CAPM estimates. When the CAPM estimate seems too high or too low, it's a good idea to check the constant growth rate model estimate.

Get Online

mhhe.com/canM

for study materials including
quizzes, iPod downloads,
and video

Your Turn...

Questions

1. Consider an asset that provides the same return no matter what economic state occurs. What would be the standard deviation (or risk) of this asset? Explain. *(LG1)*

2. Why is expected return considered "forward-looking"? What are the challenges for practitioners to utilize expected return? *(LG1)*

3. In 2000, the S&P 500 Index earned −9.1 percent while the T-bill yield was 5.9 percent. Does this mean the market risk premium was negative? Explain. *(LG2)*

4. How might the magnitude of the market risk premium impact people's desire to buy stocks? *(LG2)*

5. Describe how adding a risk-free security to modern portfolio theory allows investors to do better than the efficient frontier. *(LG3)*

6. Show on a graph like Figure 10.2 where a stock with a beta of 1.3 would be located on the security market line. Then show where that stock would be located if it is undervalued. *(LG3)*

7. Consider that you have three stocks in your portfolio and wish to add a fourth. You want to know if the fourth stock will make the portfolio riskier or less risky. Compare and contrast how this would be assessed using standard deviation versus market risk (beta) as the measure of risk. *(LG3)*

8. Describe how different allocations between the risk-free security and the market portfolio can achieve any level of market risk desired. Give examples of a portfolio from a person who is very risk averse and a portfolio for someone who is not so averse to taking risk. *(LG3)*

9. Cisco Systems has a beta of 1.88. Does this mean that you should expect Cisco to earn a return 88 percent higher than the S&P 500 Index return? Explain. *(LG4)*

10. Note from Table 10.2 that some technology-oriented firms (Intel and IBM) in the Dow Jones Industrial Average have high market risk while others (AT&T, Microsoft, and Verizon) have low market risk. How do you explain this? *(LG4)*

11. Find a beta estimate from three different sources for General Electric (GE). Compare these three values. Why might they be different? *(LG4)*

12. If you were to compute beta yourself, what choices would you make regarding the market portfolio, the holding period for the returns (daily, weekly, etc.), and the number of returns? Justify your choices. *(LG4)*

13. Explain how the concept of a positive risk-return relationship breaks down if you can systematically find stocks that are overvalued and undervalued. *(LG5)*

14. Determine what level of market efficiency each event is consistent with:

    a. Immediately after an earnings announcement the stock price jumps and then stays at the new level. *(LG5)*

    b. The CEO buys 50,000 shares of his company and the stock price does not change. *(LG5)*

    c. The stock price immediately jumps when a stock split is announced, but then retraces half of the gain over the next day. *(LG5)*

    d. An investor analyzes company quarterly and annual balance sheets and income statements looking for undervalued stocks. The investor earns about the same return as the S&P 500 Index. *(LG5)*

15. Why do most investment scams conducted over the Internet and e-mail involve penny stocks instead of S&P 500 Index stocks? *(LG5)*

16. Describe a stock market bubble. Can a bubble occur in a single stock? *(LG5)*

17. If stock prices are not strong-form efficient, then what might be the price reaction to a firm announcing a stock buyback? Explain. *(LG6)*

18. Compare and contrast the assumptions that need to be made to compute a required return using CAPM and the constant growth rate model. *(LG7)*

19. How should you handle a case where required return computations from CAPM and the constant growth rate model are very different? *(LG7)*

Problems

BASIC PROBLEMS

10-1 Expected Return Compute the expected return given these three economic states, their likelihoods, and the potential returns: *(LG1)*

Economic State	Probability	Return
Fast growth	0.3	40%
Slow growth	0.5	10
Recession	0.2	−25

10-2 Expected Return Compute the expected return given these three economic states, their likelihoods, and the potential returns: *(LG1)*

Economic State	Probability	Return
Fast growth	0.2	35%
Slow growth	0.6	10
Recession	0.2	−30

10-3 Required Return If the risk-free rate is 6 percent and the risk premium is 5 percent, what is the required return? *(LG2)*

10-4 Required Return If the risk-free rate is 3 percent and the risk premium is 7 percent, what is the required return? *(LG2)*

10-5 Risk Premium The average annual return on the S&P 500 Index from 1986 to 1995 was 15.8 percent. The average annual T-bill yield during the same period was 5.6 percent. What was the market risk premium during these 10 years? *(LG2)*

10-6 Risk Premium The average annual return on the S&P 500 Index from 1996 to 2005 was 10.8 percent. The average annual T-bill yield during the same period was 3.6 percent. What was the market risk premium during these 10 years? *(LG2)*

10-7 CAPM Required Return Hastings Entertainment has a beta of 0.24. If the market return is expected to be 11 percent and the risk-free rate is 4 percent, what is Hastings' required return? *(LG3)*

10-8 CAPM Required Return Nanometrics Inc. has a beta of 4.05. If the market return is expected to be 12 percent and the risk-free rate is 4.5 percent, what is Nanometrics' required return? *(LG3)*

10-9 Company Risk Premium Netflix, Inc. has a beta of 3.61. If the market return is expected to be 13 percent and the risk-free rate is 6 percent, what is Netflix' risk premium? *(LG3)*

10-10 Company Risk Premium Paycheck Inc. has a beta of 0.94. If the market return is expected to be 11 percent and the risk-free rate is 3 percent, what is Paycheck's risk premium? *(LG3)*

10-11 Portfolio Beta You have a portfolio with a beta of 1.2. What will be the new portfolio beta if you keep 90 percent of your money in the old portfolio and 10 percent in a stock with a beta of 1.9? *(LG3)*

10-12 Portfolio Beta You have a portfolio with a beta of 1.1. What will be the new portfolio beta if you keep 85 percent of your money in the old portfolio and 15 percent in a stock with a beta of 0.5? *(LG3)*

10-13 Stock Market Bubble The NASDAQ stock market bubble peaked at 4,816 in 2000. Two and a half years later it had fallen to 1,000. What was the percentage decline? *(LG5)*

10-14 Stock Market Bubble The Japanese stock market bubble peaked at 38,916 in 1989. Two and a half years later it had fallen to 15,900. What was the percentage decline? *(LG5)*

10-15 Required Return Paccar's current stock price is $73.10 and it is likely to pay a $2.69 dividend next year. Since analysts estimate Paccar will have a 11.2 percent growth rate, what is its required return? *(LG7)*

10-16 Required Return Universal Forest's current stock price is $54.00 and it is likely to pay a $0.23 dividend next year. Since analysts estimate Universal Forest will have a 10.0 percent growth rate, what is its required return? *(LG7)*

INTERMEDIATE PROBLEMS

10-17 Expected Return Risk For the same economic state probability distribution as in problem 10-1, determine the standard deviation of the expected return. *(LG1)*

Economic State	Probability	Return
Fast growth	0.3	40%
Slow growth	0.5	10
Recession	0.2	−25

10-18 Expected Return Risk For the same economic state probability distribution as in problem 10-2, determine the standard deviation of the expected return. *(LG1)*

Economic State	Probability	Return
Fast growth	0.2	35%
Slow growth	0.6	10
Recession	0.2	−30

10-19 Under-/Overvalued Stock A manager believes his firm will earn a 14 percent return next year. His firm has a beta of 1.5, the expected return on the market is 12 percent, and the risk-free rate is 4 percent. Compute the return the firm should earn given its level of risk and determine whether the manager is saying the firm is undervalued or overvalued. *(LG3)*

10-20 Under-/Overvalued Stock A manager believes his firm will earn a 14 percent return next year. His firm has a beta of 1.2, the expected return on the market is 11 percent, and the risk-free rate is 5 percent. Compute the return the firm should earn given its level of risk and determine whether the manager is saying the firm is undervalued or overvalued. *(LG3)*

10-21 Portfolio Beta You own $5,000 of Olympic Steel stock that has a beta of 2.9. You also own $7,000 of Rent-a-Center (beta = 1.5) and $8,000 of Lincoln Educational (beta = 0.2). What is the beta of your portfolio? *(LG3)*

10-22 Portfolio Beta You own $7,000 of Human Genome stock that has a beta of 3.5. You also own $8,000 of Frozen Food Express (beta = 1.6) and $10,000 of Molecular Devices (beta = 0.4). What is the beta of your portfolio? *(LG3)*

ADVANCED PROBLEMS

10-23 Expected Return and Risk Compute the expected return and standard deviation given these four economic states, their likelihoods, and the potential returns: *(LG1)*

Economic State	Probability	Return
Fast growth	0.30	60%
Slow growth	0.50	13
Recession	0.15	−15
Depression	0.05	−45

10-24 Expected Return and Risk Compute the expected return and standard deviation given these four economic states, their likelihoods, and the potential returns: *(LG1)*

Economic State	Probability	Return
Fast growth	0.25	50%
Slow growth	0.55	11
Recession	0.15	−15
Depression	0.05	−50

10-25 Risk Premiums You own $10,000 of Denny's Corp stock that has a beta of 2.9. You also own $15,000 of Qwest Communications (beta = 1.5) and $15,000 of Southwest Airlines (beta = 0.4). Assume that the market return will be 13 percent and the risk-free rate is 5.5 percent. What is the market risk premium? What is the risk premium of each stock? What is the risk premium of the portfolio? *(LG3)*

10-26 Risk Premiums You own $15,000 of Opsware Inc. stock that has a beta of 3.8. You also own $10,000 of Lowe's Companies (beta = 1.6) and $10,000 of New York Times (beta = 0.8). Assume that the market return will be 12 percent and the risk-free rate is 6 percent. What is the market risk premium? What is the risk premium of each stock? What is the risk premium of the portfolio? *(LG3)*

10-27 Portfolio Beta and Required Return You hold the positions in the table below. What is the beta of your portfolio? If you expect the market to earn 12 percent and the risk-free rate is 3.5 percent, what is the required return of the portfolio? *(LG3)*

	Price	Shares	Beta
Amazon.com	$40.80	100	3.8
Family Dollar Stores	30.10	150	1.2
McKesson Corp	57.40	75	0.4
Schering-Plough Corp	23.80	200	0.5

10-28 Portfolio Beta and Required Return You hold the positions in the table below. What is the beta of your portfolio? If you expect the market to earn 12 percent and the risk-free rate is 3.5 percent, what is the required return of the portfolio? *(LG3)*

	Price	Shares	Beta
Advanced Micro Devices	$ 14.70	200	4.2
FedEx Corp	120.00	50	1.1
Microsoft	28.90	150	0.7
Sara Lee Corp	17.25	200	0.5

10-29 Required Return Using the information in the table, compute the required return for each company using both CAPM and the constant-growth model. Compare and discuss the results. Assume that the market portfolio will earn 12 percent and the risk-free rate is 3.5 percent. *(LG3, LG7)*

	Price	Upcoming Dividend	Growth	Beta
US Bancorp	$36.55	$1.60	10.0%	0.8
Praxair	64.75	1.12	11.0	0.7
Eastman Kodak	24.95	1.00	4.5	2.0

10-30 Required Return Using the information in the table, compute the required return for each company using both CAPM and the constant-growth model. Compare and discuss the results. Assume that the market portfolio will earn 11 percent and the risk-free rate is 4 percent. *(LG3, LG7)*

	Price	Upcoming Dividend	Growth	Beta
Estee Lauder	$47.40	$0.60	11.7%	0.75
Kimco Realty	52.10	1.54	8.0	1.3
Nordstrom	5.25	0.50	14.6	2.2

10-31 Excel Problem As discussed in the text, beta estimates for one firm will vary depending on various factors such as the time over which the estimation is conducted, the market portfolio proxy, and the return intervals. You will demonstrate this variation using returns for Microsoft.

a. Using all 45 monthly returns for Microsoft and the three stock market indices, compute Microsoft's beta using the S&P 500 Index as the market proxy. Then compute the beta using the DJIA and the NASDAQ indices as the market portfolio proxy. Compare the three beta estimates.

b. Now estimate the beta using only the most recent 30 monthly returns and the S&P 500 Index. Compare the beta estimate to the estimate in part A when using the S&P 500 Index and all 45 monthly returns.

Date	MSFT	S&P 500	DJIA	NASDAQ	Date	MSFT	S&P 500	DJIA	NASDAQ
Jun 2007	4.45%	3.07%	4.04%	4.19%	Jul 2005	7.22%	−1.12%	−1.50%	−1.50%
May 2007	−3.98	−1.78	−1.61	−0.05	Jun 2005	3.10	3.60	3.56	6.22
Apr 2007	2.85	3.25	4.32	3.15	May 2005	−3.70	−0.01	−1.84	−0.54
Mar 2007	7.42	4.33	5.74	4.27	Apr 2005	2.28	3.00	2.70	7.63
Feb 2007	−1.07	1.00	0.70	0.23	Mar 2005	4.69	−2.01	−2.96	−3.88
Jan 2007	−8.38	−2.18	−2.80	−1.94	Feb 2005	−3.93	−1.91	−2.44	−2.56
Dec 2006	3.34	1.41	1.27	2.01	Jan 2005	−3.97	1.89	2.63	−0.52
Nov 2006	1.71	1.26	1.97	−0.68	Dec 2004	−1.66	−2.53	−2.72	−5.20
Oct 2006	2.60	1.65	1.17	2.75	Nov 2004	−0.31	3.25	3.40	3.75
Sep 2006	4.99	3.15	3.44	4.79	Oct 2004	6.80	3.86	3.99	6.17
Aug 2006	6.41	2.46	2.62	3.42	Sep 2004	1.17	1.40	−0.52	4.12
Jul 2006	7.21	2.13	1.75	4.41	Aug 2004	1.31	0.94	−0.92	3.20
Jun 2006	3.26	0.51	0.32	−3.71	Jul 2004	−3.89	0.23	0.34	−2.61
May 2006	2.86	0.01	−0.16	−0.31	Jun 2004	−0.28	−3.43	−2.83	−7.83
Apr 2006	−5.86	−3.09	−1.75	−6.19	May 2004	8.90	1.80	2.42	3.07
Mar 2006	−11.22	1.22	2.32	−0.74	Apr 2004	0.40	1.21	−0.36	3.47
Feb 2006	1.25	1.11	1.05	2.56	Mar 2004	4.82	−1.68	−1.28	−3.71
Jan 2006	−4.21	0.05	1.18	−1.06	Feb 2004	−6.05	−1.64	−2.14	−1.75
Dec 2005	7.61	2.55	1.37	4.56	Jan 2004	−4.05	1.22	0.91	−1.76
Nov 2005	−5.50	−0.10	−0.82	−1.23	Dec 2003	1.01	1.73	0.33	3.13
Oct 2005	8.01	3.52	3.50	5.31	Nov 2003	6.47	5.08	6.86	2.20
Sep 2005	−0.12	−1.77	−1.22	−1.46	Oct 2003	−1.64	0.71	−0.19	1.45
Aug 2005	−6.02	0.69	0.83	−0.02					

c. Estimate Microsoft's beta using the quarterly data returns below. Compare the estimate to the ones from parts (a) and (b).

Date	MSFT	S&P 500
Q2 2007	3.15%	4.53%
Q1 2007	−2.64	3.07
Q4 2006	7.85	4.38
Q3 2006	19.76	7.93
Q2 2006	0.00	−2.59
Q1 2006	−13.90	2.39
Q4 2005	9.84	6.05
Q3 2005	0.64	−2.20
Q2 2005	1.55	6.68
Q1 2005	−3.42	−2.07
Q4 2004	4.70	4.52
Q3 2004	−1.50	2.59
Q2 2004	9.02	−0.50
Q1 2004	−5.52	−2.11
Q4 2003	5.79	7.65

chapter eleven

calculating the cost of capital

In the previous two chapters, we discussed investors' required return given a particular risk profile. In this chapter, we examine the question from the firm's point of view: How much must the firm pay to finance its operations and expansions using debt and equity sources? Firms use a combination of debt and equity sources to fund their operations, projects, and any expansions they may undertake. In Chapter 14, we'll explore the factors that managers consider as they choose the optimal capital structure mix. For now, we'll assume that management has chosen the optimal mix for us, and that it's our job to implement it.

As we've seen in previous chapters, investors face different kinds of risks associated with debt, preferred stock, and equity. As a result, their required rates of return for each debt or equity source differ as well. So as the firm uses a combination of different financing sources, we must calculate the investors' average required rate of return. Since firms seldom use equal amounts of debt and equity capital sources, we will need to calculate a *weighted* average, with weights based on the proportion of debt and equity capital used.

One important point about the **component costs** to be used in the firm's computation of the average required rate of return is that dividends paid to either common or preferred stockholders are not tax deductible. Thus paying a certain interest rate to either costs the firm that same interest rate. On the other hand, interest paid to debt holders *is* tax deductible, implying that the firm's effective after-tax out-of-pocket interest

continued on p. 254

LEARNING GOALS

LG1 Grasp the basic intuition behind calculating the cost of capital and its relationship to the investor's required return.

LG2 Use the weighted-average cost of capital (WACC) formula to calculate a project's cost of capital.

LG3 Debate the firm's choices in estimating the appropriate capital component costs of equity, preferred stock, and debt.

LG4 Calculate and justify appropriate weights used for WACC projections.

LG5 Clarify which parts of a firmwide WACC can be used in calculating a project-specific WACC and which parts do not apply.

LG6 Note the trade-offs implicit in using either a firmwide WACC or a divisional cost of capital approach.

LG7 Differentiate between the objective and subjective approaches to computing a divisional cost of capital.

LG8 Determine the impact that flotation costs have on capital budgeting decisions and adjust the WACC to reflect flotation costs.

continued from p. 253

cost will be equal to the interest rate paid on debt multiplied by one minus the firm's relevant tax rate.

For example, if a firm pays a 10 percent coupon on $1 million in debt while it is subject to a 35 percent tax rate, then each coupon payment will be equal to .10 × $1,000,000 = $100,000, but that $100,000 in interest, being tax deductible, will reduce the firm's tax bill by .35 × $100,000 = $35,000. So paying $100,000 in interest saves the firm $35,000 in taxes, making the effective after-tax cost of debt equal to $100,000 × $35,000 = $65,000 and the effective after-tax interest rate equal to 10% × (1 − 35%) = 6.5%. ■

THE WACC FORMULA

The average cost per dollar of capital raised is called the **weighted-average cost of capital (WACC).** We calculate WACC using equation (11-1):

$$\text{WACC} = \frac{E}{E+P+D}i_E + \frac{P}{E+P+D}i_P$$
$$+ \frac{D}{E+P+D}i_D \times (1 - T_C) \qquad (11\text{-}1)$$

where

E = the market value of equity used in financing the relevant project or firm.

P = the market value of preferred stock used.

D = the market value of debt used.

i_E = the after-tax cost of equity.

i_P = the after-tax cost of preferred stock.

i_D = the before-tax cost of debt.

T_C = the appropriate corporate tax rate.

Notice that we use weights based on market values rather than book values because market values reflect investors' assessment of what they would be willing to pay for the various types of securities.

Calculating the Component Cost of Equity

We could calculate i_E using the capital asset pricing model:

$$i_E = i_f + \beta_E[E(i_M) - i_f] \qquad (11\text{-}2)$$

viewpoints

business APPLICATION

MP3 Devices, Inc. is about to launch a new project to create and market a combination MP3 player/video projector. The new project will be funded with 40 percent debt, 10 percent preferred stock, and 50 percent common stock. MP3 Devices currently has 10 million shares of common stock outstanding, selling at $18.75 per share, and expects to pay an annual dividend of $1.35 one year from now, after which future dividends are expected to grow at a constant 6 percent rate. MP3's debt consists of 20-year, 10 percent annual coupon bonds with a face value of $150 million and a market value of $165 million. The company's capital mix also includes 100,000 shares of 10 percent preferred stock selling at par. If MP3 Devices faces a marginal tax rate of 34 percent, what weighted-average cost of capital should it use as it evaluates this project?

Or we can assume that the equity in question is a constant-growth stock such as the ones we modeled in Chapter 8. Under this assumption, we can solve the constant-growth model for i_E:

$$i_E = \frac{D_1}{P_0} + g \qquad (11\text{-}3)$$

Which way is better? Well, theoretically, they should both give us the same answer, but some pragmatic reasons may dictate why we may prefer one method over the other, depending on the particular situation.

To the extent that β_E estimates *future* systematic risk, but we calculate it based on *historic* systematic risk, we obviously won't want to use the CAPM in situations in which we either don't have sufficient historic observations to estimate β_E (i.e., when the stock is fairly new), or when we suspect that the past level of the stock's systematic (or market) risk might not be a good indicator of the future. On the other hand, the constant-growth model is only going to be appropriate for the limited number of stocks that just happen to expect constant dividend growth. We can try to adjust the model to use it for those stocks without constant dividend growth, but doing so will tend to introduce potentially sizable errors. Remember that our mathematical results are only as good as their underlying assumptions and data. Under CAPM, we may have a data problem; under the constant-growth model, our assumptions may not hold.

personal APPLICATION

Mackenzie is currently finishing up her B.S. degree and is considering going back to grad school for a master's. She currently has $17,125 in student loans carrying an 8 percent interest rate from her B.S. and estimates that she will need to take out an additional $29,000 in student loans (at the same interest rate) to make it through the master's program she'd like to attend. The IRS allows taxpayers with student loans to deduct the interest on those loans, but only up to a maximum amount of $2,500 per year. Assuming that Mackenzie will face a marginal personal tax rate of 25 percent when she graduates, what will be the average after-tax interest rate that she will be paying on the student loans immediately after she graduates with her master's?

Overall, we should expect that the CAPM approach to estimating i_E will apply more accurately in most cases. However, if you do encounter a situation in which the

constant-growth model applies, then you can certainly use it. If we are really fortunate and happen to have enough information to use both approaches, then we should probably *use* both, taking an average of the resulting estimates of i_E.[1]

Calculating the Component Cost of Preferred Stock

As we discussed in Chapter 8, preferred stock represents a special case of the constant-growth model, wherein g equals zero. So we can estimate preferred stocks' component cost using a simplified version of equation 11-3:

$$i_P = \frac{D_1}{P_0} \qquad (11\text{-}4)$$

> **component costs** The individual costs of each type of capital—bonds, preferred stock, and common stock.
>
> **weighted-average cost of capital (WACC)** The weighted average after-tax cost of the capital used by a firm, with weights set equal to the relative percentage of each type of capital used.

[1]Think of taking such an average as being intuitively the same as diversifying our "portfolio" of data across the two different estimation techniques, thereby reducing the average amount of estimation error.

EXAMPLE 11-1

For interactive versions of this example visit www.mhhe.com/canM

Cost of Equity

ADK Industries' common shares sell for $32.75 per share. ADK expects to set their next annual dividend at $1.54 per share. If ADK expects future dividends to grow by 6 percent per year, indefinitely, the current risk-free rate is 3 percent, the expected return on the market is 9 percent, and the stock has a beta of 1.3, what should be the firm's cost of equity?

SOLUTION:

The cost of equity using the CAPM will be

$$i_E = i_f + \beta_E[E(i_M) - i_f]$$

$$= .03 + 1.3[.09 - .03]$$

$$= .1080, \text{ or } 10.80\%$$

The cost of equity using the constant-growth model will be

$$i_E = \frac{D_1}{P_0} + g$$

$$= \frac{\$1.54}{\$32.75} + .06$$

$$= .1070, \text{ or } 10.70\%$$

Our best estimate of ADK's equity would therefore be $\frac{10.70\% + 10.80\%}{2} = 10.75\%$.

EXAMPLE 11-2

Cost of Preferred Stock

Suppose that ADK also has 1 million shares of 7 percent preferred stock outstanding, trading at $72 per share. What is ADK's component cost for preferred equity?

SOLUTION:

The cost of the preferred stock will equal

$$i_P = \frac{D_1}{P_0}$$

$$= \frac{\$7}{\$72}$$

$$= .0972, \text{ or } 9.72\%$$

Calculating the Component Cost of Debt

Because of the tax deductibility of debt for the firm, computing the component cost of debt, unlike computing the component costs of equity and preferred stock, actually has two parts. We must estimate the before-tax cost of debt, i_D, and then adjust this figure to convert it to the post-tax residual rate of return.

To estimate i_D, we need to solve for the yield to maturity (YTM) on the firm's existing debt:

$$\text{Solve}\left\{ PV = PMT \times \left[\frac{1 - \frac{1}{(1 + i_D)^N}}{i_D} \right] + \frac{PV}{(1 + i_D)^N} \right\} \text{ for } i_D$$

(11-5)

Then we adjust this result by multiplying by $(1 - T_C)$.

EXAMPLE 11-3

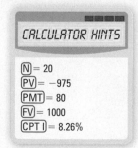

CALCULATOR HINTS

$\boxed{N} = 20$
$\boxed{PV} = -975$
$\boxed{PMT} = 80$
$\boxed{FV} = 1000$
$\boxed{CPT\ I} = 8.26\%$

Cost of Debt

ADK has 30,000 20-year, 8 percent annual coupon bonds outstanding. If the bonds currently sell for 97.5 percent of par and the firm pays an average tax rate of 35.92 percent, what will be the before-tax and after-tax component costs for debt?

SOLUTION:

The before-tax cost of debt will be the solution to

$$\text{Solve}\left\{ \$975 = \$80 \times \left[\frac{1 - \frac{1}{(1 + i_D)^{20}}}{i_D} \right] + \frac{\$1000}{(1 + i_D)^{20}} \right\} \text{ for } i_D$$

which will equal 8.26 percent. Multiplying this by one minus the tax rate will yield the after-tax cost of debt: 8.26% × (1 − .3592) = 5.2930%.

Choosing the Appropriate Tax Rate for the WACC

The interest paid on debt is tax deductible, but the benefit of that tax deductibility will vary based on the firm's marginal tax rate. The appropriate tax rate to be used in the WACC will be the weighted average of the marginal tax rates that would have been paid on the taxable income shielded by the interest deduction.

For example, if a firm had earnings before interest and taxes (EBIT) of $400,000, taxable interest deductions of $100,000, and faced the corporate tax schedule shown in Table 11.1, then the appropriate tax rate would equal a weighted average of the marginal tax rates from the fourth (i.e., "39 percent") and fifth ("34 percent") tax brackets. The weights would be determined by the relative impacts of the brackets in the computation of the post-interest tax bill:

$$\frac{\$35,000}{\$100,000} \times 39\% + \frac{\$65,000}{\$100,000} \times 34\% = 35.75\%$$

Calculating the Weights

When we calculate weights for WACC, we want to ensure that we use relevant market values of equity, preferred stock, and debt. If we're calculating WACC for a firm, then E, P, and D would be the entire market value of each source of capital; if we're calculating WACC for a project, then we would set them equal to the amount of each type used for that particular project.[2]

▼ **TABLE 11.1** Corporate Tax Rates

Taxable Income			Tax Rate
$0	–	$50,000	15%
50,001	–	75,000	25
75,001	–	100,000	34
100,001	–	335,000	39
335,001	–	10,000,000	34
10,000,001	–	15,000,000	35
15,000,001	–	18,333,333	38
18,333,334	+		35

[2]We'll discuss more about calculating WACC for a project later in the chapter.

time out!

11-1 Explain why we multiply the component cost of debt by the marginal tax rate, T_D, but don't do so for the component costs of equity or preferred stock.

11-2 How would we compute i_D if a company had multiple bond issues outstanding?

FIRM WACC VERSUS PROJECT WACC

So far, we've been defining the WACC as a weighted-average cost across the firm's different financing sources. If we think of a firm as a portfolio of different projects and products, we can also see that the WACC will be a weighted-average cost of capital across the items in that portfolio, too, and will therefore represent the cost of capital for the "typical" project that the firm is currently undertaking. So now the question we need to address is whether our firmwide WACC, calculated above, will also be appropriate to use as management evaluates new proposed projects.

The answer is: It depends. If a new project is similar enough to existing projects, then yes, the firm's WACC can be used as the project's WACC, too. But say that a firm is contemplating undertaking a significantly different project—one far different from any project that the firm is already engaged in. Then we *cannot expect* the firm's overall WACC to appropriately measure the new project's cost of capital. Let your intuition work on this: If the new project is riskier than the firm's existing projects, then it should expect to be "charged" a *higher* cost of capital. If it's safer, then the firm should assign the new project a *lower* cost of capital.

For example, consider a U.S. firm—let's call it GassUp—that currently owns a chain of gas stations. Firm management is considering a new project: opening up a series of gourmet coffee shops. Given the demand for upscale coffee in the United States, as well as the historically volatile oil markets, it's probably difficult to say exactly whether the coffee shops will

Tax Rate

Suppose that ADK expects EBIT to be approximately $20,000,000 per year for the foreseeable future. Given the 30,000 20-year, 8 percent annual coupon bonds discussed in the previous example, what would the appropriate tax rate be for use in the calculation of the debt component of ADK's WACC?

SOLUTION:

The interest payments on the bonds would total $30,000 \times \$1,000 \times .08 = \$2,400,000$ per year, resulting in earnings before tax (EBT) of $\$20,000,000 - \$2,400,000 = \$17,600,000$.

As taxable income falls from $20,000,000 to $17,600,000 after the firm pays the interest on the bonds, $1,666,667, or 69.44 percent, of the $2,400,000 reduction would fall in the highest 35 percent bracket, while the remaining $733,333, or 30.56 percent, ($733,333/$2,400,000) would occur in the 38 percent tax bracket, making the weighted average applicable tax rate equal to:

$$T_C = (.6944 \times 35\%) + (.3056 \times 38\%)$$

$$= .3592, \text{ or } 35.92\%$$

Capital Structure Weights and WACC

Let's continue the previous examples. Suppose that ADK has issued 3 million shares of common stock, 1 million shares of preferred stock, and the previously mentioned 30,000 bonds outstanding. What will ADK's WACC be, considering ADK as a firm?

SOLUTION:

Using the securities' prices given in previous examples, ADK's equity, preferred stock, and debt will have the following total market values:
- Equity: $3,000,000 \times \$32.75 = \$98,250,000$.
- Preferred stock: $1,000,000 \times \$72 = \$72,000,000$.
- Debt: $30,000 \times \$975 = \$29,250,000$.

The total combined market value for all three capital sources is $199,500,000. The applicable weights for each capital source will therefore be

$$\text{For common equity: } \frac{E}{E+P+D} = \frac{\$98,250,000}{\$199,500,000} = .4925, \text{ or } 49.25\%$$

$$\text{For preferred stock: } \frac{P}{E+P+D} = \frac{\$72,000,000}{\$199,500,000} = .3609, \text{ or } 36.09\%$$

$$\text{For debt: } \frac{D}{E+P+D} = \frac{\$29,250,000}{\$199,500,000} = .1466, \text{ or } 14.66\%$$

Tying this all in together with the answers from the previous examples, ADK will have a WACC of

$$\text{WACC} = \frac{E}{E+P+D}i_E + \frac{P}{E+P+D}i_P + \frac{D}{E+P+D}i_D \times (1-T_C)$$

$$= (.4925 \times 10.75\%) + (.3609 \times 9.72\%) + (.1466 \times 8.26\% \times [1 - .3592])$$

$$= .0958, \text{ or } 9.58\%$$

Even if GassUp's coffee venture fails, the firm's creditors would likely still collect payments from gas station operations.

be *more* or *less* risky than gas stations. We can probably say, though, that the two enterprises will face *different* risks. For example, if the coffee shops are located within the busiest and most stable gas stations—say the ones that lie along freeways— then the firm faces remodeling of existing buildings rather than starting from scratch. Locating the coffee shops within existing structures would likely mean that the risks will be lower than building new stations or new coffee shops.

attributes, but if we created all project-specific numbers, we would be ignoring a fundamental issue pertaining to all bond and preferred stock indenture contracts. Both bonds and preferred stocks create claims on the *firm*, not of any particular group of projects within that firm. Furthermore, debt claims are superior to those of common stockholders. Thus, if the new project *does* significantly increase the firm's overall risk, the increased risk will be borne disproportionately by common stockholders. Debt holders

> "Creditors understand that their repayment will likely come from continuing operations and take current cash flows into account when a firm comes seeking funds."

So, does this mean that GassUp should calculate a heterogeneous WACC for each new project using purely project-specific numbers? Well, not exactly. As we'll discuss below, some inputs to WACC should be project-specific, but others should be consistent with the firmwide values used in calculating a firmwide WACC.

Project Cost Numbers That We Should Take from the Firm

It's tempting to argue that all component inputs for a project-specific WACC should be based on the specific project

and preferred stockholders will likely face minimal impact on the risk and return that their investments give them, no matter what new project the firm undertakes—even if those claimants own bonds or preferred shares that the firm issued to fund the new project.

For example, suppose GassUp decides to build entirely separate facilities for its coffee shops, which they'll name "Bottoms Up," they partially finance their expansion into coffee shops with debt, and the project turns out to be more like "Bottoms Down"—far less successful than the firm had hoped. Though this would be an unfortunate turn of events

business risk The risk of a project arising from the line of business it is in; the variability of a firm's or division's cash flows.

proxy beta The beta (a measure of the riskiness) of a firm in a similar line of business as a proposed new project.

financial risk The risk of a project to equity holders stemming from the use of debt in the financial structure of the firm; refers to the issue of how a firm decides to distribute the business risk between debt and equity holders.

for GassUp's shareholders, the firm's creditors would likely still collect their usual interest and dividend payments from GassUp's gross revenues from gas station operations.

Creditors understand that their repayment will likely come from continuing operations and take current cash flows into account when a firm comes seeking funds. For example, if a small firm approaches a bank for a loan to finance an expansion, the bank will normally spend more time analyzing *current* cash flows to determine the probability that they will recoup their loan than it will analyzing the potential new cash flows from the proposed expansion.

Note that this situation holds true only as long as the "new" projects represent fairly small investments compared to ongoing operations. As new projects become *large* relative to ongoing cash-flow producing activities, creditors will have to examine the likelihood of being repaid from the new projects much more closely. New projects, however great their potential, inherently carry more risk than do established current operations. Changes in the proportion of new projects relative to ongoing operations will thus translate into increased risk for the creditor, who will ask for a higher rate of return to offset the risk.

Since most firms tend to grow incrementally, we will assume (unless otherwise indicated) that we're examining situations in which the number of new projects is small relative to ongoing operations. We can therefore assume that using the firm's existing WACC for both debt and preferred stock is appropriate.

Project Cost Numbers That We Should Not Take from the Firm: The Pure Play Approach

Since we've decided not to adjust the firmwide costs of debt or preferred stock for the risk of a project, where *should* we account for the new project risk brought to the firm overall? The answer lies with the residual claimant: equity.

The firm's risk will obviously change when it takes on a project that's noticeably different from its existing lines of business. Since debt holders and preferred stockholders won't notice this change in risk, the firm spreads the risks that it takes with new projects by transferring most of the risk to the common stockholders.

In response to such a change in the firm's risk profile, the stockholders will adjust their required rate of return to adjust for the new risk level. Absent any alteration to the firm's capital

structure,[3] changes in the firm's risk profile are due to differences in the firm's **business risks** based on the mix of the new and existing product lines. The firm's beta will reflect those differences in each product line.

Obviously, no proposed new project will have a history of previous returns. Without such returns data, neither analysts nor investors can calculate a project-specific beta. But to the extent that we can find other firms engaged in the proposed new line of business, we can use their betas as proxies to estimate the project's risk. Ideally, the other firms would be engaged *only* in the proposed new line of business; such monothemed firms are usually referred to as *pure plays,* with this term also in turn being applied to this approach to estimating a project's beta.

An average of *n* such **proxy betas** will give us a fairly accurate estimate of what the new project's beta will be.[4]

$$i_E = r_f + \beta_{Avg}[E(r_M) - r_f]$$

where

$$\beta_{Avg} = \frac{\sum_{j=1}^{n} \beta_j}{n} \qquad (11\text{-}6)$$

This average will *be* an estimate, in the strictest statistical sense of the word. You might recall from your statistics classes that we will need to be careful to get as large a sample as possible if we want to get as much statistical power for our estimate as possible. Ideally, we would like to find at least three or four pure-play proxies to ensure that we have a large enough sample size to safely make meaningful inferences. In reality, however, two (or even one) proxies might represent a suitable sample if their business line resembles the proposed new project closely enough. In particular, we may want to use betas from industry front-runners, and rely less on betas of any firms that the company really doesn't want to emulate.

What shall we do if we can't find *any* pure-play proxies? Well, in that case, we may want to use firms that, while not *solely* in the same business as the proposed project's venture, have a sizable proportion of revenues from that line. We may then be able to "back out" the impact of their other lines of business

---

[3]In reality, new projects are often financed with different proportions of equity, debt, and preferred stock than were used to fund the firm's existing operations. Such a change in capital structure will result in a change in **financial risk,** with increased leverage magnifying β_E.

[4]We will be able to take a straight average of the proxy firm's betas as the estimate of our beta only if the capital structures of all the proxies are identical to each other and to that of our proposed new project. If not, we will need to adjust the proxies' estimated betas for differences in capital structures before averaging them. Then we will need to readjust the average beta for our project's capital structure before using the estimate.

from their firm's beta to leave us with a good enough estimate of what the new project's beta might be.

We should also ensure that we use weights based on the *project's* sources of capital, and not necessarily the *firm's* capital structure. If the new project is going to use more or less debt than the firm's existing projects do, then the risk- and reward-sharing are going to vary across the different types of capital, and we will want to recognize this in our WACC computation.

Calculation of Project WACC

Suppose that Evita's Subs, a local shipyard, is considering opening up a chain of sandwich shops. Evita's capital structure currently consists of 2 million outstanding shares of common stock, selling for $83 per share, and a $50 million bond issue, selling at 103 percent of par. Evita's stock has a beta of 0.72, the expected market risk premium is 7 percent, and the current risk-free rate is 4.5 percent. The bonds pay a 9 percent annual coupon and mature in 20 years. The current operations of the firm produce EBIT of $100 million per year, and the new sandwich operations would add only an expected $12 million per year to that. Also, suppose that Evita's management has done some research on the sandwich shop industry, and discovered that such firms have an average beta of 1.23. If the new project will be funded with 50 percent debt and 50 percent equity, what should be the WACC for this new project?

SOLUTION:

First, note that Evita's doesn't currently have any outstanding preferred stock and doesn't plan on using any to finance the new project, so that makes our job a little simpler. Also note that, though we are given enough information to calculate the firm's current capital structure weights and component cost of equity, we won't need those figures, as this new project differs from the firmwide WACC weights. We already know the capital structure weights for the new project (50 percent debt and 50 percent equity), so we just need to calculate the appropriate component costs.

For equity, the appropriate cost will be based upon the average risk of sandwich shops:

$$i_E = r_f + \beta_{E, \text{Project}}[E(r_M) - r_f]$$

$$= .0045 + 1.23[.07]$$

$$= .1311, \text{ or } 13.11\%$$

The YTM on the new bonds issued to finance this project will be the same as the YTM on the existing bonds:

$$\text{Solve} \left\{ \$1,030 = \$90 \times \left[\frac{1 - \dfrac{1}{(1 + i_D)^{20}}}{i_D} \right] + \frac{\$1000}{(1 + i_D)^{20}} \right\} \text{ for } i_D$$

which gives us an i_D of 8.68%.

Finally, the current EBIT already puts the firm in the top 35 percent tax bracket, so the additional EBIT generated by the project will also be taxed at this same marginal 35 percent tax rate. Therefore, the WACC of the new project will be

$$\text{WACC}_{\text{Project}} = \frac{E_{\text{Project}}}{E_{\text{Project}} + P_{\text{Project}} + D_{\text{Project}}} i_{E,\text{Project}} + \frac{D_{\text{Project}}}{E_{\text{Project}} + P_{\text{Project}} + D_{\text{Project}}} i_{D,\text{Firm}} \times (1 - T_{C,\text{Firm}})$$

$$= .5 \times .1311 + .5 \times .0868 \times (1 - .35)$$

$$= .0938, \text{ or } 9.38\%$$

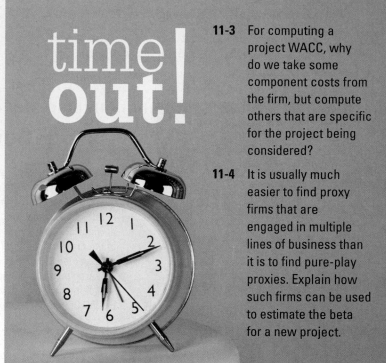

11-3 For computing a project WACC, why do we take some component costs from the firm, but compute others that are specific for the project being considered?

11-4 It is usually much easier to find proxy firms that are engaged in multiple lines of business than it is to find pure-play proxies. Explain how such firms can be used to estimate the beta for a new project.

Finally, we need to consider the appropriate corporate tax rate to use in calculating the WACC for a project. That marginal corporate tax rate will be the average marginal tax rate to which the project's cash flows will be subject. Referring back to our previous example about the appropriate marginal average tax rate to use in computing a firm's WACC, assume that the same firm with $400,000 of EBIT from current operations is considering a new project that will increase EBIT by $200,000. Since this $200,000 increase will keep the firm's marginal tax in the fifth bracket of Table 11.1, the appropriate tax rate to compute the project's WACC will simply be 34 percent.

To summarize, the component costs and weights to compute a project-specific WACC should be as shown below in equation 11-7, with the source of each part indicated by the appropriate subscript:

$$\text{WACC}_{\text{Project}} = \frac{E_{\text{Project}}}{E_{\text{Project}} + P_{\text{Project}} + D_{\text{Project}}} i_{E,\text{Project}}$$

$$+ \frac{P_{\text{Project}}}{E_{\text{Project}} + P_{\text{Project}} + D_{\text{Project}}} i_{P,\text{Firm}}$$

$$+ \frac{D_{\text{Project}}}{E_{\text{Project}} + P_{\text{Project}} + D_{\text{Project}}} i_{D,\text{Firm}}$$

$$\times (1 - T_{C,\text{Project}}) \tag{11-7}$$

DIVISIONAL WACC

Ideally, a firm would calculate a risk-appropriate WACC for every new project under consideration. Pragmatically, doing so isn't always feasible—particularly for large corporations, the managers of which must consider dozens or even hundreds of proposed new projects each year. The costs in terms of time and effort of estimating project-specific WACCs individually for each project are simply prohibitive.

Instead, large firms often take a middle-of-the-road approach to achieve many of the benefits that accrue to project-specific WACC calculations while spending much less time and resources. The key to this approach is to calculate a **divisional WACC.**

Advantages and Disadvantages of a Divisional WACC

To see the advantages and disadvantages of using divisional WACCs, let's first consider the disadvantage of using a firm's WACC to evaluate new, risk-heterogeneous projects. To make things simple, let's assume that we're looking at a firm that uses only equity finance, so that WACC is simply equal to i_E.

Similar to our discussion of the security market line in Chapter 10, required rates of return for projects with varying

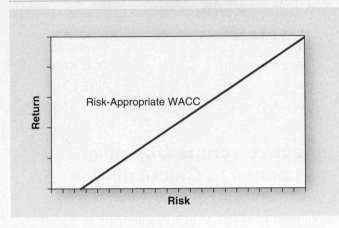

the firm's average beta. Looking at the same sample projects as before, we see that Project A would now be rejected, while Project C would be accepted.

▼ **FIGURE 11.3** Sample Project versus Firmwide WACC

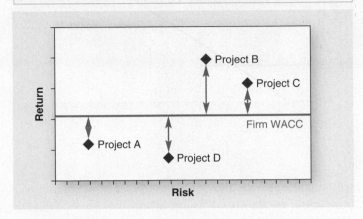

degrees of risk would lie along the sloped line shown in Figure 11.1. We could then evaluate projects with various degrees of risk based on the relationship between their expected rate of return and the required rate of return for that risk level. As Figure 11.2 shows, using risk-appropriate WACCs, projects A and B would be accepted, since their *expected* rates of return would be higher than their respective *required* rates of return. Projects C and D would be rejected because our simple scheme shows that these projects aren't expected to return enough to cover market required returns, given the projects' riskiness.

However, using a firmwide WACC would result in a comparison of the project's expected rates of return to a single, flat, firmwide cost of capital as Figure 11.3 shows. Using a simple firmwide WACC to evaluate new projects would give an unfair advantage to projects that present more risk than the firm's average beta. Using a firmwide WACC would also work against projects that involved less risk than

▼ **FIGURE 11.4** Incorrect Decisions Caused by Inappropriate Use of Firmwide WACC

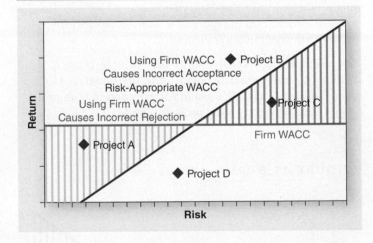

Using a firmwide WACC in this way, as an inappropriate benchmark for projects of differing risk from the firm's current operations, will result in quite a few incorrect decisions. In fact, the use of a firmwide WACC to evaluate *any* projects with risk-return coordinates lying in the two triangles indicated in Figure 11.4 will result in an incorrect accept/reject decision.

If we can divide the firm's existing projects into divisions where the different divisions proxy for systematically different average project risk levels, then calculating WACCs for each division separately, as Figure 11.5 shows,

▼ **FIGURE 11.2** Sample Projects versus Risk-Sensitive WACC

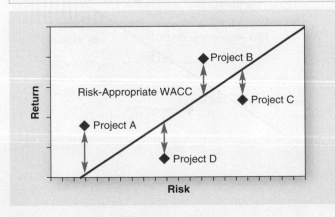

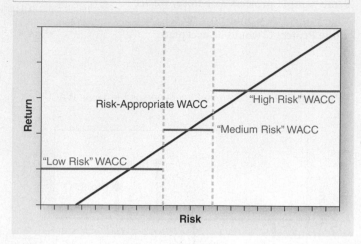

▼ **TABLE 11.2** Subjective Divisional WACCs

Risk Level	Discount Rate
Very low risk	Firm WACC − 5%
Low risk	Firm WACC − 2%
Same risk as firm	Firm WACC
High risk	Firm WACC + 3%
Very high risk	Firm WACC + 7%

Subjective versus Objective Approaches to Calculating Divisional WACCs

We can form divisional WACCs subjectively by simply considering the project's risk relative to the firm's existing lines of business. If the project is riskier (safer) than the firm average, adjust the firm WACC upward (downward) to account for our subjective opinion of project riskiness. The biggest disadvantage to this approach is that the adjustments are subjective and created just for the project at hand. For example, consider the sample subjective divisional WACCs in Table 11.2. Both the project assignments to the divisions and then the WACC adjustments for the very low risk, low risk, high risk, and very high risk are fairly arbitrary.

An objective approach to calculating divisional WACCs would be to compute the average beta per division, use these figures in the CAPM formula to calculate i_E for each division, and then, in turn, use divisional estimates of i_E to construct divisional WACCs. Though the objective approach would usually be more precise, resulting in fewer incorrect accept/reject decisions, the subjective approach is more frequently used because it is easier to implement.

will greatly reduce the problem of basing decisions on inaccurate results from using firmwide WACC for all projects.

Using divisional WACCs like this will not *eliminate* problems of incorrect acceptance and incorrect rejection as we saw in Figure 11.4, but it will greatly reduce their frequency. Instead of making errors corresponding to the two large triangular areas indicated in Figure 11.4, we will instead have six smaller areas of error shown in Figure 11.6. More acceptance/rejection regions will result in fewer errors.

For example, let's consider our four sample projects from before. We now evaluate them using divisional WACCs as shown in Figure 11.7. We would correctly accept both projects A and B and correctly reject projects C and D.

▼ **FIGURE 11.6** Divisional WACC Errors

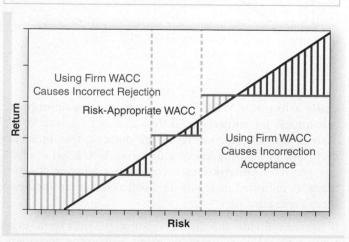

▼ **FIGURE 11.7**
Example Decisions Using Divisional WACCs

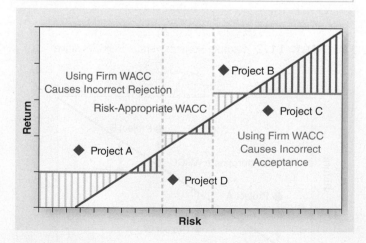

time out!

11-5 Divisions of a corporation aren't usually formed based explicitly on differences in risk between the projects in different divisions. Rather, they're normally formed along product-type or geographic differences. Explain how this division scheme may still result in divisions that *do* differ among themselves by average risk. Also explain why calculating divisional WACCs in such a situation will still improve decision making over simply using a firmwide WACC for project acceptance or rejection.

11-6 Explain why, in Example 11-7, using objectively computed divisional WACCS still resulted in an incorrect accept/reject decision for project D.

FLOTATION COSTS

If a firm uses only retained earnings or other internally generated sources of capital to finance a new project, then the component costs are exactly as discussed above. However, if a firm funds a project by issuing externally generated new capital—additional stock, bonds, and so on—then the firm will also have to pay commissions to the underwriting firm that floats the issue. Component costs will then need to integrate these **flotation costs** to figure project WACCs.

We can approach the commission costs in two basic ways. We can either increase the project's WACC to incorporate the flotation costs' impact as a percentage of WACC, or we can leave the WACC alone and adjust the project's initial investment upwards so as to reflect the "true" cost of the project. Both approaches have advantages and disadvantages. The first approach tends to understate the component cost of new equity, and the latter approach violates the **separation principle** of capital budgeting, which states that the calculations of cash flows should remain independent of financing. We'll discuss the separation principle in the next

EXAMPLE 11-7

For interactive versions of this example visit www.mhhe.com/canM

Divisional Costs of Capital

Assume that BF, Inc., an all-equity firm, has a firmwide WACC of 10 percent, and that the firm is broken into three divisions: Textiles, Accessories, and Miscellaneous. The average Textiles project has a beta of 0.7; the average Accessories project has a beta of 1.3; and the average Miscellaneous project has a beta of 1.1.

The firm is currently considering the projects shown in the table below. Their current approach is to use the firm's WACC to evaluate all projects, but they see the wisdom in adopting a subjective divisional cost of capital approach. Firm management is thus considering a divisional cost of capital scheme in which they will use the firm's WACC for Miscellaneous projects, the firm's WACC minus 1 percent for Textiles projects, and the firm's WACC plus 3 percent for Accessories projects. The current expected return to the market is 12 percent, and the current risk-free rate is 5.75 percent.

Project	Division	Expected i_E	Beta
A	$\beta_{Accessories}$	17.00%	1.3
B	$\beta_{Accessories}$	15.00	1.2
C	$\beta_{Miscellaneous}$	13.00	1.3
D	$\beta_{Miscellaneous}$	11.00	0.7
E	$\beta_{Textiles}$	9.00	0.8
F	$\beta_{Textiles}$	7.00	0.5

(continued)

For this group of projects, how much better would their accept/reject decisions be if they used this approach rather than if they continued to use the firm's WACC to evaluate all projects? Would switching to an objective divisional cost of capital approach, where the WACC for each division is based on that division's average beta, improve their accept/reject criteria any further?

SOLUTION:

Determine the required rates of return for each project assuming that the firm uses the firmwide WACC and adds the subjective adjustments to construct divisional WACCs. The objective computation of divisional WACCs using each division's average beta and the i_E computed using each project's specific beta is indicated in the table below. In each case, project acceptances appear in blue print, and project rejections appear in red print.

Project	Division	Expected i_E	Beta	Firm WACC	Subjective i_E	Objective i_E	Specific i_E
A	$\beta_{Accessories}$	17.00%	1.3	10.00%	13.00%	13.88%	13.88%
B	$\beta_{Accessories}$	15.00	1.2	10.00	13.00	13.88	13.25
C	$\beta_{Miscellaneous}$	13.00	1.3	10.00	10.00	12.63	13.88
D	$\beta_{Miscellaneous}$	11.00	0.7	10.00	10.00	12.63	10.13
E	$\beta_{Textiles}$	9.00	0.8	10.00	9.00	10.13	10.75
F	$\beta_{Textiles}$	7.00	0.5	10.00	9.00	10.13	8.88

Using the "Specific i_E" yields the "correct" accept/reject decision; that is, these accept/reject decisions would be generated exactly the same if the firm had the time and resources to compute the i_E on a project-by-project basis. In this particular situation, using the firm WACC as a benchmark for all the projects would result in projects E and F being rejected, since they both will return expected rates less than the firm's 10 percent required rate of return. By comparison to the results using the Specific i_E, both of these rejections are appropriate. We would prefer that the accept/reject criteria took account of risk; that is, both projects will be rejected because their expected returns (9 percent and 7 percent, respectively) are less than the required returns (10.75 and 8.88 percent, respectively) based on their specific levels of project risk rather than assuming that both projects carry the same risk as the firm's overall risk.

Using the subjectively adjusted approach to calculating i_E results in required rates of return of 13 percent for Accessories projects, 10 percent for Miscellaneous projects, and 9 percent for Textiles projects. The associated accept/reject decisions actually incorrectly accept project E, making the subjectively adjusted WACC approach worse (in this specific example) than simply using the firmwide WACC.

Finally, using the objective approach to constructing divisional costs of capital, along with the three divisions' average betas given above, results in required rates of return for the three divisions of

$$i_E = i_f + \beta_E[E(i_M) - i_f]$$

$$i_{E,Accessories} = .0575 + 1.3[.12 - .0575] = .1388, \text{ or } 13.88\%$$

$$i_{E,Miscellaneous} = .0575 + 1.1[.12 - .0575] = .1263, \text{ or } 12.63\%$$

$$i_{E,Textiles} = .0575 + 0.7[.12 - .0575] = .1013, \text{ or } 10.13\%$$

As the solutions above show, using these divisional cost of capital figures as required rates of return for each project results in correct rejections of projects E and F, but also results in an incorrect rejection of project D and an incorrect acceptance of project C relative to computing i_E on a project-by-project basis.

Overall, using either the objective or subjective approaches to calculating divisional costs of capital will not be as precise as using project-specific WACCs: we will wind up incorrectly accepting and/ or rejecting some projects. But this *costs.* In terms of making incorrect decisions on some of our project choices it may be worth it if the projects in question aren't large enough for project-specific calculations to be cost effective.

Flotation-Adjusted Cost of Equity

Suppose that, as in Example 11-1, ADK Industries' common shares are selling for $32.75 per share, and the company expects to set its next annual dividend at $1.54 per share. All future dividends are expected to grow by 6 percent per year, indefinitely. In addition, let's also suppose that ADK faces a flotation cost of 20 percent on new equity issues. Calculate the flotation-adjusted cost of equity.

SOLUTION:

Twenty percent of $32.75 will be $6.55, so the flotation-adjusted cost of equity will be

$$i_E = \frac{D_1}{P_0 - F} + g$$

$$= \frac{\$1.54}{\$32.75 - \$6.55} + .06$$

$$= .1188, \text{ or } 11.88\%$$

Notice that the result is 1.18 percent above the non-flotation-adjusted cost of equity, 10.70 percent, computed using the constant-growth model in Example 11-1. If we instead wanted to use the CAPM estimate, we would take the non-flotation-adjusted CAPM estimate from the same example, 10.80 percent and add the same differential of 1.18 percent to it to get the flotation-adjusted value:

$$i_E = .1080 + .0118 = .1198, \text{ or } 11.98\%$$

The adjustments for the component costs of preferred stock and debt will be similar:

$$i_P = \frac{D_1}{P_0 - F} \tag{11-9}$$

$$\text{Solve} \left\{ PV - F = PMT \times \left[\frac{1 - \dfrac{1}{(1 + i_D)^N}}{i_D} \right] + \frac{PV}{(1 + i_D)^N} \right\} \text{ for } i_D \tag{11-10}$$

chapter and so will also put off our discussion of the second approach to handling flotation costs until that time, too.

Adjusting the WACC

The first approach to adjusting for flotation costs involves adjusting the issue price of new securities by subtracting flotation cost, F, to reflect the net security price and then using this net price to calculate the component cost of capital. For equity, this approach is most commonly applied to the constant-growth model:

$$i_E = \frac{D_1}{P_0 - F} + g \tag{11-8}$$

If we instead want to apply this approach to the cost of equity obtained from the CAPM formula, we would adjust it upward by an equivalent amount. ■

time out!

11-7 Why should we expect the flotation costs for debt to be significantly lower than those for equity?

11-8 Explain how we should go about computing the WACC for a project which uses both retained earnings and a new equity issue.

Get Online

mhhe.com/canM

for study materials including quizzes, iPod downloads, and video

Your Turn...

Questions

1. How would you handle calculating the cost of capital if a firm were planning to issue two different classes of common stock? *(LG1)*

2. Why don't we multiply the cost of preferred stock by 1 minus the tax rate, as we do for debt? *(LG2)*

3. Expressing WACC in terms of i_E, i_P, and i_D, what is the theoretical minimum for the WACC? *(LG2)*

4. Under what situations would you want to use the CAPM approach for estimating the component cost of equity? The constant-growth model? *(LG3)*

5. Could you calculate the component cost of equity for a stock with nonconstant expected growth rate in dividends if you didn't have the information necessary to compute the component cost using the CAPM? Why or why not? *(LG3)*

6. Why do we use market-based weights instead of book-value-based weights when computing the WACC? *(LG4)*

7. Suppose your firm wanted to expand into a new line of business quickly, and that management anticipated that the new line of business would constitute over 80 percent of your firm's operations within three years. If the expansion was going to be financed partially with debt, would it still make sense to use the firm's existing cost of debt, or should you compute a new rate of return for debt based on the new line of business? *(LG5)*

8. Explain why the divisional cost of capital approach may cause problems if new projects are assigned to the wrong division. *(LG6)*

9. When will the subjective approach to forming divisional WACCs be better than using the firmwide WACC to evaluate all projects? *(LG7)*

10. Suppose a new project was going to be financed partially with retained earnings. What flotation costs should you use for retained earnings? *(LG8)*

Problems

11-1 **Cost of Equity** Diddy Corp. stock has a beta of 1.2, the current risk-free rate is 5 percent, and the expected return on the market is 13.5 percent. What is Diddy's cost of equity? *(LG3)*

11-2 **Cost of Equity** JaiLai Cos. stock has a beta of 1.1, the current risk-free rate is 6.2 percent, and the expected return on the market is 12 percent. What is JaiLai's cost of equity? *(LG3)*

11-3 **Cost of Debt** Oberon Inc. has a $20 million (face value) 10-year bond issue selling for 97 percent of par that pays an annual coupon of 8.25 percent. What would be Oberon's before-tax component cost of debt? *(LG3)*

11-4 **Cost of Debt** KatyDid Clothes has a $150 million (face value) 20-year bond issue selling for 104 percent of par that carries a coupon rate of 11 percent, paid semiannually. What would be Katydid's before-tax component cost of debt? *(LG3)*

11-5 **Cost of Preferred Stock** ILK has preferred stock selling for 97 percent of par that pays an 8 percent annual coupon. What would be ILK's component cost of preferred stock? *(LG3)*

11-6 **Cost of Preferred Stock** Marme Inc. has preferred stock selling for 137 percent of par that pays an 11 percent annual coupon. What would be Marme's component cost of preferred stock? *(LG3)*

11-7 **Weight of Equity** FarCry Industries, a maker of telecommunications equipment, has 2 million shares of common stock outstanding, 1 million shares of preferred stock outstanding, and 10,000 bonds. If the common shares are selling for $27 per share, the preferred shares are selling for $14.50 per share, and the bonds are selling for 98 percent of par, what would be the weight used for equity in the computation of FarCry's WACC? *(LG4)*

11-8 **Weight of Equity** OMG Inc. has 4 million shares of common stock outstanding, 3 million shares of preferred stock outstanding, and 5,000 bonds. If the common shares are selling for $17 per share, the preferred shares are selling for $26 per share, and the bonds are selling for 108 percent of par, what would be the weight used for equity in the computation of OMG's WACC? *(LG4)*

11-9 **Weight of Debt** FarCry Industries, a maker of telecommunications equipment, has 2 million shares of common stock outstanding, 1 million shares of preferred stock outstanding, and 10,000 bonds. If the common shares are selling for $27 per share, the preferred shares are selling for $14.50 per share, and the bonds are selling for 98 percent of par, what weight should you use for debt in the computation of FarCry's WACC? *(LG4)*

11-10 **Weight of Debt** OMG Inc. has 4 million shares of common stock outstanding, 3 million shares of preferred stock outstanding, and 5,000 bonds. If the common shares are selling for $17 per shares, the preferred shares are selling for $26 per share, and the bonds are selling for 108 percent of par, what weight should you use for debt in the computation of OMG's WACC? *(LG4)*

11-11 **Weight of Preferred Stock** FarCry Industries, a maker of telecommunications equipment, has 2 million shares of common stock outstanding, 1 million shares of preferred stock outstanding, and 10,000 bonds. If the common shares sell for $27 per share, the preferred shares sell for $14.50 per share, and the bonds sell for 98 percent of par, what weight should you use for preferred stock in the computation of FarCry's WACC? *(LG4)*

11-12 **Weight of Preferred Stock** OMG Inc. has 4 million shares of common stock outstanding, 3 million shares of preferred stock outstanding, and 5,000 bonds. If the common shares sell for $17 per share, the preferred shares sell for $26 per share, and the bonds sell for 108 percent of par, what weight should you use for preferred stock in the computation of OMG's WACC? *(LG4)*

11-13 WACC Suppose that TapDance, Inc.'s capital structure features 65 percent equity, 35 percent debt, and that its before-tax cost of debt is 8 percent, while its cost of equity is 13 percent. If the appropriate weighted average tax rate is 34 percent, what will be TapDance's WACC? *(LG2)*

11-14 WACC JLP Industries has 6.5 million shares of common stock outstanding with a market price of $14.00 per share. The company also has outstanding preferred stock with a market value of $10 million, and 25,000 bonds outstanding, each with a face value of $1,000 and selling at 90 percent of par value. The cost of equity is 14 percent, the cost of preferred stock is 10 percent, and the cost of debt is 7.25 percent. If JLP's tax rate is 34 percent, what is the WACC? *(LG2)*

11-15 WACC Suppose that JB Cos. has a capital structure of 78 percent equity, 22 percent debt, and that its before-tax cost of debt is 11 percent while its cost of equity is 17 percent. If the appropriate weighted-average tax rate is 25 percent, what will be JB's WACC? *(LG2)*

11-16 WACC Suppose that B2B, Inc. has a capital structure of 37 percent equity, 17 percent preferred stock, and 46 percent debt. If the before-tax component costs of equity, preferred stock, and debt are 14.5 percent, 11 percent, and 9.5 percent, respectively, what is B2B's WACC if the firm faces an average tax rate of 30 percent? *(LG2)*

11-17 WACC Suppose that MNINK Industries' capital structure features 63 percent equity, 7 percent preferred stock, and 30 percent debt. If the before-tax component costs of equity, preferred stock, and debt are 11.60 percent, 9.5 percent, and 7 percent, respectively, what is MNINK's WACC if the firm faces an average tax rate of 34 percent? *(LG2)*

11-18 WACC TAFKAP Industries has 3 million shares of stock outstanding selling at $17 per share and an issue of $20 million in 7.5 percent, annual coupon bonds with a maturity of 15 years, selling at 106 percent of par. If TAFKAP's weighted-average tax rate is 34 percent and its cost of equity is 14.5 percent, what is TAFKAP's WACC? *(LG3)*

11-19 WACC Johnny Cake Ltd. has 10 million shares of stock outstanding selling at $23 per share and an issue of $50 million in 9 percent, annual coupon bonds with a maturity of 17 years, selling at 93.5 percent of par. If Johnny Cake's weighted-average tax rate is 34 percent, its next dividend is expected to be $3 per share, and all future dividends are expected to grow at 6 percent per year, indefinitely, what is its WACC? *(LG3)*

11-20 WACC Weights BetterPie Industries has 3 million shares of common stock outstanding, 2 million shares of preferred stock outstanding, and 10,000 bonds. If the common shares are selling for $47 per share, the preferred shares are selling for $24.50 per share, and the bonds are selling for 99 percent of par, what would be the weights used in the calculation of BetterPie's WACC? *(LG4)*

11-21 Flotation Cost Suppose that Brown-Murphies' common shares sell for $19.50 per share, are expected to set their next annual dividend at $.57 per share, and that all future dividends are expected to grow by 4 percent per year, indefinitely. If Brown-Murphies faces a flotation cost of 13 percent on new equity issues, what will be the flotation-adjusted cost of equity? *(LG8)*

11-22 Flotation Cost A firm is considering a project that will generate perpetual after-tax cash flows of $15,000 per year beginning next year. The project has the same risk as the firm's overall operations and must be financed externally. Equity flotation costs 14 percent and debt issues cost 4 percent on an after-tax basis. The firm's D/E ratio is 0.8. What is the most the firm can pay for the project and still earn its required return? *(LG2)*

11-23 Risk-Free Rate in WACC A firm has 5 million shares of common stock outstanding, each with a market price of $8 per share. It has 25,000 bonds outstanding, each selling for $800. The bonds mature in 10 years, have a coupon rate of 8 percent, and pay coupons semiannually. The firm's equity has a beta of 1.4, and the expected market return is 15 percent. The tax rate is 35 percent and the WACC is 15 percent. Calculate the risk-free rate. *(LG2)*

11-24 Firmwide vs. Project-Specific WACCs An all-equity firm is considering the projects shown below. The T-bill rate is 4 percent and the market risk premium is 7 percent. If the firm uses its current WACC of 12 percent to evaluate these projects, which project(s), if any, will be incorrectly rejected? *(LG6)*

Project	Expected Return	Beta
A	8.0%	0.5
B	19.0	1.2
C	13.0	1.4
D	17.0	1.6

11-25 Firmwide vs. Project-Specific WACCs An all-equity firm is considering the projects shown below. The T-bill rate is 4 percent and the market risk premium is 7 percent. If the firm uses its current WACC of 12 percent to evaluate these projects, which project(s), if any, will be incorrectly accepted? *(LG6)*

Project	Expected Return	Beta
A	8.0%	0.5
B	19.0	1.2
C	13.0	1.4
D	17.0	1.6

11-26 Divisional WACCs Suppose your firm has decided to use a divisional WACC approach to analyze projects. The firm currently has four divisions, A through D, with average betas for each division of 0.6, 1.0, 1.3, and 1.6, respectively. If all current and future projects will be financed with half debt and half equity, and if the current cost of equity (based on an average firm beta of 1.0 and a current risk-free rate of 7 percent) is 13 percent and the after-tax yield on the company's bonds is 8 percent, what will the WACCs be for each division? *(LG7)*

estimating cash flows on
capital budgeting projects

As new capital budgeting projects arise, we must estimate when such projects will require cash flows. Estimating those cash flows isn't difficult, but it *is* complicated. As you look through this chapter's examples, questions, and problems, you'll notice that we have given you a lot more information in these types of problems than we've given you anywhere else in the text. To correctly estimate project cash flows, we need to consider quite a number of factors, such as:

- The particular new product or service's costs and revenues.
- The likely impact that the new service or product will have on the firm's *existing* products' costs and revenues.
- The use of assets or employees already employed by the firm.
- The way to handle charges such as the research and development costs incurred to develop the new product.
- A multitude of other relevant details.

Fortunately, we *do* have a way to work through all of these details systematically. In this chapter, we're going to construct a process which, if we follow it faithfully, will guide us to consider factors such as the ones listed. The process of estimating expected future cash

continued on p. 274

LEARNING GOALS

LG1 Explain why we use pro forma statements to analyze project cash flows.

LG2 Identify which cash flows we can incrementally attribute to a proposed project and which ones we can't.

LG3 Calculate a project's expected cash flows using the free cash flow approach.

LG4 Explain how accelerated depreciation affects project cash flows.

LG5 Calculate free cash flows for replacement equipment.

LG6 Calculate cash flows associated with cost-cutting proposals.

LG7 Explain and demonstrate the EAC approach to choose between alternative cash streams when projects recur.

LG8 Adjust initial project investments to account for flotation costs.

continued from p. 273

flows of a project using only the relevant parts of the balance sheet and income statements is called **pro forma analysis.** The type of *pro forma analysis* of potential projects we'll use will focus on the question, "What will be this project's impact on the firm's total cash flows if we go forward?" ■

SAMPLE PROJECT DESCRIPTION

Let's suppose that we're working for a game development company, First Strike Software (FSS). FSS is considering leasing a new plant in Gatlinburg, Tennessee, which they will use to produce copies of their new game "FinProf," a "first-person combat" game where the player battles aliens invading your local college's finance department.

FSS will price this game at $39.99, and they estimate sales for each of the next three years as shown in Table 12.1. Given buyers' rapidly changing tastes in computer games, they don't expect to be able to sell any more copies after year 3.

Variable costs per game are low ($4.25), and FSS expects fixed costs to total $150,000 per year, including rent. Start-up costs involve $75,000 for a software-duplicating machine, plus an additional $2,000 in shipping and installation costs. For our first stab at analyzing this project, we will assume that the duplicating machine will be straight-line depreciated to $5,000 over the life of the project. We'll expect that machine to bring only $2,000 on the market after we're done using it.

FinProf is an updated version of an older game sold by FSS, MktProf. FSS intends to keep selling MktProf but anticipates that FinProf will decrease sales of Mkt-Prof by 2,000 units per year throughout the life of the new game. MktProf sells for $19.99 and has variable costs of $3.50 per unit.

▼ **TABLE 12.1** Sample Project Projected Unit Sales

Year	Unit Sales
1	15,000
2	27,000
3	5,000

viewpoints

business APPLICATION

Suppose that McDonald's is considering introducing the McTurkey Dinner (MTD). They anticipate that the MTD will have unit sales, prices, and cost figures as shown below for the next five years, after which the firm will retire the MTD. Introducing the MTD will require $7 million in new assets, which will fall into the MACRS five-year class life. McDonald's expects the necessary assets to be worth $2 million in market value at the end of the project life. In addition, the company expects that NWC requirements at the beginning of each year will be approximately 13 percent of the projected sales throughout the coming year. McDonald's uses an 11 percent cost of capital for similar projects and is subject to a 35 percent marginal tax rate. What will be this project's expected cash flows?

Year	Estimated Unit Sales
1	400,000
2	1,000,000
3	$1,000,000.00
4	$1,000,000.00
5	$ 500,000.00

Development costs totaled $150,000 throughout development of the game, and First Strike estimates its NWC requirements at the beginning of each year will be approximately 10 percent of the projected sales during the coming year. First Strike is in the 34 percent tax bracket and uses a discount rate of 15 percent on projects with risk profiles such as this. The relevant question: Should FSS put FinProf into production or not?

GUIDING PRINCIPLES FOR CASH FLOW ESTIMATION

When we calculate a project's expected cash flows, we must ensure that we cover all **incremental cash flows,** that is, the cash flow changes that we would expect throughout the entire firm as the new project comes on board. Some incremental cash flow effects are fairly obvious. For example, suppose a firm has to buy a new asset to support a new project but would not be buying the asset if the project were not adopted. Clearly, the cash flows from buying the asset are obviously incremental to the project, and we should therefore count them when we calculate the cash flows associated with that project. But we can hardly expect all incremental cash flows to be so obvious. Other incremental cash flows, as discussed below, are more subtle, and we'll have to watch for them very carefully.

Opportunity Costs

As you likely remember from your microeconomics classes, an **opportunity cost** exists whenever a firm has to choose how to allocate scarce resources. If those resources go into project A, the firm must forgo using them in any other way. Those forgone choices will cost the firm in some way, and we must remember to take account of such opportunity costs in calculating cash flows attributable to project A.

For example, suppose that FSS already owned the piece of software-duplicating machinery discussed above. If the machinery was already being fully utilized by another project within the company, then obviously switching it over to the FinProf game would require that other project to find another source of software duplication. To be fair, the FinProf project should be charged for the use of the machinery.

Even if the machinery wasn't currently being used in any other projects, it could still possibly have an opportunity cost associated with using it in the FinProf project. If FSS could potentially sell the machinery on the open market for $75,000, the company would have to give up that $75,000 in order to use the piece of machinery for the FinProf game. In the end, it wouldn't really matter whether the firm had to buy the asset from outside sources or not: either way, the project will be tying up $75,000 worth of capital, and it should be charged for doing so.

The underlying concept behind charging the project for the opportunity cost of using an asset also has broader implications: overall, we should charge any new project for any assets used by that project as well as any wages and benefits paid to employees working on it. Even if the firm was already employing those people prior to starting work on the new project, they are no longer available to work on any existing projects; and if the firm didn't have any new projects, it could have laid those employees off, saving their wages and benefits.

Sunk Costs

If a firm has already paid an expense or is obligated to pay one in the future, regardless of whether a particular project is undertaken, that expense is a **sunk cost.** A firm should never count sunk costs in project cash flows.

For example, FSS incurred $150,000 in development costs in the example above. Development costs would presumably include items such as the salaries of the game's programmers, market research costs, and so forth. Since we're not told otherwise, we can sensibly assume that FSS will never recoup its development money, even if it decides not to go ahead with publishing the game. Thus those costs are sunk, and FSS wouldn't even consider them as part of its decision about whether to move forward with putting the FinProf game into production.

Substitutionary and Complementary Effects

If a new product or service will either reduce or increase sales, costs, or necessary assets for existing products or services, then those changes are incremental to the project and should rightfully be included in the project cash flows. For example, consider how FSS's FinProf game may affect the existing MktProf game. The gross sales and variable cost figures for the new game might be as shown in Table 12.2.

However, FSS also expects the MktProf game to lose yearly sales of $2,000 \times$ $19.99 = $39,980$ when FinProf comes aboard. Further, the decrease in sales of MktProf will also result in yearly variable costs of $2,000 \times $3.50 = $7,000$ per year, so the net incremental sales and variable cost figures for the project will be as shown in Table 12.3.

We see a reduction in both sales and variable costs because FinProf is a partial **substitute** for MktProf. If the new game had been a **complement,** then both sales and variable costs of the existing product would have increased instead.

Stock Dividends and Bond Interest

One final, important note concerning incremental project cash flows: We will never count any **financing costs,** including dividends paid on stock or interest paid on debt, as expenses of the project. The costs of capital are already included as component costs in the weighted average cost of capital (WACC) that we will be using to discount these cash flows in the next chapter. If we were to include them in the cash flow figures as well, we would be double-counting them.

time out!

12-1 Suppose that your manager will be devoting half of her time to a new project, with the other half devoted to currently existing projects. How would you reflect this in your calculation of the incremental cash flows of the project?

12-2 Could a new product have both substitutionary and complementary effects on existing products?

▼ **TABLE 12.2** Gross Sales and Variable Costs for FinProf

Year	Sales	Variable Costs
1	15,000 × $39.99 = $599,850	15,000 × $4.25 = $63,750
2	27,000 × $39.99 = $1,079,730	27,000 × $4.25 = $114,750
3	5,000 × $39.99 = $199,950	5,000 × $4.25 = $21,250

▼ **TABLE 12.3** Net Incremental and Variable Costs for FinProf

Year	Sales	Variable Costs
1	$599,850 − $39,980 = $559,870	$63,750 − $7,000 = $56,750
2	$1,079,730 − $39,980 = $1,039,750	$114,750 − $7,000 = $107,750
3	$199,950 − $39,980 = $159,970	$21,250 − $7,000 = $14,250

TOTAL PROJECT CASH FLOW

In Chapter 2, we discussed the concept of free cash flow (FCF), which we defined as

$$\text{FCF} = \text{Operating cash flow} - \text{Investment in operating capital} \qquad (12\text{-}1)$$
$$= [\text{EBIT} - \text{Taxes} + \text{Depreciation}]$$
$$- [\Delta\text{Gross fixed assets} + \Delta\text{Net operating working capital}]$$

In this chapter, we're going to use this variable again as a measure of the total amount of available cash flow from a project. However, we'll observe two important differences from how we used it in Chapter 2. First, since we'll be considering potential projects rather than a particular firm's actual, historic activities, the FCF numbers we calculate will be, frankly, guesses—informed guesses, surely, but guesses nonetheless. Since we'll be "calculating" guesses, we'll introduce possible estimation error into our capital budgeting decision statistics, which we'll discuss in the next chapter.

Second, we'll now calculate FCF on potential projects individually, rather than across the firm as a whole as we did in Chapter 2. In some ways, calculating FCF on individual projects will make our job much easier, since we need not worry about estimating an entire set of balance sheets for the firm. Instead, we'll only have to be concerned with the limited subset of pro forma statements necessary to keep track of the assets, expense categories, and so on that a new project will affect. Unfortunately, the elements of that limited set will vary from situation to situation, and the hard part will be identifying which parts of the balance sheets are necessary and which are not.

Calculating Depreciation

Expected depreciation on equipment used during the life of the project will affect both the operating cash flows and the change in gross fixed assets that will occur at the end of the

- Freight charges.

- Installation and testing fees.

So the depreciable basis for the new project's software-duplicating machine will be the $75,000 purchase price plus the $2,000 shipping and installation cost, for a total depreciable basis of $77,000. Since initially First Strike will depreciate this asset using the most basic form of straight-line depreciation, it will use the following formula to compute depreciation per year:

$$\text{Depreciation} = \frac{\text{Ending book value} - \text{Beginning book value}}{\text{Life of asset}} \quad (12\text{-}2)$$

$$= \frac{\$77,000 - \$5,000}{3}$$

$$= \$24,000 \text{ per year}$$

We'll discuss later in the chapter why this depreciation assumption is far too simple. Other, more-complicated depreciation methods can be much more advantageous to the company. For now, this straight-line depreciation approach will suffice for our initial go at calculating the project's cash flows.

substitute; complement A new product or service that decreases or increases sales, respectively, of an existing products or service.

financing costs Interest paid to debt holders or dividends paid to stockholders.

depreciable basis An asset's cost plus the amounts you paid for items such as sales tax, freight charges, and installation and testing fees.

> ## CALCULATING THE EXPECTED DEPRECIATION CHARGES ON ASSETS BEFORE CALCULATING THE FCF COMPONENTS IS USUALLY HELPFUL.

project. Whether an asset is sold or whether it's discarded with any remaining book value, calculating the expected depreciation charges on assets before calculating the FCF components is usually helpful.

For First Strike's proposed FinProf project, the firm will depreciate capital assets such as the software-duplicating machine using the straight-line method to an ending book value of $5,000. To calculate the annual depreciation amount, First Strike will first need to compute the machinery's **depreciable basis.** According to the Internal Revenue Service's (IRS) Publication 946, the depreciable basis for real property is:

- Its cost.

- Amounts paid for items such as sales tax.

Calculating Operating Cash Flow

We defined operating cash flow (OCF) in Chapter 2 as *EBIT − Taxes + Depreciation*. We'll still calculate OCF as being mathematically equal to *EBIT − Taxes + Depreciation*. But remember that we'll be constructing the FCF components ourselves instead of taking them off an income statement that someone else has already produced. So we'll usually find it most helpful to conduct this calculation as what we will call a "quasi-income statement" that leaves out some components like interest deductions. (Note that the process of leaving out any interest deduction is exactly in line with our discussion above of not counting interest on debt as an expense of the project, but the resulting financial statement would *not* make an accountant happy.) Such a statement is shown in Table 12.4 for First Strike's proposed project. The primary benefit of

▼ TABLE 12.4 Calculation of OCF (Tax Rate 34 percent)

	Year 1		Year 2		Year 3	
Sales of FinProf	$599,850		$1,079,730		$199,950	
Reduced sales of MktProf	39,980		39,980		39,980	
Net incremental sales		$559,870		$1,039,750		$159,970
Variable costs of FinProf	$ 63,750		$ 114,750		$ 21,250	
Reduced variable costs of MktProf	7,000		7,000		7,000	
Net increase in variable costs		56,750		107,750		14,250
Less: Fixed costs		150,000		150,000		150,000
Less: Depreciation		24,000		24,000		24,000
EBIT		329,120		758,000		−28,280
Less: Taxes		111,901		257,720		−9,615
Net income		217,219		500,280		−18,665
Plus: Depreciation		24,000		24,000		24,000
OCF		$241,219		$ 524,280		$ 5,335

calculating OCF this way instead of as an algebraic formula is that with this format, we have space to expand subcalculations, such as the impact of FinProf being a partial substitute for the MktProf product.

You may wonder why we treat EBIT as negative for tax purposes in year 3 of the project. Since we are just calculating the cash flows to a single project, we draw upon the conventional approach for handling situations where the project "loses money" (on a taxable-income basis). We would thus assume that the rest of the firm would *make* enough positive taxable income that it would need this project's loss to shelter an equivalent amount

of income from the taxing authority. Table 12.4 reflects this by the negative taxes (−$9,615) "paid" during year 3, which is conceptually equal to a tax credit of $9,615.

Calculating Change in Gross Fixed Assets

Gross fixed assets will change in almost every project at both the beginning (when assets are usually purchased) and at the end (when assets are usually sold). First Strike's proposed project is no exception.

EXAMPLE 12-1

For interactive versions of this example visit www.mhhe.com/canM

ATCF for an Asset Sold at a Gain

Suppose that a firm facing a marginal tax rate of 25 percent sells an asset for $4,000 when its depreciated book value is $2,000. What will be the ATCF from the sale of this asset?

SOLUTION:
The ATCF will equal:

ATCF = $2,000 + ($4,000 − $2,000) × (1 − .25)

    = $3,500

Calculating the change in gross fixed assets at the beginning of the project is fairly straightforward—it will simply equal the asset's depreciable basis. So, for FSS's project, we will increase gross fixed assets by $77,000 at time zero.

At the end of a project, the change in gross fixed assets is a little more complicated, because whenever a firm sells any asset, it has to consider the tax consequences of that sale. The IRS treats any sale of assets for more than depreciated book value as taxable gains and any sale for less than book value as taxable losses. In either event, we can calculate the after-tax cash flow (ATCF) from the sale of an asset using the following formula where T_C is the same appropriate corporate tax rate discussed in the previous chapter.

$$ATCF = \text{Book value} + (\text{Market value} - \text{Book value}) \times (1 - T_C) \quad \text{(12-3)}$$

Since the machinery for FSS's project will be depreciated down to $5,000 but is expected to sell for only $2,000, the ATCF for that asset's sale will equal:

$$ATCF = \$5,000 + (\$2,000 - \$5,000) \times (1 - .34)$$

$$= \$3,020$$

Note that this formula would work equally well on an asset sold at a gain.

Calculating Changes in Net Working Capital

We can make several different assumptions concerning the NWC level necessary to support a project. The most straightforward of these would be to simply assume that we add NWC at the beginning of the project and reduce it at the end. This assumption would be valid if the project is expected to have steady sales throughout its life, and in these relatively rare circumstances we will use this assumption.

FSS's proposed project, however, features a more typical product life cycle. Its unit sales will follow an approximately bell-shaped curve. When sales are timed in this way, FSS needs to give a little more thought to exactly when the firm needs to set aside net working capital to support high sales volumes and when it can reduce NWC as sales drop off.

The assumption that First Strike's NWC at any particular time will be a function of the *next* year's sales might seem odd at first glance. But a little thought about how we measure balance sheet numbers (such as NWC) and income statement items (such as sales) will show that, really, this assumption makes a lot of sense. Since income statements (and our quasi-income statement discussed above) measure what happens *during* a period, the sales show up on the statement at time 1, even though they actually

First Strike's NWC at any time will be a function of next year's sales.

start accumulating at the *beginning* of year 1, which is time 0. The balance sheet "snapshots," on the other hand, capture how much capital sits in NWC accounts *at a particular point in time.* Therefore, the sales figures that appear in time 1 OCF calculation must be supported when they start occurring, at time 0. The time 0 NWC changes need to reflect that activity. Of course, the same argument holds true in general: Any sales figures that appear in a time *N* OCF calculation need support at the beginning of year *N* by the NWC level in time *N-1* balance sheet.

Since we covered the expected changes in gross fixed assets from a new project in the previous section, we don't even really have to track all of the changes in the balance sheet here. We only need to track the change in net current assets, and any change in NWC is actually measuring exactly the total net effect of changes in gross current assets and current liabilities for this project.

So, we can use the given information for the First Strike project to compute the NWC necessary to support sales throughout the project's life, and then in turn use NWC levels to compute the necessary changes in NWC, as shown in Table 12.5. Notice that the NWC level at each time is simply 10 percent of the following year's sales figures from Table 12.4.

Year	0	1	2	3
Level of NWC	$59,985	$107,973	$19,995	$0
$NWC_t - NWC_{t-1}$ = ΔNWC_t	$59,985 − $0 = $59,985	$107,973 − $59,985 = $47,988	$19,995 − $107,973 = −$87.9789,985	$0 − $19,995 = −$19.995

This method for computing changes in NWC levels has several appealing features:

- The changes in NWC at the beginning of a project will always equal the level at time 0, as NWC will be going from a presumed zero level before the project starts up to that new, nonzero level.

- Allowing NWC to vary as a percentage of coming sales like this allows FSS to add NWC during periods when it expects sales to increase (e.g., years 0 and 1 in this example) and to decrease NWC when it expects sales to fall off (e.g., years 2 and 3 in this example). NWC levels fall off the last two years of this project precisely because FSS expects sales to fall off and is adjusting NWC to compensate.

- Finally, one especially nice feature of this approach is that it will always automatically bring NWC back down to a zero level when the project ends. Since sales in the year *after* the project ends are always zero, 10 percent of zero will also be zero. This corresponds to what we would expect to see in the real world: when a project ends, the firm sells off inventory, collects from customers, pays off accounts receivable, and so forth.

Bringing It All Together

Using the numbers that we calculated for OCF, change in gross fixed assets, and change in NWC, First Strike's expected total cash flows from the new project would be as shown in Table 12.6.

Note, in particular, that correct use of the after-tax cash flow from selling the machinery at the end of the project requires that we change the cash flows' sign to negative when we enter it for year 3. Why? Because the ATCF formula shown in equation 12-3 does a little *too* much work for us. It computes cash flow effects of selling the asset, while the formula we're using for FCF wants us to enter the change in fixed assets. Or, to put it another way, cash flow at the end of the project should go up *because* fixed assets decrease. We subtract that decrease in our FCF = OCF − (ΔFA + ΔNWC) calculation, which has the effect of "subtracting a minus." Eventually, then, we increase the final year's FCF above that which we would have generated by just combining OCF with the cash freed up from decreasing NWC.

View interactive examples at mhhe.com/canM

👍 Eric Martinez and ten others like this.

Eric Martinez The Excel run-throughs were really helpful when I was doing my homework.
9 hours ago · Like

write a comment...

▼ **TABLE 12.6** Total Cash Flows

Year	0		1	2	3
OCF		$ 0	$241,219	$524,280	$ 5,335
FA	$77,000	$ 0	$ 0	−$3,020	
NWC	59,985	47,988	−87,978	−19,995	
Less: IOC		136,985	47,988	−87,978	−23,015
FCF		−$136,985	$193,231	$612,258	$ 28,350

time out!

12-3 Explain why an increase in NWC is treated as a cash outflow rather than as an inflow.

12-4 Will OCF typically be larger or smaller than net income? Why?

ACCELERATED DEPRECIATION AND THE HALF-YEAR CONVENTION

Our FCF calculation in the previous section was complete, but we used a rather simplistic assumption concerning depreciation to complete the calculation. In reality, the IRS requires that depreciation must be calculated using the half-year convention. The IRS thus requires that all property placed in service during a given period is assumed to be placed in service at the midpoint of that period.[1] By implication, three years of asset life, such as the machinery in the First Strike example, will extend over four calendar years of the firm. Table 12.7 shows an excerpt from the IRS depreciation table for straight-line depreciation using the half-year convention.

The percentage figures denote how much of the asset's depreciable basis may be deducted in each respective firm calendar year. For example, an asset with a depreciable basis of $100,000 falling into the three-year class life would be depreciated $100,000 × 16.67 percent = $16,670 during the first calendar year the firm owned it, $33,330 during the second and third years of ownership, and another $16,670 during the fourth year of ownership.

The IRS provides guidance on which categories various assets fall into, so it's usually pretty easy to figure out which column to use. For this text, we'll assume that we're always told which class-life category an asset falls under.

Note that the IRS's interpretation of the half-year convention isn't as direct as simply taking one-half of the first year's depreciation and moving it to the end of the asset's life. For example, the column for 3.5 year depreciation shows that such an asset would have 14.29 percent of its value depreciated during the first year and 28.57 percent during each of the second, third, and fourth years. So, rather than using a formula to compute the depreciation percentage, it's preferable to look the percentages up from the appropriate IRS table. A copy of the entire table for straight-line depreciation using the half-year convention appears as Appendix 12A at the end of this chapter.

MACRS Depreciation Calculation

Though the IRS allows firms to use the straight-line method with the half-year convention to depreciate assets, most businesses probably benefit from using some form of accelerated depreciation. Accelerated depreciation allows firms to receive more of the dollars of depreciation earlier in the asset's life.

An example of this is the double-declining-balance (DDB) depreciation method, under which the depreciation rate is double that used in the straight-line method. The IRS also uses the half-year convention with DDB depreciation, so the actual yearly percentages appear in Table 12.8. The IRS allows businesses to take the most advantageous choice between straight-line and DDB depreciation methods under the modified accelerated cost recovery system (MACRS).

Section 179 Deductions

We can accelerate asset expensing even further by expensing it immediately in the year of purchase. The IRS allows most businesses to immediately expense up to $108,000 of property placed in service during

▼ **TABLE 12.7** Excerpt of Straight-Line Depreciation Table with Half-Year Convention

Year	Normal Recovery Period				
	2.5	3	3.5	4	5
1	20.00%	16.67%	14.29%	12.50%	10.00%
2	40.00	33.33	28.57	25.00	20.00
3	40.00	33.33	28.57	25.00	20.00
4	0.00	16.67	28.57	25.00	20.00
5	0.00	0.00	0.00	12.50	20.00
6	0.00	0.00	0.00	0.00	10.00

[1]There are also midmonth and midquarter conventions, which apply in special circumstances. Please refer to IRS Publication 946 for details.

each year under what is referred to as a **Section 179 deduction.** The Section 179 deduction is obviously targeted at helping small businesses, so it places a limit on the annual total of deductible property. If the cost of qualifying Section 179 property you put into service in a single tax year exceeds a statutory base of $430,000, then you can't take the full deduction.

For example, consider a manufacturer who completely reequips his facility this year, which costs $437,000. This is $7,000 more than allowed, so he must reduce his eligible deductible limit to $101,000: the current $108,000 expensing limit minus $7,000. Extending this even further, a company that spent $430,00 + $108,000 = $538,000 or more on qualifying Section 179 property would not be able to take the deduction at all, though the firm could depreciate the property using MACRS.

Property eligible for a Section 179 deduction includes:

- Machinery and equipment.
- Furniture and fixtures.
- Most storage facilities.
- Single-purpose agricultural or horticultural structures.
- Off-the-shelf computer software.

Ineligible property includes:

- Buildings and their structural components.
- Income-producing property (investment or rental property).
- Property held by an estate or trust.
- Property acquired by gift or inheritance.
- Property used in a passive activity.
- Property purchased from related parties.
- Property used outside of the United States.

▼ **TABLE 12.8** DDB Depreciation with Half-Year Convention

Year	Normal Recovery Period					
	3	5	7	10	15	20
1	33.33%	20.00%	14.29%	10.00	5.00%	3.750%
2	44.45	32.00	24.49	18.00	9.50	7.219
3	14.81	19.20	17.49	14.40	8.55	6.677
4	7.41	11.52	12.49	11.52	7.70	6.177
5	0.00	11.52	8.93	9.22	6.93	5.713
6	0.00	5.76	8.92	7.37	6.23	5.285
7	0.00	0.00	8.93	6.55	5.90	4.888
8	0.00	0.00	4.46	6.55	5.90	4.522
9	0.00	0.00	0.00	6.56	5.91	4.462
10	0.00	0.00	0.00	6.55	5.90	4.461
11	0.00	0.00	0.00	3.28	5.91	4.462
12	0.00	0.00	0.00	0.00	5.90	4.461
13	0.00	0.00	0.00	0.00	5.91	4.462
14	0.00	0.00	0.00	0.00	5.90	4.461
15	0.00	0.00	0.00	0.00	5.91	4.462
16	0.00	0.00	0.00	0.00	2.95	4.461
17	0.00	0.00	0.00	0.00	0.00	4.462
18	0.00	0.00	0.00	0.00	0.00	4.461
19	0.00	0.00	0.00	0.00	0.00	4.462
20	0.00	0.00	0.00	0.00	0.00	4.461
21	0.00	0.00	0.00	0.00	0.00	2.231

Impact of Accelerated Depreciation

So, let's return to our FSS example and FinProf. Remember that our initial, simplistic view of depreciation had us taking $24,000 per year for each of the three years of the project's life. If the software reproduction machinery fell into the three-year life class, we could instead have taken the following depreciation amounts by using either the straight-line or DDB approaches:

If First Strike could take advantage of the Section 179 deduction, that would probably be the most advantageous way to deduct the cost of the new machinery—it could deduct the entire $77,000 in year 1. If FSS couldn't use a Section 179 deduction, the DDB depreciation available under MACRS would result in the next quickest recovery of the tax breaks associated with the machinery purchase.

▼ **TABLE 12.9** FSS's Yearly Depreciation and Ending Book Values under Alternative Depreciation

	Year 1	Year 2	Year 3	Ending BV
Straight-line	$77,000 × 16.67% = $12,835.90	$77,000 × 33.33% = $25,664.10	$77,000 × 33.33% = $25,664.10	$12,835.90
DDB	$77,000 × 33.33% = $25,664.10	$77,000 × 44.45% = $34,226.50	$77,000 × 14.81% = $11,403.70	$5,705.70

Machinery is eligible for a Section 179 deduction.

"SPECIAL" CASES AREN'T REALLY THAT SPECIAL

As long as we're consistent in using incremental FCF to calculate total project cash flows, we can handle many project types that are habitually viewed as "special" cases requiring extraordinary treatment with some relatively simple revisions to the methods we used for valuing First Strike's proposed new project.

EXAMPLE 12-2

Replacement Problem

Suppose that Just-in-Time Donuts is considering replacing one of its existing ovens. The original oven cost $100,000 when purchased five years ago and has been depreciated by $9,000 per year since then. Just-in-Time thinks that they can sell the old machine for $65,000 if they sell it today, and for $10,000 if they wait another five years until its anticipated life is over. Just-in-Time is considering replacing this oven with a new one, which costs $150,000, partly because the new oven will save them $50,000 in costs per year relative to the old oven. The new oven will be subject to three-year class life DDB depreciation under MACRS, with an anticipated useful life of five years. At the end of the five years, Just-In-Time will abandon the oven as worthless. If Just-in-Time faces a marginal tax rate of 35 percent, what will be the total project cash flows if they replace the oven?

SOLUTION:

If we sell the old oven today for $65,000 when it has a remaining book value of $55,000 ($100,000 purchase price − 5 years of $9,000 per year depreciation), then the ATCF from its sale will equal:

$$\text{ATCF} = \text{Book value} + (\text{Market value} - \text{Book value}) \times (1 - T_C)$$

$$= \$55,000 + (\$65,000 - \$55,000) \times (1 - .40)$$

$$= \$61,000$$

In return for selling the old oven today, however, JIT will have to forgo both the yearly depreciation that the company would have received for it over the next five years and the $10,000 that it could get for selling it at the end of the five years. We must reflect both of these factors in our calculation of incremental FCFs so that we are reckoning the true costs of the project. In addition, switching from the old oven to the new one would apparently alter neither sales nor NWC requirements across the five-year life of the new oven:

Year	0	1	2	3	4	5
Net incremental sales		$0	$0	$0	$0	$0
Net incremental variable costs		−50,000	−50,000	−50,000	−50,000	−50,000
Depreciation on new oven		$49,995	$66,675	$22,215	$11,115	$0
Forgone depreciation on old oven		−9,000	−9,000	−9,000	−9,000	−9,000
Less: Incremental depreciation	$0	40,995	57,675	13,215	2,115	−9,000
EBIT	$0	9,005	−7,675	36,785	47,885	59,000
Less: Taxes	$0	3,152	−2,686	12,875	16,760	20,650
"Net income"	$0	5,853	−4,989	23,910	31,125	38,350
Plus: Depreciation	$0	40,995	57,675	13,215	2,115	−9,000
OCF	$0	$46,848	$52,686	$37,125	$33,240	$29,350
ΔFA for new oven	$150,000					$0
ΔFA for old oven	−$61,000					$10,000
ΔFA	$89,000	$0	$0	$0	$0	$10,000
ΔNWC	0	0	0	0	0	0
Less: Investment in operating capital	$89,000	$0	$0	$0	$0	$10,000
FCF = OCF − IOC	−$89,000	$46,848	$52,686	$37,125	$33,240	$19,350

We usually think that a positive value for ΔFA is associated with the purchase of FA. But note that in this circumstance, the $10,000 for the forgone sale of the old oven at time 5 is *not* an investment in fixed assets, but rather the opportunity cost of not getting to sell the old oven at higher than book value.

EXAMPLE 12-3

For interactive versions
of this example visit
www.mhhe.com/canM

Cost-Cutting Problem

Your company is considering a new computer system that will initially cost $1 million. It will save your firm $300,000 a year in inventory and receivables management costs. The system is expected to last for five years and will be depreciated using three-year MACRS. The firm expects that the system will have a salvage value of $50,000 at the end of year 5. This purchase does not affect net working capital; the marginal tax rate is 34 percent, and the required return is 8 percent. What will be the total project cash flows if this cost-cutting proposal is implemented?

SOLUTION:

Since the new computer falls into the three-year MACRS category, it will be fully depreciated when the project ends five years from now. As a result, the ATCF from the sale of the computer will be:

$$ATCF = BV + (MV - BV) \times (1 - T_C)$$

$$= \$0 + (\$50,000 - \$0) \times (1 - .34)$$

$$= \$33,000$$

And the FCFs for the cost-cutting proposal will be equal to:

Year	0		1	2	3	4	5	
Net incremental sales			$0	$0	$0	$0		$0
Less: Incremental variable costs			−300,000	−300,000	−300,000	−300,000		−300,000
Less: Incremental depreciation	$0		$333,300	$444,500	$148,100	$74,000		$0
EBIT	$0		−33,300	−144,500	151,900	225,900		300,000
Less: Taxes	$0		−11,322	−49,130	51,646	76,806		102,000
"Net income"	$0		−21,978	−95,370	100,254	149,094		198,000
Plus: Depreciation	$0		333,300	444,500	148,100	74,100		0
OCF	$0		$311,322	$349,130	$248,354	$223,194		$198,000
ΔFA	$1,000,000	$0		$0	$0	$0	−$33,000	
ΔNWC	0	0		0	0	0	0	
Less: Investment in operating capital		$1,000,000	$0	$0	$0	$0		−$33,000
FCF = OCF − IOC		−$1,000,000	$311,322	$349,130	$248,354	$223,194		$231,000

time out!

12-7 Explain why, in Example 12-2, the investment in operating capital in the last year of the project was positive instead of negative.

12-8 Would it ever be possible to have a project that generated net positive cash flows across all years of a project's life just by buying and depreciating assets?

CHOOSING BETWEEN ALTERNATIVE ASSETS WITH DIFFERING LIVES: EAC

Suppose a company has decided to go ahead with a project but needs to choose between two alternative assets, wherein:

- Both assets will result in the same sales.
- Both assets may have different costs and recurring expenses.

- Assets will last different lengths of time.

- When the chosen asset wears out, it will be replaced with an identical machine.

In such a situation, the firm can't really compare one iteration of each machine to the other, since they last different lengths of time. The key here is to use the fact that, since the firm will replace each machine with another identical machine when it wears out, it is really being asked to choose between two sets of infinite, but systematically varying, sets of cash flows. To handle such a situation, "smooth out" the variation in each set of cash flows so that each becomes a perpetuity. Then the company can choose between the two machines based on which will generate the highest present value of cash flows.

Since the decision will involve only a subset of a project's cash flows—the purchase of one of a choice of assets—that present value will probably be negative. If the firm were to look at all the benefits deriving from the choice of which asset to use, including expected sales and so forth, the present value of all cash flows would need to be positive for the entire project to be attractive. We will discuss this in much greater depth in the next chapter when we cover the *net present value (NPV)* rule for capital budgeting decisions.

The best approach to convert an infinite series of asset purchases into a perpetuity is known as the *equivalent annual cost* (EAC) approach. To compute and use the EACs of two or more alternative assets,

1. Find the sum of the present values of the cash flows (the net present value, or NPV, which we will cover in great detail in the next chapter) for one iteration of A and one iteration of B.

2. Treat each sum as the present value of an annuity with life equal to the life of the respective asset, and solve for each asset's payment.

3. Choose the asset with the highest (i.e., least negative) EAC.

It may seem that we have just done exactly what we said we should not do: compare the cash flows from one machine A to those from one machine B. In fact, the comparison we just did is actually much broader than that, though it will take a little explanation to see.

Visualize the cash flows to the infinitely repeated purchases of machine B (chosen simply because it has a short life, so it will be easier to see multiple iterations on a time line in the following discussion) as shown in Figure 12.1.

Notice that, after the initial purchase of the first machine B, the cash flows exhibit a systematic cycle: −$3,500 for two years, followed by −$15,500 for one year (when the next machine B is purchased), repeating this way forever. This systematic cycle, which we don't have a formula for valuing, makes it necessary to convert these cash flows into a perpetuity, which we *can* value.

When we computed the NPV of one iteration of machine B, we basically "squished" that machine's cash flows down to a single lump sum, and when we treated that as the present value of an annuity and solved for the payments, we were effectively taking that same value and spreading it evenly across the life of the first machine B. Furthermore, since subsequent machine B purchases will be identical to this first one, we can visualize doing the exact same thing to *every* machine B's cash flow. Turning each machine B's cash flow into an annuity in this manner has the net effect of turning all the machine B's cash flows into a perpetuity, as shown in Figure 12.2

In the process, we also turn the repeated purchase of machine A into a perpetuity. We *could* calculate the present values of these two perpetuities and then compare them, which is what we're really interested in doing:

▼**FIGURE 12.1** Cash Flows of Repeated Purchases of Machine B

Year	0	1	2	3	4	5	6
B	−$12,000	−$3,500	−$3,500	−$3,500			
				−$12,000	−$3,500	−$3,500	−$3,500
							−$12,000
B Total	−$12,000	−$3,500	−$3,500	−$15,500	−$3,500	−$3,500	−$15,500

▼**FIGURE 12.2** Converted Cash Flows of Repeated Purchases of Machine B

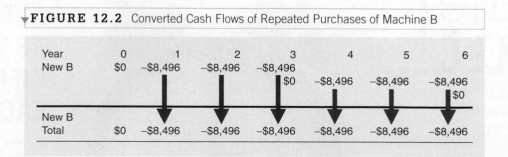

Year	0	1	2	3	4	5	6
New B	$0	−$8,496	−$8,496	−$8,496			
				$0	−$8,496	−$8,496	−$8,496
							$0
New B Total	$0	−$8,496	−$8,496	−$8,496	−$8,496	−$8,496	−$8,496

EXAMPLE 12-4

For interactive versions
of this example visit
www.mhhe.com/canM

EAC Approach

Suppose that your company has won a bid for a new project—painting highway signs for the local highway department. Based on past experience, you're pretty sure that your company will have the contract for the foreseeable future, and now you have to decide whether to use machine A or machine B to paint the signs: Machine A costs $20,000, lasts five years, and will generate annual after-tax net expenses of $2,500. Machine B costs $12,000, lasts three years, and will have after-tax net expenses of $3,500 per year. Assume that, in either case, each machine will simply be junked at the end of its useful life, and the firm faces a cost of capital of 12 percent. Which machine should you choose?

SOLUTION:

One iteration of each machine will consist of the sets of cash flows shown below:

Year	0	1	2	3	4	5
Machine A CFs	−$20,000	−$2,500	−$2,500	−$2,500	−$2,500	−$2,500
Machine B CFs	−12,000	−3,500	−3,500	−3,500		

The sum of the present values of machine A's cash flows will be

$$\sum_{t=0}^{5} \frac{CF_t}{(1+i)^t} = \frac{CF_0}{(1+i)^0} + \frac{CF_1}{(1+i)^1} + \frac{CF_2}{(1+i)^2} + \frac{CF_3}{(1+i)^3} + \frac{CF_4}{(1+i)^4} + \frac{CF_5}{(1+i)^5}$$

$$= \frac{-\$20,000}{(1.12)^0} + \frac{-\$2,500}{(1.12)^1} + \frac{-\$2,500}{(1.12)^2} + \frac{-\$2,500}{(1.12)^3} + \frac{-\$2,500}{(1.12)^4} + \frac{-\$2,500}{(1.12)^5}$$

$$= -\$29,012$$

Treating this as the present value of a five-period annuity, setting i to 12 percent, and solving for payment will yield a payment of −$8,048, which is machine A's EAC.
The sum of the present values of machine B's cash flows will be

$$\sum_{t=0}^{3} \frac{CF_t}{(1+i)^t} = \frac{CF_0}{(1+i)^0} + \frac{CF_1}{(1+i)^1} + \frac{CF_2}{(1+i)^2} + \frac{CF_3}{(1+i)^3}$$

$$= \frac{-\$12,000}{(1.12)^0} + \frac{-\$3,500}{(1.12)^1} + \frac{-\$3,500}{(1.12)^2} + \frac{-\$3,500}{(1.12)^3}$$

$$= -\$20,406$$

Treating this as the present value of a three-period annuity, setting i to 12 percent, and solving for payment will yield a payment of −$8,496, which is machine B's EAC.

Since machine A's EAC is less negative than machine B's, your firm should choose machine A.

$$PV_{\text{Perpetuity of Infinitely Repeated As}} \text{ vs. } PV_{\text{Perpetuity of Infinitely Repeated Bs}}$$

$$\frac{-\$8,048}{.12} \quad \text{vs.} \quad \frac{-\$8,496}{.12}$$

But do we really need to? No. The relationship between these two present values of the respective perpetuities is really the

same as the relationship between their payment amounts[2]—each machine's respective EAC.

[2]Because the two perpetuities have the same interest rate and the same periodicity (i.e., length between payments), the only possible source of difference in their present values would be the respective payment amounts.

time out!

12-9 Explain how the EAC approach turns uneven cash flows for infinitely repeated asset purchases into perpetuities.

12-10 What if two alternative assets would last the same length of time: would the EAC approach still work?

12-11 How would you compute the equity flotation cost if a firm were going to use a mixture of retained earnings and new equity to finance a project?

12-12 Why do we divide the initial cash flow by $(1 - f_A)$ instead of multiplying it by $(1 + f_A)$?

FLOTATION COSTS REVISITED

In the previous chapter, we talked about how to take account of flotation costs by adjusting the WACC upwards, incorporating flotation costs directly into the issue prices of the securities used to fund projects. Another way that we can account for flotation costs is to adjust the project's initial cash flow so that it will reflect the flotation costs of raising capital for the project as well as the necessary investment in assets.

In this approach, we will

1. Compute the weighted average flotation cost, f_A, using the firm's target capital weights (because the firm will issue securities in these percentages over the long term):

$$f_A = \frac{E}{E+P+D}\,f_E + \frac{P}{E+P+D}\,f_P + \frac{D}{E+P+D}\,f_D \qquad (12\text{-}4)$$

where f_E, f_P, and f_D are the percentage flotation costs for new equity, preferred stock, and debt, respectively.

2. Compute the flotation-adjusted initial investment, CF_0, using

$$\text{Adjusted } CF_0 = \frac{CF_0}{1 - f_A} \qquad (12\text{-}5)$$

EXAMPLE 12-5

For interactive versions of this example visit www.mhhe.com/canM

Adjusting CF_0 for Flotation Cost

Your company is considering a project that will cost $1 million. The project will generate after-tax cash flows of $375,000 per year for five years. The WACC is 15 percent and the firm's target D/A ratio is .375. The flotation cost for equity is 5 percent, the flotation cost for debt is 3 percent, and your firm does not plan on issuing any preferred stock within its capital structure. If your firm follows the practice of incorporating flotation costs into the project's initial investment, what will the flotation-adjusted cash flows for this project be?

SOLUTION:

Since the D/A is .375, the E/A ratio will be equal to $1 - .375 = .625$, and the weighted-average flotation cost for the firm will be:

$$f_A = \frac{E}{E+P+D}\,f_E + \frac{P}{E+P+D}\,f_P + \frac{D}{E+P+D}\,f_D$$

$$= (.625 \times 5\%) + (.375 \times 3\%)$$

$$= 4.25\%$$

(continued)

Using this, the adjusted CF_0 for the project will be:

$$\text{Adjusted } CF_0 = \frac{CF_0}{1 - f_A}$$

$$= \frac{-\$1,000,000}{1 - .0425}$$

$$= -\$1,044,386.42$$

So the flotation-adjusted cash flows for the project will be:

Year	0	1	2	3	4	5
Cash Flow	−$1,044,386.42	$375,000	$375,000	$375,000	$375,000	$375,000

> The best approach to convert an infinite series of asset purchases into a perpetuity is known as the *equivalent annual cost* (EAC) approach.

Get Online

mhhe.com/canM

for study materials including
quizzes, iPod downloads,
and video

Your Turn...

Questions

1. How is the *pro forma* statement we used in this chapter for computing OCF different from an accountant's income statement? *(LG1)*

2. Suppose you paid your old college finance professor to evaluate a project for you. If you would pay him regardless of your decision concerning whether to proceed with the project, should his fee for evaluating the project be included in the project's incremental cash flows? *(LG2)*

3. Why does a decrease in NWC result in a cash inflow to the firm? *(LG3)*

4. Everything else held constant, would you rather depreciate a project with straight-line depreciation or with DDB? *(LG4)*

5. Everything else held constant, would you rather depreciate a project with DDB depreciation or deduct it under a Section 179 deduction? *(LG4)*

6. In a replacement problem, would we ever see changes in NWC? *(LG5)*

7. In a replacement problem, will incremental net depreciation always be less than the gross depreciation on the new piece of equipment? *(LG5)*

8. In a cost-cutting proposal, what might cause you to sometimes have negative EBIT? *(LG6)*

9. How many TVM formulas do you use every time you calculate EAC for a project? *(LG7)*

10. Will an increase in flotation costs increase or decrease the initial cash flow for a project? *(LG8)*

Problems

BASIC PROBLEMS

12-1 After-Tax Cash Flow from Sale of Assets Suppose you sell a fixed asset for $109,000 when its book value is $129,000. If your company's marginal tax rate is 39 percent, what will be the effect on cash flows of this sale (i.e., what will be the after-tax cash flow of this sale)? *(LG3)*

12-2 PV of Depreciation Tax Benefits Your company is considering a new project that will require $1 million of new equipment at the start of the project. The equipment will have a depreciable life of 10 years and will be depreciated to a book value of $150,000 using straight-line depreciation. The cost of capital is 13 percent, and the firm's tax rate is 34 percent. Estimate the present value of the tax benefits from depreciation. *(LG4)*

12-3 EAC Approach You are trying to pick the least-expensive car for your new delivery service. You have two choices: the Scion xA, which will cost $14,000 to purchase and which will have OCF of −$1,200 annually throughout the vehicle's expected life of three years as a delivery vehicle; and the Toyota Prius, which will cost $20,000 to purchase and which will have OCF of −$650 annually throughout that vehicle's expected four-year life. Both cars will be worthless at the end of their life. If you intend to replace whichever type of car you choose with the same thing when its life runs out, again and again out into the foreseeable future, and if your business has a cost of capital of 12 percent, which one should you choose? *(LG7)*

12-4 EAC Approach You are evaluating two different cookie-baking ovens. The Pillsbury 707 costs $57,000, has a five-year life, and has an annual OCF (after tax) of −$10,000 per year. The Keebler CookieMunster costs $90,000, has a seven-year life, and has an annual OCF (after tax) of −$8,000 per year. If your discount rate is 12 percent, what is each machine's EAC? *(LG8)*

12-5 EAC Approach You are considering the purchase of one of two machines used in your manufacturing plant. Machine A has a life of two years, costs $80 initially, and then $125 per year in maintenance costs. Machine B costs $150 initially, has a life of three years, and requires $100 in annual maintenance costs. Either machine must be replaced at the end of its life with an equivalent machine. Which is the better machine for the firm? The discount rate is 12 percent and the tax rate is zero. *(LG8)*

INTERMEDIATE PROBLEMS

12-6 Project Cash Flows KADS, Inc. has spent $400,000 on research to develop a new computer game. The firm is planning to spend $200,000 on a machine to produce the new game.

Shipping and installation costs of the machine will be capitalized and depreciated; they total $50,000. The machine has an expected life of three years, a $75,000 estimated resale value, and falls under the MACRS seven-year class life. Revenue from the new game is expected to be $600,000 per year, with costs of $250,000 per year. The firm has a tax rate of 35 percent, an opportunity cost of capital of 15 percent, and it expects net working capital to increase by $100,000 at the beginning of the project. What will the cash flows for this project be? *(LG3)*

12-7 Depreciation Tax Shield Your firm needs a computerized machine tool lathe which costs $50,000 and requires $12,000 in maintenance for each year of its three-year life. After three years, this machine will be replaced. The machine falls into the MACRS three-year class life category. Assume a tax rate of 35 percent and a discount rate of 12 percent. Calculate the depreciation tax shield for this project in year 3. *(LG4)*

12-8 After-Tax Cash Flow from Sale of Assets If the lathe in the previous problem can be sold for $5,000 at the end of year 3, what is the after-tax salvage value? *(LG4)*

12-9 Project Cash Flows You have been asked by the president of your company to evaluate the proposed acquisition of a new special-purpose truck for $60,000. The truck falls into the MACRS three-year class, and it will be sold after three years for $20,000. Use of the truck will require an increase in NWC (spare parts inventory) of $2,000. The truck will have no effect on revenues, but it is expected to save the firm $20,000 per year in before-tax operating costs, mainly labor. The firm's marginal tax rate is 40 percent. What will the cash flows for this project be? *(LG6)*

ADVANCED PROBLEMS

12-10 Change in NWC You are evaluating a project for The Tiff-any golf club, guaranteed to correct that nasty slice. You estimate the sales price of The Tiff-any to be $400 per unit and sales volume to be 1,000 units in year 1; 1,500 units in year 2; and 1,325 units in year 3. The project has a three-year life. Variable costs amount to $225 per unit and fixed costs are $100,000 per year. The project requires an initial investment of $165,000 in assets, which will be depreciated straight-line to zero over the three-year project life. The actual market value of these assets at the end of year 3 is expected to be $35,000. NWC requirements at the beginning of each year will be approximately 20 percent of the projected sales during the coming year. The tax rate is 34 percent and the required return on the project is 10 percent. What change in NWC occurs at the end of year 1? *(LG3)*

12-11 Operating Cash Flow Continuing the previous problem, what is the operating cash flow for the project in year 2? *(LG3)*

12-12 Project Cash Flows You are evaluating a project for The Ultimate recreational tennis racket, guaranteed to correct that wimpy backhand. You estimate the sales price of The Ultimate to be $400 per unit and sales volume to be 1,000 units in year 1; 1,250 units in year 2; and 1,325 units in year 3. The project has a three-year life. Variable costs amount to $225 per unit and fixed costs are $100,000 per year. The project requires an initial investment of $165,000 in assets, which will be depreciated straight-line to zero over the three-year project life. The actual market value of these assets at the end of year 3 is expected to be $35,000. NWC requirements at the beginning of each year will be approximately 20 percent of the projected sales during the coming year. The tax rate is 34 percent and the required return on the project is 10 percent. What will the cash flows for this project be? *(LG3)*

12-13 Project Cash Flows Mom's Cookies Inc. is considering the purchase of a new cookie oven. The original cost of the old oven was $30,000; it is now five years old, and it has a current market value of $13,333.33. The old oven is being depreciated over a 10-year life toward a zero estimated salvage value on a straight-line basis, resulting in a current book value of $15,000 and an annual depreciation expense of $3,000. The old oven can be used for six more years but has no market value after its depreciable life is over. Management is contemplating the purchase of a new oven whose cost is $25,000 and whose estimated salvage value is zero. Expected before-tax cash savings from the new oven are $4,000 a year over its full MACRS depreciable life. Depreciation is computed using MACRS over a five-year life, and the cost of capital is 10 percent. Assume a 40 percent tax rate. What will the cash flows for this project be? *(LG5)*

chapter twelve appendix

MACRS depreciation tables

▼ MACRS DEPRECIATION

Year	3	5	7	10	15	20	Residential 27.5	Nonresidential 31.5	39
			Normal Recovery Period					Real Estate	
1	33.33%	20.00%	14.29%	10.00%	5.00%	3.750%	3.485%	3.0420%	2.461%
2	44.45	32.00	24.49	18.00	9.50	7.219	3.636	3.1750	2.564
3	14.81	19.20	17.49	14.40	8.55	6.677	3.636	3.1750	2.564
4	7.41	11.52	12.49	11.52	7.70	6.177	3.636	3.1750	2.564
5	0.00	11.52	8.93	9.22	6.93	5.713	3.636	3.1750	2.564
6	0.00	5.76	8.92	7.37	6.23	5.285	3.636	3.1750	2.564
7	0.00	0.00	8.93	6.55	5.90	4.888	3.636	3.1750	2.564
8	0.00	0.00	4.46	6.55	5.90	4.522	3.636	3.1750	2.564
9	0.00	0.00	0.00	6.56	5.91	4.462	3.636	3.1740	2.564
10	0.00	0.00	0.00	6.55	5.90	4.461	3.637	3.1750	2.564
11	0.00	0.00	0.00	3.28	5.91	4.462	3.636	3.1740	2.564
12	0.00	0.00	0.00	0.00	5.90	4.461	3.637	3.1750	2.564
13	0.00	0.00	0.00	0.00	5.91	4.462	3.636	3.1740	2.564
14	0.00	0.00	0.00	0.00	5.90	4.461	3.637	3.1750	2.564
15	0.00	0.00	0.00	0.00	5.91	4.462	3.636	3.1740	2.564
16	0.00	0.00	0.00	0.00	2.95	4.461	3.637	3.1750	2.564
17	0.00	0.00	0.00	0.00	0.00	4.462	3.636	3.1740	2.564
18	0.00	0.00	0.00	0.00	0.00	4.461	3.637	3.1750	2.564
19	0.00	0.00	0.00	0.00	0.00	4.462	3.636	3.1740	2.564
20	0.00	0.00	0.00	0.00	0.00	4.461	3.637	3.1750	2.564
21	0.00	0.00	0.00	0.00	0.00	2.231	3.636	3.1740	2.564
22	0.00	0.00	0.00	0.00	0.00	0.00	3.637	3.1750	2.564
23	0.00	0.00	0.00	0.00	0.00	0.00	3.636	3.1740	2.564
24	0.00	0.00	0.00	0.00	0.00	0.00	3.637	3.1750	2.564
25	0.00	0.00	0.00	0.00	0.00	0.00	3.636	3.1740	2.564
26	0.00	0.00	0.00	0.00	0.00	0.00	3.637	3.1750	2.564
27	0.00	0.00	0.00	0.00	0.00	0.00	3.636	3.1740	2.564
28	0.00	0.00	0.00	0.00	0.00	0.00	1.970	3.1750	2.564
29	0.00	0.00	0.00	0.00	0.00	0.00	0.00	3.1740	2.564
30	0.00	0.00	0.00	0.00	0.00	0.00	0.00	3.1750	2.564
31	0.00	0.00	0.00	0.00	0.00	0.00	0.00	3.1740	2.564
32	0.00	0.00	0.00	0.00	0.00	0.00	0.00	1.7200	2.564
33	0.00	0.00	0.00	0.00	0.00	0.00	0.00	0.00	2.564
34	0.00	0.00	0.00	0.00	0.00	0.00	0.00	0.00	2.564
35	0.00	0.00	0.00	0.00	0.00	0.00	0.00	0.00	2.564
36	0.00	0.00	0.00	0.00	0.00	0.00	0.00	0.00	2.564
37	0.00	0.00	0.00	0.00	0.00	0.00	0.00	0.00	2.564
38	0.00	0.00	0.00	0.00	0.00	0.00	0.00	0.00	2.564
39	0.00	0.00	0.00	0.00	0.00	0.00	0.00	0.00	2.564
40	0.00	0.00	0.00	0.00	0.00	0.00	0.00	0.00	0.107
41	0.00	0.00	0.00	0.00	0.00	0.00	0.00	0.00	0.000

SL DEPRECIATION

						Normal Recovery Period							
Year	2.5	3	3.5	4	5	6	6.5	7	7.5	8	8.5	9
1	20.00%	16.67%	14.29%	12.50%	10.00%	8.33%	7.69%	7.14%	6.67%	6.25%	5.88%	5.56%
2	40.00	33.33	28.57	25.00	20.00	16.67	15.39	14.29	13.33	12.50	11.77	11.11
3	40.00	33.33	28.57	25.00	20.00	16.67	15.38	14.29	13.33	12.50	11.76	11.11
4	0.00	16.67	28.57	25.00	20.00	16.67	15.39	14.28	13.33	12.50	11.77	11.11
5	0.00	0.00	0.00	12.50	20.00	16.66	15.38	14.29	13.34	12.50	11.76	11.11
6	0.00	0.00	0.00	0.00	10.00	16.67	15.39	14.28	13.33	12.50	11.77	11.11
7	0.00	0.00	0.00	0.00	0.00	8.33	15.38	14.29	13.34	12.50	11.76	11.11
8	0.00	0.00	0.00	0.00	0.00	0.00	0.00	7.14	13.33	12.50	11.77	11.11
9	0.00	0.00	0.00	0.00	0.00	0.00	0.00	0.00	0.00	6.25	11.76	11.11
10	0.00	0.00	0.00	0.00	0.00	0.00	0.00	0.00	0.00	0.00	0.00	5.56
11	0.00	0.00	0.00	0.00	0.00	0.00	0.00	0.00	0.00	0.00	0.00	0.00
12	0.00	0.00	0.00	0.00	0.00	0.00	0.00	0.00	0.00	0.00	0.00	0.00
13	0.00	0.00	0.00	0.00	0.00	0.00	0.00	0.00	0.00	0.00	0.00	0.00
14	0.00	0.00	0.00	0.00	0.00	0.00	0.00	0.00	0.00	0.00	0.00	0.00
15	0.00	0.00	0.00	0.00	0.00	0.00	0.00	0.00	0.00	0.00	0.00	0.00
16	0.00	0.00	0.00	0.00	0.00	0.00	0.00	0.00	0.00	0.00	0.00	0.00
17	0.00	0.00	0.00	0.00	0.00	0.00	0.00	0.00	0.00	0.00	0.00	0.00
18	0.00	0.00	0.00	0.00	0.00	0.00	0.00	0.00	0.00	0.00	0.00	0.00
19	0.00	0.00	0.00	0.00	0.00	0.00	0.00	0.00	0.00	0.00	0.00	0.00
20	0.00	0.00	0.00	0.00	0.00	0.00	0.00	0.00	0.00	0.00	0.00	0.00
21	0.00	0.00	0.00	0.00	0.00	0.00	0.00	0.00	0.00	0.00	0.00	0.00
22	0.00	0.00	0.00	0.00	0.00	0.00	0.00	0.00	0.00	0.00	0.00	0.00
23	0.00	0.00	0.00	0.00	0.00	0.00	0.00	0.00	0.00	0.00	0.00	0.00
24	0.00	0.00	0.00	0.00	0.00	0.00	0.00	0.00	0.00	0.00	0.00	0.00
25	0.00	0.00	0.00	0.00	0.00	0.00	0.00	0.00	0.00	0.00	0.00	0.00
26	0.00	0.00	0.00	0.00	0.00	0.00	0.00	0.00	0.00	0.00	0.00	0.00
27	0.00	0.00	0.00	0.00	0.00	0.00	0.00	0.00	0.00	0.00	0.00	0.00
28	0.00	0.00	0.00	0.00	0.00	0.00	0.00	0.00	0.00	0.00	0.00	0.00
29	0.00	0.00	0.00	0.00	0.00	0.00	0.00	0.00	0.00	0.00	0.00	0.00
30	0.00	0.00	0.00	0.00	0.00	0.00	0.00	0.00	0.00	0.00	0.00	0.00
31	0.00	0.00	0.00	0.00	0.00	0.00	0.00	0.00	0.00	0.00	0.00	0.00
32	0.00	0.00	0.00	0.00	0.00	0.00	0.00	0.00	0.00	0.00	0.00	0.00
33	0.00	0.00	0.00	0.00	0.00	0.00	0.00	0.00	0.00	0.00	0.00	0.00
34	0.00	0.00	0.00	0.00	0.00	0.00	0.00	0.00	0.00	0.00	0.00	0.00
35	0.00	0.00	0.00	0.00	0.00	0.00	0.00	0.00	0.00	0.00	0.00	0.00
36	0.00	3.00	3.00	4.00	5.00	6.00	6.50	7.00	7.50	8.00	8.00	9.00
37	20.00%	6.00%	0.00%	0.00%	10.00%	8.33%	7.69%	7.00%	6.67%	6.25%	5.88%	5.56%
38	0.00	33.00	0.00	0.00	20.00	0.00	15.39	14.29	13.33	12.50	0.00	0.00
39	0.00	0.00	0.00	0.00	0.00	0.00	0.00	0.00	0.00	0.00	0.00	0.00
40	0.00	0.00	0.00	0.00	0.00	0.00	0.00	0.00	0.00	0.00	0.00	0.00
41	0.00	0.00	0.00	12.50	0.00	0.00	0.00	0.00	0.00	0.00	0.00	0.00
42	0.00	0.00	0.00	0.00	0.00	0.00	0.00	0.00	0.00	0.00	0.00	0.00
43	0.00	0.00	0.00	0.00	0.00	0.00	0.00	0.00	0.00	0.00	0.00	0.00
44	0.00	0.00	0.00	0.00	0.00	0.00	0.00	7.14	13.33	12.50	0.00	0.00
45	0.00	0.00	0.00	0.00	0.00	0.00	0.00	0.00	0.00	0.00	0.00	0.00
46	0.00	0.00	0.00	0.00	0.00	0.00	0.00	0.00	0.00	0.00	0.00	0.00
47	0.00	0.00	0.00	0.00	0.00	0.00	0.00	0.00	0.00	0.00	0.00	0.00
48	0.00	0.00	0.00	0.00	0.00	0.00	0.00	0.00	0.00	0.00	0.00	0.00
49	0.00	0.00	0.00	0.00	0.00	0.00	0.00	0.00	0.00	0.00	0.00	0.00
50	0.00	0.00	0.00	0.00	0.00	0.00	0.00	0.00	0.00	0.00	0.00	0.00
51	0.00	0.00	0.00	0.00	0.00	0.00	0.00	0.00	0.00	0.00	0.00	0.00
52	0.00	0.00	0.00	0.00	0.00	0.00	0.00	0.00	0.00	0.00	0.00	0.00

▼ SL DEPRECIATION

					Normal Recovery Period								
Year	9.5	10	10.5	11	11.5	12	12.5	13	13.5	14	15	16	16.5
1	5.26%	5.00%	4.76%	4.55%	4.35%	4.17%	4.00%	3.85%	3.70%	3.57%	3.33%	3.13%	3.03%
2	10.53	10.00	9.52	9.09	8.70	8.33	8.00	7.69	7.41	7.14	6.67	6.25	6.06
3	10.53	10.00	9.52	9.09	8.70	8.33	8.00	7.69	7.41	7.14	6.67	6.25	6.06
4	10.53	10.00	9.53	9.09	8.69	8.33	8.00	7.69	7.41	7.14	6.67	6.25	6.06
5	10.52	10.00	9.52	9.09	8.70	8.33	8.00	7.69	7.41	7.14	6.67	6.25	6.06
6	10.53	10.00	9.53	9.09	8.69	8.33	8.00	7.69	7.41	7.14	6.67	6.25	6.06
7	10.52	10.00	9.52	9.09	8.70	8.34	8.00	7.69	7.41	7.14	6.67	6.25	6.06
8	10.53	10.00	9.53	9.09	8.69	8.33	8.00	7.69	7.41	7.15	6.66	6.25	6.06
9	10.52	10.00	9.52	9.09	8.70	8.34	8.00	7.69	7.41	7.14	6.67	6.25	6.06
10	10.53	10.00	9.53	9.09	8.69	8.33	8.00	7.70	7.40	7.15	6.66	6.25	6.06
11	0.00	5.00	9.52	9.09	8.70	8.34	8.00	7.69	7.41	7.14	6.67	6.25	6.06
12	0.00	0.00	0.00	4.55	8.69	8.33	8.00	7.70	7.40	7.15	6.66	6.25	6.06
13	0.00	0.00	0.00	0.00	0.00	4.17	8.00	7.69	7.41	7.14	6.67	6.25	6.06
14	0.00	0.00	0.00	0.00	0.00	0.00	0.00	3.85	7.40	7.15	6.66	6.25	6.06
15	0.00	0.00	0.00	0.00	0.00	0.00	0.00	0.00	0.00	3.57	6.67	6.25	6.06
16	0.00	0.00	0.00	0.00	0.00	0.00	0.00	0.00	0.00	0.00	3.33	6.25	6.06
17	0.00	0.00	0.00	0.00	0.00	0.00	0.00	0.00	0.00	0.00	0.00	3.12	6.07
18	0.00	0.00	0.00	0.00	0.00	0.00	0.00	0.00	0.00	0.00	0.00	0.00	0.00
19	0.00	0.00	0.00	0.00	0.00	0.00	0.00	0.00	0.00	0.00	0.00	0.00	0.00
20	0.00	0.00	0.00	0.00	0.00	0.00	0.00	0.00	0.00	0.00	0.00	0.00	0.00
21	0.00	0.00	0.00	0.00	0.00	0.00	0.00	0.00	0.00	0.00	0.00	0.00	0.00
22	0.00	0.00	0.00	0.00	0.00	0.00	0.00	0.00	0.00	0.00	0.00	0.00	0.00
23	0.00	0.00	0.00	0.00	0.00	0.00	0.00	0.00	0.00	0.00	0.00	0.00	0.00
24	0.00	0.00	0.00	0.00	0.00	0.00	0.00	0.00	0.00	0.00	0.00	0.00	0.00
25	0.00	0.00	0.00	0.00	0.00	0.00	0.00	0.00	0.00	0.00	0.00	0.00	0.00
26	0.00	0.00	0.00	0.00	0.00	0.00	0.00	0.00	0.00	0.00	0.00	0.00	0.00
27	0.00	0.00	0.00	0.00	0.00	0.00	0.00	0.00	0.00	0.00	0.00	0.00	0.00
28	0.00	0.00	0.00	0.00	0.00	0.00	0.00	0.00	0.00	0.00	0.00	0.00	0.00
29	0.00	0.00	0.00	0.00	0.00	0.00	0.00	0.00	0.00	0.00	0.00	0.00	0.00
30	0.00	0.00	0.00	0.00	0.00	0.00	0.00	0.00	0.00	0.00	0.00	0.00	0.00
31	0.00	0.00	0.00	0.00	0.00	0.00	0.00	0.00	0.00	0.00	0.00	0.00	0.00
32	0.00	0.00	0.00	0.00	0.00	0.00	0.00	0.00	0.00	0.00	0.00	0.00	0.00
33	0.00	0.00	0.00	0.00	0.00	0.00	0.00	0.00	0.00	0.00	0.00	0.00	0.00
34	0.00	0.00	0.00	0.00	0.00	0.00	0.00	0.00	0.00	0.00	0.00	0.00	0.00
35	0.00	0.00	0.00	0.00	0.00	0.00	0.00	0.00	0.00	0.00	0.00	0.00	0.00
36	0.00	0.00	0.00	0.00	0.00	0.00	0.00	0.00	0.00	0.00	0.00	0.00	0.00
37	0.00	0.00	0.00	0.00	0.00	0.00	0.00	0.00	0.00	0.00	0.00	0.00	0.00
38	0.00	0.00	0.00	0.00	0.00	0.00	0.00	0.00	0.00	0.00	0.00	0.00	0.00
39	0.00	0.00	0.00	0.00	0.00	0.00	0.00	0.00	0.00	0.00	0.00	0.00	0.00
40	0.00	0.00	0.00	0.00	0.00	0.00	0.00	0.00	0.00	0.00	0.00	0.00	0.00
41	0.00	0.00	0.00	0.00	0.00	0.00	0.00	0.00	0.00	0.00	0.00	0.00	0.00
42	0.00	0.00	0.00	0.00	0.00	0.00	0.00	0.00	0.00	0.00	0.00	0.00	0.00
43	0.00	0.00	0.00	0.00	0.00	0.00	0.00	0.00	0.00	0.00	0.00	0.00	0.00
44	0.00	0.00	0.00	0.00	0.00	0.00	0.00	0.00	0.00	0.00	0.00	0.00	0.00
45	0.00	0.00	0.00	0.00	0.00	0.00	0.00	0.00	0.00	0.00	0.00	0.00	0.00
46	0.00	0.00	0.00	0.00	0.00	0.00	0.00	0.00	0.00	0.00	0.00	0.00	0.00
47	0.00	0.00	0.00	0.00	0.00	0.00	0.00	0.00	0.00	0.00	0.00	0.00	0.00
48	0.00	0.00	0.00	0.00	0.00	0.00	0.00	0.00	0.00	0.00	0.00	0.00	0.00
49	0.00	0.00	0.00	0.00	0.00	0.00	0.00	0.00	0.00	0.00	0.00	0.00	0.00
50	0.00	0.00	0.00	0.00	0.00	0.00	0.00	0.00	0.00	0.00	0.00	0.00	0.00
51	0.00	0.00	0.00	0.00	0.00	0.00	0.00	0.00	0.00	0.00	0.00	0.00	0.00
52	0.00	0.00	0.00	0.00	0.00	0.00	0.00	0.00	0.00	0.00	0.00	0.00	0.00

▾ SL DEPRECIATION

Year	17	18	19	20	22	24	25	26.5	28	30	35	40	45	50
								Normal Recovery Period						
1	2.94%	2.78%	2.63%	2.50%	2.273%	2.083%	2.00%	1.887%	1.786%	1.667%	1.429%	1.25%	1.111%	1.00%
2	5.88	5.56	5.26	5.00	4.545	4.167	4.00	3.774	3.571	3.333	2.857	2.50	2.222	2.00
3	5.88	5.56	5.26	5.00	4.545	4.167	4.00	3.774	3.571	3.333	2.857	2.50	2.222	2.00
4	5.88	5.55	5.26	5.00	4.545	4.167	4.00	3.774	3.571	3.333	2.857	2.50	2.222	2.00
5	5.88	5.56	5.26	5.00	4.546	4.167	4.00	3.774	3.571	3.333	2.857	2.50	2.222	2.00
6	5.88	5.55	5.26	5.00	4.545	4.167	4.00	3.774	3.571	3.333	2.857	2.50	2.222	2.00
7	5.88	5.56	5.26	5.00	4.546	4.167	4.00	3.773	3.572	3.333	2.857	2.50	2.222	2.00
8	5.88	5.55	5.26	5.00	4.545	4.167	4.00	3.774	3.571	3.333	2.857	2.50	2.222	2.00
9	5.88	5.56	5.27	5.00	4.546	4.167	4.00	3.773	3.572	3.333	2.857	2.50	2.222	2.00
10	5.88	5.55	5.26	5.00	4.545	4.167	4.00	3.774	3.571	3.333	2.857	2.50	2.222	2.00
11	5.89	5.56	5.27	5.00	4.546	4.166	4.00	3.773	3.572	3.333	2.857	2.50	2.222	2.00
12	5.88	5.55	5.26	5.00	4.545	4.167	4.00	3.774	3.571	3.333	2.857	2.50	2.222	2.00
13	5.89	5.56	5.27	5.00	4.546	4.166	4.00	3.773	3.572	3.334	2.857	2.50	2.222	2.00
14	5.88	5.55	5.26	5.00	4.545	4.167	4.00	3.773	3.571	3.333	2.857	2.50	2.222	2.00
15	5.89	5.56	5.27	5.00	4.546	4.166	4.00	3.774	3.572	3.334	2.857	2.50	2.222	2.00
16	5.88	5.55	5.26	5.00	4.545	4.167	4.00	3.773	3.571	3.333	2.857	2.50	2.222	2.00
17	5.89	5.56	5.27	5.00	4.546	4.166	4.00	3.774	3.572	3.334	2.857	2.50	2.222	2.00
18	2.94	5.55	5.26	5.00	4.545	4.167	4.00	3.773	3.571	3.333	2.857	2.50	2.222	2.00
19	0.00	2.78	5.27	5.00	4.546	4.166	4.00	3.774	3.572	3.334	2.857	2.50	2.222	2.00
20	0.00	0.00	2.63	5.00	4.545	4.167	4.00	3.773	3.571	3.333	2.857	2.50	2.222	2.00
21	0.00	0.00	0.00	2.50	4.546	4.166	4.00	3.774	3.572	3.334	2.857	2.50	2.222	2.00
22	0.00	0.00	0.00	0.00	4.545	4.167	4.00	3.773	3.571	3.333	2.857	2.50	2.222	2.00
23	0.00	0.00	0.00	0.00	2.273	4.166	4.00	3.774	3.572	3.334	2.857	2.50	2.222	2.00
24	0.00	0.00	0.00	0.00	0.000	4.167	4.00	3.773	3.571	3.333	2.857	2.50	2.222	2.00
25	0.00	0.00	0.00	0.00	0.000	2.083	4.00	3.774	3.572	3.334	2.857	2.50	2.222	2.00
26	0.00	0.00	0.00	0.00	0.000	0.000	2.00	3.773	3.571	3.333	2.857	2.50	2.222	2.00
27	0.00	0.00	0.00	0.00	0.000	0.000	0.00	3.774	3.572	3.334	2.857	2.50	2.223	2.00
28	0.00	0.00	0.00	0.00	0.000	0.000	0.00	0.000	3.571	3.333	2.858	2.50	2.222	2.00
29	0.00	0.00	0.00	0.00	0.000	0.000	0.00	0.000	1.786	3.334	2.857	2.50	2.223	2.00
30	0.00	0.00	0.00	0.00	0.000	0.000	0.00	0.000	0.000	3.333	2.858	2.50	2.222	2.00
31	0.00	0.00	0.00	0.00	0.000	0.000	0.00	0.000	0.000	1.667	2.857	2.50	2.223	2.00
32	0.00	0.00	0.00	0.00	0.000	0.000	0.00	0.000	0.000	0.000	2.858	2.50	2.222	2.00
33	0.00	0.00	0.00	0.00	0.000	0.000	0.00	0.000	0.000	0.000	2.857	2.50	2.223	2.00
34	0.00	0.00	0.00	0.00	0.000	0.000	0.00	0.000	0.000	0.000	2.858	2.50	2.222	2.00
35	0.00	0.00	0.00	0.00	0.000	0.000	0.00	0.000	0.000	0.000	2.857	2.50	2.223	2.00
36	0.00	0.00	0.00	0.00	0.000	0.000	0.00	0.000	0.000	0.000	1.429	2.50	2.222	2.00
37	0.00	0.00	0.00	0.00	0.000	0.000	0.00	0.000	0.000	0.000	0.000	2.50	2.223	2.00
38	0.00	0.00	0.00	0.00	0.000	0.000	0.00	0.000	0.000	0.000	0.000	2.50	2.222	2.00
39	0.00	0.00	0.00	0.00	0.000	0.000	0.00	0.000	0.000	0.000	0.000	2.50	2.223	2.00
40	0.00	0.00	0.00	0.00	0.000	0.000	0.00	0.000	0.000	0.000	0.000	2.50	2.222	2.00
41	0.00	0.00	0.00	0.00	0.000	0.000	0.00	0.000	0.000	0.000	0.000	1.25	2.223	2.00
42	0.00	0.00	0.00	0.00	0.000	0.000	0.00	0.000	0.000	0.000	0.000	0.00	2.222	2.00
43	0.00	0.00	0.00	0.00	0.000	0.000	0.00	0.000	0.000	0.000	0.000	0.00	2.223	2.00
44	0.00	0.00	0.00	0.00	0.000	0.000	0.00	0.000	0.000	0.000	0.000	0.00	2.222	2.00
45	0.00	0.00	0.00	0.00	0.000	0.000	0.00	0.000	0.000	0.000	0.000	0.00	2.223	2.00
46	0.00	0.00	0.00	0.00	0.000	0.000	0.00	0.000	0.000	0.000	0.000	0.00	1.111	2.00
47	0.00	0.00	0.00	0.00	0.000	0.000	0.00	0.000	0.000	0.000	0.000	0.00	0.000	2.00
48	0.00	0.00	0.00	0.00	0.000	0.000	0.00	0.000	0.000	0.000	0.000	0.00	0.000	2.00
49	0.00	0.00	0.00	0.00	0.000	0.000	0.00	0.000	0.000	0.000	0.000	0.00	0.000	2.00
50	0.00	0.00	0.00	0.00	0.000	0.000	0.00	0.000	0.000	0.000	0.000	0.00	0.000	2.00
51	0.00	0.00	0.00	0.00	0.000	0.000	0.00	0.000	0.000	0.000	0.000	0.00	0.000	1.00
52	0.00	0.00	0.00	0.00	0.000	0.000	0.00	0.000	0.000	0.000	0.000	0.00	0.000	0.00

continued from p. 297

bonds, and other instruments with an emphasis on equations that had "=" signs. We will see here that most capital budgeting decision rules that we will encounter will have ">" or "<" signs. This difference arises because marketable securities are *financial* assets that trade in competitive financial markets, while capital budgeting projects usually involve the purchase of *real* assets, which typically trade in much less competitive markets. Real assets are considerably less liquid than are financial assets, and firms purchase real assets in the form of capital equipment to create value for their customers. As a result, projects and purchases that involve capital equipment typically convey at least some monopoly power (and the associated monopolistic profits) to the firm purchasing them and adopting them for long-term use. In fact, the reason for the inequality signs in the capital budgeting decision rules we'll be examining is that, rather than looking for projects that are worth "enough," we seek projects that are worth "more than enough." That is, capital budgeting equations seek projects that offer more return than they should (sometimes called *economic profits*), even after taking into account their associated risk. ■

THE SET OF CAPITAL BUDGETING TECHNIQUES

So, now we are going to apply what we've learned in the preceding two chapters about the cost of capital and cash flows that result from capital budgeting decisions to choose the projects that most deserve the scarce capital—that is, to determine which projects promise the best returns to the company. No one can perfectly predict the future, so these techniques are, by their very nature, accompanied by uncertainty. That said, commonly used capital budgeting techniques include:

- NPV (net present value).
- PB (payback).
- DPB (discounted payback).
- IRR (internal rate of return).
- MIRR (modified internal rate of return).
- PI (profitability index).

viewpoints

business APPLICATION

ADK Industries, a start-up firm in the "online social networking" industry, has run into capacity constraints with their Internet bandwidth provider. ADK management is considering building their own dedicated Web server farm at a cost of $5 million. In return, the firm expects that the increased bandwidth will generate higher demand for their services, resulting in increased cash flows of $1.2 million in the first year, $1.6 million in the second year, $2.3 million in the third year, and $2.8 million in the fourth year, for a total of $7.9 million over the next four years. At that point, the firm will scrap the server farm as obsolete. If ADK estimates that its target rate of return on such projects is 14 percent, should ADK go ahead with the project?

As we discuss each of these techniques in this chapter, we will find that, while the net present value (NPV) technique is the preferred one for most project evaluations, various situations arise in which you might wish to use one of the other decision rules, either in lieu of NPV or in conjunction with it. For example, a company or person faced with a time constraint to repay the initial capital for a project might well be more worried about a project's payback (PB) statistic, while a firm facing capital constraints might prefer to use one of the interest-rate-based decision statistics, such as the profitability index (PI), to prioritize their project choices. We will discuss the contexts for choosing one technique over another throughout the chapter.

THE CHOICE OF DECISION STATISTIC FORMAT

In general, three factors drive the choice of which decision rule(s) to use:

1. The desired format or units of measurement for the decision statistic.

2. Whether the project's cash flows are **normal** or non-normal.

3. Whether the firm is considering the project independently of other projects, or whether its project selection will be *mutually exclusive.*

We will discuss the impact of non-normal cash flows and the problems faced in using some of the techniques to choose between mutually exclusive projects as they become relevant, but the first factor, the desired decision statistic format, deserves some attention before we start.

weighing net present value +
other capital budgeting criteria

Once you've calculated the cost of capital for a project and estimated its cash flows, deciding whether or not to invest in that project basically boils down to asking the question "Is the project worth its projected future value?" To answer this question, we will, not surprisingly, turn once again to the time value of money (TVM) formulas we used to value stocks, bonds, loans, and other marketable securities in Chapters 7 and 8. But first, a caveat: Though the *mechanics* of using the TVM formulas will be the same, the *intuition* underlying our analysis of investment criteria is very different. You will recall that we used the pricing equations for stocks,

LEARNING GOALS

LG1 Develop intuition to understand the logic underlying capital budgeting decision techniques.

LG2 Calculate and use the net present value (NPV) method for evaluating capital investment opportunities.

LG3 Calculate and use the payback (PB) and discounted payback (DPB) methods for valuing capital investment opportunities.

LG4 Calculate and use the internal rate of return (IRR) and the modified internal rate of return (MIRR) methods for evaluating capital investment opportunities; understand which problems associated with IRR that MIRR can and cannot correct.

LG5 Use NPV profiles to reconcile sources of conflict between NPV and IRR methods.

LG6 Compute and use the profitability index (PI).

continued on p. 298

Decision Statistic Formats

Managers tend to focus on three general measurement units for financial decisions: currency, time, and rate of return. Of these three types, rate-based statistics usually pose the most problems.[1] Unfortunately, managers also usually prefer the seemingly concrete nature of rate-based statistics, presumably because they can then easily compare the "earned" rate of return constructed by these decision rules with the "borrowing" rates that potential lenders and the capital markets are currently quoting.

Both the popularity and the problems associated with rate-of-return-based decision rules stem from a common source: the ability to conceptualize rate relationships. The "expected rate of return per dollar invested" provides an appealingly tangible measure of a project's anticipated viability, but computing this

[1]This is true particularly when dealing with mutually exclusive projects; please see below.

measurement involves summarizing the relationship between cash inflows and cash outflows across the project's lifetime through the use of a ratio. Any time we use a ratio to create a summary statistic, some (crucial) information is lost along the way. In particular, though rate-based decision statistics tell us the rate of return *per dollar invested,* they don't reflect the *amount* of the investment on which that return is based. This omission will sometimes cause those rate-based decision statistics to incorrectly prefer projects with lower dollar returns, as we'll see in our discussion of IRR, MIRR, and PI.

PROCESSING CAPITAL BUDGETING DECISIONS

For all of our decision techniques, we need to identify how to calculate a *decision statistic;* decide on an appropriate *benchmark* for comparing the calculated statistic with; and define what relationship between the two will dictate project acceptance. When we consider one project at a time, or when we examine each of a group of independent projects, capital budgeting techniques involve two-step decision processes:

1. Compute the statistic.
2. Compare the computed statistic with the benchmark to decide whether to accept or reject the project.

However, when we deal with mutually exclusive projects, we will need to add a new step in the middle of the process:

1. Compute the statistic for each project.
2. *Have a "runoff" between the mutually exclusive projects, choosing the one with the best statistic.*
3. Compare the computed statistic from the runoff winner with the benchmark to decide whether to accept or reject.

As we'll see, the presence of this runoff step for mutually exclusive projects, as well as its placement, will create problems when we use decision statistics that either ignore or summarize critical information in the first step.

Among currency, time, and rate of return, managers usually prefer rate-based statistics.

NET PRESENT VALUE

At its heart, **net present value (NPV)** represents the "purest" of capital budgeting rules, measuring exactly the value we are interested in: the amount of wealth increase we expect from accepting a project. As we cover in more detail below, the NPV method measures this expected wealth increase by computing the difference between the present values of a project's cash inflows and outflows. Since this calculation includes the necessary capital expenditures and other start-up costs of the project as cash outflows, a positive value indicates that the project is desirable—that it more than covers all of the necessary resource costs to do the project.

NPV Statistic

We actually already know how to calculate the NPV statistic. In fact, we use a very similar approach in developing bond and stock pricing equations. The NPV statistic is simply the sum of all the cash flows' present values:

$$NPV = \frac{CF_0}{(1+i)^0} + \frac{CF_1}{(1+i)^1} + \cdots + \frac{CF_N}{(1+i)^N} \qquad (13\text{-}1)$$

$$= \sum_{n=0}^{N} \frac{CF_n}{(1+i)^n}$$

NPV Benchmark

NPV analysis includes all of the cash flows—both inflows and outflows. This inclusion implies that any required investment in the project is already factored in, so any NPV greater than zero represents value *above and beyond* that investment. Accordingly, the NPV decision rule is:

$$\text{Accept project if NPV} \geq 0 \qquad (13\text{-}2)$$

$$\text{Reject project if NPV} < 0$$

NPV Strengths and Weaknesses

One strength of the NPV rule is that the statistic is *not* a ratio as with the rate-based decision statistics. It works equally well for independent projects as it does for choosing among mutually exclusive projects. In the latter case, the mutually exclusive project with the highest NPV should add the most wealth to the firm, and so management should accept it over any competing projects.

Unfortunately, this ability to choose among projects stems from exactly what gives it its greatest weakness: the format of the statistic. Since the NPV statistic is a dollar figure, it accurately reflects the net effect of any differences in timing or scale of two projects' expected cash flows. It thus allows comparisons of two projects' NPV statistics to fully incorporate those differences. However, this same currency format often results in confusion for uninformed decision makers: managers not completely

continued on page 302

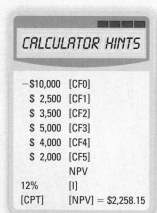
NPV for a Normal Set of Cash Flows

A company is evaluating a project with the set of normal cash flows using a risk-appropriate discount rate of 12 percent as shown in Table 13.1. Compute the NPV to determine whether the company should undertake the project.

▼ **TABLE 13.1** Sample Project with Normal Cash Flows

Year	0	1	2	3	4	5
Cash Flow	−$10,000	$2,500	$3,500	$5,000	$4,000	$2,000

CALCULATOR HINTS

−$10,000	[CF0]
$ 2,500	[CF1]
$ 3,500	[CF2]
$ 5,000	[CF3]
$ 4,000	[CF4]
$ 2,000	[CF5]
	NPV
12%	[I]
[CPT]	[NPV] = $2,258.15

SOLUTION:

The NPV statistic for this project will be:

$$NPV = \frac{-\$10,000}{(1.12)^0} + \frac{\$2,500}{(1.12)^1} + \frac{\$3,500}{(1.12)^2} + \frac{\$5,000}{(1.12)^3} + \frac{\$4,000}{(12.1)^4} + \frac{\$2,000}{(1.12)^5}$$

$$= \$2,258.15 > 0$$

The NPV decision will be to *accept* the project.

When you first start calculating NPV, it is easy to miss its deeper meaning. A relatively small NPV, such as the $2,258.15 figure in this example, raises the question of whether $2,258.15 is "worth it," in this sense: Will the project cover the opportunity cost of using the $10,000 of necessary capital? The point, of course, is that the $2,258.15 is above and beyond the recovery of that opportunity cost, so, *yes, it's worth it.*

Using a Financial Calculator—Part 2

The TVM worksheet present in most financial calculators has been fine, so far, for the types of TVM problems we've been solving. Sometimes we had to use the worksheet two or three times for a single problem, but that was usually because we needed an intermediate calculation to input into another TVM equation.

In this chapter, we will generally be using simpler TVM equations (i.e., PV and FV), but we'll find ourselves having to use them repeatedly, making only small variations in inputs over and over again within the same problem. We're also going to run up against the problem of cash flow inconsistencies in most projects. If you thought the cash flows of stocks jumped around a lot, wait until you see what project cash flows do! If we stick with the TVM worksheet, these inconsistent cash flows will be a problem for us. If we want to solve for a "common" *i* or *N* value, the TVM worksheet won't let us enter multiple cash flows unless we're solving an annuity problem. (The one notable exception to this has been when we used the TVM worksheet to simultaneously solve the annuity/lump sum problems that arise with bonds. If you recall, those problems require agreement between the inputs to the annuity and the lump sum problems. This kind of agreement is highly unlikely to occur in other circumstances.)

Luckily, most financial calculators also have built-in worksheets specifically designed for computing NPV in problems with multiple nonconstant cash flows. In many cases, they will also calculate most of the other decision rule statistics that we're going to be discussing.

To make calculator worksheets as flexible as possible, they are usually divided into two parts: one for input, which we'll refer to as the CF (for cash flow) worksheet, and one or more for calculating decision statistics. We'll go over the conventions concerning the CF worksheet here. We'll wait to cover the conventions of the various decision rules until we discuss them.

The CF worksheet is usually designed to handle inputting sets of multiple cash flows as quickly as possible. As a result, it normally consists of two sets of variables or cells—one for the cash flows and one to hold a set of frequency counts for the cash flows, so that we can tell it we have seven $1,500 cash flows in a row instead of having to enter $1,500 seven times.

Using the frequency counts to reduce the number of inputs is handy, but you must take care. Frequency counts are only good for embedded annuities of identical cash flows. You have to ensure that you don't mistake another kind of cash flow for an annuity.

Also, using frequency counts will usually affect the way that the calculator counts time periods. As an example, let's talk about how we would put the set of cash flows shown here into a CF worksheet:

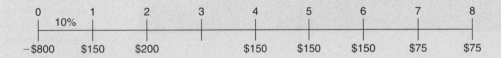

To designate which particular value we'll place into each particular cash flow cell in this worksheet, we'll note the value and the cell identifier, such as CF0, CF1, and so forth. We'll do the same for the frequency cells, using F1, F2, etc., to identify which CF cell the frequency cell goes with. (Note that, in most calculators, CF0 is treated as a unique value with an unalterable frequency of 1; we're going to make the same assumption here so you'll never see a listing for F0. For this sample time line, our inputs would be:

−$800	[CF0]		
$150	[CF1]	1	[F1]
$200	[CF2]	1	[F2]
$0	[CF3]	1	[F3]
$150	[CF4]	3	[F4]
$75	[CF5]	2	[F5]

Then, on the NPV worksheet, you would simply need to enter the interest rate and solve for the NPV:

10%	[I]
[CPT]	[NPV] = −$144.61

familiar with how the NPV statistic works often insist on comparing the NPV to the *cost* of the project, not understanding that the cost is already incorporated into the NPV.

repays in two years but is slated to last only three years, assuming that the two projects are expected to have the same yearly cash flows once payback is achieved.

Payback Statistic

The **payback** statistic remains very popular because it's easy to compute. All we have to do is keep a running subtotal of the cumulative sum of the cash flows up to the point that this sum exactly offsets the initial investment. That is, PB is determined by using this formula:

$$0 = \sum_{n=0}^{PB} CF_n \qquad (13\text{-}3)$$

Notice that this computation demands a couple of strong assumptions:

1. The whole concept of payback rests on the assumption that cash flows are normal, with all outflows occurring at the beginning of the project's life, so that we can think of the PB statistic as a type of recovery period for that initial investment. This implies that payback would be meaningless for a set of non-normal cash flows. If, for example, a project required an infusion of cash after it started, such as the cash outflows shown at times 1 and 2 in Table 13.2, we could not calculate a payback statistic.

2. Note that PB will not be very likely to occur in an exact, round number of periods, so we will need to make another assumption concerning how cash inflows occur *during* the course of a year. The usual approach to handling this condition is to assume that cash flows arrive smoothly throughout each period, allowing us to count out the months and days to estimate the exact payback statistic.

time out!

13-1 Why is a project's cost *not* an appropriate benchmark for its NPV?

13-2 Assuming that it's fairly priced, what should be the NPV of a purchase decision on a corporate bond?

PAYBACK AND DISCOUNTED PAYBACK

Both the payback and discounted payback rules carry great emotional appeal: if we assume that we are borrowing money to finance a new project, both techniques answer slightly different versions of the question, "How long is it going to take us to recoup our costs?"

So it would seem that these techniques use the same reasoning that banks and other lenders employ when they examine a potential borrower's finances to determine the probability of repayment. While at first this seems like a fairly simple question, it can actually lead to some rather sophisticated insight concerning a project's potential. For example, a project that lasts seven years but is slated to repay its initial investment within the first two years is obviously a stronger candidate than a project that also

Payback Benchmark

The payback method shows an additional weakness in that its benchmark must be exogenously specified: that is, it's not always the same value, nor is it determined by the required rate of return or any other input variable. Ideally, the maximum allowable PB for a project should be set based on some relevant external constraint, such as the number of periods until capital providers need their money back, or the time available until a project would violate a bond issue's protective covenants. As you might suspect, in real life managers often indicate the maximum allowable payback—that is, set the exogenous specification—arbitrarily.

Let's assume that we've been told that the maximum allowable payback for this project is three years. With this decision rule, we want to accept projects that show a calculated statistic less than the benchmark of three years:

$$\text{Accept project if } \frac{\text{calculated payback}}{} \leq \frac{\text{Maximum allowable}}{\text{payback}}$$

$$\text{Reject project if } \frac{\text{calculated payback}}{} > \frac{\text{Maximum allowable}}{\text{payback}} \quad (13\text{-}4)$$

Since our calculated payback is 2.8 (computed in Example 13-3) and the maximum allowable payback is three years, we should accept the project according to the payback rule.

Discounted Payback Statistic

Yet another problem that arises when we use the payback technique is that it does not recognize or incorporate the time value of money. To compensate for this exclusion, we often calculate the **discounted payback (DPB)** statistic instead, using the following formula:

$$0 = \sum_{n=0}^{DPB} \frac{CF_n}{(1+i)^n} \quad (13\text{-}5)$$

Notice that all we're doing here is summing the *present values* of the cash flows until we get a cumulative sum of zero, instead of summing the cash flows themselves as we did for the PB statistic. Other than that, we follow all the steps in the computation of DPB just as we did for the PB statistic.

Discounted Payback Benchmark

We may be tempted to assume that we should simply use the same maximum allowable payback benchmark for DPB that we used for PB. If we did so, then we would obviously have to reject this project, since its calculated DPB is 3.5581 years versus a stated maximum allowable time of only three years. However, we should be very cautious about applying the same benchmark to DPB that we did to PB. To see why, recall that payback calculations only make sense when applied to normal cash flows, so we would assume that we'll be dealing with normal cash flows here. But think about *which* cash flows are affected when we switch from calculating payback to discounted payback: Only the ones in the future will fall to lower values, because the present value of the time 0 cash flow will always be the same as its nominal value. And, if the future cash flows are all positive and the initial cash flow is negative, then it is only the positive cash

payback (PB) A capital budgeting technique that generates decision rules and associated metrics for choosing projects based on how quickly they return their initial investment.

discounted payback (DPB) A capital budgeting method that generates decision rules and associated metrics for choosing projects based on how quickly they return their initial investment plus interest.

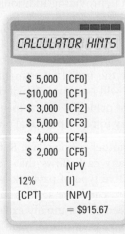

EXAMPLE 13-2

For interactive versions of this example visit www.mhhe.com/canM

CALCULATOR HINTS

$ 5,000	[CF0]
−$10,000	[CF1]
−$ 3,000	[CF2]
$ 5,000	[CF3]
$ 4,000	[CF4]
$ 2,000	[CF5]
	NPV
12%	[I]
[CPT]	[NPV]
	= $915.67

NPV for a Non-Normal Set of Cash Flows

Note that the NPV rule works equally well with non-normal cash flows, such as those for the project shown in Table 13.2. Compute the NPV for this project to determine whether it should be accepted.

▼ **TABLE 13.2** Sample Project with Non-Normal Cash Flows

Year	0	1	2	3	4	5
Cash Flow	$5,000	−$10,000	−$3,000	$5,000	$4,000	$2,000

SOLUTION:

Once again assuming a 12 percent discount rate, the NPV statistic will be:

$$NPV = \frac{\$5,000}{(1.12)^0} + \frac{-\$10,000}{(1.12)^1} + \frac{-\$3,000}{(1.12)^2} + \frac{\$5,000}{(1.12)^3} + \frac{\$4,000}{(12.1)^4} + \frac{\$2,000}{(1.12)^5}$$

$$= \$915.67 > 0$$

Based on this NPV, the project should be accepted.

EXAMPLE 13-3

For interactive versions of this example visit www.mhhe.com/canM

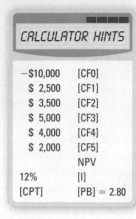

CALCULATOR HINTS

−$10,000	[CF0]
$ 2,500	[CF1]
$ 3,500	[CF2]
$ 5,000	[CF3]
$ 4,000	[CF4]
$ 2,000	[CF5]
	NPV
12%	[I]
[CPT]	[PB] = 2.80

Payback Calculation

Consider the sample project introduced in Table 13.1. To calculate this project's payback, we would first calculate the cumulative cash flows until they went from negative to positive, using the information in Table 13.3:

▼ **TABLE 13.3** Payback Calculation on Sample Project with Normal Cash Flows

Year	0	1	2	3	4	5
Cash Flow	−$10,000	$2,500	$3,500	$5,000	$4,000	$2,000
Cumulative Cash Flow	−10,000	−7,500	−4,000	1,000		

SOLUTION:

From this first step, we know that payback occurs somewhere between periods 2 and 3. To determine the exact statistic, we note that, if the magnitude of the last negative cumulative cash flow represents how much cash flow we *need* during year 3 to achieve payback, then the marginal cash flow for year 3 represents how much we will *get* over the course of the entire third year. By linear interpolation, our exact statistic is therefore where we start (year 2) plus what we need (the absolute value of the last negative cumulative cash flow, −$4,000) over what we're going to get during that year:

$$PB = 2 + \frac{\$4,000}{\$5,000} = 2.8 \text{ years}$$

---

flows that will be affected by switching to cumulative present value for DPB.

In other words, we would expect the calculated DPB statistic to always be larger than the "regular" PB statistic because DPB incorporates the interest you must pay until you reach the benchmark. Said another way, DPB will always take longer to achieve payback if you're "chipping away" at the same-sized initial cash outflow with the present values of a bunch of positive cash inflows rather than their simple nominal values. Therefore, it probably isn't fair to hold the DPB statistic up to the same benchmark we use for the PB statistic.

What benchmark should we use? Well, as with PB, management will set the DPB maximum allowable payback exogenously and, once again, often arbitrarily. Let's assume that we're told that senior management has set the maximum allowable payback for DPB as 3.5 years.

$$\text{Accept project if} \atop \text{calculated DPB} \leq {\text{Maximum allowable} \atop \text{discounted payback}}$$

$$\text{Reject project if} \atop \text{calculated DPB} > {\text{Maximum allowable} \atop \text{discounted payback}}$$ (13-6)

Since our calculated DPB is 3.5581 years and the maximum allowable amount is 3.5 years, we should reject the project.

Payback and Discounted Payback Strengths and Weaknesses

A common criticism of PB is that it doesn't account for the time value of money; the use of PV formulas in computing DPB compensates for TVM. But DPB isn't intended to really replace PB, but rather to complement it, providing additional information to analyze capital budgeting decisions.

For example, if we consider a typical, normal payback statistic based on a set of cash flows as a loan problem in which the company borrows the money for the initial investment and then pays it off over time, then PB will intuitively equal the amount of time necessary to repay just principal on the loan, and DPB will indicate the time necessary to repay principal plus interest.

Both PB and DPB have yet another serious flaw. Both decision statistics completely ignore any cash flows that accrue *after* the project reaches its respective type of payback benchmark. Ignoring this vital information can have serious implications when managers choose between two mutually exclusive projects that have very similar paybacks, but very different cash flows after payback is achieved.

EXAMPLE 13-4

For interactive versions
of this example visit
www.mhhe.com/canM

Discounted Payback Calculation

Consider the same project from Example 13-3. To calculate this project's discounted payback, we would first need to calculate the PV of each cash flow separately. Assuming the same 12 percent interest rate used when we calculated the NPV of this project, we would calculate these values as shown in Table 13.4.

▼ **TABLE 13.4** Discounted Payback Calculation: Present Values of Cash Flows

Year	0	1	2	3	4	5
Cash Flow	−$10,000.00	$2,500.00	$3,500.00	$5,000.00	$4,000.00	$2,000.00
Cash Flow Present Value	−10,000.00	2,232.14	2,790.18	3,558.90	2,542.07	1,134.85

In Table 13.5 we calculate the cumulative present value of the cash flows until they switch from negative to positive:

▼ **TABLE 13.5** Discounted Payback Calculation on Sample Project with Normal Cash Flows

Year	0	1	2	3	4	5
Cash Flow	−$10,000.00	$2,500.00	$3,500.00	$5,000.00	$4,000.00	$2,000.00
Cash Flow Present Value	−10,000.00	2,232.14	2,790.18	3,558.90	2,542.07	1,134.85
Cumulative Cash Flow PV	−10,000.00	−7,767.86	−4,977.68	−1,418.78	1,123.29	

CALCULATOR HINTS

−$10,000	[CF0]
$ 2,500	[CF1]
$ 3,500	[CF2]
$ 5,000	[CF3]
$ 4,000	[CF4]
$ 2,000	[CF5]
	NPV
12%	[I]
[CPT]	[DPB] = 3.56

SOLUTION:

As before, we can stop once the cumulative values go from negative to positive. In this case, linear interpolation will give us a DPB statistic of:

$$DPB = 3 + \frac{\$1,418.78}{\$2,542.07} = 3.5581 \text{ years}$$

EXAMPLE 13-5

For interactive versions
of this example visit
www.mhhe.com/canM

Payback Calculation for Alternative Project

Consider once again the sample project shown in Table 13.1. As we calculated in Example 13-3, that project has a PB statistic of 2.8 years. Now, compare that project to the one shown in Table 13.6:

▼ **TABLE 13.6** Payback Calculation on Alternative Sample Project with Normal Cash Flows

Year	0	1	2	3	4	5
Cash Flow	−$10,000	$2,500	$3,500	$4,000	$104,000	$102,000
Cash Flow Present Value	−10,000	−7,500	−4,000			

SOLUTION:

This project would have a slightly higher PB statistic of 3.0. Given that it still achieves payback in exactly the maximum allowable three years, it should be highly favored over the first project due to the large positive cash flows that will accrue in the later years. But managers who ignore this aspect of the PB rule and who focus only on the PB statistics of these two projects will likely incorrectly choose the first project due to its lower PB statistic.

Note that NPV will *not* suffer from this problem. Since the NPV statistic takes all of a project's cash flows into account, there aren't "remaining" cash flows to get left out of the statistic as there are with PB and DPB.

INTERNAL RATE OF RETURN AND MODIFIED INTERNAL RATE OF RETURN

The **internal rate of return (IRR)** technique is, by far, the most popular rate-based capital budgeting technique. The main reason for its popularity is that if you are considering a project with normal cash flows that is independent of other projects, the IRR statistic will give exactly the same accept/reject decision as the NPV rule does.

However, IRR runs into a lot of problems if project cash flows are not normal, or if you are using this statistic to decide among mutually exclusive projects. As we'll show below, while we can correct for the non-normal cash flows, all rate-based decision statistics will exhibit problems with deciding among mutually exclusive projects.

Internal Rate of Return Statistic

To solve for the IRR statistic, we simply solve the NPV formula for the interest rate that will make NPV equal zero:

$$0 = \sum_{n=0}^{N} \frac{CF_n}{(1 + IRR)^n} \qquad \text{(13-7)}$$

Unfortunately, we cannot solve directly for the interest rate that will set NPV equal to zero. We either have to use trial-and-error to determine the appropriate rate, or we have to rely on a calculator or computer, both of which use much the same approach.

Internal Rate of Return Benchmark

Once we calculate the IRR, we must then compare the decision statistic to the relevant cost of capital for the project—the average rate of return necessary to pay back the project's capital providers, given the risk that the project represents:

Accept project if IRR $\geq$ Cost of capital

Reject project if IRR $<$ Cost of capital   (13-8)

At this point, you may find yourself getting a little confused about which rate is *the* interest rate. The IRR statistic will equal the expected rate of return, which incorporates risk (as probabilities). We'll compare that expected rate of return to the cost of capital, which is often called the required rate of return. Up until this chapter, we've been using all of these phrases interchangeably for "*the*" interest rate. We have fudged a bit because stocks, bonds, and all other types of *financial* assets trade in relatively liquid, competitive financial markets. In such an environment, it makes sense to assume that we're not going to be able to earn any "extra" return or economic profit above and beyond what's appropriate for the amount of risk we're bearing.

Remember, though, that in this chapter, we're no longer talking about *financial* assets, but *real* assets such as land, factories with inventories, and production lines. These types of assets don't generally trade in perfectly competitive markets. Instead, they trade in quite illiquid markets in which an individual or a firm can gain at least some amount of market or monopoly power by virtue of technological, legal, or marketing expertise.

We noted this difference at the beginning of this chapter when we differentiated between formulas for financial assets such as stocks and bonds and the equations we're using in this chapter to value projects. The formulas we used to value stocks and bonds use "=" signs because those assets trade in nearly perfectly competitive markets, where what you get is (approximately, at least) equal to what you paid for it. Here, on the other hand, we examine situations in which companies seek to choose projects that are worth *more* than what they pay for them—leaving room for economic profit. That's why all of these capital budgeting rules use ">" and "<" signs.

So, when we deal with physical asset projects, we have to expect that two different rates of return will arise. The best way to think of these two rates is as the *expected* rate of return (IRR), and the *required* rate of return (*i*). We only want to invest in projects where the rate we expect to get (IRR) is larger than the rate investors require (*i*) based on the project's expected return, including risk.[2]

---

[2] As explained in earlier chapters, by definition the expected rate of return incorporates risk.

Problems with Internal Rate of Return

As we mentioned above, IRR will give the same accept/reject decision as NPV if two conditions hold true:

1. The project has normal cash flows.

2. We are evaluating the project independently of other projects—that is, we aren't considering mutually exclusive projects.

To see the problems that arise if these conditions do *not* hold, we'll make use of a tool called the **NPV profile.** This is simply a graph of a project's NPV as a function of possible capital costs. The NPV profile for our sample project with normal cash flows from Table 13.1 appears as Figure 13.1.

As you can see, the NPV profile for this normal set of cash flows slopes downward. As we noted above concerning the relationship between the PB and DPB statistics, increasing values of i with a normal set of cash flows affect the present value of positive cash flows, but not that of negative cash flows. All sets of normal cash flows will therefore share this general, downward-sloping shape.

Note that IRR appears on this graph as the intersection of the NPV profile with the x-axis (horizontal)—the intersection will represent the interest rate where NPV equals exactly zero. With

internal rate of return (IRR) A capital budgeting technique that generates decision rules and associated metrics for choosing projects based on the implicit expected geometric average of a project's rate of return.

NPV profile A graph of a project's NPV as a function of the cost of capital.

Real assets like production lines generally don't trade in perfectly competitive markets.

EXAMPLE 13-6

For interactive versions of this example visit www.mhhe.com/canM

```
CALCULATOR HINTS

−$10,000   [CF0]
$  2,500   [CF1]
$  3,500   [CF2]
$  5,000   [CF3]
$  4,000   [CF4]
$  2,000   [CF5]
           IRR
[CPT]      [IRR]
           = 20.61%
```

IRR Calculation

Looking once again at our sample set of normal cash flows from Table 13.1, IRR will be the solution to:

$$0 = \frac{-\$10,000}{(1 + IRR)^0} + \frac{\$2,500}{(1 + IRR)^1} + \frac{\$3,500}{(1 + IRR)^2} + \frac{\$3,500}{(1 + IRR)^3} + \frac{\$4,000}{(1 + IRR)^4} + \frac{\$2,000}{(1 + IRR)^5}$$

$IRR = .2062$, or 20.62%

FIGURE 13.1 NPV Profile for Sample Normal Cash Flows

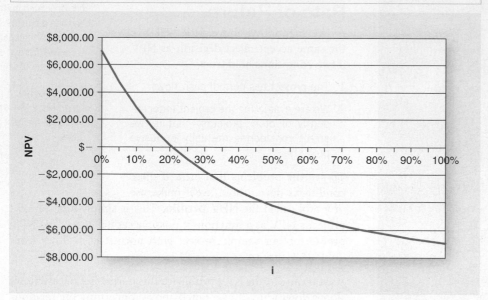

more than one interest rate. In this case we may find more than one valid IRR for which NPV equals precisely zero. An example of such an NPV profile, constructed from the cash flows in Table 13.2, appears in Figure 13.2.

In this instance, the project shows two valid IRRs: one at 23.62 percent and another at 88.62 percent. Which of these two should we use as "the" statistic? Well, it depends on what the firm pays as the actual cost of capital. If the firm pays 12 percent for capital, then using either of these two IRR values would generate a correct "accept" decision, as the project *does* have a positive NPV at $i = 12$ percent. But what if the firm paid a relatively high cost of capital, say, for example, 30 percent? Then the IRR rule would have us accept the project if we used the higher value (88.62 percent) as the project's statistic, but reject it if we used the lower IRR (23.62 percent). Of course, since the project generates a negative NPV if i is 30 percent, we would actually want to reject the project.

normal cash flows such as these, the constant downward slope of the NPV profile dictates that only one such intersection will exist for each project.

Using the IRR technique requires a bit more complicated analysis if we come across more than one valid IRR. Perhaps the best thing to do in such a situation is to simply use a decision statistic other than IRR on projects with non-normal cash flows.

If you (or, more likely, upper management) insist on using IRR with non-normal cash flows, you're going to need to use some trial and error to find all the possible IRRs. It will help to know how many there might possibly be. According to the Rule of Signs,[3] we can end up with no more different positive IRRs than the number of sign changes in the cash flows—that is, inflows to outflows or outflows to inflows. Since our non-normal cash flows set shows two sign changes (one change from positive to negative and one change from negative to positive), we know that the two IRRs we have found constitute the entire possible set.

Luckily we can solve IRR's problems associated with non-normal cash flows using the modified internal rate of return (MIRR), which also accounts for another problem associated with IRR, that of an unrealistic reinvestment rate assumption.

Differing Reinvestment Rate Assumptions of NPV and IRR

In addition to the problems associated with non-normal cash flows and handling mutually exclusive projects discussed shortly, IRR also has a different assumption than NPV concerning what we do with the cash inflows once we get them

[3]First described by René Descartes in his 1637 manuscript *La Geometrie*.

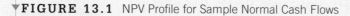

13-5 Is it possible for the NPV profile of a finite set of normal set of cash flows to never cross the x-axis?

13-6 Suppose a normal set of cash flows has an IRR equal to zero. Would NPV accept or reject such a project?

IRR and NPV Profiles with Non-Normal Cash Flows

But let's revisit what happens to the NPV profile if cash flows are *not* normal. The NPV profile will not necessarily slope continually downward and thus may cross over the x-axis at

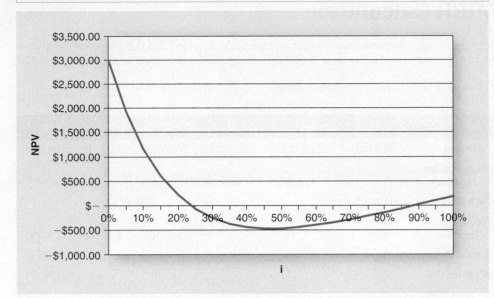

modified internal rate of return (MIRR) A capital budgeting method that converts a project's cash flows using a more consistent reinvestment rate prior to applying the IRR decision rule.

mutually exclusive projects Groups or pairs of projects where you can accept one but not all.

Two or more projects are **mutually exclusive** if management can accept one, the other, or neither, but not both, projects. As discussed below, if we compare two mutually exclusive projects using a rate-based decision statistic, problems can arise if the projects' cash flows exhibit differences in *timing* or *scale* (i.e., the size of the initial investment in each project). Over time, a "large" project that earns a slightly lower rate of return may be a better choice for the firm than a "small" project that earns a higher rate, but we will see that the rate-based decision techniques don't do well in choosing between these types of alternative projects.

What makes two or more projects mutually exclusive? Generally, mutually exclusive projects either share a common asset or target a common market, but the firm can only spare resources for one of them, or the market may only accept one product. Consider the prototypical example of mutually exclusive projects: a landowner owns two plots of land on either side of a river that people want to cross, and she is considering either building a bridge or operating a ferry for that purpose.

First, let's assume enough land on each lot to provide space for bridge footings or for pier pilings, but not for both. In this case, the two plots of land represent assets that the two projects can't share, which is the first factor making the bridge and the ferry mutually exclusive projects.

back. IRR implies that any cash inflows will be reinvested in another project with the same earning power as the first project, while NPV assumes that cash inflows will be reinvested at the cost of capital, *i*.

Which assumption is more reasonable? NPV's is because one way to "earn" the cost of capital is to pay back your capital investors. IRR's assumption doesn't make sense. Assuming that this project beat out a bunch of other projects at step 2 of the decision process, it must have had the highest possible IRR among all the alternatives, right? But now that the cash flows are rolling in, we find another project with the same, highest possible rate of return? Seems like a little too much to expect, doesn't it? Who is ever that lucky all the time?

Modified Internal Rate of Return Statistic

The name **modified internal rate of return** is a little misleading. We are going to calculate IRR the same way we did before, but we're going to *modify* the set of cash flows to account for the cost of capital before we calculate IRR. We first use the cost of capital to "move" all the negative cash flows to the initial project start date (i.e., time 0) and all the positive cash inflows to the project termination date—and only *then* will we use the regular steps to calculate IRR.

IRRs, MIRRs, and NPV Profiles with Mutually Exclusive Projects

As we have noted above, even if we use the MIRR method for a project with non-normal cash flows we can still run into problems if we try to use IRR or MIRR to choose between mutually exclusive projects.

EXAMPLE 13-7

MIRR Calculation

Turning once again to the sample non-normal project cash flows in Table 13.2, and assuming that the firm still faces a cost of capital of 12 percent, we convert the cash flows as shown in Table 13.7.

▼ **TABLE 13.7** MIRR Cash Flow Adjustments for Sample Project with Non-Normal Cash Flows

Year	0	1	2	3	4	5
Cash flow	$5,000.00	−$10,000.00	−$3,000.00	$5,000.00	$4,000.00	$2,000.00
Present value (if negative)		−8,928.57	−2,391.58			
Sum of PV	−11,320.15					
Future value (if positive)	8,811.71			6,272.00	4,480.00	2,000.00
Sum of FV						21,563.71
Modified CFs	−11,320.15					21,563.71

SOLUTION:

With this new set of modified cash flows, the (M)IRR is:

$$0 = \frac{-\$11,320.15}{(1 + IRR)^0} + \frac{\$21,563.71}{(1 + IRR)^5}$$

IRR = .1376, or 13.76%

Since our (M)IRR decision statistic exceeds the 12 percent cost of capital, we would accept the project under the MIRR method, which uses the same benchmark as the IRR rule. Notice that, regardless of how many possible IRRs a project may have, it will only ever have *one* possible MIRR. When you take a bunch of cash flows and convert them into two cash flows, one negative and one positive, you will only ever see one change in sign.

CALCULATOR HINTS

$ 5,000	[CF0]
−$10,000	[CF1]
−$ 3,000	[CF2]
$ 5,000	[CF3]
$ 4,000	[CF4]
$ 2,000	[CF5]
	IRR
12%	[I]
12%	[RI]
[CPT]	[MOD = 13.76%]

Second, even if the land provided enough room to build both ferry landing piers and bridge footings, it stands to reason that no one would take the ferry if they could simply drive across the bridge—so the two projects' inability to share a potential target market provides a second reason why the projects are mutually exclusive.

To see the problems associated with choosing between two mutually exclusive projects using a rate-based decision statistic, let's suppose that we face a choice between two mutually exclusive projects with the cash flows shown in Table 13.8.

▼ **TABLE 13.8** Sample Mutually Exclusive Projects

Year	0	1	2	3	4	5
Project A Cash Flows	$800	$600	$500	$400	$ 0	$200
Project B Cash Flows	−$400	$250	$200	$250	$50	$100

Calculating the NPVs for these two projects across a range of possible rates as shown in Table 13.9 on page 312 will yield the NPV profiles shown in Figure 13.3.

As you can see approximately (and calculate precisely), A's IRR equals 32.88 percent and B's equals 40.59 percent. You'll also notice that the two NPV profiles cross each other in the first quadrant, and that intersection is exactly what is going to cause problems for us as we try to apply an IRR decision rule.

To see why, recall our discussion of the three-step decision process necessary for mutually exclusive projects, and go through that process for both NPV and IRR using a couple of not-so-arbitrary interest rates.

First, let's suppose that the project would be subject to a 30 percent cost of capital. In that case, as per Table 13.10, the NPV for project A would be $29.47 and the NPV for project B would be

interest rate cognizant Including the cost of capital calculation into the decision-making process.

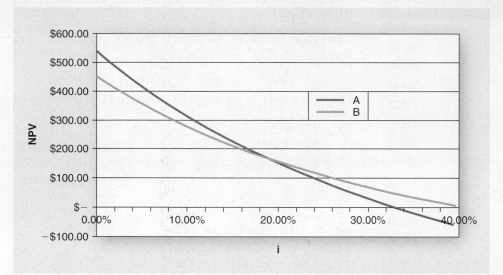

have us accept project B. These results are summarized in Table 13.11 on page 313.

Why is IRR still choosing project B, despite the 30 percent cost of capital? Well, IRR's refusal to "change its mind"[4] arises from a combination of how we calculate the statistic and how we use it in the three-step decision process. Think about it this way: The NPV statistic includes the cost of capital in its calculation, so when we get to the runoff, NPV is able to make an **interest-rate-cognizant** decision. IRR does not incorporate the cost of capital in calculating its statistic. Therefore, when it reaches step 2, it will always be comparing the same two IRRs for two particular projects, no matter what the cost of capital is.

The implication here is that, for any interest rate to the right of where the two NPV profiles cross, NPV and IRR will make the same accept/reject decision. For rates to the left of the crossover point, NPV will choose the right project but IRR will chose the wrong project. So, since it's sort of important, how do we calculate the rate at which the two NPV profiles cross? Well, we mathematically manipulate each NPV profile until one comes as close to the x-axis as possible, and then figure out the rate at which they cross each other as the IRR of the other project.

It sounds complicated, but it really isn't. All we have to do is subtract one project's cash flows from those of the other, period by period, to get a new set of cash flows that show the differences between the original two projects' cash flows,

$68.88. This means that project B would win the runoff. Since its NPV is greater than zero, the NPV decision rule would have us also accept project B.

Likewise, if we were using IRR in the same situation, project B's IRR of 40.59 percent would win the runoff over project A's IRR of 32.88 percent. But since 40.59 percent is greater than the 30 percent cost of capital, IRR would also have us accept project B. These results appear in Table 13.10 on the following page.

Now let's see what happens if the cost of capital is, say, 10 percent. In that case, as per Table 13.9, the NPV for project A would be $312.91 and the NPV for project B would be $276.63. This means that project A would now win the runoff and, ultimately, would be accepted under the NPV statistic as well.

However, if we were using IRR in the same situation, project B's IRR of 40.59 percent would *still* win the runoff over project A's IRR of 32.88 percent, and, since 40.59 percent is greater than the 30 percent cost of capital, IRR would continue to

[4]You'll sometimes hear this phenomenon referred to as IRR being "myopic," which is the technical name for nearsightedness.

i	NPV A	NPV B
0.00%	$540.00	$450.00
2.00	487.66	409.68
4.00	439.15	372.48
6.00	394.07	338.08
8.00	352.09	306.22
10.00	312.91	276.63
12.00	276.27	249.12
14.00	241.92	223.48
16.00	209.67	199.54
18.00	179.33	177.16
20.00	150.75	156.20
22.00	123.76	136.54
24.00	98.25	118.07
26.00	74.10	100.69
28.00	51.21	84.32
30.00	29.47	68.88
32.00	8.80	54.30
34.00	−10.86	40.51
36.00	−29.61	27.45
38.00	−47.49	15.07
40.00	−64.56	3.33

and then find the IRR of these differences. The values for the cash flows of "A-B," the calculated values for the NPV profile of these differences, and the resulting translated NPV profiles

(note that A' will be equal to "A-B," while B' will be the new, translated, x-axis) appear in Table 13.12, Table 13.13, and Figure 13.4.

The crossover rate will be equal to the IRR of the "A-B" cash flows:

$$0 = \frac{-\$400}{(1 + IRR)^0} + \frac{\$350}{(1 + IRR)^1} + \frac{\$300}{(1 + IRR)^2} + \frac{-\$210}{(1 + IRR)^3}$$

$$+ \frac{-\$50}{(1 + IRR)^4} + \frac{\$100}{(1 + IRR)^5}$$

$$IRR = .1856, \text{ or } 18.56\%$$

So now, IRR will give us the correct answer for these two projects if i is greater than 18.56 percent, and will choose exactly the wrong project if i is less than 18.56 percent.

You may have noticed that the set of "A-B" cash flows is *not* normal. How, then, can we feel comfortable using IRR to calculate "the" crossover rate given that we've previously decided not to use IRR with non-normal cash flows? Well, this is a special case: we knew that the two original projects' cash flows *were* normal. So we intuitively understood that their NPV profiles, while not exactly straight lines, at least sloped downward continually. So, if two "almost straight" lines do cross, they're probably only going to cross once. That is, we expect only one solution to the IRR problem for the "A-B" differences in cash flows.

CALCULATOR HINTS

−$400	[CF0]
$350	[CF1]
$300	[CF2]
−$210	[CF3]
−$ 50	[CF4]
$100	[CF5]
	IRR
[CPT]	[IRR]
	= 18.56%

▼ **TABLE 13.10** Decision Process for Projects A and B at i = 30%

NPV

1. Compute the statistic for each project.

NPV$_A$ = $29.47

NPV$_B$ = $68.88

2. Have a runoff between the mutually exclusive projects, choosing the one with the best statistic.

NPV$_B$ > NPV$_A$

3. Compare the computed statistic for the winner of the runoff to the benchmark to decide whether to accept or reject.

NPV$_B$ > 0

IRR

1. Compute the statistic for each project.

IRR$_A$ = 32.88%

IRR$_B$ = 40.59%

2. Have a runoff between the mutually exclusive projects, choosing the one with the best statistic.

IRR$_B$ > IRR$_A$

3. Compare the computed statistic for the winner of the runoff to the benchmark to decide whether to accept or reject.

IRR$_B$ > 30%

Also notice that we only have to worry about IRR giving incorrect decisions if the NPV profiles cross in the so-called "first quadrant" of the graph. If they cross outside this quadrant at a rate higher than both projects' IRRs, then we don't have to worry about problems with IRR choosing the wrong project. Any cost of capital high enough for IRR to reject the project at the third step of the IRR decision process will also result in a negative NPV.[5]

[5] Actually, in such cases the IRR rule will still choose the wrong project at step 2 of the decision process, the runoff, but the last step of the decision process, the comparison with the benchmark, will save us. The wrong project may be chosen at the runoff, but if they're both bad projects, they'll be rejected anyway.

time out!

13-7 Suppose two projects with normal cash flows, X and Y, have exactly the same required initial investment, but X has a longer payback. Can we say anything about X's IRR versus that of Y?

13-8 Assume you're evaluating a project that requires an initial investment of $5,000 at time zero, then another investment of $4,000 in one year, after which it will have cash inflows of $3,000 per year for five years. How many IRRs could this project possibly have?

revised: "That's not a bug, it's a feature!" Well, this "problem" we're experiencing with IRR and MIRR, as well as NPV, truly *is* a feature. It's a feature of all rate-based decision statistics: They tend to focus on the rate of return *per dollar invested* at the expense of ignoring *how many* dollars are getting invested in each project. IRR and MIRR chose project B all the time because, even though it sometimes had a lower NPV, it was always earning a higher rate of return *per dollar invested*.

What causes this confusion? The two cash flows differ in timing and scale. Looking back at the cash flows associated with our two mutually exclusive projects again (shown again in Table 13.14) we see that project B only costs half as much as project A.

This, together with the fact that project B's cash flows tend to be front-end loaded in terms of percentage of total cash flows, relative

MIRR Strengths and Weaknesses

As we have constructed it, the MIRR statistic explicitly corrects IRR's faulty and unreasonable reinvestment rate assumption, implicitly fixing any problems with non-normal cash flows along the way. However, it does not correct the problem of IRR choosing the wrong mutually exclusive project for a particular range of rates. For example, even if we go back to the two sample mutually exclusive projects of Table 13.8 and compute each project's MIRR, we will still see that the MIRR of project B (23.39 percent) will *always* be greater than the MIRR of project A (18.85 percent), causing the MIRR to also choose the incorrect project to the left of the crossover rate.

There's an old joke in computer programming that gets reused every time a major software product is

▼ **TABLE 13.11** Decision Process for Projects A and B at $i = 20\%$

NPV		
	1. Compute the statistic for each project.	$NPV_A = \$312.91$ $NPV_B = \$276.63$
	2. Have a runoff between the mutually exclusive projects, choosing the one with the best statistic.	$NPV_A > NPV_B$
	3. Compare the computed statistic for the winner of the runoff to the benchmark to decide whether to accept or reject.	**$NPV_A > 0$**
IRR		
	1. Compute the statistic for each project.	$IRR_A = 32.88\%$ $IRR_B = 40.59\%$
	2. Have a runoff between the mutually exclusive projects, choosing the one with the best statistic.	$IRR_B > IRR_A$
	3. Compare the computed statistic for the winner of the runoff to the benchmark to decide whether to accept or reject.	**$IRR_B > 30\%$**

▼ **TABLE 13.12** Difference in Cash Flows—Sample Mutually Exclusive Projects

Year	0	1	2	3	4	5
Project A Cash Flows	−$800	$600	$500	$ 40	$ 0	$200
Project B Cash Flows	−400	250	200	250	50	100
A-B	−400	350	300	−210	−50	100

to project A's, gives project B a "flatter," less steeply sloped, indifference curve. This, in turn, results in a higher NPV for project B when rates are relatively high.

PROFITABILITY INDEX

Another popular rate-based decision technique is the **profitability index (PI).** PI is based upon NPV, so its results will more closely resemble NPV than will IRR or PB/DPB. PI takes a project's NPV and standardizes it by simply dividing by the project's initial investment. The result: We get a decision statistic that measures "bang per buck invested." Such a measure comes in handy when the firm faces resource constraints concerning how much capital is available for new projects.

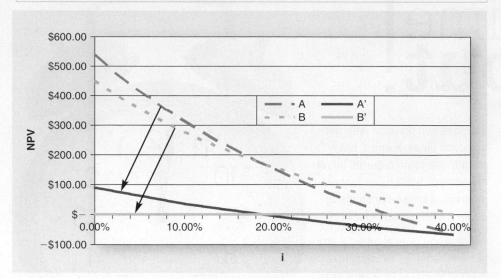

▼**FIGURE 13.4** Translated NPV Profiles

Profitability Index Statistic

The mathematics of computing the PI are straightforward:

$$PI = \frac{NPV}{CF_0}$$

(13-9)

▼ **TABLE 13.13** NPV Profile, A-B

i	NPV, A-B
0.00%	$ 90.00
2.00	77.98
4.00	66.67
6.00	55.99
8.00	45.88
10.00	36.28
12.00	27.15
14.00	18.45
16.00	10.13
18.00	2.17
20.00	−5.45
22.00	−12.77
24.00	−19.81
26.00	−26.59
28.00	−33.12
30.00	−39.41
32.00	−45.49
34.00	−51.37
36.00	−57.06
38.00	−62.56
40.00	−67.89

EXAMPLE 13-8

Calculation of Profitability Index

Turning yet again to the sample project cash flows in Table 13.1, the PI for that project will be:

$$PI = \frac{\$2,258.15}{\$10,000} = 22.58\%$$

Profitability Index Benchmark

Though we might be tempted to assume that, like IRR and MIRR, we should compare the PI to the cost of capital, such is not the case. Remember that the NPV already includes the necessary investment, so any PI above zero is "found money" or the present value of expected economic profits. In this case, the PI of 22.58 percent is telling us that the project will, roughly speaking, earn the equivalent of a 22.58 percent return on the initial investment of $10,000 above and beyond the return necessary to repay the initial cost. ∎

▼ **TABLE 13.14** Sample Mutually Exclusive Projects

Year	0	1	2	3	4	5
Project A Cash Flows	−$800	$600	$500	$400	$ 0	$200
Project B Cash Flows	−400	250	200	250	50	100

time out!

13-11 There is another version of the PI that uses the present value of just the future cash flows as its numerator instead of the NPV. How would you expect that version's benchmark to change from the version of PI we initially discussed?

13-12 Suppose you have a project whose payback is equal to its termination date. What can you say for sure about its PI? (*Hint:* what will the project's NPV be?)

Get Online

Your Turn...

Questions

1. Is the set of cash flows depicted below normal or non-normal? Explain. *(LG1)*

Time	0	1	2	3	4	5
Cash Flow	−$100	−$50	−$80	$0	$100	$100

2. Derive an accept/reject rule for IRR similar to equation 13-8 that would make the correct decision on cash flows that are non-normal but which always have one large positive cash flow at time zero followed by a series of negative cash flows. *(LG1)*

Time	0	1	2	3	4	5
Cash Flow	+	−	−	−	−	−

3. Is it possible for a company to initiate two products that target the same market and are *not* mutually exclusive? *(LG1)*

4. Suppose that your company used "APV," or "All-the-Present, Value-Except-CF_0," to analyze capital budgeting projects. What would this rule's benchmark value be? *(LG2)*

5. Under what circumstances could payback and discounted payback be equal? *(LG3)*

6. Could a project's MIRR ever *exceed* its IRR? *(LG4)*

7. If you had two mutually exclusive, normal-cash-flow projects whose NPV profiles crossed at all points, for which range of interest rates would IRR give the right accept/reject answer? *(LG5)*

8. Suppose a company wanted to double their firm's value with the next round of capital budgeting project decisions. To what would they set the PI benchmark to make this goal? *(LG6)*

9. Suppose a company faced different borrowing and lending rates: How would this range change the way that you would compute the MIRR statistic? *(LG4)*

Problems

13-1 **NPV with Normal Cash Flows** Compute the NPV for Project M and accept or reject the project with the cash flows shown below if the appropriate cost of capital is 8 percent. *(LG2)*

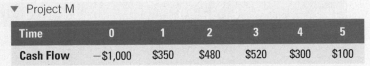

▼ Project M

Time	0	1	2	3	4	5
Cash Flow	−$1,000	$350	$480	$520	$300	$100

13-2 **NPV with Normal Cash Flows** Compute the NPV statistic for Project Y and tell whether the firm should accept or reject the project with the cash flows shown below if the appropriate cost of capital is 12 percent. *(LG2)*

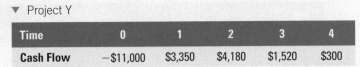

▼ Project Y

Time	0	1	2	3	4
Cash Flow	−$11,000	$3,350	$4,180	$1,520	$300

13-3 **NPV with Non-Normal Cash Flows** Compute the NPV statistic for Project U and recommend whether the firm should accept or reject the project with the cash flows shown below if the appropriate cost of capital is 10 percent. *(LG2)*

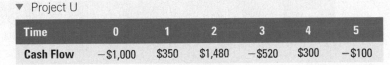

▼ Project U

Time	0	1	2	3	4	5
Cash Flow	−$1,000	$350	$1,480	−$520	$300	−$100

13-4 **NPV with Normal Cash Flows** Compute the payback statistic for Project A and recommend whether the firm should accept or reject the project with the cash flows shown below if the appropriate cost of capital is 8 percent and the maximum allowable payback is four years. *(LG3)*

▼ Project A

Time	0	1	2	3	4	5
Cash Flow	−$1,000	$350	$480	$520	$300	$100

13-5 **Payback** Compute the payback statistic for Project B and decide whether the firm should accept or reject the project with the cash flows shown below if the appropriate cost of capital is 12 percent and the maximum allowable payback is three years. *(LG3)*

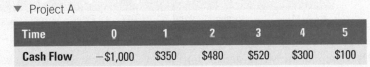

▼ Project B

Time	0	1	2	3	4	5
Cash Flow	−$11,000	$3,350	$4,180	$1,520	$0	$1,000

13-6 **Discounted Payback** Compute the discounted payback statistic for Project C and recommend whether the firm should accept or reject the project with the cash flows shown below if the appropriate cost of capital is 8 percent and the maximum allowable discounted payback is three years. *(LG3)*

▼ Project C

Time	0	1	2	3	4	5
Cash Flow	−$1,000	$350	$480	$520	$300	$100

13-7 Discounted Payback Compute the discounted payback statistic for Project D and recommend whether the firm should accept or reject the project with the cash flows shown below if the appropriate cost of capital is 12 percent and the maximum allowable discounted payback is four years. *(LG3)*

▼ Project D

Time	0	1	2	3	4	5
Cash Flow	$11,000	$3,350	$4,180	$1,520	$0	$1,000

13-8 IRR Compute the IRR statistic for Project E and note whether the firm should accept or reject the project with the cash flows shown below if the appropriate cost of capital is 8 percent. *(LG4)*

▼ Project E

Time	0	1	2	3	4	5
Cash Flow	−$1,000	$350	$480	$520	$300	$100

13-9 IRR Compute the IRR statistic for project F and note whether the firm should accept or reject the project with the cash flows shown below if the appropriate cost of capital is 12 percent. *(LG4)*

▼ Project F

Time	0	1	2	3	4
Cash Flow	−$11,000	$3,350	$4,180	$1,520	$2,000

13-10 IRR Compute the IRR statistic for Project G and note whether the firm should accept or reject the project with the cash flows shown below if the appropriate cost of capital is 10 percent. *(LG4)*

▼ Project G

Time	0	1	2	3	4	5
Cash Flow	−$1,000	$350	$1,480	−$520	$300	−$100

13-11 MIRR Compute the MIRR statistic for Project H and note whether to accept or reject the project with the cash flows shown below if the appropriate cost of capital is 8 percent. *(LG4)*

▼ Project H

Time	0	1	2	3	4	5
Cash Flow	−$1,000	$350	$480	$520	$300	$100

13-12 MIRR Compute the MIRR statistic for Project I and tell whether to accept or reject the project with the cash flows shown below if the appropriate cost of capital is 12 percent. *(LG4)*

▼ Project I

Time	0	1	2	3	4
Cash Flow	−$11,000	$3,350	$4,180	$1,520	$2,000

13-13 MIRR Compute the MIRR statistic for Project J and advise whether to accept or reject the project with the cash flows shown below if the appropriate cost of capital is 10 percent. *(LG4)*

▼ Project J

Time	0	1	2	3	4	5
Cash Flow	−$1,000	$350	$1,480	−$520	$300	−$100

13-14 PI Compute the PI statistic for Project Z and advise the firm whether to accept or reject the project with the cash flows shown below if the appropriate cost of capital is 8 percent. *(LG6)*

▼ Project Z

Time	0	1	2	3	4	5
Cash Flow	−$1,000	$350	$480	$520	$300	$100

13-15 PI Compute the PI statistic for Project Q and tell whether you would accept or reject the project with the cash flows shown below if the appropriate cost of capital is 12 percent. *(LG6)*

▼ Project Q

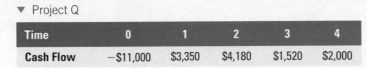

Time	0	1	2	3	4
Cash Flow	−$11,000	$3,350	$4,180	$1,520	$2,000

13-16 PI Compute the PI statistic for Project LL and decide whether to accept or reject the project with the cash flows shown below if the appropriate cost of capital is 10 percent. *(LG6)*

▼ Project LL

Time	0	1	2	3	4	5
Cash Flow	−$1,000	$350	$1,480	−$520	$300	−$100

13-17 Multiple IRRs How many possible IRRs could you find for the following set of cash flows? *(LG1)*

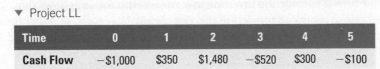

Time	0	1	2	3	4
Cash Flow	−$11,000	$3,350	$4,180	$1,520	$2,000

13-18 Multiple IRRs How many possible IRRs could you find for the following set of cash flows? *(LG1)*

Time	0	1	2	3	4
Cash Flow	−$11,000	−$39,350	$440,180	$217,520	−$2,000

Use this information to answer the next six questions. If a particular decision method should not be used, indicate why.

Suppose your firm is considering investing in a project with the cash flows shown below, that the required rate of return on projects of this risk class is 8 percent, and that the maximum allowable payback and discounted payback statistics for the project are 3.5 and 4.5 years, respectively.

Time	0	1	2	3	4	5	6
Cash Flow	−$5,000	$1,200	$1,400	$1,600	$1,600	$1,400	$1,200

13-19 Payback Use the payback decision rule to evaluate this project; should it be accepted or rejected? *(LG3)*

13-20 Discounted Payback Use the discounted payback decision rule to evaluate this project; should it be accepted or rejected? *(LG3)*

13-21 IRR Use the IRR decision rule to evaluate this project; should it be accepted or rejected? *(LG4)*

13-22 MIRR Use the MIRR decision rule to evaluate this project; should it be accepted or rejected? *(LG4)*

13-23 NPV Use the NPV decision rule to evaluate this project; should it be accepted or rejected? *(LG2)*

13-24 PI Use the PI decision rule to evaluate this project; should it be accepted or rejected? *(LG6)*

Use this information to answer the next six questions. If you should not use a particular decision technique, indicate why.

Suppose your firm is considering investing in a project with the cash flows shown below, that the required rate of return on projects of this risk class is 11 percent, and that the maximum allowable payback and discounted payback statistics for your company are 3 and 3.5 years, respectively.

Time	0	1	2	3	4	4
Cash Flow	−$235,000	$65,800	$84,000	$141,000	$122,000	$81,200

13-25 Payback Use the payback decision rule to evaluate this project; should it be accepted or rejected? *(LG3)*

13-26 Discounted Payback Use the discounted payback decision rule to evaluate this project; should it be accepted or rejected? *(LG3)*

13-27 IRR Use the IRR decision rule to evaluate this project; should it be accepted or rejected? *(LG4)*

13-28 MIRR Use the MIRR decision rule to evaluate this project; should it be accepted or rejected? *(LG4)*

13-29 NPV Use the NPV decision rule to evaluate this project; should it be accepted or rejected? *(LG2)*

13-30 PI Use the PI decision rule to evaluate this project; should it be accepted or rejected? *(LG6)*

Use the project cash flows for the two mutually exclusive projects shown below to answer the following four questions.

Time	Project A Cash Flow	Project B Cash Flow
0	−$725	−$850
1	100	200
2	250	200
3	250	200
4	200	200
5	100	200
6	100	200
7	100	200

13-31 NPV Profiles Graph the NPV profiles for both projects on a common chart, making sure that you identify all of the "crucial" points. *(LG5)*

13-32 IRR Applicability For what range of possible interest rates would you want to use IRR to choose between these two projects? For what range of rates would you NOT want to use IRR? *(LG5)*

13-33 Multiple IRRs Construct an NPV profile and determine EXACTLY how many nonnegative IRRs you can find for the following set of cash flows: *(LG5)*

Time	0	1	2	3	4	5	6	7
Cash Flow	−200	400	150	−100	−100	−300	200	−300

13-34 Multiple IRRs Construct an NPV profile and determine EXACTLY how many nonnegative IRRs you can find for the following set of cash flows: *(LG5)*

Time	0	1	2	3	4	5	6	7
Cash Flow	−150	275	150	−100	300	−300	200	−300

addressing working capital policies +
managing short-term assets and liabilities

n this chapter, we want to focus on the major trade-off implicit in funding net working capital. By and large, the trade-off involves comparing how much it costs the firm to carry an investment in current assets with the shortage costs associated with the firm's not having enough cash, inventory, or accounts receivable.

As we'll see, the firm's ideal solution to providing net working capital would be to get someone else to foot the bill. Though this may be a valid approach to fund *some* of the firm's current assets, it's usually difficult to get someone else to cover the *entire* amount of net

continued on p. 324

LEARNING GOALS

LG1 Set overall objectives of a good working capital policy.

LG2 Discuss how net working capital serves the firm.

LG3 Calculate and use the firm's operating cycle and cash cycle to discover how much funding for current assets the firm has to find.

LG4 Model the optimal trade-off between carrying costs and shortage costs that dictates the firm's current asset investment.

LG5 Compare the flexible and restrictive approaches to financing current assets.

LG6 Differentiate among sources of short-term financing available for funding current assets.

LG7 Justify the firm's need to hold cash.

LG8 Use the Baumol and Miller-Orr models for determining cash policy.

LG9 Identify sources of float and show how to control float for the firm's disbursement and collection functions.

L10 Investigate why firms have excess cash and identify their choices about what to do with it.

L11 Draw the connection between the firm's credit terms and collection policy and the amount of capital the firm has invested in accounts receivable.

continued from p. 323

working capital necessary to run the firm efficiently. We will, however, discuss how to shift those costs elsewhere as much as possible in this chapter by covering the following topics:

1. How to determine the optimal amount of investment in current assets.

2. How to measure the portion of current assets that the firm is responsible for funding.

3. How to choose the source of funding for that portion of current assets. ■

view points

business APPLICATION

Chewbacca Manufacturing expects sales of $32 million next year. CM's cost of goods sold normally runs at 55 percent of sales; inventory requirements are usually 10 percent of annual sales; the average accounts receivable balance is one-sixth of annual sales; and the average accounts payable balance is 5 percent of sales. If all sales are on credit, what will Chewbacca's level of net working capital and its cash cycle be?

REVISITING THE BALANCE-SHEET MODEL OF THE FIRM

Remember our layout of the balance sheet in Chapter 2 reproduced in Table 14.1 below:

▼ **TABLE 14.1** The Basic Balance Sheet

Total Assets		Total Liabilities and Equity
Current assets:	net working capital	Current liabilities:
Cash and marketable securities		Accrued wages and taxes
Accounts receivable		Accounts payable
Inventory		Notes payable
Fixed assets:		Long-term debt
Gross plant and equipment		Stockholders' equity:
Less: Depreciation		Preferred stock
Net plant and equipment		Common stock and paid-in surplus
Other long-term assets		Retained earnings

Earlier in the book, we discussed the fact that the current assets, while the most liquid, are also usually less profitable than fixed assets. This explains why some managers like to think of net working capital as *"the net amount of current assets that the firm has to fund, above and beyond those that someone else funds for them."*

To put it bluntly, net working capital is a necessary evil: most firms can't sell finished goods without inventory to display, or without offering to sell to customers on credit, and so forth. Therefore, those firms incur costs associated with keeping inventory on hand and with selling to customers on credit.

But just because a firm has to fund *some* net working capital doesn't mean that it should fund all of it or even a large portion of it. Instead, the firm should, to the best of its ability, ensure that the marginal benefit of each dollar tied up in net working capital equals the marginal **opportunity cost** of not having that dollar invested in positive-NPV fixed assets.

time out!

14-1 Why might a firm's creditors *not* think of net working capital as a necessary evil, but rather as a good thing?

14-2 If demand for a firm's products suddenly slows down so that inventory increases while sales decrease, how will the firm's needs for net working capital react?

TRACING CASH AND NET WORKING CAPITAL

To trace cash flows through the firm's operations, we must measure the **operating cycle**—the time necessary to acquire raw materials, turn them into finished goods, sell them, and receive payment for them—as well as the firm's **cash cycle.**

Let's think of net working capital as the portion of current assets that the firm must fund (above and beyond those assets funded by current liabilities). Then we can similarly think of the firm's cash cycle as the portion of the operating cycle that the firm must finance.

opportunity cost The cost or forgone opportunity of using an asset already in use by the firm, or a person already employed by the firm, in a new project.

cash cycle The operating cycle minus the average payment period.

The Operating Cycle

To measure the firm's operating cycle, we need to turn to some of the ratios that we discussed in Chapter 3:

$$\text{Operating cycle} = \text{Days' sales in inventory} + \text{Average collection period} \quad (14\text{-}1)$$

$$= \frac{\text{Inventory} \times 365}{\text{Cost of goods sold}} + \frac{\text{Accounts receivable} \times 365}{\text{Credit sales}}$$

> " **THINK OF NET WORKING CAPITAL AS THE PORTION OF CURRENT ASSETS THAT THE FIRM MUST FUND (ABOVE AND BEYOND THOSE ASSETS FUNDED BY CURRENT LIABILITIES).** "

EXAMPLE 14-1

For interactive versions of this example visit www.mhhe.com/canM

Calculation of Operating Cycle

Suppose that MMK Industries has annual sales of $1 million, cost of goods sold of $650,000, average inventories of $116,000, and average accounts receivable of $150,000. Assuming that all MMK's sales are on credit, what will be the firm's operating cycle?

SOLUTION:

The operating cycle will be equal to

$$\text{Operating cycle} = \frac{\text{Inventory} \times 365}{\text{Cost of goods sold}} + \frac{\text{Accounts receivable} \times 365}{\text{Credit sales}}$$

$$= \frac{\$116,000 \times 365}{\$650,000} + \frac{\$150,000 \times 365}{\$1,000,000}$$

$$= 65.14 \text{ days} + 54.75 \text{ days}$$

$$= 119.89 \text{ days}$$

So it will take MKK almost 120 days from the time they receive raw materials to produce, market, sell, and collect the cash for their finished goods.

The Cash Cycle

The firm's cash cycle will simply be the operating cycle minus the average payment period as shown in Figure 14.1:

$$\text{Cash cycle} = \text{Operating cycle} - \\ \text{Average payment period} \qquad (14\text{-}2)$$

$$= \text{Operating cycle} - \frac{\text{Accounts payable} \times 365}{\text{Cost of good sold}}$$

Note that, even though it will take MKK almost 120 days to turn their raw materials into cash, the cash cycle indicates that they will only have to foot the bill for their production cycle for 52.50 days of that time. This is the crux of managing the firm's operating and cash cycles: Minimize the number of days that the firm has to pay for its production cycle.

SOME ASPECTS OF SHORT-TERM FINANCIAL POLICY

In the last section, we derived the cash cycle by first determining the operating cycle and then subtracting the payment cycle. This derivation suggests two obvious ways that firms can reduce their net working capital needs.

time out!

14-3 How will a firm affect its operating cycle if it can reduce inventory on hand?

14-4 When we compare two firms, will the one with the longer cash cycle tend to have more or less net working capital requirements than the one with the shorter cash cycle, everything held equal? Why?

1. They can manage their need for current assets.

2. They can seek to obtain as many current liabilities as economically feasible to fund the current assets that they do need.

The Size of the Current Assets Investment

Choosing the optimal level of investment in each current asset type involves a trade-off between carrying costs and shortage costs.

Carrying costs are associated with having current assets and fall into two general categories:

1. The opportunity costs associated with having capital tied up in current assets instead of more productive fixed assets.

2. Explicit costs necessary to maintain the value of the current assets.

FIGURE 14.1 Relationship between Operating and Cash Cycles

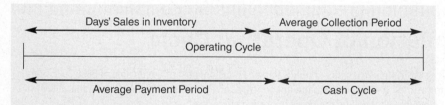

finance at work //: global

Kaizen (改善)

Kaizen is a Japanese approach to productivity improvement that aims to eliminate waste through just-in-time delivery, standardized work and equipment, and so on. The five basic elements of kaizen are:

1. Teamwork

2. Personal discipline

3. Improved morale

4. Quality circles

5. Suggestions for improvement

Studies show that the kaizen approach can reduce (sometimes dramatically) net working capital requirements, with businesses adopting the approach reporting reductions in finished-goods and in-process inventory of anywhere from 10 to 30 percent.

Want to know more?

Key Words to Search for Updates: **See the article "Off the shelf: low inventories drove down working capital last year. But will that continue as the economy improves?" at www.cfo.com.**

For example, a car dealer who purchases used vehicles and keeps them in inventory would incur the opportunity cost of not being able to invest the money paid for the used vehicles in a more lucrative opportunity, such as new cars when an exciting new hybrid come out. Our car dealer will also have to pay rental or lease payments on the piece of property where the used cars are on display and any maintenance costs necessary to keep the cars ready to sell.

Shortage costs are the costs associated with not having enough current assets and can include opportunity costs such as sales lost due to not having enough inventory on hand, as well as any explicit transaction fees paid to replenish the particular type of current asset. For example, consider a camera shop that has a reorder policy to only reorder particular lenses from their supplier if a customer comes in asking for them, and even then to only order one at a time. In today's business environment, most customers who are seeking an item want it *now*. If that item is out of stock at one store, the customer will probably turn around and order it from someone else over the Internet, resulting in lost sales to the store. If, in addition, we assume that the store pays a shipping fee for every order placed—or if they get quantity discounts if they order in bulk—then their policy will probably result in higher shipping fees. The store may also face higher costs of goods sold than it would if they ordered in quantity.

Carrying costs will increase, and shortage costs will decrease, as the firm buys more of any particular asset. Therefore, firms

carrying costs
The opportunity costs associated with having capital tied up in current assets instead of more productive fixed assets and explicit costs necessary to maintain the value of the current assets.

shortage costs
The costs associated with not having enough current assets.

Vehicles kept in inventory incur an opportunity cost.

EXAMPLE 14-2

For interactive versions of this example visit www.mhhe.com/canM

Calculation of Cash Cycle

Extending the previous example, assume that MMK's average accounts payable balance is $120,000. What will be the firm's cash cycle?

SOLUTION:

The cash cycle will be equal to

$$\text{Cash cycle} = \text{Operating cycle} - \frac{\text{Accounts payable} \times 365}{\text{Cost of good sold}}$$

$$= 119.89 \text{ days} - \frac{\$120,000 \times 305}{\$650,000}$$

$$= 119.89 \text{ days} - 67.38 \text{ days}$$

$$= 52.50 \text{ days}$$

should ideally try to choose the level of each current asset and the associated replenishment policy so that the marginal carrying and shortage costs are equal, which will result in the lowest total cost. This level is identified as CA* in Figure 14.2.

Alternative Financing Policies for Current Assets

In a perfect world, a firm would use long-term debt and equity to finance long-term (i.e., fixed) assets and short-term debt to finance current assets. Such an approach would allow the firm to maturity-match assets with their corresponding liabilities, resulting in a low or nonexistent level for net working capital. As we've previously discussed, in the real world, net working capital is usually positive for

▼FIGURE 14.2
Carrying and Shortage Costs

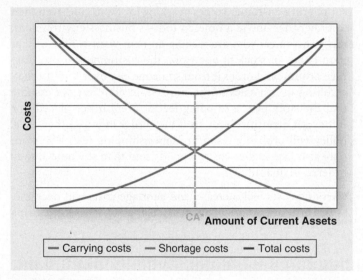

Figure 14.2 Carrying and Shortage Costs

— Carrying costs — Shortage costs — Total costs

▼FIGURE 14.3
Components of Current Assets

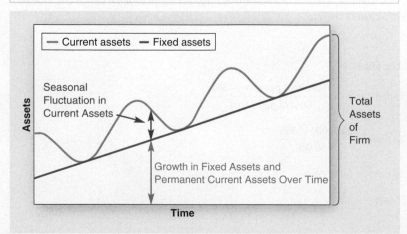

Figure 14.3 Components of Current Assets

▼FIGURE 14.4
Flexible Financing of CA

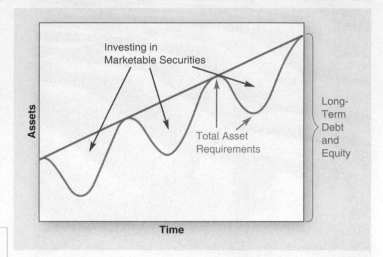

Figure 14.4 Flexible Financing of CA

most firms. The implication: at least some portion of current assets must be financed with long-term debt, equity, or a mixture of both.

Assuming that most firms can expect to have some steady, stable need for current assets throughout their calendar year and additional demand for current assets that fluctuates on some seasonal cycle, a growing firm's total demand for assets would resemble that shown in Figure 14.3.

So, a firm in such a situation faces the basic question of whether it should finance the peaks or the valleys of total asset demand (or somewhere in between) using long-term financing. Figure 14.4, Figure 14.5, and Figure 14.6 illustrate some of these choices.

We usually refer to the decision to finance the peaks of asset demand with long-term debt and equity, shown in Figure 14.4, as a *flexible financing policy*. It provides the firm with a surplus of cash and marketable securities most of the time—except during peak asset demand.

On the opposite side of the continuum, we refer to a decision to finance the troughs or valleys of asset demand with long-term debt and equity, shown in Figure 14.5, as a *restrictive financing policy*. Under this policy, the firm will have to seek short-term financing for all peak demand fluctuations for current assets, as well as for in-between demand situations. In some ways, this policy is the most "conservative"; on the other hand, it's also the least convenient for the firm, as it involves seeking some level of short-term financing almost all of the time.

A third choice is to follow a *compromise financing policy,* wherein the firm finances the seasonally adjusted average level of asset demand with long-term debt and

FIGURE 14.5
Restrictive Financing of CA

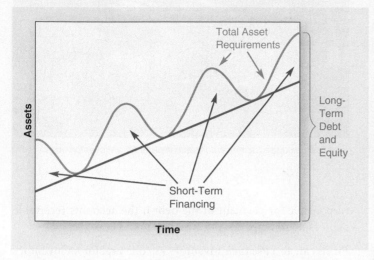

FIGURE 14.6
Compromise Financing of CA

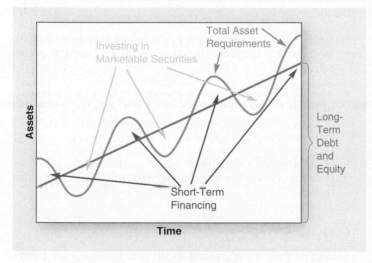

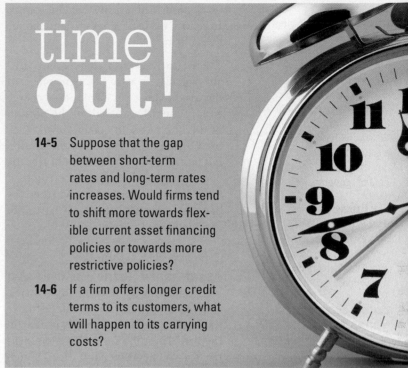

14-5 Suppose that the gap between short-term rates and long-term rates increases. Would firms tend to shift more towards flexible current asset financing policies or towards more restrictive policies?

14-6 If a firm offers longer credit terms to its customers, what will happen to its carrying costs?

• Alternative financing availability and costs, discussed below. Firms with easy and sustained access to alternative sources will want to shift towards more restrictive policies.

equity. The firm uses both short-term financing and short-term investing as needed. Figure 14.6 illustrates such a policy. Which approach works best? As is the case with almost all working capital decisions, it depends on several factors:

• Current and future expected interest rate levels. If we expect rates to rise in the future, the firm may want to lock in fixed rates for a longer time by shifting towards a flexible financing policy. With falling rates, the opposite would of course hold true.

• The spread between short- and long-term rates. Long-term borrowing usually costs more than short-term financing, but the "gap" (called the *spread*) between the two terms may be historically small or large, encouraging firms to shift to a more restrictive or flexible policy, respectively.

THE SHORT-TERM FINANCIAL PLAN

Firms that follow any financing policy other than a flexible financing plan will find themselves forced to seek short-term financing at times. Depending on their industry, they may find themselves using unsecured loans, secured loans, or other sources of short-term financing.

Unsecured Loans

For most businesses—particularly smaller ones—the most common way to cover a short-term financing need is to apply at a bank for a commercial loan. The company may expect to need such short-term loans repeatedly in the future—perhaps because they're following a restrictive financing policy but face seasonal fluctuations in asset demand, as discussed above. If the bank deems the firm creditworthy enough, the bank will usually grant the firm a *line of credit,* upon which the firm can draw and then pay off repeatedly as the firm goes through those seasonal fluctuations.

Fees for lines of credit can be both explicit (usually taking the form of an interest rate equal to the bank's prime lending rate plus a small premium) and implicit (as a compensating balance requirement and/or a bank's up-front commitment fee). A **compensating balance** is a percentage of the borrowed money (usually 5 to 10 percent) that the bank requires the firm to keep on deposit in the firm's bank accounts. In return, the bank agrees to lend money to the firm.[1]

Commitment fees, if charged, are usually calculated as a flat percentage of the credit line. But banks also charge commitment fees based on the portion of the line of credit "taken down" (i.e., used by the firm) or even of the portion *not* taken down. The amount of fees the bank charges for a line of credit and their type will depend on whether the bank is trying to encourage the use of the line of credit or not.

Secured Loans

Asset-based loans are short-term loans secured by a company's assets. Secured loans carry lower interest rates than unsecured loans, so it is usually in the firm's best interest to provide security (or collateral) when it can. Though real estate, accounts receivable, inventory, and equipment are all sometimes used to back asset-based loans, most firms seeking such a loan to finance seasonal fluctuations in current assets will typically prefer to use inventory or accounts receivable as security for the loan, as they won't wish to encumber long-term assets such as real estate or equipment.

Accounts receivable can either be sold outright to a factor or assigned. A *factor* is an entity who will buy accounts receivable on a discounted basis before they are due, with the spread between the discounted price and the receivable's face value providing the factor with expected compensation for both the time value of money and the expected level of defaults among the accounts receivable. **Assignment** is a process whereby the firm borrows money from another entity, providing them in return with both a lien on the accounts receivable as well as the right of **recourse** (i.e., the legal right to hold the firm

Firms can also use their inventory as collateral for an inventory loan.

responsible for payment of the debt if the accounts receivable debtors do not repay as promised).

Firms can also use their inventory as collateral for an inventory loan, a secured short-term loan used to purchase that inventory. Inventory loans include blanket inventory liens, trust receipts, and field warehousing financing. The major difference between the three lies with the question of who owns and keeps the inventory in question:

- Under a blanket inventory lien, the lender gets a lien against all the firm's inventory, but the firm retains ownership and possession.

- When the borrower holds the inventory in trust for the lender, with any proceed from the sale of the inventory being the property of that lender, the document acknowledging this loan commitment is referred to as the *trust receipt.*

- In field warehousing financing, a public warehouse company takes possession and supervises the inventory for the lender.

Other Sources

Two other primary sources of short-term financing are **commercial paper** issues and financing through banker's acceptances. Commercial paper is a money-market security, issued by large banks and medium-to-large corporations, that matures in nine months or less. Since these issues have such short durations, and since firms use the proceeds only for current transactions, commercial paper (or simply *paper*) is exempt from registering as a security with the SEC. The corresponding lack of paperwork and regulations to issue short-term debt, along with the fact that commercial paper is usually issued only by firms with very high credit rankings, makes commercial paper cheaper than using a bank line of credit.

A **banker's acceptance** (or **B.A.**) is a short-term promissory note issued by a corporation, bearing the unconditional guarantee (*acceptance*) of a major bank. The bank guarantee makes them very safe, and the rates are usually roughly equivalent to those charged on commercial paper.

[1] If you're sitting there wondering why the bank doesn't just lend only 95 percent or 90 percent of the money, instead of lending it all and then asking for part of it back, the answer has to do with bank regulations. Though it's too complicated to go into great detail, the simple answer is that bank regulators see a difference between a $900,000 loan and a $1,000,000 loan with a 10 percent compensating balance requirement, though they may sound the same to us.

time out!

14-7 If its bank started charging fees to a firm based upon the portion of a line of credit not taken down, how would the firm's financing policy for current assets likely change? Why would a bank take such a stance?

14-8 If a firm starts selling its accounts receivable to a factor, how will the firm's cash cycle change?

---

2. **Compensating balances:** As we previously discussed, firms must often keep a certain percentage of borrowed funds in their checking accounts with their lending institution. Since lenders are exempt from paying interest on corporate checking accounts, compensating balances become a cheap source of funds for the lender and represent opportunity costs for borrowing firms.

3. **Investment opportunities:** In some industries, investment opportunities come and go very quickly. Sometimes, this happens even too quickly for the firm to arrange a loan or seek other financing, so having excess cash on hand may allow the firm to take advantage of investment opportunities that would otherwise be impossible to transact.

banker's acceptance A short-term promissory note issued by a corporation, bearing the unconditional guarantee (*acceptance*) of a major bank.

transaction facilitation The use of cash to pay employee's wages, taxes, suppliers' bills, interest on debts, and dividends on stock.

CASH MANAGEMENT

One confusing distinction in this class is the difference between a *cash flow* and a *cash account*. Cash flows, which we've discussed in a number of contexts within this book, such as estimating cash flows for proposed new projects in Chapter 12, are a good thing. A cash account, on the other hand, is a current asset account just like all the other current asset accounts we've been discussing, and it has exactly the same attributes of high liquidity and low profitability that inventory and accounts receivable accounts have. Sure, cash may be a bit more liquid than inventory or money tied up in accounts receivable, but it's not really any more profitable.[2]

Reasons for Holding Cash

A firm may keep part of its capital tied up in cash for three primary reasons:

1. **Transaction facilitation:** Firms need cash to pay employees' wages, taxes, suppliers' bills, interest on debts, and stock dividends. Though the firm will have cash coming in from day-to-day operations and any financing activities, the inflows and outflows are not usually perfectly synchronized, so the firm will need to keep enough cash on hand to meet reasonable transaction demands.

To determine how much cash to keep on hand, firms must trade off the opportunity costs associated with holding too much cash against the shortage costs of not holding enough. The two standard models for calculating the trade-offs are the Baumol Model and the Miller-Orr Model.

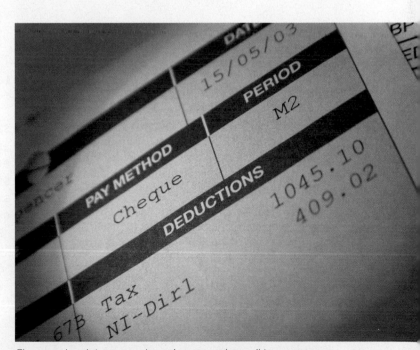

Firms need cash to pay employees' wages and payroll taxes among other things.

[2]Most students realize that cash held in the form of currency doesn't earn any interest, but they're usually surprised to learn that, by law, corporate checking accounts at commercial banks are not allowed to earn interest, either. Though firms find legal ways around that restriction, we'll leave that discussion to a more advanced text on financial institutions.

14-9 In what types of industries would firms need more cash on hand for transaction facilitation? In what industries might firms need less?

14-10 If a firm is going to take a loan with a bank that has a compensating balance requirement, how does that affect the amount of money the firm must borrow?

money than they pay out, and usually have cash inflows at all times, this assumption is obviously at odds with what we usually see.

- The model doesn't allow for any **safety stock** of extra cash to buffer the firm against unexpectedly high demand for cash.

In Baumol's model, cash is assumed to start from a **replenishment level,** C, and then decline smoothly to a value of zero. When cash declines to zero, it can be immediately replenished by selling another C worth of marketable securities, for which the firm has to pay a trading cost of F.

Thus the model implies that cash levels will follow a cyclical pattern throughout the year. For example, if a firm sells $20,000 worth of marketable securities each time it needs to replenish cash and disburses $5,000 in cash each week, then the cash balance would cycle every four weeks, as shown in Figure 14.7.

Notice another implication of the cash being disbursed at a constant rate. The average cash level should equal one-half of the replenishment level, $C/2$. If the firm can earn an interest rate i on marketable securities, then keeping an average cash balance of $C/2$ will impose an opportunity cost on the firm of

$$\text{Opportunity cost} = \frac{C}{2} \times i \qquad (14\text{-}3)$$

If we also assume that a particular firm faces an annual demand for cash of T, then the firm will need to sell marketable securities T/C times during the year, incurring in the process annual trading costs of

$$\text{Trading cost} = \frac{T}{C} \times F \qquad (14\text{-}4)$$

Determining the Target Cash Balance: The Baumol Model

William Baumol developed[3] the first model designed to minimize the sum of the opportunity costs associated with holding cash and the trading costs associated with converting other assets to cash. Baumol's model is intuitively appealing, and analysts still use it in industries for which cash outflows are fairly predictable. For other industries, its use is more problematic due to the model's rather unrealistic assumptions:

- The model assumes that the firm has a constant, perfectly predictable disbursement rate for cash. In reality, disbursement rates are much more variable and unpredictable.

- The model assumes that no cash will come in during the period in question. Since most firms hope to make more

[3]See W. S. Baumol, "The Transactions Demand for Cash: An Inventory Theoretic Approach," *Quarterly Journal of Economics* 66, no. 4 (November 1952), pp. 545–556.

▼**FIGURE 14.7**
Cash Flow Patterns of the Baumol Model

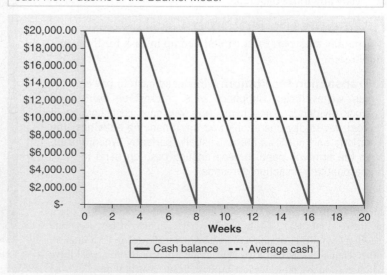

The firm's total annual costs associated with their cash management policy will therefore be:

$$\text{Total cost} = \frac{C}{2} \times i + \frac{T}{C} \times F \qquad (14\text{-}5)$$

Solving this for the value of C that minimizes annual costs, C^*, yields:

$$C^* = \sqrt{2TF/i} \qquad (14\text{-}6)$$

Determining the Target Cash Balance: The Miller-Orr Model

The Miller-Orr Model[4] takes a different approach to calculating the optimal cash management strategy. It assumes that the distribution of daily net cash flows is normally distributed and allows for both cash inflows and outflows. This model bases its computations on information about:

- The lower control limit, L.

- The trading cost for marketable securities per transaction, F.

- The standard deviation in net daily cash flows, σ.

- The daily interest rate on marketable securities, i_{day}.

Using their model, Miller and Orr show that the optimal cash return point, Z^*, and upper limit for cash balances, H^*, are equal to:

[4]See M.H. Miller and D. Orr, "A Model of the Demand for Money by Firms," *Quarterly Journal of Economics* 80, no. 3 (August 1966), pp. 413–435.

$$Z^* = \sqrt[3]{3F\sigma^2/4i_{day}} + L \qquad (14\text{-}7)$$

$$H^* = 3Z^* - 2L \qquad (14\text{-}8)$$

Note that the firm determines L, and that the firm can set it to a nonzero number to recognize the use of safety stock.

The optimal cash return point, Z^*, is analogous to the replenishment level, C^*, in Baumol's model, but with one key difference. Since Baumol's model only allowed for cash disbursements, C^* was always "replenished to" from a level of zero. In the Miller-Orr Model, Z^* will be the replenishment level to which cash is replenished when the cash level hits L, but it will also be the return level that cash is brought back *down* to when cash hits H^*.

As Figure 14.8 on the next page shows, the firm will reduce cash to $126,101.72 by buying marketable securities when the cash balance gets up to $178,305.16, and it will increase cash to $126,101.72 by selling marketable securities when the cash balance gets down to $100,000.

Other Factors Influencing the Target Cash Balance

Even the Miller-Orr Model, the more realistic of the two models because it deals with both cash inflows and outflows, still ignores fundamental factors that influence firms' cash management

---

EXAMPLE 14-3

For interactive versions of this example visit www.mhhe.com/canM

Optimal Cash Replenishment under Baumol Model

Suppose that AFS Industries faces an annual demand for cash of $2 million, incurs transaction costs of $150 every time it sells marketable securities, and can earn 6 percent on its marketable securities. What will be its optimal cash replenishment level?

SOLUTION:

The optimal cash replenishment level will be:

$$C^* = \sqrt{2TF/i}$$

$$= \sqrt{2(\$2,000,000)(\$150)/.06}$$

$$= \$100,000$$

EXAMPLE 14-4

Calculation of Optimal Return Point and Upper Limit for Miller-Orr Model

Suppose that Dandy Candy, Inc., would like to maintain its cash account at a minimum level of $100,000, but expects the standard deviation in net daily cash flows will be $5,000; the effective annual rate on marketable securities will be 8 percent per year, and the trading cost per sale or purchase of marketable securities will be $200 per transaction. What will be Dandy Candy's optimal cash return point and upper limit?

SOLUTION:

The daily interest rate on marketable securities will equal:

$$i_{day} = \sqrt[365]{1.10} - 1 = .000211$$

And the optimal cash return point and upper limit will equal:

$$Z^* = \sqrt[3]{3F\sigma^2/4i_{day}} + L$$

$$= \sqrt[3]{3(\$200)(\$5,000)^2/(4 \times .000211)} + \$100,000$$

$$= \$126,101.72$$

$$H^* = 3Z^* - 2L$$

$$= \$178,305.16$$

---

practices. First, firms also have the option of borrowing short term to meet unexpected demands for cash. Though the short-term borrowing rate faced by the firm is likely to be more expensive than the opportunity cost incurred by selling marketable securities[5], this isn't necessarily the comparison that matters. If the probability of an unexpected demand for cash causing a firm to borrow in the short term is low enough, or if the amount of interest to be earned by investing in longer-term securities is sufficiently higher than that to be earned on marketable securities, then it might be worth it for the firm to risk occasionally paying a relatively high interest rate on short-term borrowing if it can earn a substantially higher return by investing the funds that would have been tied up in marketable securities in something more lucrative.

Second, the authors of both models developed their ideas when buying and selling marketable securities was a relatively expensive and time-consuming proposition. The costs and delays of trading securities have fallen dramatically since the advent of the Internet. The cost has fallen so much that many large firms habitually

▼FIGURE 14.8
Cash Flow Patterns of the Miller-Orr Model

[5]To see why, go down to your local bank or savings and loan and see which is higher: the rate they pay on savings accounts or the rate they charge on short-term borrowing.

use all or the majority of their available cash to purchase overnight securities. If trading costs are low enough that it makes sense for the firm to incur at least two sets of trading costs each day—one for selling enough marketable securities in the morning to make it through the day, and another for purchasing marketable securities at the end of the business day—then it's also probable that any unforeseen demand for cash *during* the day can probably be met fairly cheaply by selling marketable securities as needed. Or, put another way, the transactions costs associated with trading securities have fallen so dramatically relative to the opportunity costs of not having cash invested in marketable securities that keeping any "extra" money idle in cash just doesn't make sense.

Finally, both models ignore the fact that many firms must keep compensating balances in their deposit accounts as part of borrowing agreements with their banks. If the compensating balance requirement was a constant amount or percentage, then we could adjust the Miller-Orr Model so that *L* included the compensating balance, but many firms must only keep a certain minimum compensating balance *on average*. This implies that an unforeseen demand for cash that causes a firm's deposit account to temporarily dip below the minimum compensating balance can be offset by keeping a corresponding amount of excess cash in the account in a later period. Even the more modern Miller-Orr Model doesn't allow for that.

time out!

14-11 What effect does increasing the standard deviation in daily cash flows have on the cash return point in the Miller-Orr Model?

14-12 If you were asked to adjust the Baumol Model to reflect the need to keep a minimum cash balance, how would you go about doing so?

FLOAT CONTROL: MANAGING THE COLLECTION AND DISBURSEMENT OF CASH

The economic definition of cash includes undeposited checks, but as we all know, an undeposited check isn't really as liquid as the same amount of cash sitting inside your checking account. So another component of a good cash management policy involves making sure that checks clear in a timely manner.

Accelerating Collections

The period of time between when a check is written and when it clears and is deposited is referred to as **float.** The checks sent to a firm experience three different types of collection float:

1. Mail float is the length of time that checks are en route to the firm, either through the postal system or through some sort of electronic transfer.

2. In-house processing float is the length of time that it takes the firm to process and deposit check payments from its customers once they've been received.

3. Availability float is the length of time necessary for a check to clear through the banking system once it's been deposited.

Together, these three types of float span the entire length of time between when a customer first sends in a payment and when the firm receives cash into its account.

The time elapsed when a check is written, cleared, and deposited is referred to as float.

zero-balance account A corporate checking account that keeps a zero balance, automatically transferring in just enough funds to cover any checks received on the account from another interest-bearing account.

draft Similar to a check, but payable by the issuing firm rather than by its bank.

Several different techniques can help firms reduce collection float:

- A lockbox system is a collection of geographically dispersed post office boxes, each maintained for the firm by a bank local to the respective box. For firms with hundreds or thousands of customers spread across a large region, the ideal situation is to have enough locations so that no customer is more than a couple of hundred miles from one of the firm's post office boxes. Having customers send their payments to the closest post office box, and then having the local bank pick up and handle the payment processing several times a day, the firm can reduce both mail float and in-house processing float.

- Concentration banking accelerates cash collections from customers by having funds sent to several geographically situated regional banks and then transferred to a main concentration account in another bank. The funds can be transferred through depository transfer checks and electronic transfers.

- Wire transfers are the fastest way of transmitting money from a local bank into the concentration bank. Banks within the United States utilize the Society for Worldwide Interbank Financial Telecommunication (SWIFT) system to make payments to banks in countries outside of the United States. Bank-to-bank transfers conducted within the United States take place over the Fedwire system, which uses the Federal Reserve System and its assignment of bank routing numbers.

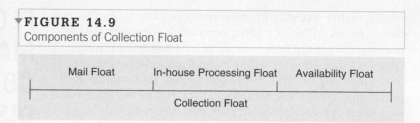

▼**FIGURE 14.9**
Components of Collection Float

Mail Float	In-house Processing Float	Availability Float
	Collection Float	

Delaying Disbursements

Disbursement float is the delay between the firm sending out a payment and the money being taken out of the firm's bank account. Two legal ways to increase disbursement float involve keeping the cash available to the firm until the very last moment:

- A **zero-balance account** is a checking account that the firm sets up so that the bank agrees to automatically transfer funds from an interest-bearing account to pay off any checks presented. Since zero-balance accounts never contain excess cash, they represent one way that firms can get around regulations against corporations having interest-bearing checking accounts.

- **Drafts** resemble checks, but differ in that they are payable by the firm issuing them rather than payable by a bank. When a draft is sent to the firm's bank for payment, the bank must present the draft to the firm *before* disbursing the funds.

finance at work //: global

Cultural Differences in Preferences for Paying Bills

Japan's Postal Savings Bank, the world's largest bank, has long been used as an example of the efficiencies available to both individuals and businesses of electronic transactions. Electronic transactions are instantaneous transactions that use security authentication rather than conventional check-clearing processes to transfer funds from a buyer to the seller.

However, in 2006, one of the Nikkei trade papers summarized the results of a survey among Japanese women regarding payment methods used for Internet shopping. Not surprisingly, the vast majority (56 percent) of respondents purchasing goods over the Internet reported that they used credit cards for their transactions. However, the distribution of the rest of the responses illustrates a vast difference between alternative payment pipelines that American and Japanese consumers use.

For example, 17.6 percent of Japanese respondents ordered online, then paid in cash at their local convenience store; 13.1 percent paid COD when the mailman delivered the goods; and 4.3 percent paid using electronic transfers from their post office savings accounts.

What implications does this have for the money management policies of firms doing business in Japan? Well, given that a far larger percentage of Americans probably pay for their online purchases with credit cards, and that the alternative methods of payment listed above could be expected to have different clearing times than do payments received through a merchant's credit card account, it's something that firms seeking to do business in Japan should consider.

Want to know more?

Key Words to Search for Updates: **See the entry "Marketing Tip: Payment Methods" on the Japan Marketing News blog at www. japanmarketingnews.com/consumer_industry_data/index.html.**

Ethical and Legal Questions

Using collected cash before actually receiving it, or continuing to use disbursed cash after you've sent a check out, can earn your firm higher returns, but this practice is illegal. The most extreme form of taking illegal advantage of disbursement float is a practice called *check kiting*, which, defined, is any sort of fraud that involves drawing out money from a bank account with insufficient funds to cover the check.

The Check Clearing for the 21st Century Act, which allows for transmitting electronic images of checks rather than the physical paper checks themselves, is expected to greatly reduce the incidence of check kiting by substantially shortening the time required for a check to be cleared from one bank to another.

INVESTING IDLE CASH

As both the Baumol and Miller-Orr models imply, firms habitually move cash into and out of marketable securities in order to partially offset the opportunity costs of having capital tied up in current assets. Most large firms will manage their marketable securities investments themselves. Smaller firms will typically invest through an independently managed money-market fund or by letting their bank transfer all available excess funds at the end of each business day into a sweep account, which will then be invested on their behalf.

Why Firms Have Surplus Cash

Firms tend to have surplus cash available either due to seasonal fluctuations in their cash flow patterns or in preparation for

> " Using collected cash before actually receiving it, or continuing to use disbursed cash after you've sent a check out, can earn your firm higher returns, but this practice is illegal. "

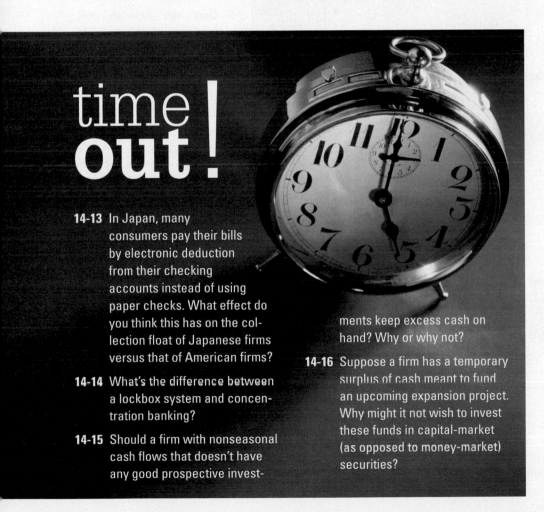

time out!

14-13 In Japan, many consumers pay their bills by electronic deduction from their checking accounts instead of using paper checks. What effect do you think this has on the collection float of Japanese firms versus that of American firms?

14-14 What's the difference between a lockbox system and concentration banking?

14-15 Should a firm with nonseasonal cash flows that doesn't have any good prospective invest-

ments keep excess cash on hand? Why or why not?

14-16 Suppose a firm has a temporary surplus of cash meant to fund an upcoming expansion project. Why might it not wish to invest these funds in capital-market (as opposed to money-market) securities?

planned expenditures. Seasonal fluctuations in the amount of cash on hand can occur as a result of either cyclical sales or cyclical purchases of raw materials. For example, a firm that produces swimming pool accessories will obviously experience higher sales from spring through late fall, and a firm that distributes fresh vegetables purchased on the spot market will have higher cash outflows during the harvest season.

Firm's cash balances may also temporarily increase immediately prior to a planned expenditure, either because the company has been "saving up" for the expenditure, or because they issued stocks or bonds in advance of the expenditure but need someplace to "park" the funds until they're needed.

What to Do with Surplus Cash

As mentioned in this chapter, firms usually put surplus cash into money-market securities. These include Treasury bills, federal funds and repurchase agreements, commercial paper, negotiable certificates of deposit, and banker's acceptances.

CREDIT MANAGEMENT

As is the case with the firm's cash management policy, the firm's optimal credit policy will trade off the opportunity cost of lost sales (if the firm does not grant credit or is too conservative in terms of the credit it does grant) against the carrying costs associated with funding the accounts receivable plus the expected costs of default on the accounts receivable.

Credit Policy: Terms of the Sale

As a minimum, the **credit terms** of sales usually contain at least the credit period, the cash discount, and a description of the type of credit instrument. The credit period is the maturity of the credit that the firm is willing to extend, which varies based on attributes of the goods being sold and the customer purchasing the goods. For example, perishable goods will usually carry a lower credit period, regardless of who is purchasing them. Creditworthy, established customers will probably be given better credit terms than customers the firm hasn't dealt with before.

To encourage early repayment, firms will often offer a percentage discount if the bill is paid within a certain time period. For example, a firm that quotes a customer terms of "2/10, net 30" is offering them the choice between paying the entire bill within 30 days or taking a 2 percent discount off the invoiced price if they pay within 10 days.

For most trade credit, the invoice is the only type of credit instrument involved. When the customer signs a copy upon receipt of the goods, the customer makes an implicit promise to pay under the terms listed on the invoice. If a firm wishes a customer to make a more explicit acknowledgement of its ability and obligation to pay, a firm can ask the customer to sign a promissory note upon delivery of the goods or to furnish a commercial draft or banker's acceptance in advance of the delivery of the goods.

Credit Analysis

Before granting a customer credit, the firm may wish to engage in **credit analysis.** Such analysis involves a systematic determination of the potential borrower's ability and willingness to pay for the goods being provided on credit. A thorough credit analysis will look at the potential borrower's past record and its present and forecasted future financial condition, which generally involves examining the "five Cs":

1. **Capacity:** Ensure that the borrower has the legal and economic capacity to borrow.

2. **Character:** Refers to the borrower's reputation and hence desire to settle debt obligations.

3. **Capital:** Having its own capital at risk makes it more likely that the borrower will repay as promised.

4. **Collateral:** Collateral that can be seized and sold, with the proceeds being used to pay the firm in the event of bankruptcy by the borrower, also makes it more likely that the customer will repay as promised.

5. **Conditions:** Any economic conditions that may affect the borrower's ability to repay the loan should also be taken into account.

Collection Policy

The firm's collection policy is aimed at collecting past-due debts from customers. The usual procedure for collecting follows a typical path of:

1. Send one or more delinquency letters informing the customer of the past-due status of the account, asking the customer to contact the firm to discuss alternative means of repayment and pointing out what legal recourse the firm has.

2. Initiate telephone calls conveying the same information as above.

3. Employ a collection agency.

4. Take legal action against the customer if all else fails.

To monitor and control this process, firms use a tool called an *aging schedule,* which stratifies a firm's accounts

▼ TABLE 14.2 Sample Aging Schedule

Age Bracket	Percentage of Ar in Bracket
0–10 days	10%
11–30 days	35
31–60 days	45
61–90 days	7
Over 90 days	3
	100%

receivable by the age of each account. For example, a firm that offers terms of 2/10, net 60 to its customers might want to measure the age of A/R using the categories shown in Table 14.2.

Such an aging schedule would allow the firm to see what percentage of its customers are still eligible to take the discount (i.e., those in the "0–10 days" category), how many are past due by less than 30 days (i.e., those in the "61–90 days" category), and how many are over 30 days past due (i.e., those in the "Over 90 days" category).

Firms often link their collection policies to their aging schedules. For example, the customers in Table 14.2 that fall into the

time out!

14-17 Why do firms offer customers discounts for paying early?

14-18 Should a firm always turn far-overdue bills from customers over to a collection agency or sue the customers? Why or why not?

"61–90 days" category might be sent a delinquency letter, while those in the "Over 90 days" category might be phoned. ■

Your Turn...

Questions

1. Is it possible for a firm to have negative net working capital? How? (LG1)

2. Would it be possible for a decision to deny credit to your customers to be value maximizing? How? (LG1)

3. Which of the following will result in an increase in net working capital? (LG2)

   a. An increase in cash.

   b. A decrease in accounts payable.

   c. An increase in notes payable.

   d. A decrease in accounts receivable.

   e. An increase in inventory.

4. Would it be possible for a firm to have a negative cash cycle? How? (LG3)

5. If a firm's inventory turnover ratio increases, what will happen to the firm's operating cycle? (LG3)

6. If a firm's inventory turnover ratio increases, what will happen to the firm's cash cycle? (LG3)

7. Everything else held constant, will an increase in the amount of inventory on hand increase or decrease the firm's profitability? (LG4)

8. Would a firm ever use short-term debt to finance permanent current assets? Why or why not? (LG5)

9. Suppose that short-term borrowing actually becomes more expensive than long-term borrowing: How would this affect the firm's choice between a flexible financing policy and a restrictive policy? (LG5)

10. If asset-backed loans are cheaper than unsecured loans, what is the disadvantage to the firm in using an asset-backed loan? (LG6)

11. Is an increase in the cash account a source of funds or a use of funds? (LG7)

12. What will be the carrying cost associated with a compensating balance requirement? (LG7)

13. What will be the shortage cost associated with a compensating balance requirement? (LG7)

14. What would be the shortage costs associated with a restaurant not having enough cash on hand to make change? (LG7)

15. If a firm needs to keep a minimum cash balance on hand and faces both cash inflows and outflows, which of the cash management models discussed in this chapter would be more appropriate for them to use? (LG8)

16. What effect will increase the trading costs associated with selling marketable securities have on the optimal replenishment level in the Baumol Model? Why? (LG8)

17. What effect will an increase in the standard deviation of daily cash flows have on the return point in the Miller-Orr Model? Why? (LG8)

18. Could a firm ever have negative collection float? Why or why not? (LG9)

19. Could a firm ever have negative disbursement float? Why or why not? (LG9)

20. Would a draft have availability float? Why or why not? (LG9)

21. From our discussion of capital markets elsewhere in this book, why would you expect a firm to have a time delay between raising funds to finance a project and the expenditure of those funds on that project? (LG9)

22. What purpose does a discount on credit terms serve? What is the cost of such a discount to the offering firm? (LG9)

Problems

BASIC PROBLEMS

14-1 **Net Working Capital Requirements** JohnBoy Industries has a cash balance of $45,000; accounts payable of $125,000; inventory of $175,000; accounts receivable of $210,000; notes payable of $120,000; and accrued wages and taxes of $37,000. How much net working capital does the firm need to fund? (LG2)

14-2 **Net Working Capital Requirements** Dandee Lions, Inc. has a cash balance of $105,000; accounts payable of $220,000; inventory of $203,000; accounts receivable of $319,000; notes payable of $65,000, and accrued wages and taxes of $75,000. How much net working capital does the firm need to fund? (LG2)

14-3 **Days' Sales in Inventory** Dabble, Inc. has sales of $980,000 and cost of goods sold of $640,000. The firm had a beginning inventory of $36,000 and an ending inventory of $46,000. What is the length of the days' sales in inventory? *(LG3)*

14-4 **Average Payment Period** If a firm has a cash cycle of 73 days and an operating cycle of 127 days, what is its average payment period? *(LG3)*

14-5 **Payables Turnover** If a firm has a cash cycle of 73 days and an operating cycle of 127 days, what is its payables turnover? *(LG3)*

14-6 **Average Payment Period** If a firm has a cash cycle of 45 days and an operating cycle of 77 days, what is its average payment period? *(LG3)*

14-7 **Payables Turnover** If a firm has a cash cycle of 45 days and an operating cycle of 77 days, what is its payables turnover? *(LG3)*

14-8 **Compensating Balance** Would it be worth it to incur a compensating balance of $10,000 in order to get a 1 percent lower interest rate on a one-year, pure discount loan of $225,000? *(LG7)*

14-9 **Compensating Balance** Would it be worth it to incur a compensating balance of $5,000 in order to get a .65 percent lower interest rate on a two-year, pure discount loan of $150,000? *(LG7)*

14-10 **Collection Float** CM Enterprises estimates that it takes, on average, five days for its customers' payments to reach the firm, one day for the payments to be processed and deposited by its bookkeeping department, and two more days for a check to clear once it's deposited. What is its collection float? *(LG9)*

14-11 **Collection Float** Smelpank, Inc., estimates that it takes, on average, four days for its customers' payments to reach the firm, three days for the payments to be processed and deposited by its bookkeeping department, and three more days for a check to clear once it's deposited. What is its collection float? *(LG9)*

INTERMEDIATE PROBLEMS

14-12 **Days' Sales in Inventory** B&B Cos. has sales of $732,000 and cost of goods sold of $347,000. The firm had a beginning inventory of $48,000 and an ending inventory of $34,000. What is the length of the days' sales in inventory? *(LG3)*

14-13 **Operating Cycle** Suppose that Dunn Industries has annual sales of $2.3 million, cost of goods sold of $1,650,000, average inventories of $1,116,000, and average accounts receivable of $750,000. Assuming that all of Dunn's sales are on credit, what will be the firm's operating cycle? *(LG3)*

14-14 **Operating Cycle** Suppose that LilyMac Photography has annual sales of $230,000, cost of goods sold of $165,000, average inventories of $4,500, and average accounts receivable of $25,000. Assuming that all of LilyMac's sales are on credit, what will be the firm's operating cycle? *(LG3)*

14-15 **Cash Cycle** Suppose that LilyMac Photography has annual sales of $230,000; cost of goods sold of $165,000; average inventories of $4,500; average accounts receivable of $25,000, and an average accounts payable balance of $7,000. Assuming that all of LilyMac's sales are on credit, what will be the firm's cash cycle? *(LG3)*

14-16 **Compensating Balance Interest Rate** Suppose your firm is seeking a seven-year, amortizing $800,000 loan with annual payments, and your bank is offering you the choice between an $850,000 loan with a $50,000 compensating balance and an $800,000 loan without a compensating balance. If the interest rate on the $800,000 loan is 8.5 percent, how low would the interest rate on the loan with the compensating balance have to be in order for you to choose it? *(LG4)*

14-17 **Compensating Balance Interest Rate** Suppose your firm is seeking a three-year, amortizing $200,000 loan with annual payments and your bank is offering you the choice between a $205,000 loan with a $5,000 compensating balance and a $200,000 loan without a compensating balance. If the interest rate on the $200,000 loan is 9.8 percent, how low would the interest rate on the loan with the compensating balance have to be in order for you to choose it? *(LG4)*

14-18 Optimal Cash Replenishment Level Rose Axels faces a smooth annual demand for cash of $5 million; incurs transaction costs of $225 every time it sells marketable securities, and can earn 4.3 percent on its marketable securities. What will be its optimal cash replenishment level? *(LG8)*

14-19 Optimal Cash Replenishment Level Watkins Resources faces a smooth annual demand for cash of $1.5 million; incurs transaction costs of $75 every time it sells marketable securities, and can earn 3.7 percent on its marketable securities. What will be its optimal cash replenishment level? *(LG8)*

ADVANCED PROBLEMS

14-20 Optimal Cash Return Point HotFoot Shoes would like to maintain its cash account at a minimum level of $25,000, but expects the standard deviation in net daily cash flows to be $2,000; the effective annual rate on marketable securities to be 6.5 percent per year; and the trading cost per sale or purchase of marketable securities to be $200 per transaction. What will be its optimal cash return point? *(LG8)*

14-21 Optimal Upper Cash Limit HotFoot Shoes would like to maintain its cash account at a minimum level of $25,000 but expects the standard deviation in net daily cash flows to be $2,000; the effective annual rate on marketable securities to be 6.5 percent per year, and the trading cost per sale or purchase of marketable securities to be $200 per transaction. What will be its optimal upper cash limit? *(LG8)*

14-22 Optimal Cash Return Point Veggie Burgers, Inc., would like to maintain its cash account at a minimum level of $245,000 but expects the standard deviation in net daily cash flows to be $12,000; the effective annual rate on marketable securities to be 4.7 percent per year; and the trading cost per sale or purchase of marketable securities to be $27.50 per transaction. What will be its optimal cash return point? *(LG8)*

14-23 Optimal Upper Cash Limit Veggie Burgers, Inc., would like to maintain its cash account at a minimum level of $245,000 but expects the standard deviation in net daily cash flows to be $12,000; the effective annual rate on marketable securities to be 4.7 percent per year; and the trading cost per sale or purchase of marketable securities to be $27.50 per transaction. What will be its optimal upper cash limit? *(LG8)*

chapter one

BUSINESS APPLICATION SOLUTION

Because Caleb is a sole proprietor of a small business, he will have trouble getting loans for large amounts of money if he wants to expand. Caleb should consider the following options.

First, Caleb can expand slowly. He can get a small loan or self-fund an expansion into one other mall. Once the new juice stand is making a profit, he can expand again. The advantage of this slow expansion is that he retains full ownership and control of his business. One significant risk is that others may copy his idea and open their own stands, thus taking the prime spots in malls before he gets there.

In order to obtain the capital to expand more quickly, Caleb may have to take on a partner. Forming a partnership with an angel investor or a venture capitalist who can provide business expertise and substantial amounts of capital would allow for much faster expansion. The disadvantage of this option is that Caleb will have to give up some ownership of his business.

PERSONAL APPLICATION SOLUTION

Dagmar should know that the market gives no guarantees against losing money investing in company stocks. These companies failed for different reasons. Enron and WorldCom went bankrupt because their managers acted unethically to falsely make their company look good. When the truth came out, the firms became so financially troubled that they had to file for bankruptcy. Delta Airlines, however, went bankrupt along with other airline companies because they had trouble competing in their business. They could not profitably deliver their product at market prices. These firms emerged out of bankruptcy court with new stockholders.

Dagmar should also know that the collapse of these firms, and others, has led to a strengthened corporate governance system monitoring managerial actions. We all hope that this new governance system will reduce the number of company failures due to managerial malfeasance. Nevertheless, she can minimize her loss from a corporate bankruptcy by not putting all her "eggs in one basket." Diversification is a finance principle discussed in detail later in this book.

chapter two

BUSINESS APPLICATION SOLUTION

If the managers of DPH Tree Farm increase the firm's fixed assets by $27 million and net working capital by $8 million in 2009, the balance sheet would look like the one below (Table 2.6). That is, fixed assets increase by $27 million, to $387 million; cash, accounts receivable, and inventory would increase by $1 million, $5 million, and $6 million, respectively. DPH Tree Farm's total assets will thus grow by $39 million to $609 million by year-end 2009. This growth in assets would be financed with $4 million in accounts payable, and the remaining $35 million will be financed with 40 percent long-term debt (.4 × $35m. = $14m.) and 60 percent with common stock (.6 × $35m. = $21m.).

PERSONAL APPLICATION SOLUTION

As Chris Ryan examines the 2008 financial statements for DPH Tree Farm, Inc. she needs to remember that the balance sheet reports a firm's assets, liabilities, and equity at a particular point in time, the income statement reports the total revenues and expenses over a specific period of time, the statement of cash flows shows the firm's cash flows over a period of time,

▼ **TABLE 2.6**

DPH TREE FARM INC. Balance Sheet as of December 31, 2009 (in millions of dollars)					
Assets	2009		**Liabilities and Equity**	2009	
Current assets:			Current liabilities:		
Cash	$ 25	($24 + $1)	Accrued wages and taxes	$ 20	
Accounts receivable	75	($70 + $5)	Accounts payable	59	($55 + $4)
Inventory	117	($111 + $6)	Notes payable	45	
Total	217		Total	124	
Fixed assets:					
Gross plant and equipment	395	($368 + $27)	Long-term debt:	209	($195 + .4($39 − $4))
Less: Depreciation	53		Stockholders' equity:		
Net plant and equipment	342		Preferred stock (5 million shares)	5	
Other long-term			Common stock and paid-in surplus (20 million shares)	61	($40 + .6($39 − $4))
assets	50		Retained earnings	210	
Total	392		Total	276	
Total assets	$609	($570 + $39)	Total liabilities and equity	$609	($570 + $39)

and the statement of retained earnings reconciles net income earned during a given period and any cash dividends paid with the change in retained earnings over the period.

GAAP procedures dictate how each financial statement is prepared. GAAP requires that the firm recognizes revenue when the firm sells the product, which is not necessarily when the firm receives the cash. Likewise, under GAAP, expenses appear on the income statement as they match sales. That is, the income statement recognizes production and other expenses associated with sales when the firm sells the product. Again, the actual cash outflow associated with producing the goods may actually occur at a very different time than that reported. In addition, the income statement contains several noncash items, the largest of which is depreciation. As a result, figures shown on an income statement may not be representative of the actual cash inflows and outflows for a firm during any particular period.

For investors like Chris Ryan, the actual cash flows are often more important than the accounting profit listed on the income statement. Cash, not accounting profit, is needed to pay the firm's obligations as they come due: to fund the firm's operations and growth and to compensate the firm's owners. So Chris is more likely to find the answers she seeks in the statement of cash flows, which shows the firm's cash flows over a given period of time. The statement of cash flows reports the amounts of cash generated and cash distributed by a firm during the time period analyzed.

Finally, Chris must remember that firms are required to prepare their financial statements according to GAAP. GAAP allows managers to have significant discretion over their reported earnings, in other words, to *manage earnings*. Indeed, managers can report their results in such a way that indicates to investors that the firm's assets are growing more steadily than may really be the case. Similarly, the choice of depreciation method—straight line or MACRS—for fixed assets may make two firms with identical fixed assets appear to have very different results. Thus, Chris may need to delve more deeply into research about this firm's—or any firm's—financial condition before she makes any final investment decision.

chapter three

BUSINESS APPLICATION SOLUTION

The managers of DPH Tree Farm, Inc. have stated that its performance surpasses that of other firms in the industry. Particularly strong are the firm's liquidity and asset management positions. The superior performance in these areas has resulted in superior overall returns for the stockholders of DPH Tree Farm, Inc., according to DPH management. Having analyzed the financial statements using ratio analysis, we could conclude that these statements are partially true. All three liquidity ratios show that DPH Tree Farm, Inc. holds more liquidity on its balance sheet than the industry average. Thus, DPH Tree Farm has more cash and other liquid assets (or current assets) available to pay its bills (or current liabilities) as they come due than the average firm in the tree farm industry. In all cases, the asset management ratios show that DPH Tree Farm, Inc. is outperforming the industry average in its asset management. The firm is turning over its inventory faster than the average

firm in the tree farm industry, thus producing more dollars of sales per dollar of inventory. It is also collecting its accounts receivable faster and paying its accounts payable slower than the average firm. Further, DPH Tree Farm is producing more sales per dollar of fixed assets, working capital, and total assets than the average firm in the industry. The profitability ratios show that DPH Tree Farm, Inc. is more profitable than the average firm in the tree farm industry. The profit margin, BEP, and ROA are all higher than the industry. Despite this, the ROE for DPH Tree Farm is much lower than the average for the industry.

What the managers do not state is that the debt management ratios show that DPH Tree Farm, Inc. holds less debt on its balance sheet than the average firm in the tree farm industry. This is a good sign in that this lack of financial leverage decreases the firm's potential for financial distress and even failure. If the firm has a bad year, it has promised relatively few payments to debt holders. Thus, the risk of bankruptcy is small. Further, the firm has more dollars of operating earnings and cash available to meet each dollar of interest obligations on the firm's debt. However, when DPH Tree Farm, Inc. does well, the low level of financial leverage dilutes the return to the stockholders of the firm. This profit dilution will likely upset the firm's common stockholders. Indeed, the market value ratios show that DPH Tree Farm's investors will not pay as much for a share of the firm's stock per dollar of book value and earnings as the average for the industry. The low debt level and high equity level used by DPH Tree Farm relative to the industry is likely a main reason for this unenthusiastic response by DPH investors.

PERSONAL APPLICATION SOLUTION

To evaluate DPH Tree Farm, Inc.'s financial statements, Chris Ryan would want to perform ratio analysis in which she uses the financial statements to calculate the most commonly used ratios. These include liquidity ratios, asset management ratios, debt management ratios, profitability ratios, and market value ratios. The values of these ratios for DPH Tree Farms and the tree farming industry are presented in Table 3.1. Chris might also want to spread the financial statements. These calculations yield common-size, easily compared financial statements that can be used to identify changes in corporate performance as well as how DPH Tree Farm compares to other firms in the industry. Having calculated these ratios, Chris can identify any interrelationships in the ratios by performing a detailed analysis of ROA and ROE using the DuPont system of analysis. A critical part of performance analysis lies in the interpretation of these numbers against some benchmark. To interpret the financial ratios, Chris will also want to evaluate the performance of the firm over time (time series analysis) and the performance of the firm against one or more companies in the same industry (cross-sectional analysis). Finally, Chris needs to exercise some cautions when reviewing data from financial statements. For example, the financial statement data are historical and may not be representative of future performance. Further, she needs to know what accounting rules DPH Tree Farm uses before making any comparisons or conclusions about its performance from ratios analysis. Finally, DPH Tree Farm's managers may have window dressed their financial statements to make them look better.

chapter four

BUSINESS APPLICATION SOLUTION

You must compare the cash flows of buying the wire now at a discount, or waiting one year. The cost of the wire should include both the supplier's bill and the storage cost, for a total of $452,000. What interest rate is implied by a $452,000 cash flow today versus $500,000 in one year? Using equation 4-2:

$$FV_N = PV \times (1 + i)^N$$

$$500,000 = 452,000 \times (1 + i)^1$$

$$i = 500,000/452,000 - 1 = 0.1062 \text{ or } 10.62\%$$

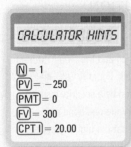

Whether your company should purchase the wire today depends on the cost of the firm's capital (discussed in Chapter 11). If it costs the firm less than 10.6 percent to obtain cash, then you should purchase the wire today. Otherwise, you should not.

PERSONAL APPLICATION SOLUTION

Since Anthony's loan of $300 requires an immediate $50 payment, the actual cash flow is $250 (= $300 − $50). He then must repay the full $300. Use equation 4-2 to compute the interest rate you pay for the period:

$$FV_N = PV \times (1 + i)^N$$

$$300 = 250 \times (1 + i)^1$$

$$i = 300/250 - 1 = 0.20 \text{ or } 20\%$$

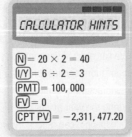

Anthony is paying 20 percent for a loan of only two weeks! This is equivalent to paying 11,348 percent per year (this is shown in Chapter 5). He will never be able to build wealth if he continues to pay interest rates like this. Indeed, many people get trapped in a continuing cycle, obtaining one payday loan after another.

chapter five

BUSINESS APPLICATION SOLUTION

Walkabout Music, Inc. pays $700,000 (= $20 million × 0.07 ÷ 2) in interest every six months on its existing debt. The new debt would require payments of $600,000 (= $20 million × 0.06 ÷ 2) every six months, which represents a $100,000 savings semiannually.

The present value of these savings over the next 20 years is computed using 40 semiannual periods and a 3 percent interest rate per period:

$$PVA_N = \$100,000 \times \left[\frac{1 - \frac{1}{(1 + 0.03)^{40}}}{0.03} \right]$$

$$= \$2,311,477.20$$

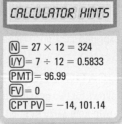

Since this savings is less than the $2.6 million cost of refinancing, the CFO should not refinance the old debt at this time. The company should wait until it can find more favorable terms.

PERSONAL APPLICATION SOLUTION

Should you switch to a new home mortgage with a lower interest rate? To answer this question, first find the monthly savings with the new mortgage. Then compare the present value of the savings to the cost of getting the new mortgage.

The current monthly mortgage payments are

$$PMT_N = \$150,000 \times \left[\frac{0.00667}{1 - \frac{1}{(1 + 0.00667)^{360}}} \right]$$

$$= \$1,100.65$$

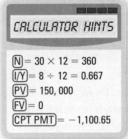 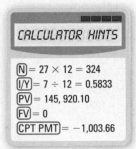

The new mortgage would payments would be

$$PMT_N = \$145,920.10 \times \left[\frac{0.00583}{1 - \frac{1}{(1 + 0.00583)^{324}}} \right]$$

$$= \$1,003.66$$

The new mortgage would save you $96.99 per month for the next 27 years. The present value of these savings at the current 7 percent interest rate is

$$PVA_N = \$96.99 \times \left[\frac{1 - \frac{1}{(1 + 0.00583)^{324}}}{0.00583} \right]$$

$$= \$14,101.14$$

Since the present value of the monthly savings is greater than the $1,000 broker fee, you should refinance the mortgage.

chapter six

BUSINESS APPLICATION SOLUTION

To raise $150 million, Beach Sand Resorts would need to issue 150,000 bonds at the customary $1,000 par value (= $150 million ÷ $1,000). The bonds will have to offer a 7 percent coupon. This means that Beach Sand Resorts will pay $35 in interest every six months for each bond issued (= 7.0% × $1,000 ÷ 2). So for all 150,000 bonds, they will pay $5.25 million semiannually (= $35 × 150,000).

PERSONAL APPLICATION SOLUTION

You can calculate that buying 10 of the Liberty Media bonds at the quoted price of 96.21 will cost $9,621 (= 96.21% × $1,000 × 10) and would generate $285 (= 5.7% × $1,000 × 10 ÷ 2) in interest payments every six months. Buying the bond in 2007, it is priced to offer a 6.48 percent yield to maturity. Ten of the Alcoa bonds would cost $10,194 (= 101.94% × $1,000 × 10) and pay $268.75 (= 5.375% × $1,000 × 10 ÷ 2) in interest payments every six months. This bond is priced to offer a 5.0 percent yield to maturity. The Liberty bonds cost less to purchase, pay more in interest, and offer a higher return than the Alcoa bonds. This is because the Liberty bonds have higher credit risk. You must decide if the higher return of the Liberty bonds is worth taking the extra risk.

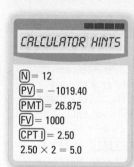

CALCULATOR HINTS

N = 12
PV = −1019.40
PMT = 26.875
FV = 1000
$CPT\ I$ = 2.50
2.50 × 2 = 5.0

chapter seven

BUSINESS APPLICATION SOLUTION

You can compute the expected return using equation 7-7 as,

$$i = \frac{\$2 \times (1 + 0.08)}{\$65} + 0.08 = 0.033 + 0.08 = 0.113$$

Investors expect an 11.3 percent return.

The P/E ratio of 16.25 and the stock price of $65 indicate that earnings were $4.00 per share (= $65 ÷ 16.25). If the P/E ratio of 16.25 continues, then the price of the stock in three years may be $81.88 [= 16.25 × $4 × (1.08)³]. However, a P/E ratio of 16.25 may seem a little high for a firm with an 8 percent growth rate. So the P/E ratio might decline a bit to 15. If so, the stock price in three years would be $75.60. On the other hand, P/E ratios in the stock market may increase in general, thereby inflating this firm's ratio to 17. In this case, the price would be $85.68.

You should report an expected stock price range of $75.60 to $85.68 with a target of $81.88.

PERSONAL APPLICATION SOLUTION

The information provided allows for two growth rate estimates for stock valuation. The dividend growth from $1.25 to $1.68 in three years implies a 10.36 percent historical growth rate (N = 3, PV = −1.25, PMT = 0, FV = 1.68, CPT I = 10.36). Since analysts' mean growth estimate is 10.1 percent, you can use either, or both, rates in the constant-growth-rate model using a 13.5 percent discount rate:

$$P_0 = \frac{\$1.68 \times (1 + 0.1036)}{0.135 - 0.1036} = \$59.05$$

$$P_0 = \frac{\$1.68 \times (1 + 0.101)}{0.135 - 0.101} = \$54.40$$

Both valuation estimates exceed the current price of $54. The current stock price does not appear overvalued, so you can consider the purchase.

chapter eight

BUSINESS APPLICATION SOLUTION

In deciding when to issue new debt, DPH Corporation needs to consider two main factors. First, what might happen to specific factors that affect interest rates on any debt the firm may issue? Such specific factors include changes in the firm's default risk, liquidity risk, any special provisions regarding the use of funds raised by the firm's security issuance, and the debt's term to maturity. An increase (decrease) in any of these risks over the next two years would increase (decrease) the rate of interest DPH Corp. would be required to pay to holders of the new debt and make the debt issue in two years less (more) attractive. Second, what might happen to the general level of interest rates in the U.S. economy over the next two years? This involves an analysis of any changes in inflation or the "real" interest rate. DPH can estimate how interest rates may change by examining the term structure of interest rates or the current yield curve. In addition to any internal analysis of these factors, DPH Corp. can get expert advice about the timing of its debt issue and get the new debt to the capital market with help from an investment bank. These financial institutions underwrite securities and engage in related activities, such as making a market in which securities can trade.

PERSONAL APPLICATION SOLUTION

In deciding which corporate bond to buy, John Adams needs to consider specific factors that affect differences in interest rates on debt. These specific factors include the general level of inflation and the "real" interest rate in the U.S. economy, as well as the default risk, liquidity risk, any special provisions regarding the use of funds raised by a security issuance, and the term to maturity of the two debt issues. While one bond earns more (10.00%) than the other (8.00%), it may be that the higher yielding bond has more default, liquidity, or other risk than the lower-yielding bond. Thus, the higher yield brings with it more risk. John Adams must consider whether he is willing to incur higher risk to get higher returns. In addition to his own analysis of these factors, John Adams can get expert advice about which bond to buy and then buy the bond with a securities firm's help. These financial institutions engage in activities such as securities brokerage, securities trading, and making markets in which securities can trade.

chapter nine

BUSINESS APPLICATION SOLUTION

We can apply diversification concepts and modern portfolio theory to many more applications than just investment portfolios. For example, a manufacturing facility can be more efficient by producing different products during the year as demand dictates the need for one product over another. Salespeople can reduce the volatility of their commission incomes by having many different products to sell.

Although new project ideas have more risk, they could actually reduce the firm's overall risk if the projects diversify the firm's current business operations. You could evaluate this possibility by determining the correlation between the expected cash flows from each project idea with the expected cash flows of the firm's current business operations. A low or negative correlation would mean that the new projects could actually reduce risk for the firm. Note that some firms may find that their position is too conservative and that they wish to increase their risk to increase the possibility of earning a higher return.

PERSONAL APPLICATION SOLUTION

Since 1950, Tables 9.2 and 9.4 show that the bond market experienced an average return and standard deviation of 6.4 percent and 10.3 percent, respectively. Stocks earned a 13.2 percent return with a 17.0 percent standard deviation. The investor is correct in the belief that the stock market is riskier than the bond market.

However, Table 9.6 shows that the correlation between the stock and bond markets is very low, at 0.11. This result allows some diversification opportunity. Indeed, a portfolio of 10 percent stocks and 90 percent bonds would have experienced an average annual return of 7.1 percent with a standard deviation of 9.7 percent since 19=0. The broker is correct; adding a small portion of stocks to a bond portfolio actually reduces total risk!

chapter ten

BUSINESS APPLICATION SOLUTION

You need to determine the firm's level of market risk. If you can obtain a beta, then you can make a required return estimate using CAPM. To assess the result, you can use the constant-growth-rate model to check the CAPM estimated required return for comparison's sake.

If you find the beta of the firm to be 1.8, assume a market return of 11 percent, and note a 5 percent T-bill rate, the CAPM computations would be:

$$5\% + 1.8 \times (11\% - 5\%) = 15.8 \text{ percent}$$

The firm will pay a $0.50 dividend next year and the current stock price is $32. Managers believe the company will grow at 13 percent per year for the foreseeable future. The constant growth rate model computation gives:

$$\$0.50 \div \$32 + 0.13 = 0.146, \text{ or } 14.6 \text{ percent}$$

You can now take these estimates to the team.

PERSONAL APPLICATION SOLUTION

You are investing 57.1 percent (= $200 ÷ $350) of your monthly contribution in stocks. You are also contributing 28.6 percent in bonds and 14.3 percent into a money market deposit. The diversified stock portfolio has a beta of 1. The long-term bond portfolio has a beta of 0.18. By definition, the money market deposit is risk-free and thus has a beta of zero.

The beta of this portfolio is therefore:

$$0.571 \times (1) + 0.286 \times (0.18) + 0.143 \times (0) = 0.62$$

With a portfolio beta of 0.62, a market return of 11 percent, and a risk-free rate of 5 percent, you can expect a return of:

$$5\% + 0.62 \times (11\% - 5\%) = 8.7 \text{ percent}$$

If you want a higher expected return, you will have to take more risk. You can do that by contributing a higher proportion of your funds to the stock portfolio.

chapter eleven

BUSINESS APPLICATION SOLUTION

MP3 Devices, Inc. faces current component costs of capital equal to:

$$i_E = \frac{D_1}{P_0} + g \qquad i_P = \frac{D_1}{P_0}$$

$$= \frac{\$1.35}{\$18.75} + .06 \qquad = \frac{\$10}{\$100}$$

$$= .1320, \text{ or } 13.20\% \qquad = .1000, \text{ or } 10.00\%$$

$$\text{Solve} \left\{ \$1,100 = \$100 \times \left[\frac{1 - \frac{1}{(1 + i_D)^{20}}}{i_D} \right] + \frac{\$1,000}{(1 + i_D)^{20}} \right\} \text{ for } i_D$$

gives $i_D = .0891$, or 8.91%

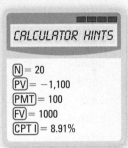

CALCULATOR HINTS

N = 20
PV = −1,100
PMT = 100
FV = 1000
CPT I = 8.91%

Using the target capital structure weights, MP3's WACC equals:

$$\text{WACC} = .5 \times 13.20\% + .1 \times 10\% + .4 \times 8.91\% \times (1 - .34)$$

$$= .0995, \text{ or } 9.95\%$$

PERSONAL APPLICATION SOLUTION

Mackenzie can expect a total of $17,125 + $29,000 = $46,125 in student loans when she graduates from her master's program. At an 8 percent rate of interest, the yearly interest charges will be $3,690 immediately after she graduates (though they will go down once she starts paying off some of the principal). Since the yearly interest will be more than the allowable $2,500 deduction, we can express her after-tax interest rate as the following weighted average:

$$\text{WACC} = \frac{D_{Nondeductible}}{D_{Nondeductible} + D_{Deductible}} i_D$$

$$+ \frac{D_{Deductible}}{D_{Nondeductible} + D_{Deductible}} i_D \times (1 - T_P)$$

$$= \frac{\$3,690 - \$2,500}{\$3,690} \times 8\% + \frac{\$2,500}{\$3,690} \times 8\% \times (1 - .25)$$

$$= .3225 \times 8\% + .6775 \times 8\% \times .75$$

$$= 6.645\%$$

chapter twelve

BUSINESS APPLICATION SOLUTION

Based on the yearly sales, levels of NWC and resulting changes in NWC for McDonald's will be:

Year	Yearly Sales	Yearly Levels of NWC	Changes in NWC
0	$ 0	$364,000	$364,000
1	2,800,000	937,300	573,300
2	7,210,000	965,900	28,600
3	7,430,000	994,500	28,600
4	7,650,000	512,200	−482,300
5	3,940,000	0	−512,200

OCF calculations, ΔNWC, and ΔFA for each year are shown below:

Year	0	1	2	3	4	5
S	0.0000	2.8000	7.2100	7.4300	7.6500	3.9400
−VC	0.0000	−1.3400	−3.5200	−3.7000	−3.8900	−2.0400
−FC	0.0000	−2.0000	−2.0000	−2.0000	−2.0000	−2.0000
−Dep	0.0000	−1.4000	−2.2400	−1.3440	−0.8064	−0.8064
EBIT	0.0000	−1.9400	−0.5500	0.3860	0.9536	−0.9064
−Tax	0.0000	0.6790	0.1925	−0.1351	−0.3338	0.3172
"NI"	0.0000	−1.2610	−0.3575	0.2509	0.6198	−0.5892
+Dep	0.0000	1.4000	2.2400	1.3440	0.8064	0.8064
OCF	0.0000	0.1390	1.8825	1.5949	1.4262	0.2172
− ΔNWC	−0.3640	−0.5733	−0.0286	−0.0286	0.4823	0.5122
− ΔFA	−7.0000	0.0000	0.0000	0.0000	0.0000	0.0000
FCF	−7.3640	−0.4343	1.8539	1.5663	1.9085	0.7294

PERSONAL APPLICATION SOLUTION

Achmed's purchase of a new computer should not be counted as an incremental cash flow to getting an MBA, as he has indicated that he would be getting one anyway. Likewise, the $250 that he paid to take the GMAT is a sunk cost, and should not be counted, either. His tuition payments constitute an annuity due, so his incremental cash flows will equal:

Years	0–3	4–23
FCF	−$15,000	$10,000

chapter thirteen

BUSINESS APPLICATION SOLUTION

ADK's project will have an NPV of:

$$NPV = \frac{-\$5m}{(1.14)^0} + \frac{\$1.2m}{(1.14)^1} + \frac{\$1.6m}{(1.14)^2}$$
$$+ \frac{\$2.3m}{(1.14)^3} + \frac{\$2.8m}{(1.14)^4}$$
$$= \$494,038.89 > 0$$

and an IRR of:

$$NPV = \frac{-\$5m}{(1 + IRR)^0} + \frac{\$1.2m}{(1 + IRR)^1} + \frac{\$1.6m}{(1 + IRR)^2}$$
$$+ \frac{\$2.3m}{(1 + IRR)^3} + \frac{\$2.8m}{(1 + IRR)^4}$$
$$IRR = 18.09\% > 14\%$$

Both the NPV and IRR support accepting the project.

We could also calculate MIRR (16.72%) and PI (9.88%), and these would provide additional support for accepting the project.

Finally, though we are not given maximum allowable payback or discounted payback, values of 2.96 and 3.70, respectively, those statistics would seem to be in an acceptable range too.

PERSONAL APPLICATION SOLUTION

First, we should note that since cash flows occur every three months, we need to convert the APR of 9 percent to an APR:

$$i_{qtr} = \left(1 + \frac{.09}{12}\right)^3 - 1 = .0227$$

With these types of cash flows, our choice of decision rules is limited to NPV, MIRR, or PI; we can't use either payback rule or IRR because of the non-normality. The NPV of this project will be:

$$NPV = \frac{-\$5,000}{(1.0227)^0} + \frac{-\$5,000}{(1.0227)^1}$$
$$+ \frac{-\$10,000}{(1.0227)^2} + \frac{\$30,000}{(1.0227)^4}$$
$$= -\$347.02 < 0$$

This NPV indicates that the project just isn't worth it.

chapter fourteen

BUSINESS APPLICATION SOLUTION

Chewbacca's operating cycle will be equal to

$$\text{Operating cycle} = \frac{.1 \times 365}{.55} + \frac{.1667 \times 365}{1}$$

$$= 127.197 \text{ days}$$

Their cash cycle will be equal to

$$\text{Cash cycle} = 127.197 - \frac{.05 \times 365}{.55}$$

$$= 94.0152 \text{ days}$$

Absent any other information about current assets or current liabilities, Chewbacca's net working capital will be

$$(.10 + .1667 - .05) \times \$32 \text{ million} = \$6,934,000$$

PERSONAL APPLICATION SOLUTION

Since Wanda will be drawing out the money smoothly from the account, she can use the Baumol Model to determine the optimal replenishment level for her personal stock of cash:

$$C^* = \sqrt{2(\$25,000)(\$9.95)/.035}$$

$$= \$3,770.18$$

P1.1, page 2, © Stockbyte/Getty Images

P1.2, page 6, © Photodisc/Getty Images

P1.3, page 10, © The McGraw-Hill Companies, Inc./John Flournoy, photographer

P1.4, page 12, © The McGraw-Hill Companies, Inc./John Flournoy, photographer

P1.5, page 14, © Getty Images/Digital Vision

P1.6, page 17, © The McGraw-Hill Companies, Inc./Christopher Kerrigan, photographer

P2.1, page 20, © Getty Images/Photographer's Choice RF

P2.2, page 25, © Royalty-Free/CORBIS

P2.3, page 33, Photo courtesy of USDA Natural Resources Conservation Service

P2.4, page 36, © Royalty-Free/CORBIS

P3.1, page 46, © Royalty-Free/CORBIS

P3.2, page 49, © Ryan McVay/Getty Images

P3.3, page 55, © Photodisc/Getty Images

P4.1, page 74, © Royalty-Free/CORBIS

P4.2, page 82, © Royalty-Free/CORBIS

P4.3, page 87, © The McGraw-Hill Companies, Inc./Ken Karp, photographer

P5.1, page 94, © Royalty-Free/CORBIS

P5.2, page 104, © Rim Light/Photo Link/Getty Images

P5.3, page 108, © Paul King/Alamy

P5.4, page 112, © The McGraw-Hill Companies, Inc./John Flournoy, photographer

P6.1, page 122, © Photodisc/Stockbyte

P6.2, page 127, © The McGraw-Hill Companies, Inc./Jill Braaten, photographer

P6.3, page 130, © The McGraw-Hill Companies, Inc./Andrew Resek, photographer

P6.4, page 134, © BananaStock/PunchStock

P6.5, page 140, © Royalty-Free/CORBIS

P7.1, page 150, © The McGraw-Hill Companies, Inc./Jill Braaten, photographer

P7.2, page 154, © Digital Vision Ltd./Getty Images

P7.3, page 157, © TongRo Image Stock/Alamy

P7.4, page 159, © Brand X Pictures

P7.5, page 160, © The McGraw-Hill Companies, Inc./Jill Braaten, photographer

P7.6, page 162, © The McGraw-Hill Companies, Inc./John Flournoy, photographer

P7.7, page 170, © The McGraw-Hill Companies, Inc./John Flournoy, photographer

P8.1, page 176, © iStockphoto

P8.2, page 182, © Diasuke Morita/Getty Images

P8.3, page 185, © The McGraw-Hill Companies, Inc./John Flournoy, photographer

P8.4, page 190, © Hisham Ibrahim/Getty Images

P9.1, page 204, © Brand X Pictures

P9.2, page 209, © Getty Images

P9.3, page 210, © Bloomberg via Getty Images

P9.4, page 213, © Dimitri Vervitsiotis

P9.5, page 215, © Getty Images

P9.6, page 216, © Photodisc/PunchStock

P10.1, page 228, © Royalty-Free/CORBIS

P10.2, page 230, © Ryan McVay/Photodisc/Getty Images

P10.3, page 235, © Lars A. Niki

P10.4, page 239, © Janis Christie/Getty Images

P10.5, page 243, © Corbis

P11.1, page 252, © Brand X Pictures

P11.3, page 259, © Ingram Publishing/SuperStock

P11.4, page 259, © Tetra Images/Alamy

P12.1, page 272, © Stockbyte/Getty Images

P12.2, page 274, © Ryan McVay/Getty Images

P12.3, page 275, © CMCD/Getty Images

P12.4, page 279, © Brand X Pictures

P12.5, page 283, © Brand X Pictures/PunchStock

P13.1, page 296, © Photodisc/Getty Images

P13.2A, page 299, © Stockbyte/Getty Images

P13.2B, page 299, © Comstock Images/JupiterImages

P13.2C, page 299, © imageshop/PunchStock

P13.3, page 307, © Royalty-Free/CORBIS

P13.4, page 309, © Photodisc/Getty Images

P14.1, page 322, © Getty Images/Stockbyte

P14.2, page 327, © Thinkstock /JupiterImages

P14.3, page 330, © Brand X Pictures/PunchStock

P14.4, page 331, Powered by Light RF/Alamy

P14.5, page 335, © Digital Vision/Getty Images

Time Out Boxes, © Ryan McVay/Getty Images; © Stockbyte/Getty Images; © Thomas Vogel/iStockphoto; © Viorika Prikhodko/iStockphoto; © Irina Tischenko/iStockphoto; © Thomas Vogel/iStockphoto

The math coach on . . . Boxes, © Royalty-Free/CORBIS; Get Online Boxes, © artparadigm/Getty Images

index

Page numbers followed by n refer to notes.

A

Accelerated depreciation, 281–283
Accounting, 8
Accounting method for fixed asset
    depreciation, 23
Accounts payable turnover, 51, 52
Accounts receivable turnover, 50, 52
Acid-test ratio, 48, 49
After-tax cash flow (ATCF), 278–279
Agency bonds, 127–128
Agency theory, 14–17
    agency problem, 14–15
    corporate governance, 15–16
    role of ethics, 16–17
Aging schedule, 338–339
Alcoa, 235
Altria, 236
Amaranth hedge fund, 239
American Bankers Association (ABA), 185
American Stock Exchange (AMEX), 155, 179
Amortized loans, 111–114
    computing the time period, 114
    loan principal, 112
    schedules for, 112, 114
Angel investors, 10
AngioDynamics Inc., 178–179
Annual percentage rate (APR), 107, 109
Annuities, 96, 97
    financial calculators and 98
    future value of multiple, 98
    ordinary, versus annuities due, 105–106
Annuity cash flows, analyzing, 95–120
    annuity loans; see Annuity loans
    compounding frequency and, 106–109
    multiple cash flows and; see Future value/
        Present value of multiple cash flows
    ordinary annuities versus annuities due,
        105–106
Annuity loans, 110–114
    finding payments on an amortized loan,
        111–114
    interest rate needed, 110–111
Apple Computer, 17, 151, 155
Ask, 158
Asset-backed securities, 128, 129
Asset-based loans, 330
Asset classes
    performance of, 208
    risk of, 210–211
Asset management ratios, 48–52
    accounts payable management, 51
    accounts receivable management, 49–50
    calculating, 52
    fixed asset and working capital
        management, 51
    inventory management, 49–50
    summary of, 60
    total asset management, 51
Asset pricing, 234
    hedge funds and, 239

Asset transformers, 186
Assets
    on the balance sheet, 22
    choosing between alternatives, 285 287
    current; see Current assets
    assignment, 330
AT&T, 236
Auditors, 15–16
Average collection period (ACP), 50, 52
Average payment period (APP), 51, 52
Average returns, 207–208
Average tax rate, 27

B

Balance sheet, 22–26
    accounting method for fixed asset
        depreciation, 23
    assets, 22
    basic, 22
    book value versus market value, 25–26
    debt versus equity financing, 24–25
    example of 23
    liabilities, 23
    liquidity, 23–24
    managing the, 23–26
    net working capital, 23, 324
    stockholders' equity, 23
Balance sheet equation, 22
Bank of America, 185
Bank of New York, 217, 218, 219
Banker acceptances (BAs), 181, 330, 331
Bankruptcy, 25
Basic earnings power ratio (BEP), 55, 56
Baumol, W. S., 332n
Baumol Model, 332–333
Beanie Babies, 87
Bearer bonds, 125
Behavioral finance, 242–243
Benartzi, Shlomo, 216
Benchmark, 299
    discounted payback, 303–305
    internal rate of return, 306
    net present value, 300
    payback, 302
    profitability index, 315
Beta, 235
    average stock, 235
    concerns about, 238
    finding, 237–238
    as a measure of market risk, 235–236
    portfolio, 236, 237
    proxy, 260
Bid, 158
Blinder, Meyer, 240
Blinder-Robinson, 240
Board of directors, 15
Bond markets, 143–145
    capital gains in, 135
    following, 144
    major indexes, 145
    trading summary, 144
Bond price, 125

Bond ratings, 140–142
    credit quality risk, 140
    debentures, 142
    equipment trust certificates, 142
    investment grade, 140, 141
    junk, 140, 141
    mortgage bonds, 142
    senior, 142
    unsecured government, 141–142
Bond valuation, 122–149
    bond ratings; see Bond ratings
    bond yields; see Bond yields
    capital gains and, 135
    interest rate risk and, 133–134
    market overview, 124–130
    present value of cash flows, 131–132
    reinvestment rate risk and, 134
    term structure of interest rates and, 134–135
Bond yields, 136–140
    current yield, 136, 137
    financial calculators and, 137
    municipal bonds, 138–139
    summarizing, 139–140
    taxable equivalent yield, 138–139
    yield to call, 137–138
    yield to maturity, 136–137
Bonds, 123–130
    agency, 127–128
    asset-backed securities, 128, 129
    calling, 138
    characteristics of, 124–125
    corporate, 126
    discount, 129
    high-yield, 142–143
    issuers of, 126
    mortgage-backed securities, 128, 129
    municipal, 126
    premium, 129
    ratings of; see Bond ratings
    reading quotes for, 128–131
    Treasury inflation-protected securities (TIPS),
        126–127
    Treasury, 126, 128
    valuing; see Bond valuation
    zero coupon, 131
Book value versus market value, 25–26
Bristol-Myers Squibb, 207
Brokers, 153
Bubbles, 242, 243
Business organization, 9–11
    corporation, 11
    hybrid, 11
    partnership, 10–11
    sole proprietorship, 9–10
    summary of, 10
Business risks, 260
Buy-side analysts, 165

C

Call, 125
Call premium, 125
Campbell, John Y., 216

Capital asset pricing model (CAPM), 234
  under- or overvalued stock and, 237
Capital budgeting, 272–321
  accelerated depreciation and, 281
  cash flow estimation; see Cash flow
    estimation
  commonly used techniques, 298
  cost-cutting problem, 285
  decision statistic formats and, 298–299
  discounted payback; see Discounted payback
    (DPB)
  equivalent annual cost and, 285–287
  estimating cash flows, 272–296
  flotation costs and, 288–289
  internal rate of return and; see Internal rate
    of return (IRR)
  net present value and; see Net present value
    (NPV)
  NPV profile and; see NPV profile
  payback and; see Payback (PB)
  processing decisions, 299
  profitability index and, 314–315
  replacement problem, 284
  sample project description, 274
  section 179 deductions and, 281–283
  total project cash flow; see Total project cash
    flow
Capital gains, 135
Capital intensity ratio, 51, 52
Capital market efficiency, 240–243
  behavioral finance, 242–243
  efficient market hypothesis, 240–242
  efficient markets, 240
  penny stocks, 240
  semistrong form, 240, 241
  stock market bubbles, 242, 243
  strong form, 240, 241–242
  weak form, 240–241
Capital market line (CML), 234–235
Capital markets, 180
  instruments of, 180, 181, 182
Capital structure, 25, 28
Carrying costs, 326–327
Cash coverage ratio, 54, 55
Cash cycle, 325, 326
  calculation of, 327
Cash flow, 4
  after-tax, 278–279
  annuity; see Annuity cash flows, analyzing
  estimation of; see Cash flow estimation
  of finance, 5–6
  financial institutions and, 18
  from financing activities, 32
  free, 32, 33–34, 276–277
  from investing activities, 32
  net present value, 300, 303
  from operations, 31–32, 277–278
  risk and, 7
  single; see Single cash flow, analyzing
  statement of; see Statement of cash flows
  stock valuation and, 160–162
  total project; see Total project cash flow
Cash flow estimation, 274–276
  complements, 276, 277
  financing costs, 276, 277
  incremental, 274–275
  opportunity costs, 275

substitutes, 276, 277
  sunk costs, 275–276
Cash management, 331–335
  compensating balances, 331
  holding cash, 331
  investing idle cash, 337
  investment opportunities, 331
  target cash balances, 332–335
  transaction facilitation, 331
Cash ratio, 48, 49
Caterpillar, 171
Charles Schwab, 179
Chase, 185
Chen, Steve, 12
Chief executive officer (CEO), 14
  compensation of, 16
Chief financial officer (CFO), 8
Citigroup, 217, 218
Coca-Cola, 160–165, 169, 171, 182
Coefficient of variation, 211–212
Coldwater Creek, 36–37
Collection policy, 338–339
Comizio, Jerry, 185
Commercial banks, 184
Commercial paper, 181, 330
Common stock, 23, 152–160
  maximizing the price of, 12–13
  purchase and sale of; see Stock markets
Compensating balance, 330
Complements, 276, 277
Component costs, 253, 255; see also Weighted
    average cost of capital (WACC)
  of debt, 256
  of equity, 254–255
  of preferred stock, 255–256
Compounding, 77
  at different interest rates over time, 79–80
  frequency of, 106–109
  future value and, 77–81
  power of 78–79
Compromise financing policy, 328–329
ConocoPhillips, 169
Consols, 105
Constant-growth model, 163, 164
  for required return, 244, 245
Consumer Price Index (CPI), 127
Controller, 8
Corporate bonds, 126, 181
  quotes for, 129, 130
Corporate goals, 11–13
Corporate governance, 15–16
  monitors of, 15
Corporate income taxes, 27–29
Cost of capital, 253–271
  component costs; see Component costs
  weighted average; see Weighted average cost
    of capital (WACC)
Costs
  carrying, 326–327
  component; see Component costs
  financing, 276, 277
  minimizing, 13
  opportunity, 275, 324, 325
  shortage, 327–328
  sunk, 275–276
Coupon rate, 125
Coverage ratios, 54–55

Credit analysis, 338
Credit analysts, 16
Credit manager, 338–339
Credit quality risk, 140, 141
Credit risk, 140–143
  bond ratings; see Bond ratings
  interest rates and, 190–191
  yield and, 142–143
Credit terms, 338
Cross-sectional analysis, 65
Current assets, 22, 23
  alternative financing policies, 328–329
  investment in, 326–328
Current liabilities, 23
Current ratio, 48, 49
Current yield, 136, 137

D

Days' sales in inventory, 50, 52
Dealers, 155
Dean Witter, 158
Debentures, 142
Debt, 256
Debt management ratios, 53–55
  calculating, 54
  coverage ratios, 54–55
  debt versus equity financing, 53–54
  summary of, 60–61
Debt ratio, 53, 54
Debt-to-equity ratio, 53, 54
Debt versus equity financing, 24–25, 28
  effect of, on funders' returns, 29
  ratios evaluating, 53–54
Decision statistic, 299
  discounted payback, 303
  internal rate of return, 306
  net present value, 300
  payback, 302–303
  profitability index, 314
Decision statistic formats, 298–299
Default risk, 188, 190–191
Default risk premium (DRP), 191
Defined benefit plans, 9
Defined contribution plans, 9
Delegated monitor, 186
Depreciable basis, 277
Depreciation
  accelerated, 281–283
  MACRS tables, 292–295
  methods of, 23, 30
  total project cash flow and, 277
Derivative securities markets, 183
Direct transfers, 184, 186
Discount bond, 129
Discount rate, 83
  increasing the, 133
Discounted payback (DPB), 303
  benchmark, 303–305
  calculation of, 305
  statistic, 303
  strengths and weaknesses, 304
Discounting
  over multiple periods, 82–83
  present value and, 81–84
  with multiple rates, 83–84
Disney, 17, 213, 214, 218, 219

Diversifiable risk, 213–214
Diversification, 212–214
    international opportunities for, 219
    portfolio risk and, 212–220
    problems with, 216
Dividend discount models, 162–163
Dividend payout ratio, 56, 57
Dividend yield, 164, 165
Divisional WACC, 262–266
    advantages and disadvantages of, 262–264
    calculation of, 265–266
    subjective versus objective, 264
Dollar return, 206
Double-declining-balance (DDB) depreciation,
    281
Double taxation, 11
Dow, Charles H., 156
Dow Jones Industrial Average (DJIA), 156
    stock market bubble and, 242
Drafts, 336
Drexel Burnham Lambert, 142
DuPont analysis system, 59, 61
    application of, 62

E

Earnings management, 35–36
EBIT (earnings before interest and taxes), 26, 27
EBT (earnings before taxes), 26, 27
Economically viable business ideas, 4–5
Effective annual rate (EAR), 107, 109
Efficient market, 240
Efficient market hypothesis (EMH), 240–242
    information and, 240–242
    levels of efficiency, 240–242
Efficient portfolio, 215
Einstein, Albert, 78, 86
Employee stock option plan (ESOP), 15
Enron, 36
Equipment trust certificates, 142
Equity, 10
    component cost of, 254–255
Equity multiplier ratio, 53, 54
Equivalent annual cost (EAC), 285–287
Ethics, 16–17
Executive compensation, 16
Executive stock options, 244
Expected returns, 230–233
    probability distribution and, 231–232
    required return and, 233
    risk and, 230–232
    risk premiums and, 232–233
    stock valuation and, 165–166
"Extra" money, 4–5

F

Fad "investments," 87
"Fallen angels," 142, 143
Fannie Mae, 128
Federal Deposit Insurance Corp. (FDIC), 185
Federal funds, 181
Fiduciary, 16
Finance, 3
    application of theory of, 7–8
    behavioral, 242–243
    in business and in life, 4–8
    financial function, 8–9

international, 7, 8
management of; see Financial management
markets, intermediaries and, 18
in other business functions, 8–9
subareas of, 6–7
what is?, 4–6
in your personal life, 9
Finance companies, 184
Financial analysts, 165
Financial asset, 7–8
Financial calculators
    annuities and, 98
    bond yields and, 137
    net present value and, 301–302
    time value of money and, 80–81
Financial institutions, 6–7, 8, 183–187; see
    also Financial markets
    cash flows of, 18
    direct transfers and, 184, 186
    indirect transfers, 186
    liquidity and, 184, 186–187
    markets and, 6–7, 177–204
    monitoring costs, 186
    price risk and, 184, 185, 186–187
    secondary securities and, 196
    types of, 184
    unique functions performed by, 186–187
Financial institutions and markets, 6–7,
    177–204
Financial leverage, 24–25, 234
    hedge funds and, 239
Financial management, 3–19; see also Finance
    agency theory and 14–17
    business organization and; see Business
        organization
    decisions involving, 6
    financial manager, 8
    firm goals, 11–13
    markets, intermediaries and, 18
    as subarea of finance, 6
Financial markets, 4, 5, 8, 18, 177–183; see
    also Financial institutions
    capital markets, 180–182
    derivative securities markets, 183
    foreign exchange markets, 182–183
    money markets, 180–181
    over-the-counter markets, 180
    primary, 178–179
    secondary, 179–180
Financial risk, 260
Financial statement analysis, 46–73
    asset management ratios, 48–52
    cautions concerning, 65–66
    cross-sectional analysis, 65
    debt management ratios, 53–55
    DuPont analysis, 59, 61–62
    internal growth rate, 63, 64
    liquidity ratios, 48
    market value ratios, 57–59
    profitability ratios, 55–57
    spreading the financial statements, 62–63
    summary of ratios, 60–61
    sustainable growth rate, 63–64
    time series analysis, 65
Financial statements, 20–45
    analysis of; see Financial statement analysis
    balance sheet; see Balance sheet

cautions in interpreting, 35–37
income statement; see Income statement
statement of cash flows; see Statement of
    cash flows
statement of retained earnings, 34–37
Financing costs, 276, 277
Firm specific risk, 213
Firm WACC, 257–262
First Albany Capital, 179
Fisher effect, 189
Fixed asset turnover ratio, 51, 52
Fixed assets, 22, 23
    accounting method for depreciating, 23
Fixed-charge coverage ratio, 54, 55
Fixed-income securities, 124, 125
Flexible financing policy, 328
Float, 335–337
    accelerating collections, 335–336
    concentration banking, 336
    delaying disbursements, 336
    drafts, 336
    ethical and legal questions, 337
    lockbox system, 336
    wire transfers, 336
    zero-balance account, 336
Flotation costs, 265, 267
    projects initial cash flow and, 288–289
Ford, 124
Foreign exchange markets, 182–183
Foreign exchange risk, 182–183
Forward P/E ratio, 170
Forward rate, 198
    estimating, 199
401k plans, 9
Freddie Mac, 128
Free cash flow, 32, 33–34, 276–277
Future value, 76–81
    compounding and, 77–81
    moving cash flows and, 85–86
    Rule of 72 and, 86–87
    single period, 76–77
Future value of multiple cash flows, 96–101
    level cash flows, 96–98
    multiple annuities, 98
    several cash flows, 96

G

GAAP (generally accepted accounting
    principles), 22
    financial statements and, 22, 33, 35, 37
General Electric, 213, 214, 218
General Motors, 95, 143, 235
General partnership, 10–11
Glass-Steagall Act, 185
Goldman Sachs, 143, 178
Google, 12, 151, 155, 169, 178
Gordon, Myron J., 163
Gordon growth model, 163
Government bonds (state and local), 181
Gross profit, 26, 27
Growth stocks, 165
Gulf Mobile & Ohio RR, 143

H

Hedge funds, 239
Hewlett-Packard, 143

High-yield bonds, 142–143
Historical cost, 25–26
Historical returns, 206–208
  asset classes and, 208
  average 207–208
  dollar, 206
  percentage, 206–208
  risk versus, 211–212
Historical risks, 208–212
  of asset classes, 210–211
  coefficient of variation and, 211–212
  computing volatility, 208–210
  return versus, 211–212
  total, 209
Home Depot, 171, 236, 245
Hurley, Chad, 12
Hybrid organizations, 11

I

IBM, 213, 214, 215, 218
Income statement, 26–30
  basic, 26
  corporate income taxes, 27–29
  example of, 27
  interest and dividends received/paid by
    corporations, 28
Incremental cash flows, 274–275
Indenture agreement, 124, 125
Independent entities, 11
Indirect transfer, 186
Individual retirement accounts (IRAs), 9
Inflation and interest rates, 187–189
Inflow, 76, 77
Initial public offerings (IPOs), 178–179
Insurance companies, 184
Interest rate cognizant, 311
Interest rate risk, 133–134
Interest rates, 76, 88, 187–199
  annuity loans and, 110–111
  compounding and; see Compounding
  computing, 88
  default risk and, 188, 190–191
  forecasting, 197–199
  forward, 198–199
  inflation and, 187–189
  key, 1972–2007, 188
  liquidity risk and, 188
  nominal, 186, 187
  real, 188, 189–190
  return asymmetries, 88
  solving for time, 88–89
  special provisions and, 188, 191–192
  term structure of; see Term structure of inter-
    est rates
  time to maturity and, 188, 192–193
  yield curves and, 192–193, 195
Internal growth rate, 63, 64
Internal rate of return (IRR), 306–314
  benchmark, 306
  calculation, of, 307
  modified; see Modified internal rate of return
    (MIRR)
  mutually exclusive projects and, 309–312
  NPV profile and, 307–313
  problems with, 307–308
  reinvestment rate assumptions, 308–309
  statistic, 306

Internal Revenue Service (IRS), 16
International finance, 7, 8
Inventory turnover ratio, 50, 52
Investment analysts, 16
Investment banks, 16, 178–179, 184
Investment grade bonds, 140, 141
Investment in operating capital (IOC), 34
Investments, 6, 7
Investors, 4–5
  angel, 10
  financial decisions and, 7–8
  psychology of, 159
Invisible hand, 12–13
Iomega, 159

J

JPMorgan, 236
Jobs, Steven, 17, 151
Johnson, Art, 185
Johnson & Johnson, 95, 236
Junk bonds, 140, 141
  Milken and, 142

K

Kaizen, 326
KeyBank Capital Markets, 179
Kohlberg Kravis Roberts, 142
Kohl's, 130

L

Lehman Brothers, 178
Leverage, 24–25, 234
  hedge funds and 239
Liabilities, 23
Limit orders, 158, 159
Limited liability, 11
Limited liability companies (LLCs), 11
Limited liability partnerships (LLPs), 11
Limited partnerships (LPs), 11
Line of credit, 329–330
Lintner, John, 234
Liquidity
  balance sheet and, 22, 23–24
  financial institutions and, 184, 186–187
Liquidity premium theory, 195–196, 197
Liquidity ratios, 48
  calculating, 49
  summary of, 60
Liquidity risk, 188, 191
Liquidity risk premium (LRP), 191
Loan principal, 112
Loans
  secured, 330
  unsecured, 329–330
Long-Term Capital Management (LTCM), 239
Long-term debt, 23
Lottery winnings, 108

M

Marginal tax rate, 27
Market capitalization, 157
Market makers, 155, 158
Market order, 158–159
Market portfolio, 234–235

Market risk, 213, 233–239
  beta and, 235–238
  hedge funds and, 239
  market portfolio, 234–235
  security market line, 236–237
Market risk premium, 233
Market segmentation theory, 196–197
Market share, 13
Market-to-book ratio, 57–58
Market value ratios, 57–59
  calculating, 58
  summary of, 61
Market value versus book value, 25–26
Markkula, Mike, 17
Markowitz, Harry, 214
Mattel, 206–216, 218, 234, 235
Maturity date, 124, 125
Maximizing shareholder wealth, 12–13
  alternatives to, 13
McCaw, Craig, 142
McDonald's, 153, 155, 159, 161, 168, 169, 171
McGowan, Bill, 142
Merck, 36, 171
Merrill Lynch, 158
Merton, Robert, 239
Microsoft, 155
Milken, Michael, 142
Miller, M. H., 333n
Miller-Orr Model, 333–335
Modern portfolio theory, 214–220
  correlation and, 217
  efficient portfolio, 215
  international diversification, 219
  operation of, 216–218
  optimal portfolio, 214, 215
  portfolio return and, 218–220
  problems with, 216
Modified accelerated cost recovery system
    (MACRS), 23, 37, 281
  depreciation tables for, 292–295
Modified internal rate of return (MIRR), 309–314
  calculation of, 310
  mutually exclusive projects and, 309–312
  strengths and weaknesses of, 313–314
Money markets, 180
  instruments of, 180, 181
Moody's, 191
Morgan Stanley, 178
Mortgage-backed securities (MBS), 128, 129,
    181
Mortgage bonds, 142
Mortgages, 181
MSCI Barra, 219
Mullins, David, 239
Multiple cash flows
  future value of, 96–101
  present value of, 101–105
Municipal bonds, 126
  quotes for, 130
  yield of, 138–139
Mutual funds, 184
Mutually exclusive projects, 309–312

N

NASDAQ, 36, 155–156, 179
  tech bubble and, 242
NASDAQ Composite Index, 156–158

Negotiable certificates of deposit, 181
Net income, 26–27
Net present value (NPV), 300–302
    benchmark, 300
    financial calculators and, 301–302
    for a non-normal set of cash flows, 303
    for a normal set of cash flows, 300
    profile; see NPV profile
    statistic, 300
    strengths and weaknesses of, 300, 302
Net working capital, 23, 323–342
    balance sheet model of the firm and, 324
    capital budgeting and changes in, 279–280
    cash management; see Cash management
    credit management, 338–339
    current assets investment, 326–329
    float control, 335
    investing idle cash, 337
    operating cycle and, 324–325
    opportunity cost and, 324, 325
    short-term financial plan; see Short-term
        financial plan
    short-term financial policy, 326–329
    tracing cash and, 324–326
Netflix, 155
New York Stock Exchange (NYSE), 153–160
    bond markets and, 143–45
    buying and selling at 153
    as secondary market, 179, 180
Newmont Mining, 213, 214, 215, 218
NeXT Computer, 17
Nikkei 225, 242
Nominal interest rates, 186, 187
Nondiversifiable risk, 214, 215
NPV profile, 307
    mutually exclusive projects and, 309–312
    non-normal cash flows and, 308
    reinvestment rate assumptions and,
        308–309
Nucor Corp., 231–232

O

Operating cash flow, 31–32
    calculating, 277–278
Operating cycle, 324–325
Opportunity costs, 275, 324, 325
Optimal portfolio, 214, 215
Options, 15
Orr, D., 333n
Outflow, 76, 77
Over-the-counter (OTC) markets, 180

P

Page, Larry, 151
Paid-in surplus, 23
Par value, 124, 125
Partnership, 10–11
Patriot Bonds, 128
Payback (PB), 302, 303
    benchmark, 302–303
    calculation of, 304, 305
    statistic, 302
    strengths and weaknesses of, 304
Penny stocks, 240
Pension funds, 184
Pension plans, 99–101, 108

Percentage returns, 206–208
Perks (perquisites), 14
Perpetuities, 105
Person life and financial decisions, 9
Pixar, 17
Polkovnichenko, Valery, 216
Portfolio beta, 236, 237
Portfolio formation, 212–220
    diversification and, 212–220
    firm-specific risk and, 213
    market risk and, 213
    modern; see Modern portfolio theory
    nondiversifiable risk and, 214, 215
Portfolios, 212, 213
    market, 234–235
Postal Savings Bank of Japan, 336
PPG Industries, 141
Preferred stock, 23
    component cost of, 255–256
    valuation of, 163–165
Premium bonds, 129
Present value (PV), 77
    of bond cash flows 131–132
    discounting and, 81–84
    moving cash flows and, 85–86
    Rule of 72 and, 86–87
Present value of multiple cash flows, 101–105
    level cash flows 102–103
    multiple annuities, 103–104
    perpetuities, 105
    several cash flows, 10
Price-earnings (PE) ratio, 57–59
    for Caterpillar, 171
    forward, 170
    stock valuation and, 168–171
    trailing, 169
Price risk, 184, 185
    liquidity and, 186–187
Primary markets, 178–179
    investment banks and, 178–179
    IPOs and 178–179
    transfer of funds in, 179
Principal, 124, 125
Privately held information, 240
Pro forma analysis, 274, 275
Probability, 231
Probability distribution, 231
Profit margin, 55, 56
Profitability index (PI), 314–315
    benchmark, 315
    calculating, 315
    statistic, 314
Profitability ratios, 55–57
    calculating, 56
    summary of, 61
Project WACC, 257–262
Proxy betas, 260
Public corporation, 11
Public information, 240

Q

Qualcomm, 155
Quick ratio, 48, 49

R

RadioShack, 206–216, 218
Rajan, Raghuram, 14n

Rate of return, 88
RBC Capital Markets, 179
Real assets, 8
Real interest rates, 188, 189–190
Real markets, 8
Recourse, 330
Reinvestment rate risk, 134, 135
Relative value, 168, 169
Replenishment level, 332, 333
Repurchase agreements (repos), 181
Required return, 233
    constant-growth model for, 244, 245
    security market line and, 236
Residual claimants, 152, 153
Restricted stock, 17, 244
Restrictive financing policy, 328, 329
Retained earnings, 5, 23
Retention ratio (RR), 63, 64
Retirement income, 99–101
Return on assets (ROA), 55, 56
    DuPont analysis of, 59, 61–62
Return on equity (ROE), 55–57
    DuPont analysis of, 59, 61–62
Returns and risk; see Risk and return
Reyes, George, 12
Risk, 7
    business, 260
    credit; see Credit risk
    default, 188, 190–191
    diversifying to reduce portfolio, 212–220
    expected return and, 230–232
    financial, 260
    historical; see Historical risks
    interest rate, 133–134
    liquidity, 188, 191
    market; see Market risk
    reinvestment rate, 134, 135
Risk and return, 205–251
    capital market efficiency; see Capital market
        efficiency
    expected returns; see Expected returns
    historical returns; see Historical returns
    historical risks; see Historical risks
    implications for financial managers,
        244–245
    market; see Market risk
    portfolio formation and; see Portfolio formation
Risk-free rate, 233
Risk premiums, 232–233
Rodriguez, Alex (A-Rod), 103–104
Rule of 72, 85, 86–87

S

S corporations, 11
Safety stock, 332, 333
Sales to working capital, 51, 52
Sarbanes-Oxley Act of 2002, 17, 36–37
Savings bonds, 128
Scholes, Myron, 239
Scott, Mike, 17
Scottrade, 158
Scully, John, 17
Secondary markets, 179–180
    trading volume in, 180
    transfer of funds in, 179
Secondary securities, 186
Section 179 deduction, 281–283

Secured loans, 330
Securities and Exchange Commission (SEC), 16, 239
Securities firms, 158, 184
Security market line (SML), 236–237
Sell-side analysts, 165
Senior bond, 142
Separation principle, 265
Sequoia Capital, 12
Shareholders, 11, 152
Sharpe, William, 234
Short-term assets and liabilities; *see* Net working capital
Short-term financial plan, 329–330
   asset-based loans, 330
   banker's acceptance, 330, 331
   commercial paper, 330
   compensating balance, 330
   line of credit, 329–330
   secured loans, 330
   unsecured loans, 329–330
Shortage costs, 327–328
Simple interest, 77–78
Single cash flows, analyzing, 75–93
   computing interest rates, 88
   future value and; *see* Future value
   organizing, 76
   present value and; *see* Present value
   solving for time, 88–89
Sirius Satellite Radio, 155
Smith, Adam, 12–13
Smith Barney, 158
Social responsibility versus profitability, 12–13
Sole proprietorship, 9–10
Sources and uses of cash, 30–33
Southwest Airlines, 129
Specialists, 153
Spreading the financial statements, 62–64
   internal growth rate, 63, 64
   sustainable growth rate, 63, 64
Stakeholders, 12, 13
Standard & Poor's (S&P)
   bond credit ratings, 141, 191
   500 index, 16, 156–158
Standard deviation, 209–210
Starbucks, 10
Statement of cash flows, 30–34
   basic, 31
   example of, 31
   free cash flow, 32, 33–34
   net change in cash and marketable securities, 32–33
   questions answered by, 33
   sources and uses of cash, 30–34
Statement of retained earnings, 34–35
Stock, 181
   common; *see* Common stock
   preferred; *see* Preferred stock
   restricted, 17, 244
Stock indices, 156–158
Stock market bubble, 242, 243
Stock markets, 152–160
   American, 152–156
   investor psychology and, 159
   tracking the, 156–158
   trading stocks, 158–160
Stock options, 244

Stock valuation, 160–171
   cash flows and, 160–162
   constant-growth model and, 163, 164
   dividend discount model and, 162–163
   dividend yield and, 164, 165
   estimating future stock prices, 171
   expected return and, 165–166
   financial analysts and, 165
   growth stocks, 165
   preferred stock, 163–165
   price/earnings (P/E) ratio and, 168–171
   value stocks, 171
   variable-growth-rate techniques 166–168
Stockbrokers, 158, 184
Stockholders, 11
   as residual claimants, 152
Stockholders' equity, 23
Straight-line depreciation, 23, 37, 281
Substitutes, 276, 277
Sunk costs, 275–276
Sunstein, Cass, 216
Sustainable growth rate, 63, 64

T

Taxable equivalent yield, 138–139
Taxes (taxation)
   after-tax cash flow, 278–279
   business organization and, 9–11
   corporate income, 27–29
   double, 11
   earnings before, 26, 27
   municipal bonds and, 126, 138–140
   triple, 28
   weighted average cost of capital and, 257, 258, 262
TD Ameritrade, 158
Term structure of interest rates, 134–135, 191, 192–193
   liquidity premium theory of, 195–196, 197
   market segmentation theory of, 196–197
   unbiased expectation theory of, 196–197
Terms of sale, 338
Thaler, Richard, 216
TheStreet.com Internet Index, 159
3M, 245
Thrifts, 184
Ticker symbol, 153, 155
Time line, 76, 77
Time series analysis, 65
Time to maturity, 124, 125
Time value of money (TVM), 8
   annuity cash flows; *see* Annuity cash flows, analyzing
   single cash flows; *see* Single cash flows, analyzing
Times interest earned, 54
Total asset turnover ratio, 51, 52
Total project cash flow, 276–280
   bringing it all together, 280
   change in gross fixed assets, 278–279
   change in net working capital, 279–280
   depreciation and 277
   free cash flow and, 276–277
   operating cash flow, 277–278
Total risk, 209
Trading post, 153

Trading volume, 180
Trailing P/E ratio, 169
Treasurer, 8
Treasury bills, 181
Treasury bonds, 126, 181
   buying, 128
   calling, 138
   quotes for, 129, 130
Treasury inflation-protected securities (TIPS), 126–127
Treasury notes, 181
Turner, Ted, 142
Type 1–Type 4 people, 4

U

Unbiased expectations theory, 193–194
Unlimited liability, 9–11
Unsecured government bonds, 141–142
Unsecured loans, 329–330
Utkus, Stephen, 216

V

Value Line Investment Survey, 237
Variable-growth-rate techniques, 166–168
Venture capitalist, 10
Verizon, 171

W

Wachovia, 185
Walmart, 143, 171, 185, 236, 244
Wall Street Journal, The, 144
Wealth of Nations, The (Smith), 12n
Weighted average cost of capital (WACC), 253–271
   business risks and, 260
   calculating the weights, 257, 258
   debt, 256
   divisional; *see* Divisional WACC
   equation, 254
   equity, 254–255
   firm versus project, 257–262
   flotation costs, 265, 267
   preferred stock, 255–256
   proxy betas and, 260
   separation principle, 265
   tax rates for, 257, 258, 262
Working capital; *see* Net working capital
WorldCom, 36
Wozniak, Stephen, 17
Wulf, Julie, 14n
Wynn, Steve, 142

Y

Yield to call, 137–138
Yield to maturity, 136–137
Yields, 136
   credit risk and, 142–143
YouTube, 12

Z

Zero-balance account, 336
Zero coupon bonds, 131
Zero-growth-rate model, 164–165

2-1 Assets = Liabilities + Equity

2-2 Earnings per share (EPS) = $\dfrac{\text{Net income available to common stockholders}}{\text{Total shares of common stock outstanding}}$

2-3 Dividends per share (DPS) = $\dfrac{\text{Common stock dividends paid}}{\text{Number of shares of common stock outstanding}}$

2-4 Book value per share (BVPS) = $\dfrac{\text{Common stockholders' equity}}{\text{Numbers of shares of common stock outstanding}}$

2-5 Market value per share (MVPS) = Market price of the firm's common stock

2-6 Average tax rate = $\dfrac{\text{Tax liability}}{\text{Taxable income}}$

2-7 FCF = [EBIT − Taxes + Depreciation] − [ΔGross fixed assets + ΔNet operating working capital]
= Operating cash flow − Investment in operating capital

3-1 Current ratio = $\dfrac{\text{Current assets}}{\text{Current liabilities}}$

3-2 Quick ratio (acid-test ratio) = $\dfrac{\text{Current assets − Inventory}}{\text{Current liabilities}}$

3-3 Cash ratio = $\dfrac{\text{Cash and marketable securities}}{\text{Current liabilities}}$

3-4 Inventory turnover ratio = $\dfrac{\text{Sales or Cost of goods sold}}{\text{Inventory}}$

3-5 Days' sales in inventory = $\dfrac{\text{Inventory} \times 365 \text{ days}}{\text{Sales or Cost of goods sold}}$

3-6 Average collection period (ACP) = $\dfrac{\text{Accounts receivable} \times 365 \text{ days}}{\text{Credit sales}}$

3-7 Accounts receivable turnover = $\dfrac{\text{Credit sales}}{\text{Accounts receivable}}$

3-8 Average payment period (APP) = $\dfrac{\text{Accounts payable} \times 365 \text{ days}}{\text{Cost of goods sold}}$

3-9 Accounts payable turnover = $\dfrac{\text{Costs of goods sold}}{\text{Accounts payable}}$

3-10 Fixed asset turnover ratio = $\dfrac{\text{Sales}}{\text{Fixed assets}}$

3-11 Sales to working capital = $\dfrac{\text{Sales}}{\text{Working capital}}$

3-12 Total assets turnover ratio = $\dfrac{\text{Sales}}{\text{Total assets}}$

3-13 Capital intensity ratio = $\dfrac{\text{Total assets}}{\text{Sales}}$

3-14 Debt ratio = $\dfrac{\text{Total debt}}{\text{Total assets}}$

3-15 Debt-to-equity ratio = $\dfrac{\text{Total debt}}{\text{Total equity}}$

3-16 Equity multiplier ratio = $\dfrac{\text{Total assets}}{\text{Total equity}}$ or $\dfrac{\text{Total assets}}{\text{Common stockholders' equity}}$

3-17 Times interest earned = $\dfrac{\text{EBIT}}{\text{Interest}}$

3-18 Fixed-charge coverage ratio = $\dfrac{\text{Earnings available to meet fixed charges}}{\text{Fixed charges}}$

3-19 Cash coverage ratio = $\dfrac{\text{EBIT + Depreciation}}{\text{Fixed charges}}$

3-20 Profit margin = $\dfrac{\text{Net income available to common stockholders}}{\text{Sales}}$

3-21 Basic earnings power ratio (BEP) − $\dfrac{\text{EBIT}}{\text{Total assets}}$

3-22 Return on assets (ROA) = $\dfrac{\text{Net income available to common stockholders}}{\text{Total assets}}$

3-23 Return on equity (ROE) = $\dfrac{\text{Net income available to common stockholders}}{\text{Common stockholders' equity}}$

3-24 Dividend payout ratio = $\dfrac{\text{Common stock dividends}}{\text{Net income available to common stockholders}}$

3-25 Market-to-book ratio = $\dfrac{\text{Market price per share}}{\text{Book value per share}}$

3-26 Price-earnings (PE) ratio = $\dfrac{\text{Market price per share}}{\text{Earnings per share}}$

3-27 ROA = Profit margin × Total asset turnover

$$\dfrac{\text{Net income available to common stockholders}}{\text{Total assets}} = \dfrac{\text{Net income available to common stockholders}}{\text{Sales}} \times \dfrac{\text{Sales}}{\text{Total assets}}$$

3-28 ROE = ROA × Equity multiplier

$$\dfrac{\text{Net income available to common stockholders}}{\text{Common stockholders' equity}} = \text{ROA} \times \dfrac{\text{Total assets}}{\text{Common stockholders' equity}}$$

3-29 ROE = Profit margin × Total asset turnover × Equity multiplier

$$\dfrac{\text{Net income available to common stockholders}}{\text{Common stockholders' equity}} = \dfrac{\text{Net income available to common stockholders}}{\text{Sales}} \times \dfrac{\text{Sales}}{\text{Total assets}} \times \dfrac{\text{Total assets}}{\text{Common stockholders' equity}}$$

3-30 Internal growth rate = $\dfrac{\text{ROA} \times \text{RR}}{1 - (\text{ROA} \times \text{RR})}$

3-31 Retention ratio (RR) = $\dfrac{\text{Addition to retained earnings}}{\text{Net income available to common stockholders}}$

3-32 Retention ratio = 1 − Dividend payout ratio

3-33 Sustainable growth rate = $\dfrac{\text{ROE} \times \text{RR}}{1 - (\text{ROE} \times \text{RR})}$

4-1 $FV_1 = PV \times (1 + i)$

4-2 Future value in N years $= FV_N = PV \times (1 + i)^N$

4-3 Future value in N periods $= FV_N = PV \times (1 + i_{\text{period 1}}) \times (1 + i_{\text{period 2}})$

$\times (1 + i_{\text{period 3}}) \times \cdots \times (1 + i_{\text{period N}})$

4-4 Present value of next period's cash flow $= PV = FV_1 \times \dfrac{1}{(1 + i)} = FV_1 / (1+i)$

4-5 Present value of cash flow made in N years $= PV = FV_N \times \dfrac{1}{(1 + i)^N} = \dfrac{FV_N}{(1 + i)^N}$

4-6 Present value with different discount rates

$= PV = \dfrac{FV_N}{(1 + i_{\text{period 1}}) \times (1 + i_{\text{period 2}}) \times (1 + i_{\text{period 3}}) \times \cdots \times (1 + i_{\text{period N}})}$

4-7 Approximate number of years to double an investment $= \dfrac{72}{\text{Interest rate}}$

5-1 FV_N = Future value of first cash flow

$+$ Future value of second cash flow

$+ \cdots +$ Future value of last cash flow

$= PMT_m \times (1 + i)^{N-m} + PMT_n \times (1 + i)^{N-n} + \cdots + PMT_p \times (1 + i)^{N-p}$

5-2 $FVA_N = PMT \times \dfrac{(1 + i)^N - 1}{i}$

5-3 PV = Present value of first cash flow + Present value of second cash flow

$+ \cdots +$ Present value of last cash flow

$= \dfrac{PMT_m}{(1 + i)^{N-m}} + \dfrac{PMT_n}{(1 + i)^{N-n}} + \cdots + \dfrac{PMT_p}{(1 + i)^{N-p}}$

5-4 $PVA_N = PMT \times \left[\dfrac{1 - \dfrac{1}{(1 + i)^N}}{i} \right]$

5-5 PV of a perpetuity $= \dfrac{PMT}{i}$

5-6 FVA_N due $= FVA_N \times (1 + i)$

6-1 Present value of bond = Present value of interest payments

$+$ Present value of par value

$= PMT \times \left[\dfrac{1 - \dfrac{1}{(1 + i)^N}}{i} \right] + \dfrac{1,000}{(1 + i)^N}$

6-2 Bond price $= PV$ of annuity $(pmt, i, N) + PV\,(FV, i, N)$

6-3 Price of a callable bond = Present value of interest payments to call date

$+$ Present value of call price

$= PMT \times \left[\dfrac{1 - \dfrac{1}{(1 + i)^N}}{i} \right] + \dfrac{\text{Call price}}{(1 + i)^N}$

6-4 Equivalent taxable yield $= \dfrac{\text{Muni yield}}{1 - \text{Tax rate}}$

7-1 $P_0 = \dfrac{D_1 + P_1}{1 + i}$

7-2 $P_0 = \dfrac{D_1}{1 + i} + \dfrac{D_2 + P_2}{(1 + i)^2}$

7-3 $P_0 = \dfrac{D_1}{1 + i} + \dfrac{D_2}{(1 + i)^2} + \cdots + \dfrac{D_n + P_n}{(1 + i)^n}$

7-4 $P_0 = \dfrac{D_1}{1 + i} + \dfrac{D_2}{(1 + i)^2} + \dfrac{D_3}{(1 + i)^3} + \cdots$

7-5 $P_0 = \dfrac{D_0(1 + g)}{1 + i} + \dfrac{D_0(1 + g)^2}{(1 + i)^2} + \dfrac{D_0(1 + g)^3}{(1 + i)^3} + \cdots$

7-6 Constant-growth model $= P_0 = \dfrac{D_0(1 + g)}{i - g} = \dfrac{D_1}{i - g}$

7-7 Expected return $= i = \dfrac{D_1}{P_0} + g$ = Dividend yield + Capital gain

7-8 $P_0 = \dfrac{D_0(1 + g_1)}{1 + i} + \dfrac{D_0(1 + g_1)^2}{(1 + i)^2} + \dfrac{D_0(1 + g_1)^3}{(1 + i)^3}$

$+ \cdots + \dfrac{D_0(1 + g_1)^n + \dfrac{D_0(1 + g_1)^n(1 + g_2)}{i - g_2}}{(1 + i)^n}$

7-9 $P/E = \dfrac{\text{Current stock price}}{\text{Per-share earnings for last 12 months}}$

7-10 $P_n = (P/E)_n \times E_n = (P/E)_n \times E_0 \times (1 + g)^n$

8-1 $\quad IP = \dfrac{CPI_{t+1} - CPI_t}{CPI_t} \times 100$

8-2 $\quad i = \text{Expected } IP + RIR$

8-3 $\quad RIR = i - \text{Expected } IP$

8-4 $\quad DRP_j = i_{jt} - i_{Tt}$

8-5 $\quad i_j^* = f(IP, RIR, DRP_j, LRP_j, SCP_j, MP_j)$

8-6 $\quad (1 + {}_1R_N)^N = (1 + {}_1R_1)[1 + E({}_2r_1)] \dots [1 + E({}_Nr_1)]$

8-7 $\quad {}_1R_N = \{[1 + {}_1R_1][1 + E({}_2r_1)] \dots [1 + E({}_Nr_1)]\}^{1/N} - 1$

8-8 $\quad {}_1R_N = \{[1 + {}_1R_1][1 + E({}_2r_1) + L_2] \dots [1 + E({}_Nr_1) + L_N]\}^{1/N} - 1$

8-9 $\quad {}_1R_2 = \{[1 + {}_1R_1][1 + ({}_2f_1)]\}^{1/2} - 1$

8-10 $\quad {}_2f_1 = [(1 + {}_1R_2)^2/(1 + {}_1R_1)] - 1$

8-11 $\quad {}_Nf_1 = [(1 + {}_1R_N)^N/(1 + {}_1R_{N-1})^{N-1}] - 1$

9-1 $\quad \text{Dollar return} = (\text{Capital gain or loss}) + \text{Income}$

$\qquad\qquad\qquad = (\text{Ending value} - \text{Beginning value}) + \text{Income}$

9-2 $\quad \text{Percentage return} = \dfrac{\text{Ending value} - \text{Beginning value} + \text{Income}}{\text{Beginning value}} \times 100\%$

9-3 $\quad \text{Average return} = \dfrac{\sum\limits_{t=1}^{N} \text{Return}_t}{N}$

9-4 $\quad \text{Standard deviation} = \sqrt{\dfrac{\sum\limits_{t=1}^{N} (\text{Return}_t - \text{Average return})^2}{N - 1}}$

9-5 $\quad \text{Coefficient of variation} = \dfrac{\text{Standard deviation}}{\text{Average return}}$

9-6 $\quad \text{Total risk} = \text{Firm-specific risk} + \text{Market risk}$

9-7 $\quad R_p = (w_1 \times R_1) + (w_2 \times R_2) + (w_3 \times R_3) + \cdots + (w_n \times R_n) = \sum\limits_{i=1}^{n} w_i R_i$

10-1

$\text{Expected return} = (p_1 \times \text{Return}_1) + (p_2 \times \text{Return}_2) + (p_3 \times \text{Return}_3)$

$\qquad\qquad + \cdots + p_s \times \text{Return}_s = \sum\limits_{j=1}^{s} p_j \times \text{Return}_j$

10-2 $\quad \text{Standard deviation} = \sqrt{\begin{array}{l} p_1 \times (\text{Return}_1 - \text{Expected return})^2 + p_2 \\ \times (\text{Return}_2 - \text{Expected return})^2 + \cdots \end{array}}$

$\qquad\qquad\qquad\qquad = \sqrt{\sum\limits_{j=1}^{s} p_j \times (\text{Return}_j - \text{Expected return})^2}$

10-3 $\quad \text{Required return} = \text{Risk-free rate} + \text{Risk premium}$

10-4 $\quad \text{Required return} = R_f + \beta(R_M - R_f)$

10-5

$\beta_p = (w_1 \times \beta_1) + (w_2 \times \beta_2) + (w_3 \times \beta_3) + \cdots + (w_n \times \beta_n) = \sum\limits_{j=1}^{n} w_j \beta_j$

10-6 $\quad i = \dfrac{D_1}{P_0} + g = \text{Dividend yield} + \text{Constant growth}$

11-1 $\quad \text{WACC} = \dfrac{E}{E + P + D} i_E + \dfrac{P}{E + P + D} i_P$

$\qquad\qquad + \dfrac{D}{E + P + D} i_D \times (1 - T_C)$

11-2 $\quad i_E = i_f + \beta_E [E(i_M) - i_f]$

11-3 $\quad i_E = \dfrac{D_1}{P_0} + g$

11-4 $\quad i_P = \dfrac{D_1}{P_0}$

11-5 $\quad \text{Solve} \left\{ PV = PMT \times \left[\dfrac{1 - \dfrac{1}{(1 + i_D)^N}}{i_D} \right] + \dfrac{PV}{(1 + i_D)^N} \right\} \text{ for } i_D$

11-6 $\quad i_E = r_f + \beta_{Avg}[E(r_M) - r_f]$

where

$\qquad \beta_{Avg} = \dfrac{\sum\limits_{j=1}^{n} \beta_j}{n}$

11-7 $WACC_{Project} = \dfrac{E_{Project}}{E_{Project} + P_{Project} + D_{Project}} i_{E, Project}$

$+ \dfrac{P_{Project}}{E_{Project} + P_{Project} + D_{Project}} i_{P, Firm}$

$+ \dfrac{D_{Project}}{E_{Project} + P_{Project} + D_{Project}} i_{D, Firm}$

$\times (1 - T_{C, Project})$

11-8 $i_E = \dfrac{D_1}{P_0 - F} + g$

11-9 $i_P = \dfrac{D_1}{P_0 - F}$

11-10 Solve $\left\{ PV - F = PMT \times \left[\dfrac{1 - \dfrac{1}{(1 + i_D)^N}}{i_D} \right] + \dfrac{PV}{(1 + i_D)^N} \right\}$ for i_D

12-1 FCF = Operating cash flow − Investment in operating capital

= [EBIT − Taxes + Depreciation]

− [ΔGross fixed assets + ΔNet operating working capital]

12-2 $Depreciation = \dfrac{\text{Ending book value} - \text{Beginning book value}}{\text{Life of asset}}$

12-3 $ATCF = \text{Book value} + (\text{Market value} - \text{Book value}) \times (1 - T_C)$

12-4 $f_A = \dfrac{E}{E + P + D} f_E + \dfrac{P}{E + P + D} f_P + \dfrac{D}{E + P + D} f_D$

12-5 Adjusted $CF_0 = \dfrac{CF_0}{1 - f_A}$

13-1 NPV Statistic

$NPV = \dfrac{CF_0}{(1 + i)^0} + \dfrac{CF_1}{(1 + i)^1} + \cdots + \dfrac{CF_N}{(1 + i)^N}$

$= \displaystyle\sum_{n=0}^{N} \dfrac{CF_n}{(1 + i)^n}$

13-2 NPV Decision Rule

Accept project if NPV ≥ 0

Reject project if NPV < 0

13-3 Payback Statistic is the solution to:

$0 = \displaystyle\sum_{n=0}^{PB} CF_n$

13-4 Payback Decision Rule

Accept project if calculated payback ≤ Maximum allowable payback

Reject project if calculated payback > Maximum allowable payback

13-5 Discounted Payback Statistic is the solution to:

$0 = \displaystyle\sum_{n=0}^{DPB} \dfrac{CF_n}{(1 + i)^n}$

13-6 Discounted Payback Decision Rule

Accept project if calculated DPB ≤ Maximum allowable discounted payback

Reject project if calculated DPB > Maximum allowable discounted payback

13-7 IRR Statistic is the solution to:

$0 = \displaystyle\sum_{n=0}^{N} \dfrac{CF_n}{(1 + IRR)^n}$

13-8 IRR Decision Rule

Accept project if IRR ≥ Cost of capital

Reject project if IRR < Cost of capital

13-9 Profitability Index Statistic

$PI = \dfrac{NPV}{CF_0}$

14-1 Operating cycle = Days' sales in inventory + Average collection period

$$= \frac{\text{Inventory} \times 365}{\text{Cost of goods sold}} + \frac{\text{Accounts receivable} \times 365}{\text{Credit sales}}$$

14-2 Cash cycle = Operating cycle − Average payment period

$$= \text{Operating cycle} - \frac{\text{Accounts payable} \times 365}{\text{Cost of good sold}}$$

14-3 Opportunity cost $= \dfrac{C}{2} \times i$

14-4 Trading cost $= \dfrac{T}{C} \times F$

14-5 Total cost $= \dfrac{C}{2} \times i + \dfrac{T}{C} \times F$

14-6 $C^* = \sqrt{2TF/i}$

14-7 $Z^* = \sqrt[3]{3F\sigma^2/4i_{day}} + L$

14-8 $H^* = 3Z^* - 2L$